W9-CFQ-038

Frommer's®
Maui 2011

By Jeanette Foster

Wiley Publishing, Inc.

Published by:
Wiley Publishing, Inc.
111 River St.
Hoboken, NJ 07030-5774

ISBN 978-0-470-63234-5 (paper); 978-0-470-42398-1 (ebk); 978-0-470-93303-9 (ebk)

Editors: Myka Carroll and Cate Latting
Production Editor: M. Faunette Johnston
Cartographer: Andrew Dolan
Photo Editor: Alden Gewirtz
Cover Photo Reasearch: Richard Fox
Design and Layout by Vertigo Design NYC
Graphics and Pre-Press by Wiley Indianapolis Composition Services

Front cover photo: Bird of Paradise flower. USA, Hawaii, Maui © Vladimir Shulevsky / AGE Fotostock, Inc. Back cover photos, *Left:* Carving honors living and ancient native Hawaiians, Pohaku Loa, Maui, Hawaiian Islands © Ken Gillham/Robert Harding Picture Library Ltd./Alamy Images. *Middle:* Palm shadows on the beach at Kihei, Maui, Hawaii, with a couple on the beach in the distance © David Olsen/Alamy Images. *Right:* Maui, windsurfer heading out from shore © Brent Bergherm/DanitaDelimont.com/Alamy Images.

For information on our other products and services or to obtain technical support, please contact our Customer Care Department within the U.S. at 877/762-2974, outside the U.S. at 317/572-3993 or fax 317/572-4002.

Wiley also publishes its books in a variety of electronic formats. Some content that appears in print may not be available in electronic formats.

Manufactured in the United States of America

5 4 3 2 1

CONTENTS

11 MOLOKAI, THE MOST HAWAIIAN ISLE 313

12 LANAI, A DIFFERENT KIND OF PARADISE 354

13 FAST FACTS 382

LIST OF MAPS

ABOUT THE AUTHORS

A resident of the Big Island, **Jeanette Foster** has skied the slopes of Mauna Kea—during a Fourth of July ski meet, no less—and gone scuba diving with manta rays off the Kona Coast. A prolific writer widely published in travel, sports, and adventure magazines, she's also the editor of *Zagat's Survey to Hawaii's Top Restaurants,* and the Hawaii chapter author of *1,000 Places to See in the USA and Canada Before You Die.* In addition to writing this guide, Jeanette is the author of *Frommer's Hawaii; Frommer's Kauai; Frommer's Hawaii with Kids; Frommer's Portable Big Island; Frommer's Honolulu, Waikiki & Oahu; Frommer's Maui Day by Day;* and *Frommer's Honolulu & Oahu Day by Day.*

HOW TO CONTACT US

In researching this book, we discovered many wonderful places—hotels, restaurants, shops, and more. We're sure you'll find others. Please tell us about them, so we can share the information with your fellow travelers in upcoming editions. If you were disappointed with a recommendation, we'd love to know that, too. Please write to:

Frommer's Maui 2011
Wiley Publishing, Inc. • 111 River St. • Hoboken, NJ 07030-5774
frommersfeedback@wiley.com

AN ADDITIONAL NOTE

Please be advised that travel information is subject to change at any time—and this is especially true of prices. We therefore suggest that you write or call ahead for confirmation when making your travel plans. The authors, editors, and publisher cannot be held responsible for the experiences of readers while traveling. Your safety is important to us, however, so we encourage you to stay alert and be aware of your surroundings. Keep a close eye on cameras, purses, and wallets, all favorite targets of thieves and pickpockets.

FROMMER'S STAR RATINGS, ICONS & ABBREVIATIONS

Every hotel, restaurant, and attraction listing in this guide has been ranked for quality, value, service, amenities, and special features using a **star-rating system.** In country, state, and regional guides, we also rate towns and regions to help you narrow down your choices and budget your time accordingly. Hotels and restaurants are rated on a scale of zero (recommended) to three stars (exceptional). Attractions, shopping, nightlife, towns, and regions are rated according to the following scale: zero stars (recommended), one star (highly recommended), two stars (very highly recommended), and three stars (must-see).

In addition to the star-rating system, we also use **seven feature icons** that point you to the great deals, in-the-know advice, and unique experiences that separate travelers from tourists. Throughout the book, look for:

Special finds—those places only insiders know about

Fun facts—details that make travelers more informed and their trips more fun

Kids—best bets for kids and advice for the whole family

Special moments—those experiences that memories are made of

Overrated—places or experiences not worth your time or money

insider tips—great ways to save time and money

Great values—where to get the best deals

The following **abbreviations** are used for credit cards:

AE	American Express	**DISC**	Discover	**V**	Visa
DC	Diners Club	**MC**	MasterCard		

TRAVEL RESOURCES AT FROMMERS.COM

Frommer's travel resources don't end with this guide. Frommer's website, **www.frommers.com**, has travel information on more than 4,000 destinations. We update features regularly, giving you access to the most current trip-planning information and the best airfare, lodging, and car-rental bargains. You can also listen to podcasts, connect with other Frommers.com members through our active-reader forums, share your travel photos, read blogs from guidebook editors and fellow travelers, and much more.

THE BEST OF MAUI

M aui, also called the Valley Isle, is just a small dot in the vast Pacific Ocean, but it has the potential to offer visitors unforgettable experiences: floating weightless through rainbows of tropical fish, standing atop a 10,000-foot volcano watching the sunrise color the sky, and listening to the raindrops in a bamboo forest.

Whether you want to experience the "real" Hawaii, go on a heart-pounding adventure, or simply relax on the beach, this book is designed to help you create the vacation of your dreams.

It can be bewildering to plan your trip with so many options vying for your attention. To make your task easier, this chapter highlights what I consider the very best that Maui has to offer.

THE best BEACHES

- **D. T. Fleming Beach Park:** This quiet, out-of-the-way beach, located north of the Ritz-Carlton hotel, starts at the 16th hole of the Kapalua golf course (Makaluapuna Point) and rolls around to the sea cliffs on the other side of the cove. Ironwood trees provide shade on the land side. Offshore, a shallow sandbar extends out to the edge of the surf. The waters are generally good for swimming and snorkeling, but sometimes, off near the sea cliffs, the waves are big enough to suit body boarders and surfers. See p. 201.

- **Kapalua Beach:** On an island of many great beaches, this one takes the prize. A golden crescent with swaying palms protected from strong winds and currents by two outstretched lava-rock promontories, Kapalua has calm waters that are perfect for snorkeling, swimming, and kayaking. Even though it borders the Kapalua Resort, the beach is long enough for everyone to enjoy. Facilities include showers, restrooms, and lifeguards. See p. 202.

D.T. Fleming Beach Park.

Maui

PACIFIC OCEAN

Pailolo Channel
Anau Channel
LANAI

WEST MAUI MOUNTAINS
West Maui Natural Area Reserve

Nakalele Pt.
Lipoa Pt.
Kapalua Beach
Kapalua
Napili
Honokowai
Kaanapali Beach
Wahikuli County Wayside
Puunoa Pt.
Lahaina
Launiupoko County Wayside
Olowalu
Hakukee Pt.
Kahakuloa
Waihee
Waiehu
Wailuku
Waikapu
Iao Valley
Maalaea
Honoapiilani Hwy
Papawai Pt.
Kapalua–West Maui Airport

Kahului Bay
Kahului
Kahului Airport
Puunene
Kealia Pond
Maalaea Bay

Hookipa Beach
H.P. Baldwin Beach Park
Paia
Haiku
Pauwela
Opana Pt.
Honokala Pt.
Huelo
Makawao
Haliimaile
Pukalani
Kula
Waiohuli
Ulupalakua
Makawao Forest Reserve
Haleakala Hwy
Kula Hwy
Kula Forest Reserve

Keanae Pt.
Keanae
Koolau Forest Reserve
Keanae Valley
Hana Hwy
Haleakala Crater HALEAKALA NATIONAL PARK
Puu Ulaula
Hanakauhi
Kuiki
Haleakala
Hanawi Natural Area Reserve
Hana Forest Reserve
Kipahulu Valley
Kipahulu Forest Reserve
Kahikinui Forest Reserve
Kanaio Natural Area Reserve
Ahihi-Kinau Natural Area Reserve

Nanu-alele Pt.
Waianapanapa State Park
Hana Airport
Hana
Kaeleku
Hamoa Beach
Muolea Pt.
Kipahulu
Kaupo
Kailio Pt.
Apole Pt.
Piilani Hwy

KANAIO COAST
La Perouse Bay

Ulua Beach
Wailea
Wailea Beach
Makena
Maluaka Beach
Makena State Park
Oneloa Beach
Molokini I.
Kamaole III Beach
Kihei
Laie

KAHOOLAWE

Alalakeiki Channel
Alenuihaha Channel

5 mi
5 km

3

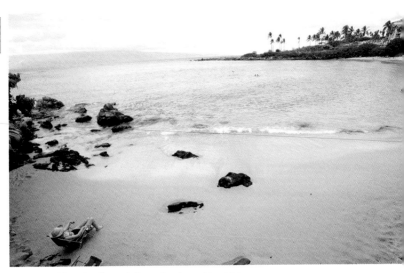

Kapalua Beach is perfect for snorkeling, swimming, and kayaking.

o **Kaanapali Beach:** Four-mile-long Kaanapali stands out as one of Maui's best beaches, with grainy gold sand as far as the eye can see. Most of the beach parallels the sea channel, and a paved beach walk links hotels and condos, open-air restaurants, and the Whalers Village shopping center. Summertime swimming is excellent. The best snorkeling is around Black Rock, in front of the Sheraton; the water is clear, calm, and populated with brilliant tropical fish. See p. 202.

o **Wailea Beach:** This is the best gold-sand, crescent-shaped beach on Maui's sun-baked southwestern coast. One of five beaches within Wailea Resort, Wailea Beach is big, wide, and protected on both sides by black-lava points. It serves as the front yard for the Four Seasons Resort, Maui's most elegant hotel, and the Grand Wailea Resort, its most outrageous. From the beach, the view out to sea is magnificent, framed by neighboring Kahoolawe and Lanai and the tiny crescent of Molokini. The clear waters tumble to shore in waves just the right size for gentle riding, with or without a board. All the beaches on the west and south coasts are great for spotting whales, but Wailea, with its fairly flat sandy beach that gently slopes down to the ocean, provides exceptionally good whale-watching from shore in season (Dec–Apr). See p. 205.

o **Maluaka Beach (Makena Beach):** On the southern end of Maui's resort coast, development falls off dramatically, leaving a wild, dry countryside punctuated by green kiawe trees. This wide, palm-fringed crescent of golden sand is set between two black-lava points and bounded by big sand dunes topped by a grassy knoll. Makena can be perfect for swimming when it's flat and placid, but it can also offer excellent bodysurfing when the waves come rolling in. Molokini and Kahoolawe can be seen off in the distance. See p. 205.

o **Waianapanapa State Park:** In east Maui, a few miles before Hana, the 120 acres of this state park offer 12 cabins, a caretaker's residence, a picnic area, a shoreline hiking trail, and, best of all, a black-sand beach (it's actually small black pebbles). Swimming is generally unsafe, though, due to strong waves and rip currents. But it's a great spot for picnicking, hiking along the shore, and simply sitting and relaxing. See p. 207.

○ **Hamoa Beach:** This half-moon-shaped, gray-sand beach (a mix of coral and lava) in a truly tropical setting is a favorite among sunbathers, snorkelers, and bodysurfers in Hana. The 100-foot-wide beach is about 900 feet long and sits below 30-foot black-lava sea cliffs. An unprotected beach open to the ocean, Hamoa is often swept by powerful rip currents. The surf breaks offshore and rolls in, making this a popular surfing and bodysurfing area. The calm left side is best for snorkeling in the summer. See p. 208.

○ **Hulopoe Beach (Lanai):** This golden, palm-fringed beach off the south coast of Lanai gently slopes down to the azure waters of a Marine Life Conservation District, where clouds of tropical fish flourish and spinner dolphins come to play. A tide pool in the lava rocks defines one side of the bay, while the other is lorded over by the Four Seasons Lanai at Manele Bay, which sits prominently on the hill above. Offshore, you'll find good swimming, snorkeling, and diving; on shore, there's a full complement of beach facilities, from restrooms to camping areas. See p. 366.

THE best MAUI EXPERIENCES

○ **Taking the Plunge:** Don mask, fins, and snorkel to explore the magical underwater world, where kaleidoscopic clouds of tropical fish flutter by exotic corals; a sea turtle might even come over to check you out. Molokini is everyone's favorite snorkeling destination (see "Snorkel Cruises to Molokini," p. 216), but the shores of Maui are lined with magical spots as well (see "Beaches," p. 201). Can't swim? No problem: Hop on a submarine with **Atlantis Adventures** (✆ **800/548-6262;** p. 218) for a plunge beneath the waves without getting wet.

A humpback whale breaches off the coast of Maui.

o **Hunting for Whales on Land:** No need to shell out megabucks to go out to sea in search of humpback whales—you can watch these majestic mammals breach and spy-hop from shore. I recommend scenic McGregor Point, at mile marker 9 along Honoapiilani Highway, just outside Maalaea in south Maui. The humpbacks arrive as early as November, but the majority travel through Maui's waters from mid-December to mid-April. See "Whale-Watching" (p. 219).

o **Watching the Windsurfers:** World-championship contests are held at Hookipa, on the north shore, one of the greatest windsurfing spots on the planet. Sit on a grassy bluff or stretch out on the sandy beach, and watch the world's top-ranked windsurfers twirling and dancing on the wind and waves like colorful butterflies. See "Windsurfing" (p. 221) and "Driving the Road to Hana" (p. 272).

o **Experiencing Maui's History:** Wander the historic streets of the old whaling town of Lahaina, where the 1800s are alive and well thanks to the efforts of the Lahaina Restoration Society. Drive the scenic Kahekili Highway, where the preserved village of Kahakuloa looks much as it did a century ago. Stand in awe at Piilanihale, Hawaii's largest *heiau* (temple), located just outside Hana. See "Lahaina & West Maui" coverage, beginning on p. 245.

o **Greeting the Rising Sun from Haleakala's Summit:** Bundle up in warm clothing, fill a Thermos full of hot java, and drive up to the summit to watch the sky turn from inky black to muted charcoal as a small sliver of orange forms on the horizon. Standing at 10,000 feet, breathing in the rarefied air, and watching the first rays of light streak across the sky is a mystical experience of the first magnitude. See "House of the Sun: Haleakala National Park" (p. 263).

o **Exploring a Different Hawaii—Upcountry Maui:** On the slopes of Haleakala, cowboys, farmers, ranchers, and other country people make their homes in

Sunrise from Haleakala's summit.

Cruising along the Hana Highway.

serene, neighborly communities such as Makawao, Kula, and Ulupalakua—worlds away from the bustling beach resorts. Acres of onions, lettuce, tomatoes, carrots, cabbage, and flowers cover the hillsides. Maui's only winery is located here, offering the perfect place for a picnic. See "More in Upcountry Maui" (p. 269).

o **Driving Through a Tropical Rainforest:** The Hana Highway is not just a drive but an adventure: Stop along the way to plunge into icy mountain ponds filled by cascading waterfalls; gaze upon vistas of waves pummeling soaring ocean cliffs; inhale the sweet aroma of blooming ginger; and take a walk back in time, catching a glimpse of what Hawaii looked like before concrete condos and fast-food joints washed ashore. See "Driving the Road to Hana" (p. 272).

o **Taking a Day Trip to Lanai:** From Lahaina, join **Trilogy** (© **888/MAUI-800** [628-4800]) for a snorkel cruise to Lanai, or take the **Expeditions Maui–Lanai Passenger Ferry** over and rent a four-wheel-drive jeep on your own. It's a two-for-one island experience: Board in Lahaina Harbor and admire Maui from offshore; then get off at Lanai and go snorkeling in the clear waters, tour the tiny former plantation island, and catch the last ferry home. See "Day Cruises to Lanai" (p. 209) and chapter 12.

THE best ADVENTURES

Branch out while you're in Maui. Do something you wouldn't normally do—after all, you're on vacation. Some of the following adventures are a bit pricey, but these splurges are worth every penny.

o **Scuba Diving:** You're in love with snorkeling and the chance to view the underwater world, but it's just not enough—you want to get closer and see even more. Take an introductory scuba dive: After a brief lesson on how to use the diving equipment, you'll plunge into the deep to swim with the tropical fish and go eyeball to eyeball with other marine critters. See "Scuba Diving" (p. 213).

○ **Skimming over the Ocean in a Kayak:** Glide silently over the water, hearing only the sound of your paddle dipping beneath the surface. This is the way the early Hawaiians traveled along the coastline. You'll be eye level and up close and personal with the ocean and the coastline, exploring areas you can't get to any other way. Venture out on your own or go with an experienced guide—either way, you won't be sorry. See "Ocean Kayaking" (p. 211).

○ **Seeing the Stars from Inside a Volcanic Crater:** Driving up to see the sunrise is a trip you'll never forget, but to *really* experience Haleakala, plan to hike in and spend the night. To get a feel for why the ancient Hawaiians considered this one of the most sacred places on the island, you simply have to wander into the heart of the dormant volcano, where you'll find some 27 miles of hiking trails, two camping sites, and three cabins. See "Hiking & Camping" (p. 222) and "House of the Sun: Haleakala National Park" (p. 263).

○ **Hiking to a Waterfall:** There are waterfalls and then there are *waterfalls:* The magnificent 400-foot Waimoku Falls, in Oheo Gulch outside of Hana, are worth the long drive and the uphill hike you have to take to get there. The falls are surrounded by lush green ferns and wild orchids, and you can even stop to take a dip in the pool at the top of Makahiku Falls on the way. See "Hiking & Camping" (p. 222).

○ **Flying over the Remote West Maui Mountains:** Your helicopter streaks low over razor-thin cliffs, then flutters past sparkling waterfalls and down into the canyons and valleys of the inaccessible West Maui Mountains. There's so much beauty to absorb that it all goes by in a rush. You'll never want to stop flying over this spectacular, surreal landscape—and it's the only way to see the dazzling beauty of the prehistoric area of Maui. See "Guided Island Adventures" (p. 239).

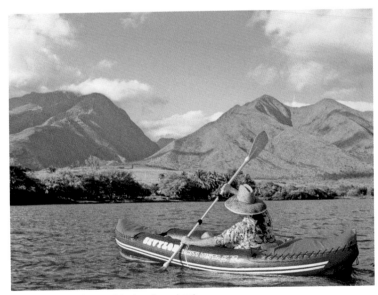

Take in the spectacular mountain views from a kayak.

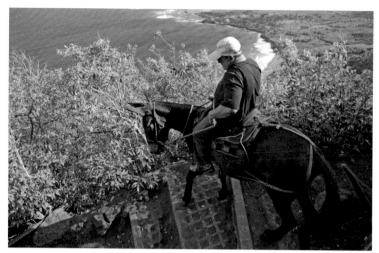

A mule ride to Kalaupapa.

o **Taking a Drive on the Wild Side:** Mother Nature's wild side, that is—on the Kahekili Highway on Maui's northeast coast. This back-to-nature experience will take you past ancient Hawaiian *heiau* (temples); along steep ravines; and by rolling pastures, tumbling waterfalls, exploding blowholes, crashing surf, and jagged lava coastlines. You'll wander through the tiny Hawaiian village of Kahakuloa and around the "head" of Maui to the Marine Life Conservation Area of Honolua-Mokuleia and on to the resort of Kapalua. You'll remember this adventure for years. See "Lahaina & West Maui," in chapter 8.

o **Riding a Mule to Kalaupapa:** Even if you have only 1 day to spend on Molokai, spend it on a mule. The **Molokai Mule Ride ★** (© **800/567-7550**) trek from "topside" Molokai to the Kalaupapa National Historical Park (Father Damien's world-famous leper colony) is a once-in-a-lifetime adventure. The cliffs are taller than 300-story skyscrapers, and the narrow 3-mile trail includes 26 dizzying switchbacks, but Buzzy Sproat has never lost one of his trustworthy mules (or any riders) on the difficult trail. The mules make the trek daily, rain or shine. See "The Legacy of Father Damien: Kalaupapa National Historical Park" (p. 342).

THE best OF UNDERWATER MAUI

An entirely different Maui greets anyone with a face mask, snorkel, and fins. Under the sea, you'll find schools of brilliant tropical fish, green sea turtles, quick-moving game fish, slack-jawed moray eels, and prehistoric-looking coral. It's a kaleidoscope of color and wonder.

o **Black Rock:** This spot, located on the Kaanapali Beach just off the Sheraton Maui Resort, is excellent for beginning snorkelers during the day and for scuba divers at night. Schools of fish congregate at the base of the rock and are so used to snorkelers that they go about their business as if no one were around. If you take the time to look closely at the crannies of the rock, you'll find lion fish in fairly shallow water. At night (when a few outfitters run night dives here), lobsters, Spanish dancers, and eels come out. See "Kaanapali Beach" (p. 202).

o **Olowalu:** When the wind is blowing and the waves are crashing everywhere else, Olowalu, the small area 5 miles south of Lahaina, can be a scene of total calm—perfect for snorkeling and diving. You'll find a good snorkeling area around mile marker 14. You might have to swim about 50 to 75 feet; when you get to the large field of finger coral in 10 to 15 feet of water, you're there. You'll see a turtle-cleaning station, where turtles line up to have small cleaner wrasses pick off small parasites. This is also a good spot to see crown-of-thorns starfish, puffer fish, and lots of juvenile fish. See "Snorkeling" (p. 214) and "Lahaina & West Maui" (p. 245).

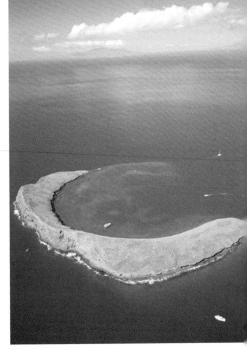

Molikini.

o **Hawaiian Reef:** Scuba divers love this area off the Kihei-Wailea coast because it has a good cross-section of topography and marine life typical of Hawaiian waters. Diving to depths of 85 feet, you'll see everything from lava formations and coral reef to sand and rubble, plus a diverse range of both shallow- and deepwater creatures. See "An Expert Shares His Secrets: Maui's Best Dives" (p. 214).

o **Third Tank:** Scuba divers looking for a photo opportunity will find it at this artificial reef, located off Makena Beach at 80 feet. This World War II tank acts like a fish magnet: Because it's the only large solid object in the area, any fish or invertebrate looking for a safe home comes here. Surrounding the tank is a cloak of schooling snappers and goatfish just waiting for a photographer with a wide-angle lens. It's small, but Third Tank is loaded with more marine life per square inch than any site off Maui. See "An Expert Shares His Secrets: Maui's Best Dives" (p. 214).

o **Molokini:** Shaped like a crescent moon, this islet's shallow concave side serves as a sheltering backstop against sea currents for tiny tropical fish; on its opposite side is a deepwater cliff inhabited by spiny lobsters, moray eels, and white-tipped sharks. Neophyte snorkelers report to the concave side; experienced scuba divers, the cliff side. Either way, the clear water and abundant marine life make this islet off the Makena coast one of Hawaii's most popular dive spots. See "Watersports" (p. 208).

o **Ahihi-Kinau Natural Preserve:** Fishing is strictly *kapu* (forbidden) in Ahihi Bay (at the end of the road in south Maui), and the fish seem to know

Snorkeling off the Molokini islet.

it—they're everywhere in this series of rocky coves and black-lava tide pools. The black, barren, lunarlike land stands in stark contrast to the green-blue water, which is home to a sparkling mosaic of tropical fish. Scuba divers might want to check out **La Pérouse Pinnacle** in the middle of La Pérouse Bay; clouds of damselfish and triggerfish will greet you on the surface. See "Snorkeling" (p. 214) and "An Expert Shares His Secrets: Maui's Best Dives" (p. 214).

THE best GOLF COURSES

o **Kaanapali Golf Resort** (𝒞 808/661-3691): All golfers, from high handicappers to near-pros, will love these two challenging courses. The North Course is a true Robert Trent Jones, Sr., design: an abundance of wide bunkers; several long, stretched-out tees; and the largest, most contoured greens on Maui. The South Course is an Arthur Jack Snyder design; although shorter than the North Course, it requires more accuracy on the narrow, hilly fairways. Just like its sibling course, it has a water hazard on its final hole, so don't tally up your score card until you sink your final putt. See p. 232.

o **Kapalua Resort** (𝒞 877/527-2582): Kapalua is probably the best nationally known golf resort in Hawaii, due to the PGA Mercedes-Benz Championship played here each January. The Bay Course and the Village Course are vintage Arnold Palmer designs; the Plantation Course is a strong entry from Ben Crenshaw and Bill Coore. All sit on Maui's wind-swept northwestern shore, at the rolling foothills of Puu Kukui, the summit of the West Maui Mountains. See p. 232.

o **Makena Golf Courses** (☏ **808/879-3344**): Here you'll find 36 holes by "Mr. Hawaii Golf"—Robert Trent Jones, Jr.—at his best. Add to that spectacular views: Molokini islet looms in the background, humpback whales gambol offshore in winter, and the tropical sunsets are spectacular. The South Course has magnificent views (bring your camera) and is kinder to golfers who haven't played for a while. The North Course is more difficult but also more stunning. The 13th hole, located partway up the mountain, has a view that makes most golfers stop and stare. The next hole is even more memorable: a 200-foot drop between tee and green. See p. 233.

o **Wailea Golf Club** (☏ **888/328-MAUI** [6284]): On the sun-baked south shore of Maui stands Wailea Resort, *the* hot spot for golf in the islands. You'll find great golf at these three resort courses: The Blue Course is an Arthur Jack Snyder design, while the Emerald and Gold courses are both by Robert Trent Jones, Jr. All boast outstanding views of the Pacific and the mid–Hawaiian Islands. See p. 233.

o **The Lanai Courses:** For quality and seclusion, nothing in Hawaii can touch Lanai's two golf-resort offerings. The **Experience at Koele** (☏ **800/321-4666**), designed by Ted Robinson and Greg Norman, and the **Challenge at Manele** (☏ **800/321-4666**), a wonderful Jack Nicklaus course, with ocean views from every hole, rate among Hawaii's best courses. Both are tremendous fun to play, with the Experience featuring the par-4 8th hole, which drops some 150 yards from tee to fairway, and the Challenge boasting the par-3 12th, which plays from one cliff side to another over a Pacific inlet—one of the most stunning holes in Hawaii. See p. 373.

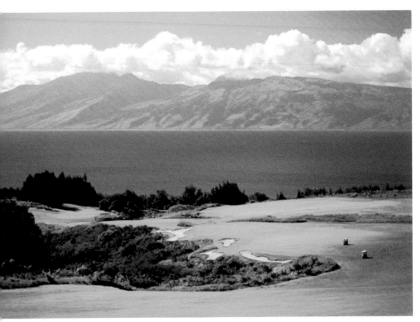

Kapalua Plantation Golf Course.

THE best LUXURY HOTELS & RESORTS

o **Hyatt Regency Maui Resort & Spa** (✆ 800/233-1234 or 808/661-1234; www.maui.hyatt.com): Spa-goers will love Hawaii's first oceanfront spa. The 806 rooms of this fantasy resort, spread out among three towers, have very comfortable separate sitting areas and private lanais with eye-popping views. This huge place covers some 40 acres; even if you don't stay here, you might want to walk through the expansive tree-filled atrium and the parklike grounds. See p. 133.

o **Kaanapali Alii** (✆ 800/642-6284 or 808/661-3330; www.kaanapali-alii. com): The height of luxury, these oceanfront condominium units (right on Kaanapali Beach) combine all the amenities of a luxury hotel (including a 24-hr. front desk) with the convenience of a condominium. The beachside recreation area includes a swimming pool, a separate children's pool, a whirl-pool, gas barbecue grills and picnic areas, exercise rooms, saunas, and tennis courts. See p. 133.

o **Sheraton Maui Resort** (✆ 866/716-8109 or 808/661-0031; www.sheraton maui.com): Offering the best location on Kaanapali Beach, recent renovations, and a great hassle-free experience, the Sheraton is my pick of Kaanapali hotels. This is the place for travelers who just want to arrive, have everything ready for them, and get on with their vacation. (Sheraton has a "no-hassle" check-in: The valet takes you and your luggage straight to your room, which means no time wasted standing in line at registration.) See p. 134.

o **Ritz-Carlton Kapalua** (✆ 800/262-8440 or 808/669-6200; www.ritz carlton.com): With its great location, style, and loads of hospitality, this is the best Ritz anywhere. Situated on the coast below the picturesque West Maui Mountains, this grand, breezy hotel overlooks the Pacific Ocean and Molokai across the channel. The natural setting, on an old coastal pineapple plantation, is the picture of tranquillity. The service is legendary, the golf courses are daunting, and the nearby beaches are perfect for snorkeling, diving, and just relaxing. See p. 142.

o **The Fairmont Kea Lani Maui** (✆ 800/659-4100 or 808/875-4100; www. fairmont.com/kealani): This all-suite luxury hotel in Wailea has 840-square-foot suites featuring kitchenettes with microwaves and coffeemakers, living rooms with high-tech media centers and pullout sofa beds (great if you have the kids in tow), marble wet bars, and spacious bedrooms. The oversize marble bathrooms have separate showers big enough for a party. Large lanais off the bedrooms and living rooms overlook the pools and lawns, with views that sweep right down to the white-sand beach. See p. 152.

o **Hotel Hana-Maui** (✆ 800/321-HANA [4262] or 808/248-8211; www.hotel-hanamaui.com): Picture Shangri-La, Hawaiian style: 66 acres rolling down to the sea in a remote Hawaiian village, with two pools and access to one of the best beaches in Hana. This is the atmosphere, the landscape, and the culture of old Hawaii set in the latest accommodations of the 21st century. A white-sand beach just a 5-minute shuttle ride away, top-notch wellness center, and numerous activities (horseback riding, mountain bicycling, tennis, pitch-and-putt golf) all add up to make this one of the top resorts in the state. See p. 160.

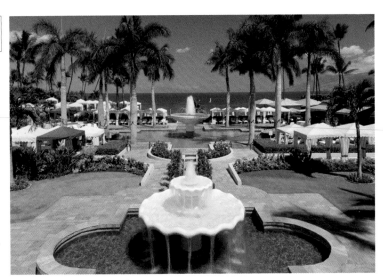

Four Seasons Resort Maui at Wailea.

○ **Grand Wailea Resort Hotel & Spa** (✆ **800/888-6100** or 808/875-1234; www.grandwailea.com): There's nothing subtle or understated about it, but many travelers adore this over-the-top fantasy resort. It has 10,000 tropical plants in the lobby; a fabulous pool with slides, waterfalls, and rapids; Hawaii's largest spa; plush oceanview rooms; and a superb location on a gorgeous stretch of beach. See p. 153.

○ **Four Seasons Resort Maui at Wailea** (✆ **800/334-MAUI** [6284] or 808/874-8000; www.fourseasons.com/maui): This is the ultimate beach hotel for latter-day royals, offering excellent cuisine, spacious rooms, gracious service, and Wailea Beach—one of Maui's best gold-sand beaches—right outside the front door. Every room has at least a partial ocean view from a private lanai. The luxury suites are as big as some Honolulu condos and full of marble and deluxe appointments. See p. 152.

○ **Four Seasons Resort Lanai at Manele Bay** (Lanai; ✆ **800/321-4666** or 808/565-2000; www.fourseasons.com/lanai): The high-end resort chain Four Seasons took over management of this 236-unit property after a multimillion-dollar makeover. Facing the deep-blue Pacific, this luxury resort has become even more luxurious. The remodeled rooms (most with an ocean view) now feature 40-inch flatscreen TVs and huge marble bathrooms. The nearly beachfront hotel (a 2-min. stroll puts you on the sands of one of Hawaii's best beaches) also has many pluses for families: child-care programs, a teen center, and an excellent fitness program and pampering spa. Add to that great golf, plenty of tennis, and all the ocean activities you can think of. See p. 360.

○ **Four Seasons Resort Lanai, The Lodge at Koele** (Lanai; ✆ **800/321-4666** or 808/565-4000; www.fourseasons.com/lanai): After some $50 million in renovations, the Four Seasons took over management of the former Lodge at Koele. All of the 102 guest rooms were totally renovated, with new

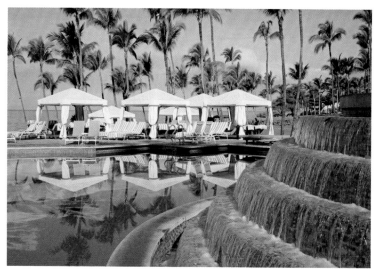

Grand Wailea Resort Hotel & Spa.

carpeting, furniture, and fabrics, plus luxuries such as signature Four Seasons beds, 42-inch flatscreen TVs, and high-speed Internet access. This inn, which resembles a grand English country estate, was built in 1991 and needed the renovation. The new look is spectacular. See p. 361.

THE best MODERATELY PRICED ACCOMMODATIONS

- **The Plantation Inn** (📞 **800/433-6815** or 808/667-9225; www.theplantation inn.com): Attention, romance-seeking couples: You need look no further. This charming Lahaina hotel looks like it's been here 100 years or more, but looks can be deceiving. The Victorian-style inn is actually of 1990s vintage—an artful deception. The rooms are romantic to the max, tastefully done with period furniture, hardwood floors, stained glass, ceiling fans, and four-poster canopy beds. The rooms wrap around the large pool and deck; also on site are a spa and an elegant pavilion lounge, where breakfast is served, all starting at $159 double. See p. 128.

- **Lahaina Inn** (📞 **800/669-3444** or 808/661-0577; www.lahainainn.com): If the romance of historic Lahaina catches your fancy, a stay here will really complete the experience. Built in 1938 as a general store, it has been restored as a charming, antiques-filled inn right in the heart of town, with room rates as low as $160. Downstairs, you'll find one of Hawaii's most popular storefront bistros, Lahaina Grill. See p. 130.

- **Kahana Sunset** (📞 **800/669-1488** or 808/669-8011; www.kahanasunset. com): This is a great choice for families, featuring a series of wooden condo units stair-stepping down the side of a hill to a postcard-perfect white-sand

Paniolo Hale offers Old Hawaii style.

beach. The units feature full kitchens, washer/dryers, large lanais with terrific views, and sleeper sofas (starting at $165 for up to four people). See p. 138.

o **Punahoa Beach Apartments** (✆ **800/564-4380** or 808/879-2720; www. punahoabeach.com): This small oceanside Kihei condo complex is hidden on a quiet side street; the grassy lawn out front rolls about 50 feet down to the beach. You'll find great snorkeling just offshore and a popular surfing spot next door, with shopping and restaurants all within walking distance. Every well-decorated unit features a lanai with fabulous ocean views, starting at $132 double for a studio. See p. 150.

o **Paniolo Hale** (Molokai; ✆ **800/367-2984** or 808/553-8334; www.molokai-vacation-rental.com or www.paniolohale.org): This is far and away Molokai's most charming lodging and probably its best value. The two-story old-Hawaii ranch-house design is airy and homey, with oak floors and walls of folding-glass doors that open to huge screened verandas. The condos start at just $120 for two. See p. 324.

o **Hotel Lanai** (Lanai; ✆ **800/795-7211** or 808/565-7211; www.hotellanai. com): This simple, down-home, plantation-era relic has recently been Laura Ashley–ized. The Hotel Lanai is homey, funky, and fun—and, best of all, a real bargain (starting at $99 for two) compared to its ritzy neighbors. See p. 362.

THE best BED & BREAKFASTS

o **Old Wailuku Inn at Ulupono** (✆ **800/305-4899** or 808/244-5897; www. mauiinn.com): Located in historic Wailuku, the most charming town in central Maui, this restored 1924 former plantation manager's home is the place to stay if you're looking for a night in the old Hawaii of the 1920s. The guest rooms are spacious, with exotic ohia-wood floors and traditional Hawaiian quilts. The morning meal is a full gourmet breakfast served on the enclosed back lanai or on a tray delivered to your room if you prefer. Rates start at $165. See p. 125.

o **Maui Guest House** (✆ **800/621-8942** or 808/661-8085; www.mauiguest house.com): This is one of the great bed-and-breakfast deals in Lahaina: a charming inn offering more amenities than the expensive Kaanapali hotels just down the road. The spacious home features floor-to-ceiling windows, parquet floors, and a large swimming pool. Guest rooms have quiet lanais and romantic Jacuzzis. Breakfasts are a gourmet affair. All units are $169 double. See p. 131.

o **Nona Lani Cottages** (✆ **800/733-2688** or 808/879-2497; www.nona lanicottages.com): Picture this: a grassy expanse dotted with eight cottages tucked among palm, fruit, and sweet-smelling flower trees, right across the street from a white-sand beach. This is one of the great hidden deals in Kihei. The cottages are tiny but contain everything you'll need. At $120 a night, this is a deal. See p. 150.

o **Pineapple Inn Maui** (✆ **877/212-MAUI** [6284] or 808/298-4403; www. pineappleinnmaui.com): This charming inn (only four rooms, plus a darling two-bedroom cottage) is not only an exquisite find, but also a terrific value (rates start at $139 a night). Located in the residential Maui Meadows area, with panoramic ocean views, the two-story inn features a giant saltwater pool and Jacuzzi overlooking the ocean. Each of the soundproof rooms is expertly decorated with a small kitchenette, comfy bed, free wireless Internet access, TV/VCR, and an incredible view off your own private lanai. See p. 150.

o **Two Mermaids on Maui B&B** (✆ **800/598-9550** or 808/874-8687; www. twomermaids.com): Two avid scuba divers are the hosts at this very friendly Kihei B&B, professionally decorated in brilliant, tropical colors, complete with hand-painted art of the island (above and below the water) in a quiet neighborhood just a short 10-minute walk from the beach. Comfy rooms start at $140, including breakfast. See p. 151.

o **What a Wonderful World B&B** (✆ **800/943-5804** or 808/879-9103; www. amauibedandbreakfast.com): Another one of Kihei's best B&Bs offers a great central location in town—just ½ mile to Kamaole II Beach Park, 5 minutes from Wailea golf courses, and convenient to shopping and restaurants. All rooms boast cooking facilities and private entrances, bathrooms, and phones. A family-style breakfast (eggs Benedict, Alaskan waffles, skillet eggs with mushroom sauce, fruit blintzes) is served on the lanai, which has views of white-sand beaches, the West Maui Mountains, and Haleakala. From $89 double. See p. 151.

o **Ekena** (✆ **808/248-7047**; www. ekenamaui.com): Situated on 8½ acres in the hills above Hana, this Hawaiian-style wooden pole house, with 360-degree views of

Old Wailuku Inn at Ulupono.

the coastline, the ocean, and Hana's verdant rainforest, is perfect for those in search of a quiet, peaceful vacation. Inside, the elegantly furnished home features floor-to-ceiling sliding-glass doors and a fully equipped kitchen (starting at $225 for two); outside, hiking trails into the rainforest start right on the property. Beaches, waterfalls, and pools are mere minutes away. See p. 161.

o **Hamoa Bay House & Bungalow** (© 808/248-7884): This enchanting retreat sits on 4 verdant acres within walking distance of Hamoa Beach, just outside Hana. The romantic 600-square-foot Balinese-style cottage has a full kitchen and hot tub. This very private place is perfect for honeymooners. The price? Just $225. See p. 161.

o **Aloha Beach House** (Molokai; © 888/828-1008 or 808/828-1100; www. molokaivacation.com): Nestled on the lush East End of Molokai is this Hawaiian-style beach house sitting right on the white-sand beach of Waialua. Perfect for families, the impeccably decorated two-bedroom, 1,600-square-foot property has a huge open living/dining/kitchen area that opens onto an old-fashioned porch for meals or just sitting in the comfy chairs and watching the clouds roll by. Just $230 for up to five people. See p. 325.

THE best RESORT SPAS

o **Spa Moana at the Hyatt Regency Maui Resort & Spa** (© 800/233-1234 or 808/661-1234; www.maui.hyatt.com): The island's first oceanfront spa, this 20,000-square-foot facility offers an open-air exercise lanai, wet-treatment rooms, massage rooms, a relaxation lounge, sauna and steam rooms, a Roman pool illuminated by overhead skylights, and a duet treatment suite for couples. See p. 133.

o **Spa at the Ritz-Carlton Kapalua** (© 800/262-8440 or 808/669-6200; www.ritzcarlton.com): Book a massage on the beach. The spa itself is welcoming and wonderful, but there is nothing like smelling the salt in the air and feeling the gentle caress of the wind in your hair while experiencing a true Hawaiian massage. See p. 142.

o **Spa Kea Lani at the Fairmont Kea Lani Maui** (© 800/659-4100 or 808/875-4100; www.fairmont.com/kealani): This intimate, Art Deco boutique spa (just a little over 5,000 sq. ft., with nine treatment rooms) is the place for personal and private attention. The fitness center next door is open 24 hours (a rarity in Hawaiian resorts) with a personal trainer on duty some 14 hours a day. See p. 152.

o **Spa at the Four Seasons Resort Maui at Wailea** (© 800/334-MAUI [6284] or 808/874-8000; www.fourseasons.com/maui): Imagine the sound of the waves rolling on Wailea Beach as you are soothingly massaged in the privacy

Go for ultimate relaxation at the Spa Kea Lani at the Fairmont Kea Lani Maui.

of your cabana, tucked in among the beachside foliage. This is the place to come to be absolutely spoiled. Yes, there's an excellent workout area and tons of great classes, but the specialty here is hedonistic indulgence. See p. 152.

PAMPERING IN paradise

Hawaii's spas have raised the art of relaxation and healing to a new level. The traditional Greco-Roman–style spas, with lots of marble and big tubs in closed rooms, have evolved into airy, open facilities that embrace the tropics. Spa-goers in Hawaii are looking for a sense of place, steeped in the culture. They want to hear the sound of the ocean, smell the salt air, and feel the caress of the warm breeze. They want to experience Hawaiian products and traditional treatments they can get only in the islands.

The spas of Hawaii, once nearly exclusively patronized by women, are now attracting more male clients. There are also special massages for children and pregnant women, and some spas have created programs to nurture and relax brides on their big day.

Today's spas offer a wide diversity of treatments. Massage options include Hawaiian lomilomi, Swedish, aromatherapy (with sweet-smelling oils), craniosacral (massaging the head), shiatsu (no oil, just deep thumb pressure on acupuncture points), Thai (another oilless massage involving stretching), and hot stone. There are even side-by-side massages for couples. The truly decadent might try a duo massage—not one, but two massage therapists working on you at once.

Body treatments, for the entire body or just the face, involve a variety of herbal wraps, masks, or scrubs using a range of ingredients from seaweed to salt to mud, with or without accompanying aromatherapy, lights, and music.

After you have been rubbed and scrubbed, most spas offer an array of water treatments—a sort of hydromassage in a tub with jets and an assortment of colored crystals, oils, and scents.

Those are just the traditional treatments. Most spas also offer a range of alternative healthcare, such as acupuncture and chiropractic, and more exotic treatments such as ayurvedic and siddha from India or reiki from Japan. Some offer specialized, cutting-edge treatments, such as the Grand Wailea Resort's full-spectrum color-light therapy pod (based on NASA's work with astronauts).

Once your body has been pampered, spas also offer a range of fitness facilities (weights, racquetball, tennis, golf, and so on) and classes (such as yoga, aerobics, spinning, tai chi, and kickboxing). Several offer adventure fitness packages (from bicycling to snorkeling). For the less active, most spas also have salons dedicated to hair and nail care.

If all this sounds a bit overwhelming, not to worry: All the spas in Hawaii have individual consultants who will help you design an appropriate treatment program to fit your individual needs.

Of course, all this pampering doesn't come cheap. Massages are generally $180 to $275 for 50 minutes and $265 to $300 for 80 minutes, body treatments are in the $150-to-$250 range, and alternative healthcare treatments can be as high as $200 to $300. But you may think it's worth the expense to banish your tension and stress.

- **Spa Grande at the Grand Wailea Resort Hotel & Spa** (© **800/888-6100** or 808/875-1234; www.grandwailea.com): This is Hawaii's biggest spa, at 50,000 square feet and with 40 treatment rooms. The spa incorporates the best of the Old World (romantic ceiling murals, larger-than-life Roman-style sculptures, mammoth Greek columns, huge European tubs), the finest Eastern traditions (a full Japanese-style traditional bath and various exotic treatments from India), and the lure of the islands (tropical foliage, ancient Hawaiian treatments, and island products). It has everything from a top fitness center to a menu of classes and is constantly on the cutting edge of the latest trends. See p. 153.

- **Spa at the Four Seasons Resort Lanai at Manele Bay** (Lanai; © **800/321-4666** or 808/565-2000; www.fourseasons.com/lanai): The spa facility here features a variety of massages, facials, wraps, and scrubs (don't miss the signature Ali'i banana-coconut scrub). In addition, the Four Seasons has added a 1,500-square-foot fitness center (with one of the best ocean views in the resort) that features the latest cardiovascular and strength-training equipment, free weights, and a wood-floor studio for classes (spinning, yoga, Pilates, and meditation). See p. 160.

THE best RESTAURANTS

- **A Saigon Cafe** (© **808/243-9560**): Jennifer Nguyen's unmarked dining room in an odd corner of Wailuku is always packed, a tribute to her clean, crisp Vietnamese cuisine—and the Maui grapevine. Grab a round of rice paper and wrap your own Vietnamese "burrito" of tofu, noodles, and vegetables. See p. 169.

- **A. K.'s Café** (© **808/244-8774**; www.akscafe.com): Chef Elaine Rothermel has a winner with this tiny cafe in the industrial district of Wailuku. It may be slightly off the tourist path, and the decor isn't much to look at, but it is well worth the effort to find this delicious eatery, with creative cuisine coming out of the kitchen—most of it healthy. Prices are so eye-poppingly cheap, you might find yourself wandering back here again during your vacation. See p. 169.

- **David Paul's Island Grill** (© **808/662-3000**): One of Hawaii's top chefs, David Paul, opened a restaurant in Lahaina, introducing a combination of American and island-style cuisine that draws heavily on local products. He dubbed this "new island cooking." See p. 173.

- **Gerard's** (© **808/661-8939**; www.gerardsmaui.com): Proving that French is fabulous, particularly in the land of sushi and sashimi, Gerard Reversade is the Gallic gastronome who delivers ecstasy with every bite. From the rack of lamb to the spinach salad and oyster mushrooms in puff pastry, every meal is memorable. The fairy lights on the veranda in the balmy outdoor Lahaina setting are the icing on the gâteau. See p. 172.

- **Mala Ocean Tavern** (© **808/667-9394**; www.malaoceantavern.com): Perched right on the ocean, this tiny "tavern" is the brainchild of Mark and Judy Ellman, owners of Maui Tacos and Penne Pasta Café. They use healthy, organically grown food and fresh fish to make intriguing dishes. The atmosphere could not be more enticing, with just a handful of tables out on the

Sansei Seafood Restaurant & Sushi Bar.

oceanfront lanai and several more tables in the warmly decorated interior. The staff is helpful and efficient, and the food is outstanding. See p. 174.

○ **Son'z Maui at Swan Court** (𝒞 808/667-4506): For 30 years, the Swan Court was *the* dining experience at the Hyatt Regency Maui Resort, and under Tri-Star Restaurant Group it's even better. The restaurant already had perhaps the most romantic location in Maui, overlooking a man-made lagoon with white and black swans swimming by and the rolling surf of the Pacific in the distance. The culinary team's creative dishes, coupled with fresh local ingredients, have made it a must for every Maui visitor. See p. 177.

○ **Roy's Kahana Bar & Grill** (𝒞 808/669-6999; www.roysrestaurant.com): This restaurant bustles with young, hip servers impeccably trained to deliver blackened ahi or perfectly seared lemon grass *shutome* (broadbill swordfish) hot to your table, in rooms that sizzle with cross-cultural tastings. See p. 181.

○ **Pineapple Grill** (𝒞 808/669-9600): If you only had a single night to eat on the island, I'd send you here. In fact, if you eat here at the beginning of your Maui trip, you might end up coming back! Chef Ryan Luckey is a genius at turning fresh local ingredients into culinary masterpieces such as the Maui-style seafood paella with Portuguese sausage and Kula herbs. See p. 183.

○ **Plantation House Restaurant** (𝒞 808/669-6299): Plantation House features teak tables, a fireplace, open sides, mountain and ocean views, and Chef Alex Stanislaw's love for Mediterranean flavors and preparations. It's a friendly, comfortable restaurant with great food, including sublime eggs Mediterranean at breakfast, and polenta, crab cakes, fish, pork tenderloin, filet mignon, and other delights at dinner. The ambience is superb. See p. 184.

○ **Ko** (𝒞 808/875-4100): The concept behind this successful restaurant in the Fairmont Kea Lani is pure genius—taking the various ethnic cuisine from Maui's old plantation days (Hawaiian, Filipino, Portuguese, Korean, Puerto

Rican, and European) and cooking them up in a gourmet fashion. There are some wonderful taste treats you are going to find only here, so don't miss them: ahi (which is tuna) "on the rocks," where the server brings you chunks of fresh ahi and you cook them on hot ishiyaki stone to the desired doneness (from barely seared on the outside to fully cooked). Or Filipino lumpia (a sort of spring roll with green papaya, shrimp, and pork [or chicken and mushroom] that you dip into a spicy sauce). See p. 188.

o **Sansei Seafood Restaurant & Sushi Bar** (☎ **808/669-6286** in Kapalua, 879-0004 in Kihei; www.sanseihawaii.com): Relentlessly popular, Sansei serves sushi and then some: hand rolls warm and cold, udon and ramen, and the signature Asian rock-shrimp cake with the oh-so-complex lime-chili butter and cilantro pesto. This place is flavor central—simplicity is not its strong suit, so be prepared for some busy tasting. See p. 184.

o **Joe's** (☎ **808/875-7767**; www.bevgannonrestaurants.com): The impressive view spans the Wailea golf course, tennis courts, ocean, and Haleakala—a worthy setting for Beverly Gannon's style of American home cooking with a regional twist (also see "Haliimaile General Store," below). The hearty staples include excellent mashed potatoes, lobster, fresh fish, and filet mignon, but the meatloaf (a whole loaf, like Mom used to make) upstages them all. See p. 191.

o **Haliimaile General Store** (☎ **808/572-2666**; www.bevgannonrestaurants. com/haliimaile): Bev Gannon, one of the 12 original Hawaii Regional Cuisine chefs, is still going strong at her foodie haven in the pineapple fields. You'll dine at tables set on old wood floors under high ceilings. The food, a blend of eclectic American with ethnic touches, bridges Hawaii and Gannon's Texas roots to put an innovative spin on Hawaii Regional Cuisine. Examples include sashimi napoleon and the house salad—island greens with mandarin oranges, onions, toasted walnuts, and blue-cheese crumble. See p. 191.

o **Moana Bakery & Cafe** (☎ **808/579-9999**): In the unlikely location of Paia, the Moana gets high marks for its stylish concrete floors, high ceilings, booths and cafe tables, and fabulous food. Don Ritchey, formerly a chef at Haliimaile General Store, has created the perfect Paia eatery, a casual bakery/cafe that highlights his stellar skills. It may not look like much from the outside, but don't be fooled. This innovative eatery serves breakfast, lunch, and dinner and offers live entertainment at night. See p. 196.

o **Colleen's at the Cannery** (☎ **808/575-9211**; www.colleensinhaiku.com): Way, way, way off the beaten path lies this chic, fabulous find in the rural Haiku Cannery Marketplace. It's worth the drive to enjoy Colleen's fabulous culinary creations, such as wild-mushroom ravioli with sautéed portobello mushrooms, tomatoes, herbs, and a roasted-pepper coulis. See p. 197.

o **Old Lahaina Luau** (☎ **800/248-5828** or 808/667-1998; www.old lahainaluau.com): It's not exactly a restaurant, but it's certainly an unforgettable dining experience. Maui's best luau serves top-quality food that's as much Pacific Rim as authentically Hawaiian, served from an open-air thatched structure. It's one-third entertainment, one-third good food, and one-third ambience. See p. 308.

- **Ihilani** (Lanai; ☏ **808/565-2296;** www.fourseasons.com/manelebay/dining): During their tenures here, a number of top Hawaii chefs (such as Philippe Padovani and Edwin Goto) have added their own style to the menu, which melds Mediterranean with Island cuisine. The result is one of Lanai's top gourmet restaurants. The latest incarnation of this classy restaurant, overlooking the resort and the ocean beyond, is traditional Italian cuisine that is actually reasonably priced. Not to be missed. See p. 363.

- **Lanai City Grille** (Lanai; ☏ **808/565-7211**): Celebrated Maui chef Bev Gannon (Haliimaile General Store, Joe's) redesigned the menu in this cute eatery, where the decor consists of pine-paneled walls, chintz curtains, and a fireplace. The menu sticks to whatever is in season and fresh that day, from the fish and seafood to the rotisserie chicken. See p. 365.

- **Pele's Other Garden** (Lanai; ☏ **808/565-9628**): You don't have to spend a fortune at the high-priced eateries in the two resorts on Lanai: This charming bistro in the heart of Lanai City has a full-scale New York deli (yummy pizzas), and you can also get box lunches and picnic baskets to go. Dinner is now served on china on cloth-covered tables—a real dining room! See p. 365.

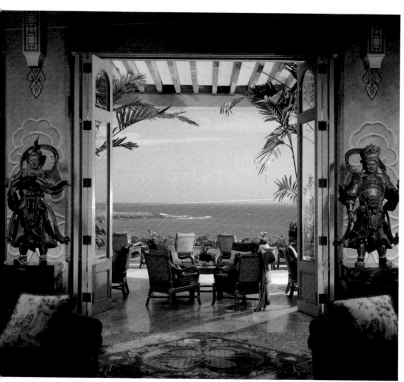

Ihilani is one of Lanai's top gourmet restaurants.

THE best SHOPS & GALLERIES

o **Sandell** (📞 808/249-0234): Since the early 1970s, artist, illustrator, and cartoonist David Sandell has been commenting on Maui through his artwork. Don't miss the opportunity to stop by this shop in old Wailuku town and "talk story" with the talented artist, who watched Maui go from undiscovered to discovered. His work—from original oils to prints to T-shirts—makes excellent souvenirs to take home. See p. 294.

o **Bailey House Museum Shop** (📞 808/244-3326): You can travel Hawaii and peruse its past with the assemblage of made-in-Hawaii items at this museum gift shop in Wailuku. Tropical preserves, Hawaiian music, pareu, prints by esteemed Hawaiian artists, cookbooks, hatbands, and magnificent wood bowls reflect a discerning standard of selection. Unequaled for Hawaiian treasures on Maui. See p. 293.

o **Brown-Kobayashi** (📞 808/242-0804): At this quiet, tasteful, and elegant Asian shop in Wailuku, the selection of antiques and collectibles changes constantly but reflects an unwavering sense of gracious living. There are old and new European and Hawaiian objects, from koa furniture (which disappears fast) to lacquerware, Bakelite jewelry, Peking glass beads, and a few priceless pieces of antique ivory. See p. 293.

o **Village Galleries** (📞 808/661-4402 in Lahaina, 808/669-1800 in Kapalua): Maui's oldest galleries have maintained high standards and the respect of a public that is increasingly impatient with clichéd island art. On exhibit are the finest contemporary Maui artists in all media, with a discerning selection of handcrafted jewelry. In Lahaina, the contemporary gallery has a larger selection of jewelry, ceramics, glass, and gift items, as well as paintings and prints. See p. 297 and 299.

o **Hui No'eau Visual Arts Center** (📞 808/572-6560): Half the experience is the center itself, one of Maui's historic treasures: a strikingly designed 1917 *kamaaina* (native-born, or old-timer) estate on 9 acres in Makawao; two of

Find one-of-a-kind works of art at Hui No'eau Visual Arts Center.

Maui's largest hybrid Cook and Norfolk pines; and an arts center with classes, exhibitions, and demonstrations. The gift shop is as memorable as the rest of it. You'll find one-of-a-kind works by local artists, from prints to jewelry and pottery. See p. 300.

o **Viewpoints Gallery** (© **808/572-5979**): I love this airy, well-designed Makawao gallery and its helpful staff, which complement the fine Maui art: paintings, sculpture, jewelry, prints, woods, and glass. This is Maui's only fine-arts cooperative, showcasing the work of dozens of local artists. See p. 301.

o **Hana Coast Gallery** (© **808/248-8636**): This gallery is a good reason to go to Hana: It's an aesthetic and cultural experience that informs as it enlightens. Tucked away in the posh hideaway Hotel Hana-Maui, the 3,000-square-foot gallery is known for its high level of curatorship and commitment to the cultural art of Hawaii. It's devoted entirely to Hawaiian artists, who display their sculptures, paintings, prints, feather work, stonework, and carvings. See p. 303.

o **Dis 'N Dat** (Lanai; © **866/DIS-N-DAT** [347-6328]): This is my favorite shop on Lanai, where Barry (Dis) and Susie (Dat) have collected the unusual, the bizarre, and the hilariously funny. You'll find everything from finely crafted teak and exotic wood sculptures and carvings to mobiles and wind chimes (the more outrageous, the better), plus an impressive line of handmade jewelry, stained glass, and more. See p. 380.

o **The Local Gentry** (Lanai; © **808/565-9130**): This wonderful Lanai boutique features clothing and accessories that are not the standard resort-shop fare. You'll find fabulous silk aloha shirts by Iolani, Putumayo separates (perfect for Hawaii) in easy-care fabrics, a fabulous line of silk aloha shirts by Tiki, top-quality hemp-linen camp shirts, inexpensive sarongs, fabulous socks, and the Tommy Bahama line for men and women. There are also great T-shirts, swimwear, jewelry, bath products, picture frames, jeans, chic sunglasses, offbeat sandals, and wonderful children's clothes. See p. 380.

Dis 'N Dat.

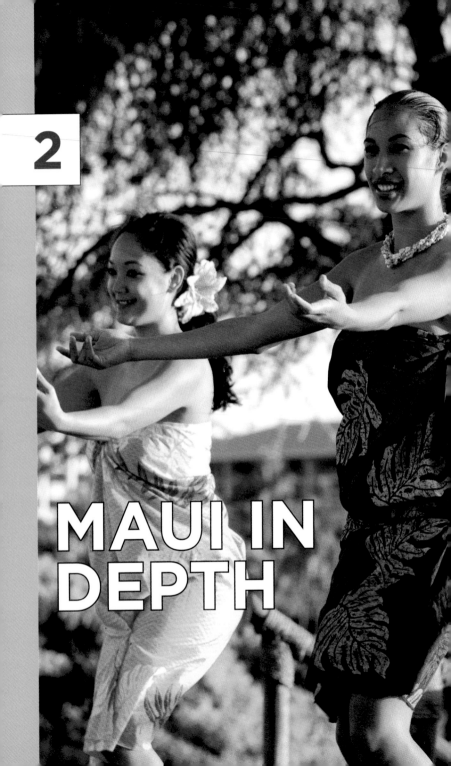

2

MAUI IN DEPTH

Since the Polynesians ventured across the Pacific to the Hawaiian Islands more than 1,000 years ago, these floating jewels have continued to call visitors from around the globe.

Located in one of the most remote and isolated places on the planet, Maui, as part of the Hawaiian Islands chain, floats in the warm waters of the Pacific, blessed by a tropical sun and cooled by gentle year-round trade winds—creating what might be the most ideal climate imaginable. Centuries of the indigenous Hawaiian culture have given the people of the islands the "spirit of aloha," a warm, welcoming attitude that invites visitors to come and share this exotic paradise. Mother Nature has carved out verdant valleys, hung brilliant rainbows in the sky, and trimmed the islands with sandy beaches in a spectrum of colors, from white to black to even green and red.

Visitors are drawn to Maui not only for its incredible beauty, but also for its opportunities for adventure: bicycling down a 10,000-foot dormant volcano, swimming in a sea of rainbow-colored fish, hiking into a rainforest, or watching whales leap out of the ocean as you tee off on one of the country's top golf courses. Others come to rest and relax in a land where the pace of life moves at a slower rate and the sun's rays soothe and allow both body and mind to regenerate and recharge.

Venturing to Maui is not your run-of-the-mill vacation, but rather an experience in the senses that will remain with you, locked into your memory, way, way, way after your tan fades. Years later, a sweet smell, the warmth of the sun on your body, or the sound of the wind through the trees will take you back to the time you spent in the islands.

Incidentally, Maui is the only island in the Hawaiian chain named after a god—well, actually a demigod (half man, half god). Hawaiian legends are filled with the escapades of Maui, who had a reputation as a trickster. In one story, Maui is credited with causing the birth of the Hawaiian Islands when he threw his "magic" fishhook down to the ocean floor and pulled the islands up from the bottom of the sea. Another legend tells how Maui lassoed the sun to make it travel more slowly across the sky so that his mother could more easily dry her clothes. Maui's status as the only island to carry the name of a deity seems fitting, considering its reputation as the perfect tropical paradise, or as Hawaiians say, *Maui no ka oi* ("Maui is the best").

MAUI TODAY

A CULTURAL RENAISSANCE A conch shell sounds, a young man in a bright feather cape chants, torchlight flickers at sunset on the beach, and hula dancers begin telling their graceful centuries-old stories. It's a cultural scene out of the past come to life once again—for Hawaii is enjoying a renaissance of hula, chant, and other aspects of its ancient culture.

The biggest, longest, and most elaborate celebrations of Hawaiian culture are the Aloha Festivals, which encompass more than 500 cultural events from August to October. "Our goal is to teach and share our culture,"

Maui's Aloha Festival.

says Gloriann Akau, a former manager of the Aloha Festivals. "In 1946, after the war, Hawaiians needed an identity. We were lost and needed to regroup. When we started to celebrate our culture, we began to feel proud. We have a wonderful culture that had been buried for a number of years. This brought it out again. Self-esteem is more important than making a lot of money."

In 1985, native Hawaiian educator, author, and *kupuna* (respected elder) George Kanahele started integrating Hawaiian values into hotels like Maui's Kaanapali Beach Hotel. "You have the responsibility to preserve and enhance the Hawaiian culture, not because it's going to make money for you, but because it's the right thing to do," Kanahele told the Hawaii Hotel Association. "Ultimately, the only thing unique about Hawaii is its Hawaiianess. Hawaiianess is our competitive edge."

From general managers to maids, resort employees went through hours of Hawaiian cultural training. They held focus groups to discuss the meaning of aloha—the Hawaiian concept of unconditional love—and applied it to their work and their lives. Now many hotels have joined the movement and instituted Hawaiian programs. No longer content with teaching hula as a joke, resorts now employ a real *kumu hula* (hula teacher) to instruct visitors and have a *kupuna* (elder) take guests on treks to visit *heiau* (temples) and ancient petroglyph sites.

THE QUESTION OF SOVEREIGNTY The Hawaiian cultural renaissance has also made its way into politics. Many *kanaka maoli* (native people) are demanding restoration of rights taken away more than a century ago when the U.S. overthrew the Hawaiian monarchy. Their demands were not lost on President Bill Clinton, who was picketed at a Democratic political fundraiser at Waikiki Beach in July 1993. Four months later, Clinton signed a document stating that the U.S. Congress "apologizes to Native Hawaiians on behalf of the people of the United States for the overthrow of the Kingdom of

Hawaii on January 17, 1893, with the participation of agents and citizens of the United States, and deprivation of the rights of Native Hawaiians to self-determination."

But even neo-nationalists aren't convinced that complete self-determination is possible. Each of the 30 identifiable sovereignty organizations (and more than 100 splinter groups) has a different stated goal, ranging from total independence to nation-within-a-nation status, similar to that of Native Indians. In 1993, the state legislature created a Hawaiian Sovereignty Advisory Commission to "determine the will of the native Hawaiian people." The commission plans to pose the sovereignty question in a referendum open to all persons over age 18 with Hawaiian blood, no matter where they live. The question still remains unanswered.

LOOKING BACK AT MAUI

Paddling outrigger canoes, the first ancestors of today's Hawaiians followed the stars and birds across the sea to Hawaii, which they called "the land of raging fire." Those first settlers were part of the great Polynesian migration that settled the vast triangle of islands stretching between New Zealand, Easter Island, and Hawaii. No one is sure exactly when they came to Hawaii from Tahiti and the Marquesas Islands, some 2,500 miles to the south, but a bone fishhook found at the southernmost tip of the Big Island has been carbon-dated to A.D. 700. Chants claim that the Mookini Heiau, also on the Big Island, was built in A.D. 480. Some recent archaeological digs at Maluuluolele Park in Lahaina even predate that.

All we have today are some archaeological finds, some scientific data, and ancient chants to tell the story of Hawaii's past. The chants, especially the *Kumulipo,* which is the chant of creation and the litany of genealogy of the *alii* (high-ranking chiefs) who ruled the islands, talk about comings and goings between Hawaii and the islands of the south, presumed to be Tahiti. In fact, the channel between Maui, Kahoolawe, and Lanai is called *Kealaikahiki,* or "the pathway to Tahiti."

Around 1300, the transoceanic voyages stopped for some reason, and Hawaii began to develop its own culture in earnest. The settlers built temples, fish ponds, and aqueducts to irrigate taro plantations. Sailors became farmers and fishermen. Each island was a separate kingdom. The *alii* created a caste system and established taboos. Violators were strangled. High priests asked the gods Lono and Ku for divine guidance. Ritual human sacrifices were common.

Maui's history, like that of the rest of Hawaii, was one of wars and conquests, with one king taking over another king's land. The rugged terrain of Maui and the water separating Maui, Molokai, Lanai, and Kahoolawe made for natural boundaries of kingdoms. In the early years, there were three kingdoms on Maui: Hana, Waikulu, and Lahaina. The chants are not just strict listings of family histories. Some describe how a ruler's pride and arrogance can destroy a community. For example, according to the chants, Hana's King Hua killed a priest in the 12th century, and as a result the gods sent a severe drought to Hana as a punishment.

Three centuries later, another ruler came out of Hana who was to change the course of Maui's history: Piilani, the first ruler to unite all of Maui. His rule was a time not only of peace but also of community construction projects. Piilani built fish ponds and irrigation fields and began creating a paved road some 4 to 6 feet wide around the entire island. Piilani's sons and grandson continued these projects and completed the *Alalou,* the royal road that circled the united island. They also completed Hawaii's largest *heiau* (temple) to the god of war, Piilanihale, which still stands today.

Maui was a part of a pivotal change in Hawaii's history: After conquering Maui in 1795, Kamehameha united all of the islands into one kingdom. It started in 1759, when yet another battle over land was going on. This time Kalaniopuu, a chief from the Big Island, had captured Hana from the powerful Maui chief Kahikili. Kahikili was busy overtaking Molokai when the Big Island chief stole Hana from him. The Molokai chief escaped and fled with his wife to Hana, where the Big Island chief welcomed him. A few years later, the Molokai chief and his wife had a baby girl in Hana, named Kaahumanu, who later married Kamehameha.

THE "FATAL CATASTROPHE" No ancient Hawaiian ever imagined a *haole* (a white person; literally, one with "no breath") would ever appear on one of these "floating islands." But then one day in 1778, just such a person sailed into Waimea Bay on Kauai, where he was welcomed as the god Lono.

The man was 50-year-old Capt. James Cook, already famous in Britain for "discovering" much of the South Pacific. Now on his third great voyage of exploration, Cook had set sail from Tahiti northward across uncharted waters to find the mythical Northwest Passage that was said to link the Pacific and Atlantic oceans. On his way, Cook stumbled upon the Hawaiian Islands quite by chance. He named them the Sandwich Islands, for the Earl of Sandwich, first lord of the admiralty, who had bankrolled the expedition.

Overnight, Stone Age Hawaii entered the age of iron. Nails were traded for fresh water, pigs, and the affections of Hawaiian women. The sailors brought syphilis, measles, and other diseases to which the Hawaiians had no natural immunity, thereby unwittingly wreaking havoc on the native population.

After his unsuccessful attempt to find the Northwest Passage, Cook returned to Kealakekua Bay on the Big Island, where a fight broke out over an alleged theft, and the great navigator was killed by a blow to the head. After this "fatal catastrophe," the British survivors sailed home. But Hawaii was now on

The Mookini Heiau.

Captain James Cook.

Captain Cook monument at Kealakekua Bay.

the sea charts, and traders on the fur route between Canada and China anchored in Hawaii to get fresh water. More trade—and more disastrous liaisons—ensued.

Two more sea captains left indelible marks on the islands. The first was American John Kendrick, who in 1791 filled his ship with sandalwood and sailed to China. By 1825, Hawaii's sandalwood forests were gone, enabling invasive plants to take charge. The second captain was Englishman George Vancouver, who in 1793 left cows and sheep, which spread out to the high-tide lines. King Kamehameha I sent for cowboys from Mexico and Spain to round up the wild livestock, thus beginning the islands' *paniolo* (cowboy) tradition.

The tightly woven Hawaiian society began to unravel after the death in 1819 of King Kamehameha I, who had used guns seized from a British ship to unite the islands under his rule. One of his successors, Queen Kaahumanu, abolished old taboos, such as that of women eating with men, and opened the door for religion of another form when she converted to Christianity.

STAYING TO DO WELL In 1819, the first whaling ship dropped anchor in Lahaina. Sailors on the *Bellina* were looking for fresh water and supplies, but they found beautiful women, mind-numbing grog, and a tropical paradise. A few years later, in 1823, the whalers met rivals for this hedonistic playground: the missionaries. The God-fearing missionaries arrived from New England bent on converting the pagans. They chose Lahaina because it was the capital of Hawaii.

Intent on instilling their brand of rock-ribbed Christianity in the islands, the missionaries clothed the natives, banned them from dancing the hula, and nearly dismantled their ancient culture. They tried to keep the whalers and sailors out of the bawdy houses, where a flood of whiskey quenched fleet-size thirsts and where the virtue of native women was never safe.

IS EVERYONE hawaiian IN HAWAII?

The plantations brought so many different people to Hawaii that the state is now a rainbow of ethnic groups: Living here are Caucasians, African Americans, American Indians, Eskimos, Japanese, Chinese, Filipinos, Koreans, Tahitians, Vietnamese, Hawaiians, Samoans, Tongans, and other Asian and Pacific Islanders. Add a few Canadians, Dutch, English, French, Germans, Irish, Italians, Portuguese, Scottish, Puerto Ricans, and Spaniards. Everyone's a minority here.

In combination, it's a remarkable potpourri. Many people retain an element of the traditions of their homeland. Some Japanese Americans in Hawaii, generations removed from the homeland, are more traditional than the Japanese of Tokyo. And the same is true of many Chinese, Koreans, Filipinos, and others, making Hawaii a kind of living museum of various Asian and Pacific cultures.

The missionaries taught reading and writing, created the 12-letter Hawaiian alphabet, started a printing press in Lahaina, and began writing the islands' history, which until then had existed only as an oral account in memorized chants. They also started the first school in Lahaina, which still exists today: the Lahainaluna High School.

Children of the missionaries became the islands' business leaders and politicians. They married Hawaiians and stayed on in the islands, causing one wag to remark that the missionaries "came to do good and stayed to do well."

In Lahaina's heyday, some 500 whaling ships a year dropped anchor in the Lahaina Roadstead. In 1845, King Kamehameha III moved the capital of Hawaii from Lahaina to Honolulu, where more commerce could be accommodated in the natural harbor there. Some whaling ships started skipping Lahaina for the larger port of Honolulu. Fifteen years later, the depletion of whales and the emergence of petroleum as a more suitable oil signaled the beginning of the end of the whaling industry.

KING SUGAR EMERGES When the capital of Hawaii moved to Honolulu, Maui might have taken a back seat in Hawaii's history had it not been for the beginning of a new industry: sugar. In 1849, George Wilfong, a cantankerous sea captain, built a mill in Hana and planted some 60 acres of sugar cane, creating Hawaii's first sugar plantation. At that time, the gold rush was on in California, and sugar prices were wildly inflated. Wilfong's harsh personality and the demands he placed on plantation workers did not sit well with the Hawaiians. In 1852, he imported Chinese immigrants to work in his fields. By the end of the 1850s, the gold rush had begun to diminish, and the inflated sugar prices dropped. When Wilfong's mill burned down, he finally called it quits.

Sugar production continued in Hana, however. In 1864, two Danish brothers, August and Oscar Unna, started the Hana Plantation. Four years later they imported Japanese immigrants to work the fields.

Some 40 miles away, in Haiku, two sons of missionaries, Samuel Alexander and Henry Baldwin, planted 12 acres of this new crop. The next year, Alexander and Baldwin added some 5,000 acres in Maui's central

Working the fields at a sugar plantation.

plains and started Hawaii's largest sugar company. They quickly discovered that without the copious amounts of rainfall found in Hana, they would need to get water to their crop, or it would fail. In 1876, they constructed an elaborate ditch system that brought water from rainy Haiku some 17 miles away to the dry plains of Wailuku, a move that cemented the future of sugar in Hawaii.

Around the same time, another sugar pioneer, Claus Spreckels, bought up property in the arid desert of Puunene from Hawaiians who sold him the "cursed" lands at a very cheap price. The Hawaiians were sure they had gotten the better part of the deal because they believed that the lands were haunted.

Spreckels was betting that these "cursed" lands could be very productive if he could get water rights up in the rainy hills and bring that water to Puunene, just as Alexander and Baldwin had done. But first he needed that water. Thus began a series of late-night poker games with the then-king Kalakaua. Spreckels's gamble paid off: Not only did he beat the king at poker (some say he cheated), but he also built the elaborate 30-mile Haiku Ditch system, which transported 50 million gallons of water a day from rainy Haiku to dry Puunene.

The big boost to sugar, not only on Maui but also across the entire state, came in 1876, when King Kalakaua negotiated the Sugar Reciprocity Treaty with the United States, giving the Hawaiian sugar industry a "sweet" deal on prices and tariffs.

In 1891, King Kalakaua visited chilly San Francisco, caught a cold, and died in the royal suite of the Sheraton Palace. His sister, Queen Liliuokalani, assumed the throne.

A SAD FAREWELL On January 17, 1893, a group of American sugar planters and missionary descendants, with the support of U.S. Marines, imprisoned Queen Liliuokalani in her own palace, where she later penned the sorrowful lyric "Aloha Oe," Hawaii's song of farewell. The monarchy was dead.

A new republic was established, controlled by Sanford Dole, a powerful sugar-cane planter. In 1898, through annexation, Hawaii became an American territory ruled by Dole. His fellow sugar-cane planters, known as the Big Five, controlled banking, shipping, hardware, and every other facet of economic life on the islands.

Planters imported more contract laborers from Puerto Rico (in 1900), Korea (in 1903), and the Philippines (1907–31). Most of the new immigrants stayed on to establish families and become a part of the islands. Meanwhile, the native Hawaiians became a landless minority in their homeland.

For nearly a century on Hawaii, sugar was king, generously subsidized by the U.S. federal government. The sugar planters dominated the territory's economy, shaped its social fabric, and kept the islands in a colonial plantation era with bosses and field hands.

WORLD WAR II & ITS AFTERMATH On December 7, 1941, Japanese Zeros came out of the rising sun to bomb American warships based at Pearl Harbor, on the island of Oahu. This was the "day of infamy" that plunged the United States into World War II.

The attack brought immediate changes to the islands. Martial law was declared, stripping the Big Five cartel of its absolute power in a single day. Japanese Americans and German Americans were interned. Hawaii was "blacked out" at night, Waikiki Beach was strung with barbed wire, and Aloha Tower was painted in camouflage.

During the postwar years, the men of Hawaii returned after seeing another, bigger world outside of plantation life and rebelled. Throwing off the mantle of plantation life, the workers struck for higher wages and improved working conditions. Within a few short years after the war, the white, Republican leaders who had ruled since the overthrow of the monarchy were voted out of office, and labor leaders in the Democratic Party were suddenly in power.

ABOVE: **King Kalakaua hosts a luau for Robert Louis Stevenson, around 1899.**

RIGHT: **Queen Liliuokalani.**

The attack at Pearl Harbor was the "day of infamy" that plunged the United States into World War II.

TOURISM & STATEHOOD In 1959, Hawaii became the last star on the Stars and Stripes, the 50th state of the union. But that year also saw the arrival of the first jet airliners, which brought 250,000 tourists to the fledgling state.

Tourism had already started on Maui shortly after World War II, when Paul I. Fagan, an entrepreneur from San Francisco who had bought the Hana Sugar Co., became the town's angel.

Fagan wanted to retire to Hana, so he focused his business acumen on this tiny town with big problems. Years ahead of his time, he thought tourism might have a future in Hana, so he built a small six-room inn, called Kauiki Inn, which later became the Hotel Hana-Maui. When he opened it in 1946, he said it was for first-class, wealthy travelers (just like his friends). Not only did his friends come, but he also pulled off a public-relations coup that is still talked about today. Fagan owned a baseball team, the San Francisco Seals. He figured they needed a spring-training area, so why not use Hana? He brought out the entire team to train in Hana, and, more important, he brought

Pidgin: 'Eh Fo' Real, Brah

If you venture beyond the tourist areas, you might hear another local tongue: pidgin English, a conglomeration of slang and words from the Hawaiian language. "Broke da mouth" (tastes really good) is the favorite pidgin phrase and one you might hear; "'Eh fo' real, brah" means "It's true, brother." You could be invited to hear an elder "talk story" (relating myths and memories). But because pidgin is really the province of the locals, your visit to Hawaii is likely to pass without your hearing much pidgin at all.

Almost everyone here speaks English. But many folks in Hawaii now speak Hawaiian as well. All visitors will hear the words *aloha* and *mahalo* (thank you). If you've just arrived, you're a *malihini*. Someone who's been here a long time is a *kamaaina*. When you finish a job or your meal, you are *pau* (finished). On Friday it's *pau hana*, work finished. You eat *pupu* (Hawaii's version of hors d'oeuvres) when you go *pau hana*.

The Hawaiian alphabet, created by the New England missionaries, has only 12 letters: the five regular vowels (*a, e, i, o,* and *u*) and seven consonants (*h, k, l, m, n, p,* and *w*). The vowels are pronounced in the Roman fashion: that is, *ah, ay, ee, oh,* and *oo* (as in "too")— not *ay, ee, eye, oh,* and *you,* as in English. For example, *huhu* is pronounced *who-who.* Most vowels are sounded separately, though some are pronounced together, as in Kalakaua: Kah-lah-*cow*-ah.

Following are some basic Hawaiian words that you'll often hear in Hawaii and see throughout this book. For a more complete list of Hawaiian words, go to **http://hawaiiandictionary.hisurf.com.**

alii	Hawaiian royalty
aloha	greeting or farewell
halau	school
hale	house or building
heiau	Hawaiian temple or place of worship
kahuna	priest or expert
kamaaina	old-timer
kapa	tapa, bark cloth
kapu	taboo, forbidden
keiki	child
kupuna	respected elder
lanai	porch or veranda
lomilomi	massage
mahalo	thank you
makai	a direction, toward the sea
mana	spirit power
mauka	a direction, toward the mountains
muumuu	loose-fitting gown or dress
ono	delicious
pali	cliff
paniolo	Hawaiian cowboy(s)
wiki	quick

A Hawaiian tourism poster promotes United Airlines' service to Hawaii.

out the sportswriters. The sportswriters penned glowing reports about the town, and one writer gave the town a name that stuck: "Heavenly Hana."

However, it would be another 3 decades before Maui became a popular visitor destination in Hawaii. Waikiki was king in the tourism industry, seeing some 16,000 visitors a year by the end of the 1960s, and some four million a year by the end of the 1970s. In 1960, Amfac, owner of Pioneer Sugar Co., looked at the area outside of Lahaina that was being used to dump sugar-cane refuse and saw another use for the beachfront land. The company decided to build a manicured, planned luxury resort in the Kaanapali area. They built it, and people came.

A decade later, Alexander & Baldwin, now the state's largest sugar company, looked at the arid land they owned south of Kihei and also saw possibilities: The resort destination of Wailea was born.

By the mid-1970s, some one million visitors a year were coming to Maui. Ten years later, the number was up to two million.

At the beginning of the 21st century, the visitor industry replaced agriculture as Maui's number-one industry. Maui is the second-largest visitor destination in Hawaii. For 13 years in a row, the readers of *Condé Nast Traveler* and *Travel + Leisure* magazines have voted Maui the "Best Island in the World."

Hawaii was at record-breaking visitor counts (6.9 million) in 2000. Then September 11, 2001, sent a blow to Hawaii—tourism dropped abruptly, sending Hawaii's economy into a tailspin. But people eventually started traveling again, and in 2003, visitor arrivals were up to 6.3 million. By 2005, Hawaii's economy was recovering, the number of visitors to the state shot up to 6.75 million, business was booming in construction, and real-estate sales were higher than ever.

Just 3 years later, the economic pendulum swung the opposite way. Real estate in Hawaii, as on the mainland, dropped in value and sales plummeted. A record number of visitors, some nine million, had come to Hawaii in 2007, but the economic downturn in 2008 saw the closure of Aloha Airlines (which had served Hawaii for 61 years before closing) and ATA Airlines, as well as the shutting down of all operations (both cattle ranch and visitor accommodations) of Molokai Ranch, that island's largest employer and land owner.

After more than a decade in the new century, Maui is still climbing out of the recession and the tourism industry has not yet recovered to its former healthy state.

THE LAY OF THE LAND

The first Hawaiian islands were born of violent volcanic eruptions that took place deep beneath the ocean's surface about 70 million years ago—more than 200 million years after the major continental landmasses had been formed. As soon as the islands emerged, Mother Nature's fury began to carve beauty from barren rock. Untiring volcanoes spewed forth rivers of fire that cooled into stone. Severe tropical storms, some with hurricane-force winds, battered and blasted the cooling lava rock into a series of shapes. Ferocious earthquakes flattened, shattered, and reshaped the islands into precipitous valleys, jagged cliffs, and recumbent flatlands. Monstrous surf and gigantic tidal waves rearranged and polished the lands above and below the reaches of the tide.

It took millions of years for nature to shape the familiar form of Diamond Head on Oahu, Maui's majestic peak of Haleakala, the waterfalls of Molokai's northern side, the reefs of Hulopoe Bay on Lanai, and the lush rainforests of the Big Island. The result is an island chain like no other—a tropical dreamscape of a landscape rich in flora and fauna, surrounded by a vibrant underwater world.

The Flora of the Islands

Hawaii is filled with sweet-smelling flowers, lush vegetation, and exotic plant life.

African Tulip Trees Even from afar, you can see the flaming red flowers on these large trees, which can grow to be more than 50 feet tall. The buds hold water, and Hawaiian children use the flowers as water pistols.

Angel's Trumpets These small trees can grow up to 20 feet tall, with an abundance of large (up to 10-in. diameter) pendants—white or pink flowers that resemble, well, trumpets. The Hawaiians call them *nana-honua,* which means "earth gazing." The flowers, which bloom continually from early spring to late fall, have a musky scent. ***Warning:*** All parts of the plant are poisonous and contain a strong narcotic.

Anthuriums Anthuriums originally came from the tropical Americas and the Caribbean islands. There are more than 550 species, but the most popular are the heart-shaped red, orange, pink, white, and purple flowers with tail-like spathes. Look for the heart-shaped green leaves in shaded areas. These exotic plants have no scent but will last several weeks as cut flowers. Anthuriums are particularly prevalent on the Big Island.

Banyan Trees Among the world's largest trees, banyans have branches that grow out and away from the trunk, forming descending roots that grow down to the ground to feed and form additional trunks, making the tree very stable during tropical storms. The banyan in the courtyard next to the old courthouse in Lahaina, Maui, is an excellent example of a spreading banyan—it covers ⅔ acre.

Birds-of-Paradise These natives of Africa have become something of a trademark of Hawaii. They're easily recognizable by the orange and blue flowers nestled in gray-green bracts, looking somewhat like birds in flight.

Bougainvillea Originally from Brazil, these vines feature colorful, tissue-thin bracts, ranging in color from majestic purple to fiery orange, that hide tiny white flowers.

Breadfruit Trees A large tree—more than 60 feet tall—with broad, sculpted, dark-green leaves, the famous breadfruit produces a round, head-size green fruit that's a staple in the diets of all Polynesians. When roasted or baked, the whitish-yellow meat tastes somewhat like a sweet potato.

Bromeliads There are more than 1,400 species of bromeliads, of which the pineapple plant is the best known. "Bromes," as they're affectionately called, are generally spiky plants ranging in size from a few inches to several feet in diameter. They're popular not only for their unusual foliage, but also for their strange and wonderful flowers. Used widely in landscaping and interior decoration, especially in resort areas, bromeliads are found on every island.

Coffee Hawaii is the only state that produces coffee commercially. Coffee is an evergreen shrub with shiny, waxy, dark-green pointed leaves. The flower is a small, fragrant white blossom that develops into ½-inch berries that turn bright red when ripe. Look for coffee at elevations above 1,500 feet on the Kona side of the Big Island and on large coffee plantations on Kauai, Molokai, Oahu, and Maui.

Ginger White and yellow ginger flowers are perhaps the most fragrant in Hawaii. Usually found in clumps growing 4 to 7 feet tall in areas blessed by rain, these sweet-smelling, 3-inch-wide flowers are composed of three dainty petal-like stamens and three long, thin petals. Ginger was introduced to Hawaii in the 19th century from the Indonesia-Malaysia area. Look for white and yellow ginger from late spring to fall. If you see ginger on the side of the road, stop and pick a few blossoms—your car will be filled with a divine fragrance the rest of the day.

Other members of the ginger family frequently seen in Hawaii include red, shell, and torch ginger. Red ginger consists of tall green stalks with foot-long red "flower heads." The red "petals" are actually bracts, which protect the 1-inch-long white flowers. Red ginger, which does not share the heavenly smell of white ginger, lasts a week or longer when cut. Look for red ginger from spring through late fall. Shell ginger, which originated in India and Burma, thrives in cool, wet mountain forests. These plants, with their pearly white, clamshell-like blossoms, bloom from spring to fall.

Perhaps the most exotic ginger is the red or pink torch ginger. Cultivated in Malaysia as seasoning, torch ginger rises directly out of the ground. The flower stalks, which are about 5 to 8 inches in length, resemble the fire of a lighted torch. This is one of the few types of ginger that can bloom year-round.

Heliconia Some 80 species of the colorful heliconia family came to Hawaii from the Caribbean and Central and South America. The bright yellow, red, green, and orange bracts overlap and appear to unfold like origami birds. The most obvious heliconia to spot is the lobster claw, which resembles a string of boiled crustacean pincers. Another prolific heliconia is the parrot's beak: Growing to about hip height, it's composed of bright-orange flower bracts with black tips. Look for parrot's beaks in spring and summer.

Hibiscus The 4- to 6-inch hibiscus flowers bloom year-round and come

Hawaiian coffee beans.

in a range of colors, from lily white to lipstick red. The flowers resemble crepe paper, with stamens and pistils protruding spirelike from the center. Hibiscus hedges can grow up to 15 feet tall. The yellow hibiscus is Hawaii's official state flower.

Jacaranda Beginning around March and sometimes lasting until early May, these huge lacy-leaved trees metamorphose into large clusters of spectacular lavender-blue sprays. The bell-shaped flowers drop quickly, leaving a majestic purple carpet beneath the tree.

Macadamia A transplant from Australia, macadamia nuts have become a commercial crop in recent decades in Hawaii, especially on the Big Island and Maui. The large trees—up to 60 feet tall—bear a hard-shelled nut encased in a leathery husk, which splits open and dries when the nut is ripe.

Monkeypod Trees The monkeypod is one of Hawaii's most majestic trees; it grows more than 80 feet tall and 100 feet across. Seen near older homes and in parks, the leaves of the monkeypod drop in February and March. Its wood is a favorite of woodworking artisans.

Hibiscus.

Plumeria.

Night-Blooming Cereus Look along rock walls for this spectacular night-blooming flower. Originally from Central America, this vinelike member of the cactus family has green scalloped edges and produces foot-long white flowers that open as darkness falls and wither as the sun rises. The plant also bears an edible red fruit.

Orchids To many minds, nothing says Hawaii more than orchids. The most widely grown variety—and the major source of flowers for leis and garnish for tropical libations—is the vanda orchid. The vandas used in Hawaii's commercial flower industry are generally lavender or white, but they grow in a rainbow of colors, shapes, and sizes. The orchids used for corsages are the large, delicate cattleya; the ones used in floral arrangements—you'll probably see them in your hotel lobby—are usually dendrobiums.

Pandanus (Hala) Called *hala* by Hawaiians, pandanus is native to Polynesia. Thanks to its thick trunk, stiltlike supporting roots, and crown of long, swordlike leaves, the hala tree is easy to recognize. In what is quickly becoming a dying art, Hawaiians weave the *lau* (leaves) of the hala into hats, baskets, mats, bags, and the like.

Plumeria Also known as frangipani, this sweet-smelling, five-petal flower, found in clusters on trees, is the most popular choice of lei makers. The Singapore plumeria has five creamy-white petals, with a touch of yellow in the center. Another popular variety, ruba—with flowers from soft pink to flaming red—is also used in leis. When picking plumeria, be careful of the sap from the flower—it's poisonous and can stain clothes.

Protea Originally from South Africa, this unusual oversize shrub comes in more than 40 different varieties. The flowers of one species resemble pincushions; those of another look like a bouquet of feathers. Once dried, proteas will last for years.

Silversword This very uncommon and unusual plant is seen only on the Big Island and in the Haleakala Crater on Maui. The rare relative of the sunflower family blooms between July and September. The silversword in bloom is a fountain of red-petaled, daisylike flowers that turn silver soon after blooming.

Taro Around pools, near streams, and in neatly planted fields, you'll see these green heart-shaped leaves, whose dense roots are a Polynesian staple. The ancient Hawaiians pounded the roots into poi. Originally from Sri Lanka, taro not only is a food crop, but is also grown for ornamental reasons.

The Fauna of the Islands

When the first Polynesians arrived in Hawaii between A.D. 500 and 800, scientists say they found some 67 varieties of endemic Hawaiian birds, a third of which are now believed to be extinct. They did not find any reptiles, amphibians, mosquitoes, lice, fleas, or even a cockroach.

There were only two endemic mammals: the hoary bat and the monk seal. The **hoary bat** must have accidentally blown to Hawaii at some point, from either North or South America. It can still be seen during its early evening forays, especially around the Kilauea Crater on the Big Island.

The **Hawaiian monk seal,** a relative of warm-water seals found in the Caribbean and the Mediterranean, was nearly slaughtered into extinction for its skin and oil during the 19th century. These seals have recently experienced a minor population explosion; sometimes they even turn up at various beaches throughout the state. They're protected under federal law by the Marine Mammals Protection Act. If you're fortunate enough to see a monk seal, just look; don't disturb one of Hawaii's living treasures.

Protea.

Aeo, or Hawaiian stilt.

Pueo.

The first Polynesians brought a few animals from home: dogs, pigs, and chickens (all were for eating), as well as rats (stowaways). All four species are still found in the Hawaiian wild today.

BIRDS

More species of native birds have become extinct in Hawaii in the last 200 years than anywhere else on the planet. Of 67 native species, 23 are extinct and 30 are endangered. Even the Hawaiian crow, the **alala,** is threatened.

The **aeo,** or Hawaiian stilt—a 16-inch-long bird with a black head, black coat, white underside, and long pink legs—can be found in protected wetlands such as the Kanaha Wildlife Sanctuary (where it shares its natural habitat with the Hawaiian coot) and Kealia Pond on Maui.

The **nene** is Hawaii's state bird. It's being brought back from the brink of extinction through strenuous protection laws and captive breeding. A relative of the Canada goose, the nene stands about 2 feet high and has a black head and yellow cheeks. The approximately 500 nene in existence can be seen in only three places: on Maui at Haleakala National Park, on the Big Island at Mauna Kea State Recreation Area bird sanctuary, and on the slopes of Mauna Kea.

The Hawaiian short-eared owl, the **pueo,** which grows to between 12 and 17 inches, can be seen at dawn and dusk. According to legend, spotting a pueo is a good omen.

SEA LIFE

Approximately 680 species of fish are known to inhabit the waters

> ### Leapin' Lizards!
>
> **Geckos** are harmless, soft-skinned, insect-eating lizards that come equipped with suction pads on their feet, enabling them to climb walls and windows to reach tasty insects such as mosquitoes and cockroaches. You'll see them on windows outside a lighted room at night or hear their cheerful chirp.

around the Hawaiian Islands. Of those, approximately 450 species stay close to the reef and inshore areas.

Coral The reefs surrounding Hawaii are made up of various coral and algae. The living coral grows through sunlight that feeds specialized algae, which, in turn, allow the development of the coral's calcareous skeleton. The reef, which takes thousands of years to develop, attracts and supports fish and crustaceans, which use it for food and habitat. Mother Nature can batter the reef with a strong storm, but humans have proven far more destructive.

The corals most frequently seen in Hawaii are hard, rocklike formations named for their familiar shapes: antler, cauliflower, finger, plate, and razor coral. Some coral appears soft, such as tube coral; it can be found in the ceilings of caves. Black coral, which resembles winter-bare trees or shrubs, is found at depths of more than 100 feet.

Reef Fish Of the approximately 450 types of reef fish here, about 27% are native to Hawaii and are found nowhere else in the world. During the millions of years it took for the islands to sprout up from the sea, ocean currents—mainly from Southeast Asia—carried thousands of marine animals and plants to Hawaii's reef; of those, approximately 100 species adapted and thrived. You're likely to spot one or more of the following fish while underwater.

Angelfish can be distinguished by the spine, located low on the gill plate. These fish are very shy; several species live in colonies close to coral.

Blennies are small, elongated fish, ranging from 2 to 10 inches long, with the majority in the 3- to 4-inch range. Blennies are so small that they can live in tide pools; you might have a hard time spotting one.

Butterflyfish, among the most colorful of the reef fish, are usually seen in pairs (scientists believe they mate for life) and appear to spend most of their day feeding. There are 22 species of butterflyfish, of which three (bluestripe; lemon, or milletseed; and multiband, or pebbled butterflyfish) are endemic. Most butterflyfish have a dark band through the eye and a spot near the tail resembling an eye, meant to confuse their predators (moray eels love to lunch on them).

Moray and **conger eels** are the most common eels seen in Hawaii. Morays are usually docile except when provoked or when there's food around. Unfortunately, some morays have been fed by divers and now associate divers with food; thus, they can become aggressive. But most morays like to keep to themselves. While morays may look menacing, conger eels look downright happy, with big lips and pectoral fins (situated so that they look like big ears) that give them the appearance of a perpetually smiling face. Conger eels have crushing teeth so they can feed on crustaceans; because they're sloppy eaters, they usually live with shrimp and crabs that feed off the crumbs they leave.

Parrotfish, one of the largest and most colorful of the reef fish, can grow up to 40 inches long. They're easy to spot—their front teeth are fused together, protruding like buck teeth that allow them to feed by scraping algae from rocks and coral. The rocks and coral pass through the parrotfish's system, resulting in fine sand. In fact, most of the white sand found in Hawaii is parrotfish waste; one large parrotfish can produce a ton of sand a year. Native parrotfish species include yellowbar, regal, and spectacled.

Scorpion fish are what scientists call "ambush predators": They hide under camouflaged exteriors and ambush their prey. Several kinds sport a venomous dorsal spine. These fish don't have a gas bladder, so when they stop swimming, they sink—that's why you usually find them "resting" on ledges and on the ocean

Parrotfish.

bottom. They're not aggressive, but be very careful where you put your hands and feet in the water so as to avoid those venomous spines.

Surgeonfish, sometimes called *tang,* get their name from the scalpel-like spines located on each side of the body near the base of the tail. Several surgeonfish, such as the brightly colored yellow tang, are boldly colored; others are adorned in more conservative shades of gray, brown, or black. The only endemic surgeonfish—and the most abundant in Hawaiian waters—is the convict tang, a pale white fish with vertical black stripes (like a convict's uniform).

Wrasses are a very diverse family of fish, ranging in length from 2 to 15 inches. Wrasses can change gender from female to male. Some have brilliant coloration that changes as they age. Several types of wrasse are endemic to Hawaii: Hawaiian cleaner, shortnose, belted, and gray (or old woman).

Game Fish Hawaii is known around the globe as *the* place for big-game fish—marlin, swordfish, and tuna. Six kinds of **billfish** are found in the offshore waters around the islands: Pacific blue marlin, black marlin, sailfish, broadbill swordfish, striped marlin, and shortbill spearfish. Hawaii billfish range in size from the 20-pound shortbill spearfish and striped marlin to the 1,805-pound Pacific blue marlin, the largest marlin ever caught with rod and reel in the world.

Tuna ranges in size from small (1 lb. or less) mackerel tuna used as bait (Hawaiians call them *oioi*) to 250-pound yellowfin ahi tuna. Other local species of tuna are big-eye, albacore, kawakawa, and skipjack.

Other types of fish, also excellent for eating, include **mahimahi** (also known as dolphin fish or dorado), in the 20- to 70-pound range; **rainbow runner,** from 15 to 30 pounds; and **wahoo** (ono), from 15 to 80 pounds. Shoreline fishermen are always on the lookout for **trevally** (the state record for a giant trevally is 191 lb.), **bonefish, ladyfish, threadfin, leatherfish,** and **goatfish.** Bottom fishermen pursue a range of **snapper**—red, pink, gray, and others—as well as **sea bass** (the state record is a whopping 563 lb.) and **amberjack** (which weigh up to 100 lb.).

Mahimahi.

Whales Humpback whales are popular visitors who come to Hawaii to mate and calve every year, beginning in November and staying until spring—April or so—when they return to Alaska. On every island, you can take winter whale-watching cruises that will let you observe these magnificent leviathans up close. You can also spot them from shore—humpbacks grow to up to 45 feet long, so when one breaches (jumps out of the water), you can see it for miles.

Humpbacks are among the biggest whales found in Hawaiian waters, but other whales—such as pilot, sperm, false killer, melon-headed, pygmy killer, and beaked—can be seen year-round, especially in the calm waters off the Big Island's Kona Coast.

Sharks Yes, there *are* sharks in Hawaii, but you more than likely won't see one unless you're specifically looking. About 40 different species of sharks inhabit the waters surrounding Hawaii, ranging from the totally harmless whale shark (at 60 ft., the world's largest fish), which has no teeth and is so docile that it frequently lets divers ride on its back, to the not-so-docile, extremely uncommon great white shark. The most common sharks seen in Hawaii are white-tip or gray reef sharks (about 5 ft. long) and black-tip reef sharks (about 6 ft. long).

Hawaii's Ecosystem Problems

Officials at Hawaii Volcanoes National Park on the Big Island saw a potential problem a few decades ago with people taking a few rocks home with them as "souvenirs." To prevent this problem from escalating, the park rangers created a legend that the fiery volcano goddess, Pele, would punish these souvenir-seekers with bad luck. There used to be a display case in the park's visitor center filled with letters from people who had taken rocks from the volcano, relating stories of all the bad luck that followed. Most begged Pele's forgiveness and instructed the rangers to please return the rock to the exact location that was its original home.

Unfortunately, Hawaii's other ecosystem problems can't be handled as easily.

Marine Life Hawaii's beautiful and abundant marine life has attracted so many visitors that they threaten to overwhelm it. A great example of this is **Molokini,** a small crater off the coast of Maui. Twenty-five years ago, one or two small six-passenger boats made the trip once a day to Molokini; today it's not uncommon to sight 20 or more boats, each carrying 20 to 49 passengers, moored inside the tiny crater. One tour operator has claimed that, on some days, it's so crowded that you can actually see a slick of suntan oil floating on the surface of the water.

Hawaii's **reefs** have faced increasing impact over the years as well. Runoff of soil and chemicals from construction, agriculture, and erosion can blanket and choke a reef, which needs sunlight to survive. Human contact with the reef can also upset the ecosystem. Coral, the basis of the reef system, is very fragile; snorkelers and divers grabbing onto it can break off pieces that took decades to form. Feeding the fish can also upset the balance of the ecosystem (not to mention upsetting the digestive systems of the fish). In areas where they're fed, the normally shy reef fish become more aggressive, surrounding divers and demanding food.

Flora The rainforests are among Hawaii's most fragile environments. Any intrusion—from hikers carrying seeds on their shoes to the rooting of wild boars—can upset the delicate balance of these complete ecosystems. In recent years, development has moved closer and closer to the rainforests. On the Big Island, people have protested the invasion of bulldozers and the drilling of geothermal wells in the Wao Kele O Puna rainforest for years.

Fauna The biggest impact on the fauna in Hawaii is the decimation of native birds by feral animals, which have destroyed the bird's habitats, and by mongooses that have eaten the birds' eggs and young. Government officials are vigilant about snakes because of the potential damage they can do to the remaining bird life.

A recent pest introduced to Hawaii is the coqui frog. That loud noise you hear after dark, especially on the eastern side of the Big Island and various parts of Maui, including the Kapalua Resort area and on the windward side of the island, is the cry of the male coqui frog looking for a mate. A native of Puerto Rico, where the frogs are kept in check by snakes, the coqui frog came to Hawaii in some plant material, found no natural enemies, and has spread across the Big Island and Maui. A chorus of several hundred coqui frogs is deafening (it's been measured at 163 decibels, or the noise level of a jet engine from 100 ft.). In some places, like Akaka Falls, on the Big Island, there are so many frogs that they are now chirping during daylight hours.

MAUI IN POPULAR CULTURE

In addition to the books discussed below, you may want to peruse *Frommer's Maui Day by Day.* Those planning an extended trip to Hawaii should check out *Frommer's Honolulu, Waikiki & Oahu; Frommer's Honolulu & Oahu Day by Day; Frommer's Kauai; Frommer's Hawaii;* and *Frommer's Hawaii with Kids* (all published by Wiley Publishing, Inc.).

Books

FICTION

The first book people think about is James A. Michener's *Hawaii* (Fawcett Crest, 1974). This epic novel manages to put the island's history into chronological order, but remember, it is still fiction, and very sanitized fiction, too. For a more contemporary look at life in Hawaii today, one of the best novels is *Shark Dialogues,* by Kiana Davenport (Plume, 1995). The novel tells the story of Pono, the larger-than-life matriarch, and her four daughters of mixed races. Davenport skillfully weaves legends and myths of Hawaii into the "real life" reality that Pono and her family face in the complex Hawaii of today. Lois-Ann Yamanaka uses a very "local" voice and stark depictions of life in the islands in her fabulous novels *Wild Meat and the Bully Burgers* (Farrar, Straus, Giroux, 1996), *Blu's Hanging* (Avon, 1997), and *Heads by Harry* (Avon, 1999).

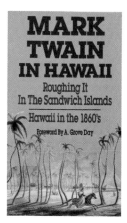

NONFICTION

Mark Twain's writing on Hawaii in the 1860s offers a wonderful introduction to Hawaii's history. One of his best books is *Mark Twain in Hawaii: Roughing It in the Sandwich Islands* (Mutual Publishing, 1990). A great depiction of the Hawaii of 1889 is *Travels in Hawaii,* by Robert Louis Stevenson (University of Hawaii Press, 1973).

For contemporary voices on Hawaii's unique culture, one of the best books to get is *Voices of Wisdom: Hawaiian Elders Speak,* by M. J. Harden (Aka Press, 1999). Some 24 different *kahuna* (experts) in their fields were interviewed about their talent, skill, or artistic practice. These living treasures talk about how Hawaiians of yesteryear viewed nature, spirituality and healing, preservation and history, dance and music, arts and crafts, canoes, and the next generation.

Mark Twain's writing on Hawaii offers a wonderful introduction to Hawaiian history.

Native Planters in Old Hawaii: Their Life, Lore, and Environment (Bishop Museum Press, Honolulu, 2004) was originally published in 1972 but is still one of the most important ethnographic works on traditional Hawaiian culture, portraying the lives of the common folk and their relationship with the land before the arrival of Westerners. This revised edition, with a great index that allows you to find anything, is an excellent resource for anyone interested in Hawaii.

The just-released *Honolulu Stories: Two Centuries of Writing,* edited by Gavan Daws and Bennett Hymer (Mutual Publishing, 2008), is a fascinating 1,000-plus-page book filled with the writings of various authors over the past 200 years. More than 350 selections—ranging from short stories, excerpts from novels, and scenes from plays, musicals, and operas to poems, songs, Hawaiian chants, cartoons, slams, and even stand-up comedy routines—are contained in this must-read for anyone interested in Hawaii. The authors range from Hawaiian kings and queens to Hawaiian chefs and commoners, including some well-known writers (translated from seven different languages)—all telling their own stories about Honolulu.

Flora & Fauna Because Hawaii is so lush with nature and blessed with plants, animals, and reef fish seen nowhere else on the planet, a few reference books can help you identify what you're looking at and make your trip more interesting. In the botanical world, Angela Kay Kepler's *Hawaiian Heritage Plants* (A Latitude 20 Book, University of Hawaii Press, 1998) is the standard for plant reference. In a series of essays, Kepler weaves culture, history, geography, botany, and even spirituality into her vivid descriptions of plants. You'll never look at plants the same way. There are great color photos and drawings to help you sort through the myriad species. Another great resource is *Tropicals,* by Gordon Courtright (Timber Press, 1988), which is filled with color photos identifying everything from hibiscus and heliconia to trees and palms.

The other necessary reference to have in Hawaii is one that identifies the colorful reef fish you will see snorkeling. The best of the bunch is John E. Randall's *Shore Fishes of Hawaii* (University of Hawaii Press, 1998). Two other books on reef-fish identification, with easy-to-use spiral bindings, are *Hawaiian Reef Fish: The Identification Book,* by Casey Mahaney (Blue Kirio Publishing, 1993), and *Hawaiian Reef Fish,* by Astrid Witte and Casey Mahaney (Island Heritage, 1998).

To learn everything you need to identify Hawaii's unique birds, try H. Douglas Pratt's *A Pocket Guide to Hawaii's Birds* (Mutual Publishing, 1996).

For fans of the Hawaiian lei, *Na Lei Makamae: The Treasured Lei,* by Marie McDonald and Paul Weissich (University of Hawaii Press, 2003), is a comprehensive work on this incredible art form. McDonald is one of Hawaii's top lei makers, and Weissich is the director emeritus of Honolulu Botanical Gardens; together they cover some 88 flowers and plants used for leis.

For a complete rundown on where to see the best botanical gardens on Maui (and other Hawaiian islands), get Kevin Whitton's *A Pocket Guide to Hawaii's Botanical Gardens* (Mutual Publishing, 2009).

History   There are many great books on Hawaii's history, but one of the best places to start is with the formation of the Hawaiian Islands, vividly described in David E. Eyre's *By Wind, By Wave: An Introduction to Hawaii's Natural History* (Bess Press, 2000). In addition to chronicling the natural history of Hawaii, Eyre describes the complex interrelationships among the plants, animals, ocean, and people. He points out that Hawaii has become the "extinction capital of the world," but rather than dwelling on that fact, he urges readers to do something about it and carefully spells out how.

For an even more complete tome, get the University of Hawaii Press's *Hawaiian Natural History, Ecology, and Evolution* (2002), by Alan C. Ziegler. Readers can trace the natural history of the Hawaiian archipelago through the book's 28 chapters, or focus on specific topics such as island formation by plate tectonics, plant and animal evolution, flightless birds and their fossil sites, Polynesian migrational history and ecology, the effects of humans and exotic animals on the environment, current conservation efforts, and the contributions of the many naturalists who visited the islands over the centuries and the stories behind their discoveries.

For a history of "precontact" Hawaii (before Westerners arrived), David Malo's *Hawaiian Antiquities* (Bishop Museum Press, 1976) is the preeminent source. Malo was born around 1793 and wrote about the Hawaiian lifestyle at that time, as well as the beliefs and religion of his people. It's an excellent reference book, but not a fast read. For more readable books on old Hawaii, try *Stories of Old Hawaii,* by Roy Kakulu Alameida (Bess Press, 1997), on myths and legends; *Hawaiian Folk Tales,* by Thomas G. Thrum (Mutual Publishing, 1998); and *The Legends and Myths of Hawaii,* by His Hawaiian Majesty King David Kalakaua (Charles E. Tuttle Company, 1992).

The best story of the 1893 overthrow of the Hawaiian monarchy is told by Queen Liliuokalani, in her book *Hawaii's Story by Hawaii's Queen, Liliuokalani* (Mutual Publishing, 1990). When it was written, it was an international plea for justice for her people, but it is a poignant read even today. It's also a must-read for people interested in current events and the recent rally for sovereignty in the 50th state. Two contemporary books on the question of Hawaii's sovereignty are Tom Coffman's *Nation Within: The Story of America's Annexation of the Nation of Hawaii* (Epicenter, 1998) and Thurston Twigg-Smith's *Hawaiian Sovereignty: Do the Facts Matter?* (Goodale, 2000), which explores the opposite view. Twigg-

Smith, former publisher of the statewide newspaper *The Honolulu Advertiser,* is the grandson of Lorrin A. Thurston, one of the architects of the 1893 overthrow of the monarchy. His so-called "politically incorrect" views present a different look on this hotly debated topic.

For more recent history, Lawrence H. Fuchs's *Hawaii Pono* (Bess Press, 1991) is a carefully researched tome on the contributions of each of Hawaii's main immigrant communities (Chinese, Japanese, and Filipino) between 1893 and 1959.

An insightful look at history and its effect on the Hawaiian culture is *Waikiki, A History of Forgetting & Remembering,* by Andrea Feeser (University of Hawaii Press, 2006). A beautiful art book (designed by Gaye Chan), this is not your typical coffee-table book, but a different look at the cultural and environmental history of Waikiki. Using historical texts, photos, government documents, and interviews, this book lays out the story of how Waikiki went from a self-sufficient agricultural area to a tourism mecca, detailing the price that was paid along the way.

Another great cultural book recently released is Davianna Pomaikai McGregor's *Na Kua'aina: Living Hawaiian Culture* (University of Hawaii Press, 2007). I love this book for so many reasons—first, it focuses not on the Hawaiian royalty, but on the common people of Hawaii and how they lived. McGregor, a professor of ethnic studies at UH, examines how people lived in rural lands and how they kept the Hawaiian traditions alive. She describes the cultural significance of each area (the island of Molokai; Hana, Maui; and Puna, HI), the landscape, the Hawaiian gods who lived there, the chants and myths about the area, and how the westernization of the area has changed the land and the Hawaiian people.

Film

My favorite films made in Hawaii but about other places are:

- **Bird of Paradise:** Delmer Daves's 1951 remake of the 1932 film stars Debra Paget as an island princess who falls in love with a visiting Frenchman (Louis Jourdan) against the wishes of the princess's people. It was filmed on the island of Kauai with a new technology called Technicolor.

- **The Devil at Four O'Clock:** Mervyn LeRoy directed this 1961 story about faith and redemption (filmed on Maui), which tells the story of an alcoholic priest (Spencer Tracy) who enlists the aid of three condemned convicts (one played by Frank Sinatra) to help in the rescue of native children threatened by an erupting volcano.

- **Donovan's Reef:** John Ford directed this 1963 John Wayne romantic comedy about two ex-Navy men who remain on a South Seas island (played by Kauai) after World War II. "Guns" Donovan (Wayne) runs the local bar, while Doc Dedham (Jack Warden) has married a local princess. A former shipmate (Lee Marvin) arrives, followed by a high-society Bostonian (Elizabeth Allen).

- **The Enemy Below:** This classic story (released in 1957) of a U.S. destroyer chasing a German submarine during World War II stars Robert Mitchum and Curt Jurgens in the lead roles as the American and German captains. While all of the ocean scenes take place in the North Atlantic, they were actually filmed in Hawaii.

- *Islands in the Stream:* Filmed on Kauai, this 1977 movie tells the story of Ernest Hemingway's last published novel. Set on the island of Bimini in the Caribbean, it is about artist Thomas Hudson's renewed relationship with his three young sons and former wife.

- *Joe Versus the Volcano:* This least well-known of the Tom Hanks/Meg Ryan movies is a romantic comedy filmed in 1990. John Shanley's film tells the tale of a hypochondriac who, when told that he is dying, accepts an offer to throw himself into the volcano of a remote tropical island. En route, however, he learns that there are many reasons to keep on living.

- *Jurassic Park:* Filmed on the islands of Kauai and Oahu, Steven Spielberg's 1993 megahit, which was billed as "an adventure 65 million years in the making," is the story of dinosaurs on the loose at the site of the world's only dinosaur farm and theme park, where creatures from the past are produced using harvested DNA.

- *The Karate Kid, Part II:* In one of those instances where the sequel is actually better than the original, this 1986 movie takes our hero Daniel LaRusso (Ralph Macchio) and his mentor, Mr. Miyagi (Pat Morita), to Miyagi's homeland, Okinawa, to visit his dying father and confront his old rival. An entire Okinawan village was re-created on Oahu's Windward Coast.

- *King Kong:* John Guillermin's 1976 version of the classic story of the great ape and the girl (Jessica Lange) was filmed on parts of Kauai rarely seen by visitors or residents.

- *The Lost World: Jurassic Park:* In Steven Spielberg's 1997 follow-up to *Jurassic Park,* dinosaurs have been bred and then escaped following the abandonment of the project in the first installment. The sequel features much more Hawaiian scenery than the original.

- *Mister Roberts:* John Ford's 1955 comedy-drama, set aboard an insignificant ship stationed in the Pacific during World War II, was nominated for three Academy Awards, including Best Picture. Jack Lemmon won the Oscar for Best Supporting Actor for his role as Ensign Pulver. The film also stars Henry Fonda in the title role and James Cagney as Captain Morton.

- *None But the Brave:* Frank Sinatra directed and starred in this 1965 story of American and Japanese soldiers who, when stranded on a tiny Pacific island during World War II (filmed on Kauai), must make a temporary truce and cooperate to survive. This was the only film directed by Sinatra.

- *Outbreak:* Wolfgang Petersen directed this 1995 tale of a lethal virus that is transported to the United States by an African monkey host. Federal agencies rush to find an antidote before the planet's population is wiped out. The scenes of the African village were filmed near the Wailua River on Kauai.

- *Planet of the Apes:* Tim Burton's 2001 remake of the 1968 science-fiction classic, which starred Charlton Heston, is more faithful to the original Pierre Boulle novel, but also much more dark and sinister. Exterior battle scenes were filmed on lava fields on the Big Island of Hawaii.

- *Raiders of the Lost Ark:* Filmed on Kauai, Steven Spielberg's 1981 film follows archaeologist Indiana Jones on a search for the Ark of the Covenant, which is also sought by the Nazis under orders from Hitler.

- **Six Days Seven Nights:** Ivan Reitman's 1998 adventure-comedy is about a New York magazine editor and a gruff pilot who are forced to put aside their dislike for each other in order to survive after crash-landing on a deserted South Seas island (filmed on Kauai). It stars Harrison Ford and Anne Heche.

- **South Pacific:** The 1958 motion-picture adaptation of the Rodgers and Hammerstein musical was filmed on Kauai. The film has an all-star cast, with Rossano Brazzi and Mitzi Gaynor in the lead roles. It was nominated for three Academy Awards but won only for Best Sound.

- **Uncommon Valor:** Ted Kotcheff's 1983 story tells of a retired Marine colonel (Gene Hackman) who reunites his son's former unit to organize a secret raid on a Vietnamese prison camp, where he hopes to rescue his son and other American MIAs. The climactic scenes set in Laos were filmed on the island of Kauai.

- **The Wackiest Ship in the Army:** Richard Murphy directed this 1960 comedy set during World War II and filmed on Kauai and Oahu. The crew and captain (played by Jack Lemmon) are sent on a secret mission in waters patrolled by the Japanese. The film was based on the true story of a mission ordered by Army Gen. Douglas MacArthur.

- **Waterworld:** Kevin Costner directed and starred in this 1995 film about a future in which the polar ice caps have melted, leaving most of the world's surface deep beneath the oceans. The survivors live poorly on the water's surface, dreaming of finding "dry land." Some of the water scenes were filmed off Kauai. The final and most beautiful scenes in the movie were filmed in the Waipio Valley on the Big Island.

My favorite films made in Hawaii and about Hawaii are:

- **Blue Hawaii:** Chad Gates (Elvis Presley), upon discharge from the Army, returns to Hawaii to enjoy life with his buddies and girlfriend, against the wishes of his parents, who want him to work for the family business. Presley, Joan Blackman, and Angela Lansbury make this 1961 film a classic, with great music and beautiful Hawaiian scenery from the early 1960s.

- **50 First Dates:** This 2004 romantic comedy stars Drew Barrymore and Adam Sandler in a story about a young woman (Barrymore) who has lost her short-term memory in a car accident and who now relives each day as if it were October 13. She follows the same routine

A poster for Elvis Presley's film Blue Hawaii.

every day, until she meets Henry Roth (Sandler), who falls in love with her and seeks a way to forge a long-term relationship.

o **From Here to Eternity:** Fred Zinnemann's 1953 multiple-Oscar winner, set in pre–World War II Hawaii, tells the story of several Army soldiers stationed on Oahu on the eve of Pearl Harbor. The film won Best Picture, Best Supporting Actor (Frank Sinatra), Best Supporting Actress (Donna Reed), and five other awards.

o **Hawaii:** George Roy Hill's 1966 adaptation of the James Michener novel features amazing island scenery and stars Julie Andrews, Max von Sydow, and Richard Harris. It is a great introduction to the early history of Hawaii.

o **Honeymoon in Vegas:** Andrew Bergman's 1992 comedy starring James Caan, Nicolas Cage, Sarah Jessica Parker, and Pat Morita is primarily set in Las Vegas, but has a wonderful segment shot on Kauai at the fictional home of millionaire Tommy Korman (Caan).

o **In Harm's Way:** Otto Preminger's 1965 classic drama of the war in the Pacific focuses on several Navy officers (and the women in their lives) who are suddenly catapulted into the war following the Japanese attack on Pearl Harbor. It stars John Wayne, Kirk Douglas, Patricia Neal, Tom Tryon, and Paula Prentiss.

o **Molokai: The Story of Father Damien:** This 1999 film follows the life of Belgian priest Damien de Veuster from 1872, the year before his arrival in Kalaupapa, through his years ministering to the patients with Hansen's disease at Kalaupapa, until his death at the Molokai settlement in 1889.

o **Pearl Harbor:** Michael Bay's 2001 film depicts the time before, during, and after the December 7, 1941, Japanese attack (with the best re-creation of the Pearl Harbor attack ever put on film) and tells the story of two best friends and the woman they both love.

o **Picture Bride:** Japanese director Kayo Hatta presents this 1995 film about a Japanese woman who travels to Hawaii to marry a man whom she has never met but has seen only through photos and letters. She soon discovers that he is twice her age and that much turmoil awaits her in her new home. Beautifully filmed on the North Shore of

St. Joseph's Church, where Father Damien treated Kalaupapa's leper community.

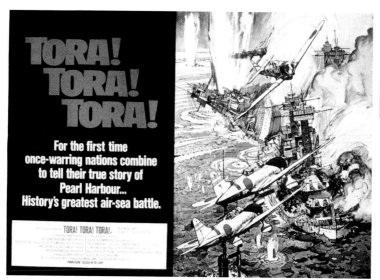

A promotional poster for Tora! Tora! Tora!.

Oahu and the Hamakua Coast of the Big Island, with a special appearance by Toshiro Mifune.

o **Tora! Tora! Tora!:** This 1970 film tells the story of the Japanese attack on Pearl Harbor as seen from both the American and the Japanese perspectives.

Music

Hawaiian music ranges from traditional ancient chants and hula to slack-key guitar, to contemporary rock and a new genre, Jawaiian, a cross of reggae, Jamaican, and Hawaiian. To listen to Hawaiian music, check out Hawaiian 105 (www.hawaiian105.com). Below are my picks for Hawaiian music.

o **Best of the Gabby Band,** by Gabby Pahinui (traditional Hawaiian)

o **Gently Weeps,** by Jake Shimabukuro (contemporary Hawaiian)

o **Hapa,** by Hapa (contemporary Hawaiian)

o **Hawaiian Blossom,** by Raiatea Helm (traditional Hawaiian)

o **Hawaiian Tradition,** by Amy Hanaiali'i Gilliom (traditional Hawaiian)

o **Honolulu City Lights,** by Keola & Kapono Beamer (contemporary Hawaiian)

o **Legends of Hawaiian Slack Key Guitar,** by various artists (a collection of slack-key guitar music and a 2007 Grammy winner)

o **Masters of Hawaiian Slack Key Guitar, Vol. 1,** by various artists (a collection of slack-key guitar music and a 2006 Grammy winner)

o **Na Leo Hawaii Kaniko,** by the Master Chanters of Hawaii (chanting)

o **Na Pua O Hawaii,** by Makaha Sons (contemporary Hawaiian)

o **Wonderful World,** by Israel Kamakawiwo'ole (contemporary Hawaiian)

EATING & DRINKING ON MAUI

Tried & True: Hawaii Regional Cuisine

Peter Merriman, a founding member of Hawaii Regional Cuisine (HRC) and a recipient of the James Beard Award for Best Chef: Northwest/Hawaii (along with George Mavrothalassitis of Chef Mavro Restaurant), describes the current trend in Hawaii as a refinement, a tweaking upward, of everything from fine dining to down-home local cooking. This means sesame- or nori-crusted fresh catch on plate-lunch menus, and *huli-huli* chicken at five-diamond eateries, paired with Beaujolais and leeks and gourmet long rice.

At the same time, says Merriman, HRC, the style of cooking that put Hawaii on the international culinary map, has become watered down, a buzzword: "A lot of restaurants are paying lip service."

As it is with things au courant, it is easy to make a claim but another thing to live up to it. As Merriman points out, HRC was never solely about technique; it is equally about ingredients and the chef's creativity and integrity. "We continue to get local inspiration," says Merriman. "We've never restricted ourselves." If there is a fabulous French or Thai dish, chefs like Merriman will prepare it with local ingredients and add a creative edge that makes it distinctively Hawaii Regional.

HRC was established in the mid-1980s in a culinary revolution that catapulted Hawaii into the global epicurean arena. The international training, creative vigor, fresh ingredients, and cross-cultural menus of the 12 original HRC chefs have made the islands a dining destination applauded nationwide. (In a tip of the toque to island tradition, *ahi*—a word ubiquitous in Hawaii—has replaced *tuna* on many chic New York menus.)

Here's a sampling of what you can expect to find on a Hawaii Regional Cuisine menu: seared Hawaiian fish with *lilikoi* shrimp butter; taro-crab cakes; Pahoa corn cakes; Molokai sweet-potato or breadfruit vichyssoise; Ka'u orange sauce and Kahua Ranch lamb; fern shoots from Waipio Valley; Maui onion soup and Hawaiian bouillabaisse, with fresh snapper, Kona crab, and fresh aquacultured shrimp; blackened ahi summer rolls; herb-crusted onaga; and gourmet Waimanalo greens, picked that day. You may also encounter locally made cheeses, squash and taro risottos, Polynesian *imu*-baked foods, and guava-smoked meats. If there's pasta or risotto or rack of lamb on the menu, it could be nori (red algae) linguine with opihi (limpet) sauce, or risotto with local seafood served in taro cups, or rack of lamb in cabernet and hoisin sauce (fermented soybean, garlic, and spices). Watch for ponzu sauce, too; it's lemony and zesty, much more flavorful than the soy sauce it resembles.

Plate Lunches & More: Local Food

At the other end of the spectrum is the vast and endearing world of "local food." By that, I mean plate lunches and poke, shave ice and saimin, bento lunches and manapua—cultural hybrids all.

Reflecting a polyglot population of many styles and ethnicities, Hawaii's idiosyncratic dining scene is eminently inclusive. Consider surfer chic: Barefoot in the sand, in a swimsuit, you chow down on a **plate lunch** ordered from a lunch wagon, consisting of fried mahimahi, "two scoops rice," macaroni salad, and a few leaves of green, typically julienned cabbage. (Generally, teriyaki beef and shoyu chicken are options.) Heavy gravy is often the condiment of choice, accompanied by a soft drink in a paper cup or straight out of the can. Like **saimin**—the local version of noodles in broth topped with scrambled eggs, green onions, and sometimes pork—the plate lunch is Hawaii's version of high camp.

But it was only a matter of time before the humble plate lunch became a culinary icon in Hawaii. These days, even the most chichi restaurant has a version of this modest island symbol (not at plate-lunch prices, of course), while vendors selling the real thing—carb-driven meals served from wagons—have queues that never end.

Because this is Hawaii, at least a few licks of poi—cooked, pounded taro (the traditional Hawaiian staple crop)—are a must. Other **native foods** include those from before and after Western contact, such as laulau (pork, chicken, or fish steamed in ti leaves), kalua pork (pork cooked in a Polynesian underground oven known here as an *imu*), lomi salmon (salted salmon with tomatoes and green onions), squid luau (cooked in coconut milk and taro tops), poke (cubed raw fish seasoned with onions and seaweed and the occasional sprinkling of roasted kukui nuts), haupia (creamy coconut pudding), and kulolo (steamed pudding of coconut, brown sugar, and taro).

Traditional Hawaiian foods include taro, poi, and kalua pork.

Bento, another popular quick meal available throughout Hawaii, is a compact, boxed assortment of picnic fare usually consisting of neatly arranged sections of rice, pickled vegetables, and fried chicken, beef, or pork. Increasingly, however, the bento is becoming more health conscious, as in macrobiotic or vegetarian brown-rice bentos. A derivative of the modest lunch box for Japanese immigrants who once labored in the sugar and pineapple fields, bentos are dispensed everywhere, from department stores to corner delis and supermarkets.

Also from the plantations comes *manapua,* a bready, doughy sphere filled with tasty fillings of sweetened pork or sweet beans. In the old days, the Chinese "manapua man" would make his rounds with bamboo containers balanced on a rod over his shoulders. Today you'll find white or whole-wheat manapua containing chicken, vegetables, curry, and other savory fillings.

The daintier Chinese delicacy **dim sum** is made of translucent wrappers filled with fresh seafood, pork hash, and vegetables, served for breakfast and lunch in Chinatown restaurants. The Hong Kong–style dumplings are ordered fresh and hot from bamboo steamers rolled on carts from table to table. Much like hailing a taxi in Manhattan, you have to be quick and loud for dim sum.

For dessert or a snack, particularly on Oahu's North Shore, the prevailing choice is **shave ice,** the Island version of a snow cone. Particularly on hot, humid days, long lines of shave-ice lovers gather for heaps of finely shaved ice topped with sweet tropical syrups. (The sweet-sour *li hing mui* flavor is a current favorite.) The fast-melting mounds, which require prompt, efficient consumption, are quite the local summer ritual for sweet tooths. Aficionados order shave ice with ice cream and sweetened adzuki beans plopped in the middle.

Ahi, Ono & Opakapaka: A Hawaiian Seafood Primer

The seafood in Hawaii has been described as the best in the world. And why not? Without a doubt, the islands' surrounding waters, including the waters of the remote northwestern Hawaiian Islands, and a growing aquaculture industry contribute to the high quality of the seafood here.

The reputable restaurants in Hawaii buy fresh fish daily at predawn auctions or from local fishermen. Some chefs even catch their ingredients themselves. "Still wiggling" and "just off the hook" are the ultimate terms for freshness in Hawaii.

Although some menus include the Western description for the fresh fish used, most often the local nomenclature is listed, turning dinner into a confusing, quasiforeign experience for the uninitiated. To help familiarize you with the menu language of Hawaii, here's a basic glossary of Island fish:

ahi   yellowfin or big-eye tuna, important for its use in sashimi and poke at sushi bars and in Hawaii Regional Cuisine

aku   skipjack tuna, heavily used by local families in home cooking and poke

ehu   red snapper, delicate and sumptuous, yet lesser known than opakapaka

hapuupuu   grouper, a sea bass whose use is expanding

hebi   spearfish, mildly flavored, and frequently featured as the "catch of the day" in upscale restaurants

kajiki   Pacific blue marlin, also called *au,* with a firm flesh and high fat content that make it a plausible substitute for tuna

kumu   goatfish, a luxury item on Chinese and upscale menus, served *en papillote* or steamed whole, Oriental style, with scallions, ginger, and garlic

mahimahi   dolphin fish (the game fish, not the mammal) or dorado, a classic sweet, white-fleshed fish requiring vigilance among purists because it's often disguised as fresh when it's actually "fresh-frozen"—a big difference

monchong   bigscale or sickle pomfret, an exotic, tasty fish, scarce but gaining a higher profile on Hawaiian Island menus

nairagi   striped marlin, also called *au,* good as sashimi and in poke, and often substituted for ahi in raw-fish products

onaga   ruby snapper, a luxury fish, versatile, moist, and flaky

ono   wahoo, firmer and drier than the snappers, often served grilled and in sandwiches

opah   moonfish, rich and fatty, and versatile—cooked, raw, smoked, and broiled

opakapaka   pink snapper, light, flaky, and luxurious, suited for sashimi, poaching, sautéing, and baking; the best-known upscale fish

papio   jack trevally, light, firm, and flavorful, and favored in Island cookery

shutome   broadbill swordfish, of beeflike texture and rich flavor

tombo   albacore tuna, with a high fat content, suitable for grilling

uhu   parrotfish, most often encountered steamed, Chinese style

uku   gray snapper of clear, pale-pink flesh, delicately flavored and moist

ulua   large jack trevally, firm-fleshed and versatile

PLANNING YOUR TRIP TO MAUI

aui has so many places to explore, things to do, and sights to see that it's hard to know where to start—that's where I come in. In the pages that follow, I've compiled everything you need to know to plan your ideal trip to Maui: information on airlines, seasons, a calendar of events, how to make camping reservations, and much more (even how to tie the knot).

A couple of suggestions: First, if you can fly direct to Maui (the airport is Kahului and the airport code is OGG), do it! If you fly to Honolulu, you will have a 2-hour layover, and then have to take an interisland plane to Maui (not a great way to start your dream vacation). And second—don't plan to go island-hopping. This is not the Caribbean, where the islands are close together and easy to get to. You can consider going from Maui to either Molokai or Lanai, two close islands. Save the other fabulous Hawaiian islands for another trip; otherwise, you will spend your precious vacation time touring our state airport facilities waiting for your plane.

For additional help in planning your trip and for more on-the-ground resources in Maui, please turn to chapter 13.

WHEN TO GO

Most visitors don't come to Maui when the weather's best in the islands; rather, they come when it's at its worst everywhere else. Thus, the **high season**—when prices are up and resorts are often booked to capacity—is generally from mid-December through March or mid-April. The last 2 weeks of December, in particular, are the prime time for travel to Maui. If you're planning a holiday trip, make your reservations as early as possible, expect crowds, and prepare to pay top dollar for accommodations, car rentals, and airfare.

The **off-season,** when the best rates are available and the islands are less crowded, is spring (mid-Apr to mid-June) and fall (Sept to mid-Dec)—a paradox because these are the best seasons to be in Maui, in terms of reliably great weather. If you're looking to save money, or if you just want to avoid the crowds, this is the time to visit. Hotel rates and airfares tend to be significantly lower, and good packages are often available.

Note: If you plan to come to Maui between the last week in April and early May, be sure you book your accommodations, interisland air reservations, and car rentals in advance. In Japan, the last week of April is called **Golden Week** because three Japanese holidays take place one after the other. Waikiki is especially busy with Japanese tourists during this time, but the neighboring islands also see dramatic increases.

Due to the large number of families traveling in **summer** (June–Aug), you won't get the fantastic bargains of spring and fall. However, you'll still do much better on packages, airfare, and accommodations than you will in the winter months.

PREVIOUS PAGE: **A bird's eye view of Maui.**

Climate

Travel Tip

Because Hawaii lies at the edge of the tropical zone, it techni- cally has only two seasons, both of them warm. There's a dry sea- son that corresponds to **summer** (Apr–Oct) and a rainy season in

Your best bets for total year-round sun are Kihei and Wailea on the south coast, and Lahaina and Kapalua on the west coast of Maui.

winter (Nov–Mar). It rains every day somewhere in the islands any time of the year, but the rainy season sometimes brings enough gray weather to spoil your tanning opportunities. Fortunately, it seldom rains in one spot for more than 3 days straight.

The **year-round temperature** doesn't vary much. At the beach, the aver- age daytime high in summer is 85°F (29°C), while the average daytime high in winter is 78°F (26°C); nighttime lows are usually about 10°F cooler. But how warm it is on any given day really depends on *where* you are on the island.

Each island has a leeward side (the side sheltered from the wind) and a windward side (the side that gets the wind's full force). The **leeward** sides (the west and south) are usually hot and dry, while the **windward** sides (east and north) are generally cooler and moist. When you want arid, sun-baked, desert- like weather, go leeward. When you want lush, wet, junglelike weather, go windward.

Hawaii is also full of **microclimates,** thanks to its interior valleys, coastal plains, and mountain peaks. Kauai's Mount Waialeale is the wettest spot on earth, yet Waimea Canyon, just a few miles away, is almost a desert. On the Big Island, Hilo is one of the wettest cities in the nation, with 180 inches of rainfall a year, but at Puako, only 60 miles away, it rains less than 6 inches a year. If you travel into the mountains, the climate can change from summer to winter in a matter of hours because it's cooler the higher you go. So if the weather doesn't suit you, just go to the other side of the island—or head into the hills.

On rare occasions, the weather can be disastrous, as when Hurricane Iniki crushed Kauai in September 1992 with 225-mph winds. Tsunamis have swept Hilo and the South Shore of Oahu. But those are extreme exceptions. Mostly, one day follows another here in glorious, sunny procession, each quite like the other.

Average Monthly High/Low Temperature, Water Temperature & Precipitation in Lahaina

	JAN	FEB	MAR	APR	MAY	JUNE	JULY	AUG	SEPT	OCT	NOV	DEC
HIGH (°F)	81	80	82	84	85	86	87	88	88	87	85	83
HIGH (°C)	27	27	28	29	29	30	31	31	31	31	29	29
LOW (°F)	66	63	64	65	64	68	69	70	69	69	67	65
LOW (°C)	19	17	18	18	18	20	21	21	21	21	19	18
WATER TEMP. (°F)	75	74	74	75	76	77	78	79	80	79	77	76
WATER TEMP. (°C)	24	23	23	24	24	25	26	26	27	26	25	24
AVG. PRECIP. (IN INCHES)	3.3	2	2	1	0.5	0.1	.02	0.3	0.3	1	2	3

3

PLANNING YOUR TRIP TO MAUI | When to Go

Average Monthly High/Low Temperatures, Water Temperature & Precipitation in Kihei

	JAN	FEB	MAR	APR	MAY	JUNE	JULY	AUG	SEPT	OCT	NOV	DEC
HIGH (°F)	80	81	81	82	86	86	87	87	88	87	84	82
HIGH (°C)	27	27	27	28	30	30	31	31	31	31	29	28
LOW (°F)	63	63	65	66	69	69	66	71	70	69	68	65
LOW (°C)	17	17	18	19	20	21	19	22	21	21	20	18
WATER TEMP. (°F)	75	74	74	75	76	77	78	79	80	79	77	76
WATER TEMP. (°C)	24	23	23	24	24	25	26	26	27	26	25	24
AVG. PRECIP. (IN INCHES)	4	3	2	2	0.6	0.1	0.1	0.3	0.3	1	2	3

Holidays

When Maui observes holidays (especially those over a long weekend), travel between the islands increases, interisland airline seats are fully booked, rental cars are at a premium, and hotels and restaurants are busier.

Federal, state, and county government offices are closed on all federal holidays; for a list, go to "Holidays" in chapter 13.

State and county offices are also closed on local holidays, including Prince Kuhio Day (Mar 26), honoring the birthday of Hawaii's first delegate to the U.S. Congress; King Kamehameha Day (June 11), a statewide holiday commemorating Kamehameha the Great, who united the islands and ruled from 1795 to 1819; and Admissions Day (third Fri in Aug), which honors the admittance of Hawaii as the 50th state on August 21, 1959.

Other special days celebrated in Hawaii by many people but which involve no closing of federal, state, and county offices are the Chinese New Year (which can fall in Jan or Feb; in 2011, it's Feb 3; 2012 it's Jan. 23), Girls' Day (Mar 3), Buddha's Birthday (Apr 8), Father Damien's Day (Apr 15), Boys' Day (May 5), Samoan Flag Day (in Aug), Aloha Festivals (Sept–Oct), and Pearl Harbor Day (Dec 7).

 Hey, No Smoking in Hawaii

Well, not *totally* no smoking, but Hawaii has one of the toughest laws against smoking in the U.S. It's against the law to smoke in public buildings, including airports, shopping malls, grocery stores, retail shops, buses, movie theaters, banks, convention facilities, and all government buildings and facilities. There is no smoking in restaurants, bars, or nightclubs. Most bed-and-breakfasts prohibit smoking indoors, and more and more hotels and resorts are becoming smoke-free even in public areas. Also, there is no smoking within 20 feet of a doorway, window, or ventilation intake (so no hanging around outside a bar to smoke—you must go 20 ft. away). Even some beaches have no-smoking policies (and at those that do allow smoking, you'd better pick up your butts and not use the sand as your own private ashtray—or else face stiff fines). Breathing fresh, clear air is "in," while smoking in Hawaii is "out."

Maui, Molokai & Lanai Calendar of Events

Please note that, as with any schedule of upcoming events, the following information is subject to change; always confirm the details before you plan your trip around an event.

For an exhaustive list of events beyond those listed here, check **www.visitmaui.com**, **www.molokai-hawaii.com**, or **www.visitlanai.net** for events throughout Maui, Molokai, and Lanai. Also consult **http://events.frommers.com**, where you'll find a searchable, up-to-the-minute roster of what's happening in destinations all over the world.

JANUARY

PGA SBS Championship, Kapalua Resort. Top PGA golfers compete for $1 million. Call ✆ **808/669-2440** or go to www.kapaluamaui.com. Generally in early January.

EA Sports Maui Invitational Basketball Tournament, Lahaina Civic Center, Lahaina. Top college teams vie in this annual preseason tournament. Call ✆ **847/850-1818,** or go to www.maui invitational.com. Early January.

Ka Molokai Makahiki, Kaunakakai Town Baseball Park, Mitchell Pauole Center, Kaunakakai, Molokai. Makahiki, a traditional time of peace in ancient Hawaii, is re-created with performances by Hawaiian music groups and hula *halau* (schools), ancient Hawaiian games, a sporting competition, and Hawaiian crafts and food. It's a wonderful chance to experience the Hawaii of yesteryear. Call ✆ **800/800-6367** or 808/553-3876, or go to www.molokai-hawaii.com. Late January.

Wendy's Champions Skins ProAm Golf Tournament, Royal Kaanapali Golf Course. Several of PGA's most legendary professionals play along side amateurs on Royal Kaanapali's Golf Course. Call ✆ **808/661-3271**, or www.kaanapali resort.com. Mid- to late January.

Chinese New Year. Lahaina town rolls out the red carpet for this important event with a traditional lion dance at the historic Wo Hing Temple on Front Street, accompanied by fireworks, food booths, and a host of activities. Call ✆ **888/310-1117** or 808/667-9175. Also on Market Street in Wailuku; call ✆ **808/244-3888.** Chinese New Year can fall in January or February; in 2011, the year of the rabbit, it's February 3. In 2012, the year of the dragon, it's on January 23.

FEBRUARY

Whale Day Celebration, Kalama Park, Kihei. A daylong celebration in the park, with a parade of whales, entertainment, a crafts fair, games, and food. Call ✆ **808/249-8811,** or go to www. pacificwhale.org. Early or mid-February.

MARCH

Ocean Arts Festival, Lahaina. The entire town of Lahaina celebrates the annual migration of Pacific humpback whales

---

 Daylight Saving Time

Since 1966, most of the United States has observed daylight saving time from the first Sunday in April to the last Sunday in October. In 2007, these dates changed, and now daylight saving time lasts from 2am on the second Sunday in March to 2am on the first Sunday in November. Note that Hawaii does *not* observe daylight saving time. So when daylight saving time is in effect in most of the U.S., Hawaii is 3 hours behind the West Coast and 6 hours behind the East Coast. When the U.S. reverts to standard time in November, Hawaii is 2 hours behind the West Coast and 5 hours behind the East Coast.

with this festival in Banyan Tree Park. Artists display their best ocean-themed art for sale, while Hawaiian musicians and hula troupes entertain. Enjoy marine-related activities, games, and a Creature Feature touch-pool exhibit for children. Call ☎ **888/310-1117** or 808/667-9194, or go to www.visitlahaina. com. Mid-March.

Molokai Hawaiian Paniolo Heritage Rodeo, Molokai Rodeo Arena, Maunaloa, Molokai. A celebration of Hawaii's *paniolo* (cowboy) heritage. Call ☎ **877/88-TRAIL** (888-7245).

APRIL

East Maui Taro Festival, Hana. Here's your chance to taste taro in many different forms, from poi to chips. The Hawaiian staple food is celebrated through exhibits, music, hula, arts, crafts, and, of course, food. Call ☎ **808/264-3336,** or go to www.tarofestival.org. Varying dates in April.

Buddha Day, Lahaina Jodo Mission, Lahaina. Each year on the first Saturday in April, this historic mission holds a flower festival pageant honoring the birth of Buddha. Call ☎ **808/661-4303.** April 2, 2011.

Celebration of the Arts, Ritz-Carlton Kapalua, Kapalua Resort. Contemporary and traditional artists give free hands-on lessons during this 4-day festival, which begins the Thursday before Easter. Call ☎ **808/669-6200,** or go to www. celebrationofthearts.org. Easter is April 24, 2011 and April 8, 2012.

Polo Spring Season Begins. For a complete list of all the polo matches in the cool, upcountry area of Maui, call ☎ **808/877-7744** or go to www.maui poloclub.com.

David Malo Day, Lahainaluna High School, Lahaina. This daylong event, with hula and other Hawaiian cultural celebrations, commemorates Hawaii's famous scholar and ends with a luau. Call ☎ **808/662-4000.** Mid- or late April.

Banyan Tree Birthday Party, Lahaina. Come celebrate the birthday of Lahaina's famous Banyan Tree with a weekend of activities. Call ☎ **888/310-1117** or 808/667-9175, or go to www.visitlahaina. com. Generally the end of April.

MAY

Maui Onion Festival, Whalers Village, Kaanapali. Everything you ever wanted to know about the sweetest onions in the world. Food, entertainment, tastings, and the Maui Onion cook-off. Call ☎ **808/661-4567,** or go to www.whalers village.com. Early May.

Outrigger Canoe Season, all islands. From May to September, canoe paddlers across the state participate in outrigger canoe races nearly every weekend. Call ☎ **808/383-7790,** or go to www. y2kanu.com for this year's schedule of events.

Lei Day Celebration, Fairmont Kea Lani Maui, Wailea. May Day is Lei Day in Hawaii, celebrated with lei-making contests, pageantry, arts and crafts, and concerts throughout the islands. The Fairmont Kea Lani hosts its own royal court procession. Call ☎ **808/224-6042,** or go to www.visitmaui.com. May 1.

Kapalua Jr. Vet/Sr. Tennis Championships, Kapalua Resort. Men and women ages 35 and older compete in singles and doubles championship tournaments. Call ☎ **808/669-5677** or go to www.kapaluamaui.com. Early May.

International Festival of Canoes, West Maui. At this celebration of the Pacific islands' seafaring heritage, events include canoe paddling and sailing regattas, a luau feast, cultural demonstrations, canoe-building exhibits, and music. Call ☎ **888/310-1117.** Mid- to late May.

Molokai Ka Hula Piko Festival, Papohaku Beach Park, Kaluakoi, Molokai. This daylong celebration of the hula takes place in mid-May on the island where it was born. It features performances by hula schools, musicians, and singers from across Hawaii, as well as local food and Hawaiian crafts, including quilting, woodworking, feather work, and deer-horn scrimshaw. Call ☎ **800/800-6367** or 808/553-3876, or go to www.molokaievents.com.

Da Kine Classic Windsurfing Event, Kanaha Beach Park, Kahului. This annual windsurfing slalom race takes place at Kanaha Beach Park, west of Kahului Airport in central Maui. Call ☎ **808/877-2111.** Early June.

Maui Film Festival, Wailea Resort. Five days and nights of screenings of premieres and special films, along with traditional Hawaiian storytelling, chants, hula, and contemporary music. It begins the Wednesday before Father's Day. Call ☎ **808/572-3456** or go to www.mauifilmfestival.com.

King Kamehameha Celebration, statewide. This state holiday (officially June 11, but celebrated on different dates on each island) features a massive floral parade, *hoolaulea* (parties), and much more. Call ☎ **888/310-1117** or 808/667-9194, or go to www.visitlahaina.com for Maui events; call ☎ **808/567-6361** for Molokai events.

Hawaiian Slack Key Guitar Festival, Maui Arts & Cultural Center, Kahului. Great music performed by the best musicians in Hawaii. It's 5 hours long and absolutely free. Call ☎ **808/226-2697,** or go to www.slackkeyfestival.com. Late June.

Kapalua Clambake Pro-Am Golf Tournament, Kapalua Resort. This tournament, which has taken place every year for more than 2 decades, ends with a giant clambake on the beach. Call ☎ **808/669-8802** or go to www.kapalua.com. Late June.

Kapalua Wine & Food Festival, Kapalua Resort. Famous wine and food experts and oenophiles gather at the Ritz-Carlton hotel for formal tastings, panel discussions, and samplings of new releases. Call ☎ **800/KAPALUA** (527-2582), or go to www.kapaluaresort.com. June or early July.

Polo Season, Olinda Polo Field, Makawao. Polo matches featuring Hawaii's top players, often joined by famous international players, are held every Sunday at 1pm throughout the summer. Call ☎ **808/877-7744,** or go to www.mauipolo.com.

Lanai Pineapple Festival, Lanai City, Lanai. This festival on the first Saturday in July celebrates Lanai's history of pineapple plantations and ranching, including a pineapple-eating contest, a pineapple-cooking contest, entertainment, arts and crafts, food, and fireworks. Call ☎ **808/565-7600,** or go to www.visitlanai.net. Generally close to July 4.

Fourth of July. Lahaina holds an old-fashioned Independence Day celebration with fireworks lighting the night sky over Lahaina's roadstead. Call ☎ **888/310-1117** or 808/667-9194, or go to www.visitlahaina.com. Kaanapali puts on a grand old celebration with live music, children's activities, and fireworks. Call ☎ **808/661-3271.**

Makawao Parade & Rodeo, Makawao. The annual parade and rodeo event has been taking place in this upcountry cowboy town for generations. Call ☎ **808/572-9565,** or go to www.makawaotowncenter.com. July 4.

Bon Dance & Lantern Ceremony, Lahaina. This colorful Buddhist ceremony honors the souls of the dead. Call ☎ **808/661-4304.** Usually early July.

Rainbow Sandals Molokai to Oahu Paddleboard Race, starts on Molokai and finishes on Oahu. Some 70 participants from an international field journey to Molokai to compete in this 32-mile race, considered to be the world championship of long-distance paddleboard racing. The race begins at Kaluakoi Beach on Molokai at 7am and finishes at Maunaloa Bay on Oahu around 12:30pm. Call ☎ **808/638-8208,** or go to www.molokai-hawaii.com. Mid- to late July.

ONGOING EVENTS ON maui

Every Friday night from 7 to 10pm, as part of **Friday Night Is Art Night** in Lahaina, the town's galleries open their doors for special shows, demonstrations, and refreshments. There are even strolling musicians wandering the streets.

If you're hungry for Hawaiian music, the **Masters of Hawaiian Slack Key Guitar Series** (☎ 888/669-3858; www.slackkey.com) features some of the great masters (and some Grammy award winners) of this guitar style unique to the Hawaiian Islands. Concerts are held every Wednesday night at 7:30pm at the Napili Kai Beach Resort. Tickets are $40; call in advance for reservations.

On the first and third weekends of the month, Hawaiian artists sell and share culture, arts, and crafts under the famous landmark **Banyan Tree** in Lahaina. On the other weekends, the Lahaina Arts Society holds an exhibit and sale of various works of art in the same place.

Every Wednesday at 5:30 and 7:30pm, the **Maui Film Festival** (☎ 808/572-3456 or 579-9244; www.mauifilmfestival.com) presents outstanding contemporary and art films at the Maui Arts & Cultural Center, 1 Cameron Way (just off Kahului Beach Rd.), in Kahului.

There are **free hula performances** every week. In **Lahaina,** they take place Saturday and Sunday at 1pm and Tuesday and Thursday at 7pm in the Lahaina Cannery Mall. In **Kaanapali,** they're held nightly, at 7 and 8pm at the Whalers Village; and every night at 6:30pm at the Kaanapali Beach Hotel. If you would like to try the hula yourself, there are free hula lessons at Whalers Village every Thursday from 3 to 4pm.

AUGUST

Hawaii State Windsurfing Championship, Kanaha Beach Park, Kahului. Top windsurfers compete. Call ☎ 808/877-2111. Early August.

Tahiti Fete, War Memorial Gym, Wailuku. An annual festival with Tahitian dance competition, arts and crafts, and food. Call ☎ 808/244-8088. Two days in August.

SEPTEMBER

Aloha Festivals, various locations. Parades and other events celebrate Hawaiian culture. Call ☎ 800/852-7690 or 808/545-1771, or go to www.aloha festivals.com for a schedule of events.

A Taste of Lahaina, Lahaina Civic Center, Lahaina. Some 30,000 people show up to sample 40 signature entrees from Maui's premier chefs during this weekend festival, which includes cooking demonstrations, wine tastings, and live entertainment. The event begins Friday night with Maui Chefs Present,

a themed dinner/cocktail party featuring about a dozen of Maui's best chefs. Call ☎ 888/310-1117, or go to www.visitlahaina.com. Second weekend in September.

Hana Relays, Hana Highway. Hundreds of runners, in relay teams, crowd the Hana Highway from Kahului to Hana (you might want to avoid the road on this day). Call ☎ 808/243-9636, or go to www.virr.com. Early September.

Maui Marathon, Kahului to Kaanapali. Runners line up at the Maui Mall before daybreak and head off for Kaanapali. Call ☎ 866/577-8379, or go to www.virr.com or www.mauimarathon.com. Mid- to late September.

Na Wahine O Ke Kai, Molokai. The top women canoe paddlers from across the state will arrive at Hale Lono Harbor on Molokai and paddle across the ocean to Oahu. Call ☎ 808/259-7112, or go to www.molokai-hawaii.com. Mid-September.

Maui County Fair, War Memorial Complex, Wailuku. The oldest county fair in Hawaii features a parade, amusement rides, live entertainment, and exhibits. Call ☎ **800/525-MAUI** (6284; in July, 808/242-2721), or go to www.mauicountyfair.com. Last week in September or first week in October.

Aloha Festivals Hoolaulea, Lahaina. This all-day cultural festival, which marks the end of Maui's Aloha Festivals Week, is held at Banyan Tree Park and features Hawaiian food, music, and dance, along with arts and crafts on display and for sale. Call ☎ **888/310-1117** or 808/667-9194, or go to www.visitlahaina.com. September or October.

Molokai Hoe, Molokai to Oahu. This men's 40-mile outrigger contest starts in Molokai and finishes at Fort DeRussy Beach in Waikiki. Call ☎ **808/259-7112,** or go to www.molokai-hawaii.com or www.holoholo.com.

Hula O Na Keiki, Kaanapali Beach Hotel, Kaanapali. This solo hula competition for children ages 5 to 17 has been held for 2 decades. The weekend festival celebrates Hawaiian dance, arts, and music. Call ☎ **808/661-0011,** or go to www.kbhmaui.com. Early November.

Hawaii International Film Festival, various locations. This cinema festival with a cross-cultural spin features filmmakers from Asia, the Pacific Islands, and the United States. Call ☎ **808/550-8457,** or go to www.hiff.org. Late October or early November.

Hui Noeau Christmas House, Makawao. The festivities in the beautifully decorated Hui mansion include shopping, workshops and art demonstrations, visits with Santa, holiday music, and local foods. Call ☎ **808/572-6560,** or go to www.huinoeau.com. Late November and early December.

Na Mele O Maui, Kaanapali Beach Resort. Children from Maui and Molokai participate in this traditional Hawaiian song competition. Call ☎ **808/661-3271,** or go to www.kaanapaliresort.com. Mid-November to early December.

Festival of Lights, island-wide. Festivities include parades and tree-lighting ceremonies. Marching bands, floats, and Santa roll down Lahaina's Front Street. Call ☎ **808/667-9175** on Maui, or 552-2800 on Molokai. Early December.

Festival of Trees, Lahaina Cannery Mall, Lahaina. Look for decorated trees as well as entertainment. Call ☎ **808/661-5304.** Early December.

Lighting of the Banyan Tree, Lahaina. At 6:30pm, Lahaina's historic Banyan Tree is lit up with thousands of Christmas lights for the entire holiday season. Santa Claus makes an appearance, and choirs sing Christmas carols accompanied by hula. Call ☎ **808/667-9194** or 667-9194, or go to www.visitlahaina.com. Early December.

Tree Lighting Ceremony, Ritz-Carlton Kapalua, Kapalua Resort. With the flick of a switch, more than 250,000 sparkling lights illuminate the 25-foot tree and dozens of pine and palm trees around the courtyards of the Ritz-Carlton Kapalua and throughout the resort. Call ☎ **808/669-6200,** or go to www.kapaluaresort.com. Early December.

Christmas Light Parade, Kaunakakai, Molokai. A light parade with music and holiday arts and crafts. Call ☎ **808/552-2800.** Mid-December.

First Light, Maui Arts & Cultural Center, Kahului. The Academy of Motion Pictures holds major screenings of top films. Call ☎ **808/572-3456,** or go to www.mauifilmfestival.com. Late November, throughout December and early January.

ENTRY REQUIREMENTS

Passports

Virtually every air traveler entering the U.S. is required to show a passport. All persons, including U.S. citizens, traveling by air between the United States and Canada, Mexico, Central and South America, the Caribbean, and Bermuda are required to present a valid passport. **Note:** U.S. and Canadian citizens entering the U. S. at land and sea ports of entry from within the Western Hemisphere must now also present a passport or other documents compliant with the Western Hemisphere Travel Initiative (WHTI; see www.getyouhome.gov for details). Children 15 and under may continue entering with only a U.S. birth certificate, or other proof of U.S. citizenship.

It is advised to always have at least one or two consecutive blank pages in your passport to allow space for visas and stamps that need to appear together. It is also important to note when your passport expires. Many countries require your passport to have at least 6 months left before its expiration in order to allow you into the destination.

Visas

For information on obtaining a visa, please visit "Fast Facts," on p. 386.

The U.S. State Department has a **Visa Waiver Program (VWP)** allowing citizens of the following countries to enter the United States without a visa for stays of up to 90 days: Andorra, Australia, Austria, Belgium, Brunei, Czech Republic, Denmark, Estonia, Finland, France, Germany, Hungary, Iceland, Ireland, Italy, Japan, Latvia, Liechtenstein, Lithuania, Luxembourg, Malta, Monaco, the Netherlands, New Zealand, Norway, Portugal, San Marino, Singapore, Slovakia, Slovenia, South Korea, Spain, Sweden, Switzerland, and the United Kingdom. (**Note:** This list was accurate at press time; for the most up-to-date list of countries in the VWP, consult http://travel.state.gov/visa.) Even though a visa isn't necessary, in an effort to help U.S. officials check travelers against terror watch lists before they arrive at U.S. borders, visitors from VWP countries must register online through the Electronic System for Travel Authorization (ESTA) before boarding a plane or a boat to the U.S. Travelers will complete an electronic application providing basic personal and travel eligibility information. The Department of Homeland Security recommends filling out the form at least 3 days before traveling. Authorizations will be valid for up to 2 years or until the traveler's passport expires, whichever comes first. Currently, there is no fee for the online application. **Note:** Any passport issued on or after October 26, 2006, by a VWP country must be an **e-Passport** for VWP travelers to be eligible to enter the U.S. without a visa. Citizens of these nations also need to present a round-trip air or cruise ticket upon arrival. e-Passports contain computer chips capable of storing biometric information, such as the required digital photograph of the holder. If your passport doesn't have this feature, you can still travel without a visa if it is a valid passport issued before October 26, 2005, and includes a machine-readable zone, or between October 26, 2005, and October 25, 2006, and includes a digital photograph. For more information, go to **http://travel.state.gov/visa.** Canadian citizens may enter the United States without visas; they will need to show passports (if traveling by air) and proof of residence, however.

Citizens of all other countries must have (1) a valid passport that expires at least 6 months later than the scheduled end of their visit to the U.S., and (2) a tourist visa.

Customs

WHAT YOU CAN BRING INTO THE U.S.

Every visitor 21 years of age or older may bring in, free of duty, the following: (1) 1 U.S. quart of alcohol; (2) 200 cigarettes, 50 cigars (but not from Cuba), or 3 pounds of smoking tobacco; and (3) $100 worth of gifts. These exemptions are offered to travelers who spend at least 72 hours in the United States and who have not claimed them within the preceding 6 months. It is forbidden to bring into the country almost any meat products (including canned, fresh, and dried meat products such as bouillon, soup mixes, etc.). Generally, condiments including vinegars, oils, pickled goods, spices, coffee, tea, and some cheeses and baked goods are permitted. Avoid rice products, as rice can often harbor insects. Bringing fruits and vegetables is prohibited since they may harbor pests or disease. International visitors may carry in or out up to $10,000 in U.S. or foreign currency with no formalities; larger sums must be declared to U.S. Customs on entering or leaving, which includes filing form CM 4790. For details regarding U.S. Customs and Border Protection, consult your nearest U.S. embassy or consulate, or **U.S. Customs** (www.customs.gov).

WHAT YOU CAN TAKE HOME FROM MAUI

For information on what you're allowed to bring home, contact one of the following agencies:

U.S. Citizens: U.S. Customs & Border Protection (CBP), 1300 Pennsylvania Ave., NW, Washington, DC 20229 (✆ **877/287-8667;** www.cbp.gov).

Canadian Citizens: Canada Border Services Agency, Ottawa, Ontario, K1A 0L8 (✆ **800/461-9999** in Canada, or 204/983-3500; www.cbsa-asfc.gc.ca).

U.K. Citizens: HM Customs & Excise, Crownhill Court, Tailyour Road, Plymouth, PL6 5BZ (✆ **0845/010-9000;** from outside the U.K., 020/8929-0152; www.hmce.gov.uk).

Australian Citizens: Australian Customs Service, Customs House, 5 Constitution Ave., Canberra City, ACT 2601 (✆ **1300/363-263;** from outside Australia, 612/6275-6666; www.customs.gov.au).

New Zealand Citizens: New Zealand Customs, The Customhouse, 17–21 Whitmore St., Box 2218, Wellington, 6140 (✆ **04/473-6099** or 0800/428-786; www.customs.govt.nz).

Medical Requirements

Unless you're arriving from an area known to be suffering from an epidemic (particularly cholera or yellow fever), inoculations or vaccinations are not required for entry into the United States.

GETTING THERE & GETTING AROUND

Getting To Maui

If you think of the island of Maui as the shape of a head and shoulders of a person, you'll probably arrive at its neck, at **Kahului Airport** (OGG). If you're headed for Molokai or Lanai, you'll have to connect through Honolulu.

For complete airline contact information, see chapter 13.

At press time, the following airlines fly directly from the U.S. mainland to Kahului: **United Airlines** offers daily nonstop flights from San Francisco and Los Angeles; **Hawaiian Airlines** has direct flights from San Diego, Portland, and Seattle; **Alaska Airlines** offers flights from Anchorage to Seattle to Kahului; **American Airlines** flies direct from Los Angeles and San Jose; **Northwest Airlines** flies direct from Oakland, California, and **Delta Air Lines** offers direct flights from San Francisco via Los Angeles.

The other carriers—including **Continental Airlines**—fly to Honolulu, where you'll have to pick up an interisland flight to Maui. (The airlines listed in the preceding paragraph also offer many more flights to Honolulu from additional cities on the mainland.) **Hawaiian Airlines** offers jet service from Honolulu.

INTERISLAND FLIGHTS The major interisland carriers have cut way, way, way back on the number of interisland flights. The airlines warn you to show up at least 90 minutes before your flight, and believe me, with all the security inspections, you will need all 90 minutes to catch your flight. Also, be sure to book your interisland connection from Honolulu to Maui in advance.

In 2008, Hawaii lost one of its major interisland carriers, Aloha Airlines, but three other carriers remain: **Hawaiian Airlines** (🕾 800/367-5320; www.hawaiianair.com), **Mokulele Airlines** (🕾 866/260-7070; www.mokuleleairlines.com), and **go!** (🕾 888/I-FLY-GO-2 [435-9462]; www.iflygo.com).

Visitors to Molokai and Lanai have commuter airlines to choose from: **Mokulele Airlines** (🕾 866/260-7070; www.mokuleleairlines.com); **go!** (🕾 888/I-FLY-GO-2 [435-9462]; www.iflygo.com); **Pacific Wings' PW Express** services (🕾 888/866-5022 or 808/873-0877; www.pacificwings.com), with daily nonstop flights between Honolulu and Molokai and Lanai, plus flights from Kahului, Maui; and **Island Air** (🕾 800/323-3345 or 808/484-2222; www.islandair.com), which serves Hawaii's small interisland airports on Maui, Molokai, and Lanai. However, I have to warn you that I have not had stellar service on Island Air.

IMMIGRATION & CUSTOMS

International visitors arriving by air should cultivate patience and resignation before setting foot on U.S. soil. Clearing Customs and Immigration can take as long as 2 hours.

LANDING AT KAHULUI AIRPORT

If there's a long wait at baggage claim, step over to the state-operated **Visitor Information Center,** where you can ask about island activities and pick up brochures and the latest issue of *This Week Maui,* which features great regional maps of the islands. After collecting your bags from the poky, automated carousels, step out, take a deep breath, proceed to the curbside rental-car pickup area, and wait for the appropriate rental-agency shuttle van to take you a half-mile away to the rental-car checkout desk. (All major rental companies have branches at Kahului; see "Getting Around Maui," later in this chapter.)

If you're not renting a car, the cheapest way to get to your hotel is via **SpeediShuttle** (🕾 877/242-5777; www.speedishuttle.com), which can take you between Kahului Airport and all the major resorts between 6am and 11pm daily. Rates vary, but figure on $39 for one person to Wailea (round-trip), $51 to Kaanapali, and $75 to Kapalua. Be sure to call ahead of time to arrange for pickup.

You'll see taxis outside the airport terminal, but note that they are quite expensive—expect to spend around $70 to $85 for a ride from Kahului to Kaanapali and $60 to Wailea.

If possible, avoid landing on Maui between 3 and 6pm, when the working stiffs on Maui are "pau work" (finished with work) and a major traffic jam occurs at the first intersection getting out of the airport.

AVOIDING KAHULUI

If you're planning to stay in Kapalua or Kaanapali, you might consider flying **Island Air** (© 800/323-3345; www.islandair.com) from Honolulu to the **Kapalua–West Maui Airport.** From this airport, it's only a 10- to 15-minute drive to most hotels in west Maui, as opposed to an hour from Kahului.

Pacific Wings (© 888/575-4546 or 808/873-0877; www.pacificwings. com) flies eight-passenger, twin-engine Cessna 402C aircraft into tiny **Hana Airport,** in east Maui, and also flies into Kahului.

AGRICULTURAL SCREENING

Note that at all airports in Hawaii, baggage and passengers bound for the mainland must be screened by agricultural officials. Officials will confiscate local produce like fresh avocados, bananas, and mangoes, in the name of fruit-fly control.

 THE WELCOMING lei

Nothing makes you feel more welcome than a **lei.** The tropical beauty of the delicate garland, the deliciously sweet fragrance of the blossoms, the sensual way the flowers curl softly around your neck—there's no doubt about it: Getting lei'd in Hawaii is a sensuous experience.

Leis are much more than just a decorative necklace of flowers—they're also one of the nicest ways to say "hello," "goodbye," "congratulations," "I salute you," "my sympathies are with you," or "I love you."

During ancient times, leis given to *alii* (royalty) were accompanied by a bow, since it was *kapu* (forbidden) for a commoner to raise his arms higher than the king's head. The presentation of a kiss with a lei didn't come about until World War II; it's generally attributed to an entertainer who kissed an officer on a dare and then quickly presented him with her lei, saying it was an old Hawaiian custom. It wasn't then, but it sure caught on fast.

Lei-making is a tropical art form. All leis are fashioned by hand in a variety of traditional patterns; some are sewn with hundreds of tiny blooms or shells, or bits of ferns and leaves. Some are twisted, some braided, some strung. Every island has its own special flower lei—the lei of the land, so to speak. On Maui, it's the *lokelani,* a small rose; on Molokai, it's the *kukui,* the white blossom of a candlenut tree; and on Lanai it's the *kaunaoa,* a bright yellow moss. Leis are available at the Kahului Airport, from florists, and even at supermarkets.

Leis are the perfect symbol for the islands: They're given in the moment, and their fragrance and beauty are enjoyed in the moment, but even after they fade, their spirit of aloha lives on. Welcome to Hawaii!

Coping with Jet Lag

Jet lag is a pitfall of traveling across time zones. If you're flying north–south and you feel sluggish when you touch down, your symptoms will be the result of dehydration and the general stress of air travel. When you travel east–west or vice versa, however, your body becomes thoroughly confused about what time it is, and everything from your digestive system to your brain is knocked for a loop. Traveling east—say, from San Francisco to Boston—is more difficult on your internal clock than traveling west—say from Atlanta to Hawaii—because most people's bodies are more inclined to stay up late than to fall asleep early.

Here are some tips for combating jet lag:

o **Reset your watch** to Maui time before you board the plane.

o **Drink lots of water** before, during, and after your flight. Avoid alcohol.

o **Exercise and sleep well** for a few days before your trip.

o If you have trouble sleeping on planes, **fly eastward on morning flights.**

o **Daylight** is the key to resetting your body clock. At the website for **Outside In** (www.bodyclock.com), you can get a customized plan of when to seek and avoid light.

Pineapples, coconuts, and papayas inspected and certified for export; boxed flowers; leis without seeds; and processed foods (macadamia nuts, coffee, jams, dried fruit, and the like) will pass.

LONG-HAUL FLIGHTS: HOW TO STAY COMFORTABLE

o Your choice of airline and airplane will definitely affect your legroom. Find more details about U.S. airlines at **www.seatguru.com**. For international airlines, the research firm Skytrax has posted a list of average seat pitches at **www.airlinequality.com**.

o Emergency-exit seats and bulkhead seats typically have the most legroom. Emergency-exit seats are usually left unassigned until the day of a flight (to ensure that someone able-bodied fills the seats); it's worth checking in online at home (if the airline offers that option) or getting to the ticket counter early to snag one of these spots for a long flight. Many passengers find that bulkhead seating offers more legroom, but keep in mind that bulkhead seats have no storage space on the floor in front of you.

o To have two seats for yourself in a three-seat row, try for an aisle seat in a center section toward the back of coach. If you're traveling with a companion, book an aisle and a window seat. Middle seats are usually booked last, so chances are good you'll end up with three seats to yourselves. And in the event that a third passenger is assigned the middle seat, he or she will probably be more than happy to trade for a window or an aisle.

o To sleep, avoid the last row of any section or the row in front of an emergency exit, as these seats are the least likely to recline. Avoid seats near highly trafficked toilet areas. Avoid seats in the back of many jets—these can be narrower than those in the rest of coach. Or reserve a window seat so you can rest your head and avoid being bumped in the aisle.

- Get up, walk around, and stretch every 60 to 90 minutes to keep your blood flowing. This helps avoid **deep-vein thrombosis,** or "economy-class syndrome." See "Avoiding 'Economy-Class Syndrome,'" p. 77.

- Drink water before, during, and after your flight to combat the lack of humidity in airplane cabins. Avoid caffeine and alcohol, which will dehydrate you.

- If you're flying with kids, don't forget to carry on toys, books, pacifiers, and snacks and chewing gum to help them relieve ear pressure buildup during ascent and descent.

Getting Around Maui

The only way to really see Maui is by rental car. There's no real island-wide public transit.

Maui has only a handful of major roads, and you can expect to encounter a traffic jam or two in the major resort areas. Two of the roads follow the coastline around the two volcanoes that form the island, Haleakala and Puu Kukui (the West Maui Mountains), one road goes up to Haleakala's summit, one road goes to Hana, one goes to Wailea, and one goes to Lahaina. It sounds simple, right? Well, it isn't because the names of the few roads change en route. Study a map before you set out.

BY CAR

Since the downturn in the economy, all of Hawaii's major car agencies have reduced their fleets. So it is imperative that you book your car in advance. (Or you may not get a car at any price!) Hawaii has some of the lowest car-rental rates in the country—about $51 a day (including all state tax and fees); the national average is about $56. (An exception is the island of Lanai, where they're very expensive.) To rent a car in Hawaii, you must be at least 25 years of age and have a valid driver's license and credit card. *Note:* If you're visiting from abroad and

---

 Traffic Advisory

The road from central Maui to Kihei and Wailea, **Mokulele Highway (Hwy. 311),** is a dangerous strip that's often the scene of head-on crashes involving intoxicated and speeding drivers. Be careful.

Also be alert on the **Honoapi-ilani Highway (Hwy. 30)** en route to Lahaina—drivers who spot whales in the channel between Maui and Lanai often slam on the brakes and cause major tie-ups and accidents.

Note that all highways on Maui are packed, bumper-to-bumper, between 7 and 9am and 4 and 6pm, so plan accordingly.

If you get into trouble on Maui's highways, look for the flashing blue strobe lights on 12-foot poles; at the base are emergency solar-powered call boxes (programmed to dial © **911** as soon as you pick up the handset). There are 29 emergency call boxes on the island's busiest highways and remote areas, including along the Hana and Haleakala highways and on the north end of the island in the remote community of Kahakuloa.

Another traffic note: Buckle up your seat belt—Hawaii has stiff fines for noncompliance.

plan to rent a car in the United States, keep in mind that foreign driver's licenses are usually recognized in the U.S., but you should get an international one if your home license is not in English. Also, international visitors should note that insurance and taxes are almost never included in quoted rental car rates in the U.S. Be sure to ask your rental agency about additional fees for these. They can add a significant cost to your car rental.

All major car-rental agencies have offices on Maui, usually at both Kahului and West Maui airports. They include **Alamo, Avis, Budget, Dollar, Hertz,** and **National.** For complete rental-agency contact information, see chapter 13.

There are also a few frugal car-rental agencies offering older cars at discount prices. **Word of Mouth Rental Car ★**, in Kahului (© **800/533-5929** or 808/877-2436; www.mauirentacar.com), has older cars (1995–2007 Toyotas and Nissans, air-conditioned). Rates include free airport pickup and drop-off. **Maui Cruisers,** in Wailuku (© **877/749-7889** or 808/249-2319; www.mauicruisers. net), also offers free airport pickup and return on its 8- to 10-year-old Nissan Sentras, with rentals starting at $23 a day (3-day minimum) or $161 a week (including tax and insurance).

INSURANCE Hawaii is a no-fault state, which means that if you don't have collision-damage insurance, you are required to pay for all damages before you leave the state, whether or not the accident was your fault. Your personal car insurance may provide rental-car coverage; check before you leave home. Bring your insurance identification card if you decline the optional insurance, which usually costs from $12 to $20 a day. Obtain the name of your company's local claim representative before you go. Some credit card companies also provide collision-damage insurance for their customers; check with yours before you rent.

DRIVING RULES Hawaii state law mandates that all car passengers must wear a **seat belt** and all infants must be strapped into a car seat. You'll pay a $50 fine if you don't buckle up. **Pedestrians** always have the right of way, even if they're not in the crosswalk. You can turn **right on red** after a full and complete stop, unless otherwise posted.

ROAD MAPS The best and most detailed road maps are published by *This Week* magazine, a free visitor publication available on Maui. Most rental-car maps are pretty good, too.

BY MOTORCYCLE

Don black denim and motorcycle boots, feel the wind on your face, and smell the salt air by riding a Harley, available for rent from **Island Riders,** 126 Hinau St., Lahaina, or 2463 South Kihei Rd., Kihei (© **800/529-2925** or 808/661-9966; www.islandriders.com).

BY MOPED

Mopeds are available for rent from **Discount Scooters** (www.mauimoped rentals.com), with locations at 252 Lahainaluna Rd., Lahaina (© **808/667-7000**), and 1455 Kihei Rd., at Lipoa Street, Kihei (© **808/667-7000**). Smaller scooters, which start at $30 for 2 hours and $75 for all day, are little more than motorized bicycles that get up to around 35 mph (with a good wind at your back), so I suggest using them only locally (to get to the beach or to go shopping). Don't take them out on the highway—they can't keep up with the traffic.

BY TAXI & SHUTTLE

For island-wide 24-hour service, call **Alii Cab Co.** (✆ 808/661-3688 or 667-2605). You can also try **Kihei Taxi** (✆ 808/879-3000), **Wailea Taxi** (✆ 808/874-5000), or **Maui Central Cab** (✆ 808/244-7278) if you need a ride.

SpeediShuttle (✆ 877/242-5777; www.speedishuttle.com) can take you between Kahului Airport and all the major resorts from 5am to 11pm daily (for details, see "Landing at Kahului Airport," p. 68).

Maui Public Transit is a public/private partnership that has convenient, economical, and air-conditioned shuttle buses on 11 routes, all operated by Roberts Hawaii (✆ 808/871-4838; www.mauicounty.gov/bus). These routes are funded by the County of Maui and provide service in and between various central, west, south, and upcountry Maui communities (including the airport). All routes operate daily. The routes go from as far south as Wailea up to as far north as Kapalua. Fares range from free to $1.

 WHAT TO pack

Maui is very informal: You'll get by with shorts, T-shirts, and sneakers at most attractions and restaurants; a casual sundress or a polo shirt and khakis are fine even in the most expensive places. Dinner jackets for men are required only in some of the fine-dining rooms of a very few ultraexclusive resorts, such as the Lodge at Koele on Lanai—and they'll cordially provide you with a jacket if you don't bring your own. Aloha wear is acceptable everywhere, so you may want to plan on buying an aloha shirt or a muumuu (a Hawaiian-style dress) while you're in Maui.

So bring T-shirts, shorts, long pants, a couple of bathing suits, tennis shoes, and rubber water shoes or flip-flops. Don't forget a long-sleeved cover-up (to throw on at the beach when you've had enough sun for the day). If you plan on hiking, bring hiking boots and several pairs of good socks. You might also want to bring binoculars for whale-watching.

The tropical sun poses the greatest threat to anyone who ventures into the great outdoors, so be sure to pack **sun protection:** a good pair of sunglasses, strong sunscreen, a light hat, and a canteen or water bottle if you'll be hiking—you'll easily dehydrate in the tropical heat, so figure on carrying 2 liters of water per day on any hike. Campers should bring water-purification tablets or devices. Also see "Staying

Healthy" and "Crime & Safety," later in this chapter.

Don't bother overstuffing your suitcase with 2 whole weeks' worth of clothes: Maui has **laundry facilities** almost everywhere (except Hana). If your accommodations don't have a washer and dryer or laundry service (most do), there will most likely be a laundry nearby.

One last thing: **It really can get cold on Maui.** If you plan to see the sunrise from the top of Haleakala, bring a warm jacket. Even in summer when it's 80°F (27°C) at the beach, 40°F (4°C) upcountry temperatures are not uncommon. It's always a good idea to bring long pants and a windbreaker, sweater, or light jacket. And be sure to toss some **rain gear** in your suitcase if you'll be in Maui any time between November and March.

MONEY & COSTS

The most common bills are the $1 (a "buck"), $5, $10, and $20 denominations. There are also $2 bills (seldom encountered), $50 bills, and $100 bills (the last two are usually not welcome as payment for small purchases).

Coins come in seven denominations: 1¢ (1 cent, or a penny); 5¢ (5 cents, or a nickel); 10¢ (10 cents, or a dime); 25¢ (25 cents, or a quarter); 50¢ (50 cents, or a half-dollar); the gold-colored Sacagawea and presidential coins, worth $1; and the rare silver dollar.

It's always advisable to bring money in a variety of forms on a vacation: a mix of cash, credit cards, and traveler's checks. You should also exchange enough petty cash to cover airport incidentals, tipping, and transportation to your hotel before you leave home, or withdraw money upon arrival at an airport ATM.

WHAT THINGS COST ON MAUI	US$/C$	EURO€	UK£
Hamburger	6.00	4.63	4.33
Movie ticket (adult)	9.00	5.63	6.50
Movie ticket (child)	5.50	3.44	3.97
Entry to Maui Ocean Center (adult)	25.00	18.54	16.84
Entry to Maui Ocean Center (child)	18.50	11.57	13.35
Entry to Maui Tropical Plantation (adult)	14.00	8.76	10.11
Entry to Maui Tropical Plantation (child)	5.00	3.13	3.61
Entry to Haleakala National Park	5.00	3.13	3.61
Old Lahaina Luau (adult)	96.00	60.04	69.26
Old Lahaina Luau (child)	65.00	40.65	46.90
20-ounce soft drink at convenience store	2.50	1.56	1.81
16-ounce apple juice	3.50	2.19	2.53
Cup of coffee	3.00	1.88	2.16
Moderate three-course dinner without alcohol	50.00	31.21	36.07
Moderately priced hotel	125.00	78.18	90.18

ATMs

Nationwide, the easiest and best way to get cash away from home is from an ATM (automated teller machine), sometimes referred to as a "cash machine" or "cashpoint." ATMs are everywhere in Maui—at banks, supermarkets, Longs Drugs, and in some resorts and shopping centers. The **Cirrus** (© **800/424-7787**; www.mastercard.com) and **PLUS** (© **800/843-7587**; www.visa.com) networks span the country; you can find them even in remote regions. Go to your bank card's website to find ATM locations on Maui. Be sure you know your daily withdrawal limit before you depart.

Note: Many banks impose a fee every time you use a card at another bank's ATM, and that fee is often higher for international transactions (up to $5 or more) than for domestic ones (where they're rarely more than $2). In addition, the bank from which you withdraw cash may charge its own fee. To compare banks' ATM fees within the U.S., use **www.bankrate.com**. Visitors from outside the U.S. should also find out whether their bank assesses a 1% to 3% fee on charges incurred abroad.

Credit Cards & Debit Cards

Credit cards are the most widely used form of payment in the United States: **Visa** (Barclaycard in Britain), **MasterCard** (Eurocard in Europe, Access in Britain, Chargex in Canada), **American Express, Diners Club,** and **Discover.** They also provide a convenient record of all your expenses and offer relatively good exchange rates. You can withdraw cash advances from your credit cards at banks or ATMs, but high fees make credit card cash advances a pricey way to get cash.

It's highly recommended that you travel with at least one major credit card. You must have a credit card to rent a car, and hotels and airlines usually require a credit card imprint as a deposit against expenses.

ATM cards with major credit card backing, known as **"debit cards,"** are now a commonly acceptable form of payment in most stores and restaurants. Debit cards draw money directly from your checking account. Some stores enable you to receive cash back on your debit card purchases as well. The same is true at most U.S. post offices.

Beware of hidden credit card fees while traveling. Check with your credit or debit card issuer to see what fees, if any, will be charged for overseas transactions. Recent reform legislation in the U.S., for example, has curbed some exploitative lending practices. But many banks have responded by increasing fees in other areas, including fees for customers who use credit and debit cards while out of the country—even if those charges were made in U.S. dollars. Fees can amount to 3% or more of the purchase price. Check with your bank before departing to avoid any surprise charges on your statement.

STAYING HEALTHY
Regional Health Concerns
INSECTS & SCORPIONS

Like any tropical climate, Hawaii is home to lots of bugs. Most of them won't harm you. However, watch out for mosquitoes, centipedes, and scorpions, which do sting and may cause anything from mild annoyance to severe swelling and pain.

MOSQUITOES These pesky insects are not native to Hawaii but arrived as larvae stowed away in water barrels on the ship *Wellington* in 1826, when it anchored in Lahaina. There's not a whole lot you can do about them, except to apply commercial repellent, which you can pick up at any drugstore.

CENTIPEDES These segmented bugs with a jillion legs come in two varieties: 6- to 8-inch-long brown ones and 2- to 3-inch-long blue guys. Both can really pack a wallop with their sting. Centipedes are generally found in damp, wet places, such as under wood piles or compost heaps; wearing closed-toe shoes can help prevent stings. If you're stung, apply ice at once to prevent swelling. See a doctor if you experience extreme pain, swelling, nausea, or any other severe reaction.

SCORPIONS Rarely seen, scorpions are found in arid, warm regions; their stings can be serious. Campers in dry areas should always check their boots before putting them on and shake out sleeping bags and bed rolls. Symptoms of a scorpion sting include shortness of breath, hives, swelling, and nausea. In the unlikely event that you're stung, apply diluted household ammonia and cold compresses to the area of the sting and seek medical help immediately.

HIKING SAFETY

While it may seem obvious to recommend hikers take appropriate precautions regarding Hawaii's bug population and sun, a few quick hiking tips can help prevent an adventure from turning into a disaster.

- Wear comfortable, closed-toed, sturdy shoes with good soles. No slippers.

- Be informed before you set out. Know about the route and the trail you will follow. Don't rely on information being available at the site. Also know how strenuous the hike is—don't overestimate your ability.

- Let someone know where you are hiking and when you should be back. If you are staying at a hotel, tell the concierge the name of the trail and when you plan to return.

- Check the weather. Do not hike if rain or a storm is predicted. Flash floods are common in Hawaii.

DON'T GET BURNED: smart tanning tips

Hawaii's Caucasian population has the highest incidence of malignant melanoma (deadly skin cancer) in the world. And nobody is completely safe from the sun's harmful rays: All skin types and races can burn. To ensure that your vacation won't be ruined by painful sunburn, here are some helpful tips:

- **Wear a strong sunscreen at all times.** Use a sunscreen with an SPF of 15 or higher; people with light complexions should use SPF 30. Apply it liberally (1 tablespoon for each limb), and reapply every 2 hours. The best sunscreens block both UVA and UVB rays. Look for zinc oxide, benzophenone, oxybenzone, sulisobenzone, titanium dioxide, or avobenzone (also known as Parsol 1789) in the list of ingredients.

- **Wear a hat and sunglasses.** Your hat should have a brim all the way around, to cover not only your face but also the sensitive back of your neck. Make sure your sunglasses have UV filters.

- **Protect children from the sun.** Keep infants under 6 months out of the sun completely, and slather older babies and children with strong sunscreen frequently.

- **If it's too late:** The best remedy for sunburn is to stay out of the sun until all the redness is gone. Aloe vera, cool compresses, cold baths, and anesthetic benzocaine also help with the pain.

Deep-vein thrombosis, or "economy-class syndrome" as it's known in the world of flying, is a blood clot that develops in a deep vein. It's a potentially deadly condition that can be caused by sitting in cramped conditions—such as an airplane cabin—for too long. During a flight (especially a long-haul flight), get up, walk around, and stretch your legs every 60 to 90 minutes to keep your blood flowing. Other preventive measures include frequent flexing of the legs while sitting, drinking lots of water, and avoiding alcohol and sleeping pills. If you have a history of deep-vein thrombosis, heart disease, or another condition that puts you at high risk, some experts recommend wearing compression stockings or taking anticoagulants when you fly; always ask your physician about the best course for you. Symptoms of deep-vein thrombosis include leg pain or swelling, or even shortness of breath.

- Carry a small day pack with more water than you think you will need, insect repellant, sun block, basic first aid, a snack, a trash bag to take your rubbish out, and a cellphone. Remember to pack out what you pack in.

- Plan to finish your hike an hour before sunset. Because Hawaii is so close to the equator, it does not have a twilight period. The sun sets, and then it gets dark quickly.

- If you're planning a trek to the top of 10,000-foot Haleakala, you'll need to watch for signs of **altitude sickness.** If you experience dizziness, drowsiness, or a sudden headache, consider heading back down the mountain. Pregnant women, heavy smokers, and people with asthma and/or heart conditions should be especially careful.

VOG

The volcanic haze dubbed *vog* is caused by gases released when molten lava—from the continuous eruption of Kilauea volcano on the Big Island—pours into the ocean. As we went to press, Kilauea had not one but two eruptions going on, spewing out sulfur dioxide. Some people claim that long-term exposure to the hazy, smoglike air has caused bronchial ailments, but it's highly unlikely to cause you any harm in the course of your visit.

There actually is a vog season in Hawaii: the fall and winter months, when the trade winds that blow the fumes out to sea die down. The vog is felt not only on the Big Island, but also as far away as Maui and Oahu.

OCEAN SAFETY

Because most people coming to Hawaii are unfamiliar with the ocean environment, they're often unaware of the natural hazards it holds. With just a few precautions, your ocean experience can be a safe and happy one. An excellent book is *All Stings Considered: First Aid and Medical Treatment of Hawaii's Marine Injuries,* by Craig Thomas and Susan Scott (University of Hawaii Press, 1997).

Note that sharks are not a big problem in Hawaii; in fact, they appear so infrequently that locals look forward to seeing them. Since records have been kept, starting in 1779, there have been only about 100 shark attacks in Hawaii, of which 40% have been fatal. Most attacks occurred after someone fell into the ocean from the shore or from a boat; in these cases, the sharks probably attacked after the person was dead. But general rules for avoiding sharks are: Don't swim at sunrise, at sunset, or where the water is murky due to stream runoff—sharks may mistake you for one of their usual meals. And don't swim where there are bloody fish in the water, as sharks become aggressive around blood.

SEASICKNESS The waters in Hawaii can range from as calm as glass (off the Kona Coast on the Big Island) to downright frightening (in storm conditions); they usually fall somewhere in between. In general, expect rougher conditions in winter than in summer. Some 90% of the population tends toward seasickness. If you've never been out on a boat, or if you've been seasick in the past, you might want to heed the following suggestions:

o   The day before you go out on the boat, avoid alcohol, caffeine, citrus and other acidic juices, and greasy, spicy, or hard-to-digest foods.

o   Get a good night's sleep the night before.

o   Take or use whatever seasickness prevention works best for you—medication, an acupressure wristband, ginger-root tea or capsules, or any combination. But do it **before you board;** once you set sail, it's generally too late.

o   While you're on the boat, stay as low and as near the center of the boat as possible. Avoid the fumes (especially if it's a diesel boat); stay out in the fresh air and watch the horizon. Do not read.

o   If you start to feel queasy, drink clear fluids, such as water, and eat something bland such as a soda cracker.

STINGS The most common stings in Hawaii come from Portuguese man-of-war and box jellyfish. Because the poisons they inject are very different, you need to treat each type of sting differently.

A bluish-purple floating bubble with a long tail, the **Portuguese man-of-war** is responsible for some 6,500 stings a year on Oahu alone. These stings, although painful and a nuisance, are rarely harmful; fewer than 1 in 1,000 requires medical treatment. The best prevention is to watch for these floating bubbles as you snorkel (look for the hanging tentacles below the surface). Get out of the water if anyone near you spots one of these.

Reactions to stings range from mild burning and reddening to severe welts and blisters. *All Stings Considered* recommends the following treatment: First, pick off any visible tentacles with a gloved hand, a stick, or anything handy; then rinse the sting with salt- or fresh water, and apply ice to prevent swelling and to help control pain. Avoid such folk remedies as vinegar, baking soda, or urinating on the wound, which may actually cause further damage. Most Portuguese man-of-war stings will disappear by themselves within 15 to 20 minutes if you do nothing at all to treat them. Still, be sure to see a doctor if pain persists or a rash or other symptoms develop.

Transparent, square-shaped **box jellyfish** are nearly impossible

Everything You've Always Wanted to Know about Sharks

The Hawaii State Department of Land and Natural Resources has launched a website, **www.hawaiisharks.com,** that covers the biology, history, and culture of these carnivores. It also provides safety information and data on shark bites in Hawaii.

> ### Enjoying the Ocean & Avoiding Mishaps
>
> The Pacific Whale Foundation has a free brochure called *Enjoying Maui's Unique Ocean Environment* that introduces visitors to Hawaii's ocean, beaches, tide pools, and reefs; it even has maps showing Maui's beaches. It's a great general resource on how to stay safe around the ocean, with hints on how to assess weather before you jump into the water and the best ways to view marine wildlife. To get the brochure, call ✆ 808/244-8390 or visit www.pacificwhale.org.

to see in the water. Fortunately, they seem to follow a monthly cycle: 8 to 10 days after the full moon, they appear in the waters on the leeward side of each island and hang around for about 3 days. Also, they seem to sting more in the morning hours, when they're on or near the surface.

The stings can cause anything from no visible marks to hivelike welts, blisters, and pain lasting from 10 minutes to 8 hours. *All Stings Considered* recommends the following treatment: First, pour regular household vinegar on the sting; this will stop additional burning. Do not rub the area. Pick off any vinegar-soaked tentacles with a stick. For pain, apply an ice pack. Seek additional medical treatment if you experience shortness of breath, weakness, palpitations, muscle cramps, or any other severe symptoms. Most box jellyfish stings disappear by themselves without any treatment.

PUNCTURES Most sea-related punctures come from stepping on or brushing against the needlelike spines of sea urchins (known locally as *wana*). Be careful when you're in the water; don't put your foot down (even if you have booties or fins on) if you can't clearly see the bottom. Waves can push you into *wana* in a surge zone in shallow water. The spines can even puncture a wet suit.

A sea-urchin puncture can result in burning, aching, swelling, and discoloration (black or purple) around the area where the spines entered your skin. The best thing to do is to pull any protruding spines out. The body will absorb the spines within 24 hours to 3 weeks, or the remainder of the spines will work themselves out. Again, contrary to popular wisdom, do not urinate or pour vinegar on the embedded spines—this will not help.

CUTS All cuts obtained in the marine environment must be taken seriously because the high level of bacteria present in the water can quickly cause the cut to become infected. The best way to prevent cuts is to wear a wet suit, gloves, and reef shoes. Never touch coral; not only can you get cut, but you can also damage a living organism that took decades to grow.

The symptoms of a coral cut can range from a slight scratch to severe welts and blisters. *All Stings Considered* recommends gently pulling the edges of the skin open and removing any embedded coral or grains of sand with tweezers. Next, scrub the cut well with fresh water. If pressing a clean cloth against the wound doesn't stop the bleeding, or the edges of the injury are jagged or gaping, seek medical treatment.

If You Get Sick

If you suffer from a chronic illness, consult your doctor before your departure. Pack prescription medications in your carry-on luggage, and carry them in their original containers, with pharmacy labels—otherwise, they won't make it through airport security. Visitors from outside the U.S. should carry generic names of prescription drugs. For U.S. travelers, most reliable health-care plans provide coverage if you get sick away from home. Foreign visitors may have to pay all medical costs upfront and be reimbursed later.

See "Medical Insurance," under "Insurance," in chapter 13. Doctors, dentists, and emergency numbers are also listed in chapter 13.

CRIME & SAFETY

General Safety

Although tourist areas are generally safe, visitors should always stay alert, even in laid-back Hawaii. It's wise to ask the island tourist office if you're in doubt about which neighborhoods are safe. Avoid deserted areas, especially at night. Don't go into any city park at night unless there's an event that attracts crowds, such as a concert. Generally speaking, you can feel safe in areas where there are many people and open establishments.

Avoid carrying valuables with you on the street, and don't display expensive cameras or electronic equipment. Hold on to your pocketbook, and place your billfold in an inside pocket. In theaters, restaurants, and other public places, keep your possessions in sight.

Remember also that hotels are open to the public and that in a large property, security may not be able to screen everyone entering. Always lock your room door—don't assume that once inside your hotel, you're automatically safe.

Driving Safety

Recently, burglaries of tourists' rental cars in hotel parking structures and at beach parking lots have become more common. Park in well-lighted and well-traveled areas, if possible. Never leave any packages or valuables visible in the car. If someone attempts to rob you or steal your car, do not try to resist the thief or carjacker—report the incident to the police department immediately. Ask your rental agency about personal safety, and get written directions or a map with the route to your destination clearly marked.

What Is Illegal

Generally, Maui has the same laws as the mainland United States. Nudity is illegal in Maui. There are NO legal nude beaches (I don't care what you have read). If you are nude on a beach (or anywhere) in Hawaii, you can be arrested.

Smoking marijuana also is illegal. Yes, there are lots of "stories" claiming that marijuana is grown in Maui, but the drug is illegal; if you attempt to buy it or light up, you can be arrested.

SPECIALIZED TRAVEL RESOURCES

Gay & Lesbian Travelers

Hawaii is known for its acceptance of all groups. The number of gay- or lesbian-specific accommodations on the islands is limited, but most properties welcome gays and lesbians like any other travelers. For the latest information on the gay marriage issue, contact the **Hawaii Marriage Project** (© 808/532-9000).

Pacific Ocean Holidays, P.O. Box 88245, Honolulu, HI 96830 (© 800/735-6600 or 808/944-4700; www.gayhawaiivacations.com), offers vacation packages that feature gay-owned and gay-friendly lodgings. It also has a website (www.gayhawaii.com) with a list of gay-owned and gay-friendly businesses and links throughout the islands.

For more gay and lesbian travel resources, visit Frommers.com.

Travelers with Disabilities

Most disabilities shouldn't stop anyone from traveling in the U.S. Thanks to provisions in the Americans with Disabilities Act, most public places are required to comply with disability-friendly regulations. There are more options and resources out there than ever before.

Travelers with disabilities are made to feel very welcome in Maui. Hotels are usually equipped with wheelchair-accessible rooms, and tour companies provide many special services. The **Hawaii Center for Independent Living,** 414 Kauwili St., Ste. 102, Honolulu, HI 96817 (© 808/522-5400; fax 808/586-8129; www.hisilc.org), can provide information.

The only travel agency in Hawaii specializing in needs for travelers with disabilities is **Access Aloha Travel** (© 800/480-1143; www.accessalohatravel.com), which can book anything, including rental vans, accommodations, tours, cruises, airfare, and anything else you can think of.

If you plan to see Haleakala National Park, check out the **America the Beautiful—National Parks and Federal Recreational Lands Pass—Access Pass** (formerly the **Golden Access Passport**), which gives visually impaired people or persons with permanent disabilities (regardless of age) free lifetime entrance to federal recreation sites administered by the National Park Service, including the Fish and Wildlife Service, the Forest Service, the Bureau of Land Management, and the Bureau of Reclamation. This may include national parks, monuments, historic sites, recreation areas, and national wildlife refuges.

The America the Beautiful Access Pass can be obtained only in person at any NPS facility that charges an entrance fee. You need to show proof of medically determined disability. Besides free entry, the pass offers a 50% discount on some federal-use fees charged for such facilities as camping, swimming, parking, boat launching, and tours. For more information, go to www.nps.gov/fees_passes.htm or call the United States Geological Survey (USGS), which issues the passes, at © 888/275-8747.

For more on organizations that offer resources to travelers with disabilities, go to Frommers.com.

Family Travel

Maui is paradise for children: beaches to run on, water to splash in, and unusual sights to see. To locate accommodations, restaurants, and attractions that are particularly child-friendly, refer to the "Kids" icon throughout this guide, and check out the "Especially for Kids" box in chapter 8. And look for *Frommer's Hawaii with Kids* (Wiley Publishing, Inc.).

The larger hotels and resorts offer supervised programs for children and can refer you to qualified babysitters. By state law, hotels can accept only children ages 5 to 12 in supervised activities programs, but they often accommodate younger kids by simply hiring babysitters to watch over them. You can also contact **People Attentive to Children (PATCH),** which can refer you to babysitters who have taken a training course on child care. On Maui, call ✆ **808/242-9232;** on Molokai and Lanai, call ✆ **800/498-4145;** or visit www.patchhawaii.org.

Baby's Away (✆ **800/942-9030** or 808/875-9030; www.babysaway.com) rents cribs, strollers, highchairs, playpens, infant seats, and the like. The staff will deliver whatever you need to wherever you're staying and pick it up when you're done.

Recommended family-travel websites include **Family Travel Forum** (www.familytravelforum.com), a comprehensive site that offers customized trip planning; **Family Travel Network** (www.familytravelnetwork.com), an online magazine providing travel tips; and **TravelWithYourKids.com** (www.travelwithyourkids.com), a comprehensive site written by parents for parents offering sound advice for long-distance and international travel with children. For a list of more family-friendly travel resources, turn to the experts at Frommers.com.

Senior Travel

Discounts for seniors are available at almost all of Maui's major attractions and occasionally at hotels and restaurants. Always ask when making hotel reservations or buying tickets. And always carry identification with proof of your age—it can really pay off.

If you're planning to visit Haleakala National Park, pick up an **America the Beautiful—National Parks and Federal Recreational Lands Pass—Senior Pass** (formerly the **Golden Age Passport**), which gives seniors 62 years or older lifetime entrance to all properties administered by the National Park Service—national parks, monuments, historic sites, recreation areas, and national wildlife refuges—for a one-time processing fee of $10. The pass must be purchased in person at any NPS facility that charges an entrance fee. Besides free entry, the America the Beautiful Senior Pass offers a 50% discount on some federal-use fees charged for such facilities as camping, swimming, parking, boat launching, and tours. For more information, go to www.nps.gov/fees_passes.htm or call the United States Geological Survey (USGS), which issues the passes, at ✆ **888/275-8747.**

Frommers.com offers more information and resources on travel for seniors.

RESPONSIBLE TOURISM

If there is one place on the planet that seems ideally suited for ecotourism and sustainable travel, it's Hawaii, a place people visit because of the ecology—the ocean, the beach, the mountains, and overall beauty of the place. It seems only natural that the maintenance of its environment would be a concern, both to the people who live there and the visitors who come to enjoy all its ecosystem has to offer.

In fact, Hawaii has a long history of environmental stewardship. The ancient Hawaiians not only knew about sustainability, but also practiced it in their daily lives. They had to! When the ancient Hawaiians occupied the islands they did not have the luxury of "importing" goods from anywhere else. They had the land under their feet and the ocean to gain subsistence from, and those resources had to last not only for their own lifetime, but also for the lifetimes of generations to come. So these ancient people lived in harmony with the land and sea, and had a complex social structure that managed resources and forbade the taking of various resources during certain times of the year, to allow those resources to replenish themselves.

Now fast-forward to the 21st century. Today we, the current stewards of the islands of Hawaii, are just beginning to appreciate just how wise and advanced the ancient Hawaiians were. In some ways, the state of Hawaii is a pioneer when it comes to the various ways it protects and saves its natural resources (for example, Hawaii is second only to California in the number of marine reserves in the National System of Marine Protected Areas). And yet in other ways, modern Hawaii still falls short of the ancient Hawaiians, whose unique system sustained, without imports, the entire population.

Ongoing Environmental Initiatives

The State of Hawaii has several excellent stewardship programs to preserve the ocean environment and its resources, such as Marine Life Conservation Districts (an ocean version of parks; Kealakekua, on the Big Island of Hawaii, and Hanauma Bay, on Oahu, are two examples), Fishery Management Areas (where what you can take from the ocean is restricted), Fishery Replenishment Areas, and Estuarine Reserves. On land, there are corresponding programs to protect the environment from the Soil and Water Conservation District to Watershed Reserves.

In the visitor industry, the majority of hotels have adopted green practices, not only to save the environment, but also to save them money. Nearly every hotel in the state will have a card in your room asking you to really consider if you need a new towel or if you can hang it up and use it one more day. Various state-wide organizations have numerous programs recognizing hotels that are helping the environment, such as the Green Business Awards Program, which recently awarded the **Maui Prince Hotel** its top award for the steps the hotel took to modify equipment and work practices to reduce energy use by more than 10%, reduce water consumption by some 10 million gallons, and to increase recycling to 560 tons of its total 880 tons of annual waste.

Every island has recycling centers (varying from collection of recyclable bottles only to places that take everything); for a list of recycling centers close to where you will be staying, visit the website of the **Hawaii State Department of Health** (http://hi5deposit.com/redcenters.html).

Restaurants across the state are using more local products and produce than ever. Many proudly report that all of their products were grown, grazed, or caught within 100 miles of their restaurant. You can support this effort by ordering local (drink Kona coffee, not a coffee from Central America; eat local fish, not imported seafood), and asking the restaurant what items on its menu are grown or raised on the island, and then ordering the local items.

Below are some helpful hints travelers to Hawaii may want to keep in mind during their adventure to the islands, so that their ecological footprint on Hawaii will be minimal.

WHAT VISITORS CAN DO IN & AROUND THE OCEAN

- Do not touch anything in the ocean. In fact, unless you are standing on the sandy bottom where the waves roll into shore, try not to walk or stand on the ocean floor. The no-touch rule is not only for your protection—there are plenty of stinging, stabbing things out there that could turn your vacation into a nightmare—but also for the protection of the marine environment. Coral is composed of living things, which take years to grow, and a careless brush of your hand or foot could destroy them. Fragile habitats for marine critters can be damaged forever by your heavy foot.

- Do not feed the fish, or any other marine creature. They have their own food and diet, and they can be irreparably harmed by your good intentions if you feed them "people food" or, even worse, some "fish food" you have purchased.

- Leave the ocean and beach area clearer than you found it. If you see trash in the ocean (plastic bags, bottles, and so on), remove it. You may have saved the life of a fish, turtle, marine mammal, or even a seabird by removing that trash, which kills hundreds of marine inhabitants every year. The same thing is true of the beach: Pick up trash, even if it's not yours.

- The beach is not an ashtray. Do not use the sand for your cigarette butts. How would you like someone using your living room carpet as his ashtray?

- Look at, but don't approach, turtles or Hawaiian monk seals resting on the shoreline. The good news is that the number of turtles and Hawaiian monk seals on the main Hawaiian Islands is increasing. While visitors may not know it, both are protected by law. You must stay 100 feet away from them. So take photos, but do not attempt to get close to the resting sea creatures (and no, they are not dead or injured, just resting).

- If you plan to go fishing, practice "catch and release." Let the fish live another day. Ask your charter boat captains if they practice catch and release; if they say no, book with someone else.

 ## Volunteering on Vacation

If you are looking for a different type of experience during your next vacation to Hawaii, you might want to consider becoming a volunteer and leaving the islands a little nicer than when you arrived. People interested in volunteering at beach and ocean cleanups can contact the **University of Hawaii Sea Grant College Program** (☎ **808/397-2651**, ext. 256) or **Hawaii Wildlife Fund** (☎ **808/756-1808**). For eco-volunteering on land, contact **Malama Hawaii,** (www.malamahawaii.org/get_involved/volunteer.php), a statewide organization dedicated to *malama* (taking care) of the culture and environment of Hawaii. At this site you will find a range of opportunities on Maui as well as other islands, such as weeding gardens and potting plants in botanical gardens, restoring taro patches, cleaning up mountain streams, bird-watching, and even hanging out at Waikiki Beach to helping with a reef project. If you are interested in other areas, check out the book *Preserving Paradise, Opportunities in Volunteering for Hawaii's Environment* by Kirsten Whatley (Island Heritage Publishing, 2008).

- If you are environmentally conscious, we do not recommend that you rent jet skis, which have a significant negative environmental impact.

WHAT VISITORS CAN DO ON LAND

- Avoid littering (this includes throwing a cigarette butt out of your car).
- Before you go hiking, in addition to the safety tips outlined on p. 76, scrub your hiking shoes (especially the soles) to get rid of seeds and soil.
- When hiking, carry a garbage bag so you can carry out everything you carried in, including your litter (and if you see other garbage on the trail, carry it out, too).
- Stay on the trail. Wandering off a trail is not only dangerous to you (you can get lost, fall off overgrown cliffs, or get injured by stepping into a hidden hole), but you also could possibly carry invasive species into our native forests.
- Do not pick flowers or plants along your hike. Just leave the environment the way you found it.

TRANSPORTATION CONCERNS

RENTAL CARS   Most visitors coming to Hawaii seem to think "convertible" when they think of renting a car, or they think "SUV" for off-road adventures. If you're thinking "hybrid," you'll have to check your budget, because hybrids from car-rental agencies are not only hard to find, but also extremely expensive in Hawaii. Car-rental agencies do have a variety of cars to rent, though, and you can make a point of selecting a car that gets the best gas mileage. Also, ask for a white car, as they use less energy to air-condition than a dark colored car.

INTERISLAND TRANSPORTATION   The only option for interisland travel between most islands is via air. There are two exceptions, however. If you're traveling between Maui and Lanai, you may want to consider taking the passenger-only Lanai Ferry. If you're traveling between Maui and Molokai, you can take the passenger-only Molokai Princess. Not only are these ferries cheaper than air travel, but their impact on the environment is also less, especially when you consider that most airlines will route you from Maui to Honolulu, and then from Honolulu on to either Molokai or Lanai.

Hawaiian Culture

One of Hawaii's most cherished resources is the Hawaiian culture. After years of being ignored, the Hawaiian culture is flourishing today more than ever. Part of the Hawaii school system are the Hawaiian emersion schools, where all children (not just Hawaiians) can attend schools from kindergarten through college taught in the Hawaiian language. And cultural events in Hawaii are very popular. If you want to see the **Masters of Hawaiian Slack Key Guitar Series** (p. 305), for example, which is held every Wednesday night at 7:30pm at the Napili Kai Beach Resort, you had better call ahead to get your tickets early.

If you want to support Hawaiian culture, plan to attend cultural events like Hawaiian music and dance performances (see the Calendar of Events, p. 61).

Search out locally owned establishments (look for our recommendations in this book). Attempt to buy souvenirs made in Hawaii by local residents (we have many recommendations in chapter 9).

questions **TO PONDER**

One of the toughest questions in Hawaii is "what is the carrying capacity of the islands?" How much can be built before Hawaii becomes overbuilt, or unable to support the increased infrastructure and increased population? How many people can Hawaii hold, and how many visitors, before the beaches are too crowded, the lifestyle is gone, and the islands have more concrete than open green spaces?

Along those same lines, the people of Hawaii are constantly debating cultural issues vs. social issues. For example, currently laws regarding ancient burial sites can stop, reroute, or delay construction projects ranging from building roads to shopping centers. How much do we protect and preserve vs. how much do we allow new infrastructure or buildings to be built to meet modern wants and needs?

If you visit a cultural site, like an ancient *heiau* (temple), the protocol calls for reverence. Be as respectful as you would at a cathedral or church. Never climb or sit on rock walls at a *heiau*. Never take anything from a *heiau*, even rocks, and never pick flowers there. You may see offerings of flowers or fruit—do not disturb them.

HOW TO FIT IN LIKE A LOCAL

Most visitors to Hawaii want to fit in, and be respectful of the local residents. The best way to do that is to be friendly and practice the same common courtesy that you do in your own neighborhood. If you smile and are polite to local residents, chances are they will smile back at you. There are a few things you may want to think about:

o Be super polite when driving. People in Hawaii do not use their car horn as a comment on other people's driving. Most Hawaii residents use their car horn only as a greeting to a friend.

o Another driving comment—you may be on vacation, but not everyone here is, so check your rearview mirror. If you are impeding traffic by driving slowly, pull off the road. If you want to watch the sunset, pull off the road. If you have a long line of cars behind you, pull off the road.

o Dress respectfully. Just because it's Hawaii and warm does not mean that it is acceptable to wear your swimwear into a restaurant. A good rule of thumb is to ask yourself: Would I wear this outfit to a restaurant or retail store at home?

o Remember, Hawaii is part of the United States, and is, in fact, a state. A good way to alienate local residents is to say something such as, "I'm from the States . . . . or "Back in the States, we do it this way."

GENERAL RESOURCES FOR green travel

The following websites provide valuable, wide-ranging information on sustainable travel. For a list of even more sustainable resources, as well as tips and explanations on how to travel greener, visit www.frommers.com/planning.

o **Responsible Travel** (www. responsibletravel.com) is a great source of sustainable travel ideas; the site is run by a spokesperson for ethical tourism in the travel industry. **Sustainable Travel International** (www. sustainabletravelinternational.org) promotes ethical tourism practices, and manages an extensive directory of sustainable properties and tour operators around the world.

o **Carbonfund** (www.carbonfund.org), **TerraPass** (www.terrapass.org), and **Carbon Neutral** (www.carbonneutral. org) provide info on "carbon offsetting," or offsetting the greenhouse gas emitted during flights.

o **Greenhotels** (www.greenhotels.com) recommends green-rated member hotels around the world that fulfill the company's stringent environmental requirements. **Environmentally Friendly Hotels** (www.

environmentallyfriendlyhotels.com) offers more green accommodations ratings.

o **Sustain Lane** (www.sustainlane.com) lists sustainable eating and drinking choices around the U.S.; also visit **www.eatwellguide.org** for tips on eating sustainably in the U.S. and Canada.

o For information on animal-friendly issues throughout the world, visit **Tread Lightly** (www.treadlightly.org). For information about the ethics of swimming with dolphins, visit the **Whale and Dolphin Conservation Society** (www.wdcs.org).

o **Volunteer International** (www. volunteerinternational.org) has a list of questions to help you determine the intentions and the nature of a volunteer program. For general info on volunteer travel, visit **www.volunteer abroad.org** and **www.idealist.org**.

PACKAGES FOR THE INDEPENDENT TRAVELER

Package tours are simply a way to buy the airfare, accommodations, and other elements of your trip (such as car rentals, airport transfers, and sometimes even activities) at the same time and often at discounted prices.

One good source of package deals is the airlines themselves. Most major airlines offer air/land packages, including **American Airlines Vacations** (✆ 800/321-2121; www.aavacations.com), **Continental Airlines Vacations** (✆ 800/301-3800; www.covacations.com), **Delta Vacations** (✆ 800/654-6559; www.deltavacations.com), and **United Vacations** (✆ 888/854-3899; www.unitedvacations.com). Several big online travel agencies—Expedia, Travelocity, Orbitz, Site59, and Lastminute.com—also do a brisk business in packages.

Before you invest in a package deal:

o Always ask about the **cancellation policy.** Can you get your money back? Is there a deposit required?

o Ask about the **accommodations choices** and **prices** for each. Then look up the hotels' reviews in a Frommer's guide and check their

rates online for your specific dates of travel. Also find out what types of rooms are offered.

o Look for **hidden expenses.** Ask whether airport departure fees and taxes, for example, are included in the total cost—they rarely are.

Some packagers specialize in Hawaiian vacations. **Travelzoo** (www.travelzoo.com) often lists package deals to Hawaii. By far the biggest and most comprehensive packager to Hawaii is **Pleasant Holidays** (✆ 800/2-HAWAII [242-9244]; www.pleasantholidays.com), which offers an extensive, high-quality collection of 50 condos and hotels in every price range. At press time, Pleasant Holidays featured a package deal that included airfare from Los Angeles to Maui, 3 nights in a hotel in Kaanapali (double occupancy), and a 3-day car rental starting at $465 per person.

Hawaii's top hotel chains offer package deals and special rates as well. Packages may be available for families, seniors, honeymooners, and golfers, and some offer discounts on rental cars or multinight stays. Check with **Ohana Hotels & Resorts** (✆ 800/462-6262; www.ohanahotels.com) and its more upscale sibling, **Outrigger Hotels & Resorts** (✆ 800/OUTRIGGER [688-7444]; www.outrigger.com); **ResortQuest** (✆ 800/GO-RELAX [467-3529]; www.resortquest.com); **Marc Resorts Hawaii** (✆ 800/535-0085); and **Castle Resorts & Hotels** (✆ 800/367-5004; www.castleresorts.com).

Travel packages are also listed in the travel section of your local Sunday newspaper. Or check ads in national travel magazines such as *Arthur Frommer's Budget Travel, Travel + Leisure, National Geographic Traveler,* and *Condé Nast Traveler.*

For more information on package tours and for tips on booking your trip, see Frommers.com.

SPECIAL-INTEREST TRIPS

If all you want is a fabulous beach and a perfectly mixed mai tai, then Maui has what you're looking for. But the island's wealth of natural wonders is equally hard to resist; the year-round tropical climate and spectacular scenery tend to inspire almost everyone to get outside and explore.

If you don't have your own snorkel gear or other watersports equipment, or if you just don't feel like packing it, don't fret: Everything you'll need is available for rent. I discuss all kinds of places to rent or buy gear in chapter 7.

Setting Out on Your Own Vs. Using an Outfitter

There are two ways to go: Plan all the details before you leave and either rent gear or schlep your stuff 2,500 miles across the Pacific, or go with an outfitter or a guide and let someone else worry about the details.

Experienced outdoors enthusiasts may head to coastal campgrounds or even trek into the rainforest on their own. But in Hawaii, it's often preferable to go with a local guide who is familiar with the conditions at both sea level and summit peaks, knows the land and its flora and fauna in detail, and has all the gear you'll need. It's also good to go with a guide if time is an issue or if you have specialized interests. If you really want to see native birds, for instance, an experienced guide will take you directly to the best areas for sightings. And many forests and valleys in the interior of the islands are either on private property or in wilderness preserves accessible only on guided tours. The downside? If you go with a guide, plan on spending at least $100 a day per person. I recommend the best local outfitters and tour-guide operators in chapter 7.

Don't Let the Sun Go Down on You

When planning sunset activities, be aware that Maui, like other places close to the equator, has a very short (5–10 min.) twilight period after the sun sets. After that, it's dark. If you hike out to watch the sunset, be sure you can make it back quickly, or else take a flashlight.

But if you have the time, already own the gear, and love doing the research and planning, try exploring on your own. Chapter 7 discusses the best spots to set out on your own, from the top offshore snorkel and dive spots to great day-long hikes, as well as the federal, state, and county agencies that can help you with hikes on public property. In chapter 2, see "The Lay of the Land" (p. 38) for an overview of birds, plants, and sea life; and "Maui in Popular Culture" (p. 46) for some reference books to help you identify what you're seeing. I recommend that you always use the resources available to inquire about weather, trail, or surf conditions; water availability; and other conditions before you take off on your adventure.

For hikers, a great alternative to hiring a private guide is taking a guided hike offered by the **Nature Conservancy of Hawaii,** Pukalani Square, 81 Makawao Ave., Ste. 203A, Makawao, HI 96768 (✆ **808/572-7849** on Maui, 808/621-2008; www.nature.org/hawaii; on Oahu, or 808/553-5236 on Molokai), or the **Hawaii Chapter of the Sierra Club,** P.O. Box 2577, Honolulu, HI 96813 (✆ **808/579-9802** on Maui; www.hi.sierraclub.org). Both organizations offer guided hikes in preserves and special areas during the year, as well as day- to weeklong work trips to restore habitats and trails and to root out invasive plants. It might not sound like a dream vacation to everyone, but it's a chance to see the "real" Maui—including wilderness areas that are ordinarily off-limits.

All Nature Conservancy hikes and work trips are free (donations are appreciated). However, you must reserve a spot for yourself, and a deposit is required for guided hikes to ensure that you'll show up; your deposit is refunded once you do. The hikes are generally offered once a month on Maui, Molokai, and Lanai. For all islands, call the Oahu office for reservations. Write for a schedule of guided hikes and other programs.

The Sierra Club offers weekly hikes on Maui. They are led by certified Sierra Club volunteers and are classified as easy, moderate, or strenuous. These half- or all-day affairs cost $1 for Sierra Club members and $3 for nonmembers (bring exact change). For a copy of the club newsletter, which lists all outings and trail-repair work, send $2 to the address above.

Using Activities Desks to Book Your Island Fun

If you're unsure of which activity or which outfitter or guide is the right one for you and your family, you might want to consider booking through a discount activities center or activities desk. Not only will they save you money, but good activities centers should also be able to help you find, say, the snorkel cruise that's right for you, or the luau that's most suitable for both you *and* the kids.

Remember, however, that it's in the activities agent's best interest to sign you up with outfitters from which they earn the most commission. Some agents have no qualms about booking you into any activity if it means an extra buck for them. If an agent tries to push a particular outfitter or activity too hard, be skeptical. Conversely, they'll try to steer you away from outfitters who don't offer big commissions. For example, Trilogy, the company that offers Maui's most popular snorkel cruises to Lanai (and the only one with rights to land at Lanai's Hulopoe Beach), offers only minimum commissions to agents and does not allow agents to offer any discounts at all. As a result, most activities desks will automatically try to steer you away from Trilogy.

Outdoor Etiquette

Act locally, think globally, and carry out what you carry in. Find a trash container for all your litter (including cigarette butts; it's *very* bad form to throw them out of your car window or to use the beach as an ashtray). Observe KAPU (taboo) and NO TRESPASSING signs. Don't climb on ancient Hawaiian *heiau* (temple) walls or carry home rocks, all of which belong to the Hawaiian volcano goddess Pele. Some say it's just a silly superstition, but each year the national and state park services get boxes of lava rocks in the mail that have been sent back to Hawaii by visitors who've experienced unusually bad luck.

DON'T LEAVE HOME WITHOUT YOUR
gold card

Almost any activity you can think of, from submarine rides to Polynesian luau, can be purchased at a discount by using the **Activities & Attractions Association of Hawaii Gold Card,** 355 Hukilike St., No. 202, Kahului, HI 96732 (✆ **800/398-9698** or 808/871-7947; fax 808/877-3104; www.hawaiifun.org). The Gold Card, accepted by members on all islands, offers a discount of 10% to 25% off activities and meals for up to four people. It's good for a year from the purchase date and costs $30.

Your Gold Card can lower the regular $149 price of a helicopter ride to only $119, saving you almost $120 for a group of four. And there are hundreds of activities to choose from: dinner cruises, horseback riding, watersports, and more—plus savings on rental cars, restaurants, and golf.

Contact Activities & Attractions to purchase your card. You then contact the outfitter, restaurant, rental-car agency, or other proprietor directly; supply your card number; and receive the discount.

Another word of warning: Stay away from activities centers that offer discounts as fronts for timeshare sales presentations. Using a free or discounted snorkel cruise or luau tickets as bait, they'll suck you into a 90-minute presentation—and try to get you to buy into a Hawaii timeshare in the process. Because their business is timeshares, not activities, they won't be as interested, or as knowledgeable, about which activities might be right for you. These shady deals seem to be particularly rampant on Maui.

On Maui, your best bet is **Tom Barefoot's Tours,** 250 Alamaha St., Kahului (*©* **800/895-2040** or 808/661-8889; www.tombarefoot.com). Tom offers a 10% discount on all tours, activities, and adventures if you pay using cash, a personal check, or traveler's checks. If you use a credit card, you'll get a 7% discount.

Note that you can reserve activities yourself and save the commission by booking via the Internet. Most outfitters offer 10% to 25% off their prices if you book online.

STAYING CONNECTED
Telephones

Generally, hotel surcharges on both long-distance and local calls are astronomical, so you're better off using your **cellphone** or a **public pay phone.** Many convenience groceries and packaging services sell **prepaid calling cards** in denominations up to $50; for international visitors, these can be the least expensive way to call home. Many public pay phones at airports now accept American Express, MasterCard, and Visa credit cards. In most locales, **local calls** made from pay phones cost 50¢ (no pennies, please).

Most long-distance and international calls can be dialed directly from any phone. All calls on Maui are local calls, whereas calls between the islands are long distance. For **calls from one Hawaiian island to another,** dial 1 followed by the Hawaii area code, 808, and the seven-digit phone number.

For **calls within the United States and to Canada,** dial 1 followed by the area code and the seven-digit number. For **other international calls,** dial 011 followed by the country code, city code, and number you are calling.

Calls to area codes **800, 888, 877,** and **866** are toll-free. However, calls to area codes **700** and **900** (chat lines, bulletin boards, "dating" services, and so on) can be very expensive—usually a charge of 95¢ to $3 or more per minute, and they sometimes have minimum charges that can run as high as $15 or more.

For **reversed-charge** or **collect calls,** and for **person-to-person calls,** dial the number 0 and then the area code and number; an operator will come on the line, and you should specify whether you are calling collect, person-to-person, or both. If your operator-assisted call is international, ask for the overseas operator.

For **local directory assistance** ("information"), dial 411; for long-distance information, dial 1, then the appropriate area code, and 555-1212.

Cellphones

Just because your cellphone works at home doesn't mean it'll work everywhere in the U.S. (thanks to our nation's fragmented cellphone system). It's a good bet that your phone will work in major cities, but take a look at your wireless company's coverage map on its website before heading out; T-Mobile, Sprint, and Nextel are particularly weak in rural areas. If you need to stay in touch at a destination where you know your phone won't work, rent a phone that does from **InTouch USA** (☎ **800/872-7626;** www.intouchglobal.com) or a rental-car location, but be aware that you'll pay $1 or more a minute for airtime.

If you're not from the U.S., you'll be appalled at the poor reach of our **GSM (Global System for Mobile Communications) wireless network,** which is used by much of the rest of the world. Your phone will probably work in most major U.S. cities; it definitely won't work in many rural areas. To see where GSM phones work in the U.S., check out www.t-mobile.com/coverage. And you may or may not be able to send SMS (text messaging) home.

Voice-Over Internet Protocol (VOIP)

If you have Web access while traveling, consider a broadband-based telephone service (in technical terms, **Voice-over Internet Protocol,** or **VoIP**) such as Skype (www.skype.com) or Vonage (www.vonage.com), which allows you to make free international calls from your laptop or in a cybercafe. Neither service requires the people you're calling to also have that service (though there are fees if they do not). Check the websites for details.

Internet & E-mail
WITH YOUR OWN COMPUTER

More and more hotels, resorts, airports, cafes, and retailers are going wireless, becoming hot spots that offer free high-speed Wi-Fi (wireless fidelity) access or charge a small fee for usage. Wi-Fi is even found in campgrounds, RV parks, and entire towns. Most laptops sold today have built-in wireless capability.

Every **Starbucks** in Hawaii has Wi-Fi; for a list of locations, go to www.starbucks.com/retail/find/default.aspx. To find other public Wi-Fi hot spots on Maui, go to **www.jiwire.com**; its Hotspot Finder holds the world's largest directory of public wireless hot spots.

For dial-up access, most business-class hotels in the U.S. offer dataports for laptop modems, and a few thousand hotels in the U.S. and Europe now offer free high-speed Internet access.

Wherever you go, bring a **connection kit** of the right power and phone adapters, a spare phone cord, and a spare Ethernet network cable—or find out whether your hotel supplies them to guests.

For information on electrical currency conversions, see "Electricity" in chapter 13.

WITHOUT YOUR OWN COMPUTER

Most major airports have **Internet kiosks** that provide basic access for a per-minute fee that's usually higher than cybercafe prices. Check out copy shops, such as **FedEx Office** (formerly Kinko's), which offer computer stations with fully loaded software (as well as Wi-Fi). **Hotel business centers** generally provide access, but most charge exorbitant rates.

On every island, branches of the **Hawaii State Public Library System** have free computers with Internet access. To find your closest library or to reserve a computer, check www.librarieshawaii.org/services/pcreservation.htm. There is no charge for use of the computers, but you must have a Hawaii library card, which is free to Hawaii residents and members of the military. Visitors have a choice of two types of cards: a $25 nonresident card that is good for 5 years (and may be renewed for an additional $25) or a $10 visitor card ($5 for children 18 and under) that is good for 3 months but may not be renewed. To download an application for a library card, go to www.librarieshawaii.org/services/libcard.htm.

TIPS ON ACCOMMODATIONS

Maui offers a tremendous variety of accommodations, from ritzy resorts to simple bed-and-breakfasts. Each type has its pluses and minuses, so before you book, make sure you know what you're getting into. I've also included some tips on how to get the best rates.

Types Of Accommodations

HOTELS In Hawaii, the term "hotel" can indicate a wide range of options, from few or no on-site amenities to enough extras to qualify as a resort. Generally, a hotel offers daily maid service and has a restaurant, on-site laundry facilities, a pool, and a sundries/convenience-type shop (as opposed to the shopping arcades that most resorts have). Top hotels also have activities desks, concierge and valet services, room service, business centers, airport shuttles, bars and/or lounges, and perhaps a few more shops.

The advantages of staying in a hotel are privacy and convenience; the disadvantage is generally noise (either thin walls between rooms or loud music from a lobby lounge late into the night).

RESORTS In Hawaii, a resort offers everything a hotel does—and more. You can expect direct beach access, with beach cabanas and lounge chairs; pools and a Jacuzzi; a spa and fitness center; restaurants, bars, and lounges; a 24-hour front desk; concierge, valet, and bellhop services; room service (often 24-hr.); an activities desk; tennis and golf; ocean activities; a business center; kids' programs; and more.

The advantages of a resort are that you have everything you could possibly want in the way of services and things to do; the disadvantage is that the price generally reflects this. And don't be misled by a name—just because a place is called "ABC Resort" doesn't mean it actually *is* a resort. Make sure you're getting what you pay for.

CONDOS The roominess and convenience of a condo—which is usually a fully equipped, multiple-bedroom apartment—makes this a great choice for families. Condominium properties in Hawaii generally consist of several apartments set in either a single high-rise or a cluster of low-rise units.

Nickel-and-Dime Charges at High-Priced Hotels

Several upscale resorts in Hawaii engage in a practice that I find distasteful and dishonest: charging a so-called resort fee. This daily fee is added on to your bill for such "complimentary" items as a daily newspaper, local phone calls, and use of the fitness facilities—amenities that the resort has been happily providing free to its guests for years. In most cases, you do not have an option to decline the resort fee—in other words, this is a sneaky way to increase the nightly rate without telling you.

WHAT IF YOUR dream hotel BECOMES A NIGHTMARE?

To avoid any unpleasant surprises, find out when you make your reservation exactly what the accommodations are offering you: cost, minimum stay, and included amenities. Ask if there's any penalty for leaving early. Discuss what the cancellation policy is if the accommodations fail to meet your expectations—and get this policy in writing.

Upon checking in, if you're not satisfied with your room, notify the front desk or booking agency immediately. Approach the management in a calm, reasonable manner, and suggest a solution (such as moving to another unit). Be willing to compromise. Do not leave; if you do, you may not get your deposit back.

If all else fails, when you get home, write to any association the establishment may be a member of (such as the Hawaii Visitors & Convention Bureau or a resort association). Describe your complaint and why the issue was not resolved to your satisfaction. And be sure to let us know if you have a problem with a place recommended in this book!

Condos usually have amenities such as some maid service (ranging from daily to weekly; it may or may not be included in your rate), a pool, and an on-site front desk or a live-in property manager. Condos tend to be clustered in resort areas. There are some very high-end condos, but most are quite affordable, especially if you're traveling in a group.

The advantages of a condo are privacy, space, and conveniences—which usually include a full kitchen, a washer and dryer, a private phone, and more. The downsides are the standard lack of an on-site restaurant and the density of the units (vs. the privacy of a single-unit vacation rental).

BED & BREAKFASTS Hawaii has a wide range of places that call themselves B&Bs: everything from a traditional B&B—several bedrooms in a home, with breakfast served in the morning—to what is essentially a vacation rental on an owner's property that comes with fixings for you to make your own breakfast. Make sure that the B&B you're booking matches your own mental picture. Note that laundry facilities and private phones are not always available. I review lots of wonderful B&Bs in the chapters that follow. If you have to share a bathroom, I spell it out in the listings; otherwise, you can assume that you will have your own.

The advantages of a traditional B&B are its individual style and congenial atmosphere, with a host who's often happy to act as your own private concierge. In addition, B&Bs are usually an affordable way to go. The disadvantages are lack of privacy, usually a set time for breakfast, few amenities, and generally no maid service. Also, B&B owners typically require a minimum stay of 2 or 3 nights, and it's often a drive to the beach.

VACATION RENTALS This is another great choice for families and for long-term stays. "Vacation rental" usually means that there will be no one on the property where you're staying. The actual accommodations can range from an apartment to an entire fully equipped house. Generally, vacation rentals allow you to settle in and make yourself at home for a while. They have kitchen facilities (at least a kitchenette), on-site laundry facilities, and a phone; some also come with such extras as a TV, VCR or DVD player, and stereo.

The advantages of a vacation rental are complete privacy, your own kitchen (which can save you money on meals), and lots of conveniences. The disadvantages are a lack of an on-site property manager and generally no maid service; often a minimum stay is required (sometimes as much as a week). If you book a vacation rental, be sure that you have a 24-hour contact to call if the toilet won't flush or you can't figure out how to turn on the air-conditioning.

Using a Booking Agency vs. Doing It Yourself

If you don't have the time to call several places yourself to make sure they offer the amenities you'd like, you might consider a booking agency.

A statewide booking agent for B&Bs is **Bed & Breakfast Hawaii** (© **800/733-1632** or 808/822-7771; fax 808/822-2723; www.bandb-hawaii. com), offering a range of accommodations from vacation homes to bed-and-breakfast inns, starting at $65 a night. For vacation rentals, contact **Hawaii Beachfront Vacation Homes** (© **808/247-3637;** fax 808/235-2644). **Hawaii Condo Exchange** (© **800/442-0404;** www.myhawaiibeachfront.com) acts as a consolidator for condo and vacation-rental properties.

Surfing for Hotels

In addition to the online travel booking sites **Travelocity, Expedia, Orbitz, Priceline,** and **Hotwire,** you can book hotels through **Hotels.com, Quikbook. com,** and **Travelaxe.com.**

HotelChatter.com is a daily webzine offering smart coverage and critiques of hotels worldwide. **TripAdvisor.com** and **HotelShark.com** offer helpful independent consumer reviews of hotels and resort properties.

It's a good idea to get a confirmation number and make a printout of any online booking transaction.

For more tips on surfing for hotel deals online, visit Frommers.com.

Saving on Your Hotel Room

The **rack rate** is the maximum rate that a hotel charges for a room. Hardly anybody pays this price, however, except in high season or on holidays.

Rates can sometimes be bargained down, but it depends on the place. The best bargaining can be had at **hotels** and **resorts.** If business is slow and you book directly, some places may give you at least part of the commission they'd normally pay a travel agent. Most hotels and resorts also have local rates for islanders, which they may extend to visitors during slow periods. It never hurts to ask about discounted or local rates; a host of special rates are available for the military, seniors, members of the travel industry, families, corporate travelers, and long-term stays. Also ask about **package deals,** which might include a car rental or free breakfast for the same price as a room by itself. Hotels and resorts offer packages for everyone: golfers, tennis players, families, honeymooners, and more (see "Packages for the Independent Traveler," earlier in this chapter). I've found that it's worth the extra few cents to make a local call to the hotel; sometimes the local reservations person knows about package deals that the toll-free operators are unaware of. If all else fails, try to get the hotel or resort to upgrade you to a better room for the same price as a budget room, or to waive the parking fee or extra fees for children. Persistence and polite inquiries can pay off.

It's harder to bargain at **bed-and-breakfasts.** You may be able to negotiate down the minimum stay or get a discount if you're staying a week or longer. But generally, a B&B owner has only a few rooms and has already priced the property at a competitive rate; expect to pay what's asked.

You have somewhat more leeway to negotiate at **vacation rentals** and **condos.** In addition to asking for a discount on a multinight stay, ask if they can throw in a rental car to sweeten the deal; believe it or not, they often will.

To lower the cost of your room:

o **Ask about special rates or other discounts.** You may qualify for corporate, student, military, senior, frequent-flier, trade-union, or other discounts.

o **Dial direct.** When booking a room in a chain hotel, you'll often get a better deal by calling the individual hotel's reservation desk rather than the chain's main number.

o **Book online.** Many hotels offer Internet-only discounts or supply rooms to Priceline, Hotwire, or Expedia at rates much lower than the ones you can get through the hotel itself.

o **Remember the law of supply and demand.** Resort hotels are most crowded and, therefore, most expensive on weekends, so discounts are usually available for midweek stays. Business hotels in downtown locations are busiest during the week, so you can expect big discounts over the weekend.

o **Look into group or long-stay discounts.** If you come as part of a large group, you should be able to negotiate a bargain rate. Likewise, if you're planning a long stay (at least 5 days), you might qualify for a discount. As a general rule, expect 1 night free after a 7-night stay.

o **Sidestep excess surcharges and hidden costs.** Many hotels have the unpleasant practice of nickel-and-diming their guests with opaque surcharges (see "Nickel-and-Dime Charges at High-Priced Hotels," earlier in this chapter). When you book a room, ask what is included in the room rate and what costs extra. Avoid dialing direct from hotel phones, which can have exorbitant rates. And don't be tempted by the room's minibar offerings: Most hotels charge through the nose for water, soda, and snacks. Finally, ask about local taxes and service charges, which can increase the cost of a room by 15% or more.

o **Carefully consider your hotel's meal plan.** If you enjoy eating out and sampling the local cuisine, it makes sense to choose a **Continental Plan (CP),** which includes breakfast only, or a **European Plan (EP),** which doesn't include any meals and allows you maximum flexibility. If you're more interested in saving money, opt for a **Modified American Plan (MAP),** which includes breakfast and one meal, or the **American Plan (AP),** which includes three meals. If you must choose a MAP, see if you can get a free lunch at your hotel if you decide to do dinner out.

- **Book an efficiency.** A room, usually a studio, just a single room, with a kitchenette allows you to shop for groceries and cook your own meals. This is a big money saver, especially for families on long stays.

- **Consider enrolling in hotel frequent-guest programs,** which are upping the ante lately to win the loyalty of repeat customers. Frequent guests can now accumulate points or credits to earn free hotel nights, airline miles, in-room amenities, merchandise, tickets to concerts and events, and discounts on sporting facilities. Perks are awarded by not only many chain hotels and motels (Hilton HHonors, Marriott Rewards, Wyndham ByRequest, to name a few), but also individual inns and B&Bs. Many chain hotels partner with other hotel chains, car-rental firms, airlines, and credit card companies to give consumers additional incentive to do repeat business.

Landing the Best Room

Somebody has to get the best room in the house. It might as well be you. You can start by joining the hotel's frequent-guest program, which may make you eligible for upgrades. A hotel-branded credit card usually gives its owner "silver" or "gold" status in frequent-guest programs for free. Always ask about a corner room. They're often larger and quieter, with more windows and light, and they often cost the same as standard rooms. When you make your reservation, ask if the hotel is renovating; if it is, request a room away from the construction. If you're a light sleeper, request a quiet room away from vending or ice machines, elevators, restaurants, bars, and discos. Ask for a room that has most recently been renovated or redecorated.

If you aren't happy with your room when you arrive, notify the front desk or booking agency immediately. Approach the management in a calm, reasonable manner and suggest a solution (such as moving to another unit). Be willing to compromise. Do not leave; if you do, you may not get your deposit back. See "What if Your Dream Hotel Becomes a Nightmare?" earlier in this chapter.

In resort areas, particularly in warm climates, ask the following questions before you book a room:

- What's the view like? Cost-conscious travelers may be willing to pay less for a back room facing the parking lot, especially if they don't plan to spend much time in their room.

- Does the room have air-conditioning or ceiling fans? Do the windows open? If they do, and the nighttime entertainment takes place alfresco, you may want to find out when the show is over.

- What's included in the price? Your room may be moderately priced, but if you're charged for beach chairs, towels, sports equipment, and other amenities, you could end up spending more than you bargained for.

- How far is the room from the beach and other amenities? If it's far, is there transportation to and from the beach, and is it free?

GETTING MARRIED ON MAUI

Maui is a great place for a wedding. Not only does the entire island exude romance and natural beauty, but after the ceremony, you're also already on your honeymoon. And the members of your wedding party will most likely be delighted, as you've given them the perfect excuse for their own island vacation.

More than 20,000 marriages are performed annually on the islands, mostly on Oahu; nearly half are for couples from somewhere else. The booming wedding business has spawned dozens of companies that can help you organize a long-distance event and stage an unforgettable wedding, Hawaiian style or your style.

The easiest way to plan your wedding is to let someone else handle it at the resort or hotel where you'll be staying. Most Maui resorts and hotels have wedding coordinators who can plan everything from a (relatively) simple low-cost wedding to an extravaganza that people will talk about for years. Resorts can be pricey, though, so be frank with your wedding coordinator if you want to keep costs down. And remember, you don't have to use a coordinator: You can also plan your own island wedding, even from afar, and not spend a fortune doing it.

The Paperwork

The state of Hawaii has some very minimal procedures for obtaining a marriage license. The first thing you should do is contact the **Marriage License Office,** State Department of Health Bldg., 54 S. High St., Wailuku, HI 96793 (*©* **808/984-8210;** www.state.hi.us/doh/records/vr_marri.html), which is open Monday through Friday from 8am to 4pm. You can download the office's brochure *Getting Married* from the website, which also lists the marriage-licensing agent closest to where you'll be staying on Maui.

Once on Maui, the prospective bride and groom must go together to the marriage-licensing agent to get the license, which costs $60 and is good for 30 days. Both parties must be 15 years of age or older (couples 15–17 years old must have proof of age, written consent of both parents, and written approval of the judge of the family court) and not more closely related than first cousins. That's it.

At this time, gay couples cannot marry in Hawaii. After a protracted legal battle and much discussion in the state legislature, in late 1999 the Hawaii Supreme Court ruled that the state will not issue marriage licenses to same-sex couples, and the 2010 state legislature refused to consider a bill for a civil union for same-sex couples.

Planning the Wedding
DOING IT YOURSELF

The marriage-licensing agents, who range from employees of the governor's satellite office to private individuals, are usually friendly, helpful people who can steer you to a nondenominational minister or marriage performer who's licensed by the state of Hawaii. These marriage performers are great sources of information for budget weddings. They usually know wonderful places to have the ceremony for free or for a nominal fee. For the names and addresses of marriage-licensing agents on Maui, call *©* **808/984-8210;** on Molokai, *©* **808/553-3663;** and on Lanai, *©* **808/565-6411.**

If you don't want to use a wedding planner (see below), but you do want to make arrangements before you arrive on Maui, my best advice is to get a copy of the daily newspaper, the ***Maui News,*** P.O. Box 550, Wailuku, HI 96793 (*©* **808/244-7691;** www.mauinews.com). People willing and qualified to conduct weddings advertise in the classifieds. They're great sources of information, as they know the best places to have the ceremony and can recommend caterers, florists, and everything else you'll need.

USING A WEDDING PLANNER

Wedding planners—many of whom are marriage-licensing agents as well—can arrange everything for you, from a small, private outdoor affair to a full-blown formal ceremony in a tropical setting. They charge anywhere from $150 to a small fortune—it all depends on what you want.

Planners on Maui include **First Class Weddings** (© **800/262-8433** or 808/877-1411; www.firstclassweddings.com), **A Dream Wedding: Maui Style** (© **800/743-2777** or 808/661-1777; fax 808/667-2042; www.adream wedding.net), **Romantic Maui Weddings** (© **800/808-4144** or 808/874-6444; fax 808/879-5525; www.justmauied.com), and **Dolphin Dream Weddings** (© **800/793-2-WED** [793-2933] or 808/661-8535; www. dolphindreamweddings.com). For a more complete list, contact the Maui Visitors Bureau (www.visitmaui.com). Many of the big resorts have their own coordinators on staff as well.

Getting Married on Maui

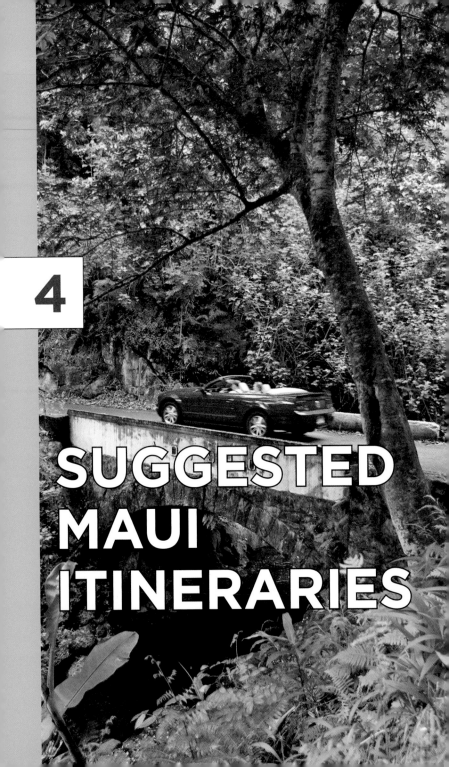

4

SUGGESTED MAUI ITINERARIES

Your vacation time is precious—you have only so many days and you don't want to waste a single one. That's where I come in. Below are several suggestions for what to do and how to spend your time on Maui. I've included ideas if you have 1 week or 2, are traveling with kids, or want a more active vacation. I've also included the best things to see and do on the islands of Molokai and Lanai.

The number-one thing I suggest is this: Don't max out your days. This is Hawaii—allow some time to do nothing but relax. Remember that you most likely will arrive jet-lagged, so it's a good idea to ease into your vacation. In fact, exposure to sunlight can help reset your internal clock, so I include time at the beach on the first day of most of these itineraries.

Also, if this is your first trip to Maui, think of it as a "scouting" trip. Maui is too beautiful, too sensual, too enticing to see just once in a lifetime. You'll be back. You don't need to see and do everything on this trip.

Keep in mind that the following itineraries are designed to appeal to a wide range of travelers. If you're a golf fan or a scuba diver, check out the best golf courses and dive spots in chapter 1 to plan your trip around your passion.

One last thing—you will need a car to get around the island. But plan to get out of the car as much as possible—to smell the sweet perfume of plumeria, to hear the sound of the wind through a bamboo forest, and to plunge into the gentle waters of the Pacific.

THE ISLAND IN BRIEF

See the "Maui" map on p. 3 to locate the following regions

Central Maui

This flat, often windy corridor between Maui's two volcanoes is where you'll most likely arrive—it's the site of the main airport. It's also home to the majority of the island's population, the heart of the business community, and the local government (courts, cops, and county/state government agencies). You'll find good shopping and dining bargains here but very little in the way of accommodations.

KAHULUI This is "Dream City," home to thousands of former sugar-cane workers whose dream in life was to own their own homes away from the sugar plantations. There's wonderful shopping here (especially at discount stores), and a couple of small hotels near the airport are convenient for 1-night stays if you have a late arrival or early departure, but this is not a place to spend your entire vacation.

WAILUKU Wailuku is like a time capsule, with its faded wooden storefronts, old plantation homes, shops straight out of the 1940s and 1950s, and relaxed way of life. While most people race through on their way to see the natural

FACING PAGE: **Driving the Hana Highway.**

Kaahumanu Church in Wailuku.

beauty of **Iao Valley** ★, this quaint little town is worth a brief visit, if only to see a real place where real people actually appear to be working at something other than a suntan. This is the county seat, so you'll see people in suits on important missions in the tropical heat. Beaches surrounding Wailuku are not great for swimming, but the town has a spectacular view of Haleakala Crater, great budget restaurants, some interesting bungalow architecture, a Frank Lloyd Wright building, a wonderful historic B&B, and the always-endearing Bailey House Museum.

West Maui

This is the fabled Maui you see on postcards. Jagged peaks, green velvet valleys, a wilderness full of native species—the majestic West Maui Mountains are the epitome of earthly paradise. The beaches here are some of Hawaii's best. And it's no secret: This stretch of coastline along Maui's "forehead," from Kapalua to the historic port of Lahaina, is the island's most bustling resort area (with south Maui close behind). Expect a few mainland-style traffic jams.

If you want to book into a resort or condo on this coast, first consider what community you'd like to base yourself in. Starting at the southern end of west Maui and moving northward, the coastal communities look like this:

LAHAINA This old seaport is a tame version of its former self, a raucous whaling town where sailors swaggered ashore in search of women and grog. Today, the vintage village teems with restaurants, T-shirt shops, and a gallery on nearly every block, and parts of it are downright tacky, but there's still a lot of real history to be found amid the tourist development. Lahaina makes a great base for visitors: A few old hotels (such as the restored 1901 Pioneer

Inn on the harbor), quaint bed-and-breakfasts, and a handful of oceanfront condos offer a variety of choices. This is the place to stay if you want to be in the center of things—restaurants, shops, and nightlife—but parking can be a problem.

KAANAPALI ★ Farther north along the west Maui coast is Hawaii's first master-planned family resort. Pricey midrise hotels line nearly 3 miles of lovely gold-sand beach; they're linked by a landscaped parkway and a walking path along the sand. Golf greens wrap around the slope between beachfront and hillside properties. **Whalers Village**—a seaside mall with 48 shops and restaurants, plus the best little whale museum in Hawaii—and other restaurants are easy to reach on foot along the oceanfront walkway or by resort shuttle, which also serves the small West Maui Airport just to the north. Shuttles also go to Lahaina (see above), 3 miles to the south, for shopping, dining, entertainment, and boat tours. Kaanapali is popular with convention groups and families—especially those with teenagers, who like all the action.

HONOKOWAI, KAHANA & NAPILI In the building binge of the 1970s, condominiums sprouted along this gorgeous coastline like mushrooms after a rain. Today, these older ocean-side units offer excellent bargains for astute travelers. The great location—along sandy beaches, within minutes of both the Kapalua and Kaanapali resort areas, and close enough to the goings-on in Lahaina—makes this area a great place to stay for value-conscious travelers. It feels more peaceful and residential than either Kaanapali or Lahaina.

In **Honokowai** and **Mahinahina,** you'll find mostly older units that tend to be cheaper. There's not much shopping here (mostly convenience stores), but you'll have easy access to the shops and restaurants of Kaanapali.

Kahana is a little more upscale than Honokowai and Mahinahina. Most of its condos are big high-rise types, newer than those immediately to the south. You'll find a nice selection of shops and restaurants (including the Maui branch of Roy's) in the area, and Kapalua–West Maui Airport is nearby.

Napili is a much-sought-after area for condo seekers: It's quiet; has great beaches, restaurants, and shops; and is close to Kapalua. Units are generally more expensive here (although I've found a few hidden gems at affordable prices; see the Napili Bay listing on p. 141).

KAPALUA ★★ North beyond Kaanapali and the shopping centers of Napili and Kahana, the road starts to climb and the vista opens up to fields of golden-green pineapple and manicured golf fairways. A country lane lined with Pacific pines that leads toward the sea brings you to Kapalua. It's the very exclusive domain of the luxurious Ritz-Carlton Kapalua and expensive condos and villas, set on one of Hawaii's best white-sand beaches, next to two bays that are marine-life preserves (with fabulous surfing in winter).

Even if you don't stay here, you're welcome to come and enjoy Kapalua. The fancy hotel here provides public parking and beach access. The resort has an art school where you can learn local crafts, as well as a golf school, three golf courses, historic features, swanky condos and homes (many available for vacation rental at astronomical prices), and wide-open spaces that include a rainforest preserve—all open to the general public.

Kapalua is a great place to stay put. However, if you plan to "tour" Maui, know that it's a long drive from here to get to many of the island's highlights. You might want to consider a more central place to stay—even Lahaina is a 15-minute drive away.

South Maui

This is the hottest, sunniest, driest, most popular coastline on Maui for sun lovers—Arizona by the sea. Rain rarely falls here, and temperatures stick around 85°F (29°C) year-round. On this former scrubland from Maalaea to Makena, where cacti once grew wild and cows grazed, there are now four distinctive areas—Maalaea, Kihei, Wailea, and Makena—and a surprising amount of traffic.

MAALAEA If west Maui is the island's head, Maalaea is just under the chin. This windy oceanfront village centers on a small boat harbor (with a general store, a couple of restaurants, and a huge new mall) and the **Maui Ocean Center ★★**, an aquarium/ocean complex. This quaint region offers several condominium units to choose from, but visitors staying here should be aware that it's almost always very windy. All the wind from the Pacific is funneled between the West Maui Mountains and Haleakala, and comes out in Maalaea.

KIHEI Kihei is less a proper town than a nearly continuous series of condos and minimalls lining South Kihei Road. This is Maui's best vacation bargain: Budget travelers swarm like sun-seeking geckos over the eight sandy beaches along this scalloped, condo-packed 7-mile stretch of coast. Kihei is neither

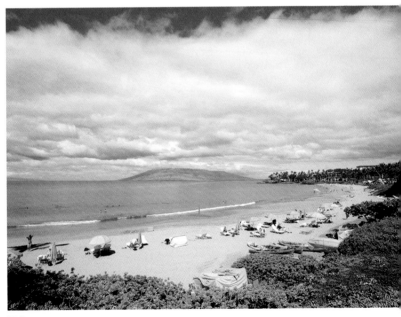

Wailea.

Kayaking is popular along Makena's gorgeous, pristine beach.

charming nor quaint; what it lacks in aesthetics, though, it more than makes up for in sunshine, affordability, and convenience. If you want a latte in the morning, fine beaches in the afternoon, and Hawaii Regional Cuisine in the evening—all at reasonable prices—head to Kihei.

WAILEA ★★ Just 3 decades ago, this was wall-to-wall scrub kiawe trees, but now Wailea is a manicured oasis of multimillion-dollar resort hotels along 2 miles of palm-fringed gold coast. It's like Beverly Hills by the sea, except California never had it so good: Wailea has warm, clear water full of tropical fish; year-round golden sunshine and clear blue skies; and hedonistic pleasure palaces on 1,500 acres of black-lava shore indented by five beautiful beaches. It's amazing what a billion dollars can do.

This is the playground of the stretch-limo set. The planned resort development—practically a well-heeled town—has a shopping village, three prized golf courses of its own and three more in close range, and a tennis complex. A growing number of large homes sprawl over the upper hillside, some offering excellent bed-and-breakfast units at reasonable prices. The resorts along this fantasy coast are spectacular, to say the least. Next door to the Four Seasons, the most elegant, is the Grand Wailea Resort Hotel & Spa, a public display of ego by Tokyo mogul Takeshi Sekiguchi, who dropped $600 million in 1991 to create his own mini city. Stop in and take a look—it's so gauche, you've gotta see it.

Appealing natural features include the coastal trail, a 3-mile round-trip path along the oceanfront with pleasing views everywhere you look—out to sea and to the neighboring islands, or inland to the broad lawns and gardens of the hotels. The trail's south end borders an extensive garden of native coastal plants, as well as the ruins of ancient lava-rock houses juxtaposed with elegant oceanfront condos. But the chief attractions, of course, are those five outstanding beaches (the best is Wailea Beach).

MAKENA ★★ After passing through well-groomed Wailea, suddenly the road enters raw wilderness. After Wailea's overdone density and overmanicured development, the thorny landscape is a welcome relief. Although beautiful,

this is an end-of-the-road kind of place: It's a long drive from Makena to anywhere on Maui. If you're looking for an activities-filled vacation or you want to tour a lot of the island, you might want to try somewhere else, or you'll spend most of your time in the car. But if you crave a quiet, relaxing respite, where the biggest trip of the day is from your bed to the gorgeous, pristine beach, Makena is the place.

Beyond Makena, you'll discover Haleakala's last lava flow, which ran to the sea in 1790; the bay named for French explorer La Pérouse; and a chunky lava trail known as the King's Highway, which leads around Maui's empty south shore past ruins and fish camps. Puu Olai stands like Oahu's Diamond Head on the shore, where a sunken crater shelters tropical fish and empty gold-sand beaches stand at the end of dirt roads.

Upcountry Maui

After a few days at the beach, you'll probably take notice of the 10,000-foot mountain in the middle of Maui. The slopes of Haleakala ("House of the Sun") are home to cowboys, growers, and other country people who wave at you as you drive by. They're all up here enjoying the crisp air, emerald pastures, eucalyptus, and flower farms of this tropical Olympus—there's even a misty California redwood grove. You can see a thousand tropical sunsets reflected in the windows of houses old and new, strung along a road that runs like a loose hound from Makawao, an old cowboy–turned–New Age village, to Kula, where the road leads up to the crater and **Haleakala National Park ★★★**. The rumpled, two-lane blacktop of Hwy. 37 narrows on the other side of Tedeschi Winery, where wine grapes and wild elk flourish on the Ulupalakua Ranch, the biggest on Maui. A stay upcountry is usually affordable, a chance to commune with nature, and a nice contrast to the sizzling beaches and busy resorts below.

MAKAWAO ★★ Until recently, this small, two-street upcountry town consisted of little more than a post office, gas station, feed store, bakery, and restaurant/bar serving the cowboys and farmers living in the surrounding community; the hitching posts outside storefronts were really used to tie up horses. As the population of Maui started expanding in the 1970s, a health-food store sprang up, followed by boutiques, a chiropractic clinic, and a host of health-conscious restaurants. The result is an eclectic amalgam of old *paniolo* (cowboy) Hawaii and the baby-boomer trends of transplanted mainlanders. **Hui No'eau Visual Arts Center ★**, Hawaii's premier arts collective, is definitely worth a peek. The only accommodations here are reasonably priced bed-and-breakfasts, perfect for those who enjoy great views and don't mind slightly chilly nights.

KULA ★ A feeling of pastoral remoteness prevails in this upcountry community of old flower farms, humble cottages, and newer suburban ranch houses with million-dollar views that take in the ocean, the isthmus, the West Maui Mountains, and, at night, the lights that run along the gold coast like a string of pearls from Maalaea to Puu Olai. Everything flourishes at a cool 3,000 feet (bring a jacket), just below the cloud line, along a winding road on the way up to Haleakala National Park. Everyone here grows something— Maui onions, carnations, orchids, and proteas (those strange-looking blossoms that look like *Star Trek* props). The local B&Bs cater to guests seeking cool tropic nights, panoramic views, and a rural upland escape. Here you'll

find the true peace and quiet that only rural farming country can offer—yet you're still just 30 to 40 minutes away from the beach and an hour's drive from Lahaina.

East Maui

ON THE ROAD TO HANA ★★★ When old sugar towns die, they usually fade away in rust and red dirt. Not **Paia ★★**. The tangled spaghetti of electrical, phone, and cable wires hanging overhead symbolizes the town's ability to adapt to the times—it may look messy, but it works. Here, trendy restaurants, eclectic boutiques, and high-tech windsurf shops stand next door to a ma-and-pa grocery, a fish market, and storefronts that have been serving customers since plantation days. Hippies took over in the 1970s; although their macrobiotic restaurants and old-style artists' co-ops have made way for Hawaii Regional Cuisine and galleries featuring the works of renowned international artists, Paia still manages to maintain a pleasant granola vibe. The town's main attraction, though, is **Hookipa Beach Park ★**, where the wind that roars through the isthmus of Maui brings windsurfers from around the world. A few B&Bs are located just outside Paia in the tiny community of **Kuau.**

Ten minutes down the road from Paia and up the hill from the Hana Highway—the connector road to the entire east side of Maui—is **Haiku.** Once a pineapple-plantation village, complete with a cannery (now a shopping complex), Haiku offers vacation rentals and B&Bs in a quiet, pastoral setting: the perfect base for those who want to get off the beaten path and experience the quieter side of Maui, but don't want to feel too removed (the beach is only 10 min. away).

About 15 to 20 minutes past Haiku is the largely unknown community of **Huelo ★**. Every day, thousands of cars whiz by on the road to Hana; most barely glance at the double row of mailboxes overseen by a fading Hawaii Visitors Bureau sign. But if you take the time to stop and head down the gun-metal road, you'll discover a hidden Hawaii—a Hawaii of an earlier time, where Mother Nature is still sensual and wild, where ocean waves pummel soaring lava cliffs, and where an indescribable sense of serenity prevails. Huelo is not for everyone, but those who hunger for a place still largely untouched by "progress" should check in to a B&B or vacation rental here.

HANA ★★★ Set between an emerald rainforest and the blue Pacific is a village probably best defined by what it lacks: golf courses, shopping malls, and McDonald's. Except for a gas station and a bank with an ATM, you'll find little of what passes for progress here. Instead, you'll discover the simple joys of fragrant tropical flowers, the sweet taste of backyard bananas and papayas, and the easy calm and unabashed small-town aloha spirit of old Hawaii. What saved "Heavenly" Hana from the inevitable march of progress? The 52-mile **Hana Highway,** which winds around 600 curves and crosses more than 50 one-lane bridges on its way from Kahului. You can go to Hana for the day—from Kihei and Lahaina, it's a 3-hour drive (and a half-century away)—but 3 days are better. The tiny town has one hotel, a handful of great B&Bs, and some spectacular vacation rentals.

A WEEK ON MAUI

I've outlined the highlights of Maui for those who have just 7 days and want to see everything. Two suggestions: First, spend 2 nights in Hana, a decision you will not regret, and second, take the Trilogy boat trip to Lanai for the day. I've designed this itinerary assuming you'll stay in west Maui for 5 days. If you are staying elsewhere (such as Wailea or Kihei), allow extra driving time.

DAY 1: Arriving & Seeing Kapalua Beach ★★★

After checking in to your hotel, head for **Kapalua Beach** (p. 202). Don't overdo the sun on your first day. After an hour or two at the beach, drive to **Lahaina** (p. 245) and spend a couple of hours walking the historic old town. Go to the **Old Lahaina Luau** (p. 308) at sunset to immerse yourself in Hawaiian culture.

DAY 2: Going Up a 10,000-foot Volcano & Down Again

You'll likely wake up early on your first day in Hawaii, so take advantage of it and head up to the 10,000-foot dormant volcano, **Haleakala.** You can **hike in the crater** (p. 224), **speed down the mountain on a bicycle** (p. 234), or just wander about the national park. You don't have to be at the top for sunrise; in fact, it has gotten so congested at sunrise that you may be too busy fighting the crowds to have an awe-inspiring experience. Instead, I'd suggest heading up any time during the day. On your way back down, stop and tour **Upcountry Maui** (p. 269), particularly the communities of **Kula, Makawao,** and **Paia.** Plan for a sunset dinner in Paia or Kuau.

Hiking in Haleakala.

1A Kapalua Beach
1B Lahaina
2 Haleakala National Park
3 Hana Highway
4 Hana
5A Ulapalakua Ranch, the Tedeschi Winery & Grandma's Coffee House
5B Haliimaile General Store
5C Maui Ocean Center
6 Lanai
7 Iao Valley

DAY 3: Driving the Hana Highway ★★★

Pack a lunch and spend the entire day driving the scenic **Hana Highway** (p. 272). Pull over often and get out to take photos, smell the flowers, and jump in the mountain-stream pools. Wave to everyone, move off the road for those speeding by, and breathe in Hawaii. Plan to spend at least 2 nights in Hana (hotel recommendations start on p. 160).

DAY 4: Spending a Day in Heavenly Hana ★★★

You have an entire day in paradise and plenty of things to see. Take an early-morning hike along the black sands of **Waianapanapa State Park** (p. 281); then explore the tiny town of **Hana.** Be sure to see the **Hana Cultural Center & Museum** (p. 283), **Hasegawa General Store** (p. 303), and **Hana Coast Gallery** (p. 303). Get a picnic lunch and drive out to the Kipahulu end of Haleakala National Park at **Oheo Gulch** (p. 288). Hike to the waterfalls and swim in the pools. Splurge on dinner at the dining room at the **Hotel Hana-Maui** (p. 160). Spend another night in Hana.

DAY 5: Enjoying Wine, Food & (Hawaiian) Song

Check to see if the road past Hana is open; if it is, continue driving around the island, past Kaupo and up to the **Ulupalakua Ranch** (p. 271) and the **Tedeschi Vineyards and Winery** (p. 271). Stop at **Grandma's Coffee**

ABOVE: **Stop in for a tasting at the Tedeschi Vineyards and Winery.**

LEFT: **Trilogy offers the best sailing & snorkeling trips in Hawaii.**

House (p. 194) for a cup of java, and then head down the mountain, with a stop for lunch at **Haliimaile General Store** (p. 191). Spend the afternoon at the **Maui Ocean Center,** in Maalaea (p. 260), checking out the sharks and other marine life. Have dinner in Lahaina and see the drama/dance/ music show **Ulalena** (p. 309). If the road past Hana is closed, go back along the Hana Highway the way you came, stopping for lunch at Haliimaile, and then follow the rest of the itinerary from there.

DAY 6: Sailing to Lanai ★★★

Trilogy (p. 369) offers the best sailing/snorkeling trip in Hawaii, so don't miss it. You'll spend the day (breakfast and lunch included) sailing to Lanai, snorkeling, touring the island, and sailing back to Lahaina. Plus, you still have the afternoon free to shop or take a nap.

DAY 7: Relaxing & Shopping

Depending on how much time you have on your final day, you can decide to relax on the beach, get pampered in a spa, or shop for souvenirs. Spa-goers have a range of terrific spas to choose from, and shopping aficionados should check out some of my favorite stores (recommendations start on p. 290). If you have a late flight, you might want to check out **Iao Valley** (p. 243).

TWO WEEKS ON MAUI

Lucky travelers will get 2 weeks to totally relax on the Valley Isle. I'd suggest adding lots of naps, vegging out on the beach, and stopping to smell all the exotic flowers to the 1-week itinerary above. Below are suggestions for your second week on Maui.

DAYS 1 TO 7

Follow 1-week itinerary as outlined above.

1A Kapalua Beach
1B Lahaina
2 Haleakala National Park
3 Hana Highway
4 Hana
5A Ulapalakua Ranch, the Tedeschi Winery
& Grandma's Coffee House
5B Haliimaile General Store
5C Maui Ocean Center
6 Lanai
7 Iao Valley

8 Molokai
9 Molokini Crater
10 Makena
11 O'o Farm tour, Surfing Goat Dairy
tour, or Alii Kula Lavender tour
12 Wailuku
13A Lahaina
13B Whalers Village Museum
13C Kahakuloa
13D Halekii and Pihanakalani Heiau

DAY 8: Flying or Ferrying to Molokai for a Mule Ride ★★★

If you have a spare day or two, head over to the "Friendly Isle" to experience the **Molokai Mule Ride** down into the **Kalaupapa Peninsula** (p. 343). This is an all-day experience that you will remember for the rest of your life. You can either take the ferry over or fly; either way, don't miss this opportunity.

DAY 9: Snorkeling in an Old Volcanic Crater ★★★

Take a day to see the fish inside the **Molokini Crater.** Go in the morning before the wind comes up. If it's whale season and you're lucky, you may spot whales on the way over or back. You'll have to go as part of a tour—my recommendations start on p. 216.

DAY 10: Gliding Over the Water in a Kayak ★★★

Kayaking is so easy that you will be paddling away within a few minutes of lessons. One of the best kayak places is **Makena**—it's calm, the water is so clear you can see the fish, and you're protected from the wind. See "Ocean Kayaking" (p. 211) for more suggestions. After a couple hours of kayaking and snorkeling, stop for a picnic lunch at **Makena Landing,** and then explore this area. If you still have energy to spare, hike over to **La Pérouse Monument,** along the rugged shoreline. For coverage of Makena, see p. 262.

A sign near Surfing Goat Dairy.

DAY 11: Taking an Offbeat Tour ★

Plan at least one off-the-beaten-path tour while you're on Maui. If you love good food, book the tour of Chef James McDonald's **O'o Farm** (p. 178), which includes lunch. Cheese aficionados will love visiting **Surfing Goat Dairy** (p. 271) and sampling its cheeses. For a really exotic experience, take the Combo Tour at **Alii Kula Lavender** (p. 270), which includes a tour of the farm and lunch made with lavender products.

DAY 12: Seeing Maui from a Helicopter ★★★

The feeling of suddenly lifting off straight up in the air and then floating over the island of Maui in a helicopter is a memory that will stay with you forever. Of all the helicopter companies, I recommend booking with **Blue Hawaiian Helicopters** (p. 239) for the most comfortable, informative, and fun tour in the air. After the tour, take some time to explore old **Wailuku** town, wander through the shops (p. 292), stop at the **Bailey House Museum** (p. 243), and then take in **Waikapu** (p. 242), **Kahului** (p. 241), and **Puunene** (p. 241).

DAY 13: Walking Back in Time in Lahaina ★★

Plan to arrive in this historic town early, before the crowds. Eat a big breakfast, and then put on your walking shoes and take the self-guided **historic walking tour** (p. 250) of the old town. Plan to do some browsing in the quaint stores (recommendations start on p. 295), watch the surfers skim the waves in front of the library, and pop over to Kaanapali to the **Whalers Village Museum** (p. 257). Then drive around the head of the island on the **Kahekili Highway** (p. 258), stopping to see the ancient Hawaiian village of **Kahakuloa** and the **Halekii** and **Pihanakalani Heiau** on the Wailuku side.

DAY 14: Enjoying your Last Day

After 13 days of exploring Maui, spend your last day doing what you loved best: beachcombing, snorkeling, hiking, shopping, or whatever your favorite Maui activity is. Pick up a lei before you go to the airport, so you will have a little bit of Maui with you as you say aloha.

MAUI WITH KIDS

Your itinerary is going to depend on the ages of your kids. The number-one rule is don't plan too much, especially with young children, who will be fighting jet lag, trying to get adjusted to a new bed (and most likely new food), and possibly dealing with excitement to the point of exhaustion. The 7-day itinerary below is a guide to the various family-friendly activities available on Maui. Pick and choose the ones everyone in your family will enjoy.

DAY 1: Arriving & Enjoying Pool Time ★★

If you have young kids who are not used to the waves, you might consider taking them to the swimming pool at your hotel. They'll be happy playing in the water, and you won't have to introduce them to ocean safety after that long plane ride. Plan an early dinner, with food your kids are used to. If you're in Lahaina, go to **Cheeseburger in Paradise** (p. 175); if you're in Kihei, consider either **Shaka Sandwich & Pizza** (p. 188) or **Stella Blues Cafe** (p. 186). Get to bed early.

DAY 2: Going Up a 10,000-foot Volcano & Down Again ★★★

Your family will likely be up early, so take advantage of it and head up to the 10,000-foot dormant volcano, **Haleakala.** Depending on the age of your children, you can either **hike in the crater** (p. 224), **speed down the mountain on a bicycle** (p. 234), or just wander about the national park. On your way back down, stop and tour the upcountry communities of **Kula, Makawao,** and **Paia.** Plan to visit the **Surfing Goat Dairy** (p. 271), stop and look at the strange flowers at the **Kula Botanical Garden** (p. 271), or take the 40-minute narrated tram tour at **Maui Tropical Plantation** (p. 242). Grab an early dinner—try **A. K.'s Café** in Wailuku (p. 169).

The tide pool at Maui Ocean Center.

DAY 3: Seeing Sharks, Stingrays & Starfish Without Getting Wet ★★★

After a lazy breakfast, wander over to the **Maui Ocean Center** (p. 260) in Maalaea so your kids can see the fabulous underwater world without having to get wet. Plan to spend the morning immersed in the 5-acre oceanarium. Eat something fishy for lunch. Then head out to **Lahaina,** where you can take the kids underwater in a Jules Verne–type submarine at **Atlantis Adventures** (p. 241); or, if they are too small, hop aboard the **Lahaina/Kaanapali Sugar Cane Train** (p. 240), or rent some snorkel equipment and hit one of the terrific beaches in west Maui (recommendations start on p. 201). Book ahead for the **Old Lahaina Luau** (p. 308) in the evening.

DAY 4: Sailing to Lanai ★★★

Now that the kids have seen the underwater world, take them sailing to Lanai. **Trilogy** (p. 369) offers the best sailing/snorkeling trip in Hawaii, so don't miss it. In the afternoon, wander around Lahaina and see the giant **Banyan Tree** (p. 247), the old **Lahaina Courthouse** (p. 253), and the **old prison** (p. 256).

DAY 5: Driving the Hana Highway ★★★

Pack a lunch and spend the entire day driving the **Hana Highway** (p. 272), the world's most scenic tropical road. Pull over often and get out to take photos, smell the flowers, and jump in the mountain-stream pools. Wave to everyone, move off the road for those speeding by, and breathe in Hawaii. Plan to spend at least 2 nights in Hana (hotel recommendations start on p. 160).

DAY 6: Spending a Day in Heavenly Hana ★★★

You have an entire day in paradise and plenty of things to see. Take an early-morning hike along the black sands of **Waianapanapa State Park** (p. 281); then explore the tiny town of **Hana.** Be sure to see the **Hana Cultural Center & Museum** (p. 283), **Hasegawa General Store** (p. 303), and **Hana Coast Gallery** (p. 303). Get a picnic lunch and drive out to the Kipahulu end of Haleakala National Park at **Oheo Gulch** (p. 288). Hike to the waterfalls and swim in the pools. Splurge on dinner at the dining room at the **Hotel Hana-Maui** (p. 160). Spend another night in Hana.

Oheo Gulch.

Maui with Kids

1A Lahaina
1B Kihei
2A Haleakala National Park
2B Surfing Goat Dairy
2C Kula Botanical Garden
2D Maui Tropical Plantation
3A Maui Ocean Center
3B Lahaina
4 Lanai
5 Hana Highway
6 Hana

7A Ulupalakua Ranch and the Tedeschi Winery
7B Grandma's Coffee House
7C Haliimaile General Store
7D Maui Nature Center and the Iao Valley State Park

0   5 mi
0   5 km

DAY 7: Seeing the World from a Dragonfly's Point of View ★★

Check to see if the road past Hana is open; if it is, continue driving around the island, past Kaupo and up to the **Ulupalakua Ranch** (p. 271) and the **Tedeschi Vineyards and Winery** (p. 271). Stop at **Grandma's Coffee House** (p. 194) for a cup of java and head down the mountain, with a stop for lunch at **Haliimaile General Store** (p. 191). Spend the afternoon at the **Hawaii Nature Center** (p. 244) and the **Iao Valley State Park** (p. 244) next door. If the road past Hana is closed, go back along the Hana Highway the way you came, stopping for lunch at Haliimaile, and then follow the rest of the itinerary from there.

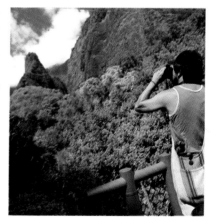

The Iao Needle juts an impressive 2,250 feet above sea level.

MAUI FOR THE ADVENTUROUS

If you can't stand the thought of just lazing around the beach all day, and your idea of the perfect vacation is to be up, active, and trying new adventures, then Maui is the place for you. This itinerary covers all the basics of what to see on Maui, with added adventures that active people like you will love.

DAY 1: Arriving in Maui & Hitting the Beach ★★

Your first stop after you get off the plane should be **Snorkel Bob's** (p. 201) to pick up snorkel gear (the staff will even show you how to use it). Check in to your hotel, and then head for the beach. Great snorkeling spots in west Maui include **D. T. Fleming Beach Park, Kapalua Beach, Black Rock on Kaanapali Beach,** and **Wahikuli County Wayside Park.** In south Maui, wonderful snorkeling beaches include the north end of **Oneloa (Big) Beach** in Makena (by the cinder cone), **Ulua Beach** and **Wailea Beach** in Wailea, and **Kamaole III Beach** in Kihei. Beach coverage begins on p. 201. Remember not to overdo the sun on your first day. If you just can't get enough of the underwater world, take a submarine trip with **Atlantis Adventures** (p. 241).

DAY 2: Going Up a 10,000-foot Volcano & Down Again ★★★

You'll likely wake up early on your first day in Hawaii, so take advantage of it and head up to the 10,000-foot dormant volcano, **Haleakala.** Plan to either **hike in the crater** (p. 224), **speed down the mountain on a bicycle** (p. 234), see the crater on horseback with **Pony Express Tours** (p. 236), or just wander about the national park. You don't have to be at the top for sunrise; in fact, it has gotten so congested at sunrise that you may be too busy fighting the crowds to have an awe-inspiring experience. Instead, I'd suggest heading up any time during the day.

On your way back down, stop and take **Skyline Eco-Adventures' Zipline Haleakala Tour** (p. 223)—not for the faint of heart.

Experiencing Haleakala's crater on horseback.

Maui for the Adventurous

1A West Maui beaches
1B South Maui beaches
2A Haleakala National Park
2B Skyline Eco-Adventures'
   Zipline Haleakala Tour
3 Hana Highway
4 Hana
5A Kaupo
5B Ulupalakua Ranch and the
   Tedeschi Winery
5C Grandma's Coffee House
5D Haliimaile General Store
6 Lanai
7 Molokini Crater

DAY 3: Driving the Hana Highway ★★★

Pack a lunch and spend the entire day driving the scenic **Hana Highway** (p. 272). Pull over often and get out to take photos, smell the flowers, and jump in the mountain-stream pools. Wave to everyone, move off the road for those speeding by, and breathe in Hawaii. Plan to spend at least 2 nights in Hana (hotel recommendations start on p. 160).

DAY 4: Spending a Day in Heavenly Hana ★★★

You have an entire day in paradise and plenty of things to see. Take an early-morning hike along the black sands of **Waianapanapa State Park** (p. 281) and explore the **Piilanihale Heiau** in the **Kahanu Garden** (p. 281). Set up a spelunking tour with **Hana Lava Tube** (p. 237). Get a picnic lunch and drive out to the Kipihulu end of Haleakala National Park at **Oheo Gulch** (p. 288). Hike to the waterfalls and swim in the pools. While you're out there, book a horseback tour with **Maui Stables** (p. 236). Spend another night in Hana.

DAY 5: Trying Something New & Exciting

Check to see if the road past Hana is open. If it is, continue driving around the island, past Kaupo and up to the **Ulupalakua Ranch** (p. 271) and the **Tedeschi Winery** (p. 271). Stop at **Grandma's Coffee House** (p. 194) for a cup of java and head down the mountain. Plan to do something you've never tried before, such as **learning how to surf** with **Rivers to the Sea** (p. 218), **ocean rafting** with **Capt. Steve's Rafting Excursions** (p. 216), or **windsurfing** (p. 221). If the road past Hana is closed, go back along the Hana Highway the way you came, stopping for lunch at **Haliimaile General Store** (p. 191), and then follow the rest of the itinerary from there.

DAY 6: Sailing to Lanai ★★★

Trilogy (p. 369) offers the best sailing/snorkeling trip in Hawaii, so don't miss it. You'll spend the day (breakfast and lunch included) sailing to Lanai, snorkeling, touring the island, and sailing back to Lahaina. The really adventurous can also try **scuba diving.**

DAY 7: Enjoying your Last Chance at Adventure

It's your last chance to do something out of the ordinary. My first pick would be to book a helicopter ride on **Blue Hawaiian Helicopters** (p. 239) to discover what Maui looks like from above. Or if you're a fan of the underwater world, sign up for a **sailing/snorkel tour of Molokini** (p. 216). Even a **guided hike into Maui's rainforest** (p. 223) will remain etched in your memory.

A WEEK ON MOLOKAI

The island of Molokai is for people trying to get away from everything or those looking for adventure. There are no direct flights from the mainland to Molokai, so you will have to fly into Honolulu, and then take a commuter plane to Molokai.

DAY 1: Arriving & Stopping in Kaunakakai

If you're staying in a condo or vacation rental, head into **Kaunakakai** and stock up on groceries. While you're here, wander around the old two-street town and check out the stores. Be sure to stop at the **Kapuaiwa Coconut Grove/Kiowea Park** (p. 338) and watch the sunset.

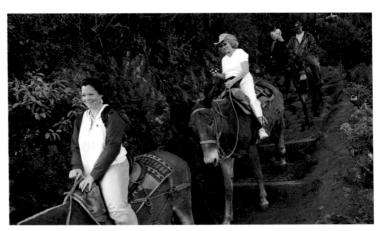

Descending the switchbacks on a mule ride to Kalaupapa.

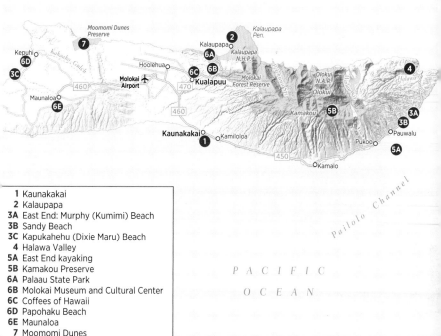

0 5 mi
0 5 km

Moomomi Dunes Preserve
7

Kepuhi
6D
3C

Kaluapapa Pen.
2
Kalaupapa
6A
Kalaupapa N.H.P.

Hoolehua
6C **6B**
Kualapuu
Molokai Airport
Molokai Forest Reserve
470

Maunaloa
6E
460

460

Olokui N.A.R.
Olokui

Halawa
4

Kamakou
5B
3A
Pauwalu
3B

Kaunakakai
1
Kamiloloa

Pukoo
5A
450

Kamalo

Pailolo Channel

1 Kaunakakai
2 Kalaupapa
3A East End: Murphy (Kumimi) Beach
3B Sandy Beach
3C Kapukahehu (Dixie Maru) Beach
4 Halawa Valley
5A East End kayaking
5B Kamakou Preserve
6A Palaau State Park
6B Molokai Museum and Cultural Center
6C Coffees of Hawaii
6D Papohaku Beach
6E Maunaloa
7 Moomomi Dunes

P A C I F I C

O C E A N

DAY 2: Riding a Mule to Kalaupapa ★★★

Your internal clock will still be set to mainland time, so you should have no problem waking up early for the **Molokai Mule Ride** (p. 344). This adventure will take you through 26 switchbacks on a 1,600-foot cliff and give you a chance to tour the **Kalaupapa Peninsula,** where people suffering from leprosy lived for decades.

DAY 3: Heading for the Beach

Molokai has terrific beaches—and on weekdays they are generally empty! Depending on the time of year and the weather, great beaches for snorkeling are **Murphy Beach Park (Kumimi Beach Park)** and **Sandy Beach** (p. 331) on the East End, and **Kapukahehu (Dixie Maru) Beach** (p. 335) on the West End. Pack a picnic lunch or stop by **Outpost Natural Foods** (p. 328) or the **Sundown Deli** (p. 328), both in Kaunakakai. Stay all day. Relax.

DAY 4: Hiking in a Tropical Valley ★

After a day at the beach, you'll be ready for a hike into the tropical jungle of **Halawa Valley** (p. 348). Bring a picnic lunch for after the hike, and then spend the rest of the day on the beach at Halawa. Stop to see the **fishponds** (p. 347) before you leave the East End.

Molokai Palaau State Park.

DAY 5: Exploring the Outdoors ★

Spend a day kayaking, biking, or hiking.

My choice would be kayaking along the shallow waters of the East
End. Hikers should check out **Pepeopae Trail** (p.335) or the **Kamakou
Preserve** (p. 346).

DAY 6: Touring the West End ★★

Because you've already seen the East End, spend a day exploring the rest
of the island. Start out with a tour of the central part of Molokai by driving out to **Palaau State Park** (p. 341), which overlooks the Kalaupapa
Peninsula, and then stop at the **Molokai Museum and Cultural Center**
(p. 340) and take a coffee break at **Coffees of Hawaii Plantation Store
and Espresso Bar** (p. 351). Next head to the 3-mile-long, white-sand
Papohaku Beach (p. 330). After an hour or so at the beach, drive up to
the cool air in Maunaloa town to see the best store on the island: the **Big
Wind Kite Factory & Plantation Gallery** (p. 352).

DAY 7: Seeing Moomomi Dunes: Archaeology
Heaven

Before your flight back, stop by the **Moomomi Dunes** (p. 344), located
close to the Hoolehua Airport. This wild, sand-covered coast is a treasure
trove for archaeologists. Buried in the mounds are ancient Hawaiian burial
sites, fossils, Hawaiian artifacts, and even the bones of prehistoric birds. If
you have time, take the 20-minute easy walk west to **Kawaaloa Bay,** the
perfect place to say aloha to Molokai.

A WEEK ON LANAI

The smallest of all the Hawaiian Islands, Lanai was once a big pineapple planta-tion and is now home to two exclusive resorts, hundreds of years of history, and just one small town with some of the friendliest people you will ever meet. Like the island of Molokai, there are no direct flights from the mainland to Lanai. You will have to fly into Honolulu and then take a commuter plane to Lanai.

DAY 1: Arriving & Seeing Hulopoe Bay ★★

After you settle into your hotel, head for the best beach on the island: the marine preserve at **Hulopoe Bay** (p. 366). It's generally safe for swimming, the snorkeling is terrific, and the fish are so friendly you practically have to shoo them away.

DAY 2: Touring the Island in a Four-Wheel-Drive Vehicle

Lanai is a fantastic place to go four-wheeling. Generally, you won't need a car if you're staying at one of the two resorts or at the Hotel Lanai (they provide shuttle service), so splurge and rent a four-wheel-drive vehicle for 2 or 3 days. Get a picnic lunch from **Pele's Other Garden** (p. 365) and head out of Lanai City to the **Kanepuu Preserve** (p. 378), a 590-acre dry-land forest. Next stop is **Garden of the Gods** (p. 375) and a picnic lunch at **Polihua Beach** (p. 367), Lanai's largest white-sand beach. The beach generally is not safe for swimming and can be windy, but it will probably

Polihua Beach.

Pele's Other Garden.

be deserted and you'll have a great view of Molokai in the distance. After lunch, reverse directions and head to **Shipwreck Beach** (p. 368) and then on to **Keomoku Village** (p. 379).

DAY 3: Spending a Day at the Beach

Plan a lazy day at **Hulopoe Beach** (p. 366). Grab a book, watch the kids play in the surf, or take a long walk around the crescent-shaped bay. For lunch, wander over to the **Four Seasons Resort at Manele Bay** and sit poolside at the **Ocean Grill** (p. 364), or else head to the resort's **Challenge at Manele Clubhouse** (p. 364). In the afternoon, plan a nap or try your hand at some Island crafts at the **Lanai Art Center** (p. 380).

DAY 4: Hiking (or Driving) the Munro Trail

If it has not been raining and the ground is dry, do a little exploring. The adventurous can spend the day (plan on at least 7 hr.) climbing to the top of Lanai on the **Munro Trail** (p. 376). The not-so-adventurous can take a four-wheel-drive vehicle. Soak in a hot tub on your return.

DAY 5: Enjoying a Day on the Water ★★

Ring up **Trilogy Lanai Ocean Sports** (p. 369) and book a sailing/snorkeling, whale-watching, or scuba trip.

1 Hulopoe Beach
2A Kanepuu Preserve
2B Garden of the Gods
2C Polihua Beach
2D Shipwreck Beach
2E Keomoku Village
3A Hulopoe Beach
3B Ocean Grill
3C Challenge at Manele Clubhouse
3D Lanai Art Center
4 Munro Trail
5 A day on the water
6 Kaunolu Village
7 Lanai City

A Week on Lanai

DAY 6: Kayaking or Horseback Riding, Followed by a Trip Back in Time

If you can't get enough time on the water, plan a morning kayaking tour with **Trilogy Lanai Ocean Sports** (p. 369). A picnic lunch is included. Horse lovers should arrange a tour of Lanai through the **Stables at Koele** (p. 374). In the afternoon, take a four-wheel-drive vehicle to the historic ruins of the old **Kaunolu Village** (p. 378), on the southwestern side of the island.

DAY 7: Biking & Shopping

The best way to get around the tiny village of Lanai City is via bicycle. Rent one from the **Four Seasons Resort Lanai, The Lodge at Koele** (p. 361), and ride (downhill) into town. Lanai City has some terrific boutiques that you'll find nowhere else (descriptions of my favorites start on p. 379).

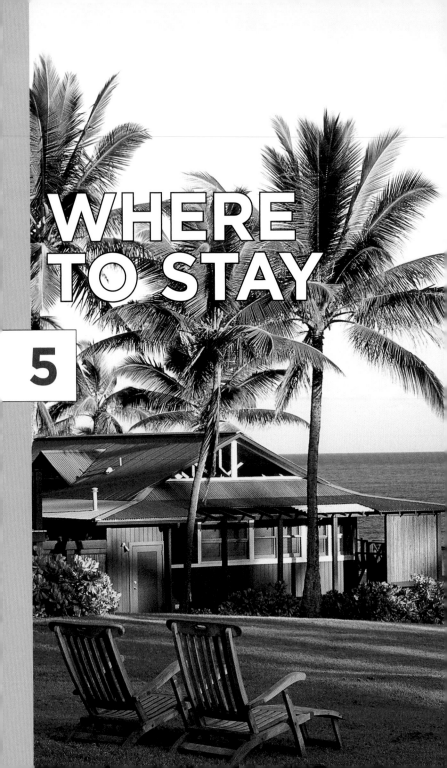

WHERE TO STAY

5

M aui has accommodations to fit every taste and budget, from luxury oceanfront suites and historic bed-and-breakfasts to reasonably priced condos that will sleep a family of four. The high season, during which rooms are always booked and rates are at the top end, runs from mid-December to March. A second high season, when rates are high but reservations are somewhat easier to get, is summer (late June to early Sept). The off seasons, with fewer tourists and cheaper rates, are April to early June and late September to mid-December. Remember to add Hawaii's 11.42% accommodations tax to your final bill. Parking is free unless otherwise noted. *Important note:* Before you book, be sure to read "The Island in Brief" (p. 101), which will help you choose your ideal location, as well as "Tips on Accommodations" (p. 93). Also check out p. 13 – 20 in chapter 1 for a quick look at my favorite accommodations.

CENTRAL MAUI

Kahului

If you're arriving late at night or you have an early-morning flight out, the best choice near Kahului Airport is the **Maui Beach Hotel,** 170 Kaahumanu Ave., Kahului, HI 96732 (© **800/367-5004** or 808/877-0051; fax 808/871-5797; www.mauibeachhotel.net). The nondescript, motel-like rooms (the standard room is so small, you can barely walk around the queen-size bed) start at $117 and include free airport shuttle service (6am–9pm only). It's okay for a night, but it's not a place to spend your entire vacation.

Wailuku

MODERATE

Old Wailuku Inn at Ulupono ★★ 🎁 This 1924 former plantation manager's home, lovingly restored by innkeepers Janice and Thomas Fairbanks with their daughter Shelly, offers a genuine old Hawaii experience. The theme is Hawaii of the 1920s and 1930s, with decor, design, and landscaping to match. The spacious rooms are gorgeously outfitted with exotic ohia-wood floors, high ceilings, and traditional Hawaiian quilts. The mammoth bathrooms (some with claw-foot tubs, others with Jacuzzis) have plush towels and earth-friendly toiletries on hand. The owners recently added the Vagabond House, a modern three-room complex in the inn's lavishly landscaped backyard. These rooms are decorated in Island designer Sig Zane's floral prints with rare framed prints of indigenous Hawaiian flowers, plus plenty of modern amenities (including an ultraluxurious

FACING PAGE: **Hotel Hana-Maui.**

multihead shower). You'll feel right at home lounging on the living-room sofa or in an old wicker chair on the enclosed lanai, where a full gourmet breakfast is served in the morning. The inn is located in the historic area of Wailuku, just a few minutes' walk from the Maui County Seat Government Building, the court-house, and a wonderful stretch of antiques shops.

2199 Kahookele St. (at High St., across from the Wailuku School), Wailuku, HI 96732. © **800/305-4899** or 808/244-5897. Fax 808/242-9600. www.mauiinn.com. 10 units. $165–$195 double. Rates include full breakfast. 2-night minimum. MC, V. **Amenities:** Jacuzzi. *In room:* A/C, TV/VCR, high-speed Internet access.

INEXPENSIVE

Backpackers should head to **Banana Bungalow Maui,** a funky Happy Valley hostel at 310 N. Market St., Wailuku, HI 96793 (© **800/846-7835** or 808/244-5090; www.mauihostel.com), with $25 dorm rooms and some private rooms ($59 single, $68 double). It provides many free amenities not often found in hostel-type accommodations, such as tours of Maui, high-speed Internet access, and a Jacuzzi out back. Dorm-style accommodations ($26) and private rooms ($59 single, $69 double) are also available in old Wailuku at the **Northshore Hostel,** 2080 West Vineyard St., Wailuku, HI 96793 (© **866/946-7835** or ©/fax 808/986-8095; www.northshorehostel.com). Note, however, that women travel-ing alone might not feel safe here after dark.

Happy Valley Hale ♠ The Kong family, owners of Nona Lani Cottages in Kihei (p. 150), have with loving care turned this old plantation home into a tiny oasis in the midst of an economically challenged area. Keep in mind these are budget accommodations—really an alternative to a youth hostel. However, the place is immaculately clean, and the Kongs have made extensive renovations. The four bedrooms—each with twin beds, small fridge, dresser, and closet—share two bathrooms. It's like staying in a family home, with a shared kitchen (no stove, but microwave, griddle, coffeemaker, and so on) and common room with TV. The front yard sports a barbecue and picnic area. The only drawback is that Happy Valley is not exactly a resort area—public housing is just across the street. But for those on extremely tight budgets, it's a good option.

332 N. Market St., Wailuku, HI 96793. © **800/733-2688** or 808/870-9100. www.nonalani cottages.com. 4 units. $33 per bed in shared room; $65 double private room; $99 triple private room. 3-night minimum. MC, V. *In room:* Small fridge, no phone; kitchen in cottages.

WEST MAUI
Lahaina
VERY EXPENSIVE

Ho'oilo House ★ Located just outside Lahaina, about a mile up the West Maui Mountains from Launiupoko Wayside Park, this six-bedroom house is con-structed and furnished with materials and furniture from Bali, but the view is all Maui. The atmosphere is relaxing, the rooms are custom decorated with tradi-tional Bali doors and custom beds, there's a private lanai, and the big, big bath-rooms have huge tubs and outdoor showers. My favorite rooms are the Kohola and the Nalu (great ocean views). There's also a small swimming pool on the property. My only complaint is that $229 to $369 a night seems a bit high for a double room with no hot tub and no fridge. Just a few blocks away is the Guest House (see below), with private hot tubs on private lanais in every room for just $169.

Where to Stay in Lahaina & Kaanapali

Train Depot

Puukolii Rd.

Kaanapali Royal (North) Golf Course

KAANAPALI

PACIFIC OCEAN

Area of detail

Kahului

M A U I

Haleakala National Park

Whalers Village

Kaanapali Kai (South) Golf Course

LK & PR Sugar Cane Train

Honoapiilani Hwy.

Hanakao'o Beach Park

Lahaina Civic Center

Wahikuli Beach Park

Kaniau Rd.
Lokia St.
Rd.
Malanai St.
Wahikuli Rd.
Fleming Rd.
Anakea St.
Kapunakea St.

Lahaina Cannery Mall

Mala Wharf

Puunoa Point

PACIFIC OCEAN

Front St.
Kenui St.
Baker St.
Pababaua St.

Train Depot

Pioneer Sugar Mill

Kahoma Stream

Lahainaluna Rd.

LAHAINA

Lahaina Center
Lahaina Square Shopping Center

Dickenson
Liakini St.
Wainee St.
Honoapiilani Hwy.

Lahaina Small Boat Harbor

505 Front St. (Shops & Restaurants)

Shaw St.

0   1/2 mi
0   1/2 km

138 Awaiku St., Lahaina, HI 96761. © **808/667-6669.** Fax 808/661-7857. www.hooilohouse.com. 6 units. $229–$369 double. Rates include continental breakfast. 3-night minimum. AE, MC, V. **Amenities:** Pool. *In room:* A/C, TV/VCR, Wi-Fi.

Puunoa Beach Estates ★★ ☺ If you're taking a family to Maui, consider these 10 gorgeous town houses in an exclusive 3-acre enclave on a white-sand beach. The individually owned and decorated two-bedroom units (1,700 sq. ft. and up) all have private beachfront lanais, hardwood floors, marble bathrooms, and modern kitchens. Prices are high, but the amenity list has everything you should want for a first-class vacation rental in a dream location. It's within walking distance of the center of Lahaina, but the residential location makes you feel miles away.

45 Kai Pali Place, Lahaina, HI 96761. Managed by Classic Resorts. © **866/504-9465** or 808/661-3339. Fax 808/667-5631. www.puunoabeachestates.com. 10 units. $800–$1,000 2-bedroom unit (sleeps 4). 3-night minimum. AE, MC, V. **Amenities:** Barbecues; concierge; free Internet; fitness center; outdoor pool; sauna; whirlpool; complimentary snorkeling equipment; video library. *In room:* A/C, TV/VCR/DVD, Internet access, full kitchen, fridge, hair dryer.

EXPENSIVE

Outrigger Aina Nalu ★ Set on 9 acres in the middle of Lahaina, this property was totally renovated in 2005. Then the units were sold off to private owners and put into a rental pool. The result is a first-class property, with all the latest appliances, new furniture, and 21st-century conveniences. The property is on a quiet side street (a rarity in Lahaina) and within walking distance of restaurants, shops, attractions, and the beach (just 3 blocks away). All of the good-size rooms, decorated in tropical-island style, are comfortable and quiet. The complex includes a sun deck and pool, a barbecue, and a picnic area. The aloha-friendly staff will take the time to answer all of your questions.

660 Wainee St. (btw. Dickenson and Prison sts.), Lahaina, HI 96761. © **800/OUTRIGGER** (688-7444) or 808/667-9766. Fax 808/661-3733. www.outrigger.com. 197 units. $119–$139 studio with kitchenette; $165–$185 1-bedroom with kitchen (sleeps up to 4); $165–$185 2-bedroom with 1 bathroom and kitchen (sleeps 6); $175–$195 2-bedroom with 2 bathrooms and kitchen (sleeps 6). AE, DC, DISC, MC, V. Parking $15. **Amenities:** Outdoor pool whirlpool. *In room:* A/C, TV/DVD, fridge, hair dryer, high-speed Internet access, kitchenette (in studio), full kitchen (in 1- and 2-bedroom units).

The Plantation Inn ★★ 🛏 Attention, romance-seeking couples: Look no further. This charming Victorian-style inn, located a couple of blocks from the water, looks like it's been here 100 years or more, but it's actually of 1990s vintage—an artful deception. The rooms are romantic to the max, tastefully done with period furniture, hardwood floors, stained glass, and ceiling fans. There are four-poster canopy beds in some rooms, brass beds and wicker beds in others. All units are soundproof (a plus in Lahaina) and come with a private lanai; the suites have kitchenettes. The rooms wrap around the large pool and deck. Breakfast is served around the pool and in an elegant pavilion lounge. Also on the property is an outstanding French restaurant, Gerard's (p. 172).

174 Lahainaluna Rd. (btw. Wainee and Luakini sts., 1 block from Hwy. 30), Lahaina, HI 96761. © **800/433-6815** or 808/667-9225. Fax 808/667-9293. www.theplantationinn.com. 19 units (some with shower only). $159–$245 double; from $239 suite. Check the website for great package deals. Rates include full breakfast. Extra person $30. AE, DC, DISC, MC, V. **Amenities:** Acclaimed restaurant and bar; concierge; Jacuzzi; large outdoor pool. *In room:* A/C, TV/DVD, fridge, hair dryer, kitchenette (in suites), Wi-Fi.

B&B Etiquette

In Hawaii, it is traditional and customary to remove your shoes before entering anyone's home. The same is true for most bed-and-breakfast facilities. Most hosts post signs or will politely ask you to remove your shoes before entering the B&B. Not only does this keep the place clean, but you'll also be amazed at how relaxing it is to walk around barefoot. If this custom is unpleasant to you, a B&B may not be for you.

If you've never stayed at a B&B before, here are a few other hints:

Generally the hosts live on the property, and their part of the house is off-limits to guests (you do not have the "run of the house"). Most likely there will be a common area that you can use. Don't expect daily maid service. Your host may tidy up, but will not do complete maid service. Also don't expect amenities like little bottles of shampoo and conditioner—this is a B&B, not a resort. Remember you are sharing your accommodations with other guests, so be considerate when you come in late at night.

Puamana These 28 acres of town houses set right on the water are ideal for those who want to be able to retreat from the crowds and cacophony of downtown Lahaina into the serene quiet of an elegant neighborhood. Private and peaceful are apt descriptions for this complex: Each unit is a privately owned individual home, with no neighbors above or below. Most are exquisitely decorated, and all come with full kitchen, lanai, barbecue, and at least two bathrooms. Puamana was once a private estate in the 1920s, part of the sugar plantations that dominated Lahaina; the plantation manager's house has been converted into a clubhouse with an oceanfront lanai, library, card room, sauna, table-tennis tables, and office. I've found the best rates by booking through Klahani Travel (see below for contact information), but its office is not on-site, which has caused some problems with guests getting assistance. If you'd rather book directly with the Puamana association office, contact Puamana Community Association, 34 Puailima Place, Lahaina, HI 96761 (© **808/661-3423;** fax 808/667-0398; info@puamana.info).

Front St. (at the extreme southern end of Lahaina, ½ mile from downtown), Lahaina, HI 96761. Reservations c/o Klahani Travel, 159 Halelo St., Lahaina, HI 96761. © **800/669-6284** or 808/667-2712. Fax 808/661-5875. www.klahani.com. 40 units. $140–$250 1-bedroom; $160–$350 2-bedroom; $350–$500 3-bedroom. 3-night minimum. AE, DISC, MC, V. **Amenities:** 3 pools (1 for adults only); Jacuzzi; tennis court. *In room:* TV, fridge, hair dryer, kitchen.

MODERATE

Best Western Pioneer Inn This once-rowdy home away from home for sailors now seems respectable—even charming. The hotel is a two-story plantation-style structure with big verandas that overlook the streets of Lahaina and the harbor, which is just 50 feet away. All rooms have been totally remodeled, with vintage bathrooms and new curtains and carpets. The quietest units face either the garden courtyard—devoted to refined outdoor dining accompanied by live (but quiet) music—or the square-block-size banyan tree next door. I recommend room no. 31, over the banyan court, with a view of the ocean and the harbor. If you want a front-row seat for all the Front Street action, book no. 36 or 49.

658 Wharf St. (in front of Lahaina Pier), Lahaina, HI 96761. ☎ **800/457-5457** or 808/661-3636. Fax 808/667-5708. www.pioneerinnmaui.com. 34 units. $145–$205 double; from $185 suite. Extra person (12 or older) $20. AE, DC, DISC, MC, V. Parking included in room rates. **Amenities:** Restaurant (good for breakfast); bar w/live music; outdoor pool. *In room:* A/C, TV, fridge, hair dryer, high-speed Internet access.

Garden Gate Bed & Breakfast This oasis of a B&B, located on a quiet residential street just outside Lahaina town, is 5 minutes from the beach by car. The six units all have private entrances and a garden or ocean view; the deluxe suites have a deck and a separate pullout sofa for kids. Continental breakfast is served in the garden (Mon–Fri), and hosts Jamie and Bill Mosley are available to answer any questions about things to do or places to eat. Bicycles, boogie boards, beach chairs, and mats are available at no charge. The barbecue area and adjacent laundry facilities are available for guests' use.

67 Kaniau Rd., Lahaina, HI 96761. ☎ **800/939-3217** or 808/661-8800. Fax 808/661-0209. www.gardengatebb.com. 6 units. $99–$169 double. Extra person $10. 3-night minimum. Rates include continental breakfast. AE, DC, DISC, MC, V. *In room:* A/C, TV, VCR (on request), fridge, hair dryer, Wi-Fi, microwave.

House of Fountains Bed & Breakfast 🎁 This 7,000-square-foot contemporary home, in a quiet residential subdivision at the north end of town, is popular with visitors from around the world. Hostess Daniela Atay keeps the place immaculate; in 2002, she won the prestigious "Most Hawaiian Accommodation" award from the Hawaii Visitors & Convention Bureau. The oversize rooms are fresh and quiet, with white ceramic-tile floors, handmade koa furniture, Hawaiian quilt bedspreads, and a Hawaiian theme; the four downstairs rooms all open onto flower-filled private patios. Guests share a fully equipped kitchen and barbecue area, and are welcome to curl up on the living-room sofa with a book from the library. The nearest beach is about a 5-minute drive away; tennis courts are nearby. Around the pool is a Hawaiian *hale* (house), an *imu* pit for luau, and an area that's perfect for Hawaiian weddings (arrangements available).

1579 Lokia St. (off Fleming Rd., north of Lahaina town), Lahaina, HI 96761. ☎ **800/789-6865** or 808/667-2121. Fax 808/667-2120. www.alohahouse.com. 6 units (all with shower only). $150–$170 double (2 people per room). Rates include full breakfast. AE, MC, V. From Hwy. 30, take the Fleming Rd. exit; turn left on Ainakea; after 2 blocks, turn right on Malanai St.; go 3 blocks, and turn left onto Lokia St. **Amenities:** Jacuzzi; outdoor pool. *In room:* A/C, TV/VCR, fridge, hair dryer, Wi-Fi.

Lahaina Inn ★ If you like old hotels that have genuine historic touches, you'll love this place. As in many older hotels, some of these antiques-stuffed rooms are small; if that's a problem for you, ask for a larger unit. All come with private bathrooms and lanais. The best room in the house is no. 7, which overlooks the beach, the town, and the island of Lanai. There's an excellent, though unaffiliated, restaurant in the same building (David Paul's Lahaina Grill, p. 172) and a bar downstairs.

127 Lahainaluna Rd. (near Front St.), Lahaina, HI 96761. ☎ **800/669-3444** or 808/661-0577. Fax 808/667-9480. www.lahainainn.com. 12 units (most with shower only). $160–$180 double; from $205 suite. AE, MC, V. Next-door parking $7 per day. **Amenities:** Bar; concierge; Wi-Fi. *In room:* A/C, hair dryer.

Lahaina Roads 🤿 If you dream of an oceanfront condo but your budget is on the slim side, here's your place. This condominium complex offers small, reasonably priced units in an older building located in the quiet part of Lahaina, away from the noisy, crowded downtown area, overlooking the boats in the Mala Wharf roadstead (a protected place to anchor near the shore). The compact units have full kitchens and soundproof walls—a real plus. The bedrooms face the road, while the living rooms and lanais overlook the ocean and the island of Lanai. The building is nearly 40 years old but well maintained. The only drawbacks are no air-conditioning (it can be boiling hot in the summer in Lahaina) and no laundry facilities.

1403 Front St. (1 block north of Lahaina Cannery Mall), Lahaina, HI 96761. Reservations c/o Klahani Travel, 159 Halelo St., Lahaina, HI 96761. ☏ **800/669-MAUI** (6284) or 808/667-2712. Fax 808/661-5875. www.klahani.com. 5 units. $150 1-bedroom (sleeps up to 4); 3-night minimum. AE, DISC, MC, V. **Amenities:** Oceanside outdoor pool. *In room:* TV, fridge, hair dryer, kitchen.

Lahaina Shores Beach Resort ★ First there's the location, right on the beach; second there's the location, away from the hustle and bustle of downtown Lahaina; and third there's the location, next door to the 505 Front Street restaurants and shops. This recently upgraded condominium project (of studios and one-bedroom units) resembles an old plantation home, with arched colonnades at the entry and an open-air, beachfront lobby. From the moment you step into the airy units (ranging in size from 550–1,430 sq. ft.), you'll feel like you are home. The units all have full kitchens, large lanais, and ocean or mountain views. Ask for an oceanfront unit for that terrific view of the water with the island of Lanai in the distance.

475 Front St., Lahaina, HI 96761. ☏ **866/934-9176** or 808/661-4835. www.lahainashores.com. 199 units. $218–$290 studio double; $266–$355 1-bedroom double; from $355 1-bedroom penthouse double. Extra person $20. AE, MC, V. Parking $8. **Amenities:** Concierge; outdoor pool; tennis courts (across the street); whirlpool; barbecue grill. *In room:* A/C, TV, fridge, hair dryer, high-speed Internet access ($11), kitchen.

Maui Guest House ★★ 🏠 This is one of Lahaina's great bed-and-breakfast deals: a charming house with more amenities than the expensive Kaanapali hotels just down the road. The roomy home features parquet floors and floor-to-ceiling windows; its swimming pool—surrounded by a deck and comfortable lounge chairs—is larger than some at high-priced condos. Every unit has a quiet lanai and a romantic Jacuzzi. Guests share the large, well-equipped kitchen, barbecue, and computers with high-speed Internet access. Scuba divers are welcome here (and provided with places to wash and store their gear). The Guest House also operates Trinity Tours and offers discounts on car rentals and other island activities. Tennis courts are nearby, and the nearest beach is about a block away.

1620 Ainakea Rd. (off Fleming Rd., north of Lahaina town), Lahaina, HI 96761. ☏ **800/621-8942** or 808/661-8085. Fax 808/661-1896. www.mauiguesthouse.com. 4 units. $149 single; $169 double. Extra person $15. Rates include expanded continental breakfast. MC, V. Take Fleming Rd. off Hwy. 30; turn left on Ainakea; it's 2 blocks down. **Amenities:** Huge outdoor pool; free use of watersports equipment; concierge. *In room:* A/C, TV/VCR/DVD, fridge, Wi-Fi, Jacuzzi.

Wai Ola Vacation Paradise on Maui ★ Just 2 blocks from the beach, in a quiet residential development behind a tall concrete wall, lies this lovely retreat, with shade trees, sitting areas, gardens, a pool, an ocean mural, and a range of accommodations. You can book a small studio, a couple of suites inside the home, a separate honeymoon cottage, a one-bedroom apartment, or the entire

5,000-square-foot house. Hosts Kim and Jim Wicker will gladly provide any information you need to make your vacation fabulous. Every unit has a welcome fruit basket when you arrive, plus coffee beans for the coffeemaker. Kim often surprises her guests with "a little something" from her kitchen, like cheesecake or heavenly brownies. You'll also find a deck, barbecue facilities, and an outdoor wet bar on the property; a great beach and tennis courts are nearby.

1565 Kuuipo St. (P.O. Box 12580), Lahaina, HI 96761. © **800/492-4652** or 808/661-7901. Fax 808/661-1119. www.waiola.com. 4 units. $169–$235 studio; from $179 suite; from $209 1-bedroom honeymoon cottage for 2. AE, DISC, MC, V. **Amenities:** Jacuzzi; outdoor pool; free use of watersports equipment. *In room:* A/C, TV/DVD/VCR, fridge, hair dryer, kitchenette, Wi-Fi.

INEXPENSIVE

In addition to the following choices, consider value-priced **Old Lahaina House** (© **800/847-0761** or 808/667-4663; fax 808/669-9199; www.oldlahaina.com), which features comfy twin- and king-bedded doubles for just $89 to $139. It's about a 2-minute walk to the water just across Front Street.

Makai Inn 🏄 Budget travelers, take note: Here's a small apartment complex located right on the water (okay, no white-sand beach out front, but what do you want at these eye-popping prices?). You can take a 10-minute stroll from this quiet neighborhood to the closest white-sand beach, or walk 20 minutes to the center of Lahaina town. The units are small (400 sq. ft.) but clean and have full kitchens, views of the ocean (from most units), and separate bedrooms. There are no phones or TVs, but there's a public phone by the office. In the middle of the complex is a tropical garden. I recommend the Paradise Found unit, which has windows on two sides overlooking the ocean, for just $180. Families will like the Pineapple "Sweet," the only two-bedroom unit (800 sq. ft.), also priced at $180.

1415 Front St., Lahaina, HI 96761. © **808/662-3200.** Fax 808/661-9027. www.makaiinn.net. 18 units. $105–$180 double. Extra person $15. AE, MC, V. *In room:* Kitchen, no phone, Wi-Fi.

Penny's Place Inn Paradise ★ 🏠 No attention to detail has been spared in this Victorian-style bed-and-breakfast, just 50 feet from the water with a fabulous view from the front porch of Molokai and Lanai. Each of the four rooms is uniquely decorated, with themes ranging from contemporary Hawaiian to formal Victorian. Guests are welcome to use the balcony kitchenette (fridge, microwave, toaster, coffeemaker, and ice machine). The only problem is the location—a small island bounded by Honoapiilani Highway on one side and busy Front Street on the other. The house is soundproof, and air-conditioning in each room drowns out the noise inside. Penny recently enclosed the outdoor lanai area, so you can enjoy your breakfast without the highway noise.

1440 Front St., Lahaina, HI 96761. © **888/329-0777** or 808/661-1068. Fax 808/667-7102. www.pennysplace.net. 4 units. $98–$147 double. Rates include continental breakfast Mon–Sat. 3-night minimum. DISC, MC, V. *In room:* A/C, TV/DVD, Wi-Fi.

Kaanapali

Another option to consider, in addition to those below, is the **Royal Lahaina Resort** (© **800/222-5642** or 808/661-3611; fax 808/661-6150; www. hawaiianhotelsandresorts.com). But skip the overpriced hotel rooms: Only stay here if you can get one of the 132 cottages tucked among the well-manicured grounds. Book online, where rates are $199 to $650 (50% off the rack rates).

VERY EXPENSIVE

Hyatt Regency Maui Resort & Spa ★★ ☺ Spa-goers will love this resort. Hawaii's first oceanfront spa, the Spa Moana, opened here in 2000 and boasts 20,000 square feet of facilities, including an exercise floor with an ocean view, 15 treatment rooms, sauna and steam rooms, and a huge menu of massages, body treatments, and therapies. Book your treatment before you leave home—this place is popular.

The management has poured some $19 million in renovations into this fantasy resort, the southernmost of the Kaanapali beachfront properties. It certainly has lots of imaginative touches: a collection of exotic species (pink flamingos, unhappy-looking penguins, and an assortment of loud parrots and macaws in the lobby), nine waterfalls, and an eclectic Asian and Pacific art collection. This huge place covers some 40 acres; even if you don't stay here, you might want to walk through the expansive tree-filled atrium and the parklike grounds, which contain a ½-acre outdoor pool with a 150-foot lava-tube slide, a cocktail bar under the falls, a "honeymooners' cave," and a swinging rope bridge. There's even a kids-only pool with its own beach, tidal pools, and fountains.

The rooms, spread out among three towers, are pleasantly outfitted with an array of amenities and have very comfortable separate sitting areas and private lanais with eye-popping views. The latest, most comfortable bedding (including fluffy feather beds) is now standard in every room. Two Regency Club floors offer a private concierge, complimentary breakfast, sunset cocktails, and snacks.

Families will appreciate Camp Hyatt, a year-round program offering young guests a range of activities, from "Olympic Games" to a scavenger hunt. There's also a game room for kids with video games, pool, Ping-Pong, and air hockey.

200 Nohea Kai Dr., Lahaina, HI 96761 ℭ **800/233-1234** or 808/661-1234. Fax 808/667-4498. www.maui.hyatt.com. 806 units. $311–$485 double; $461–$785 Regency Club double; from $1,000 suite. Extra person $75 ($125 in Regency Club rooms). Children 18 and under stay free in parent's room using existing bedding. Daily $15 resort fee for access to Moana Athletic Club, local newspaper delivery, local and toll-free calls, and 1-hr. tennis-court time per day. Packages available. AE, DC, DISC, MC, V. Valet parking $12; free self-parking. **Amenities:** 5 restaurants (including Son'z Maui at Swan Court, p. 177); 2 bars; babysitting; year-round children's program ($70 full day, $45 half day per child); concierge; concierge-level rooms; 36-hole golf course; health club w/ weight room; Jacuzzi; half-acre outdoor pool; room service; state-of-the-art spa; 6 tennis courts; watersports equipment rentals. *In room:* A/C, TV, fridge, hair dryer, high-speed Internet access ($10 per day), minibar.

Kaanapali Alii ★★ ☺ These luxurious oceanfront condominiums sit on 8 landscaped acres right on Kaanapali Beach. Kaanapali Alii combines the amenities of a luxury hotel (including a 24-hr. front desk) with the conveniences of a condominium. Each of the one-bedroom (1,500 sq. ft.) and two-bedroom (1,900 sq. ft.) units is impeccably decorated and comes with all the comforts of home (fully equipped kitchen, washer/dryer, lanai, two full bathrooms) and then some (room service from the Westin next door, daily maid service, complimentary local newspaper). The beachside recreation area includes a swimming pool, a separate children's pool, a whirlpool, gas barbecue grills and picnic areas, exercise rooms, saunas, and tennis courts. You can even take yoga classes on the lawn.

50 Nohea Kai Dr., Lahaina, HI 96761. ℭ **866/664-6410** or 808/667-1400. Fax 808/661-5686. www.kaanapali-alii.com. 264 units. $295–$480 1-bedroom for 4; $390–$897 2-bedroom for 6 near by golf course. **Amenities:** Babysitting; children's program (seasonally at the Westin next door for

a fee); concierge; fitness center; Jacuzzi; room service; 3 lighted tennis courts; watersports equipment rentals. *In room:* A/C, TV/DVD, fridge, hair dryer, high-speed Internet ($11), kitchen.

Sheraton Maui Resort and Spa ★★ ☺ Terrific facilities for families and fitness buffs and a premier beach location make this beautiful resort an all-around great place to stay. The grande dame of Kaanapali Beach is built into the side of a cliff on the curving, white-sand cove next to Black Rock (a lava formation that rises 80 ft. above the beach), where there's excellent snorkeling. The resort comprises six buildings of six stories or fewer set in well-established tropical gardens. The lobby has been elevated to take advantage of panoramic views, and a lagoon-like pool features lava-rock waterways, wooden bridges, and an open-air whirlpool. Cliff divers swan-dive off the torch-lit lava-rock headland in a traditional sunset ceremony—a sight to see. And the views of Kaanapali Beach, with Lanai and Molokai in the distance, are some of the best around.

Every unit is outfitted with amenities galore, right down to toothbrushes and toothpaste. Other pluses include the Sweet Sleeper Bed, a private balcony, and a "no-hassle" check-in policy: The valet takes you and your luggage straight to your room. There's also a new emphasis on family appeal, with a class of rooms dedicated to those traveling with kids. These "family suites" have three beds, a sitting room with full-size couch, and two TVs, both equipped with Nintendo. In addition, there's the Keiki Aloha program, with fun activities ranging from Hawaiian games to visits to nearby attractions. Children 12 and younger eat free when dining with one adult.

2605 Kaanapali Pkwy., Lahaina, HI 96761. ☎ **866/716-8109** or 808/661-0031. Fax 808/661-0458. www.sheraton-maui.com. 510 units. $230–$560 double; from $560 suite. Extra person $80. Children 17 and under stay free in parent's room using existing bedding. Daily $26 resort fee for in-room Internet access, self-parking, local calls and credit-card calls up to 60 minutes. AE, DC, DISC, MC, V. Valet parking $5. **Amenities:** 2 restaurants; poolside bar; indoor lounge; babysitting; children's program (at the Westin); lobby and poolside concierge; 36-hole golf course; fitness center; Jacuzzi; lagoon-style pool; room service; day spa; 3 tennis courts; watersports equipment rentals. *In room:* A/C, TV, fridge, hair dryer, high-speed Internet access, PlayStation.

The Westin Ka'anapali Ocean Resort Villas ★★ ☺ Not to be confused with the other Westin in Kaanapali (see West Maui Resort & Spa, below), this oceanfront condominium project, located at the very serene north end of Kaanapali, features full kitchens with marble counters in the kitchen and bathrooms, big living rooms, spacious bedrooms and whirlpool tubs in all guest rooms. The individually owned units are all managed by the Westin Resort people, who maintain top standards. Everything in the units are top draw, from the kitchen appliances to the comfy beds. The units range from 440-square-foot studios with complete kitchen to 960-square-foot one-bedroom units (with a pullout couch for the kids). In addition to all the amenities of the Kaanapali Resort (golf course, tennis courts, restaurants, and shops), the Westin also has three restaurants on the property, plus a general store, a fresh food market, and the terrific Heavenly Spa (not to be missed).

6 Kai Ala Dr., Kaanapali Resort. HI 96761 ☎ **866/716-8112** or 808/667-3200. Fax 808/667-3201. www.westinkaanapali.com. 1,021 units. $380–$770 double studio; $540–$1,184 double 1-bedroom; $720–$870 double 2-bedroom. Extra person $75. Shuttle services to Lahaina. AE, DC, DISC, MC, V. Valet parking $9; self-parking $7. **Amenities:** 3 restaurants; 2 bars; babysitting; children's program; concierge; 36-hole golf course; health club; Jacuzzi; 3 outdoor pools; separate

children's pool; room service; spa; tennis courts. *In room:* A/C, TV, fridge, hair dryer, high-speed Internet access, kitchen.

Westin Maui Resort & Spa ★★ ☺ The 758-room Westin Maui has added a $5-million spa and gym, and in the spirit of having a healthy environment, smoking is no longer allowed in guest rooms. I love the fabulous pillow-top Westin Heavenly Beds, with your choice of five different pillows. If that doesn't give you sweet dreams, nothing will. Once you get up, head to the aquatic playground— an 87,000-square-foot pool area with five free-form heated pools joined by swim-through grottoes, waterfalls, and a 128-foot-long water slide. This is the Disney World of water-park resorts, and your kids will be in water-hog heaven. The fantasy theme extends from the estatelike grounds into the interior's public spaces, which are filled with the shriek of tropical birds and the splash of waterfalls. The oversize architecture and $2-million art collection make a pleasing backdrop for all the action. Most of the rooms in the two 11-story towers overlook the aquatic playground, the ocean, and the island of Lanai in the distance.

2365 Kaanapali Pkwy., Lahaina, HI 96761. ☏ **866/716-8112** or 808/667-2525. Fax 808/661-5764. www.westinmaui.com. 758 units. $329–$800 double; from $800 suite (Starwood members receive a 35% discount). Extra person $75. Daily $25 resort fee for local calls, use of fitness center and spa, a souvenir shopping bag, a 4 x 6-in. photo, shuttle services to golf and tennis facilities, in-room high-speed Internet access, self-parking, and local newspaper delivery. AE, DC, DISC, MC, V. Valet parking $10; free self-parking. **Amenities:** 4 restaurants; 3 bars; babysitting; bike rental; children's program; concierge; 36-hole golf course; health club; Jacuzzi; 5 free-form outdoor pools; room service; spa; tennis courts; watersports equipment rentals. *In room:* A/C, TV, fridge, hair dryer, high-speed Internet access, minibar.

EXPENSIVE

Honua Kai Resort & Spa ★★ Recently opened in 2009, this North Kaanapali Beach resort, on 38 acres facing the ocean, features luxury condominium units, ranging from 590-square-foot studios to 2,800-square-foot three-bedroom units, with top-of-the-line appliances, lanais, and ocean views. The property has a full-service restaurant (Duke's Beach House) plus a deli with takeout. Every unit is fully furnished and has daily housekeeping. If you are looking for a relaxing vacation for your family, this is the place. A second tower and a spa are slated to open by the time you read this review.

130 Kai Malina Pkwy., North Kaanapali Beach, HI 96761. ☏ **800/877-7654** or 808/662-2800. Fax 808/667-5544. www.honua-kai-maui.com. 628 units. $175–$250 studio double; $225–$295 1-bedroom (up to 4 people); $350–$525 2-bedroom (up to 6 people); $550–$975 3-bedroom (up to 8 people). AE, DC, DISC, MC, V. $25 daily resort fee for unlimited local calls, fitness center, pool and beach services, resort charging privileges, in-room and resort-wide Internet access, daily housekeeping, and parking. **Amenities:** Restaurant; deli; bar; 5 barbecue areas; nearby 36-hole golf course; 5 outdoor pools; nearby tennis courts; whirlpool. *In room:* A/C, TV/DVD, full kitchen.

The Whaler on Kaanapali Beach ★ In the heart of Kaanapali, right on the world-famous beach, lies this oasis of elegance, privacy, and luxury. The relaxing atmosphere strikes you as soon as you enter the open-air lobby, where light reflects off the dazzling koi in the meditative lily pond. No expense has been spared on these gorgeous accommodations; every unit has a full kitchen, marble bathroom, 10-foot beamed ceilings, and blue-tiled lanai—and spectacular views of Kaanapali's gentle waves or the humpback peaks of the West Maui

Mountains. Next door is Whalers Village, with numerous restaurants, bars, and shops; Kaanapali Golf Club's 36 holes are across the street.

2481 Kaanapali Pkwy. (next to Whalers Village), Lahaina, HI 96761. © **877/997-6667** or 808/661-4861. Fax 808/661-8315. www.astonhotels.com. 360 units. $195–$345 studio double; $288–$455 1-bedroom (up to 4 people); $443–$800 2-bedroom (up to 6 people). Check website for specials. AE, DC, DISC, MC, V. Parking $12 per day. **Amenities:** Concierge; refurbished fitness room; Jacuzzi; outdoor pool; Hina Mana Salon & Spa; tennis courts. *In room:* A/C, TV/VCR/DVD, fridge, hair dryer, free high-speed Internet access, kitchen.

MODERATE

Kaanapali Beach Hotel ★ 🦟 It's older and less high-tech than its upscale neighbors, but the Kaanapali Beach Hotel has an irresistible local style and a real Hawaiian warmth that's missing from many other Maui properties. Three low-rise wings, bordering a fabulous stretch of beach, are set around a wide, grassy lawn with coco palms and a whale-shaped pool. The spacious, spotless motel-like rooms are done in wicker and rattan, with Hawaiian-style bedspreads and a lanai facing the courtyard and the beach. The beachfront rooms are separated from the water only by Kaanapali's landscaped walking trail.

Old Hawaii values and customs are always close at hand, and the service is some of the friendliest around. Tiki torches, hula, and Hawaiian music create a festive atmosphere every night in the expansive courtyard. As part of the hotel's extensive Hawaiiana program, you can learn to cut pineapple, weave lauhala, and even dance the hula. The children's program is complimentary. There's also an arts-and-crafts fair 4 days a week, a morning welcome reception Monday through Saturday, and a farewell lei ceremony when you depart.

2525 Kaanapali Pkwy., Lahaina, HI 96761. © **800/262-8450** or 808/661-0011. Fax 808/667-5978. www.kbhmaui.com. 430 units. $237–$357 double; from $475 suite. Extra person $30. Car, golf, bed-and-breakfast, and romance packages available, as well as senior discounts. AE, DC, DISC, MC, V. Valet parking $11; self-parking $9. **Amenities:** 2 restaurants; poolside bar (where you can get a mean piña colada); babysitting; children's program; concierge/guest services; 36-hole golf course nearby; outdoor pool; access to tennis courts; watersports equipment rentals. *In room:* A/C, TV, fridge, high-speed Internet ($10).

Outrigger Maui Eldorado ★ ☺ These spacious condominium units—each with full kitchen, washer/dryer, and daily maid service—were built at a time when land in Kaanapali was cheap, contractors took pride in their work, and visitors expected spacious units with views from every window. You'll find it hard to believe that this was one of Kaanapali's first properties in the late 1960s; this first-class choice still looks like new. The Outrigger chain has managed to keep prices reasonable, especially in spring and fall. This is a great choice for families, with its big units, grassy areas that are perfect for running off excess energy, and a beachfront (with beach cabanas and a barbecue area) that's usually safe for swimming. Tennis courts are nearby.

2661 Kekaa Dr., Lahaina, HI 96761. © **888/339-8585** or 808/661-0021. Fax 808/667-7039. www.outrigger.com. 204 units (87 managed by Outrigger). $129–$149 studio double; $169–$179 1-bedroom (up to 4); $199–$219 2-bedroom (up to 6). Numerous packages available, including 5th night free, rental-car deals, senior rates, and more. Parking $7. AE, DC, DISC, MC, V. **Amenities:** Concierge; 36-hole golf course; 3 outdoor pools. *In room:* A/C, TV, fridge, hair dryer, high-speed Internet access, kitchen.

Honokowai, Kahana & Napili

EXPENSIVE

Napili Kai Beach Resort ★★ 🎁 This comfortable oceanfront complex lies just south of the Kapalua Resort, nestled in a small white-sand cove. The one- and two-story units, with double-hipped Hawaii-style roofs, face a gold-sand beach that's safe for swimming. Many units have a view of the Pacific, with Molokai and Lanai in the distance. Those who prefer air-conditioning should book into the Honolua Building, where you'll get a room set back from the shore around a grassy, parklike lawn and pool. Every unit (except eight hotel rooms) has a fully stocked kitchenette with full-size fridge, cooktop, microwave, toaster oven, washer/dryer, and coffeemaker; some have dishwashers. On-site pluses include daily maid service, even in the condo units; two shuffleboard courts; barbecue areas; complimentary morning coffee and afternoon tea; weekly lei making, hula lessons, and horticultural tours; and a free weekly mai tai party. There are three nearby championship golf courses and excellent tennis courts at the adjacent Kapalua Resort.

5900 Honoapiilani Rd. (at the extreme north end of Napili, next to Kapalua), Lahaina, HI 96761. ℭ **800/367-5030** or 808/669-6271. Fax 808/669-5740. www.napilikai.com. 162 units. $240–$345 hotel room double; $310–$455 studio double (sleeps 3–4); $475–$670 1-bedroom suite (sleeps up to 5); $685–$995 2-bedroom suite (sleeps up to 7). Packages available. AE, DISC, MC, V. **Amenities:** Restaurant (Sea House Restaurant, p. 181); bar; babysitting; free children's activities at Easter, June 15–Aug 31, and Christmas; concierge; good-size fitness room; 2 18-hole putting greens (w/free use of golf putters); Jacuzzi; 4 outdoor pools; tennis courts nearby (and complimentary use of tennis rackets); complimentary watersports equipment. *In room:* A/C (in most units), TV/DVD, fridge, hair dryer, high-speed Internet access, kitchenette (in most units).

MODERATE

In addition to the choices below, consider **Polynesian Shores,** 3975 Lower Honoapiilani Rd. (near Kahana and just 2 min. from the Kapalua–West Maui Airport), Lahaina, HI 96761 (ℭ **800/433-6284** or 808/669-6065; fax 808/669-0909; www.polynesianshores.com). Every unit (one to three bedrooms, $125–$290) has floor-to-ceiling sliding-glass doors that open onto a private lanai with an ocean view. There's great snorkeling off the beach out front.

Hale Kai ★ ☺ This small two-story condo complex is ideally located, right on the beach and next door to a county park—a great location for those traveling with kids. Shops, restaurants, and ocean activities are all within a 6-mile radius. The units are older but in excellent shape; they come with well-equipped kitchens (with dishwasher, disposal, microwave, and blender) and louvered windows that open to the trade winds. Lots of guests clamor for the oceanfront pool units, but I find the park-view units cooler, and they still have ocean views (upstairs units also have cathedral ceilings). This place fills up fast, so book early; repeat guests make up most of the clientele.

3691 Lower Honoapiilani Rd. (in Honokowai), Lahaina, HI 96761. ℭ **800/446-7307** or 808/669-6333. Fax 888/831-0122. www.halekai.com. 40 units. $160 1-bedroom double; $210 2-bedroom (sleeps up to 4); $350 3-bedroom (sleeps up to 6). Extra person $10. 5-night minimum. MC, V. **Amenities:** Concierge; outdoor pool. *In room:* TV/VCR, fridge, hair dryer, high-speed Internet access, kitchen.

Honokeana Cove 🏄 These large, secluded units—cozily set around a pool in a lush tropical setting—have fabulous views of Honokeana Cove. The beach here isn't sandy (it's composed of smooth round rocks), but the water just offshore is excellent for snorkeling (turtles have been spotted here) and for whale-watching in winter. The well-appointed units all come with full kitchens and lanais. Amenities include barbecues and deck chairs. The management holds weekly *pupu* parties so you can meet the other guests. All in all, a well-priced option in an expensive neighborhood.

5255 Lower Honoapiilani Rd. (in Napili), Lahaina, HI 96761. © **800/237-4948** or 808/669-6441. Fax 808/669-8777. www.honokeana-cove.com. 33 units. $189–$205 1-bedroom; $218–$305 2-bedroom (sleeps up to 4); $310 3-bedroom. Extra person $10–$15. 3- to 5-night minimum (Christmas/New Year's 7- to 14-night min.). MC, V. **Amenities:** Concierge; outdoor pool. *In room:* TV/VCR, kitchen, Wi-Fi ($7/day plus $3 set-up).

Kahana Sunset ★★ ☺ Lying in the crook of a sharp horseshoe curve on Lower Honoapiilani Road is this series of wooden condo units, stair-stepping down the side of a hill to a postcard-perfect white-sand beach. The unique location, nestled between the coastline and the road above, makes this a very private place to stay. In the midst of the buildings sits a grassy lawn with a small pool and Jacuzzi; down by the sandy beach are gazebos and picnic areas. The units feature full kitchens (complete with dishwashers), washer/dryers, large lanais with terrific views, and sleeper sofas. This is a great complex for families: The beach is safe for swimming, the grassy area is away from traffic, and the units are roomy.

4909 Lower Honoapiilani Hwy. (at the northern end of Kahana, almost in Napili), Lahaina, HI 96761. Reservations c/o Premier Properties, P.O. Box 10219, Lahaina, HI 96761. © **800/669-1488** or 808/669-8700. Fax 808/669-4466. www.kahanasunset.com. 79 units. $165–$290 1-bedroom (sleeps up to 4); $225–$465 2-bedroom (sleeps up to 6). 2-night minimum. AE, MC, V. From Hwy. 30, turn makai (toward the ocean) at the Napili Plaza (Napilihau St.), and then left on Lower Honoapiilani Rd. **Amenities:** Concierge; 2 outdoor pools (1 for children). *In room:* TV/DVD/VCR, high-speed Internet access, kitchen.

Mauian Hotel on Napili Beach ★ The Mauian is perched above a beautiful ½-mile-long white-sand beach with great swimming and snorkeling; there's a pool with lounges, umbrellas, and tables on the sun deck; and the verdant grounds burst with tropical color. The rooms feature Indonesian-style furniture, and big lanais with great views. The floorings and furnishings were redone in 2008. Thoughtful touches include fresh flowers, plus chilled champagne for guests celebrating a special occasion. There are no phones or TVs in the rooms, but the large *ohana* (family) room does have a TV with a VCR and an extensive library if you need entertainment. There's a barbecue area, great restaurants are just a 5-minute walk away, and Kapalua Resort is up the street. The nightly sunsets off the beach are spectacular.

5441 Lower Honoapiilani Rd. (in Napili), Lahaina, HI 96761. © **800/367-5034** or 808/669-6205. Fax 808/669-0129. www.mauian.com. 44 units. $150–$165 double room; $165–$280 double studio (sleeps up to 4). Extra person $10. Children under 5 stay free in parent's room. AE, DISC, MC, V. **Amenities:** Golf course nearby; free Wi-Fi in family room; outdoor pool; tennis courts nearby. *In room:* Fridge, kitchen (most units), no phone.

Napili Sunset *✦* Housed in three buildings (two on the ocean, one across the street) and located just down the street from Napili Bay (see below), these clean, older, well-maintained units offer good value. At first glance, the plain two-story structures don't look like much, but the location, the moderate prices, and the

Where to Stay from Kapalua to Honokowai

0 1/2 mi
0 1/2 km

Plantation Club Dr.

Plantation Golf Course

Honokahua Bay

Makaluapuna Pt.

Fleming Beach Park

❶

Oneloa Bay

Office Rd.

Hawea Pt.

❷

Kapalua Dr.

KAPALUA

Village Golf Course

Namalu Bay

Bay Golf Course

Pailolo Channel

Kapalua Beach

❸
❹

Napili Beach

❺

Napili Bay

❻
❼

Honoapiilani Hwy.

Honokeana Bay

❽

NAPILI

Napilihau St.

❾

Alaeloa Pt.

Haukoe Pt.

Kaia Pt. Omaikai Pl.

KAHANA

Hoohui Rd.

Kapalua–West Maui Airport

❿

Akahele St.

⓫
⓬

Lower Honoapiilani Rd.

⓭

Honoapiilani Hwy.

⓮
⓯

HONOKOWAI

30

⓰ To Kaanapali & Lahaina

Area of detail

Laihaina oKahului

M A U I

Haleakala National Park

Aston at Papakaea **16**
Hale Kai **15**
Hale Maui Apartment Hotel **14**
Honokeana Cove **8**
Hoyochi Nikko **13**
Kahana Sunset **9**
Kaleialoha **12**
Kapalua Villas **2**
Mauian Hotel on Napili Beach **4**
Napili Bay **6**
Napili Kai Beach Resort **3**
Napili Sunset **5**
Napili Surf Beach Resort **7**
Noelani Condominium Resort **10**
Polynesian Shores **11**
Ritz-Carlton Kapalua **1**

friendly staff are the real hidden treasures here. In addition to daily maid service, the units all have full kitchens (with dishwashers), ceiling fans (no air-conditioning), sofa beds, small dining rooms, and small bedrooms. The studio units are located in the building off the beach and a few steps up a slight hill; they're a good size, with a full kitchen and either a sofa bed or a Murphy bed, and they overlook the small pool and garden. The one- and two-bedroom units are all on the beach (the downstairs units have lanais that lead right to the sand). The staff makes sure each unit has the basics (paper towels, dishwasher soap, coffee filters, condiments) to get your stay off to a good start. There are restaurants within walking distance. The beach—one of Maui's best—can get a little crowded because the public beach access is through this property (and everyone on Maui seems to want to come here).

46 Hui Rd. (in Napili), Lahaina, HI 96761. ✆ **800/447-9229** or 808/669-8083. Fax 808/669-2730. www.napilisunset.com. 42 units. $135–$398 studio double; $239–$310 1-bedroom double (sleeps 5-6); $245–$419 2-bedroom (sleeps up to 7). Check website for specials. Extra person $15. Children under 3 stay free in parent's room. MC, V. **Amenities:** Small outdoor pool. *In room:* TV, fridge, kitchen, Wi-Fi.

Napili Surf Beach Resort ★ 🏠 This well-maintained, superbly landscaped condo complex has a great location on Napili Beach. The well-furnished units (all with full kitchens) were renovated several with new carpeting, beds, and (in some units) kitchens. Free daily maid service, a rarity in condo properties, keeps the place clean. Management encourages socializing: In addition to weekly mai tai parties and coffee socials, the resort hosts annual shuffleboard and golf tournaments, as well as get-togethers on July 4th, Thanksgiving, Christmas, and New Year's. Facilities include three shuffleboard courts and three gas barbecue grills.

50 Napili Place (off Lower Honoapiilani Rd., in Napili), Lahaina, HI 96761. ✆ **888/627-4547** or 808/669-8002. Fax 808/669-8004. www.napilisurf.com. 53 units (some with shower only). $116–$249 studio double (sleeps up to 3); $200–$353 1-bedroom double (sleeps up to 4). Extra person $15. No credit cards. **Amenities:** 2 outdoor pools. *In room:* TV/VCR, fridge, kitchen, Wi-Fi.

Noelani Condominium Resort ★★ This oceanfront condo is a great value, whether you stay in a studio or a three-bedroom unit (ideal for large families). Everything is first class, from the furnishings to the oceanfront location. Though it's on the water, there's no sandy beach here (despite the photos posted on the website)—but right next door is a sandy cove at the county park. There's good snorkeling off the cove, which is frequented by spinner dolphins and turtles in summer and humpback whales in winter. All units feature complete kitchens, entertainment centers, and spectacular views (all except the studio units also have their own washer/dryers and dishwashers). My favorites are in the Anthurium Building, where the condos have oceanfront lanais just 20 feet from the water. Frugal travelers will love the deluxe studios in the Orchid Building, with great ocean views. Guests are invited to a continental breakfast orientation on their first day and mai tai parties at night; there are also oceanfront barbecue grills for guest use.

4095 Lower Honoapiilani Rd. (in Kahana), Lahaina, HI 96761. ✆ **800/367-6030** or 808/669-8374. Fax 808/669-7904. www.noelani-condo-resort.com. 45 units. $125–$175 studio double; $175–$197 1-bedroom (sleeps up to 4); $245–$290 2-bedroom (sleeps up to 6); $330–$357 3-bedroom (sleeps up to 8). Rates include continental breakfast on 1st morning. Extra person $20. Children under 18 stay free in parent's room. Packages for honeymooners, seniors, and

AAA members available. 3-night minimum. AE, MC, V. **Amenities:** Concie〔...〕 health club; oceanfront Jacuzzi; 2 freshwater pools (1 heated for night sw〔...〕 VCR, fridge, hair dryer, high-speed Internet access, kitchen.

INEXPENSIVE

In addition to the choices below, consider **Hale Maui** (☎ **808/669-6312;** fax 808/669-1302; www.halemaui.com), a wonderful, 〔...〕 place run by Hans and Eva Zimmerman and daughter Marika, whose spirit is 100% aloha. The one-bedroom suites, which start at around $115 for a double, come with ceiling fans, private lanais, and complete kitchens (the kitchens were remodeled and new furniture added in 2008). There's no pool, but a private path leads to a great swimming beach.

Another option is **Hoyochi Nikko,** 3901 Lower Honoapiilani Rd. (in Honokowai), Lahaina, HI 96761 (☎ **800/487-6002,** ext. 1, or 808/669-0089, ext. 1; fax 808/669-3937; www.mauilodging.com), which has 17 older (but well-maintained) one- bedroom units (and a few one-bedroom with separate loft) sharing 180 feet of oceanfront ($130–$190 one-bedroom double). There's a surcharge for stays of less than 10 nights.

Aston at Papakea Resort ✦ Just a mile down the beach from Kaanapali lie these low-rise buildings, surrounded by manicured grounds and ocean views galore. Palm trees and tropical plants dot the property, a putting green wraps around two kidney-shaped pools, and a footbridge arches over a lily pond brimming with carp. Each pool has its own private cabana with sauna, Jacuzzi, and barbecue grills; a poolside shop rents snorkel gear for exploring the offshore reefs. All units have dishwashers, big lanais, and washer/dryers. The studios have pull-down beds to save space during the day. Definitely a good value.

3543 Lower Honoapiilani Rd. (in Honokowai), Lahaina, HI 96761. ☎ **877/997-6667** or 808/669-4848. Fax 808/665-0662. www.astonhotels.com. 364 units. $141–$229 studio double; $157–$273 1-bedroom (sleeps up to 4); $187–$395 2-bedroom (sleeps up to 6). AE, DISC, MC, V. **Amenities:** 2 Jacuzzis; 2 outdoor pools; 3 tennis courts; watersports equipment rental. *In room:* A/C, TV/VCR, fridge, kitchen, Wi-Fi.

Kaleialoha This condo complex for the budget-minded has recently been upgraded, with new paint, bedspreads, and drapes in each apartment. Each one-bedroom unit has a sofa bed in the living room, which allows you to comfortably sleep four. All of the Island-style units feature fully equipped kitchens, with everything from dishwashers to washer/dryers (but bring your own beach towels). There's great ocean swimming just off the rock wall (no sandy beach); a protective reef mows waves down and allows even timid swimmers to relax.

3785 Lower Honoapiilani Rd. (in Honokowai), Lahaina, HI 96761. ☎ **800/222-8688** or 808/669-8197. Fax 808/669-2502. www.mauicondosoceanfront.com. 18 units. $99–$250 1-bedroom double. Cleaning fee $95 for less than 7-night stay. Extra person $10. Children under 4 stay free in parent's room. 3- to 5-night minimum. DISC, MC, V. **Amenities:** Concierge; outdoor pool. *In room:* TV/DVD, fridge, high-speed Internet access, kitchen.

Napili Bay Resort ★ 🏨 One of Maui's best bargains is this small two-story complex right on Napili's beautiful ½-mile white-sand beach. It's perfect for a romantic getaway: The atmosphere is comfortable and relaxing, the ocean lulls you to sleep at night, and birdsong wakes you in the morning. The beach here is one of the best on the coast, with great swimming and snorkeling—in fact, it's so ul that people staying at much more expensive resorts down the road frequently come here. The studio apartments are definitely small, but they pack in everything you need to feel at home, from a full kitchen to a comfortable queen-size bed, plus a roomy lanai that's great for watching the sun set over the Pacific. There's no air-conditioning, but louvered windows and ceiling fans keep the units fairly cool during the day. There are lots of restaurants and a convenience store within walking distance, and you're about 10 to 15 minutes away from Lahaina and some great golf courses.

33 Hui Dr. (off Lower Honoapiilani Hwy., in Napili), Lahaina, HI 96761. © **877/877-5758** or 808/930-1830. www.alohacondos.com. 28 units. $120–$325 double. Cleaning fee $85–$110. 1- to 3-night minimum. AE, DC, MC, V. *In room:* TV, fridge, high-speed Internet access (most units), kitchen.

Kapalua

VERY EXPENSIVE

Ritz-Carlton Kapalua ★★★ ☺ This Ritz is a complete universe, one of those resorts where you can happily sit by the ocean with a book for 2 whole weeks and never leave the grounds. It rises proudly on a knoll, in a singularly spectacular setting between the rainforest and the sea. During construction, the burial sites of hundreds of ancient Hawaiians were discovered in the sand, so the hotel was moved inland to avoid disrupting the graves. The setback gives the hotel a commanding view of Molokai.

In 2008, the Ritz reopened after an extensive $160-million renovation that transformed the place into an even more elegant property, with a focus on a Hawaiian (vs. the former European) theme. All guest rooms now have the latest technology, including flatscreen TVs, DVD players, iPod docking stations, and Wi-Fi (included in the resort fee). Marble bathrooms and private lanais are other nice touches. The penthouse floor has been converted into Residential Suites (with kitchens, living rooms, and separate bedrooms), available for guests. If you can afford it, stay on the **Club Level** ★★★—it offers the best amenities in the state, from French-roast coffee in the morning to a buffet at lunch, from cookies in the afternoon to *pupu* and drinks at sunset.

Other transformations include upgrades to the signature 10,000-square-foot, three-tiered pool; a new children's pool; an Ambassadors of the Environment Education Center (by Jean-Michel Cousteau); and a new 17,500-square-foot Waihua Spa, with 15 treatment rooms, saunas, whirlpool with lava-stone walls, and fitness center. Your children will enjoy the Ritz Kids program's wide variety of activities, plus the weekly "Ritz Kids Night Out" that allows parents to spend a quiet evening alone.

1 Ritz-Carlton Dr., Kapalua, HI 96761. © **800/262-8440** or 808/669-6200. Fax 808/669-1566. www.ritzcarlton.com. 463 units. $299–$750 double; $595–$895 Club Level double; from $545 suite; from $995 Club Level suite; residential suites from $545 1-bedroom, $875 2-bedroom. Extra person $50 ($150 in Club Level rooms). Daily $20 resort fee for use of fitness center, steam room, and sauna; selected wellness classes; Aloha Friday festivities; cultural-history tours; in-room Wi-Fi; self-parking; resort shuttle service; morning coffee at the Lobby Lounge; preferred tee times; 9-hole putting green; tennis and basketball courts; and games of bocce ball on the lawn. Wedding/honeymoon, golf, and other packages available. AE, DC, DISC, MC, V. Valet parking $18; free self-parking. **Amenities:** 6 restaurants (including the Banyan Tree, p. 183); 4 bars (including 1 serving drinks and light fare next to the beach); babysitting; bike rentals; children's

program; concierge; concierge-level rooms (some of Hawaii's best); fitness room; access to the Kapalua Resort's 3 championship golf courses (each w/its own pro shop), golf academy, and deluxe tennis complex; outdoor pool; room service; spa; watersports equipment rentals; 2 outdoor hot tubs. *In room:* A/C, TV, hair dryer, Wi-Fi.

EXPENSIVE

If you're interested in a luxurious condo or town house, consider **Kapalua Villas** (*© 800/545-0018* or 808/669-8088; www.kapaluavillas.com). The palatial units dotting the oceanfront cliffs and fairways of this idyllic coast are a (relative) bargain, especially if you're traveling with a group. In 2009 the locally respected Outrigger resort chain took over the management of this property. The one-bedroom condos run $299 to $449, two-bedroom condos $399 to $659, and three-bedroom condos from $599, plus a $25 daily recreation fee which covers parking; unlimited local, national, and international calls; high-speed Internet access; use of in-villa safe; delivery of newspaper Mon–Fri; use of computer at Kapalua Resort Center; access to Ritz-Carlton pools and pool towels; access to Ritz-Carlton Spa; preferred guest rates at the Kapalua Golf Courses and tennis courts; and resort-wide charging privileges). Numerous package deals (which include golf, tennis, honeymoon amenities, and car) can save you even more money.

SOUTH MAUI

A new trend has sprouted up in south Maui, especially in the Kihei area: Properties (especially condominiums) have started adding a booking fee, ranging from $25 to $35 and most of the time nonrefundable. The reasons for this fee seem to stem from the depressed economy (oh great, times are bad so charge your clients a new fee!). I am totally opposed to this new fee; if you book at a condo with this fee and are unhappy about it, let them know.

Unfortunately, **Kihei Maui Vacations** (*© 808/879-4000;* www.kmvmaui.com) and **Condominium Rentals Hawaii** (*© 800/367-5242* or 808/879-2778; www.crhmaui.com)—the two booking agencies I have recommended for years because they are reliable and offer a host of condominiums and unique vacation homes in the Kihei/Wailea/Maalaea area—now charge a nonrefundable $35 booking fee.

Kihei

EXPENSIVE

In addition to the choices below, consider the **Aston at the Maui Banyan** (*© 877/997-6667* or 808/924-2924; www.astonhawaii.com), a condo property across the street from Kamaole Beach Park II. The large one- to three-bedroom units are very nicely done and feature full kitchens, air-conditioning, and washer/dryers. Rates start at $189 for hotel rooms ($171 if you book online), $223 for one-bedroom units ($200 online), and $280 for two-bedroom units ($252 online); be sure to ask about packages.

Aston Maui Hill ★ If you can't decide between the privacy of a condo and the conveniences of a hotel, try this place. Maui Hill gives you the best of both worlds. Located on a hill above the heat of Kihei town, this large Spanish-style resort (with stucco buildings, red-tile roofs, and arched entries) combines all the amenities and activities of a hotel—pool, hot tub, tennis courts, Hawaiiana classes, maid service, and more—with large luxury condos that have full kitchens and plenty of privacy. Nearly all units have ocean views, dishwashers, washer/dryers, queen-size sofa beds, and big lanais. Beaches, restaurants, and shops are within easy walking distance; a golf course is nearby; and barbecue grills are provided for guests' use. The management here goes out of its way to make sure your stay is perfect. *Note:* Some of the units have converted to timeshares, although no timeshare salesperson bothered me during my stay.

2881 S. Kihei Rd. (across from Kamaole Park III, btw. Keonekai St. and Kilohana Dr.), Kihei, HI 96753. ℂ **877/997-6667** or 808/879-6321. Fax 808/879-8945. www.astonhotels.com. 140 units. $240–$255 1-bedroom ($180–$191 if you book online); $289–$320 2-bedroom (from $217 online); $479 3-bedroom (from $431 online). AE, DC, DISC, MC, V. **Amenities:** Concierge; putting green; Jacuzzi; outdoor pool; tennis courts. *In room:* A/C, TV/VCR, fridge, hair dryer, high-speed Internet access, kitchen.

Hale Pau Hana Resort ★ ☺ Located on the sandy shores of Kamaole Beach Park but separated from the white-sand beach by a velvet-green manicured lawn, this is a great condo resort for families. Each of the large units has a private lanai, a terrific ocean view, and a complete kitchen. The management goes above and beyond, personally greeting each guest and acting as your own concierge service. Guests can mingle at the free coffee hour every morning, or at the *pupu* parties with local Hawaiian entertainment held twice a week at sunset. The location is in the heart of Kihei, close to shopping, restaurants, and activities.

2480 S. Kihei Rd., Kihei, HI 96753. ℂ **800/367-6036** or 808/879-2715. Fax 808/875-0238. www.hphresort.com. 79 units. $245–$355 1-bedroom; $340–$505 2-bedroom. Extra person $15–$25. 7-night minimum in Dec. DISC, MC, V. **Amenities:** Concierge; outdoor pool. *In room:* A/C in bedrooms, TV, fridge, hair dryer, high-speed Internet access, full kitchen.

Maalaea Surf Resort ★ Enjoy a quiet, relaxing vacation on this well-landscaped property, with a beautiful white-sand beach right outside. Located at the quiet end of Kihei Road, this two-story complex sprawls across 5 acres of lush tropical gardens. The luxury town houses all have ocean views, big kitchens (with dishwashers), cable TV, and VCRs. Amenities include maid service 3 times per week (Mon–Sat), shuffleboard, barbecue grills, and discounts on tee times at nearby golf courses; restaurants and shops are within a 5-minute drive.

12 S. Kihei Rd. (at S. Kihei Rd. and Hwy. 350), Kihei, HI 96753. ℂ **800/423-7953** or 808/879-1267. Fax 808/874-2884. www.maalaeasurfresort.com. 34 units. $285–$335 1-bedroom (sleeps up to 4); $380–$450 2-bedroom (sleeps up to 6). MC, V. **Amenities:** Concierge; 2 outdoor pools; 2 tennis courts. *In room:* A/C, TV/VCR/DVD, fridge, hair dryer, high-speed Internet access, kitchen.

Maui Coast Hotel ★ This place stands out as one of the few hotels in Kihei (which is largely full of affordable condo complexes rather than traditional hotels or resorts). The Extra Value Package gives you a rental car for just a few dollars more than your room rate. The other chief advantage of this hotel is its location, about a block from Kamaole Beach Park I, with plenty of bars, restaurants, and shopping within walking distance, plus a golf course nearby. Guest rooms offer extras such as sitting areas, whirlpool tubs, ceiling fans, and private lanais.

2259 S. Kihei Rd. (1 block from Kamaole Beach Park I), Kihei, HI 96753. ℂ **800/895-6284** or 808/874-6284. Fax 808/875-4731. www.mauicoasthotel.com. 265 units. $179 double; from $199 suite; $245 1-bedroom (sleeps up to 4). Children 17 and under stay free in parent's room using existing bedding. Rollaway bed $30. Packages available. AE, DC, DISC, MC, V. **Amenities:**

Where to Stay in South Maui

KIHEI

Lahaina • Kahului

M A U I

Area of detail

Haleakala National Park

Kihei Beach

Piilani Hwy.

Kulanihakoi St.

Kihei Rd.

Keonoulu Beach

Waipuilani Rd.

Kulanihakoi Gulch

PACIFIC

OCEAN

Lipoa St.

L A I E

Halama St.

Kalama Beach Park

KAMAOLE

Kamaole Beach Park I

Kamaole Beach Park II

Kamaole Beach Park III

Keonekai Rd.

Piilani Hwy.

Kilohana Dr.

Keawakapu Beach

WAILEA

MAUI MEADOWS

Mokapu Beach

Ulua Beach

Wailea Ike Dr.

Wailea Beach

Polo Beach

Kaukahi St.

Palauea Beach

Makena Rd.

Poolenalena Beach

MAKENA

Makena Rd.

Maluaka Beach

Makena State Park

Makena Rd.

0   1 mi

0   1 km

Restaurant; pool bar w/nightly entertainment; concierge; fitness room; outdoor pool (plus children's wading pool); 2 lighted tennis courts. *In room:* A/C, TV, fridge, hair dryer, high-speed Internet access ($10).

MODERATE

The **Kihei Beach Resorts,** 36 S. Kihei Rd., Kihei, HI 96753 (© **800/367-6034** or 808/879-2744; fax 808/875-0306; www.kiheibeachresort.com), has spacious condos right on the beach. The downside is the constant traffic noise from Kihei Road. Rates are $155 to $200 for a one-bedroom double, $260 to $295 for a two-bedroom (sleeps four); there's a 4- to 10-night minimum and a $10 charge per extra person.

Eva Villa ★★ 🏠 This three-unit bed-and-breakfast is located on ½ acre of lushly landscaped property at the top of the Maui Meadows subdivision. From the rooftop lanai, guests have a spectacular view of the sunset behind Kahoolawe and Lanai, and in the distance the West Maui Mountains. Hosts Rick and Dale Pounds have done everything to make this one of Maui's classiest vacation rentals. From the continental breakfast stocked in the unit's kitchen (fresh fruit, juice, bread, muffins, jam, coffee, and tea) to the decor of the suites, from the heated pool and Jacuzzi to the individual barbecue facilities, this is a great place to stay. The location couldn't be better—just a few minutes' drive to Kihei's sunny beaches, restaurants in Kihei and Wailea, golf courses, and plenty of tennis and shopping. Each unit is a roomy 600 square feet. The separate cottage has a living room, full kitchen, bedroom, and washer/dryer; the poolside studio is a one-room unit with a huge kitchen; and the poolside suite has two bedrooms and a kitchenette. You can't go wrong booking here.

815 Kumulani Dr., Kihei, HI 96753. © **800/884-1845** or 808/874-6407. Fax 808/874-6407. www.mauibnb.com. 3 units. $135–$175 double. 4-night minimum. No credit cards. **Amenities:** Jacuzzi; heated outdoor pool; barbecue grill. *In room:* AC, TV/DVD, CD player, fridge, kitchen or kitchenette, Wi-Fi.

Kamaole Nalu Resort This six-story condominium complex is located between two beach parks, Kamaole I and Kamaole II, and right across the street from a shopping complex. Units have fabulous ocean views, large living rooms, and private lanais; the kitchens are a bit small but come fully equipped. I recommend no. 306 for its wonderful bird's-eye view. The property also has an oceanside pool and great barbecue facilities. Restaurants, bars, a golf course, and tennis courts are nearby. *Warning:* Because the building is right on Kihei Road, it can be noisy.

2450 S. Kihei Rd. (btw. Kanani and Keonekai rds., next to Kamaole Beach Park II), Kihei, HI 96753. © **800/767-1497** or 808/879-1006. Fax 808/879-8693. www.kamaolenalu.com. 28 units. High season $250–$350 double; low season $190–$275 double. $30 booking fee. Extra person $20. Children 12 and under stay free in parent's room using existing bedding. 5-night minimum (2-week min. over Christmas and New Year's). MC, V. **Amenities:** Outdoor pool. *In room:* TV, fridge, hair dryer, high-speed Internet access, kitchen.

Kealia Resort 🤿 This oceanfront property at the northern end of Kihei is well maintained and nicely furnished—and the prices are excellent. But as tempting as the lower-priced units may sound, don't give in: They face noisy Kihei Road and are near a major junction, so you'll be listening to big trucks downshifting all night. Instead, go for one of the oceanview units, which all have full kitchens and private lanais. The grounds face a 5-mile stretch of white-sand beach. Social gatherings include free coffee-and-doughnut get-togethers every Friday morning and *pupu* parties on Wednesdays.

191 N. Kihei Rd. (north of Hwy. 31, at the Maalaea end of Kihei), Kihei, HI 96753. 📞 **800/265-0686** or 808/280-1192. Fax 808/875-1540. www.kealiaresort.com. 51 units. $115–$130 studio double; $150–$190 1-bedroom double; $215–$250 2-bedroom (sleeps up to 4). $25 reservation fee. Children 12 and under stay free in parent's room. 4-night minimum (10-night min. Dec 15–Jan 10). Cleaning fees $65–$95. AE, MC, V. **Amenities:** Outdoor pool. *In room:* TV, fridge, hair dryer, high-speed Internet access (some units), kitchen.

Leinaala ★ From Kihei Road, you can't see Leinaala amid the jumble of buildings, but this oceanfront boutique condo offers excellent accommodations at moderate prices. The building is set back from the water, with a county park—an oasis of green grass and tennis courts—in between. A golf course is nearby. The units are compact but filled with everything you need: a full kitchen, sofa bed, and oceanview lanai. (Hideaway beds are available if you need one.)

998 S. Kihei Rd., Kihei, HI 96753. 📞 **800/822-4409.** Fax 808/874-6144. www.mauicondo.com. 24 units. $132–$190 1-bedroom double; $168–$240 2-bedroom (sleeps up to 4). $35 reservation fee. 4-night minimum. Check for Internet specials. AE, MC, V. **Amenities:** Outdoor pool. *In room:* A/C, TV, fridge, high-speed Internet access ($10), kitchen.

Mana Kai Maui Resort ★ ☺ This eight-story complex, situated on a beautiful white-sand cove, is an unusual combination of hotel and condominium. The hotel rooms, which account for half of the total number of units, are small but nicely furnished. Families should consider the condo units, which feature full kitchens and open living rooms with sliding-glass doors that lead to small lanais overlooking the sandy beach and ocean. Some units are beginning to show their age (the building is more than 30 years old), but they're all clean and comfortable. One of the best snorkeling beaches on the coast is just steps away; a golf course and tennis courts are nearby.

2960 S. Kihei Rd. (btw. Kilohana and Keonekai rds., at the Wailea end of Kihei), Kihei, HI 96753. 📞 **800/367-5242** or 808/879-2778. Fax 808/879-7825. www.crhmaui.com. 105 units. $125–$185 hotel room double; $205–$365 1-bedroom (sleeps up to 4); $240–$430 2-bedroom (up to 6). $30 reservation fee. 4-night minimum Christmas. Extra person $12. AE, MC, V. **Amenities:** Restaurant (Five Palms, p. 185); bar; concierge; outdoor pool. *In room:* A/C (in hotel rooms only), TV, fridge, high-speed Internet access (in condo units), kitchen (in condo units).

Maui Kamaole You'll find this condo complex right across the street from the Kihei Public Boat Ramp and beautiful Kamaole Beach Park III, which is great for swimming, snorkeling, and beachcombing. Each roomy, fully furnished unit comes with a private lanai, two bathrooms (even in the one-bedroom units), and an all-electric kitchen. The one-bedroom units—which can comfortably accommodate four—are quite a deal, especially if you're traveling in low season. The grounds are nicely landscaped and offer barbecues. Restaurants and bars are within walking distance; a golf course and tennis courts are also nearby.

2777 S. Kihei Rd. (btw. Keonekai and Kilohana rds., at the Wailea end of Kihei), Kihei, HI 96753. 📞 **800/822-4409** or 808/879-5445. Fax 808/874-6144. www.mauikamaole.com. 62 out of the 210 units are in the rental pool. $205–$280 1-bedroom (sleeps up to 4); $265–$350 2-bedroom (sleeps up to 6). $35 reservation fee. ($100 cleaning fee for less than 4 nights). AE, MC, V. **Amenities:** Jacuzzi; 2 outdoor pools; tennis courts. *In room:* A/C, TV, fridge, high-speed Internet access ($10), kitchen.

INEXPENSIVE

In addition to the choices below, also check out **Luana Kai Resort,** 940 S. Kihei Rd., Kihei, HI 96753 (ⓒ **800/669-1127** or 808/879-1268; fax 808/879-1455; www.luanakai.com). This older condo complex has 113 units ($109–$179 one-bedroom; $129–$229 two-bedroom; $249–$299 three-bedroom; 4- to 7-night min.).

Kihei Kai Resort, 61 N. Kihei Rd., Kihei, HI 96753 (ⓒ **888/778-7717** or 808/891-0780; fax 808/891-9403; www.kiheikai.com), has one-bedroom apartments ($125–$190 double; 4- to 7-night min.) that are ideal for families.

Dreams Come True on Maui ✦ This bed-and-breakfast (where "you are never just renting a room") was a dream come true for hosts Tom Croly and Denise McKinnon, who, after several years of vacationing to Maui, opened this three-unit property in 2002. It's centrally located in the Maui Meadows subdivision, just a few minutes' drive to golf courses, tennis courts, white-sand beaches, shopping, and restaurants in Kihei and Wailea. The one-bedroom oceanview cottage has its own gourmet kitchen, two TVs, a washer/dryer, a computer with high-speed Internet access, and wraparound decks. Also available are two rooms in the house (one with king-size bed, one with queen-size), each with TV, private entrance, kitchenette, use of washer/dryer, and lots of other amenities not usually found in B&Bs. Guests are invited to use the centrally located oceanview deck; the house living room, which has a computer with high-speed Internet connection; and an outdoor cooking area with barbecue grill, sink, and microwave. Every guest is given personal concierge treatment, from the lowdown on good snorkeling to a tour of the property. In the evenings, Tom shows movies on an 8-foot-wide movie screen and frequently helps guests transfer their digital images to a CD so they can go out and shoot more photos of Maui. The owners recently acquired a one- and two-bedroom condo, across the street from the beach, which they rent for $135 to $169 a night.

3259 Akala Dr., Kihei, HI 96753. ⓒ **877/782-9628** or 808/879-7099. Fax 808/879-7099. www.dreamscometrueonmaui.com. 3 units. $89–$109 room double (3- to 4-night min.); $135–$169 cottage double (6-night min.; extra person $15). Room rates include continental breakfast (except in cottage). MC, V. **Amenities:** Concierge. *In room:* A/C ($3–$5 per day), TV/VCR, CD player, fridge, hair dryer, kitchen or kitchenette.

Hale Alana ★ 🏠 There was new management (with plans for complete renovation) in 2010 for this large vacation home, tucked into the residential neighborhood of Maui Meadows (and a 5-min. drive from the nearest good beach). This three-bedroom, three-bathroom Polynesian-style home comes complete with air-conditioning, three TVs, VCR, stereo, CD player, three cordless phones and an answering machine, full kitchen, open dining room, breakfast bar, and laundry room. It's a terrific deal for a large family or three couples traveling together. The master bedrooms have California-king-size beds, walk-in closets, and dual sinks and showerheads; the third bedroom has two double beds and a large closet. Skylights, ceiling fans, and an interior lava-rock wall add to the tropical environment. The deck has outdoor tables and chairs, a barbecue grill, and a fabulous hot tub.

490 Mikioi Place (in Maui Meadows), Kihei, HI 96753. ⓒ **800/871-5032** or 808/875-4840. Fax 808/879-3998. www.halealana.com or www.beachbreeze.com. 1 unit. $300 3-bedroom for 2. Cleaning fee $200. Extra person $20. 7-night minimum. MC, V. **Amenities:** Jacuzzi. *In room:* A/C, TV/VCR/DVD, fridge, hair dryer, kitchen.

Koa Resort ★ ☺ Located just across the street from the ocean, Koa Resort comprises five two-story wooden buildings on more than 5½ acres of landscaped grounds. There's plenty of room for families, who can enjoy the tennis courts, pool, and putting green. The spacious, privately owned one-, two-, and three-bedroom units are decorated with care and come fully equipped, right down to the dishwasher and disposal in the kitchens. The larger condos have both showers and tubs; the smaller units have showers only. All feature large lanais, ceiling fans, and washer/dryers. For maximum peace and quiet, ask for a unit far from Kihei Road. Bars, restaurants, and a golf course are nearby.

811 S. Kihei Rd. (btw. Kulanihakoi St. and Namauu Place), Kihei, HI 96753. Reservations c/o Bello Realty, P.O. Box 1776, Kihei, HI 96753. ℂ **800/541-3060** or 808/879-3328. Fax 808/875-1483. www.bellomaui.com. 54 units (some with shower only). High season $115–$120 1-bedroom, $120–$145 2-bedroom, $180–$275 3-bedroom; low season $99 1-bedroom, $100–$125 2-bedroom, $160–$240 3-bedroom. MC, V. **Amenities:** 18-hole putting green; Jacuzzi; outdoor pool; 2 tennis courts. *In room:* TV, fridge, high-speed Internet access (most units), kitchen.

Maui Sunseeker 🏖 This former budget property, located just across the street from a terrific white-sand beach, has a new management team that has spiffed up the studio and one-bedroom units by adding custom furniture, air-conditioning, and other amenities not usually seen at small properties (like high-speed Internet access and concierge services). This property is geared for adults, so families with children, this is not the place for you. The redone units have been tastefully decorated. The one-bedrooms, which have a pullout sofa in the living room and new appliances in the kitchen, are a deal during low season. All units have private oceanview lanais and the beach just a few steps away, plus there's a gas barbecue for guests' use. The new owners also bought the apartment complex next door, where they've revamped everything, put slate in the bathrooms and new tile on the floor, bought new furniture, and repainted. The units are small, but the lanais are large and the price is right—and there's even a rooftop lanai where you can sit in the hot tub and enjoy great ocean views

551 S. Kihei Rd. (P.O. Box 276), Kihei, HI 96753. ℂ **800/532-6284** or 808/879-1261. Fax 808/874-3877. www.mauisunseeker.com. 16 units. $105–$185 hotel room double; $110–$195 studio double; $125–$235 junior suite double; $145–$245 premium junior suite double; $145–$265 1-bedroom double; $275–$395 penthouse apt. Extra person $45. AE, DISC, MC, V. **Amenities:** Concierge; hot tub. *In room:* A/C, TV/VCR, hair dryer, kitchen or kitchenette, Wi-Fi.

Menehune Shores ⚓ If you plan to stay on Maui for a week, you might want to look into the car/condo packages here; they're a real deal, especially for families on a budget. The six-story Menehune Shores is more than 4 decades old and is showing its age in some places, but all units are well maintained and have ocean views and lanais. The design is straight out of the 1970s, but the view is timeless. The kitchens are fully equipped, all units have washer/dryers, and the oceanfront location guarantees a steady breeze that keeps the rooms cool (there's no air-conditioning). The building sits in front of the ancient Hawaiian fishponds of Kalepolepo. Some Hawaiians still fish them using traditional throw nets, but generally the pond serves as protection from the ocean waves, making it safe for children (and those unsure of their ability) to swim in the relatively calm waters. There's also a heated pool, shuffleboard courts, and a whale-watching platform on the roof garden. Don't expect the Ritz, but this budget option offers oceanfront units at affordable prices in the heart of Kihei.

760 S. Kihei Rd. (btw. Kaonoulu and Hoonani sts.), P.O. Box 1327, Kihei, HI 96753. © **800/558-9117** or 808/879-3428. Fax 808/879-5218. www.menehunereservations.com. 64 units. $150–$180 1-bedroom double ($1,219 per week with car); $190–$215 2-bedroom for up to 4 ($1,419–$1,529/week with car); $240–$285 3-bedroom for up to 6 ($1,909/week with car). $20 booking fee. 3-night minimum. Extra person $7.50. No credit cards. **Amenities:** Restaurant; bar; outdoor pool; gas grills. *In room:* TV/VCR, fridge, kitchen.

Nona Lani Cottages ★ 👜 Picture this: a grassy expanse dotted with eight cottages tucked among palm, fruit, and sweet-smelling flower trees, right across the street from a white-sand beach. This is one of the great hidden deals in Kihei. The cottages are tiny but contain everything you'll need: a small but complete kitchen, twin beds that double as couches in the living room, a separate bedroom with a queen-size bed, and a lanai with table and chairs. The real attraction, however, is the garden setting next to the beach. There are no phones in the cabins, but there's a public one by the check-in area. There's also a barbecue area. Your hosts, the industrious Kong family, also run Happy Valley Hale (p. 126), hostel accommodations on the other side of the island in Happy Valley, next to Wailuku.

455 S. Kihei Rd. (just south of Hwy. 31), P.O. Box 655, Kihei, HI 96753. © **800/733-2688** or 808/879-2497. www.nonalanicottages.com. 11 units. $120–$150 cottage double. Extra person $15. 7-night minimum in high season. No credit cards. *In room:* A/C, TV, fridge, kitchen, no phone.

Pineapple Inn Maui ★★ 👜 This charming inn (four rooms, plus a two-bedroom cottage) is not only an exquisite find, but also a terrific value. Located in the residential Maui Meadows area, with panoramic ocean views, the two-story inn is expertly landscaped, with a lily pond in the front and a giant saltwater pool and Jacuzzi overlooking the ocean. Each of the expertly decorated, soundproof rooms (you won't hear the traffic from nearby Piilani Hwy.) has a private lanai with incredible view, plus a small kitchenette stocked with juice, pastries, and drinks on your arrival. There's also a darling two-bedroom, one-bathroom cottage (wood floors, beautiful artwork) that's landscaped for maximum privacy and has a full kitchen (even a dishwasher), separate bedrooms, phone and answering machine, and private lanai. There's a barbecue area for guests.

3170 Akala Dr., Kihei, HI 96753. © **877/212-MAUI** (6284) or 808/298-4403. www.pineappleinnmaui.com. 5 units. $139–$149 double; $215 cottage for 4. 3-night minimum for rooms, 6-night minimum for cottage. No credit cards. **Amenities:** Jacuzzi; large saltwater pool. *In room:* A/C, TV/VCR, fridge, hair dryer, kitchenette or kitchen, no phone (in rooms), Wi-Fi.

Punahoa Beach Apartments ★ 🏄 Book this place! I can't put it any more simply than that. The location—off noisy, traffic-ridden Kihei Road, on a quiet side street with ocean frontage—is fabulous. A grassy lawn rolls about 50 feet down to the beach, where there's great snorkeling just offshore and a popular surfing spot next door; shopping and restaurants are all within walking distance. All of the beautifully decorated units in this small four-story building have fully equipped kitchens and lanais with great ocean views. Rooms go quickly in winter, so reserve early.

2142 Iliili Rd. (off S. Kihei Rd., 300 ft. from Kamaole Beach I), Kihei, HI 96753. © **800/564-4380** or 808/879-2720. Fax 808/875-9147. www.punahoabeach.com. 13 units. $132–$159 studio double; $164–$244 1-bedroom double; $204–$274 2-bedroom double; $199–$269 1-bedroom penthouse. $35 reservation fee. Extra person $15. 5-night minimum. AE, MC, V. *In room:* A/C (some units), TV, fridge, Internet access, kitchen.

Two Mermaids on Maui B&B ★ 🎁 The two mermaids, Juddee and Miranda, both avid scuba divers, offer a friendly B&B, professionally decorated with brilliant colors and hand-painted art of the island. It sits in a quiet neighborhood just a 10-minute walk from the beach. My favorite unit is the Ocean Ohana, a large one-bedroom apartment (with the option of a separate connecting bedroom), complete with kitchenette, huge private deck, private entry, and your own giant hot tub. Equally cute is the Poolside Suite, with private entry next to the outdoor pool. This studio (with the option of a separate connecting bedroom) is a living room during the day; at night it converts to a bedroom with a pull-down bed. Continental breakfast, with some of the best homemade bread on the island, is placed on your doorstep every morning (so you can sleep in). Amenities include guitars in every unit, a range of complimentary beach equipment, microwave popcorn, and a barbecue area. If the spirit moves you, Juddee is a licensed minister who can perform weddings.

2840 Umalu Place, Kihei, HI 96753. ℂ **800/598-9550** or 808/874-8687. Fax 808/875-1833. www.twomermaids.com. 2 units. $115 studio double; $140 double 1-bedroom apt; 2-bedroom double $175–$200. Rates include continental breakfast. 3-night minimum. No credit cards, but will do credit cards through PayPal. **Amenities:** Babysitting; golf nearby; outdoor pool; hot tub; tennis courts nearby. *In room:* TV, DVD (on request), fridge, hair dryer, kitchenette, Wi-Fi.

Wailana Kai ★ 🏄 Bello Realty has added this renovated two-story apartment building to its collection. Located at the end of a cul-de-sac, and just a 1-minute walk to the beach, the property was totally renovated several years ago. All units have full kitchens and concrete soundproof walls, and the second floor has ocean views. There's also a barbecue area for guests.

34 Wailana Place, Kihei, HI 96753. Reservations c/o Bello Realty, P.O. Box 1776, Kihei, HI 96753. ℂ **800/541-3060** or 808/879-3328. Fax 808/875-1483. www.bellomaui.com. 10 units. $110–$120 1-bedroom; $115–$150 2-bedroom. MC, V. **Amenities:** Outdoor pool. *In room:* TV/VCR, fridge, high-speed Internet access (in some units), kitchen.

What a Wonderful World B&B ★ 🏄 I couldn't believe what I'd discovered here: an impeccably done B&B with a great location, excellent rates, and thought and care put into every room. Hostess Eva Tantillo has not only a full-service travel agency, but also a master's degree—along with several years of experience—in hotel management. The result? One of Maui's finest bed-and-breakfasts, centrally located in Kihei (½ mile to Kamaole II Beach Park, 5 min. from Wailea golf courses, and convenient to shopping and restaurants). Choose from one of four units: the master suite (with a barbecue grill on the lanai), a studio apartment, or two one-bedroom apartments. Eva serves a gourmet expanded continental breakfast on her lanai, which boasts views of white-sand beaches, the West Maui Mountains, and Haleakala. You're also welcome to use the communal barbecue.

2828 Umalu Place (off Keonakai St., near Hwy. 31), Kihei, HI 96753. ℂ **800/943-5804** or 808/879-9103. Fax 808/879-5340. www.amauibedandbreakfast.com. 4 units. $89–$150 double. Rates include breakfast. Children 11 and under stay free in parent's room. AE, MC, V. **Amenities:** Hot tub. *In room:* TV, fridge, hair dryer, kitchen (in apartment units), Wi-Fi.

Wailea

For a complete selection of condo units throughout Wailea and Makena, contact **Destination Resorts** (ℂ **866/384-1366** or 808/891-6200; fax 808/874-3554; www.drhmaui.com). Its luxury units include studio doubles starting at $275, one-bedroom doubles from $275, two bedrooms from $350, and three bedrooms from $475. At most properties, those rates include free long-distance calls, high-speed Internet access, and parking; all properties are nonsmoking. Children under 12 stay free; minimum stays vary by property.

VERY EXPENSIVE

The Fairmont Kea Lani Maui ★★★ At first glance, this blinding-white complex of arches and turrets may look a bit out of place in tropical Hawaii (it's a close architectural cousin of Las Hadas, the *Arabian Nights* fantasy resort in Manzanillo, Mexico). But once you enter the flower-filled lobby and see the big blue Pacific outside, there's no doubt you're in Hawaii.

It's not cheap, but for the price of a hotel room in other luxury resorts, you get an entire suite here—plus a few extras. Each unit in the all-suite hotel has a kitchenette, a living room with entertainment center and sofa bed (great if you have the kids in tow), a wet bar, an oversize marble bathroom (with separate shower big enough for a party), a spacious bedroom, and a large lanai that overlooks the pools, lawns, and white-sand beach. The small boutique spa offers the latest in body work in intimate, relaxing surroundings—not to be missed, even if you're staying elsewhere.

The rich and famous stay in the villas—2,000-square-foot two- and three-bedroom fantasy beach bungalows, each with its own plunge pool and gourmet kitchen (and includes a luxury car rental).

4100 Wailea Alanui Dr., Wailea, HI 96753. ℂ **866/540-4456** or 808/875-4100. Fax 808/875-1200. www.fairmont.com/kealani. 450 units. $369–$1,100 suite (sleeps up to 4); from $1,300 villa. Valet parking $20; free self-parking. AE, DC, DISC, MC, V. **Amenities:** 4 restaurants (including Nick's Fishmarket Maui, p. 189), plus gourmet bakery and deli; 3 bars (w/sunset cocktails and entertainment at the Caffè Ciao Restaurant); babysitting; year-round children's program; concierge; fine 24-hr. fitness center; nearby Wailea Golf Club's 3 18-hole championship golf courses, as well as the Makena and Elleair golf courses; 2 large swimming lagoons connected by a 140-ft. water slide and swim-up bar, plus an adults-only pool; room service; excellent full-service spa; use of Wailea Tennis Center's 11 courts (3 lit for night play) and pro shop; watersports equipment rentals; 2 whirlpools. *In room:* A/C, TV/DVD/VCR, CD player, fridge, hair dryer, high-speed Internet access ($14 per day), kitchenette, microwave. (*Tip:* If you join the President's Club, which is free, there is no charge for the Internet access.)

Four Seasons Resort Maui at Wailea ★★★ ☺ If money's no object, this is the place to spend it. It's hard to beat this modern version of a Hawaiian palace by the sea, with a relaxing, casual atmosphere. Although it sits on a glorious beach between two other hotels, you won't feel like you're on resort row: The Four Seasons inhabits its own world, thanks to an open courtyard of pools and gardens. Amenities are first-rate here, including outstanding restaurants and an excellent spa. This may also be the most kid-friendly resort on the island: There's a complete activities program for *keiki* (complimentary, of course), plus other perks like milk and cookies on arrival, kids' menus in all restaurants, infant gear (cribs, strollers, and even toilet-seat locks), and a game room (video games, foosball, and more). You can even prepurchase necessities like diapers and baby food; the hotel will have them waiting for you when you arrive.

The spacious (about 600 sq. ft.) guest rooms feature furnished lanais, nearly all with ocean views, that are great for watching whales in winter and sunsets year-round. The grand bathrooms contain deep marble tubs and showers for two.

Service is attentive but not cloying. At the pool, guests lounge in casbahlike tents, pampered with iced Evian and chilled towels. And you'll never see a housekeeping cart in the hall: The cleaning staff works in teams, so they're as unobtrusive as possible and in and out of your room in minutes.

The fabulous spa—which is smaller than the one at the Grand Wailea but has more intimate service—features an incredible menu of treatments ranging from traditional Hawaiian to craniosacral to ayurvedic massage, offered in 13 treatment rooms and three oceanside *hale.*

The ritzy neighborhood surrounding the hotel is home to great restaurants and shopping, the Wailea Tennis Center (known as Wimbledon West), and six golf courses—not to mention that great beach, with gentle waves and islands framing the view on either side.

3900 Wailea Alanui Dr., Wailea, HI 96753. © **800/311-0630** or 808/874-8000. Fax 808/874-2244. www.fourseasons.com/maui. 380 units. $425–$970 double; $1,120–$1,220 Club Floor double; from $1,025 suite. Packages available. Extra person $100 ($300 in Club Floor rooms). Children under 18 stay free in parent's room. Valet parking $20. AE, DC, MC, V. **Amenities:** 3 restaurants (including Spago, p. 190, and Ferraro's at Seaside, p. 190); 3 bars (w/nightly entertainment); babysitting; free use of bikes; fabulous year-round children's program; one of Maui's best concierge desks; concierge-level rooms; putting green; use of Wailea Golf Club's 3 18-hole championship golf courses, as well as the nearby Makena and Elleair golf courses; health club featuring outdoor cardiovascular equipment (w/individual TV/VCRs); 3 fabulous outdoor pools; room service; excellent spa; 2 on-site tennis courts (lit for night play); use of Wailea Tennis Center's 11 courts (3 lit for night play); beach pavilion w/water equipment rentals and 1-hr. free use of snorkel equipment; 2 whirlpools (1 for adults only); . *In room:* A/C, TV, fridge, hair dryer, minibar, Wi-Fi ($13/day except Club Level).

Grand Wailea Resort Hotel & Spa ★★★ Spa aficionados, take note: Hawaii's largest (50,000 sq. ft.) and most elaborate spa is located here, with every kind of body treatment you can imagine. Treatments include use of the numerous baths, hot tubs, mineral pools, saunas, steam rooms, and other relaxation amenities in the his-and-hers spa area.

Built at the pinnacle of Hawaii's brief fling with fantasy megaresorts, the Grand Wailea is extremely popular with families, incentive groups, and conventions; it's the grand prize in Hawaii vacation contests and the dream of many honeymooners. Some 10,000 tropical plants in the lobby; an intricate pool system with slides, waterfalls, rapids, and a water-powered elevator to take you up to the top; a restaurant in a man-made tide pool; a floating New England–style wedding chapel; and nothing but oceanview, amenity-filled guest rooms. It's all crowned with a $30-million collection of original art, much of it created expressly for the hotel by Hawaii artists and sculptors. Though minimalists may be put off, there's no denying that the Grand Wailea is plush, professional, and pampering, with all the diversions you could imagine. Oh, and did I mention the fantastic beach out front?

Note: Smoking is limited to the private lanais outside the rooms.

3850 Wailea Alanui Dr., Wailea, HI 96753. © **800/888-6100** or 808/875-1234. Fax 808/874-2442. www.grandwailea.com. 780 units. $429–$925 double; from $1,100 suite; from $729 Napua Club Room (in Napua Tower). Daily $25 resort fee for lei greeting on arrival, welcome drink, local calls, use of spa, admission to scuba-diving clinics and water aerobics, art and garden tours, nightly turndown service, in-room high-speed Internet access, self-parking, and shuttle service to Wailea area. Extra person $50 ($100 in Napua Tower). Valet parking $20; free self-parking. AE, DC, DISC, MC, V. **Amenities:** 6 restaurants; 7 bars (including a nightclub w/ laser-light shows); babysitting; children's program; concierge; concierge-level rooms; complete fitness center; use of Wailea Golf Club's 3 18-hole championship golf courses, as well as the nearby Makena and Elleair golf courses; Jacuzzi; 2,000-ft.-long Activity Pool, featuring a swim/ ride through mountains and grottoes; room service; Hawaii's largest spa; use of Wailea Tennis Center's 11 courts (3 lit for night play) and pro shop; watersports equipment rentals; diving and windsurfing lessons. *In room:* A/C, TV, fridge (fee of $25 per stay), hair dryer, high-speed Internet access, kitchenette, minibar.

EXPENSIVE

Wailea Beach Marriott Resort & Spa ★★ This classic, open-air, 1970s-style hotel in a tropical garden by the sea gives you a sense of what Maui was like before the big resort boom. It was the first resort built in Wailea (in 1976), and it remains the most Hawaiian of them all. Airy and comfortable, with touches of Hawaiian art throughout and a terrific aquarium that stretches forever behind the front desk, it just feels right. What's truly special about this hotel is how it fits into its environment without overwhelming it. Eight buildings, all low-rise except for an eight-story tower, are spread along 22 gracious acres of lawns and gardens spiked by coco palms, with lots of open space and a half-mile of oceanfront property on a point between Wailea and Ulua beaches. The vast, parklike expanses are a luxury on this now-crowded coast.

The small Mandara Spa offers a long list of treatments, from relaxing massages to aromatherapy wraps to rejuvenating facials in a very Zen atmosphere. My only criticism is the lack (at this time) of a shower facility in the spa.

3700 Wailea Alanui Dr., Wailea, HI 96753. © **800/367-2960** or 808/879-1922. Fax 808/874-8331. www.waileamarriott.com. 545 units. $299–$735 double; from $400 suite. Extra person $40. Packages available. Parking $18 valet, $15 self. Daily $25 resort fee for local calls, discounts on luau and snorkel-gear rental, and free kids' meals with purchase of adult entree. AE, DC, DISC, MC, V. **Amenities:** 2 restaurants; 2 bars; babysitting; concierge; fitness center; use of Wailea Golf Club's 3 18-hole championship golf courses; outdoor pools (including 1 for kids only); room service; full-service Mandara Spa w/steam rooms and whirlpools; use of Wailea Tennis Center's 11 courts (3 lit for night play) and pro shop; watersports equipment rentals; recreation center. *In room:* A/C, TV, hair dryer, high-speed Internet access ($14), 4-outlet technology console.

Makena

EXPENSIVE

Makena Beach and Golf Resort ★★ If you're looking for a vacation in a beautiful, tranquil spot with a golden-sand beach, here's your place. But if you plan to tour Maui, you might try another hotel. The Makena Beach Resort is at the end of the road, far, far away from anything else on the island, so sightseeing in other areas would require a lot of driving.

Originally, owned and built by the exclusive Prince Resorts, the property was designed for the Japanese market. In 2009, Benchmark Hospitality took over the management. In Hawaii, Benchmark did wonders with the Turtle Bay Resort on Oahu, so we expect that they will also bring this property up to luxury standards. The location, on one of Maui's best beaches is beautiful, the interior atrium, filled with tropical plants and a koi-filled waterfall stream is gorgeous.

5400 Makena Alanui, Makena, HI 96753. © **800/321-6284** or 808/874-1111. Fax 808/879-8763. www.makenaresortmaui.com. 310 units. $425–$600 double; from $560 suite. Extra person $60. Packages available. AE, DC, MC, V. **Amenities:** 4 restaurants; 2 bars (w/local Hawaiian music nightly); babysitting; children's program; concierge; fitness room; 36-hole golf course (designed by Robert Trent Jones, Jr.); Jacuzzi; 2 outdoor pools (1 for adults, 1 for children); room service; 6 Plexipave tennis courts (2 lit for night play); watersports equipment rentals. *In room:* A/C, TV, fridge, hair dryer, high-speed Internet access.

UPCOUNTRY MAUI
Makawao, Olinda & Haliimaile

When you stay in the cooler upcountry climate of Makawao, Olinda, and Haliimaile, on the slopes of Maui's 10,000-foot Haleakala volcano, you'll be (relatively) close to Haleakala National Park. Makawao and Olinda are approximately 90 minutes from the entrance to the park at the 7,000-foot level (you still have 3,000 ft. and another 30–45 min. to get to the top). Staying in Haliimaile adds another 10 to 15 minutes to your drive up to the summit. Accommodations in Kula (reviewed in the next section) are the closest to the summit.

EXPENSIVE

Aloha Cottage ★★ 🏠 Hidden in the secluded rolling hills of Olinda on a 5-acre parcel of manicured, landscaped tropical foliage features a tropical cottage, designed and decorated by hosts Ron and Ranjana Serle. The Thai Tree House resembles an upscale Thai home with high vaulted ceilings, teak floors, and a king-size cherrywood bed in the center of the room. The private deck and private soaking tub make this a very romantic lodging. In fact, Ranjana can arrange weddings, prepare a private dinner, set up personal massages, and even organize a private yoga session for two.

1879 Olinda Rd., Makawao, HI 96765. © **888/328-3330** or 808/573-8555. Fax 808/573-2551. www.alohacottage.com. 1 cottage. $245 double. 3-night minimum preferred. MC, V. *In room:* TV/ VCR, CD player, fridge, hair dryer, kitchen.

MODERATE

Banyan Tree House ★ 🏠 Huge monkeypod trees (complete with swing and hammock) extend their branches over this 2½-acre property like a giant green canopy. The restored 1920s plantation manager's house is decorated with Hawaiian furniture from the 1930s. The house can accommodate a big family or a group of friends; it has three spacious bedrooms and three private marble bathrooms. A fireplace stands at one end of the huge living room, a large lanai runs the entire length of the house, and the hardwood floors shine throughout. The four smaller guest cottages have been totally renovated and also feature hardwood floors and marble bathrooms. Floor plans vary; one has one queen-size bed, the others have two beds (a mix of queen-size, doubles, and twins). The quiet neighborhood and old Hawaii ambience give this place a comfortable, easygoing atmosphere. Restaurants and shops are just minutes away in Makawao, and the beach is a 15-minute drive—but this place is so relaxing that you may want to do nothing but lie in a hammock and watch the clouds float by. Recently they've added a yoga and meditation center.

3265 Baldwin Ave. (next to Veterans' Cemetery, less than a mile below Makawao), Makawao, HI 96768. © **808/572-9021.** Fax 808/573-5072. www.banyantreehouse.com. 7 units. $165–$175 double room in house; $145–$190 cottage for 2. Extra person $25. Children 12 and under stay in parent's room for $10. Cleaning fee $20. AE, DC, DISC, MC, V. **Amenities:** Babysitting; Jacuzzi; outdoor pool. *In room:* TV (in some cottages), fridge, kitchen or kitchenette, Wi-Fi.

INEXPENSIVE

If you'd like your own private cottage, consider **Peace of Maui,** 1290 Haliimaile Rd. (just outside Haliimaile town), Haliimaile, HI 96768 (© **888/475-5045** or 808/572-5045; www.peaceofmaui.com), which has a full kitchen, two bedrooms, a day bed, and a large deck. The cottage goes for $150, (plus a $75 cleaning fee) and children are welcome. The owners also have rooms in the main house (with shared bathroom and kitchen facilities) from $65 single and $70 double.

Hale Ho'okipa Inn Makawao ★ 🎁 Step back in time at this 1924 plantation-style home, rescued by owner Cherie Attix in 1996 and restored to its original charm (and listed on the State and National Historic Registers). Cherie lovingly refurbished the old wooden floors, filled the rooms with furniture from the 1920s, and hung works by local artists on the walls. The result is a charming, serene place to stay, just a 5-minute walk from the shops and restaurants of Makawao, 15 minutes from beaches, and an hour's drive from the top of Haleakala. The guest rooms have separate outside entrances and private bathrooms. The house's front and back porches are wonderful spots for sipping tea and watching the sun set. The Kona Wing is a two-bedroom suite with private bathroom and use of the kitchen.

32 Pakani Place, Makawao, HI 96768. © **877/572-6698** or ©/fax 808/572-6698. www.maui-bed-and-breakfast.com. 4 units (2 with shower only). $125–$180 double. Rates include continental breakfast. Extra person $20. MC, V. From Haleakala Hwy., turn left on Makawao Ave., and turn right on the 5th street on the right off Makawao Ave. (Pakani Place); it's the 2nd-to-last house on the right (green house with white picket fence and water tower). *In room:* A/C, TV, hair dryer, Wi-Fi.

Kula

Lodgings in Kula are the closest options to the entrance of Haleakala National Park (about a 60-min. drive away).

INEXPENSIVE

In addition to the options below, consider **Gildersleeve's Bed & Breakfast,** formerly known as Elaine's Upcountry Guest Rooms (© **808/878-6623**). The warm and welcoming hosts rent three rooms in their spacious pole house ($85 double; 3-night minimum).

Kula Cottage ★ 🎁 I can't imagine having a less-than-fantastic vacation here. Tucked away on a quiet street amid a large grove of blooming papaya and banana trees, Cecilia and Larry Gilbert's romantic honeymoon cottage is very private—it even has its own driveway and carport. The 700-square-foot cottage has a full kitchen (complete with dishwasher) and three huge closets that offer enough storage space for you to move in permanently. The lanai is outfitted with a gas barbecue and an umbrella-covered table and chairs. Cecilia delivers a continental breakfast daily. Groceries and a small takeout lunch counter are within walking distance; it's a 30-minute drive to the beach.

40 Puakea Place (off Lower Kula Rd.), Kula, HI 96790. © **808/878-2043** or 808/871-6230. Fax 808/871-9187. www.kulacottage.com. 1 unit. $110 double. Rate includes continental breakfast. 3-night minimum. Extra person $15. No credit cards. *In room:* TV, fridge, kitchen.

Kula View Bed & Breakfast 🎁 Hostess and gardener extraordinaire Susan Kauai has this cute private suite (with its own deck and private entrance)

Where to Stay in Upcountry & East Maui

Aloha Cottage **10**
Banyan Tree House **7**
Cliff's Edge **4**
Gildersleeve's Vacation Rentals **13**
Hale Ho'okipa Inn Makawao **9**
Huelo Point Flower Farm **5**
The Inn at Mama's Fish House **2**

Kula Cottage **12**
Kula View B&B **11**
Maui Dream Cottage **3**
Paia Inn **1**
Peace of Maui **8**
Piialoha B&B Cottage **6**
Tea Houses Cottage **5**

upstairs in her home. The roomy studio has a huge deck with a panoramic view of Haleakala and a private bath, which she renovated in 2009. Inside, there's a reading area with a comfy lounge chair and an eating area with table and chairs, toaster oven, coffeemaker, and electric teakettle. Susan serves breakfast in your suite (or will pack a picnic breakfast if you are out early) of tasty breads or muffins, fruit, juice, and tea and coffee. She has plenty of warm jackets, sweaters, and blankets you can borrow if you plan to make the trip to the top of Haleakala. Be sure to take a stroll through her magical garden.

P.O. Box 322, Kula, HI 96790. © **808/878-6736.** sue@kulaview.com. 1 suite. $125 double. Rates include continental breakfast. No credit cards. 2-night minimum. *In room:* Fridge.

EAST MAUI: ON THE ROAD TO HANA

Paia

EXPENSIVE

Paia Inn I really wanted to love this boutique inn (only 5 rooms), which opened in 2009 in the middle of the tiny, funky town of Paia. But the main problems here are that the rooms are tiny (almost claustrophobic) and noisy (not only from the street outside, but also from other guest rooms), and combined with very expensive rack rates and virtually no parking, I'd suggest you can find better deals in this area (see below). The inn features bamboo wood floors and a common living room where guests can gather (which can be a problem late at night if you want to sleep and the other guests want to talk and listen to music). Each of the guest rooms has 500-thread-count sheets, tiny travertine bathrooms, high-definition flatscreen televisions, iPod docking stations, and very limited space to unpack your clothes. There is a complimentary coffee and tea with muffins and scones every morning.

93 Hana Hwy., Paia, HI 96779. © **800/721-4000** or 808/579-6000. 5 rooms. $189–$500 double. AE, MC, V. **Amenities**: Bicycle, surfboard, and stand-up paddle board rentals; concierge; room service. *In room:* A/C, fridge, free Wi-Fi.

Kuau

MODERATE

The Inn at Mama's Fish House ★★ The fabulous location (nestled in a coconut grove on secluded Kuau Beach), beautifully decorated interior (with rattan furniture and works by Hawaiian artists), and extras (gas barbecue, 27-in. TVs, and beach toys) make this place a gem for those seeking a centrally located vacation rental. All this, and the fabulous Mama's Fish House restaurant is just next door. The one-bedrooms are nestled in a tropical jungle (red ginger surrounds the garden patio), while the two-bedrooms face the beach. All have wood or terracotta floors, kitchenettes or complete kitchens (some even have dishwashers), sofa beds, and laundry facilities.

799 Poho Place (off the Hana Hwy. in Kuau), Paia, HI 96779. © **800/860-HULA** (4852) or 808/579-9764. Fax 808/579-8594. www.mamasfishhouse.com. 12 units. $175 garden studio double; $225 1-bedroom (sleeps up to 4); $275–$575 2-bedroom (up to 6); $575 Beachfront cottages; Junior suite from $325. 3-night minimum in Dec and Jan. AE, DISC, MC, V. **Amenities:** Restaurant. *In room:* A/C, TV/VCR, fridge, hair dryer, kitchen, Wi-Fi.

Haiku

MODERATE

Pilialoha B&B Cottage ★ At press time, this fabulous B&B was still trying to get a "new" B&B permit; after more than a year, they were still caught in the bureaucratic process (and lots of dollars in renovations). I'm sure they will get the permit—eventually. Call them, because this is a great place to stay. The minute you arrive at this split-level country cottage, set on a large lot with half-century-old eucalyptus trees, you'll see owner Machiko Heyde's artistry at work. Just in front of the quaint cottage is a garden blooming with some 200 varieties of roses. There's a queen-size bed in the master bedroom, from which a large lanai extends. There's a great movie collection for rainy days or cool country nights, plus a garage. If you plan on an early-morning ride to the top of Haleakala, Machiko will make sure you go with a Thermos of coffee and her homemade bread. The property is not appropriate for children.

2512 Kaupakalua Rd. (½ mile from Kokomo intersection), Haiku, HI 96708. © **808/572-1440.** 1 unit. $150 double. 3-night minimum. No credit cards. **Amenities:** Complimentary use of beach toys (including snorkel equipment). *In room:* TV, fridge, kitchenette,Wi-Fi.

INEXPENSIVE

Maui Dream Cottage Essentially a vacation rental, this country estate is located atop a hill overlooking the ocean. The grounds are dotted with fruit trees (bananas, papayas, and avocados, all free for the picking), and the front lawn is comfortably equipped with a double hammock, chaise longues, and table and chairs. The cottage has two bedrooms, and is very well maintained and comfortably outfitted with furniture that's attractive but casual. The Haiku location is quiet and restful, offering the opportunity to see how real islanders live. However, you'll have to drive a good 20 to 25 minutes to restaurants in Makawao or Paia. Hookipa Beach is about a 20-minute drive, and Baldwin Beach (good swimming) is 25 minutes away.

265 W. Kuiaha Rd. (1 block from Pauwela Cafe), HI 96708. © **808/575-9079.** Fax 808/575-9477. www.mauidreamcottage.com. 1 units (with shower only). $770 per week double. Extra person $10. 7-night minimum. MC, V. *In room:* TV, fridge, kitchen, Wi-Fi.

Twin Falls

INEXPENSIVE

Hidden in a secluded jungle, powered by alternative energy (no utility poles!), the off-the-beaten-path **Tea House Cottage** (© **800/215-6130** or 808/572-5610; www.mauiteahouse.com) gives you the chance to get away from it all while still having electricity, phone, and TV—you can even plug in your laptop. Your private cottage has two decks, a screened lanai, a bedroom, a small kitchen, and a unique bathhouse. Rates of $135 single (2-night minimum) and $150 double (2-night minimum) include taxes and complimentary breakfast. Owner Ann DeWeese is on the property and can provide any helpful tips you need during your vacation. Discounts available for 4 or more nights.

Huelo/Wailua

EXPENSIVE

Cliff's Edge ★ This B&B and vacation rental couldn't be much closer to the ocean without being underwater. The saltwater swimming pool perches on the edge of a 300-foot cliff in Huelo. The tropically landscaped 2-acre property also has a hot tub and 600-square-foot sun deck. Accommodations include two bedrooms in the main house, a two-bedroom 900-square-foot guesthouse, and a 600-square-foot cottage. The rooms in the B&B range in size from 300 to 600 square feet, all with awesome ocean views, private entries, private lanais, private bathrooms, small kitchenettes (with microwave, coffeemaker, and refrigerator), and ceiling fans. Restaurants and shopping are about 30 minutes away in Paia.

P.O. Box 1095, Haiku, HI 96708. © **866/262-6284** or 808/268-4530. www.cliffsedge.com. 4 units. $185–$225 double room in house; $350 cottage. Extra person $25. 3-night minimum. Rates include continental breakfast. No credit cards. **Amenities:** Pool; hot tub; Wi-Fi. *In room:* TV (in cottages), stereo/CD player, fridge, kitchenette or kitchen, microwave.

Huelo Point Flower Farm 🏕 Here's a little Eden by the sea on a spectacular, remote, 300-foot sea cliff near a waterfall stream. This estate overlooking Waipio Bay has a guest cottage, a guesthouse, and a main house available for rent. The studio-size Gazebo Cottage has three glass walls that make the most of the oceanfront location, a koa-wood captain's bed, a private oceanside patio, a private hot tub, and a half-bathroom with outdoor shower. The two-bedroom main house contains an exercise room, a fireplace, a sunken Roman bath, cathedral ceilings, and other extras. On the property is a natural pool with a waterfall and an oceanfront hot tub. You're welcome to pick fruit, vegetables, and flowers from the extensive garden. Homemade scones, tree-ripened papayas, and fresh-roasted coffee start your day. The secluded location, off the crooked road to Hana, is just a half-hour from Kahului, or about 20 minutes from Paia's shops and restaurants.

P.O. Box 791808 (off Hana Hwy., btw. mile markers 3 and 4), Paia, HI 96779. © **808/572-1850.** www.mauiflowerfarm.com. 3 units. $350 cottage double; $450 guesthouse double; $600 main house for 4. Extra person $35–$40. 2-night minimum. AE, MC, V. **Amenities:** 3 Jacuzzis; outdoor pool. *In room:* TV, fridge, hair dryer, kitchenette or kitchen.

AT THE END OF THE ROAD IN EAST MAUI: HANA

Note: To locate the following accommodations, see the "Hana" map on p. 283.

Expensive

Hotel Hana-Maui ★★★ ☺ This hotel sits on 66 rolling seaside acres and offers a wellness center, two pools, and access to one of the best beaches in Hana. This is the atmosphere, the landscape, and the culture of old Hawaii set in 21st-century accommodations. Every unit is excellent, but my favorites are the Sea Ranch Cottages (especially units 215–218 for the best views), where individual duplex bungalows look out over the craggy shoreline to the rolling surf. You step out of the oversize, airy units (with floor-to-ceiling sliding doors) onto a huge lanai with views that will stay with you long after your tan has faded. These comfy units have been totally redecorated with every amenity you can think of, and you won't be nickel-and-dimed for things like coffee and water—everything provided, from the homemade banana bread to the bottled water, is complimentary. Cathedral ceilings, a plush feather bed, a giant soaking tub, Hawaiian artwork, bamboo floors—this is luxury. The white-sand beach (just a 5-min. shuttle away), top-notch wellness center with some of the best massage therapists in Hawaii, and numerous activities (horseback riding, mountain biking, tennis, pitch-and-putt golf) all add up to make this one of the top resorts in the state. There's no TV in the rooms, but the Club Room has a giant-screen TV, plus VCR and Internet access. I highly recommend this little slice of paradise.

5031 Hana Hwy. (P.O. Box 9), Hana, HI 96713. © **800/321-HANA** (4262) or 808/248-8211. Fax 808/248-7202. www.hotelhanamaui.com. 66 units. $495 Bay Cottage double; $595–$1,675 Sea Ranch Cottage double; $1,800 3-bedroom suite for 6; from $4,000 2-bedroom Plantation House. Extra person $140. AE, DC, DISC, MC, V. **Amenities:** Restaurant (w/Hawaiian entertainment Fri); bar (entertainment 5 times a week); babysitting; concierge; fitness center; complimentary use of the 3-hole practice golf courses (complimentary use of clubs); 2 outdoor pools; room service; full-service spa; tennis courts. *In room:* Fridge, hair dryer, kitchenette.

Moderate

Bamboo Inn This inn shares the same historic site as the Hana Hale Inn (p. 162), and guests have full access to Hana Hale Inn's ancient fishponds and cave. There's access to a nearby rocky beach, which isn't good for swimming but makes a wonderful place to watch the sunset. All accommodations include fully equipped kitchens, bathrooms, bedrooms, living/dining areas, and private lanais. The oceanfront Bamboo Inn contains three units (two studios and a convertible one- or two-bedroom unit).

P.O. Box 374, Hana, HI 96713. © **808/248-7718.** www.bambooinn.com. 3 units. $175–$240 double (includes continental breakfast). Extra person $15. 2-night minimum. MC, V. **Amenities:** Jacuzzi. *In room:* TV/DVD, fridge, kitchen, Jacuzzi.

Ekena ★ Just one glance at the 360-degree view, and you can see why hosts Robin and Gaylord gave up their careers on the mainland and moved here. This 8½-acre piece of paradise in rural Hana boasts ocean and rainforest vistas; the floor-to-ceiling glass doors in the spacious Hawaiian-style pole house bring the outside in. The elegant two-story home is exquisitely furnished, from the comfortable U-shaped couch that invites you to relax and take in the view to the top-of-the-line mattress on the king-size bed. The fully equipped kitchen has everything you should need to cook a gourmet meal. Only one floor (and one two-bedroom unit) is rented at any given time to ensure privacy. The grounds are impeccably groomed and dotted with tropical plants and fruit trees. Hiking trails into the rainforest start right on the property, and beaches and waterfalls are just minutes away. Robin places fresh flowers in every room and makes sure you're comfortable; after that, she's available to answer questions, but she also respects your privacy.

P.O. Box 728 (off Hana Hwy., above Hana Airport), Hana, HI 96713. © **808/248-7047.** Fax 808/248-7853. www.ekenamaui.com. 2 units. $225 for 2; $295–$400 for 4. 3-night minimum. Children must be 14 or older. MC, V. *In room:* TV/DVD, CD player, fridge, kitchen, free Wi-Fi.

Hamoa Bay House & Bungalow ★ 🏠 Down a country lane guarded by two Balinese statues stands a little bit of Indonesia in Hawaii: a carefully crafted bungalow and an Asian-inspired two-bedroom house overlooking Hamoa Bay. This enchanting retreat is just 2 miles beyond Hasegawa General Store on the way to Kipahulu. It sits on 4 verdant acres within walking distance of Hamoa Beach (which James Michener considered one of the most beautiful in the Pacific). The 600-square-foot Balinese-style cottage is distinctly tropical, with elephant-bamboo furniture from Indonesia, batik prints, a king-size bed, a full kitchen, and a screened porch with hot tub and shower. Hidden from the cottage is a 1,300-square-foot home with a soaking tub and private outdoor stone shower. It offers an elephant-bamboo king-size bed in one room, a queen-size bed in another, a screened-in sleeping porch, a full kitchen, and wonderful ocean views.

P.O. Box 773, Hana, HI 96713. *C* **808/248-7884.** Fax 808/248-7853. E-mail: hamoabay@maui. net. 2 units. $225 cottage (sleeps only 2); $285 house for 2; $395 house for 4. 3-night minimum. MC, V. **Amenities:** Hot tub. *In room:* TV/DVD, CD player, fridge, kitchen, Wi-Fi (house only).

Hana Hale Inn 🎁 Hana Hale Inn sits on a historic site with ancient fishponds and a cave mentioned in ancient chants. Host John takes excellent care of the ponds (you're welcome to watch him feed the fish at 5pm daily) and is fiercely protective of the hidden cave ("It's not a tourist attraction, but a sacred spot"). There's access to a nearby rocky beach, which isn't good for swimming but makes a wonderful place to watch the sunset. All accommodations include fully equipped kitchens, bathrooms, bedrooms, living/dining areas, and private lanais. Next to the fishpond, the Royal Lodge, a 2,600-square-foot architectural masterpiece built entirely of Philippine mahogany, has large skylights the entire length of the house and can be rented as a house or two separate units. The cottages range from the separate two-level Tree House Cottage (with Jacuzzi for two, a Balinese bamboo bed, small kitchen/living area, and deck upstairs) to the Pond View Bungalow (with private outdoor Jacuzzi and shower).

P.O. Box 374, Hana, HI 96713. *C* **808/248-7641.** www.hanahaleinn.com. 5 units. $160–$260 double. Extra person $15. 2-night minimum. MC, V. **Amenities:** Jacuzzi. *In room:* TV/DVD, fridge, kitchen, Jacuzzi (in all but 1 unit).

Hana Kai Maui Resort Hana's only vacation condo complex, Hana Kai offers studio and one-bedroom units overlooking Hana Bay. All units have large kitchens and private lanais. Each of the one-bedroom units has a sliding door that separates the bedroom from the living room, plus a sofa bed that sleeps two additional guests. Ask for a corner unit with wraparound ocean views.

1533 Uakea Rd. (P.O. Box 38), Hana, HI 96713. *C* **800/346-2772** or 808/248-8426. Fax 808/248-7482. www.hanakaimaui.com. 17 units. $185–$235 studio double; $210–$260 1-bedroom (sleeps up to 4); $450 2-bedroom. Extra person $15. $20 service fee for less than 3 nights. Children 6 and under stay free in parent's room. MC, V. *In room:* Fridge, kitchen, Wi-Fi.

Hana Oceanfront Cottages ★★ Just across the street from Hamoa Bay, Hana's premier white-sand beach, lie these two plantation-style units, impeccably decorated in old Hawaii decor. My favorite unit is the romantic cottage, complete with front porch where you can sit and watch the ocean; a separate bedroom (with a bamboo sleigh bed), plus pullout sofa for extra guests; top-notch kitchen appliances; and comfy living room. The 1,000-square-foot vacation suite, located downstairs from hosts Dan and Sandi's home (but totally soundproof—you'll never hear them), has an elegant master bedroom with polished bamboo flooring, a spacious bathroom with custom hand-painted tile, and a fully appointed gourmet kitchen. Outside is a 320-square-foot lanai. The units sit on the road facing Hana's most popular beach, so there is traffic during the day. At night the traffic disappears, the stars come out, and the sound of the ocean lulls you to sleep.

P.O. Box 843, Hana, HI 96713. © **808/248-7558.** Fax 808/248-8034. www.hanaoceanfront cottages.com. 2 units. $250–$275 double. 3-night minimum. MC, V. **Amenities:** Barbecue area. *In room:* TV/VCR/DVD, stereo/CD player, fridge, hair dryer, kitchen.

Heavenly Hana Inn ★★ 🏨 This place on the Hana Highway, just a stone's throw from the center of Hana town, is a little bit of heaven, where no attention to detail has been spared. Each suite has a sitting room with futon and couch, polished hardwood floors, and separate bedroom with a raised platform bed (with an excellent, firm mattress). The black-marble bathrooms have huge tubs. Flowers are everywhere, and ceiling fans keep the rooms cool. The grounds are done in Japanese style with a bamboo fence, tiny bridges over a meandering stream, and Japanese gardens.

P.O. Box 790, Hana, HI 96713. ©/fax **808/248-8442.** 3 units. $350–$600 suite. Full gourmet breakfast available for $16 per person. 2-night minimum. AE, DISC, MC, V. Children must be 15 or older. *In room:* TV, no phone.

Inexpensive

Mrs. Nakamura has been renting her **Aloha Cottages** (© **808/248-8420**) since the 1970s. Located in residential areas near Hana Bay, these five budget rentals are simply but adequately furnished, varying in size from a roomy studio with kitchenette to a three-bedroom, two-bathroom unit. They're all fully equipped, clean, and fairly well kept. Rates run from $75 to $105 double (rate includes the taxes). Not all units have TVs, and none have phones, but Mrs. N is happy to take messages.

Baby Pigs Crossing Bed & Breakfast ★ 🏨 If you're looking for a quiet, romantic little cottage, nestled away from it all in old Hawaii but close enough to Hana to drive in for dinner, this is your place. International artist Arabella Gail Ark (formerly known as Gail Bakutis) has created a lovely retreat on her 1-acre parcel of land, which is landscaped in a "fragrance" garden carefully planted with Hawaii's best sweet-smelling plants. The separate guesthouse, with an ocean view from the lanai, is professionally decorated with comfort in mind, from the very cozy rattan furniture to the king-size sofa bed. There's a separate bedroom with a queen-size bed and a small but utilitarian kitchenette. The surprise is the unique bathroom with glass ceiling and walls (with privacy curtains), which opens onto a garden area. Even if you are not staying here, stop by and see the Ark Ceramics Gallery (daily 11am–4pm).

P.O. Box 667, Hana, HI 96713. © **808/248-8890.** Fax 808/248-4865. www.mauibandb.com. 1 unit. $250 double for 1 night ($225/night for 2 nights; $200/night for 3 nights). AE, MC, V. *In room:* TV/VCR, fridge, kitchenette.

Hana's Tradewind Cottages ★ 🖋 ☺ Nestled among the ginger and heliconias on a 5-acre flower farm are two separate cottages, each with carport, barbecue, private hot tub, ceiling fans, and sofa bed. The studio cottage sleeps up to four; a bamboo shoji blind separates the sleeping area (with queen-size bed) from the sofa bed in the living room. The Tradewinds Cottage has two bedrooms (with a queen-size bed in one room and two twins in the other), one bathroom (shower only), and a huge front porch. The atmosphere is quiet and relaxing, and hostess Rebecca Buckley, who has been in business for more than a decade, welcomes families. You can use the laundry facilities if staying 3 or more nights.

135 Alalele Place (the airport road), P.O. Box 385, Hana, HI 96713. 📞 **800/327-8097** or 808/248-8980. Fax 808/248-7735. www.hanamaui.net. 2 units. $175 studio double; $175 2-bedroom double. Extra person $15. 2-night minimum. AE, DISC, MC, V. *In room:* TV, fridge, kitchen, no phone, Wi-Fi.

Joe's Rentals 🏷 This is as close to a hostel as you can get in Hana. Joe's is a large, rambling house located just spitting distance from Hana Bay. Seven spartan but immaculately clean bedrooms share showers and bathroom; one has private facilities. All guests are welcome to use the large living room with TV and adjoining communal kitchen (free coffee available all day). Other amenities include a rec room, barbecue, and owner Ed Hill himself. He'll tell you the long story about the name if you ask and can also talk about what to do and see in Hana all day if you let him.

4870 Uakea Rd. (P.O. Box 746), Hana, HI 96713. 📞 **808/248-7033.** www.joesrentals.com. 8 units (7 with shared bathroom). $50 double with shared bathroom; $60 double with private bathroom. Extra person $10. MC, V. *In room:* No phone.

Waianapanapa State Park Cabins 🏷 These 12 rustic cabins are the best lodging deal on Maui. Everyone knows it, too—so make your reservations early (up to 6 months in advance). The cabins are warm and dry, and come complete with kitchen, living room, bedroom, and bathroom with hot shower; furnishings include linens, towels, dishes, and very basic cooking and eating utensils. Don't expect luxury—this is a step above camping, albeit in a beautiful tropical jungle setting. The key attraction at this 120-acre state beach park is the unusual horseshoe-shaped black-sand beach on Pailoa Bay, popular for shore fishing, snorkeling, and swimming. There's an on-site caretaker, along with restrooms, showers, picnic tables, shoreline hiking trails, and historic sites. Bring mosquito protection—this *is* the jungle, after all.

Off Hana Hwy. Reservations c/o State Parks Division, 54 S. High St., Room 101, Wailuku, HI 96793. 📞 **808/984-8109.** 10 units. $45 for 4 (sleeps up to 6). Extra person $5. 5-night maximum. No credit cards. *In room:* Fridge, kitchen, no phone.

6

WHERE
TO DINE

With soaring visitor statistics and a glamor-ous image, the Valley Isle is fertile ground not only for an international name or two (Wolfgang Puck of Spago) but also for Hawaii's famous enterprising chefs, such as Roy Yamaguchi of Roy's; Gerard Reversade of Gerard's; James McDonald of I'O and Pacific'O; Peter Merriman of Peter Merriman Kapalua; Mark Elman of Maui Tacos, Mala Ocean Tavern, and Mala Wailea; D. K. Kodama of Sansei Seafood Restaurant; and Beverly Gannon of Haliimaile General Store, Joe's, and Gannon's—a Pacific View Restaurant. There are also a few newcomers who are cook-ing up a storm and getting a well-deserved following, including Ryan Luckey of Pineapple Grill, Dana Pastula of the Cafe O'Lei res-taurants, and Don Ritchey of Moana Bakery & Cafe.

In this dizzying scenario, some things haven't changed: You can still dine well at Lahaina's open-air waterfront watering holes, where the view counts for 50% of the experience. There are still budget eateries, but not many; Maui's old-fash-ioned, multigenerational mom-and-pop diners are disappearing, eclipsed by the flashy newcomers, or clinging to the edge of existence in the older neighborhoods of central Maui, such as lovable Wailuku. Although you'll have to work harder to find them in the resort areas, you won't have to go far to find creative cuisine, pleasing style, and stellar dining experiences.

In the listings below, reservations are not necessary unless otherwise noted.

CENTRAL MAUI

Kahului

MODERATE

Bistro Casanova ★ 🎁 MEDITERRANEAN From the same group that brought interesting and delicious Italian food to Casanova Italian Restaurant & Deli (p. 191) in Makawao is this cosmopolitan bistro in the heart of Kahului serving tapas, pastas, steaks, and seafood for lunch and dinner. The space—located in a Kahului office complex formerly housing the restaurant The Manana Garage—has been totally renovated and now sports a nautical theme (everything is blue) with a great outdoor dining area. Packed with a business crowd at lunch and a more relaxed atmosphere at dinner (when mainly local residents dine), Bistro Casanova has some interesting items such as sweet and savory crepes,

PREVIOUS PAGE: Grilled seafood is popular island-wide.

166

quinoa salads, and Maui-raised beef, in addition to traditional Italian pastas, a tasty osso buco, and fresh fish.

33 Lono Ave., Kahului. ℭ **808/873-3650.** www.casanovamaui.com. Main courses $7-$14 lunch, $12-$36 dinner. AE, DISC, MC, V. Mon 11am-2:30pm; Tues-Sat 11am-2:30pm and 5-9:30pm.

Ichiban 🍴 JAPANESE/SUSHI What a find: an informal neighborhood restaurant that serves inexpensive, home-cooked Japanese food *and* good sushi at realistic prices. Local residents consider Ichiban a staple for breakfast, lunch, or dinner and a haven of comforts: egg-white omelets; great saimin; combination plates of teriyaki chicken, teriyaki meat, *tonkatsu* (pork cutlet), rice, and pickled cabbage; chicken yakitori; and sushi—everything from unagi and scallop to California roll. The sushi items may not be cheap, but like the specials, such as steamed opakapaka, they're a good value. I love the tempura, miso soup, and spicy ahi hand roll.

At the Kahului Shopping Center, 47 Kaahumanu Ave., Kahului. ℭ **808/871-6977.** Main courses $6-$7 breakfast, $10-$13 lunch (combination plates $13), $10-$30 dinner (combination dinner $15, dinner specials from $10). AE, DC, MC, V. Mon-Fri 7am-2pm and 5-9pm; Saturday 10:30am-2pm and 5-9pm. Closed 2 weeks around Christmas and New Year's.

Marco's Grill & Deli ITALIAN Located in the thick of central Maui, where the roads to upcountry, west, and south Maui converge, Marco's is popular among area residents for its homemade Italian fare and friendly informality. Everything—from the meatballs, sausages, and burgers to the sauces, salad dressings, and raviolis—is made in-house. The 35 different choices of hot and cold sandwiches and entrees are served all day; some favorites include vodka rigatoni with imported prosciutto and simple pasta with marinara sauce. The antipasto salad and roasted peppers are taste treats, but the meatballs and Italian sausage are famous in central Maui. This is one of those comfortable neighborhood fixtures favored by all generations. It also has a full bar.

At the Dairy Center, 444 Hana Hwy., Kahului. ℭ **808/877-4446.** Main courses $6-$33. AE, DISC, MC, V. Daily 7:30am-10pm.

INEXPENSIVE

The **Queen Kaahumanu Center** (www.queenkaahumanucenter.com)—the structure that looks like a white *Star Wars* umbrella in Kahului at 275 Kaahumanu Ave. (a 10-min drive from Kahului Airport on Hwy. 32)—has a very popular food court. Eateries include **Edo Japan,** whose flat Benihana-like grill dispenses marvelous, flavorful teppanyaki; **Panda Express,** which serves tasty Chinese food; and **Alexander's Fish and Chips,** a great place for fast takeout. Outside of the food court, but still in the shopping center, are **Ruby's,** dishing out burgers, fries, and shakes; and **Starbucks.** There's also a branch of **Maui Tacos** (p. 182). When you leave Kaahumanu Center, take a moment to gaze at the West Maui Mountains to your left from the parking lot.

Down to Earth 🍴 ORGANIC HEALTH FOOD If you are looking for a healthy alternative to fast foods, here's your place. Healthful organic ingredients, 90% vegan, appear in scrumptious salads, lasagna, chili, curries, and dozens of tasty dishes, presented at hot and cold self-serve stations. Stools line the counters in the simple dining area, where a few tables are available for those who don't want takeout. The food is great: millet cakes, mock tofu chicken, curried tofu, and Greek salad, nearly everything organic and tasty, with herb-tamari marinades

ROSELANI: MAUI'S BEST ice cream

For the culinary highlight of your trip to Maui, try **Roselani Ice Cream,** Maui's only made-from-scratch, old-fashioned ice cream. In fact, be sure to try it early in your trip so you can eat your way through this little bit of heaven at restaurants and scooping parlors, or get your own stash at grocery stores. There are more than 40 different flavors, divided into two different brands under the Roselani label: the Premium Parlour Flavors (ranging from the traditional vanilla to the unique black cherry, cappuccino chip, fresh-brewed coffee, and choco-cookie crunch) and the Tropics (with delicious varieties like the best-selling haupia, made from coconut and macadamia nut, or the popular choco-

late macadamia nut, Kona mud pie, mango and cream, coconut pineapple, and luau fudge pie). Each rich, creamy flavor contains 12% to 16% butterfat. For a list of hotels, restaurants, ice-cream parlors, and grocery stores that carry Roselani, either call Maui Soda & Ice Works ℭ **808/244-7951** or check online at www.roselani.com.

and pleasing condiments such as currants or raisins, apples, and cashews. (The fabulous tofu curry has apples, raw cashews, and raisins.) The food is sold by the pound, but you can buy a hearty, wholesome plate for $7. Vitamin supplements, health-food products, fresh produce, and cosmetics fill the rest of the store.

305 Dairy Rd., Kahului. ℭ **808/877-2661.** www.downtoearth.org. Self-serve hot buffet and salad bar and deli; sandwiches $8, food sold by the pound, average $7–$9 for a plate. AE, MC, V. Mon–Sat 7am–7:45pm; Sun 8am–6:45pm.

Restaurant Matsu JAPANESE/LOCAL Customers have come from Hana (more than 50 miles away) just for Matsu's California rolls, while regulars line up for the cold saimin (julienned cucumber, egg, Chinese-style sweet pork, and red ginger on noodles) and for the bento plates (various assemblages of chicken, teriyaki beef, fish, and rice). The nigiri sushi items are popular, especially among the don't-dally lunch crowd. The *katsu* pork and chicken, breaded and deep fried, are other specialties of this casual Formica-style diner. I love the tempura udon and the saimin, steaming mounds of wide and fine noodles swimming in homemade broths and topped with condiments. The daily specials are a changing lineup of home-cooked classics: oxtail soup, roast pork with gravy, teriyaki ahi, miso butterfish, and breaded mahimahi.

161 Alamaha St., Kahului. ℭ **808/871-0822.** Most items under $8. MC, V. Mon–Thurs 10am–3pm and 5–7:30pm; Fri 10am–3pm and 5–8pm.

Wailuku

MODERATE

Class Act ★ 🎁 GLOBAL Part of a program run by the distinguished Food Service Department of Maui Community College, now housed in a state-of-the-art, $15-million culinary facility (with floor-to-ceiling windows at one end, exhibition kitchen at the other end), Class Act is a "classroom" restaurant with a huge following. Student chefs show their stuff with a flourish and pull out all the stops to give you a dining experience you will long remember. Linen, china, servers in ties and white shirts, and a four-course lunch make this a unique value. The appetizer, soup, salad, and dessert are set, but you can choose between the regular entrees and a heart-healthy main course prepared in the culinary tradition of the week. The menu roams the globe, with highlights of Italy, Mexico, Maui, Napa Valley, France, New Orleans, and other locales. The filet mignon of French week is popular, as are the New Orleans gumbo and Cajun shrimp, the sesame-crusted mahimahi on taro-leaf pasta, the polenta flan with eggplant, and the bean and green-chile chilaquile.

At Maui Community College, 310 Kaahumanu Ave., Wailuku. ℂ **808/984-3280.** www.maui culinary.com/academy/class_act.cfm. Reservations recommended. 4-course lunch $30. MC, V. Wed and Fri 11am–12:30pm (last seating). Closed June–Aug for summer vacation and parts of Dec and Jan. Menu and cuisine type change weekly.

A Saigon Cafe ★★ 🏠 VIETNAMESE Jennifer Nguyen has stuck to her guns and steadfastly refused to erect a sign, but diners find their way here anyway. That's how good the food is. Fans drive from all over the island for her crisp spiced Dungeness crab, steamed opakapaka with ginger and garlic, and wok-cooked Vietnamese specials tangy with spices, herbs, and lemon grass. There are a dozen different soups, cold and hot noodles (including the popular beef noodle soup called *pho*), and chicken and shrimp cooked in a clay pot. You can create your own Vietnamese "burritos" from a platter of tofu, noodles, and vegetables that you wrap in rice paper and dip in garlic sauce. Among my favorites are the shrimp lemon grass, savory and refreshing, and the tofu curry, swimming in herbs and vegetables straight from the garden. The Nhung Dam—a hearty spread of basil, cucumbers, mint, romaine, bean sprouts, pickled carrots, turnips, and vermicelli, wrapped in rice paper and dipped in a legendary sauce—is cooked at your table.

1792 Main St., Wailuku. ℂ **808/243-9560.** Main courses $6.50–$21. MC, V. Daily 10am–9:30pm. Heading into Wailuku from Kahului, go over the bridge and take the 1st right onto Central Ave.; then take the 1st right on Nani St. At the next stop sign, look for the building with the neon sign that says OPEN.

INEXPENSIVE

A. K.'s Café ★★ 🍃 HEALTHFUL/PLATE LUNCHES Chef Elaine Rothermel has a winner with this tiny cafe in the industrial district of Wailuku. It may be slightly off the tourist path, but the creative cuisine coming out of the kitchen makes it well worth the effort to find this delicious eatery. Prices are so eye-poppingly cheap, you might find yourself wandering back here during your vacation. Lunches feature everything from linguini with roasted chicken and basil to fish tacos, from hamburger steak to garlic-crusted ono or mahi. Dinner specials include pot roast with mushroom gravy, crab cakes with papaya beurre blanc, or sometimes a tofu Napoleon with ginger-basil sauce or Hunan lamb chops. There are plenty of heart-healthy options to choose from (low in sugar, salt, and fat).

1237 Lower Main St., Wailuku. ℂ **808/244-8774.** www.akscafe.com. Plate lunches $7.50–$16; dinners $14–$18. MC, V. Tues–Fri 11am–1:30pm; Tues–Sat 5:30–8:30pm. Live Hawaiian music Fri nights.

Main Street Bistro 🔔 AMERICAN Formerly Who's the Boss restaurant and, before that, Iao Café, this popular eatery, located on the main street of Wailuku, is now owned by Chef Tom Selman, well known in culinary circles on Maui. He was formerly the chef de cuisine at David Paul's Lahaina Grill and was also corporate chef for the Sansei/Vino restaurants. Main Street Bistro is open for lunch and *pau hana* (after-work) menu of tapas like crispy crab and shrimp *gau gee,* mini hamburgers, and barbecued ribs. He calls his cuisine "refined comfort food," with signature items that include onion rings with house-made smoky ketchup, roasted Chinese chicken salad, "mother's roast beef sandwich" (served open-faced on a French roll), Southern-fried chicken, Maryland-style crab cake, and a roasted-veggie sandwich. The chef will happily customize any menu item for those who prefer low-calorie, low-fat, or low-carbohydrate options. Daily specials range from grilled steak to Asian risotto with shrimp, crab, and veggies.

2051 Main St., Wailuku. ☎ **808/244-6816.** www.msbmaui.com. Main courses $7–$13 lunch, $5–$23 tapas, daily specials $9–$17. MC, V. Mon–Fri 11am–7pm; tapas menu 3–7pm. Live music Fri evenings.

Sam Sato's NOODLES/PLATE LUNCHES Sam Sato's is a Maui institution, not only for its noodles (saimin, dry noodles, chow fun), but also for its flaky baked *manju,* a pastry filled with sweetened lima beans or adzuki beans. Sam opened his family eatery in 1933, and his daughter, Lynne Toma, makes the broth from scratch. The saimin and the dry noodles, with broth that comes in a separate bowl, are big sellers. Eat at the counter, with well-worn wooden stools and homemade salt and pepper shakers. Try the plate lunch with two barbecued meat sticks, two scoops of rice, and macaroni salad. The peach, apple, coconut, and pineapple turnovers fly out the door, as do takeout noodles. *Tip:* If you want them to hold the MSG, be sure to make your request early.

At the Millyard, 1750 Wili Pa Loop, Wailuku. ☎ **808/244-7124.** Plate lunches $7–$7.50. No credit cards. Mon–Sat 7am–2pm (from 2–4pm they do takeout for pre-ordered items).

WEST MAUI

Lahaina

There's a **Maui Tacos** (p. 182) in Lahaina Square (☎ **808/661-8883**). Maui's branch of the **Hard Rock Cafe** is at 900 Front St., in Lahaina (☎ **808/667-7400**).

VERY EXPENSIVE

The Feast at Lele ★★ POLYNESIAN The owners of the Old Lahaina Luau (see "A Night to Remember: Luau, Maui Style," p. 308) have recruited the culinary prowess of chef James McDonald (I'O and Pacific'O), found the perfect outdoor oceanfront setting, and added the exquisite dancers of the Old Lahaina Luau. The result: a culinary and cultural experience that sizzles. As if the sunset weren't heady enough, dances from Hawaii, New Zealand, Tahiti, and Samoa are presented, up close and personal, in full costumed splendor. Chanting, singing, drumming, dancing, the swish of ti-leaf skirts, the scent of plumeria—it's a full adventure, even for the most jaded luau aficionado. Guests sit at white-clothed, candlelit tables set on the sand (unlike the luau, where seating is en masse) and dine on entrees from each island: imu-roasted kalua pig from Hawaii, Maori fishcake from New Zealand, *poisson cru* from Tahiti, and beef with breadfruit from

Where to Dine in Lahaina & Kaanapali

PACIFIC OCEAN

KAANAPALI

Kaanapali Royal (North) Golf Course

Whalers Village ❹

Kaanapali Kai (South) Golf Course

LK & PR Sugar Cane Train

Train Depot

Puukolii Rd.

Kekaa Dr.

Kaanapali Pkwy.

Nohea Kai Dr.

Honoapiilani Hwy.

Hanakao'o Beach Park

Lahaina Civic Center

Wahikuli Beach Park

Kaniau Rd.

Lokia St.

Malanai St.

Wahikuli Rd.

Fleming Rd.

Anakea Rd.

Kapunakea St.

Lahaina Cannery Mall

Mala Wharf

Puunoa Point

Front St.

Kenui St.

Baker St.

Papalaua St.

Train Depot

Pioneer Sugar Mill

Lahaina Center

Dickenson St.

Liakin St.

Wainee St.

Honoapiilani Hwy.

Kahoma Stream

Lahainaluna Rd.

LAHAINA

Lahaina Small Boat Harbor

505 Front St. (Shops & Restaurants) ❷⓿

Shaw St.

PACIFIC OCEAN

Area of detail

Kahului

MAUI

Haleakala National Park

Samoa. Particularly mesmerizing is the evening's opening: A softly lit canoe carries three people ashore to the sound of conch shells.

505 Front St. ☎ **866/244-5353** or 808/667-5353. www.feastatlele.com. Reservations required. Set 5-course menu (including all beverages) $110 adults, $80 children 2–12. AE, MC, V. Apr–Sept daily 6–9pm; Oct–Mar daily 5:30–8:30pm.

Lahaina Grill ★★ NEW AMERICAN Despite David Paul Johnson's departure, this Lahaina hot spot has maintained its popularity. It's still filled with chic, tanned diners in stylish aloha shirts, and there's still attitude aplenty at the entrance. The signature items remain: tequila shrimp and firecracker rice, Kona coffee–roasted rack of lamb, Maui onion–crusted seared ahi, and kalua-duck quesadilla. As always, a special custom-designed chef's table can be arranged with 72 hours' notice for larger parties. The ambience—black-and-white tile floors, pressed-tin ceilings, eclectic 1890s decor—is striking, and the bar, despite not having an ocean view, is the busiest spot in Lahaina.

127 Lahainaluna Rd. ☎ **808/667-5117.** www.lahainagrill.com. Reservations required. Main courses $33–$52. AE, DC, DISC, MC, V. Daily 6–10pm. Bar daily 6–10pm (earlier if it's slow).

EXPENSIVE

Gerard's ★★★ 🗝 FRENCH The charm of Gerard's—soft lighting, excellent service, Edith Piaf on the sound system—is matched by a menu of uncompromising standards. After more than 2½ decades in Lahaina, Gerard Reversade never runs out of creative offerings, yet stays true to his French roots. Roasted opakapaka with star anise, fennel fondue, and hints of orange and ginger is a stellar entree on a menu of winners. Quail with foie gras stuffing and truffle sauce promises ecstasy, and the spinach salad with scallops is among the finest I've tasted. Gerard's has an excellent appetizer menu, with oyster mushrooms and prosciutto ham in puff pastry, fresh ahi and smoked salmon carpaccio, and a very rich, highly touted escargot ragout with burgundy butter and garlic cream. The restaurant is a frequent winner of the *Wine Spectator* Award of Excellence.

At the Plantation Inn, 174 Lahainaluna Rd. ☎ **808/661-8939.** www.gerardsmaui.com. Reservations recommended. Main courses $33–$54. AE, DC, DISC, MC, V. Daily 6–9pm.

I'O ★ PACIFIC RIM I'O is a fantasy of sleek curves and etched glass, co-owned by chef James McDonald. He offers an impressive selection of appetizers (his strong suit) and some lavish Asian-Polynesian interpretations of seafood, such as his "rainbow catch"—fresh fish of the day topped with lemon-grass pesto, tomatoes, truffle oil, and goat-cheese fondue sauce—or his "scallops ala bondage"— scallops wrapped in sage and jalapeño bacon, served with roasted Japanese eggplant and a ponzu-cream sauce. Unless you're sold on a particular entree, my advice is to go heavy on the superb appetizers, especially the blackened-ahi tower (a tower of ahi, avocado, fruit, and tomatoes), shredded pork in a quesadilla with pepper-jack cheese, or the Siamese shashi rolls (spicy tempura portobello with an orange-mint dipping sauce). McDonald also owns Pacific'O Restaurant (reviewed below) and is the chef for the Feast at Lele (reviewed above).

505 Front St. ☎ **808/661-8422.** www.iomaui.com. Reservations recommended. Main courses $32–$39. AE, DC, DISC, MC, V. Daily 5:30–9pm.

Pacific'O Restaurant ★ CONTEMPORARY PACIFIC RIM You can't get any closer to the ocean than the tables here, which are literally on the beach.

With good food complementing this sensational setting, foodies and aesthetes have much to enjoy. The split-level dining starts near the entrance, with a long bar (where you can also order lunch or dinner) and a few tables along the railing. Steps lead down to the outdoor tables, where the award-winning seafood dishes come to you with the backdrop of Lanai across the channel. Favorites include the fresh island catch crusted in Indian spices topped with a subtle coconut Wana (sea urchin), or the hapa hapa tempura with white miso dressing and lime basil sauce. If you like seafood, sunsets, and touches of India and Indonesia in your fresh-from-the-sea dining choices, you should be happy here.

505 Front St. ⓒ **808/667-4341.** www.pacificomaui.com. Reservations recommended. Main courses $13–$16 lunch, $32–$40 dinner. AE, MC, V. Daily 11:30am–4pm and 5:30–9pm.

MODERATE

David Paul's Island Grill ★★ NEW ISLAND CUISINE One of Hawaii's top chefs, David Paul, opened yet another restaurant in Lahaina in 2008 introducing his "new island cooking," a combination of his latest American cuisine and island products—items such as slow-braised roasts, seared fresh fish, macadamia nut–smoked and fire-grilled meals, brick-pressed chicken, and olive oil–poached Keahole lobster. Although his menu changes daily, my picks are the roasted island snapper in Parmesan brood with sautéed upcountry field greens and house-cured pork shoulder, the pot roast scented with five Chinese spices, or the grilled pork chops with shiitake reduction and lobster cream. Chef David has an exhibit kitchen, so you can watch all the action. The Lanai Lounge has cocktails and a "tasting" menu of small plate versions of his entrees. Great wine deals too: 50 to 60 wines by the glass, most $10 or less.

Lahaina Center, 900 Front St., Ste. A-101, Lahaina. ⓒ **808/662-3000.** www.davidpaulsisland grill.com. Main courses $20–$47, "nine item" tasting menu $40–$45. AE, DC, DISC, MC, V. Daily 5–9:30pm; lounge 5pm–midnight.

Kimo's STEAK/SEAFOOD Kimo's has a loyal following that keeps it from falling into the faceless morass of waterfront restaurants serving surf and turf with great sunset views. It's a formula restaurant (sibling to Leilani's on the Beach, Hula Grill, and Duke's Beach House) that works not only because of its oceanfront patio and upstairs dining room, but also because, for the price, there are some satisfying choices. It's always crowded, buzzing with people on a deck offering views of Molokai, Lanai, and Kahoolawe. Burgers and sandwiches are affordable and consistent, and the fresh catch in sweet-basil glaze is a top seller. The waistline-defying hula pie— macadamia-nut ice cream in a chocolate-wafer crust with fudge and whipped cream—originated here.

 The Ultimate Cookies

Looking for the ultimate taste treat to bring the folks back home? Try mouth-watering **Broke da Mouth Cookies,** 190 Alamaha St., Kahului (ⓒ 808/873-9255), open Monday through Friday from 6am to 7pm, Saturday from 7am to 5pm (get here early before the locals buy everything up). These terrific cookies range from chocolate mac-nut, oatmeal raisin, and shortbread to almond, peanut butter, and coconut crunch. While you're here, take a look at the other goodies—the sweet potato-haupia pie is to die for, and the *lilikoi* (passion fruit) cake will make your taste buds stand up and applaud.

845 Front St. ℭ **808/661-4811.** www.kimosmaui.com. Reservations recommended for dinner. Main courses $8–$13 lunch, $18–$35 dinner. AE, DC, DISC, MC, V. Daily 11am–3:30pm and 5–10pm. Bar 11am–12:30am; light menu 3:30–5pm.

Lahaina Fish Company SEAFOOD The open-air dining room is literally over the water, with flickering torches after sunset and an affordable menu that covers the seafood-pasta basics. Head to an oceanside table and order a cheeseburger, chicken burger, fish burger, generous basket of peel-and-eat shrimp, or sashimi— lingering is highly recommended. The light lunch/grill menu offers appetizers (sashimi, seared ahi, spring rolls, and pot stickers), salads, sandwiches, and soups. The restaurant has spiffed up its dinner selections to include hand-carved steaks, several pasta choices, and local fare such as stir-fry dishes, teriyaki chicken, and luau-style ribs. The specialty, though, remains the fresh seafood: Four types of fresh fish are offered nightly, in three preparations. Pacific Rim specials include fresh ahi, seared spicy or cooked in a sweet ginger-soy sauce.

831 Front St. ℭ **808/661-3472.** www.lahainafishcompany.com. Main courses $9–$15 lunch, $10–$30 dinner. AE, MC, V. Daily 11am–10pm.

Mala Ocean Tavern ★★ 🐟 LOCAL/SEAFOOD Perched right on the ocean, this tiny "tavern" is the brainchild of Mark and Judy Ellman, owners of Maui Tacos and Penne Pasta Café. They use healthy, organically grown food and fresh fish to make intriguing dishes. The atmosphere could not be more enticing, with just a handful of tables out on the oceanfront lanai and several more tables in the warmly decorated interior. The staff is helpful and efficient, and the food is out- standing. If you're in the mood, ask for the exotic martini menu. You can opt for "tavern food" like an ahi burger or a cheeseburger, one of the tempting salads (the beet and Kula goat cheese is divine), or something off the "big plate" menu (like wok-fried fresh catch or hoisin-glazed baby back ribs). Don't miss the weekend brunches (I recommend the "killer" French toast). This is a popular place, so try to avoid prime lunch and dinner hours.

1307 Front St. (across from the Lahaina Cannery Mall's Safeway grocery store). ℭ **808/667- 9394.** www.malaoceantavern.com. Main courses $13–$24 lunch,; $17–$40 dinner; brunch $8–$16. AE, DISC, MC, V. Mon–Fri 11am–9:30pm; Sat and Sun 9am–9pm "or so."

Melting Pot FONDUE If you simply cannot eat another Pacific rim fish dinner and are tired of burgers, this well-known mainland chain offers a different type of dinner experience, where you cook your own food. You first select your cheese for the fondue or appetizer portion of the meal (from a traditional cheddar to a non-traditional spinach artichoke type dip), then you select your salad (spinach mushroom, house, Caesar or California greens) and finally you select your entree (from seafood to chicken to lobster to steak, even vegetarian) and cooking style. If you are still game, select your chocolate fondue for dipping desserts. Bring a gang—it's more fun with several people.

Lahaina Gateway Shopping Center, 325 Keawe St., Ste. A202. ℭ **808/661-6181.** www.meltingpot. com. Reservations recommended. Main courses $26–$42. AE, DC, DISC, MC, V. Daily 5–9pm.

INEXPENSIVE

Aloha Mixed Plate ★ 🐟 PLATE LUNCHES/BEACHSIDE GRILL Look for the festive turquoise-and-yellow, plantation-style front with the red corrugated-iron roof and adorable bar, tiny and busy, directly across from the Lahaina Cannery Mall. Grab a picnic table at ocean's edge, in the shade of large kiawe and milo trees, where you can watch the bobbing sailboats and two islands on the near horizon. (On the upper level, there are umbrellas and plumeria trees—just as charming.) Then tuck into inexpensive mahimahi, kalua pig and cabbage, shoyu chicken, teriyaki beef, and other local plate-lunch specials, all at budget-friendly prices, served with macaroni salad and rice. The shoyu chicken is the best I've had, fork-tender and tasty, and the spicy chicken drumettes come from a fabled family recipe. (The bestsellers are the coconut prawns and Aloha Mixed Plate of shoyu chicken, teriyaki beef, and mahimahi.) I don't know of anywhere else where you can order a mai tai with a plate lunch and enjoy table service with an ocean view.

1285 Front St. (C) **808/661-3322.** www.alohamixedplate.com. Main courses $5–$14. MC, V. Daily 10:30am–10pm.

Cheeseburger in Paradise AMERICAN Wildly successful, always crowded, highly visible, and very noisy (especially when live music plays in the evenings), Cheeseburger is a shrine to the American classic. The home of three-napkin cheeseburgers with attitude, this is burger country, tropical style, with everything from tofu and garden burgers to the biggest, juiciest beef and chicken burgers, served on whole-wheat and sesame buns baked fresh daily. There are good reasons why the two-story green-and-white building next to the sea wall is always packed: good value, good grinds, and a great ocean view. The Cheeseburger in Paradise—a hefty hunk with jack and cheddar cheeses, sautéed onions, lettuce, fresh tomatoes, and Thousand Island dressing—is a paean to the basics. You can build your own burger by adding sautéed mushrooms, bacon, grilled Ortega chiles, and other condiments for an extra charge. Onion rings, chili-cheese fries, and cold beer complete the carefree fantasy.

811 Front St. (C) **808/661-4855.** www.cheeseburgerland.com. Burgers $9–$16. AE, DISC, MC, V. Daily 8am–10pm.

EAT LIKE A local

Are you the type of visitor who feels you haven't "experienced" a destination unless you've hit the restaurants where the local residents eat? Or do you enjoy National Public Radio's "Road Food," or any of the Food Network's on-the-road culinary shows? Then sign up for **Tour da Food** ★★★ ((C) **808/242-8383;** www.tourda-food.com). Pastry chef (and food writer, restaurant publicist, and cookbook author) Bonnie Friedman takes foodies off the tourist path to discover the culinary treasures—from snack shacks to restaurants to markets and manufacturers—that make up Maui's unique cuisine. You will laugh your way across the island with Bonnie's wonderful commentary about Maui's multicultural food options and its colorful history—and you'll also eat some of the island's most yummy food (which you never would have discovered on your own). Check out her website to read about the different tours (from breakfast at an old inn to "lunch like a local" to "plate lunch and picnic with poke"); prices begin at $280 per couple, which includes transportation, a main meal, snacks, an island traditional dessert, a bag of goodies to take home, and Bonnie's personal list of under-the-radar eating places. *Tip:* Book this tour early in your trip, so you have time to follow Bonnie's terrific suggestions of places to eat on Maui. (Best to book at least one week in advance).

Cilantro: Fresh Mexican Grill ★ 🎁 ☺ MEXICAN This is Maui's best bet for fabulous Mexican food at frugal prices. And, believe it or not, this fast-food restaurant serves fresh, healthy food. The chef and owner is Paris Nabavi, creator of Maui's Pizza Paradiso Italian Kitchen. He wanted the "challenge of something different," so he took off to Mexico to find out how the Mexicans used to cook in "the old days." He's back on Maui with this unbelievably delicious eatery where everything is made from scratch. Even the corn tortillas are handmade daily. Signature dishes include the citrus-and-herb-marinated chipotle rotisserie chicken, the veggie Mariposa salad, the popular mother-clucker flautas, and lip-smacking "al pastor"-style adobo pork. All this at budget-pleasing prices. It's a great place to take the kids; Los Niños menu items are under $5.

170 Papalaua Ave. ℂ **808/667-5444.** www.cilantrogrill.com. Main courses $8–$14. MC, V. Daily 11am–10pm.

Lahaina Coolers ★ AMERICAN/INTERNATIONAL A huge marlin hangs above the bar, epic wave shots and wall sconces made of surfboard fins fill the walls, and open windows line three sides of this ultracasual indoor/outdoor restaurant. This is a great breakfast joint, with feta-cheese Mediterranean omelets; huevos rancheros; and fried rice made with jasmine rice, Kula vegetables, and Portuguese sausage. There are three types of eggs Benedict: the classic, a vegetarian version (with Kula vegetables—excellent), and the Local, with kalua pork and sweetbread. At lunch, burgers rule and the sandwiches, from grilled fresh fish to the Cajun wrap, are ideal for casual Lahaina. The pasta, made fresh daily, is prepared Asian style (with chicken and spicy Thai peanut sauce), with pesto, or vegetarian (in a spicy Creole sauce). Pizzas, fresh catch, steak, and enchiladas round out the entrees. Everything can be prepared vegetarian upon request.

180 Dickenson St. ℂ **808/661-7082.** www.lahainacoolers.com. Main courses $9–$12 breakfast, $10–$16 lunch, $18–$27 dinner. AE, DC, DISC, MC, V. Daily 8am–1am.

Maui Sunrise Café 🍴 GOURMET DELI/CAFE If you want to know where to find the best breakfasts or the most filling lunches on a budget, follow the surfers to this teeny-tiny cafe located on Front Street, next door to the library. Eat in the patio garden out back or take your lunch to the beach. You'll find huge breakfasts, delicious gourmet sandwiches, and filling lunch plates all at bargain prices. It's tough to find a parking spot nearby (and you can't park at the library), but you'll probably want a brisk walk after eating here anyway.

693A Front St. ℂ **808/661-8558.** Breakfast items under $10; lunch items $7–$12. No credit cards. Daily 6am–4:30pm.

Maui Swiss Cafe SANDWICHES/PIZZA Recently renovated and double its original size (which was tiny), Swiss Cafe continues to serve excellent sandwiches and continental breakfast. Having gone from a sandwich-and-pizza shop to a European-style sidewalk Internet cafe, it still serves $6 lunch specials and two scoops of Roselani ice cream for $4 (and sometimes the ice cream is free with the lunch special). Top-quality breads baked fresh daily, Dijon mustard, good Swiss cheese, and keen attention to sandwich fillings and pizza toppings make this a very special sandwich shop. The Swiss owner, Rolf Egli, bought the cafe from Dominique Martin several years ago, and has maintained the European flavor in this corner of Lahaina, down to the menus printed in English and German and the Swiss breakfast of sliced ham, cheese, hard-boiled egg, and freshly baked croissant. *Tip:* The "signature melt" sandwiches, with imported Emmenthal cheese baked on an Italian Parmesan crust, are something to watch for, and there are excellent vegetarian and turkey sandwiches as well.

640 Front St. ✆ **808/661-6776.** www.swisscafe.net. Sandwiches and 8-in. pizzas $6–$8. AE, DISC, MC, V. Daily 9am–6pm.

Penne Pasta Café ★ 🍴 ITALIAN/MEDITERRANEAN Bargain hunters head for this neighborhood cafe, under the helm of chef Mark Ellman (of Maui Tacos and Mala fame). It features delicious Italian and Mediterranean cuisine. You'll get a sit-down meal at takeout prices, and *mamma mia!*—those are big plates of pasta, pizzas, salads, and sandwiches. So, what's the catch? No wait help. You order at the counter and the manager delivers your order to your table. Favorites include the *molto bene* linguine pesto, baked penne, and pizza with olives, capers, basil, and roasted pepper. Wine (from $6.50 a glass) and beer are available, too.

180 Dickenson St. ✆ **808/661-6633.** www.pennepastacafe.com. Basic menu items under $10; specials up to $15. AE, DISC, MC, V. Mon–Fri 11am–9:30pm; Sat–Sun 5–9:30pm.

Kaanapali
EXPENSIVE

Son'z Maui at Swan Court ★★★ CONTEMPORARY EUROPEAN/ HAWAII REGIONAL For 30 years, the Swan Court was *the* dining experience at the Hyatt Regency Maui Resort. When Tri-Star Restaurant Group CEO Aaron Placourakis (who also owns Nick's Fishmarket Maui; p. 189) took over this restaurant a few years ago, he and executive chef Geno Sarmiento knew they wanted to hit a home run every night with the cuisine. The restaurant already had perhaps the most romantic location in Maui, overlooking a man-made lagoon with white and black swans swimming by and the rolling surf of the Pacific in the distance. Now the combination of the culinary team's creative dishes, fresh local ingredients (Kula corn and strawberries, Ono Farms avocados, Hana hearts of palm, Maui Cattle Company beef, fresh Hawaiian fish, and sweet Maui onions), top-notch service, and relaxing atmosphere makes this one of Maui's best restaurants. My personal picks from the very tempting menu are the escargot profiterole appetizer (with baby spinach, Ali'I oyster mushrooms, and Gorgonzola foam) and, for a main course, either the Hawaiian opakapaka piccata (with artichokes, caperberries, Lisbon lemon, sweet-potato hash browns, and tomato purée) or the seared scallops BLT (with bacon and poached cherry tomatoes in a Caesar-salad emulsion, served with truffled potato chips). A beautiful breakfast buffet is also served.

At the Hyatt Regency Maui Resort, 200 Nohea Kai Dr. ✆ **808/667-4506.** www.tristar restaurants.com. Reservations required for dinner. Main courses $31–$50. AE, DC, DISC, MC, V. Daily 5:30–10pm.

MODERATE

Beachside Grill/Leilani's on the Beach STEAK/SEAFOOD The Beachside Grill is the informal, less expensive room downstairs on the beach, where folks wander in off the sand for a frothy beer and a beachside burger. Leilani's is the dinner-only room, with more expensive but still not outrageously priced steak and seafood offerings. At Leilani's, you can order everything from fresh fish to

Chef McDonald Has a Farm, E-I-E-I-O

Here's your chance to see where those delicious greens, sweet basil, and wonderful tropical fruits that make up your dinner at Pacific'O and I'O restaurants (p. 172) come from. James McDonald was the first chef in the state to own and operate a farm for the purpose of supplying his own restaurants. Your visit to **O'o Farm** begins with hot apple cider and pastries. The tour is led by a culinary specialist who helps you handpick items for your lunch. At the end of the tour, lunch is served. The cost is $50 per person. For more information, call ℂ **808/667-4341** or go to www.oofarm. com.

filet mignon to fried coconut prawns. All of this, of course, comes with an ocean view. There's live music Friday, Saturday, and Sunday from 3 to 5pm.

At Whalers Village, 2435 Kaanapali Pkwy. ℂ **808/661-4495.** www.leilanis.com. Reservations suggested for dinner. Lunch and dinner (Beachside Grill) $9–$19, dinner (Leilani's) $19–$33. AE, DC, DISC, MC, V. Beachside Grill daily 11am–11pm; Leilani's daily 5–9:30pm.

Cane & Taro ★ ASIAN FUSION Another winner in Chef D. K. Kodama's growing list of fabulous restaurants (Sansei Seafood Restaurant & Sushi Bar on Maui, Oahu, and the Big Island, and d.k. Steakhouse, Hiroshi, and Vino on Oahu), Cane & Taro, opened in 2009 and marks a departure from the chef's creative sushi, steaks, and tapas (although you can find his best sellers on the menu here) into a hybrid Asian-pasta-steaks-seafood eatery in the Whalers Village Shopping Center. Located oceanside in the former Rusty Harpoon Restaurant, it has fantastic panoramic views that quickly become secondary when the meal arrives. Breakfast includes five different kinds of eggs Benedict; lunch and dinner feature award-winning items such as rock shrimp dynamite (crispy tempura rock shrimp with a masago aioli and unagi glaze), crunchy noodle crab and shrimp cake (with ginger-lime-chili and cilantro pesto), and Kona coffee baby back ribs (roasted with coffee-mango barbecue sauce and served with a smoked tomato slaw), as well as pastas (including kid's portions), sushi rolls, sashimi, fish, chicken, and steaks. The new restaurant is always packed.

Whaler's Village, 2435 Kaanapali Pkwy., Kaanapali. © **808/662-0668.** www.dkrestaurants.com. Reservations recommended for dinner, especially at sunset. Main courses $10–$14 lunch, $10–$37 dinner. AE, DC, DISC, MC, V. Daily 8am–10pm.

Duke's Beach House ★★ PACIFIC RIM Perched on the side of the ocean, facing the beautiful Kaanapali Beach and housed in what appears to be an open-air plantation home, the latest of TS Restaurants (which include Kimo's and Leilani's on Maui) opened in late 2009. It was a winner from the start, with a fabulous beachfront location and great decor (the authentic memorabilia of Hawaii's Duke Kahanamoku, who was an award-winning Olympic swimmer, famous surfer, movie star, and un-official Hawaii Ambassador of Aloha), but more importantly, the food is fabulous. Following the new locavore tradition, the staff is committed to a "farm to fork" dining experience and stresses that ingredients are obtained on Maui. Breakfast features a host of omelets, eggs, pancakes, and even a "beach boy burrito" (with eggs, sausage, bacon, potatoes, chipotle cream, and avocado salsa); the lunch menu features creative salads, sandwiches, burgers, and fresh fish. Dinner adds steaks, chicken, and a seafood risotto. Leave room for the hula pie—Oreo cookie crust topped with macadamia nut ice cream, hot fudge, and whipped cream—for dessert.

Honua Kai Resort & Spa, 130 Kai Malina Pkwy., North Kaanapali Beach. © **808/662-2900.** www. dukesmaui.com. Breakfast items $6.25–$12; main courses $10–$14 lunch, $18–$29 dinner. AE, MC, V. Daily 7am–8pm.

Umalu ★ PACIFIC RIM This is the kind of restaurant that visitors dream about. Located oceanside, next to the Hyatt Regency Maui's pool with a great view of the islands of Molokai and Lanai in the distance, you will be happy way before you get your first exotic cocktail or even the menu. Umalu translates into "the shade cast by a cliff" and that is a great description of the relaxed casual atmosphere of this outdoor restaurant (with plenty of huge umbrellas for shade). Lunch is very casual with sandwiches such as the Maui Waui–style fish tacos with beer-battered mahimahi on warm flour tortillas and the chicken sandwich with jalapeño jack cheese, crispy bacon, and avocado to the angus burger (a half-pound grilled burger) and pizzas (from a sausage and pepperoni pie to a ham-pineapple and Maui onion pie). By dinner, the atmosphere is still open-air but more upscale with prime rib, seared ahi steaks, and sesame-orange chicken stir-fry, plus pizza, burgers, and sandwiches.

Hyatt Regency Maui Resort & Spa, 200 Nohea Kai Dr., Kaanapali. © **808/661-1234.** Main courses $10–$19 lunch, $16–$41 dinner. AE, DC, MC, V. Daily 11am–9:30pm. Live entertainment every evening.

INEXPENSIVE

Whalers Village, 2435 Kaanapali Pkwy. in Kaanapali (www.whalersvillage.com/ restaurants.htm), has a food court where you can buy pizza, Chinese, ice cream, sandwiches, wraps, and burgers at self-serve counters and courtyard tables. It's an inexpensive alternative and a quick, handy stop for shoppers and Kaanapali beachgoers.

CJ's Deli & Diner ★ 🥄 AMERICAN/DELI If you're staying in Kaanapali, this restaurant is within walking distance from your resort; if you're not staying in Kaanapali, it's worth the drive to sample the "comfort food" (as they call it) at this hip, happening eatery with prices so low you won't believe you're still on Maui.

179

A huge billboard menu hangs from the yellow-and-gold textured wall, and highly polished wooden floors give the roadside eatery a homey feeling. You can eat in or take out (you can even get a "chef-to-go" to come to your accommodations

THE TIKI *terrace*

Bravo to the Kaanapali Beach Hotel for the low-salt, employee-tested Native Hawaiian diet served in its **Tiki Terrace Restaurant,** 2525 Kaanapali Pkwy. (✆ **808/667-0124**). The Native Hawaiian Combination features the healthy, traditional diet of fresh fish (you can also order it with chicken breast) and taro greens and tomato, flavored with ginger and herbs. Fresh mild *limu* (seaweed) adds some natural saltiness, and you can always add your own salt and pepper to taste. The Native Hawaiian menu also includes a salad made from *pohole* fern shoots and Ogo marinated with sweet Maui onions and tomatoes tossed with a lime-soy vinaigrette and served with papaya. (With their freshness, pleasing crunch, and mild flavor, fern shoots are one of the most underused greens of Hawaii.) Entree choices are accompanied by steamed purple sweet potato, taro, and fresh poi made on the premises. The dessert is half a chilled Hana papaya with lemon, grilled bananas, and pineapple slices. The cost for the Hawaiian Combination is $23.

The use of fresh local ingredients is a noteworthy touch in the a la carte menu as well. My favorites are the baked crab and shrimp with artichoke hearts and the coconut shrimp. Try Chef Muromoto's signature Sesame Shoyu dressing on the Kula greens salad—it's a house favorite. The a la carte menu entrees are headed up by the Huki Hukilau, a combination of fresh catch, jumbo prawn, and baby lobster tail. The menu also includes steak, ribs, teriyaki grilled chicken, and rack of lamb.

The dining room is old-fashioned Hawaii, not fancy, with tables on a terrace ringed with plumeria and palm trees. Nightly entertainment is a hula show from 6:30 to 7:30pm and music for dancing under the stars until 9pm.

The regular Tiki Terrace breakfast menu presents all the old favorites along with the opportunity to sample Hawaiian food in a familiar context: taro hash browns; three-egg lomi salmon omelet with sweet-potato home fries; a fruit plate of banana baked in ti leaf with lehua honey and macadamia nuts, served with yogurt; and French toast

made with taro bread. There are even Hawaiian taro pancakes, and they're wonderful. The Hawaiian **Sunday Champagne Brunch** ($37) features more than 50 items on the buffet, plus stir-fry, carving, and omelet stations, along with Belgian waffles and great desserts, all accompanied by Hawaiian music (9am–1pm).

The hotel also serves guests a complimentary **Ohana Welcome Breakfast** on their first morning at 8am Monday through Saturday, with live music, hula, a buffet breakfast, and advice on how to make the most of a Maui vacation. The hotel's staff greets guests, then takes to the stage for one of their specialties—singing and dancing hulas. Then they are off to work while guests enjoy a tour of hotel events and island activities.

The emphasis on Hawaiian food is only one part of a pervasive spirit of aloha that distinguishes this hotel. Reservations are recommended for dining in the Tiki Terrace (✆ **808/667-0124**). Dinner is served daily from 6 to 9pm.

and cook for you), the atmosphere is friendly, and there's a computer with high-speed Internet access to keep the techies humming. Huge, delicious breakfasts are served from 7 to 11am (check out the $5.95 early-bird special of two eggs, bacon or sausage, rice, and coffee). There's a wide selection of egg dishes, plus pancakes and waffles, and don't forget the tempting delights from the bakery. Lunch ranges from deli sandwiches and burgers to pot roast, ribs, and fish dishes. If you are on your way to Hana or up to the top of Haleakala, stop by and get a box lunch. CJ's even has a menu for the kids.

At the Fairway Shops at Kaanapali, 2580 Kekaa Dr. (just off the Honoapiilani Hwy.), Kaanapali. © **808/667-0968.** www.cjsmaui.com. Breakfast items $4–$9.50, lunch items $8.50–$15, Hana Lunch Box and Air Travel Lunch Box $12 each. AE, MC, V. Daily 7am–8pm.

Nikki's Pizza PIZZA Formerly Pizza Paradiso, Nikki's has a full menu of pastas, pizzas, and desserts, including smoothies, coffee, and ice cream. This is a welcome addition to the Kaanapali scene, where casual is king and good food doesn't have to be fancy. The pizzas reflect a simple and effective formula that has won acclaim through the years: good crust, true-blue sauces, and toppings loyal to tradition but with just enough edge for those who want it. Create your own pizza with roasted eggplant, mushrooms, anchovies, artichoke hearts, sausage, and a slew of other toppings. Nikki's offers some heroic choices, from the Hawaiian (ham and Maui pineapple) to the Sopranos (roasted chicken, artichoke hearts, sun-dried tomatoes).

At Whalers Village, 2435 Kaanapali Pkwy. © **808/667-0333.** Gourmet pizza $4–$5 by the slice, whole pizzas $18–$28. AE, DISC, MC, V. Daily 8am–9pm.

Honokowai, Kahana & Napili

Note: You'll find the following restaurants on the "Where Dine from Kapalua to Honokowai" map on p. 185.

EXPENSIVE

Roy's Kahana Bar & Grill ★★★ EURO-ASIAN Despite the lack of dramatic view and an upstairs location in a shopping mall, Roy's remains crowded and extremely popular for one reason: fabulous food. It bustles with young, hip, impeccably trained servers delivering Szechuan BBQ–grilled ahi steak, basil seared opakapaka with wild mushroom and asparagus risotto, and glazed honey-mustard short ribs. You could make a meal of the incredibly creative appetizers, such as Roy's original Kai style ahi, crab cakes, lobster and shrimp potstickers, crispy shrimp and pork lumpia, or lemon grass–poached pear salad. Large picture windows open up Roy's Kahana but don't quell the noise, another tireless trait long ago established by Roy's Restaurant in Honolulu, the flagship of Yamaguchi's burgeoning empire. Don't get your heart set on anything, as Roy changes his menu frequently.

At the Kahana Gateway Shopping Center, 4405 Honoapiilani Hwy. © **808/669-6999.** www.roysrestaurant.com. Reservations strongly recommended. Main courses $30–$46. AE, DC, DISC, MC, V. Daily 5:30–9:30pm.

Sea House Restaurant ASIAN/PACIFIC RIM The Sea House is not glamorous, famous, or hip, but it's worth mentioning for its spectacular view of Napili Bay. The Napili Kai Beach Resort, where the Sea House is located, is a charming throwback to the days when hotels blended in with their surroundings, had lush tropical foliage, and were sprawling rather than vertical. Dinner entrees range from taro-crusted sea bass with green papaya salad to seafood cioppino to mustard and Poha berry crusted rack of lamb. There's even a menu for the *keiki* (kids), with items such as hamburgers and chicken nuggets.

At the Napili Kai Beach Resort, 5900 Honoapiilani Hwy. © **808/669-1500.** Reservations required for dinner. Main courses $6–$12 breakfast, $11–$16 lunch, $26–$39 dinner; appetizer menu $9–$14. AE, DISC, MC, V. Daily 7am–9pm.

MODERATE

Maui Brewing Co. SEAFOOD/STEAK This restaurant consists of a bar, a retail section, and tables. The small retail section sells fresh seafood, while the sit-down menu covers basic tastes: salads, fish and chips, fresh-fish sandwiches, cheeseburgers, and beer—lots of it. At dinner, count on heavier meats and the fresh catch of the day (maybe ahi, mahimahi, or ono), with rotisserie items such as grilled chicken, steaks, and duck. The late-night menu offers shrimp, cheese fries, quesadillas, and lighter fare.

At the Kahana Gateway Shopping Center, 4405 Honoapiilani Hwy. © **808/669-3474.** www. mauibrewingco.com. Reservations recommended for dinner. Main courses $11–$29. AE, DC, DISC, MC, V. Daily 11am–9:30pm; late-night menu 9:30pm–midnight. Sun brunch 8am–11pm during football season (Sept–Jan).

INEXPENSIVE

Maui Tacos MEXICAN Mark Ellman's Maui Tacos chain has grown faster than you can say "Haleakala." Ellman put gourmet Mexican on paper plates and on the island's culinary map long before Maui became known as Hawaii's center for salsa and chimichangas. Barely more than a takeout counter with a few tables, this and the six other Maui Tacos in Hawaii (five on Maui alone) are popular with hungry surfers, discerning diners, burrito buffs, and Hollywood glitterati like Sharon Stone, whose picture adorns a wall or two. Choices include excellent fresh-fish tacos (garlicky and flavorful), chimichangas, and mouth-breaking compositions such as the Hookipa (a personal favorite): a "surf burrito" of fresh fish, black beans, and salsa. The spinach burrito contains four kinds of beans, rice, and potatoes—it's a knockout, requiring a siesta afterward. Expect good food but not very fast service.

At Napili Plaza, 5095 Napili Hau St. © **808/665-0222.** www.mauitacos.com. All items $3–$10. AE, DISC, MC, V. Daily 10:30am–7:30pm. Also in Lahaina Sq., Lahaina (© **808/661-8883**); Kamaole Beach Center, Kihei (© **808/879-5005**); Piilani Village shopping Center, Kihei (© **808/875-9340**); and Kaahumanu Center, Kahului (© **808/871-7726**).

Pizza Paradiso Italian Kitchen PIZZA/ITALIAN Order at the counter (pastas, gourmet pizza whole or by the slice, paninis, salads, and desserts) and find a seat at one of the few tables. The pasta sauces—marinara, pescatore, Alfredo, Florentine, and pesto, with options and add-ons—are as popular as the pizzas (which took best pizza in a recent *Maui News'* reader poll). The Massimo, a pesto sauce with artichoke hearts, sun-dried tomatoes, and capers, comes with a choice of chicken, shrimp, or clams, and is so good it was a Taste of Lahaina Festival winner. Recent additions to the menu include gyros, souvlaki, hummus, and cheesesteak sandwiches. Takeout, dine-in, or delivery (free!), this is a hot spot in the neighborhood.

At the Honokowai Marketplace, 3350 Lower Honoapiilani Rd. © **808/667-2929.** www.pizzaparadiso.com. Pastas $10–$11; pizzas $16–$28. MC, V. Daily 10am–9pm.

Kapalua

Note: You'll find the following restaurants on the "Where Dine from Honokowai" map on p. 185.

VERY EXPENSIVE

The Banyan Tree ★★ ASIAN-INSPIRED The most recent chef de cuisine here, in a long line of outstanding chefs chosen from the stables of the Ritz-Carlton resorts around the globe, is Ryan Urig. His distinctive menu includes Kona lobster with ginger-carrot risotto, tarragon-coral butter; chorizo crusted opah, cauliflower florets, oyster mushrooms, yellow curry; and grilled lamb loin, lentil dahl. They are currently doing a "50/50 Menu": a three-course dinner for $50 and a bottle of selected wine for $50. The atmosphere is extremely romantic, overlooking the ocean with the island of Molokai in the distance—make reservations for sunset.

At the Ritz-Carlton Kapalua, 1 Ritz-Carlton Dr. ℂ **808/669-6200.** Reservations recommended. Main courses $38–$65. AE, DC, DISC, MC, V. Tues–Sat 5:30–9:30pm.

Merriman's ★★★ PACIFIC RIM This is probably the most beautiful location for a restaurant in the state. On a point jetting out into the ocean, overlooking Kapalua Bay on one side and the island of Molokai in the distance, the former location of the Kapalua Bay Club, well-known local chef Peter Merriman, who is a James Beard award winner, opened this spectacular restaurant in 2008. His fantastic menu, where he pioneered the "farm-to-table" concept of serving only fresh products from local farmers, fishermen, and ranchers, is on display here with Haleakala Ranch–raised lamb, his well-known wok-charred ahi (served with pumpkin puree and tangerine-green peppercorn jus), and even locally grown fresh vegetable pot pie for the vegetarians. To really experience Merriman's culinary genius, order the *pupu* (appetizer) taster; the night I dined, the taster (which changes daily) included crudo of fresh fish and avocado, local kalua pig with sweet onion quesadilla, baked local goat cheese with beet chutney and herbed tartines, and ahi sashi with miso-marinated calamari salad. *Insider tip:* Book your reservation for sunset to really experience this incredible vista. If sunset tables are booked, come for sunset anyway and sit on the large open-air patio and enjoy a cocktail and an appetizer.

One Bay Club Pl., Kapalua Resort. ℂ **808/669-6400.** www.merrimanshawaii.com. Reservations recommended. Main courses $24–$44. AE, MC, V. Daily 5:30–9pm; Point Bar menu daily 5–9pm.

EXPENSIVE

Pineapple Grill ★★★ PACIFIC ISLAND If you had only a single night to eat on the island of Maui, this would be the place to go. Up-and-coming young chef Ryan Luckey (a local Lahaina boy) has taken the helm and is winning high praise from both critics and the local residents who flock here nightly. My picks on this creative menu would be ahi steak crusted with pistachios and wasabi peas (served with coconut-scented "forbidden" rice, Makawao mushrooms, and wasabi-soy butter), candied macadamia-crusted roast mahimahi (in a poha berry beurre blanc), or the wonderful lemon porcini-dusted Monchong (served with mashed potatoes and tomato lomi-lomi). An excellent list of wine pairings by the glass is available. Save room for the Maui gold-pineapple upside-down cake (with Whaler dark-rum sauce and Maui-made Roselani gourmet mac-nut ice cream). There are lots of tasty sandwiches and salads at lunch. Plus, it's all served in a very Maui-like atmosphere, overlooking the rolling hills of the Kapalua golf course out to the Pacific Ocean.

At the Kapalua Golf Club Bay Course, 200 Kapalua Dr. ℂ **808/669-9600.** www.pineapple kapalua.com. Reservations recommended for dinner. Main courses $10–$18 lunch, $25–$50 dinner. AE, MC, V. Mon–Sat 11am–2:30pm, grill menu 2:30–5:30pm, and dinner 5:30–10pm; Sun 10am–10pm.

Plantation House Restaurant ★★ SEAFOOD/HAWAIIAN-MEDITER-RANEAN With its teak tables, fireplace, and open sides, Plantation House gets stellar marks for atmosphere. The 360-degree view from high among the resort's pine-studded hills takes in Molokai and Lanai, the ocean, the rolling fairways and greens, the northwestern flanks of the West Maui Mountains, and the daily sunset spectacular. Readers of the *Maui News* have deemed this the island's "Best Ambience"—a big honor on an island of wonderful views. It's the best place for breakfast in west Maui, hands down, and one of my top choices for dinner. The eggs Mediterranean makes a superb start to your day, and at lunch, sandwiches (open-faced smoked turkey, roasted vegetable, and goat-cheese wrap) and salads rule. When the sun sets, the menu expands to marvelous starters such as polenta and scampi-style shrimp, crab cakes, and Kula and Mediterranean salads. The menu changes constantly but may include fresh fish prepared several ways—among them, Mediterranean (on roasted Maui onions with couscous), Venice (pressed in panko, with a golden-raisin/pine-nut butter), Maui (pistachio-crusted), and Italy (pepper-dusted with olives and caper-berry salsa). Don't forget the numerous vegetarian entrees and wonderful Australian lamb, New Zealand lobster, and a roast pork tenderloin you'll long remember.

At the Kapalua Golf Club Plantation Course, 2000 Plantation Club Dr. ℂ **808/669-6299.** www. theplantationhouse.com. Reservations recommended. Main courses $7.75–$15 breakfast, $12–$18 lunch, $20–$42 dinner. AE, DC, MC, V. Daily 8am–3pm and 5:30–9pm (6–9pm May 1–Sept 30).

MODERATE

Sansei Seafood Restaurant & Sushi Bar ★★★ PACIFIC RIM/SUSHI Perpetual award-winner Sansei offers an extensive menu of Japanese and East-West delicacies. Part fusion, part Hawaii Regional Cuisine, Sansei is tirelessly creative, with a menu that scores higher with adventurous palates than with purists (although there are endless traditional choices as well). If you don't like cilantro, watch out for those complex mango/crab-salad rolls. Other choices include panko-crusted ahi sashimi, sashimi trio, ahi carpaccio, noodle dishes, lobster, Asian shrimp cakes, and sauces that surprise, in creative combinations such as ginger-lime chile butter and cilantro pesto. But there's simpler fare as well, such as shrimp tempura, noodles, and wok-tossed upcountry vegetables. Desserts are not to be missed. If it's autumn, don't pass up the Granny Smith apple tart with vanilla ice cream and homemade caramel sauce. In other seasons, opt for tempura-fried ice cream with chocolate sauce. There's karaoke Thursday nights from 10pm to 1am. *Money-saving tip:* Eat early; all food is 25% off between 5:30 and 6pm (be aware that the line for this budget deal starts forming before 5pm).

600 Office Rd. ℂ **808/669-6286.** www.sanseihawaii.com. Reservations recommended. Main courses $16–$43. AE, DISC, MC, V. Daily 5:30–10pm. Also at Kihei Town Center, Kihei (ℂ **808/879-0004**).

Where to Dine from Kapalua to Honokowai

Plantation Club Dr.
30
❶

Plantation Golf Course

Honokahua Bay

Makaluapuna Pt.

Fleming
Beach
Park
❷

Oneloa Bay

Office Rd.

Hawea Pt.

❸
Kapalua Dr.

KAPALUA

Village Golf Course

Namalu Bay

Bay Golf Course

❹

Kapalua Beach

❺ ❻

Lower Honoapiilani Rd.

Napili Beach

Napili Bay

Honoapiilani Hwy.

Honokeana Bay

NAPILI

Napilihau St. ❼

Alaeloa Pt.

Haukoe Pt.

Kaia Pt. Omaikai Pl.

KAHANA

❽ Hoohui Rd.
❾

Kapalua–
West Maui
Airport

Akahele St.

Lower Honoapiilani Rd.

Honoapiilani Hwy.

HONOKOWAI

30

❿

To Kaanapali & Lahaina
↓

Scale

0 — 1/2 mi
0 — 1/2 km

Area of detail

Laihaina · Kahului
M A U I
Haleakala National Park

Restaurant List

The Banyan Tree **2**
Maui Brewing Co. &
    Fish & Game Rotisserie **8**
Maui Tacos **7**
Merriman's **5**
Pineapple Grill Kapalua **4**
Pizza Paradiso Italian Caffe **10**
Plantation House Restaurant **1**
Roy's Kahana Bar & Grill **9**
Sensei Seafood Restaurant and Sushi Bar **3**
Sea House Restaurant **6**

SOUTH MAUI
Kihei/Maalaea

There's a **Maui Tacos** at Kamaole Beach Center, in Kihei (✆ **808/879-5005**).

EXPENSIVE

Buzz's Wharf AMERICAN Buzz's is another formula restaurant that offers a superb view, substantial sandwiches, meaty french fries, and surf-and-turf fare—in a word, satisfying but not sensational. Still, this bright, airy dining room makes a fine way station for whale-watching over a cold beer and a mahimahi sandwich. Consider opting for several appetizers (stuffed mushrooms, steamer clams, clam chowder, onion soup) and a salad, and then splurge on dessert—try the bananas wrapped in pastry and fried, topped with vanilla ice cream, cinnamon, macadamia nuts, and raspberry and caramel syrups.

50 Hauoli St., Maalaea Harbor. ✆ **808/244-5426.** www.buzzswharf.com. Reservations recommended. Main courses $11–$25 lunch, $21–$38 dinner. AE, DC, DISC, MC, V. Daily 11am–9pm.

Five Palms ★ PACIFIC RIM This is the best lunch spot in Kihei—open air, with tables a few feet from the beach and up-close-and-personal views of Kahoolawe and Molokini. You'll have to walk through a nondescript parking area and the modest entrance of the Mana Kai Maui Resort to reach this unpretentious place. It features a menu of breakfast and lunch items served from 8am to 2:30pm, so if you're jet-lagged and your stomach isn't on Hawaiian time, you can get a crab omelet at 2 in the afternoon or a juicy Kobe beef hamburger at 8 in the morning. At dinner, with the torches lit on the beach and the main dining room open, the ambience shifts to evening romantic, but still casual. Just-caught fish is the star of the dinner menu.

At the Mana Kai Maui Resort, 2960 S. Kihei Rd., Kihei. ✆ **808/879-2607.** www.fivepalms restaurant.com. Reservations recommended for dinner. Main courses $8–$20 breakfast and lunch, $28–$45 dinner. AE, DC, MC, V. Daily 8am–2:30pm and 5–9pm; *pupu* menu daily 2–7pm.

The Waterfront at Maalaea ★★ SEAFOOD The family-owned Waterfront has won many prestigious awards for wine excellence, service, and seafood, but its biggest boost is word of mouth. Loyal diners rave about the friendly staff and seafood, fresh off the boat in nearby Maalaea Harbor and prepared with care. The bay and harbor view is one you'll never forget, especially at sunset. There are nine choices of preparations for the several varieties of fresh Hawaiian fish, ranging from *en papillote* (baked in buttered parchment) to Southwestern (smoked chile and cilantro butter) to Island style (sautéed, broiled, poached, or baked and paired with tiger prawns). Other choices: Kula onion soup, an excellent Caesar salad, the signature lobster chowder, and grilled eggplant layered with Maui onions, tomatoes, and spinach, served with red-pepper coulis and feta ravioli. Like the seafood, it's superb.

50 Hauoli St., Maalaea Harbor. ✆ **808/244-9028.** www.waterfrontrestaurant.net. Reservations recommended. Main courses $21–$46. AE, DC, DISC, MC, V. Daily 5pm–closing (last seating at 8:30pm).

MODERATE

Cafe O'Lei Kihei ★★ STEAK/SEAFOOD Chefs Michael and Dana Pastula have had a host of Cafe O'Lei restaurants on Maui, and I've loved every one of them. Their latest is in an out-of-the-way location, the not-very-attractive Rainbow Mall. Nevermind—you come here for the food, not the view (which is of congested Kihei Rd. and a small bit of ocean between the fence of high-rise condos across the street). Inside, the open and airy room has floor-to-ceiling windows, hardwood floors, a big circular bar in the middle, and, on one side, an exhibition kitchen. The atmosphere is relaxing and inviting. The food is, as usual, not only outstanding, but also a real bargain. You can't beat lunch with fresh fish, rice, and salad for under $10 (arrive early, as the locals will book all the tables in advance). Dinners range from fresh fish to prime rib, mac-nut-crusted chicken breast to roast duck, and even a mushroom-asparagus-pine-nut linguine for the vegetarians. Save room for dessert, such as pineapple upside-down cake or a fudge brownie sundae (yum, yum).

2439 S. Kihei Rd., Kihei. © **808/891-1368.** www.cafeoleirestaurants.com. Reservations recommended. Main courses $7–$13 lunch, $17–$35 dinner. AE, DC, DISC, MC, V. Tues–Sun 10:30am–3:30pm and 5–9pm.

Stella Blues Cafe ★ AMERICAN Stella Blues gets going at breakfast and continues through to dinner with something for everyone—vegetarians, kids, pasta and sandwich lovers, hefty steak eaters, and sensible diners who go for the inexpensive salad of fresh Maui greens. Grateful Dead posters line the walls, and a covey of gleaming motorcycles is invariably parked outside. It's loud and lively, irreverent and unpretentious. Sandwiches are the highlight, ranging from the half-pound Maui Beef Company Blues burger to grilled chicken to the kalua pork and cabbage plate lunch. Mountain-size salads are popular, as are large coffee shakes with mounds of whipped cream. Daily specials include fresh seafood and other surprises—all home-style cooking, made from scratch, down to the pesto mayonnaise and herb bread. At dinner, selections are geared toward good-value family dining, from affordable full dinners to pastas and burgers. There's live music from 4 to 6pm Tuesday through Friday.

At the Azeka Place II Shopping Center, 1279 S. Kihei Rd., Kihei. © **808/874-3779.** www.stellablues.com. Main courses $6–$13 breakfast, $9–$15 lunch, $15–$28 dinner. AE, DC, DISC, MC, V. Daily 7:30am–11pm.

INEXPENSIVE

The Coffee Store COFFEEHOUSE This simple, classic coffeehouse for caffeine connoisseurs serves two dozen types of coffee and coffee drinks, from mochas and lattes to cappuccinos, espressos, and toddies. Breakfast items include smoothies, lox and bagels, quiches, granola, and assorted pastries. Salads and sandwiches (tuna, turkey, ham, grilled veggie panini) also move briskly from the takeout counter. The turkey-and-veggie wraps are a local legend. There are only a few small tables, and they fill up fast, often with musicians and artists who've spent the previous evening entertaining at the Wailea and Kihei resorts.

At the Azeka Place II Shopping Center, 1279 S. Kihei Rd., Kihei. © **808/875-4244.** www.mauicoffee.com. All items under $10. AE, MC, V. Mon–Sat 6am–6pm; Sun 6am–5pm.

Joy's Place ✦ HEALTHY DELI/SANDWICHES If you're in Kihei and looking for a healthy, delicious lunch at a rock-bottom price, it's worth hunting around for Joy's Place. This tiny hole in the wall has humongous sandwiches (turkey and avocado, tuna salad), wheat-free wraps, fresh salads, hot items (falafel burger, veggie burger), soups, and desserts. Most items are organic.

In the Island Surf Building, 1993 S. Kihei Rd. (entrance on Auhana St.). © **808/879-9258.** All items under $12. AE, DC, DISC, MC, V. Mon–Sat 8am–3pm.

Peggy Sue's AMERICAN Just for a moment, forget that diet and take a leap. This 1950s-style diner has oodles of charm and is a swell place to spring for the best chocolate malt on the island. You'll also find sodas, shakes, floats, egg creams, milkshakes, and made-on-Maui Roselani-brand gourmet ice cream. Old-fashioned soda-shop stools, an ELVIS PRESLEY BOULEVARD sign, and jukeboxes on every Formica table serve as a backdrop for the famous burgers (and garden burgers), brushed with teriyaki sauce and served with all the goodies. The fries are great, too.

At the Azeka Place II Shopping Center, 1279 S. Kihei Rd., Kihei. ✆ **808/875-8944.** www.peggy-sues-maui.com. Burgers (with fries) $9.45–$11, plate lunches $7–$9. AE, DISC, MC, V. Sun–Thurs 11am–9pm; Sat–Sun 11am–10pm.

Shaka Sandwich & Pizza PIZZA How many "best pizzas" are there on Maui? It depends on which shore you're on, the west or the south. This south-shore old-timer recently moved to a new (and much larger) location, but the award-winning pizzas, New York–style heroes, Philly cheesesteaks, calzones, salads, and home-made garlic bread haven't changed. Shaka uses fresh Maui produce, long-sim-mered sauces, and homemade Italian bread. Choose thin or Sicilian thick crust with gourmet toppings: Maui onions, spinach, anchovies, jalapeños, and a spate of other vegetables. Try the white pizza; with the perfectly balanced flavors of olive oil, garlic, and cheese, you won't even miss the tomato sauce. My favorite, the spinach pizza (with olive oil, spinach, garlic, and mozzarella), is a real treat.

1770 S. Kihei Rd., Kihei. ✆ **808/874-0331.** www.shakapizza.com. Sandwiches $7–$15, pizzas $18–$27. MC, V. Sun–Thurs 10:30am–9pm; Fri–Sat 10:30am–10pm.

Wailea

The **Shops at Wailea** (www.shopsatwailea.com), with a sprawling location between the Grand Wailea Resort and Outrigger Wailea Resort, has added a spate of shops and restaurants to this stretch of South Maui. Five restaurants and dozens of shops, most of them upscale, are among the new tenants of this complex. Ruth's Chris Steak House is here, as well as Tommy Bahama's Tropical Cafe & Emporium, Honolulu Coffee Company, Kai Wailea, Longhi's (reviewed below), Cheeseburger Island Style, and Lappert's Ice Cream. Next door at the Wailea Beach Marriott Resort is **Mala Wailea** (reviewed below). *Note:* You'll find the restaurants in this section on the "Where to Dine in South Maui" map (p. 193).

VERY EXPENSIVE

Ko ★★★ GOURMET PLANTATION CUISINE The concept behind this successful restaurant in the Fairmont Kea Lani is pure genius: taking the various ethnic cuisines from Maui's old plantation days (Hawaiian, Filipino, Portuguese, Korean, Puerto Rican, and European) and cooking them up in a gourmet fashion. Quicker than you can say "humuhumukununukuapua'a" (Hawaii's state fish), you have a culinary success. Many of the recipes they use come from old fam-ily recipes. The word *ko* means cane, as in sugar cane, back to the days when the sugar cane plantations had "camp" housing for each ethnic group. Among the wonderful taste treats you won't want to miss is ahi "on the rocks," where the server brings you chunks of fresh ahi to cook on a hot ishiyaki stone to your desired doneness and then dip into an orange-ginger-miso sauce. Other options include Filipino *lumpia* (a sort of spring roll with green papaya, shrimp, and pork [or chicken and mushroom], accompanied by a spicy sauce); Paniolo (cowboy) rib-eye steak with fern shoots; Korean-style spicy chicken served with Maui lavender honey; and a wonderful Portuguese bean soup.

Fairmont Kea Lani, 4100 Wailea Alanui Dr., Wailea. © **808/875-4100.** www.fairmont.com. Reservations recommended. Main courses $21–$50. AE, DC, DISC, MC, V. Daily 5:30–10pm.

Longhi's ★ ITALIAN Unfortunately, the ocean view is now blocked by yet another high-rise, but Longhi's open-air room and its trademark black-and-white checkered floor still make a great backdrop to start the day. Breakfasts here are worth waking up for: perfect baguettes, fresh-baked cinnamon rolls (one is enough for two people), and eggs Benedict or Florentine. Lunch is either an Italian banquet (ahi torino, prawns amaretto, and a wide variety of pastas) or fresh salads and sandwiches. Dinner is where Longhi's shines, with a long list of fresh-made pasta dishes, seafood platters, and beef and chicken dishes (filet mignon with basil, veal scaloppine). Leave room for the daily dessert specials.

At the Shops at Wailea, 3750 Wailea Alanui Dr., Wailea. © **808/891-8883.** www.longhi-maui. com. Reservations recommended for dinner. Breakfast items $8.50–$21, lunch items $9.50–$38, dinner main courses $17–$120. AE, DC, DISC, MC, V. Mon–Fri 8am–10pm; Sat–Sun 7:30am–10pm.

Mala Wailea ★★★ HAWAIIAN REGIONAL CUISINE/SEAFOOD This upscale version of Mala Ocean Tavern in Lahaina (p. 174) occupies the prime restaurant location at the Wailea Beach Marriott Resort & Spa. Serving breakfast and wonderful dinners, this is not to be missed as a food experience. Created by Chef Mark Ellman, one of the original founders of the Hawaiian Regional Cuisine movement (his other restaurants on Maui include Maui Tacos, Penne Pasta Café, and Mala Ocean Tavern), this is a great place to enjoy island food in a casual atmosphere. Chef Ellman has created a menu that rivals the spectacular ocean view for your attention: Balinese stir-fry with fresh island fish, ginger-garlic black bean sauce over a whole wok-fried fish, and hoisin-glazed baby back ribs. Or you can choose from the lighter "tavern" menu of ahi burger, fresh island fish sandwich, or Kobe beef cheeseburger. Breakfast features both a la carte items (don't miss the "killer" French toast or the *chilaquiles*—salsa, corn tortillas, eggs, sour cream, and feta cheese) and a full (more than full) buffet.

Wailea Beach Marriott Resort & Spa, 3700 Wailea Alanui Dr. © **808/875-9394.** www.mala oceantavern.com. Reservations recommended. Breakfast buffet $27; main courses $19–$39 dinner. AE, DC, DISC, MC, V. Mon–Sat 6:30am–9:30pm; Sun 6:30am–9pm.

Nick's Fishmarket Maui ★★ SEAFOOD Here's the place to bring your sweetie to enjoy the moon rise and the sweet smell of the stephanotis growing on the terrace. Fans love this classic seafood restaurant that sticks to the tried and true. The few detractors complain that the food is too old style (circa 1970s), but most agree that there is a high degree of professionalism in both service and preparation, and it's hard to beat the fantasy setting on the south Maui shoreline. The Greek Maui Wowie salad gets my vote as one of the top salads in Hawaii. The rest of the menu features great fresh fish like opakapaka (one of the signature dishes), grilled opah, and Hawaiian spiny lobster. There are ample choices for the nonfish-eaters as well, including rack of lamb, roasted chicken, and dry-aged New York steak.

At the Fairmont Kea Lani Maui, 4100 Wailea Alanui Dr. © **808/879-7224.** www.tristar restaurants.com. Reservations recommended. Main courses $30–$120. AE, DC, DISC, MC, V. Daily 5:30–9:45pm.

Spago ★★ HAWAIIAN/CALIFORNIA/PACIFIC REGIONAL California meets Hawaii in this contemporary eatery featuring fresh, local Hawaii ingredients prepared under the culinary watch of master chef Wolfgang Puck. The room, formerly Seasons Dining Room, has been stunningly transformed into a sleek modern layout using stone and wood in the open-air setting overlooking the Pacific. The cuisine lives up to Puck's reputation of tweaking traditional Hawaiian dishes with his own brand of cutting-edge innovations. The menu changes daily and can feature Hawaiian Moi steamed Hong Kong style; pineapple grilled mahi; grilled Chinois-style lamb chops; and roast Cantonese duck with pineapple and papaya. The wine and beverage list is well thought out and extensive. Make reservations as soon as you land on the island (if not before); this place is popular. And bring plenty of cash or your platinum card.

At the Four Seasons Resort Maui at Wailea, 3900 Wailea Alanui Dr. ✆ **808/879-2999.** www. fourseasons.com/maui. Reservations required. Main courses $39–$68. AE, DC, DISC, MC, V. Daily 6–9:30pm; bar with *pupu* daily 6–11pm.

EXPENSIVE

Ferraro's Bar e Ristorante ★ ITALIAN This was a master stroke for the Four Seasons: authentic Italian fare in a casual outdoor tropical setting, with a drop-dead gorgeous view of the ocean and the West Maui Mountains. Ferraro's is not inexpensive, but the food is first rate. Lunch in the open-air restaurant features fabulous salads (my pick is the seared Hawaiian tuna and Niçoise salad), sandwiches (from a chicken pita to pizza), and some Hawaiian classics (try the kalua eggrolls). At dinner, the romantic setting, with the sound of the ocean waves, makes for a memorable evening. The fish selection is noteworthy: fennel-dusted snapper with eggplant and Yukon gold potato puree, or roasted sea bass, pepper cress butter sauce and toasted pine nuts. Make room for dessert; my favorite is the citrus angel food cake with mascarpone mousse and roasted fruit.

At the Four Seasons Resort Maui at Wailea, 3900 Wailea Alanui Dr. ✆ **808/874-8000.** www. fourseasons.com/maui. Reservations recommended. Main courses $19–$25 lunch, $30–$52 dinner. AE, DC, DISC, MC, V. Daily 11am–5:30pm, 4–9pm (*pupu* menu), and 6–9pm.

MODERATE

Gannon's—A Pacific View Restaurant ★★ LOCAL/AMERICAN Award-winning chef Bev Gannon has taken over the former Sea Watch restaurant, perched high on a hill above the Wailea Golf Course with a spectacular ocean view and Molokini in the distance. Chef Gannon (of Haliimaile General Store and Joe's on Maui plus Lanai City Grille on Lanai) is known for her American home cooking with a regional twist—in this case a Hawaiian twist, such as miso-glazed black cod with Asian slaw and wasabi mashed potatoes, ahi scallopini with lemon capers and an eggplant terrine, and venison loin with Parmesan risotto with smoked corn nage. For breakfast, don't miss the smoked salmon pate with Maui onions, sliced tomato, cream cheese, and bagel, or the Hawaiian sweet bread French toast. A must-try at lunch is the lobster salad with butter lettuce, jicama, zucchini, fresh corn, truffle vinaigrette, and lemon cream fraiche. Make reservations to watch the sunset for dinner.

Wailea Golf Course, 100 Wailea Golf Club Dr., Wailea Resort. ✆ **808/875-8080.** www.bev gannonrestaurants.com. Reservations recommended for dinner. Main courses $10–$14 breakfast, $10–$19 lunch, $26–$38 dinner. AE, DC, DISC, MC, V. Daily 8:30am–9pm.

Joe's ★★ AMERICAN/GRILL The 270-degree view spans the golf course, tennis courts, ocean, and Haleakala—a worthy setting for Beverly Gannon's style of American home cooking. The hearty staples include excellent mashed potatoes, jambalaya fresh fish, and prime rib, but the meatloaf (a whole loaf, like Mom used to make) seems to upstage them all. The Tuscan white-bean soup is superb, and the roasted pork shank with goat cheese grits and dried fruit compote, is American home cooking at its best. Daily specials could be grilled ahi with white-truffle Yukon gold mashed potatoes or sautéed mahimahi with shrimp bisque and sautéed spinach. If chocolate cake is on the menu, you should definitely spring for it.

At the Wailea Tennis Club, 131 Wailea Ike Place. © **808/875-7767.** www.bevgannonrestaurants. com. Reservations recommended. Main courses $12–$42. AE, DC, DISC, MC, V. Daily 5:30–9pm.

Haliimaile (on the Way to Upcountry Maui)

EXPENSIVE

Haliimaile General Store ★★★ HAWAII REGIONAL/AMERICAN For more than 2 decades, Bev Gannon, one of the original Hawaii Regional Cuisine chefs, has been going strong at her foodie haven in the pineapple fields. You'll dine at tables set on old wood floors under high ceilings (sound ricochets fiercely here), in a peach-colored room emblazoned with works by local artists. The food, a blend of eclectic American with ethnic touches, puts an innovative spin on Hawaii Regional Cuisine. Even the fresh-catch sandwich on the lunch menu is anything but prosaic. Sip the *lilikoi* lemonade and nibble the sashimi napoleon or the house salad (Island greens with mandarin oranges, onions, toasted walnuts, and blue-cheese crumble)—all are notable items on a menu that bridges Hawaii and Gannon's Texas roots.

Haliimaile Rd. © **808/572-2666.** www.haliimailegeneralstore.com. Reservations recomended. Main courses $14–$22 lunch, $26–$42 dinner. AE, DC, MC, V. Mon–Fri 11am–2:30pm; daily 5:30–9pm.

Makawao & Pukalani

MODERATE

Casanova Italian Restaurant & Deli ★ ITALIAN Look for the tiny veranda with a few stools, always full, in front of a deli at Makawao's busiest intersection— that's the most visible part of the Casanova restaurant and lounge. Makawao's nightlife center contains a stage, dance floor, restaurant, and bar—and food to love and remember. This is pasta heaven; try the spaghetti *fra diavolo* or the spinach gnocchi in a Gorgonzola sauce. Other options include a huge pizza selection, grilled lamb chops in an Italian mushroom marinade, lots more pasta dishes, and luscious desserts. My personal picks on a stellar menu: garlic spinach topped with Parmesan and pine nuts, and tiramisu, the best on the island. Check their website for a schedule of top entertainment, such as Willie K and his band.

1188 Makawao Ave. © **808/572-0220.** www.casanovamaui.com. Reservations recommended for dinner. Lunch items $8–$18, dinner main courses $22–$36, 12-in. pizzas $12–$20, pastas $12–$18. AE, DC, DISC, MC, V. Mon–Sat 11:30am–2pm and 5:30–9:30pm; Sun 5:30–9:30pm. Dancing Wed, Fri–Sat 10pm–1:30am. Lounge daily 5:30pm–1:30am (closing time varies depending on entertainment). Deli daily 7:30am–5:30pm.

Market Fresh Bistro ★★ 🎁 LOCAL/MEDITERRANEAN Attention foodies: Plan to eat dinner here at least once during your stay on Maui. Yes, it is a long drive from a resort area, and yes, parking is on the street and you may have to walk a block or two, but Chef Justin Pardo (formerly of the Union Square Café in New York City and the Wailea Grand on Maui) is a culinary genius and he uses 80% to 90% local products and is having fun creating menus at this off-the-beaten path restaurant, hidden in a minimall complex, behind the Makawao Steak House. You will be well rewarded for your efforts to get here. The menu changes daily, the chef's wonderful creations include an appetizer of pan-seared sea scallops with a watermelon curried gazpacho or a spice-crusted duck breast in a port wine marinade with local figs and micro-greens. Entrees range from taro-crusted fish with roasted carrots and asparagus in a fennel-saffron tomato jus to a pork loin wrapped in applewood-smoked bacon with sweet potatoes and mushrooms to a free-range chicken croquette with Maui onion and manchezo cheese with organic eggplant and smoked paprika tomato chutney. If you have time, call ahead for their once- or twice-monthly farm dinners, featuring the best from local farmers in a four-course dinner plus dessert for $50.

3620 Baldwin Ave., Makawao. 𝄯 **808/572-4877.** Reservations recommended for dinner. Main courses $29–$30. MC, V. Mon–Wed 8–11am and 11:30am–4pm; Thurs–Sat 8–11am, 11:30am–3pm, and 6–8:30pm; Sun 9am–2:30pm.

Kula (at the Base of Haleakala National Park)

MODERATE

Kula Lodge ★ HAWAII REGIONAL/AMERICAN Don't let the dinner prices scare you: The Kula Lodge is equally enjoyable, if not more so, at breakfast and lunch, when the prices are lower and the views through the picture windows have an eye-popping intensity. The million-dollar vista spans the flanks of Haleakala, rolling 3,200 feet down to central Maui, the ocean, and the West Maui Mountains. The Kula Lodge has always been known for its breakfasts: fabulous eggs Benedict, including a vegetarian version with Kula onions, shiitake mushrooms, and scallions; legendary banana/mac-nut pancakes; and a highly recommended tofu scramble with green onions, Kula vegetables, and garlic chives. If possible, go for sunset cocktails and watch the colors change into deep end-of-day hues. When darkness descends, a roaring fire and lodge atmosphere add to the coziness of the room. The dinner menu features "small plates" of Thai summer rolls, seared ahi, and other starters. Fresh catch with a choice of preparations and sauces leads the seafood attractions, but there's also pasta, rack of lamb, filet mignon, and free-range chicken breast.

15200 Haleakala Hwy. (Hwy. 377). 𝄯 **808/878-2517.** www.kulalodge.com. Reservations recommended for dinner. Main courses $10–$18 breakfast, $12–$22 lunch, $25–$35 dinner. AE, DC, DISC, MC, V. Daily 7am–9pm.

INEXPENSIVE

Cafe 808 AMERICAN/LOCAL Despite its out-of-the-way location (or perhaps because of it), Cafe 808 has become the universal favorite among upcountry residents of all ages. The breakfast coffee group, the lunchtime crowd, and dinner regulars all know it's the place for tasty home-style cooking with no pretensions: beloved burgers (teriyaki, hamburger, cheeseburger, garden burger, mahimahi, taro), roast pork, smoked turkey, and a huge selection of local-style specials. Regulars rave about the chicken *katsu*, saimin, and beef stew. The few tables are

Where to Dine in South Maui

sprinkled around a room with linoleum floors, hardwood benches, plastic patio chairs, and old-fashioned booths—rough around the edges in a pleasing way, and very camp.

Lower Kula Rd., past Holy Ghost Church, across from Morihara Store. ✆ **808/878-6874.** Burgers from $5, main courses $8–$12. MC, V. Daily 6am–8:30pm.

Grandma's Coffee House COFFEEHOUSE/AMERICAN Alfred Franco's grandmother started what is now a fifth-generation coffee business back in 1918, when she was 16 years old. Today, this tiny wooden coffeehouse, still fueled by homegrown Haleakala coffee beans, is the quintessential roadside oasis. Grandma's offers espresso, hot and cold coffees, home-baked pastries, inexpensive pasta, sandwiches (including sensational avocado garden burgers), homemade soups, fresh juices, and local plate-lunch specials that change daily. Rotating specials include Hawaiian beef stew, ginger chicken, chicken curry, lentil soup, and sandwiches piled high with Kula vegetables. The coffee is legendary, but the real standouts are the lemon squares and the pumpkin bread.

At the end of Hwy. 37, Keokea (about 6 miles before the Tedeschi Vineyards in Ulupalakua). ✆ **808/878-2140.** www.grandmascoffee.com. Most items under $9.50. DISC, MC, V. Daily 7am–5pm.

Kula Sandalwoods Restaurant ★ AMERICAN Chef Eleanor Loui, a graduate of the Culinary Institute of America, makes hollandaise sauce every morning from fresh upcountry egg yolks, sweet butter, and Meyer lemons, which her family grows in the yard above the restaurant. This is Kula cuisine, with produce from the backyard and everything made from scratch, including French toast with home-baked Portuguese sweet bread; hotcakes or Belgian waffles with fresh fruit; open-faced country omelets; hamburgers drenched in a special cheese sauce made with grated sharp cheddar; a killer kalua-pork sandwich; a grilled ono sandwich; and an outstanding veggie burger. The grilled chicken-steak sandwich is marvelous, served with soup of the day and Kula mixed greens. Dine in the gazebo or on the terrace, with dazzling views in all directions—including, in the spring, a yard dusted with lavender jacaranda flowers and a hillside ablaze with fields of orange akulikuli blossoms.

15427 Haleakala Hwy. (Hwy. 377). ✆ **808/878-3523.** www.kulasandalwoods.com. Breakfast $8–$14, lunch $9–$14, Sun brunch $7–$14. MC, V. Mon–Fri 7:30am–3pm; Sun 7:30–11:30am.

EAST MAUI: ON THE ROAD TO HANA

Paia

MODERATE

Charley's Restaurant ★★ AMERICAN/MEXICAN Although Charley's (named after Charley P. Woofer, a Great Dane) serves three meals a day, breakfast is really the time to come here. Located in downtown Paia, Charley's is a cross between a 1960s hippie hangout, a windsurfers' power-breakfast spot, and a honky-tonk bar that gets going after dark. Before you head out to Hana, stop at Charley's for a larger-than-life breakfast (eggs, potatoes, toast, and coffee will set you back about $9.50). There are plenty of espresso drinks, but the regular coffee is excellent. Lunch is burgers, sandwiches, calzones, and pizza (after 2pm).

Where to Dine in Upcountry & East Maui

PACIFIC
OCEAN

Pauwela Pt.   Opana Pt.

Uaoa Kealii Pt.
Bay

Hookipa Beach

Kuau

Pauwela

H.P. Baldwin
Beach Park

Hana Hwy.

Haiku

Huelo

Spreckelsville

Sugar Mill   Paia

EAST MAUI

To Hana

To Kahului

Baldwin Ave.

Haliimaile

Makawao

Pukalani

Koolau
Forest Reserve

Makawao
Forest
Reserve

UPCOUNTRY
MAUI

Lower
Kula Rd.

Kula

Kula Botanical Garden

HALEAKALA
NATIONAL
PARK

Alii Kula Lavender

Puu Ulaula

Area of
detail

Lahaina
Kahului

MAUI

Hana

Haleakala
National Park

Keokea

Kula
Forest Reserve

Cafe 808 **13**
Café des Amis **2**
Casanova Italian Restaurant **10**
Charley's Restaurant **5**
Colleen's at the Cannery **7**
Grandma's Coffee House **14**
Haliimaile General Store **8**

Kula Lodge **11**
Kula Sandalwoods Restaurant **12**
Mama's Fish House **6**
Market Fresh Bistro **9**
Milagros Food Co. **4**
Moana Bakery & Café **3**
Paia Fish Market **1**

Dinner is grilled fish and steak. The current chef is featuring a menu with stir-fry, a variety of pasta dishes, a meatloaf, and fresh fish. You'll see all walks of life here, from visitors on their way to Hana at 7am to buff windsurfers chowing down at noon to Willie Nelson on his way to the bar to play a tune.

142 Hana Hwy. © **808/579-8085.** www.charleysmaui.com. Breakfast items $7.75–$13, lunch items $8.50–$14, dinner main courses $13–$22. AE, DISC, MC, V. Daily 7am–10pm; food served at the bar until 10pm.

Milagros Food Company ★ SOUTHWESTERN/SEAFOOD Milagros has gained a following with its great home-style cooking, upbeat atmosphere, and highly touted margaritas. Sit outdoors and watch the parade of Willie Nelson look-alikes ambling by as you tuck into the ahi creation of the evening, a combination of Southwestern and Pacific Rim styles and flavors accompanied by fresh veggies and Kula greens. For breakfast, I recommend the Popeye spinach omelet or the huevos rancheros. Lunch ranges from ahi burgers to honey and mac-nut grilled salmon salad. For dinner, options include a grilled ahi burrito, seafood enchiladas, New York strip steak, shrimp pasta, and sometimes Chesapeake Bay crab cakes. I love Paia's tie-dyes, beads, and hippie flavor, and this is the front-row seat for it all. Watch for happy hour, with cheap and fabulous margaritas.

Hana Hwy. and Baldwin Ave. © **808/579-8755.** Breakfast items $7–$10, lunch items $10–$13, dinner main courses $13–$20. AE, MC, V. Daily 8am–10pm.

Moana Bakery & Cafe ★★ LOCAL/EURO-ASIAN Moana gets high marks for its stylish concrete floors, high ceilings, booths and cafe tables, and fabulous food. Don Ritchey, formerly a chef at Haliimaile General Store, has created the perfect Paia eatery, a casual bakery/cafe that highlights his stellar skills. All the bases are covered: saimin, omelets, wraps, pancakes, and fresh-baked goods in the morning; soups, sandwiches, pasta, and satisfying salads for lunch; and, at dinner, varied selections with Asian and European influences and fresh Island ingredients. The lemon grass grilled prawns with green-papaya salad are an explosion of flavors and textures; the roasted vegetable napoleon is gourmet fare; and the Thai red curry with coconut milk, served over vegetables, seafood, or tofu, comes atop jasmine rice with crisp rice noodles and fresh sprouts to cool the fire. Ritchey's Thai-style curries are richly spiced and intense. I also vouch for his special gift with fish: The nori-sesame-crusted mahimahi with miso-garlic tapioca pearls is cooked, like the curry, to perfection. There's live jazz Wednesday nights.

71 Baldwin Ave. © **808/579-9999.** www.moanacafe.com. Reservations recommended for dinner. Breakfast items $7–$12, lunch items $9–$17, dinner main courses $22–$34. MC, V. Tues–Sat 8am–9pm; Sun–Mon 8am–2:30pm and 4–9pm. Sun and Mon 4–9pm Indian menu available; sushi after noon daily.

INEXPENSIVE

Cafe des Amis ★★ 🏠 CREPES/MEDITERRANEAN/INDIAN This tiny eatery is a hidden delight: healthy and tasty breakfasts, lunches, and dinners that are easy on the wallet. Crepes are the star here, and they are popular: spinach with feta cheese, shrimp curry with coconut milk, and dozens more choices, including breakfast crepes and dessert crepes (like banana and chocolate or strawberries and cream). Equally popular are the Greek salads and smoothies. Dinners feature authentic Indian curries (served with rice, mango chutney, and tomato chutney), such as a vegetable curry with spinach, carrots, cauliflower, and potato with Tamil spices and tomato. You'll also find the best coffee in Paia here.

42 Baldwin Ave. © **808/579-6323.** Breakfast crepes $9–$10, lunch crepes $9–$11, dinner main courses $12–$17. MC, V. Daily 8:30am–8:30pm.

Paia Fish Market SEAFOOD This is a true fish market, with fresh fish to take home and cooked seafood, salads, pastas, fajitas, and quesadillas to take out or enjoy at the few picnic tables inside the restaurant. It's an appealing selection: Cajun-style fresh catch, fresh-fish specials (usually ahi or salmon), fresh-fish tacos and quesadillas, and seafood and chicken pastas. You can also order hamburgers, cheeseburgers, fish and chips (or shrimp and chips), and wonderful lunch and dinner plates that are cheap and tasty. Photos of the number-one sport here, windsurfing, adorn the walls.

110 Hana Hwy. © **808/579-8030.** www.paiafishmarket.com. Lunch and dinner $8.50–$19. DISC, MC, V. Daily 11am–9:30pm.

Haiku

MODERATE

Colleen's at the Cannery ★★ 🎁 ECLECTIC Way, way, way off the beaten path lies this fabulous find in the rural Haiku Cannery Marketplace. Once through the doors, you'll swear you've dropped down in the middle of a hot, chic boutique restaurant in SoHo in Manhattan (only, when you look around at the patrons, they are pure Haiku upcountry residents). It's worth the drive to enjoy Colleen's fabulous culinary creations, like a wild-mushroom ravioli with sautéed portobello mushrooms, tomatoes, herbs, and a roasted-pepper coulis for $17 (not New York City prices); pan-seared ahi for $21; or filet mignon with a side salad for $30. Colleen also serves up smaller meals, such as burgers and fish and chips. Breakfast includes wonderful omelets ($11) and mouth-watering French toast made with Colleen's own homemade bread ($7.75). Lunch stars baguette sandwiches, wraps, salads, and burgers and fries. I only wish Colleen's would take reservations.

At the Haiku Cannery Marketplace, 810 Haiku Rd. © **808/575-9211.** www.colleensinhaiku.com. Reservations not accepted. Breakfast $6.50–$14, lunch $8–15, dinner main courses $10–$33. AE, DISC, MC, V. Daily 6am–10pm.

Elsewhere on the Road to Hana

VERY EXPENSIVE

Mama's Fish House ★★★ SEAFOOD Okay, it's expensive (maybe the most expensive seafood house on Maui), but if you love fish, this is the place for you. The restaurant's entrance, a cove with windsurfers, tide pools, white sand, and a canoe resting under palm trees, is a South Seas fantasy worthy of Gauguin. The interior features curved lauhala-lined ceilings, walls of split bamboo, lavish arrangements of tropical blooms, and picture windows to let in the view. With servers wearing Polynesian prints and flowers behind their ears, and the sun setting in Kuau Cove, Mama's mood is hard to beat. The fish is fresh (the fishermen are even credited by name on the menu) and prepared either Hawaiian style, with tropical fruit or baked in a crust of macadamia nuts and vanilla beans, or in a number of dishes involving ferns, seaweed, Maui onions, and roasted *kukui* nut. My favorite is mahimahi laulau with luau leaves (taro greens) and Maui onions, baked in ti leaves and served with kalua pig and Hanalei poi. You can get deepwater ahi seared with coconut and lime, or perhaps the ono "caught by Keith Nakamura along the 40-fathom ledge near Hana" with a ginger teriyaki with mac nuts and crisp Maui onion. Other special touches include the use of Molokai sweet potato, organic lettuces, Haiku bananas, and fresh coconut, which evoke the mood and tastes of old Hawaii.

799 Poho Place, just off the Hana Hwy., Kuau. ✆ **808/579-8488.** www.mamasfishhouse.com. Reservations recommended for lunch, required for dinner. Main courses $27–$54 lunch, $27–$57 dinner. AE, DC, DISC, MC, V. Daily 11am–9pm (last seating).

INEXPENSIVE

Nahiku Coffee Shop, Smoked Fish Stand, and Ti Gallery ★ 🎁 SMOKED KABOBS What a delight to stumble across this trio of comforts on the long drive to Hana! The small coffee shop purveys locally made baked goods, several flavors of Maui-grown coffee, organic tropical-fruit smoothies, and the Original and Best Coconut Candy made by Hana character Jungle Johnny. Next door, the Ti Gallery sells locally made Hawaiian arts and crafts, such as pottery and koa-wood vessels.

The barbecue smoker, though, is my favorite part of the operation. It puts out superb smoked and grilled fish, fresh and locally caught, sending seductive aromas out into the moist Nahiku air. These are not jerkylike smoked meats: The process keeps the kabobs moist while retaining the smoke flavor. The bread-fruit—sliced, wrapped in banana leaf, and baked—can be bland and starchy (like a baked potato), but it's a stroke of genius to give visitors a taste of this important Polynesian staple. The teriyaki-based marinade, made by the owner, adds a special touch to the fish (such as ono, ahi, and marlin). Among the biggest sellers are the kalua-pig sandwich and the Island-style, two-hand tacos of fish, beef, and chicken, served with about six condiments, including cheese, jalapeños, and salsa. When available, fresh corn on the cob from Kipahulu is grabbed up apace. There are a few roadside picnic tables, or you can take your lunch to go for a beachside picnic in Hana.

Hana Hwy., ½ mile past mile marker 28. No phone. Kabobs $3 each. No credit cards. Fish stand Fri–Wed 10am–5pm. Coffee shop daily 9am–5:30pm. Gallery daily 10am–5pm.

AT THE END OF THE ROAD IN EAST MAUI: HANA

Expensive

Hotel Hana-Maui ★★★ LOCAL/ECLECTIC Although the restaurant's official name is Ka'uiki, everyone in Hana just calls it the Hotel Hana-Maui. Breakfast features eggs Benedict with local fish, wilted Okinawa spinach and roasted tomato hollandaise, kalua pig hash and eggs, or local papaya with yogurt and homemade granola. Lunch ranges from Maui Cattle Company burgers to just-caught fish sandwiches. Dinner, which changes daily, can include just-picked lettuce for salads (Kula-grown baby romaine with Gruyère crostini and sherry-thyme vinaigrette, or baby greens with Kula citrus, local radishes, and kalamata olives); a range of soups (such as a chilled Kula cucumber soup); and entrees like seared rare Hana-caught ahi with smoked bacon, forest mushrooms, and wilted greens, or oven-roasted chicken breast with crispy polenta, Nihiku bush beans, and mole sauce. Try the four-course Chef's Table

Hana Hwy. ✆ **808/248-8212.** Reservations recommended for Fri–Sat dinner. Main courses $18–$23 breakfast, $26–$33 dinner. AE, DISC, MC, V. Daily 7:30–10:30am and 6–9pm. Fri 6–9pm Hawaiian show and buffet $50, under 12 years $35.

Moderate

Hana Ranch Restaurant ✋ AMERICAN Part of the Hotel Hana-Maui operation, the Hana Ranch Restaurant is the informal alternative to the hotel's dining room for lunch. The menu is burgers and a chicken and a fish sandwich. There are indoor tables as well as two outdoor pavilions that offer distant ocean views. At the adjoining takeout stand, fast-food classics prevail: teriyaki plate lunch, mahimahi sandwich, cheeseburgers, hot dogs, and ice cream.

Hana Hwy. ✆ **808/270-5280.** www.hotelhanamaui.com. Main courses $14–$18. AE, DISC, MC, V. Daily 11:30am–8pm; happy hour 4–7pm; takeout counter daily 11am–4pm.

FUN ON & OFF THE BEACH

This is why you've come to Maui—the sun, the sand, and the surf. In this chapter, I'll tell you about the best beaches, from where to soak up the rays to where to plunge beneath the waves. I've covered a range of ocean activities on Maui, as well as my favorite places and outfitters for these marine adventures. Also in this chapter are things to do on dry land, including the best spots for hiking and camping and the greatest golf courses.

BEACHES

Maui has more than 80 accessible beaches of every conceivable description, from rocky black-sand beaches to powdery golden ones; there's even a rare red-sand beach. What follows is a personal selection of the finest of Maui's beaches, carefully chosen to suit a variety of needs and interests.

Hawaii's beaches belong to the people. All beaches, even those in front of exclusive resorts, are public property, and you are welcome to visit. Hawaii state law requires all resorts and hotels to offer public right-of-way access to the beach, along with public parking. So just because a beach fronts a hotel doesn't mean that you can't enjoy the water. Generally, hotels welcome nonguests to their facilities. They frown on nonguests using the beach chairs reserved for guests, but if a nonguest has money and wants to rent gear, buy a drink, or eat a sandwich, well, money is money, and they will gladly accept it from anyone.

For snorkel gear, boogie boards, and other ocean toys, head to one of **Snorkel Bob's** (www.snorkelbob.com) four locations: Dickenson and Wainee streets, Lahaina (☏ **808/662-0104**); Napili Village, 5425-C Lower Honoapiilani Hwy., Napili (☏ **808/669-9603**); in North Kihei at Azeka Place II, 1279 S. Kihei Rd. #310 (☏ **808/875-6188**); and in South Kihei/Wailea at Kamaole Beach Center, 2411 S. Kihei Rd. (☏ **808/879-7449**). All locations are open daily from 8am to 5pm. If you're island hopping, you can rent from a Snorkel Bob's location on one island and return to a branch on another.

West Maui

D. T. FLEMING BEACH PARK ★★

This quiet, out-of-the-way beach cove, named after the man who started the commercial growing of pineapples on the Valley Isle, is a great place to take the family. The crescent-shaped beach, located north of the Ritz-Carlton hotel, starts at the 16th hole of the Kapalua golf course (Makaluapuna Point) and rolls around to the sea cliffs at the other side. Ironwood trees provide shade on the land side. Offshore, a shallow sandbar extends to the edge of the surf. The waters are generally good for swimming and snorkeling; sometimes, off on the right side near the sea cliffs, the waves build enough for body boarders and surfers to get a few good rides in. This park has lots of facilities: restrooms, showers, picnic tables, barbecue grills, and a paved parking lot.

FACING PAGE: **The beach at Waianapanapana State Park.**

Kapalua Beach.

Kaanapali Beach.

KAPALUA BEACH ★★★

The beach cove that fronts the Coconut Grove Villas and the former Kapalua Bay hotel (now in the process of being replaced by condos) is the stuff of dreams: a golden crescent bordered by two palm-studded points. The sandy bottom slopes gently to deep water at the bay mouth; the water's so clear that you can see it turn to green and then deep blue. Protected from strong winds and currents by the lava-rock promontories, Kapalua's calm waters are ideal for swimmers of all ages and abilities, and the bay is big enough to paddle a kayak around in without getting into the more challenging channel that separates Maui from Molokai. Waves come in just right for riding, and fish hang out by the rocks, making it great for snorkeling.

The sandy beach isn't so wide that you'll burn your feet getting in or out of the water, and the inland side is edged by a shady path and cool lawns. Facilities include outdoor showers, restrooms, lifeguards, a rental shack, and plenty of shade. Parking is limited to about 30 spaces in a small lot off Lower Honoapiilani Road, by Napili Kai Beach Resort, so arrive early. Next door is a nice but pricey oceanfront restaurant, Kapalua's Bay Club.

KAANAPALI BEACH ★★

Four-mile-long Kaanapali is one of Maui's best beaches, with grainy gold sand as far as the eye can see. The beach parallels the sea channel through most of its length, and a paved beach walk links hotels and condos, open-air restaurants, and Whalers Village shopping center. Because Kaanapali is so long, and because most hotels have adjacent swimming pools, the beach is crowded only in pockets—there's plenty of room to find seclusion. Summertime swimming is excellent. There's fabulous snorkeling around **Black Rock,** in front of the Sheraton.

HIKES
Fagan's Cross **21**
Halemauu Trail **16**
Hana-Waianapanapa
Coast Trail **22**
Hosmer Grove
Nature Trail **14**
Kaupo Gap **19**
Keanae Arboretum **24**
Polipoli Loop **10**
Skyline Trail **12**
Sliding Sands Trail **13**
Waihee Ridge **3**

CABINS & CAMPGROUNDS
Holua Cabin & Campground **15**
Hosmer Grove Campground **14**
Kanaha Beach Park **5**
Kapalaoa Cabin **17**
Oheo Campground **20**
Paliku Cabin & Campground **18**
Polipoli Spring State Recreation Area Campground **11**
Polipoli State Park Cabin & Campground **11**
Waianapanapa State Park Cabins & Campground **23**

GOLF COURSES
Elleair Maui Golf Club **6**
Kaanapali Golf Resort **2**
Kapalua Resort **1**
Makena Golf Courses **8**
Pukalani Country Club **9**
Waiehu Municipal Golf Course **4**
Wailea Golf Club **7**

Beaches & Outdoor Activities

203

The water is clear, calm, and populated with clouds of tropical fish. You might even spot a turtle or two.

Facilities include outdoor showers; you can use the restrooms at the hotel pools. Various beach-activity vendors line up in front of the hotels, offering nearly every type of water activity and equipment. Parking is a problem, though. There are two public entrances: At the south end, turn off Honoapiilani Highway into the Kaanapali Resort and pay for parking there, or continue on Honoapiilani Highway, turn off at the last Kaanapali exit at the stoplight near the Maui Kaanapali Villas, and park next to the beach signs indicating public access (this is a little tricky to find and limited to only a few cars, so to save time, you might want to just head to the Sheraton or Whalers Village and plunk down your money).

WAHIKULI COUNTY WAYSIDE PARK

This small stretch of beach, adjacent to Honoapiilani Highway between Lahaina and Kaanapali, is one of Lahaina's most popular beach parks. It's packed on weekends, but during the week it's a great place for swimming, snorkeling, sunbathing, and picnics. Facilities include paved parking, restrooms, showers, and small covered pavilions with picnic tables and barbecue grills.

LAUNIUPOKO STATE WAYSIDE PARK

Families with children will love this small park off Honoapiilani Highway, just south of Lahaina. A large wading pool for kids fronts the shady park, with giant boulders protecting the wading area from the surf outside. Just to the left is a small sandy beach with good swimming when conditions are right. Offshore, the waves are occasionally big enough for surfing. The view from the park is one of the best: You can see the islands of Kahoolawe, Lanai, and Molokai in the distance. Facilities include a paved parking lot, restrooms, showers, picnic tables, and barbecue grills. It's crowded on weekends.

South Maui

KAMAOLE III BEACH PARK ★

Three beach parks—Kamaole I, II, and III—stand like golden jewels in the front yard of the funky seaside town of Kihei, which is exploding with suburban sprawl. The beaches are the best thing about Kihei; these three are popular with local residents and visitors alike because they're easily accessible. On weekends, they're jam-packed with fishermen, picnickers, swimmers, and snorkelers.

The most popular is Kamaole III, or "Kam-3," as locals say. The biggest of the three beaches, with wide pockets of gold sand, it's the only one with a children's playground and a grassy lawn that meets the sand. Swimming is safe here, but scattered lava rocks are toe-stubbers at the water line, and parents should make sure kids don't venture too far out, as the bottom slopes off quickly. Both the north and south shores are rocky fingers with a surge big enough to attract fish and snorkelers; the winter waves appeal to bodysurfers. Kam-3 is also a wonderful place to watch the sunset. Facilities include restrooms, showers, picnic tables, barbecue grills, and lifeguards. There's plenty of parking on South Kihei Road, across from the Maui Parkshore condos.

ULUA BEACH ★

One of the most popular beaches in Wailea, Ulua is a long, wide, crescent-shaped gold-sand beach between two rocky points. When the ocean's calm, Ulua offers

Kamaole III.

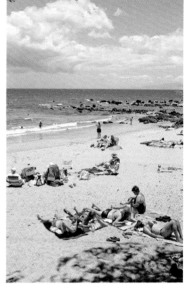
Ulua Beach.

Wailea's best snorkeling; when it's rough, the waves are excellent for bodysurfers. The ocean bottom is shallow and gently slopes down to deeper waters, making swimming generally safe. The beach is usually occupied by guests of nearby resorts; in high season (Christmas–Mar and June–Aug), it's carpeted with beach towels and packed with sunbathers like sardines in cocoa butter.

Facilities include showers and restrooms. Beach equipment is available for rent at the nearby Wailea Ocean Activity Center. To find Ulua, look for the blue SHORELINE ACCESS sign on South Kihei Road, near the Renaissance Wailea Beach Resort. There's a tiny parking lot nearby.

WAILEA BEACH ★★

Wailea is the best golden-sand crescent on Maui's sun-baked southwestern coast. One of five beaches within Wailea Resort, Wailea is big, wide, and protected on both sides by black-lava points. It's the front yard of the Four Seasons Resort and the Grand Wailea Resort, Maui's most elegant and outrageous beach hotels, respectively. From the beach, the view out to sea is magnificent, framed by neighboring Kahoolawe and Lanai and the tiny crescent of Molokini, probably the most popular snorkel spot in these parts. The clear waters tumble to shore in waves just the right size for gentle riding, with or without a board. From shore, you can see Pacific humpback whales in season (Dec–Apr) and unreal sunsets nightly. Facilities include restrooms, outdoor showers, and limited free parking at the blue SHORELINE ACCESS sign, on Wailea Alanui Drive, the main drag of this resort.

MALUAKA BEACH (MAKENA BEACH) ★★

On the southern end of Maui's resort coast, development falls off dramatically, leaving a wild, dry countryside of green kiawe trees. The Maui Prince sits in

Maluaka Beach.

isolated splendor, sharing Makena Resort's 1,800 acres with only a couple of first-rate golf courses and a necklace of perfect beaches. The strand nearest the hotel is Maluaka Beach, often called Makena, notable for its beauty and its views of Molokini Crater, the offshore islet, and Kahoolawe, the so-called "target" island (it was used as a bombing target from 1945 until the early 1990s). This is a short, wide, palm-fringed crescent of golden, grainy sand set between two black-lava points and bounded by big sand dunes topped by a grassy knoll. The swimming in this mostly calm bay is considered the best on Makena Bay, which is bordered on the south by Puu Olai cinder cone and historic Keawalai Congregational Church. The waters around Makena Landing, at the north end of the bay, are particularly good for snorkeling. Facilities include restrooms, showers, a landscaped park, lifeguards, and roadside parking. Along Makena Alanui, look for the SHORELINE ACCESS sign near the hotel, turn right, and head down to the shore.

ONELOA BEACH (BIG BEACH) ★★

Oneloa, meaning "long sand" in Hawaiian, is one of the most popular beaches on Maui. Locals call it Big Beach—it's 3,300 feet long and more than 100 feet wide. Mauians come here to swim, fish, sunbathe, surf, and enjoy the view of Kahoolawe and Lanai. Snorkeling is good around the north end, at the foot of Puu Olai, a 360-foot cinder cone. During storms, however, big waves lash the shore and a strong rip current sweeps the sharp drop-off, posing a danger for inexperienced open-ocean swimmers. There are no facilities except for portable toilets, but there's plenty of parking. To get here, drive past the Maui Prince Hotel to the second dirt road, which leads through a kiawe thicket to the beach.

On the other side of Puu Olai is **Little Beach,** a small pocket beach where assorted nudists work on their all-over tans, to the chagrin of uptight authorities. You can get a nasty sunburn and a lewd-conduct ticket, too.

East Maui

BALDWIN PARK

Located off the Hana Highway between Spreckelsville and Paia, this beach park draws lots of Maui residents, especially body-board enthusiasts. It's easy to see why this place is so popular: The surf breaks along the entire length of the white-sand beach, creating perfect conditions for body boarding. On occasion, the waves get big enough for surfing. A couple of swimming areas are safe enough for children: one in the lee of the beach rocks near the large pavilion, and another at the opposite end of the beach, where beach rocks protect a small swimming area. There's a large pavilion with picnic tables and kitchen facilities, barbecue grills, additional picnic tables on the grassy area, restrooms, showers, a semi-paved parking area, a baseball diamond, and a soccer field. The park is well used on weekends; weekdays are much quieter.

HOOKIPA BEACH PARK ★

Two miles past Paia, on the Hana Highway, is one of the most famous windsurfing sites in the world. Due to its constant winds and endless waves, Hookipa attracts top windsurfers and wave jumpers from around the globe. Surfers and fishermen also enjoy this small gold-sand beach at the foot of a grassy cliff, which provides a natural amphitheater for spectators. Except when competitions are being held, weekdays are the best time to watch the daredevils fly over the waves. When the water is flat, snorkelers and divers explore the reef. Facilities include restrooms, showers, pavilions, picnic tables, barbecue grills, and a parking lot.

WAIANAPANAPA STATE PARK ★

Four miles before Hana, off the Hana Highway, is this beach park, which takes its name from the legend of the Waianapanapa Cave. Chief Kaakea, a jealous and cruel man, suspected his wife, Popoalaea, of having an affair. Popoalaea left her husband and hid herself in a chamber of the Waianapanapa Cave. A few days later, when Kaakea was passing by the cave, the shadow of a servant gave

Hookipa Beach.

Waianapanapa State Park.

away Popoalaea's hiding place, and Kaakea killed her. During certain times of the year, the water in the tide pool turns red, commemorating Popoalaea's death. (Scientists claim, less imaginatively, that the water turns red due to the presence of small red shrimp.)

Waianapanapa State Park's 120 acres contain 12 cabins (p. 164), a caretaker's residence, a beach park, picnic tables, barbecue grills, restrooms, showers, a parking lot, a shoreline hiking trail, and a black-sand beach (it's actually small black pebbles). This is a wonderful area for shoreline hikes (mosquitoes are plentiful, so bring insect repellent) and picnicking. Swimming is generally unsafe due to strong waves and rip currents. Waianapanapa is crowded on weekends; weekdays are generally a better bet.

HAMOA BEACH ★★

This half-moon-shaped, gray-sand beach (a mix of coral and lava) in a truly tropical setting is a favorite among sunbathers seeking rest and refuge. The Hotel Hana-Maui maintains the beach and acts as though it's private, which it isn't—so just march down the lava-rock steps and grab a spot on the sand. James Michener called it "a beach so perfectly formed that I wonder at its comparative obscurity." The 100-foot-wide beach is three football fields long and sits below 30-foot black-lava sea cliffs. Surf on this unprotected beach breaks offshore and rolls in, making it a popular surfing and bodysurfing area. Hamoa is often swept by powerful rip currents, so be careful. The calm left side is best for snorkeling in summer. The hotel has numerous facilities for guests; there are outdoor showers and restrooms for nonguests. Parking is limited. Look for the Hamoa Beach turnoff from Hana Highway.

WATERSPORTS

Snorkel Bob's (www.snorkelbob.com) rents snorkel gear, boogie boards, and other ocean toys; see p. 201 for four locations. If you're island hopping, you can rent from a Snorkel Bob's location on one island and return to a branch on another.

Boss Frog's Dive and Surf Shops (www.bossfrog.com) has eight locations for rental and other gear: Napili, 5059 Napilihau St. (✆ 808/669-4949); Kahana Manor Shops, 4310 Lower Honapiilani Rd., Kahana (✆ 808/669-6700); Kaanapali, 3636 Lower Honoapiilani Rd. (✆ 808/665-1200); Lahaina Cannery Mall, 1221 Honoapiilani Hwy. (✆ 808/661-5995); 150 Lahainaluna Rd., in Lahaina (✆ 808/661-3333);

Hamoa Beach.

Longs Drugs Shopping Center, 1215 Kihei Rd., in North Kihei (© 808/891-0077); Dolphin Plaza, 2395 S. Kihei Rd., behind Pizza Hut, in South Kihei (© 808/875-4477); and 1770 S. Kihei Rd., Shaka Pizza Building (© 808/874-5225).

Safety Tip

Be sure to see the "Staying Healthy" and "Crime & Safety" sections in chapter 3 before setting out on your Maui adventures. You'll find useful information on hiking, camping, and ocean safety, plus how to avoid seasickness and sunburn, and what to do should you get stung by a jellyfish.

Boating & Sailing

To really appreciate Maui, you need to get off the land and get on the sea. Trade winds off the Lahaina coast and the strong wind that rips through Maui's isthmus make sailing around the island exciting. Many different boats, from a three-masted schooner to spacious trimarans, offer day cruises from Maui.

Later in this section, you can find information on snorkel cruises to Molokini under "Snorkeling," fishing charters under "Sportfishing," and trips that combine snorkeling with whale-watching under "Whale-Watching Cruises."

Scotch Mist Sailing Charters This 50-foot Santa Cruz sailboat offers 2-hour sailing adventures. Prices include snorkel gear, juice, fresh fruit, beer, wine (on some cruises), and soda. Sunset sails are also available.

Lahaina Harbor, slip 2. © **808/661-0386.** www.scotchmistsailingcharters.com. Sailing trips $50; sail and snorkel $90; whale-watching trips $50.

DAY CRUISES TO MOLOKAI

You can travel across the seas by ferry from Maui's Lahaina Harbor to Molokai's Kaunakakai Wharf on the *Molokai Princess* (© 800/275-6969 or 808/667-6165; www.mauiprincess.com). The 100-foot yacht, certified for 149 passengers, is fitted with the latest generation of gyroscopic stabilizers, making the ride smoother. The ferry makes the 90-minute journey from Lahaina to Kaunakakai daily; the round-trip cost is $109 for adults and $52 for children 3 to 12. Or you can choose to tour the island on one of two different package options: Cruise-Drive, which includes round-trip passage and a rental car for $230 for the driver, $100 per additional adult passenger, and $50 for children; or the Alii Tour, which is a guided tour in an air-conditioned van plus lunch for $230 per adult and $160 per child.

DAY CRUISES TO LANAI

Expeditions Maui–Lanai Passenger Ferry The cheapest way to Lanai is the ferry, which runs five times a day, 365 days a year. It leaves Lahaina at 6:45am, 9:15am, 12:45pm, 3:15pm, and 5:45pm; the return ferry from Lanai's Manele Bay leaves at 8am, 10:30am, 2pm, 4:30pm, and 6:45pm. The 9-mile channel crossing takes between 45 minutes and an hour, depending on sea conditions. Reservations are strongly recommended. Baggage is limited to two checked bags and one carry-on. Call **Lanai City Service** (© 800/800-4000 or 808/565-7227) to arrange a car rental or bus ride when you arrive.

Ferries depart from Lahaina Harbor; office: 658 Front St., Ste. 127, Lahaina. © **800/695-2624** or 808/661-3756. www.go-lanai.com. Round-trip fares from Maui to Lanai $60 adults, $40 children 2–11.

7

FUN ON & OFF THE BEACH

Watersports

Molokai Princess.

Trilogy ★★★ ☺ Trilogy offers my favorite **snorkel-sail trips.** Hop aboard one of the fleet of custom-built catamarans, from 54 to 64 feet long, for a 9-mile sail from Lahaina Harbor to **Lanai's Hulopoe Beach,** a terrific marine preserve, for a fun-filled day of sailing, snorkeling, swimming, and **whale-watching** (in season, of course). This is the only cruise that offers a personalized ground tour of the island and the only one with rights to take you to Hulopoe Beach. The full-day trip costs $189 for adults and $95 for children 3 to 12. Ask about overnighters to Lanai, too.

Trilogy also offers snorkel-sail trips to **Molokini,** one of Hawaii's best snorkel spots. This half-day trip leaves from Maalaea Harbor and costs $110 for adults, $55 for kids 3 to 12, including breakfast and a barbecue lunch. Other options include a late-morning half-day snorkel-sail off Kaanapali Beach for the same price, plus a host of other trips.

These are the most expensive sail-snorkel cruises on Maui, but they're worth every penny. The crews are fun and knowledgeable, and the boats comfortable and well equipped. All trips include breakfast (Mom's homemade cinnamon buns) and a very good barbecue lunch (onboard on the half-day trip, on land on the Lanai trip). Note, however, that you will be required to wear a flotation device no matter how good your swimming skills are; if this bothers you, go with another outfitter.

☎ **888/225-MAUI** (225-6284) or 808/TRILOGY (874-5649). www.sailtrilogy.com. Prices and departure points vary depending on cruise.

Body Boarding (Boogie Boarding) & Bodysurfing

Bodysurfing—riding the waves without a board, becoming one with the rolling water—is a way of life in Hawaii. Some bodysurfers just rely on their hands to ride the waves; others use hand boards (flat, paddlelike gloves). For additional maneuverability, try a boogie board or body board (also known as belly boards

Trilogy snorkel-sail trips are expensive, but worth every penny.

or *paipo* boards). These 3-foot-long boards support the upper part of your body and are easy to carry and very maneuverable in the water. Both bodysurfing and body boarding require a pair of open-heeled swim fins to help propel you through the water.

Baldwin Beach, just outside of Paia, has great bodysurfing waves nearly year-round. In winter, Maui's best body-surfing spot is **Mokuleia Beach,** known locally as Slaughterhouse because of the cattle slaughterhouse that once stood here, not because of the waves—although they are definitely for expert bodysurfers only. To get to Mokuleia, take Honoapiilani Highway just past Kapalua Resort; various hiking trails will take you down to the pocket beach. Storms from the south bring fair bodysurfing conditions and great boo-

Maui offers excellent waves for boogie boarding.

gie boarding to the lee side of Maui: **Oneloa Beach (Big Beach)** in Makena, **Ulua Beach** and **Kamaole III Beach Park** in Kihei, and **Kapalua Beach** are all good choices.

Ocean Kayaking

Gliding silently over the water, propelled by a paddle, seeing Maui from the sea the way the early Hawaiians did—that's what ocean kayaking is all about. One of Maui's best kayak routes is along the **Kihei Coast,** where there's easy access to calm water. Early mornings are always best, as the wind comes up around 11am, making seas choppy and paddling difficult.

Kayaking is a great way to see Maui the way early Hawaiians did, from the sea.

For beginners, my favorite kayak-tour operator is **Makena Kayak & Tours** ★ (© 808/879-8426; www.makenakayaks.com). Professional guide Dino Ventura leads a 2½-hour trip from Makena Landing for $55, and loves taking first-timers over the secluded coral reefs and into remote coves. His wonderful tour will be a highlight of your vacation. The 4-hour tour (with lunch) costs $85. Prices include refreshments and snorkel and kayak equipment. Check the website for discounts.

South Pacific Kayaks, 2439 S. Kihei Rd., Kihei (© 800/776-2326 or 808/875-4848; www.southpacifickayaks.com), is Maui's oldest kayak-tour company. Its experts lead ocean-kayak trips that include lessons, a guided tour, and snorkeling. Tours run from 2½ to 5 hours and range in price from $65 to $99.

Ocean Rafting

If you're semiadventurous and looking for a more intimate experience with the sea, try ocean rafting. The inflatable rafts hold 6 to 24 passengers. Tours usually include snorkeling and coastal cruising. One of the best (and most reasonable) outfitters is **Hawaii Ocean Rafting** (© 888/677-RAFT [7238] or 808/667-2191; www.hawaiioceanrafting.com), which operates out of Lahaina Harbor. The best deal is the 5-hour morning tour, which is $74 for adults and $53 for children 5 to 12 (book online and save $11). It includes three snorkeling stops and time spent searching for dolphins, plus continental breakfast and midmorning snacks.

Parasailing

Soar high above the crowds (at around 400 ft.) for a bird's-eye view of Maui. This ocean adventure sport, which is something of a cross between sky diving and water-skiing, involves sailing through the air, suspended under a large parachute attached by a towline to a speedboat. Keep in mind, though, that parasailing tours don't run during whale season, which is roughly December through May.

I recommend **UFO Parasailing** (© **800/FLY-4-UFO** [359-4836] or 808/661-7-UFO [7836]; www.ufoparasail.net), which picks you up at Kaanapali Beach. UFO offers parasail rides daily from 8am to 2pm. The cost is $60 for the standard flight of 7 minutes of airtime at 600 feet, $70 for a 10-minute ride at 1,200 feet. You can go up alone or with a friend; no experience is necessary. The company operates in Maui only from May 16 to December 14.

Scuba Diving

Some people come to Maui for the sole purpose of plunging into the tropical Pacific and exploring the underwater world. You can see the great variety of tropical marine life (more than 100 endemic species found nowhere else on the planet), explore sea caves, and swim with sea turtles and monk seals in the clear tropical waters off the island. I recommend going early in the morning. Trade winds often rough up the seas in the afternoon, so most dive operators schedule early-morning dives that end at noon, and then take the rest of the day off.

Unsure about scuba diving? Take an introductory dive: Most operators offer no-experience-necessary dives, ranging from $119 to $150. You can learn from this glimpse into the sea world whether diving is for you.

Everyone dives **Molokini,** a marine-life park and one of Hawaii's top dive spots. This crescent-shaped crater has three tiers of diving: a 35-foot plateau inside the crater basin (used by beginning divers and snorkelers), a wall sloping to 70 feet just beyond the inside plateau, and a sheer wall on the outside and backside of the crater that plunges 350 feet. This underwater park is very popular, thanks to calm, clear, protected waters and an abundance of marine life, from manta rays to clouds of yellow butterflyfish.

For personalized diving, **Ed Robinson's Diving Adventures** ★ (© **800/635-1273** or 808/879-3584; www.mauiscuba.com) is the only Maui company rated one of *Scuba Diver* magazine's top five best dive operators for 7 years straight. Ed, a widely published underwater photographer, offers specialized charters for small groups. Two-tank dives are $130; his dive boats depart from Kihei Boat Ramp.

If Ed is booked, call **Mike Severns Diving** (© **808/879-6596;** www.mikesevernsdiving.com) for small (maximum 12 people, divided into two groups of six), personal diving tours on a 38-foot Munson/Hammerhead boat with freshwater shower. Mike and his wife, Pauline Fiene-Severns, are both biologists who make diving in Hawaii educational as well as fun (they have a spectacular underwater photography book called *Molokini Island*). In their 30 years of operation, they have been accident-free. Two-tank dives are $145, including equipment rental, or $130 if you have your own equipment.

The best time for scuba diving is early in the morning, before trade winds rough up the seas.

Watersports

AN EXPERT SHARES HIS SECRETS:
maui's best dives

Ed Robinson, of Ed Robinson's Diving Adventures (see above), knows what makes a great dive. Here are some of his favorites on Maui:

Hawaiian Reef This area off the Kihei-Wailea Coast is so named because it hosts a good cross-section of Hawaiian topography and marine life. Diving to depths of 85 feet, you'll see everything from lava formations and coral reef to sand and rubble, plus a diverse range of both shallow- and deepwater creatures. It's clear why this area was so popular with ancient Hawaiian fishermen: Large helmet shells, a healthy garden of antler coral heads, and big schools of snapper are common.

Third Tank Located off Makena Beach at 80 feet, this World War II tank is one of the most picturesque artificial reefs you're likely to see around Maui. It acts like a fish magnet: Because it's the only large solid object in the area, any fish or invertebrate looking for a safe home comes here. Surrounding the tank is a cloak of schooling snappers and goat-fish just waiting for a photographer with a wide-angle lens. Despite its small size, Third Tank is loaded with more marine life per square inch than any site off Maui.

Molokini Crater The backside of the crater is always done as a live boat-drift dive. The vertical wall plummets from more than 150 feet above sea level to around 250 feet below. Looking down to unseen depths gives you a feeling for the vastness of the open ocean. Pelagic fish and sharks are often sighted, and living coral perches on the wall, which is home to lobsters, crabs, and a number of photogenic black-coral trees at 50 feet.

There are actually two great dive sites around Molokini Crater. Named after common chub or rudderfish, **Enenue Side** gently slopes from the surface to about 60 feet and then drops

Stop by any location of **Maui Dive Shop ★** (www.mauidiveshop.com), Maui's largest diving retailer, with everything from rentals to scuba-diving instruction to dive-boat charters, for a free copy of the 24-page *Maui Dive Guide* (you can also order a copy online). Inside are maps of and details on the 20 best shoreline and offshore dives and snorkel sites, each ranked for beginner, intermediate, or advanced snorkelers/divers. Maui Dive Shop has branches in Kihei at Azeka Place II Shopping Center, 1455 S. Kihei Rd. (© 808/879-3388); Kamaole Shopping Center (© 808/879-1533); and Shops at Wailea (© 808/875-9904). In Lahaina, the branches are at Lahaina Gateway Mall (© 808/661-5388) and in the Honokowai Marketplace (© 808/661-6166). In Maalaea, they are located at the Maalaea Village (© 808/244-5514); Whalers Village, Kaanapali (© 808/661-5117); and Kahana Gateway (© 808/669-3800).

Snorkeling

Snorkeling is the main attraction in Maui—and almost anyone can do it. All you need are a mask, a snorkel, fins, and some basic swimming skills. Floating over underwater worlds through colorful clouds of tropical fish is like a dream. In many places all you have to do is wade into the water and look down. If you've rapidly to deeper waters. The shallower area is an easy dive, with lots of tame butterflyfish. It's also the home of Morgan Bentjaw, one of our friendliest moray eels. Enenue Side is often done as a live boat-drift dive to extend the range of the tour. Diving depths vary. Divers usually do a 50-foot dive, but on occasion advanced divers drop to the 130-foot level to visit the rare boarfish and the shark condos.

Almost every kind of fish found in Hawaii can be seen in the crystalline waters of **Reef's End.** It's an extension of the rim of the crater, which runs for about 600 feet underwater, barely breaking the surface. Reef's End is shallow enough for novice snorkelers and exciting enough for experienced divers. The end and outside of this shoal drop off in dramatic terraces to beyond diving range. In deeper waters, there are shark ledges at varying depths and dozens of eels (some of which are tame), including moray, dragon, snowflake, and garden eels. The shallower inner side is home to Garbanzo, one of the largest and first eels to be tamed. The reef is covered with cauliflower coral; in bright sunlight, it's one of the most dramatic underwater scenes in Hawaii.

La Pérouse Pinnacle In the middle of scenic La Pérouse Bay, site of Haleakala's most recent lava flow, is a pinnacle rising from the 60-foot bottom to about 10 feet below the surface. Getting to the dive site is half the fun: The scenery above water is as exciting as that below the surface. Underwater, you'll enjoy a very diversified dive. Clouds of damselfish and triggerfish will greet you on the surface. Divers can approach even the timid bird wrasse. There are more porcupine puffers here than anywhere else, as well as schools of goatfish and fields of healthy finger coral. La Pérouse is good for snorkeling and long, shallow second dives.

never snorkeled before, most resorts and excursion boats offer instruction, but it's plenty easy to figure it out for yourself.

Some snorkeling tips: Always go with a buddy. Look up every once in a while to see where you are, how far offshore you are, and whether there's any boat traffic. Don't touch anything; not only can you damage coral, but camouflaged fish and shells with poisonous spines also might surprise you. Always check with a dive shop, lifeguards, and others on the beach about the area in which you plan to snorkel: Are there any dangerous conditions you should know about? What are the current surf, tide, and weather conditions? If you're not a good swimmer, wear a life jacket or other flotation device, which you can rent at most places offering watersports gear.

Snorkel Bob's ★ (www.snorkelbob.com) or **Boss Frog's Dive and Surf Shops** (www.bossfrog.com) will rent you everything you need; see the introduction to this section for locations. Also see "Scuba Diving" (above) for Maui Dive Shop's free booklet on great snorkeling sites.

Maui's best snorkeling spots include **Kapalua Beach;** at **Black Rock at Kaanapali Beach,** in front of the Sheraton; along the Kihei coastline, especially at **Kamaole III Beach Park;** and along the Wailea coastline, particularly at **Ulua Beach.** Mornings are best because local winds don't kick in until around noon. **Olowalu** has great snorkeling around **mile marker 14,** where there is a turtle-cleaning station about 150 to 225 feet out from shore. Turtles line up here to have cleaner wrasses pick off small parasites.

Ahihi-Kinau Natural Preserve is another terrific place. I recommend going there, even though it requires more effort to get here, but it's worth it because it's home to Maui's tropical marine life at its best. You can't miss in Ahihi Bay, a 2,000-acre state natural area reserve in the lee of Cape Kinau, on Maui's rugged south coast, where Haleakala spilled red-hot lava that ran to the sea in 1790. Fishing is strictly *kapu* (forbidden) here, and the fish know it; they're everywhere in this series of rocky coves and black-lava tide pools. The black, barren, lunar-like land stands in stark contrast to the

Almost anyone can enjoying snorkeling. All you need are a mask, a snorkel, fins, and some basic swimming skills.

green-blue water. After you snorkel, check out La Pérouse Bay on the south side of Cape Kinau, where the French admiral La Pérouse became the first European to set foot on Maui. A lava-rock pyramid known as Pérouse Monument marks the spot. To get here, drive south of Makena past Puu Olai to Ahihi Bay, where the road turns to gravel (and sometimes seems like it will disappear under the waves). At Cape Kinau, three four-wheel-drive trails lead across the lava flow; take the shortest one, nearest La Pérouse Bay. If you have a standard car, drive as far as you can, park, and walk the remainder of the way. For information on the preserve, go to **www.dofaw.net**, scroll down to "Programs" then "Natural Area Reserve Systems," then select "Natural Area Reserve Systems" and click on Maui on the map. The DLNR/Division of Forestry and Wildlife (© **808/984-8100**) has a printed brochure to mail.

When the whales aren't around, **Capt. Steve's Rafting Excursions** (© **808/667-5565;** www.captainsteves.com) offers 5½-hour snorkel trips from Mala Wharf in Lahaina to the waters around **Lanai** (you don't actually land on the island). Discounted online rates of $124 for adults and $89 for children 12 and under include breakfast, lunch, snorkel gear, and wet suits.

If you'd like to head over to Lanai for a day of snorkeling in its pristine waters, see "Day Cruises to Lanai," above.

SNORKEL CRUISES TO MOLOKINI

Like a crescent moon fallen from the sky, the crater of **Molokini** ★ sits almost midway between Maui and the uninhabited island of Kahoolawe. Tilted so that only the thin rim of its southern side shows above water in a perfect semicircle, Molokini stands like a scoop against the tide, and it serves, on its concave side, as a natural sanctuary for tropical fish and snorkelers, who commute daily in a fleet of dive boats to this marine-life preserve. Note that in high season, Molokini can be crowded with dozens of boats, each carrying scores of snorkelers.

Maui Classic Charters ★★ Maui Classic Charters offers morning and afternoon **snorkel-sail cruises to Molokini** on *Four Winds II*, a 55-foot glass-bottom catamaran. Rates for the morning sail are $89 adults and $59 children 3 to 12; in the afternoon, $42 adults and $30 children (book online to save 15%). *Four Winds* trips include continental breakfast and a hot lunch (lunch is optional on the afternoon cruise); complimentary beer, wine, and soda; snorkeling gear and instruction; and sportfishing along the way. Those looking for speed should book a trip on the state-of-the-art catamaran *Maui Magic*. A 5-hour snorkel journey to both Molokini and La Pérouse costs $112 adults and $92 children 5 to 12, including continental breakfast; barbecue lunch; beer, wine, and soda; snorkel gear; and instruction. During whale season (Dec 22–Apr 22), the *Four Winds* has a 3½-hour **whale-watch cruise** that goes for $42 adults and $30 children 3 to 12 (including beverages).

Maalaea Harbor, slip 55 and slip 80. © **800/736-5740** or 808/879-8188. www.mauicharters.com. Prices vary depending on cruise.

Pacific Whale Foundation This not-for-profit foundation supports its whale research, public education and conservation programs by offering **whale-watch cruises, wild dolphin encounters,** and **snorkel tours,** some to Molokini and Lanai. There are 17 daily trips to choose from, offered from December through May, out of both Lahaina and Maalaea harbors.

300 Ma'alaea Rd., Ste. 211, Wailuku. © **800/942-5311** or 808/879-8811. www.pacificwhale.org. Trips from $20 adults, $17 children 7–12, free for ages 6 and under (one free child per paying adult). They have stores at 612 Front St., Lahaina and at the Harbor Shops at Ma'alaea.

Pride of Maui For a high-speed, action-packed snorkel-sail experience, consider the *Pride of Maui*. These 5-hour **snorkel cruises to Molokini** also stop at Turtle Bay and Makena; the cost is $90 for ages 13 and up ($80 if you book online) and $56 for children 3 to 12 ($50 online). Rates include continental breakfast, barbecue lunch, beverages and open bar, gear, and instruction. Other options include an afternoon Molokini cruise ($42 for ages 13 and up, $27 for children 3–12, with discounts online), an evening sunset cruise ($70 for ages 13 and up, $27 for children 3–12), and, during whale season, a whale-watching cruise ($42 for ages 13 and up, $30 for children 3–12; book on their website for $33 adults and $27 children).

Maalaea Harbor. © **877/TO-PRIDE** (867-7433) or 808/875-0955. www.prideofmaui.com. Prices vary depending on cruise.

Sportfishing

Marlin (as big as 1,200 lb.), tuna, ono, and mahimahi await the baited hook in Maui's coastal and channel waters. No license is required; just book a sportfishing vessel out of Lahaina or Maalaea harbor. Most charter boats that troll for big-game fish carry a maximum of six passengers. You can walk the docks, inspect boats, and talk to captains and crews, or book through an activities desk or one of the outfitters recommended below.

Shop around: Prices vary widely according to the boat, the crowd, and the captain. A shared boat for a half-day of fishing starts at $100; a shared full day of fishing starts at around $250. A half-day exclusive (you get the entire boat) starts at $600; a full-day exclusive starts at $900. Also, many boat captains tag and release marlin or keep the fish for themselves (sorry, that's Hawaii style). If you want to eat your mahimahi for dinner or have your marlin mounted, tell the captain before you go.

The best way to book a sportfishing charter is through the experts; the top booking desk in the state is **Sportfish Hawaii ★** (© **877/388-1376** or 808/396-2607; www.sportfishhawaii.com), which books boats on all the islands. These fishing vessels have been inspected and must meet rigorous criteria to guarantee that you'll have a great time. Prices range from $999 to $1,100 for a full-day exclusive charter (you, plus five friends, get the entire boat to yourself); from $599 for a half-day exclusive.

Submarine Dives

Plunging 100 feet below the surface of the sea in a state-of-the-art, high-tech submarine is a great way to experience Maui's magnificent underwater world, especially if you're not a swimmer. **Atlantis Adventures ★**, 658 Front St., Lahaina (© **800/548-6262** or 808/667-2224; www.atlantisadventures.com), offers trips out of Lahaina Harbor every hour on the hour from 9am to 2pm; prices are $99 for adults and $45 for children under 12 (children must be at least 3 ft. tall). Book online and save 10%. Allow 2 hours for this underwater adventure. *Warning:* This is not a good choice if you're claustrophobic.

Surfing

The ancient Hawaiian sport of *hee nalu* (wave sliding) is probably the sport most people picture when they think of the islands. If you'd like to give it a shot, just sign up at any one of the recommended surfing schools listed below.

Tide and Kiva Rivers, two local boys (actually twins) who have been surfing since they could walk, operate **Rivers to the Sea** (© **808/280-8795** or 280-6236; www.riverstothesea.com), one of the best surfing schools on Maui. Rates are $75 each for a 2-hour class for a group of three or more, $220 for a couple for

The submarine *Atlantis*.

If you want to participate in Hawaii's ancient sport of *hee nalu* (wave sliding) just sign up for lessons at one of Maui's myriad surfing schools.

a 2-hour class, and $160 to $200 for a 2-hour private lesson. All lessons include equipment. The instructor decides where the lesson will take place based on the client's ability and where the surf is on that day. Tide, who has been surfing for over 25 years, says he has beginners standing up in their first lesson.

Well-known surfer Nancy Emerson can also teach you how to surf—just call the **Nancy Emerson School of Surfing,** 505 Front St., Ste. 224B, Lahaina (© **808/244-SURF** [7873] or 662-4445; www.mauisurfclinics.com). Nancy has been surfing since 1961 and has even been a stunt performer for various movies such as *Waterworld.* She's pioneered a new instructional technique called "Learn to Surf in One Lesson" (you can, really). It's $78 per person for a 2-hour group lesson; private 2-hour classes are $165. All instructors are certified lifeguards.

Whale-Watching

Every winter, pods of Pacific humpback whales make the 3,000-mile swim from the chilly waters of Alaska to bask in Maui's summery shallows, fluking, spy hopping, spouting, and having an all-around swell time.

The humpback is the star of the annual whale-watching season, which usually begins in December or January and lasts until April or sometimes May. About 1,500 to 3,000 humpback whales appear in Hawaii waters each year. Adults grow to be about 45 feet long and weigh a hefty 40 tons. Humpbacks are officially an endangered species: In 1997, some of the waters around the state were designated the Hawaiian Islands Humpback Whale National Marine Sanctuary, the country's only federal single-species sanctuary.

WHALE-WATCHING FROM SHORE

Between mid-December and April, you can just look out to sea. There's no best time of day for whale-watching, but the whales seem to appear when the sea is glassy and the wind calm. Once you see one, keep watching in the same vicinity; they might stay down for 20 minutes. Bring a book—and binoculars, if you can. Some good whale-watching points on Maui include:

McGregor Point On the way to Lahaina, there's a scenic lookout at mile marker 9 (just before you get to the Lahaina Tunnel); it's a good viewpoint to scan for whales.

Olowalu Reef Along the straight part of Honoapiilani Highway, between McGregor Point and Olowalu, you'll sometimes see whales leap out of the water. Their appearance can bring traffic to a screeching halt: People abandon their cars and run down to the sea to watch, causing a major traffic jam. If you stop, pull off the road so others may pass.

Wailea Beach Marriott Resort & Spa On the Wailea coastal walk, stop at this resort to look for whales through the telescope installed as a public service by the Hawaii Island Humpback Whale National Marine Sanctuary.

Puu Olai It's a tough climb up this coastal landmark near the Maui Prince Hotel, but you're likely to be well rewarded: This is the island's best spot for off-shore whale-watching. On the 360-foot cinder cone overlooking Makena Beach, you'll be at the right elevation to see Pacific humpbacks as they dodge Molokini and cruise up Alalakeiki Channel between Maui and Kahoolawe. If you don't see one, you'll at least have a whale of a view.

WHALE-WATCHING CRUISES

For a closer look, take a whale-watching cruise. The **Pacific Whale Foundation,** 101 N. Kihei Rd., Kihei (✆ **800/942-5311** or 808/879-8811; www.pacificwhale.org), is a nonprofit foundation in Kihei that supports its whale research by offering cruises and snorkel tours, some to Molokini and Lanai. It operates a 65-foot power catamaran called the *Ocean Explorer,* a 50-foot sailing catamaran

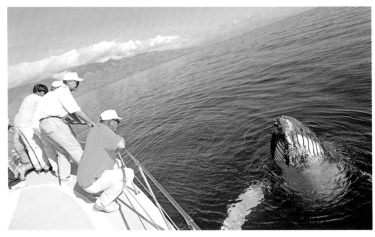

Get up close and personal with whales off the coast of Maui.

called the *Manute'a*, and other boats. There are 15 daily trips from which to choose, and the rates for a 2-hour whale-watching cruise would make Captain Ahab smile (starting at $18 for adults, $15 for children). Cruises are offered from December to May, out of both Lahaina and Maalaea harbors.

If you want to combine ocean activities, then a snorkel or dive cruise to Molokini, the sunken crater off Maui's south coast, might be just the ticket. You can see whales on the way there, at no extra charge. See "Scuba Diving" and "Boating & Sailing," earlier in this section.

WHALE-WATCHING BY KAYAK & RAFT

Seeing a humpback whale from an ocean kayak or raft is awesome. **Capt. Steve's Rafting Excursions** (📞 **808/667-5565**; www.captainsteves.com) offers 2-hour whale-watching excursions out of Lahaina Harbor from $39 for adults, $29 for children 5 to 12.

Windsurfing

Maui has Hawaii's best windsurfing beaches. In winter, windsurfers from around the world flock to the town of **Paia** to ride the waves. **Hookipa Beach,** known all over the globe for its brisk winds and excellent waves, is the site of several world-championship contests. **Kanaha Beach,** west of Kahului Airport, also has dependable winds. When the winds turn northerly, **Kihei** is the spot to be; some days, you can spot whales in the distance behind the windsurfers. The northern end of Kihei is best: **Ohukai Park,** the first beach as you enter South Kihei Road from the northern end, has not only good winds, but also parking, a long strip of grass to assemble your gear, and good access to the water. Experienced windsurfers here are found in front of the **Maui Sunset** condo, 1032 S. Kihei Rd., near Waipuilani Street (a block north of McDonald's), which has great windsurfing conditions but a very shallow reef (not good for beginners).

Hawaiian Island Surf & Sport, 415 Dairy Rd., Kahului (📞 **800/231-6958** or 808/871-4981; www.hawaiian-island.com), offers lessons (from $89), rentals, and repairs. Other shops that offer rentals and lessons are **Hawaiian Sailboarding Techniques,** 425 Koloa St., Kahului (📞 **800/968-5423** or

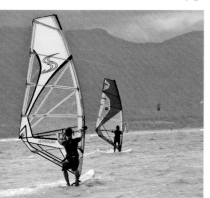
Maui has Hawaii's best windsurfing beaches.

808/871-5423; www.hstwindsurfing.com), with 2½-hour lessons from $79; and **Maui Windsurf Co.,** 22 Hana Hwy., Kahului (© **800/872-0999** or 808/877-4816; www.maui-windsurf.com), which has complete equipment rental (board, sail, rig harness, and roof rack) from $49, plus 1- or 2-hour lessons ranging from $60 to $99.

For daily reports on wind and surf conditions, call the **Wind and Surf Report** at © **808/877-3611.**

HIKING & CAMPING

In the past 3 decades, Maui has grown from a rural island to a fast-paced resort destination, but its natural beauty remains largely inviolate; there are still many places that can be explored only on foot. Those interested in seeing the backcountry—complete with virgin waterfalls, remote wilderness trails, and quiet, meditative settings—should head for Haleakala's upcountry or the tropical Hana Coast.

Camping on Maui can be extreme (inside a volcano) or benign (by the sea in Hana). It can be wet, cold, and rainy, or hot, dry, and windy—often all on the same day. If you're heading for Haleakala, remember that U.S. astronauts trained for the moon inside the volcano: Bring survival gear. Don't forget both your swimsuit and your rain gear if you're bound for Waianapanapa. Bring your own gear, as there are no places to rent camping equipment on Maui.

For more information on Maui camping and hiking trails, and to obtain free maps, contact **Haleakala National Park,** P.O. Box 369, Makawao, HI 96768 (© **808/572-4400;** www.nps.gov/hale); or the **State Division of Forestry and Wildlife,** 54 S. High St., Wailuku, HI 96793 (© **808/984-8100;** www.hawaiistateparks.org). For information on trails, hikes, camping, and permits for state parks, contact the **Hawaii State Department of Land and Natural Resources,** State Parks Division, P.O. Box 621, Honolulu, HI 96809 (© **808/587-0300;** www.hawaiistateparks.org/camping/fees.cfm); note that you can get information from the website but cannot obtain permits there. For Maui County Parks, contact the **Maui County Department of Parks and Recreation,** 200 S. High St., Wailuku, HI 96793 (© **808/270-7230;** www.co.maui.hi.us/departments/parks).

TIPS ON SAFE HIKING & CAMPING Water might be everywhere in Hawaii, but it more than likely isn't safe to drink. Most stream water must be treated because cattle, pigs, and goats have probably contaminated the water upstream. The Department of Health continually warns campers of bacterium leptospirosis, which is found in freshwater streams throughout the state and enters the body through breaks in the skin or through the mucous membranes. It produces flulike symptoms and can be fatal. Make sure that your drinking water is safe by vigorously boiling it, or if boiling is not an option, use tablets with hydroperiodide; portable water filters will not screen out bacterium leptospirosis. Firewood isn't always available, so it's a good idea to carry a small, light backpacking stove, which you can use both to boil water and to cook meals.

Remember, the island is not crime-free: Never leave your valuables (wallet, airline ticket, and so on) unprotected. Carry a day pack if you have a campsite, and never camp alone. Some more dos and don'ts: Do bury personal waste away from streams. Don't eat unknown fruit. Do carry your trash out. And don't forget there is very little twilight in Maui when the sun sets—it gets dark quickly.

See "Staying Healthy" and "Crime & Safety" in chapter 3 for more hiking and camping tips.

GUIDED HIKES If you'd like a knowledgeable guide to accompany you on a hike, call **Maui Hiking Safaris ★** (*©* **888/445-3963** or 808/572-3037; www. mauihikingsafaris.com). Owner Randy Warner takes visitors on half- and full-day hikes into valleys, rainforests, and coastal areas. Randy's been hiking around Maui for more than 25 years and is wise in the ways of Hawaiian history, native flora and fauna, and volcanology. His rates are $59 to $79 for a half-day and $105 to $139 for a full day, which include day packs, rain parkas, snacks, water, and, on full-day hikes, sandwiches.

Maui's oldest hiking-guide company is **Hike Maui ★** (*©* **866/324-6284** or 808/879-5270; www.hikemaui.com), headed by Ken Schmitt, who

zipping **OVER THE FOREST CANOPY**

For those looking for a different perspective of Haleakala, try **Skyline Eco-Adventures' Zipline Haleakala Tour** (*©* **808/878-8400;** www.zipline.com/locations/haleakala), which blends a short hike through a eucalyptus forest with four "zipline" crossings. During the zipline crossing, you'll be outfitted with a seat harness and connected to a cable, then launched from a 70-foot-high platform to "zip" along the cable suspended over the slopes of Haleakala. From this viewpoint, you fly over treetops, valleys, gulches, and waterfalls at 10 to 35 mph. These bird's-eye tours operate daily and take riders from ages 10 and up, weighing between 80 and 260 pounds. The cost is $80, if you book on their website.

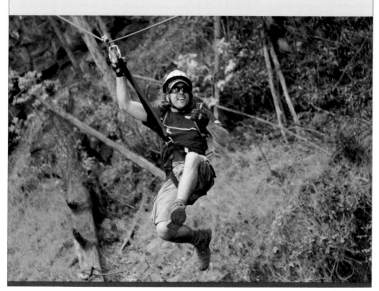

pioneered guided hikes on the Valley Isle. Hike Maui offers five different hikes a day, ranging from an easy 1-mile, 3-hour hike to a waterfall ($75) to a strenuous full-day waterfall and rainforest hike ($150). All prices include equipment and transportation.

Venture into the lush West Maui Mountains with an experienced guide on one of the numerous hikes offered by **Maui Eco-Adventures** (*Ⓒ* **877/661-7720** or 808/661-7720; www.ecomaui.com). I love the Rainforest/Waterfall Hike: After a continental breakfast, you'll hike by streams and waterfalls, through native trees and plants, and on to breathtaking vistas. The tour includes a picnic lunch, swims in secluded pools, and memorable photo ops. The 6-hour excursion costs $125 per person, $63 children ages 5 to 12, including meals, a fanny pack with bottled water, and rain gear if necessary. Age restrictions for children differ for each hike. An easier jaunt costs just $104.

For information on hikes given by the **Hawaii Sierra Club** on Maui, call *Ⓒ* **808/573-4147** or go to www.hi.sierraclub.org.

Haleakala National Park ★★★

For complete coverage of the national park, see "House of the Sun: Haleakala National Park" (p. 263).

HIKING INTO THE WILDERNESS: SLIDING SANDS & HALEMAUU TRAILS

Hiking into Maui's dormant volcano is the best way to see it. The terrain inside the wilderness area of the volcano, which ranges from burnt-red cinder cones to ebony-black lava flows, is simply spectacular. Inside the crater there are some 27 miles of hiking trails, two camping sites, and three cabins.

Hiking into Haleakala's crater is the best way to experience it.

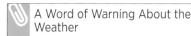

A Word of Warning About the Weather

The weather at nearly 10,000 feet can change suddenly and without warning. Come prepared for cold, high winds, rain, and even snow in winter. Temperatures can range from 77°F (25°C) down to 26°F (-3°C), and high winds (which make it feel even colder) are frequent. Rainfall varies from 40 inches a year on the west end of the crater to more than 200 inches on the eastern side. Bring boots, waterproof gear, warm clothes, extra layers, and lots of sunscreen—the sun shines very brightly up here.

Try to arrange to stay at least 1 night in the park; 2 or 3 nights will allow you more time to explore the fascinating interior of the volcano (see below for details on the cabins and campgrounds in the wilderness area of the valley). If you want to venture out on your own, the best route takes in two trails: into the crater along **Sliding Sands Trail** ★, which begins on the rim at 9,800 feet and descends into the belly of the beast, to the valley floor at 6,600 feet; and back out along **Halemauu Trail** ★. Hardy hikers can consider making the 11-mile one-way descent, which takes 9 hours, and the equally long return ascent in a day. The rest of us will need to extend this steep but wonderful hike to 2 days. The descending and ascending trails aren't loops; the trail heads are miles (and several thousand feet in elevation) apart, so you'll need to make advance transportation arrangements to get back to your car, which you'll leave at the beginning of the hike, about a 30- to 45-minute drive from where the Halemauu Trail ends. You either arrange with someone to pick you up, hitchhike back up to your car, or hook up with other people doing the same thing and drop off one car at each trail head. Before you set out, stop at park headquarters to get camping and hiking updates. See below for details on the cabins and campgrounds in the wilderness area in the valley. There is no registration for day hikers.

The trail head for Sliding Sands is well marked, and the trail is easy to follow over lava flows and cinders. As you descend, look around: The view is breathtaking. In the afternoon, waves of clouds flow into the Kaupo and Koolau gaps. Vegetation is sparse to nonexistent at the top, but the closer you get to the crater floor, the more growth you'll see: bracken ferns, pili grass, shrubs, even flowers. On the floor, the trail travels across rough lava flows, passing by rare silversword plants, volcanic vents, and multicolored cinder cones.

The Halemauu Trail goes over red and black lava and past vegetation such as evening primrose as it begins its ascent up the crater wall. Occasionally, riders on horseback use this trail as an entry and exit from the park. The proper etiquette is to step aside and stand quietly next to the trail as the horses pass.

DAY HIKES FROM THE MAIN ENTRANCE

In addition to the difficult hike into the crater, the park has a few shorter and easier options. Anyone can take a .5-mile walk down the **Hosmer Grove Nature Trail** ★, or you can start down **Sliding Sands Trail** for a mile or two to get a hint of what lies ahead (even this short hike can be exhausting at the high altitude). A good day hike is **Halemauu Trail** to Holua Cabin and back, an 8-mile, half-day trip.

A 20-minute orientation presentation is given daily in the Summit Building at 9:30, 10:30, and 11:30am. The park rangers offer two **guided hikes.** The 2-hour, 2-mile **Cinder Desert Hike** takes place Tuesday and Friday at 10am and starts from the Sliding Sands trail head at the end of the Haleakala Visitor Center parking lot. The 3-hour, 3-mile **Waikamoi Cloud Forest Hike** leaves every Monday and Thursday at 9am; it starts at the Hosmer Grove, just inside the park entrance, and traverses through the Nature Conservancy's Waikamoi Preserve. *Always call in advance:* The hikes and briefing sessions may be canceled, so check first. For details, call the park at © **808/572-4400** or visit www.nps.gov/hale.

CAMPING NEAR THE MAIN ENTRANCE

Most people stay at one of two tent campgrounds, for more information, contact **Haleakala National Park,** P.O. Box 369, Makawao, HI 96768 (© **808/572-4400;** www.nps.gov/hale).

CABINS It can get really cold and windy down in the valley (see "A Word of Warning About the Weather," above), so try for a cabin. They're warm, provide protection from the elements, and are reasonably priced. Each has 12 padded bunks (but no bedding; bring your own), a table, chairs, cooking utensils, a two-burner propane stove, and a wood-burning stove with firewood (you might also have a few cockroaches). The cabins are spaced so that each one is an easy walk from the other: Holua cabin is on the Halemauu Trail, Kapalaoa cabin on Sliding Sands Trail, and Paliku cabin on the eastern end by the Kaupo Gap. The rates are $75 a night if you book more than 3 weeks in advance or $60 a night if you book less than 3 weeks in advance.

The cabins are so popular, requests for cabins must be made 3 months in advance (be sure to request alternate dates). You can request all three cabins at once; you're limited to 2 nights in one cabin and 3 nights total within the wilderness per month. Visit **www.fhnp.org/wcr** for complete rules and regulations, as well as an online application.

CAMPGROUNDS If you don't win the cabin lottery, all is not lost—there are three tent-camping sites that can accommodate you: two in the wilderness area, and one just outside at Hosmer Grove. There is no charge for tent camping.

If you want to stay in a cabin, be sure to book way in advance.

Hosmer Grove, located at 6,800 feet, is a small, open, grassy area surrounded by a forest. Trees protect campers from the winds, but nights still get quite cold—sometimes there's ice on the ground up here. This is the best place to spend the night in a tent if you want to see the Haleakala sunrise. Come up the day before, enjoy the park, take a day hike, and then turn in early. The enclosed-glass summit building opens at sunrise for those who come to greet the dawn—a welcome windbreak. Facilities at Hosmer Grove include a covered pavilion with picnic tables and grills, chemical toilets, and drinking water. No permits are needed, and there's no charge—but you can stay for only 3 nights in a 30-day period.

The two tent-camping areas inside the volcano are **Holua,** just off Halemauu at 6,920 feet; and **Paliku,** just before the Kaupo Gap at the eastern end of the valley, at 6,380 feet. Facilities at both campgrounds are limited to pit toilets and nonpotable catchment water. Water at Holua is limited, especially in summer. No open fires are allowed inside the volcano, so bring a stove if you plan to cook. Tent camping is restricted to the signed area. No camping is allowed in the horse pasture. The inviting grassy lawn in front of the cabin is off-limits. Camping is free but limited to 2 consecutive nights, and no more than 3 nights a month inside the volcano. Permits are issued at park headquarters daily from 8am to 3pm on a first-come, first-served basis on the day you plan to camp. Occupancy is limited to 25 people in each campground.

HIKING & CAMPING AT KIPAHULU (NEAR HANA)

In the east Maui section of Haleakala National Park, you can set up at **Oheo Campground,** a first-come, first-served, drive-in campground with tent sites for 100 near the ocean. It has a few tables, barbecue grills, and chemical toilets. No permit is required, but there's a 3-night limit. No food or drinking water is available, so bring your own. Bring a tent as well—it rains 75 inches a year here. Contact **Kipahulu Ranger Station,** Haleakala National Park, HI 96713 (✆ **808/248-7375;** www.nps.gov/hale/planyourvisit/wilderness-camping.htm) for information.

HIKING FROM THE SUMMIT If you hike from the crater rim down **Kaupo Gap** to the ocean, more than 20 miles away, you'll pass through climate zones ranging from arctic to tropical. On a clear day, you can see every island except Kauai on the trip down.

APPROACHING KIPAHULU FROM HANA If you drive to Kipahulu, you'll have to approach it from the Hana Highway—it's not accessible from the summit. Always check in at the ranger station before you begin your hike; the staff can inform you of current conditions and share their wonderful stories about the history, culture, flora, and fauna of the area. The entry fee is $10 a car, the same as for the summit atop Haleakala.

There are two hikes you can take here. The first is a short, easy .5-mile loop along the **Kaloa Point Trail** (Kaloa Point is a windy bluff overlooking **Oheo Gulch**), which leads toward the ocean along pools and waterfalls and back to the ranger station. The clearly marked path leaves the parking area and rambles along the flat, grassy peninsula. Along the way you'll see the remnants of an ancient fishing shrine, a house site, and a lauhala-thatched building depicting an earlier time. The pools are above and below the bridge; the best for swimming are usually above the bridge.

The second hike is for the hardier. Although just a 4-mile round-trip, the trail is steep and you'll want to stop and swim in the pools, so allow 3 hours. You'll be climbing over rocks and up steep trails, so wear hiking boots. Take water, snacks, swim gear, and insect repellent. Always be on the lookout for flash-flood conditions. This walk will pass two magnificent waterfalls, the 181-foot **Makahiku Falls** and the even bigger 400-foot **Waimoku Falls ★**. The trail starts at the ranger station, where you'll walk uphill for .5 mile to a fence overlook at the thundering Makahiku Falls. If you're tired, you can turn around here; true adventurers should press on. Behind the lookout, the well-worn trail picks up again and goes directly to a pool on the top of the Makahiku Falls. The pool is safe to swim in as long as the waters aren't rising; if they are, get out and head back to the ranger station. The rest of the trail takes you through a meadow and bamboo forest to Waimoku Falls.

GUIDED HIKES The rangers at Kipahulu conduct a 1-mile hike to the **Bamboo Forest ★** at 9:30am daily; and a 4-mile round-trip hike to **Waimoku Falls** on Saturday at 9:30am. All programs and hikes begin at the ranger station; they may be canceled, so check in advance by contacting the **Kipahulu Ranger Station,** Haleakala National Park, HI 96713 (🕾 **808/248-7375;** www.nps.gov/hale).

Skyline Trail, Polipoli Spring State Recreation Area ★

This is some hike—strenuous but worth every step. It's 8 miles, all downhill, with a dazzling 100-mile view of the islands dotting the blue Pacific, plus the West Maui Mountains, which seem like a separate island.

The trail is located just outside Haleakala National Park at Polipoli Spring State Recreation Area; however, you access it by going through the national park to the summit. The Skyline Trail starts just beyond the Puu Ulaula summit building on the south side of Science City and follows the southwest rift zone of Haleakala from its lunarlike cinder cones to a cool redwood grove. The trail drops 3,800 feet on a 4-hour hike to the recreation area in the 12,000-acre Kahikinui Forest Reserve. If you'd rather drive, you'll need a four-wheel-drive vehicle.

There's a **campground** at the recreation area, at 6,300 feet. Permits and reservations are required, fees are $5 per campsite per night, and your stay must be limited to 5 nights. One 10-bunk cabin is available for $45 a night for one to four guests ($5 for each additional guest); it has a cold shower and a gas stove, but no electricity or drinking water (bring your own). To reserve, contact the **State Parks Division,** 54 S. High St., Room 101, Wailuku, HI 96793 (🕾 **808/984-8109;** www.hawaiistateparks.org/camping/fees.cfm).

Polipoli State Park ★

You'll find one of the most unusual hiking experiences in the state at Polipoli State Park, part of the 21,000-acre Kula and Kahikinui Forest Reserve on the slope of Haleakala. At Polipoli, it's hard to believe that you're in Hawaii. First of all, it's cold, even in summer, because the loop is up at 5,300 to 6,200 feet. Second, this former forest of native koa, ohia, and mamane trees, which was overlogged in the 1800s, was reforested in the 1930s with introduced species: pine, Monterey cypress, ash, sugi, red alder, redwood, and several varieties of eucalyptus.

The **Polipoli Loop ★** is an easy 3.5-mile hike that takes about 3 hours; dress warmly for it. To get here, take the Haleakala Highway (Hwy. 37) to Keokea and turn right onto Hwy. 337; after less than ½ mile, turn on Waipoli Road, which climbs swiftly. After 10 miles, Waipoli Road ends at the Polipoli State Park campground. The well-marked trail head is next to the parking lot, near a stand of Monterey cypress; the tree-lined trail offers the best view of the island.

The Polipoli Loop is really a network of three trails: Haleakala Ridge, Plum Trail, and Redwood Trail. After .5 mile of meandering through groves of eucalyptus, blackwood, swamp mahogany, and hybrid cypress, you'll join the Haleakala Ridge Trail, which, about a mile in, joins with the Plum Trail (named for the plums that ripen in June–July). This trail passes through massive redwoods and by an old Conservation Corps bunkhouse and a run-down cabin before joining up with the Redwood Trail, which climbs through Mexican pine, tropical ash, Port Orford cedar, and, of course, redwood.

Camping is allowed in the park with a $5-per-night permit from the **State Parks Division,** 54 S. High St., Room 101, Wailuku, HI 96793 (© **808/984-8109;** www.hawaiistateparks.org/camping/fees.cfm). There's one cabin, which is available by reservation.

Kanaha Beach Park Camping

One of the few Maui County camping facilities on the island is at Kanaha Beach Park, located next to the Kahului Airport. The county has two separate areas for camping: 7 tent sites on the beach and an additional 10 tent sites inland. This well-used park is a favorite of windsurfers, who take advantage of the strong winds that roar across this end of the island. Facilities include a paved parking lot, portable toilets, outdoor showers, barbecue grills, and picnic tables. Camping is open 5 days a week (closed Mon and Tues) and limited to no more than 3 consecutive days. Per-night permits fees are Wednesday and Thursday $5 per adult and $2 per child under 18 years; and Friday through Sunday $8 adults and $3 children under 18 years. Permits can be obtained from the **Maui County Parks and Recreation Department,** 700 Halia Nakoa St., Unit 2, Wailuku, HI 96793 (© **808/270-7389;** www.mauimapp.com/information/campingcounty. htm). The 17 sites book up quickly; reserve your dates far in advance (the county will accept reservations a year in advance).

Waianapanapa State Park ★★

Tucked in a tropical jungle on the outskirts of the little coastal town of Hana is Waianapanapa State Park, a black-sand beach set in an emerald forest.

Hana-Waianapanapa Coast Trail ★ This is an easy 6-mile hike that takes you back in time. Allow 4 hours to walk along this relatively flat trail, which parallels the sea, along lava cliffs and a forest of lauhala trees. The best time to take the hike is either early morning or late afternoon, when the light on the lava and surf makes for great photos. Midday is the worst time; not only is it hot (lava intensifies the heat), but there's also no shade or potable water available. There's no formal trail head; join the route at any point along the Waianapanapa Campground and go in either direction.

Along the trail, you'll see remains of an ancient *heiau* (temple), stands of lauhala trees, caves, a blowhole, and a remarkable plant, naupaka, that flourishes along the beach. Upon close inspection, you'll see that the naupaka has only half-blossoms; according to Hawaiian legend, a similar plant living in the mountains has the other half of the blossoms. One ancient explanation is that the two plants represent never-to-be-reunited lovers: As the story goes, the couple bickered so much that the gods, fed up with their incessant quarreling, banished one lover to the mountain and the other to the sea.

Camping Waianapanapa has 12 cabins and a tent campground. Go for the cabins (reviewed on p. 164), as it rains torrentially here, sometimes turning the campground into a mud-wrestling arena. Tent camping is $5 per night but limited to 5 nights in a 30-day period. Permits are available from the **State Parks Division,** 54 S. High St., Room 101, Wailuku, HI 96793 (© **808/984-8109;** www.hawaiistateparks.org/camping/fees.cfm). Facilities include restrooms, outdoor showers, drinking water, and picnic tables.

Hana: The Hike to Fagan's Cross

This 3-mile hike to the cross erected in memory of Paul Fagan, the founder of Hana Ranch and Hotel Hana-Maui, offers spectacular views of the Hana Coast, particularly at sunset. The uphill trail starts across Hana Highway from the Hotel Hana-Maui. Enter the pastures at your own risk; they're often occupied by glaring bulls and cows with new calves. Watch your step as you ascend this steep hill on a jeep trail across open pastures to the cross and the breathtaking view.

Keanae Arboretum ★

About 47 miles from Kahului, along the Hana Highway and just after the Keanae YMCA Camp (and just before the turnoff to the Keanae Peninsula), is an easy family walk through the Keanae Arboretum, which is maintained by the State Department of Land and Natural Resources, Division of Forestry and Wildlife. The walk, which is just over 2 miles, passes through a forest with both native and introduced plants. Allow 1 to 2 hours, longer if you take time out to swim. Take rain gear and mosquito repellent.

Park at the Keanae Arboretum and pass through the turnstile. Walk along the fairly flat jeep road to the entrance. For .5 mile, you will pass by plants introduced to Hawaii (ornamental timber, pomelo, banana, papaya, hibiscus, and more), all with identifying tags. At the end of this section is a taro patch showing the different varieties that Hawaiians used as their staple crop. After the taro, a 1-mile trail leads through a Hawaiian rainforest. The trail crisscrosses a stream as it meanders through the forest. My favorite swimming hole is just to the left of the first stream crossing, at about 300 feet.

Waihee Ridge ★

This strenuous 3- to 4-mile hike, with a 1,500-foot climb, offers spectacular views of the valleys of the West Maui

A cross erected in memory of Paul Fagan, founder of Hana Ranch and Hotel Hana-Maui.

Keanae Arboretum is an ideal spot for an easy family walk.

Mountains. Allow 3 to 4 hours for the round-trip hike. Pack a lunch, carry water, and pick a dry day, as this area is very wet. There's a picnic table at the summit with great views.

To get here from Wailuku, turn north on Market Street, which becomes the Kahekilii Highway (Hwy. 340) and passes through Waihee. Go just over 2.5 miles from the Waihee Elementary School and look for the turnoff to the Boy Scouts' Camp Maluhia on the left. Turn into the camp and drive nearly a mile to the trail head on the jeep road. About ⅓ mile in, there will be another gate, marking the entrance to the West Maui Forest Reserve. A foot trail, kept in good shape by the State Department of Land and Natural Resources, begins here. The trail climbs to the top of the ridge, offering great views of the various valleys. The trail is marked by a number of switchbacks and can be extremely muddy and wet. In some areas, it's so steep that you have to grab onto the trees and bushes for support. The trail takes you through a swampy area, then up to **Lanilili Peak,** where a picnic table and magnificent views await.

GREAT GOLF

In some circles, Maui is synonymous with golf. The island's world-famous golf courses start at the very northern tip of the island and roll right around to Kaanapali, jumping down to Kihei and Wailea in the south. There are also some lesser-known municipal courses that offer challenging play for less than $100.

Golfers new to Maui should know that it's windy here, especially between 10am and 2pm, when winds of 10 to 15 mph are the norm. Play two to three clubs up or down to compensate for the wind factor. I also recommend bringing extra balls—the rough is thicker here and the wind will pick your ball up and drop it in very unappealing places (like water hazards).

If your heart is set on playing on a resort course, book at least a week in advance. For the ardent golfer on a tight budget, consider playing in the afternoon, when discounted twilight rates are in effect. There's no guarantee you'll get 18 holes in, especially in winter when it's dark by 6pm, but you'll have an opportunity to experience these world-famous courses at half the usual fee.

For last-minute and discount tee times, call **Hawaii Stand by Golf** (✆ **888/645-2665;** www.hawaiistandbygolf.com), which offers savings of up to 50% off greens fees, plus guaranteed tee times for same-day or next-day golfing.

Golf Club Rentals (✆ **808/665-0800;** www.mauiclubrentals.com) has custom-built clubs for men, women, and juniors (both right- and left-handed), which can be delivered island-wide; the rates are $25 a day for steel clubs, a full graphite set is $30 a day.

Central Maui

Waiehu Municipal Golf Course ⛳ This public, oceanside par-72 golf course is like playing two different courses: The first 9 holes, built in 1930, are set along the dramatic coastline, while the back 9 holes, added in 1966, head toward the mountains. It's a fun course that probably won't challenge your handicap. The only hazard here is the wind, which can rip off the ocean and play havoc with your ball. The only hole that can raise your blood pressure is the 511-yard, par-5 4th hole, which is very narrow and very long. Facilities include a snack bar, driving range, practice greens, club rentals, and clubhouse. Because this is a public course, the greens fees are low—but getting a tee time is tough.

Lower Waiehu Beach Rd., Wailuku. ✆ **808/244-5934.** www.co.maui.hi.us/parks/maui/central/ waiehugolfcourse.htm. Greens fees $50 Mon–Fri; $55 Sat–Sun and holidays. From the Kahului Airport, turn right on the Hana Hwy. (Hwy. 36), which becomes Kaahumanu Ave. (Hwy. 32). Turn right at the stoplight at the junction with Waiehu Beach Rd. (Hwy. 340). Go another 1½ miles and you'll see the entrance on your right.

West Maui

Kaanapali Golf Resort ★ Both courses at Kaanapali offer a challenge to all golfers, from high handicappers to near-pros. The par-71, nearly 6,700-yard **Royal Kaanapali Course** is a true Robert Trent Jones, Sr., design: an abundance of wide bunkers; several long, stretched-out tees; and the largest, most contoured greens on Maui. The par-70, 6,400-yard **Kaanapali Kai** is an Arthur Jack Snyder design; although shorter than the North Course, it requires more accuracy on the narrow, hilly fairways. Facilities include a driving range, putting course, and clubhouse with dining. You'll have a better chance of getting a tee time on weekdays.

Off Hwy. 30, Kaanapali. ✆ **808/661-3691.** www.kaanapali-golf.com. Greens fees: Royal Kaanapali Course $235 ($190 for Kaanapali guests), twilight rates $120; Kaanapali Kai Course $195 ($150 for Kaanapali guests), twilight rates $95. At the 1st stoplight in Kaanapali, turn onto Kaanapali Pkwy.; the 1st building on your right is the clubhouse.

Kapalua Resort ★★★ The views alone from these two championship courses are worth the greens fees. The par-72, 6,761-yard **Bay Course** (✆ **808/669-8820**) was designed by Arnold Palmer and Ed Seay. This course is a bit forgiving, with its wide fairways; the greens, however, are difficult to read. The often-photographed 5th overlooks a small ocean cove; even the pros have trouble with this rocky par-3, 205-yard hole. The **Plantation Course** (✆ **808/669-8877**), site of the PGA Mercedes-Benz Championship, is a Ben Crenshaw/Bill Coore design. This par-73, 6,547-yard course, set on a rolling hillside, is excellent for developing your low shots and precise chipping. Facilities for all two courses include locker rooms, a driving range, and excellent dining. Weekdays are your best bet for tee times.

Off Hwy. 30, Kapalua. ✆ **877/KAPALUA** (527-2582). www.kapaluamaui.com. Greens fees: Bay Course $220 ($183 for hotel guests), midday $176, twilight rates $138; Plantation Course $298 ($218 for guests), midday $238, twilight rates $150.

South Maui

Elleair Maui Golf Club Sitting in the foothills of Haleakala, just high enough to afford spectacular ocean vistas from every hole, Elleair (formerly Silversword Golf Club) is a course for golfers who love the views as much as the fairways and greens. It's very forgiving. *Just one caveat:* Go in the morning. Not only is it cooler, but, more important, it's also less windy. In the afternoon, the winds bluster down Haleakala with great gusto. This is a fun course to play, with some challenging holes: The par-5 2nd hole is a virtual minefield of bunkers, and the par-5 8th hole shoots over a swale and then uphill. Facilities include a clubhouse, driving range, putting green, pro shop, and lessons.

1345 Piilani Hwy. (near Lipoa St. turnoff), Kihei. ✆ **808/874-0777.** www.elleairmauigolfclub. com. Greens fees $120; twilight rates $95.

Makena Golf Courses ★★ Here you'll find 36 holes of "Mr. Hawaii Golf"— Robert Trent Jones, Jr.—at its best. Add to that spectacular views: Molokini islet looms in the background, humpback whales gambol offshore in winter, and the tropical sunsets are spectacular. The par-72, 6,876-yard **South Course** has a couple of holes you'll never forget. The view from the par-4 15th, which shoots from an elevated tee 183 yards downhill to the Pacific, is magnificent. The 16th hole has a two-tiered green that's blind from the tee 383 yards away (that is, if you make it past the gully off the fairway). The par-72, 6,823-yard **North Course** is more difficult and more spectacular. The 13th hole, located partway up the mountain, has a view that makes most golfers stop and stare. The next hole is even more memorable: a 200-foot drop between tee and green. Facilities at Makena include a clubhouse, a driving range, two putting greens, a pro shop, lockers, and lessons. Beware of weekend crowds.

On Makena Alanui Dr., just past the Makena Beach and Golf Resort. ✆ **808/891-4000.** www. makenagolf.com. Greens fees $129 and $99 after noon ($99 and $79 for Makena Resort guests); twilight rate $60.

Wailea Golf Club ★★ There are three courses to choose from at Wailea. The **Blue Course,** a par-72, 6,758-yard course designed by Arthur Jack Snyder and dotted with bunkers and water hazards, is for duffers and pros alike. The wide fairways appeal to beginners, while the undulating terrain makes it a course everyone can enjoy. A little more difficult is the par-72, 7,078-yard championship **Gold Course,** with narrow fairways, several tricky dogleg holes, and the classic Robert Trent Jones, Jr., challenges: natural hazards, like lava-rock walls, and native Hawaiian grasses. The **Emerald Course,** also designed by Robert Trent Jones, Jr., is Wailea's newest, with tropical landscaping and a player-friendly design. With 54 holes to play, getting a tee time is slightly easier on weekends than at other resorts, but weekdays are still best (the Emerald Course is usually the toughest to book). Facilities include two pro shops, restaurants, locker rooms, and a complete training facility.

Wailea Alanui Dr. (off Wailea Iki Dr.), Wailea. © **888/328-MAUI** (6284) or 808/875-7450. www.waileagolf.com. Greens fees: $225 ($190–$199 for resort guests); twilight rates $90.

Upcountry Maui

Pukalani Country Club This cool par-72, 6,962-yard course at 1,100 feet offers a break from the resorts' high greens fees, and it's really fun to play. The 3rd hole offers golfers two different options: a tough (especially into the wind) iron shot from the tee, across a gully (yuck!) to the green; or a shot down the side of the gully across a second green into sand traps below. (Most people choose to shoot down the side of the gully; it's actually easier than shooting across a ravine.) High handicappers will love this course, and more experienced players can make it more challenging by playing from the back tees. Facilities include club and shoe rentals, practice areas, lockers, a pro shop, and a restaurant.

360 Pukalani St., Pukalani. © **808/572-1314.** www.pukalanigolf.com. Greens fees for 18 holes (including cart) $79 before 11am; $74 11am–1pm; $60 after 1pm; $27 after 2:30pm. Take the Hana Hwy. (Hwy. 36) to Haleakala Hwy. (Hwy. 37) to the Pukalani exit; turn right onto Pukalani St. and go 2 blocks.

BIKING, HORSEBACK RIDING & OTHER OUTDOOR ACTIVITIES

Biking

It's not even close to dawn, but here you are, rubbing your eyes awake, riding in a van up the long, dark road to the top of Maui's dormant volcano. It's colder than you ever thought possible for a tropical island. The air is thin. The place is crowded, packed with people. You stomp your chilly feet while you wait, sipping hot coffee. Then comes the sun, exploding over the yawning Haleakala Crater, which is big enough to swallow Manhattan whole—it's a mystical moment you won't soon forget. Now you know why Hawaiians named the crater the House of the Sun. But there's no time to linger: Decked out in your screaming-yellow parka, you mount your mechanical steed and test its most important feature, the brakes—because you're about to coast 37 miles down a 10,000-foot volcano.

Cruising down Haleakala, from the lunarlike landscape at the top past flower farms, pineapple fields, and eucalyptus groves, is quite an experience—and you don't have to be an expert cyclist to do it. This is a safe trip that requires some stamina in the colder, wetter winter months but is fun for everyone in the warmer months—the key word being *warmer*. In winter and the rainy season, conditions can be harsh, especially on the top, with below-freezing temperatures and 40 mph winds.

Maui's oldest downhill company is **Maui Downhill ★ (© 800/535-BIKE** [2453] or 808/871-2155; www.mauidownhill.com), which offers a sunrise safari bike tour, including continental breakfast and a stop for lunch (not hosted), starting at $129 ($89 if booked online). If it's all booked up, try **Maui Mountain Cruisers (© 800/232-6264** or 808/871-6014; www.mauimountaincruisers.com), which has sunrise and midday trips for $170 ($135 if booked on the website). **Mountain Riders Bike Tours (© 800/706-7700** or 808/242-9739; www.mountainriders.com) offers sunrise rides for $150 ($120 if booked online) and midday trips for $130 ($104 online). All rates include hotel pickup, transport to the top, bicycle, safety equipment, and continental breakfast (there is a stop

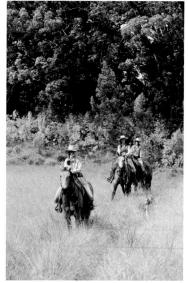

You don't have to be an expert cyclist to tour Haleakala by bike.

Maui offers spectacular adventure rides through rugged ranchlands, into tropical forests, and to remote swimming holes.

for food down the mountain that guests pay for themselves). Wear layers of warm clothing—there may be a 30°F (17°C) change in temperature from the top of the mountain to the ocean. Generally, tour groups will not take riders under 12, but younger children can ride along in the van that accompanies the groups, as can pregnant women.

If you want to avoid the crowds and go down the mountain at your own pace, call **Haleakala Bike Company** (*(C)* **888/922-2453;** www.bikemaui. com), which will outfit you with the latest gear and take you up Haleakala.

Note: Not all tours go to the summit. If you want to start your bike ride at the summit, be sure to confirm. The cheapest trip starts at around the 6,500-foot level (about two-thirds up the mountain). After making sure you are secure on the bike, they will let you ride down by yourself at your own pace. Trips range from $70 to $115; bicycle rentals (from $35 a day) are also available if you'd like to tour other parts of Maui on your own.

Horseback Riding

Maui offers spectacular adventure rides through rugged ranchlands, into tropical forests, and to remote swimming holes. I recommend riding with **Mendes Ranch & Trail Rides ★**, 3530 Kahekili Hwy., 4 miles past Wailuku (*(C)* **808/244-7320;** www.mendesranch.com). The 300-acre Mendes Ranch is a real-life working cowboy ranch that has the essential elements of an earthly paradise—rainbows, waterfalls, palm trees, coral-sand beaches, lagoons, tide pools, a rainforest, and its own volcanic peak (more than a mile high). Allan Mendes, a third-generation wrangler, will take you from the edge of the rainforest out to the sea. On the way, you'll cross tree-studded meadows where Texas longhorns sit in the shade and pass a dusty corral. Allan keeps close watch, turning often in his

MORATORIUM ON bike tours INSIDE HALEAKALA NATIONAL PARK

As we went to press, the National Park Service issued a moratorium on commercial bicycle tours inside Haleakala National Park due to a September 26, 2007, death of a tourist who lost control of her bicycle and struck a van inside the park.

Some operators of Haleakala's "downhill bike tours" have circumvented this moratorium by staging their bicycle tours outside the park's boundaries. There are also a handful of companies who have "road-based" tour permits, which allows them to transport their clients within the park boundaries by van, but does not allow their clients to bike inside the park. If you want to see the sunrise from the Haleakala Crater, be sure to ask your tour operator if it has a road-based permit; otherwise, you will not be able to get inside the park.

The moratorium does not affect private citizens riding their bikes inside the park boundaries. For information on bikeways and maps, get a copy of the *Maui County Bicycle Map,* which has details on road suitability, climate, trade winds, mileage, elevation changes, bike shops, safety tips, and various bicycling routes. The map is available at bike shops all over the island. A great book for mountain bikers who want to venture out on their own is John Alford's *Mountain Biking the Hawaiian Islands,* published by Ohana Publishing (www. bikehawaii.com).

saddle to make sure everyone is happy. He points out flora and fauna and fields questions, but generally just lets you soak up Maui's natural splendor in golden silence. A 2-hour morning or afternoon ride costs $110; add on a barbecue lunch at the corral for an additional $20.

Another one of my favorites is **Piiholo Ranch,** in Makawao (© **866/572-5544** or 808/357-5544; www.piiholo.com). A working cattle ranch owned by the *kamaaina* (longtime resident) Baldwin family, it offers horseback-riding adventures with a variety of different options to suit your ability, rates start at $120 for a 2-hour country ride through a working cattle ranch.

If you're out in Hana, don't pass up **Maui Horseback Tours at Maui Stables ★★**, a mile past Oheo Gulch in Kipahulu (© **808/248-7799;** www. mauistables.com). It offers two rides daily (9:30am and 1pm) through the mountains above Kipahulu Valley—and you get a fantastic historical and cultural tour through the unspoiled landscape, to boot. It is an experience you will not forget. Both rides are $150. If you enjoy your ride, remember to kiss your horse and tip your guide.

For horse lovers looking for the ultimate, check out Frank Levinson's **Maui Horse Whisperer Experience** (© **808/572-6211;** www.mauihorses.com), which includes a seminar on the language of the horse. Prices are $200 for half-day and $300 for full-day workshops. No horse aficionado should pass it up.

HALEAKALA ON HORSEBACK If you'd like to ride down into Haleakala's crater, contact **Pony Express Tours ★** (© **808/667-2200** or 878-6698; www. ponyexpresstours.com), which leads a variety of rides down to the crater floor and back up, from $182 per person. Shorter 1- and 2-hour rides are also offered at Haleakala Ranch, located on the beautiful lower slopes of the volcano, for $95 to $110. If you book via the website, you get 10% off. Pony Express provides well-trained horses and experienced guides, and accommodates all riding levels. You must be at least 10 years old, weigh no more than 230 pounds, and wear long pants and closed-toe shoes.

Spelunking

Don't miss the opportunity to see how the Hawaiian Islands were made by exploring a million-year-old underground lava tube/cave. Chuck Thorne, of **Hana Lava Tube ★** (© 808/248-7308; www.mauicave.com), offers several tours of this unique geological feature. After more than 10 years of leading scuba tours through underwater caves around Hawaii, Chuck discovered some caves on land that he wanted to show visitors. When the land surrounding the largest cave on Maui went on the market in 1996, Chuck snapped it up and started his own tour company. Daily, between 10:30am and 4pm, you can take a self-guided 30- to 45-minute tour for just $12 (free for kids 5 and under).

If you want to combine caving with a tour of Hana, contact **Temptation Tours** (© 808/877-8888; www.temptationtours.com). Its Cave Quest option costs $219, which covers a 1¼-hour cave tour, an air-conditioned van tour from your hotel to Hana, continental breakfast, beachside picnic lunch, and a stop for a swim.

Tennis

Maui has excellent public tennis courts; all are free and available from daylight to sunset (a few are even lit for night play until 10pm). The courts are available on a first-come, first-served basis; when someone's waiting, limit your play to 45 minutes. For a complete list of public courts, call **Maui County Parks and Recreation** (© 808/270-7383). Because most public courts require a wait and are not conveniently located near the major resort areas, most visitors are likely to pay a fee to play at their own hotels. The exceptions to this are in Kihei (which has courts in Kalama Park on South Kihei Rd., and in Waipualani Park on West Waipualani Rd., behind the Maui Sunset condo), in Lahaina (which has courts in Malu'uou o lele Park, at Front and Shaw sts.), and in Hana (which has courts in Hana Park, on the Hana Hwy.).

Private tennis courts are available at most resorts and hotels on the island. The **Kapalua Tennis Garden and Village Tennis Center,** Kapalua Resort (© 808/669-5677; www.kapaluamaui.com), is home to the Kapalua Open, which features the largest purse in the state, on Labor Day weekend. Court rentals are $14 per person for resort guests and $16 per person for nonguests. The staff will match you up with a partner if you need one. In Wailea, try the **Wailea Tennis Club,** 131 Wailea Iki Place (© 808/879-1958; www.wailea tennis.com), with 11 Plexipave courts. Court fees are $15 per player.

8

SEEING THE SIGHTS

A fter a few days of just relaxing on the beach, the itch to explore the rest of Maui sets in: What's on top of Haleakala, looming in the distance? Is the road to Hana really the tropical jungle everyone raves about? What does the inside of a 19th-century whaling boat look like?

There is far more to the Valley Isle than just sun, sand, and surf. Get out and see for yourself the otherworldly interior of a 10,000-foot volcanic crater, watch endangered sea turtles make their way to nesting sites in a wildlife sanctuary, wander back in time to the days when whalers and missionaries fought for the soul of Lahaina, and feel the energy of a thundering waterfall cascade into a serene mountain pool.

GUIDED ISLAND ADVENTURES

The adventures below aren't cheap. However, each one offers such a wonderful opportunity to see Maui from a unique perspective that, depending on your interests, you might make one of them the highlight of your trip. It'll be worth every penny.

Flying High: Helicopter Rides

Only a helicopter can bring you face-to-face with remote sites like Maui's little-known Wall of Tears, near the summit of Puu Kukui in the West Maui Mountains. You'll glide through canyons etched with 1,000-foot waterfalls and over dense rainforests; you'll climb to 10,000 feet, high enough to glimpse the summit of Haleakala, and fly by the dramatic vistas at Molokai.

The first chopper pilots in Hawaii were good ol' boys on their way back from Vietnam—hard-flying, hard-drinking cowboys who cared more about the ride than the scenery. But not anymore. Today's pilots, like the ones at Blue Hawaiian (see below), are an interesting hybrid: part Hawaiian historian, part DJ, part tour guide, and part amusement-ride operator. As you soar through the clouds, you'll learn about the island's flora, fauna, history, and culture.

Among the many helicopter-tour operators on Maui, the best is **Blue Hawaiian Helicopters ★★**, at Kahului Airport (© **800/745-BLUE**

Come face-to-face with Maui's remote sites when you take a helicopter ride over the island.

[2583] or 808/871-8844; www.bluehawaiian.com), which not only takes you on the ride of your life but also entertains, educates, and leaves you with an experience you'll never forget. Blue Hawaiian is also the only helicopter company in the state to have the latest high-tech, environmentally friendly (and quiet) Eco-Star helicopters, specially designed for air-tour operators. Flight times range from 30 to 90 minutes and cost $206 to $413 (if you book on their website, rates start at $139).

ESPECIALLY FOR kids

Taking a Submarine Ride Climb aboard a real sub with **Atlantis Adventures** (© **800/548-6262**), which will take you down into the shallow coastal waters off Lahaina to see plenty of fish (maybe even a shark!). Kids will love it, and you'll stay dry the entire time. See "Going Under: Submarine Rides," below, for details.

Riding the Sugar Cane Train This ride will appeal to small kids as well as train buffs of all ages. A steam engine pulls open passenger cars of the Lahaina/Kaanapali & Pacific Railroad on a 30-minute, 12-mile round-trip through sugar-cane fields between Lahaina and Kaanapali. The conductor sings and calls out the landmarks, and along the way you can see Molokai, Lanai, and the hidden parts of Kaanapali. Tickets are $23 for adults, $16 for kids 3 to 12. Call © **808/661-0080** or visit www.sugar canetrain.com for details.

Tour of the Stars The stars over Kaanapali shine big and bright because the tropical sky is almost entirely free of pollutants and the interference of big-city lights. Amateur astronomers can probe the Milky Way, see Saturn's rings and Jupiter's moons, and scan the Sea of Tranquillity in a 60-minute star search on the world's first recreational computer-driven telescope. This cosmic adventure takes place nightly at the **Hyatt Regency Maui Resort,** 200 Nohea Kai Dr. (© **808/661-1234;** www.maui. hyatt.com/hyatt/hotels/activities;

p. 133), at 8, 9, and 10pm. The cost is $30 for adults and $15 for children 5 to 12 (under 5 are free).

Seeing Sharks, Stingrays & Starfish Hawaii's largest aquarium, the **Maui Ocean Center** (© **808/270-7000;** p. 260), has a range of sea critters—from tiger sharks to tiny starfish—that are sure to fascinate kids of all ages. At this 5-acre facility in Maalaea, visitors can take a virtual walk from the beach down to the ocean depths via the three dozen tanks, countless exhibits, and 100-foot-long main oceanarium.

Getting a Dragonfly's View Kids will think this is too much fun to be educational. Don a face mask and get the dizzying perspective of what a dragonfly sees as it flies over a mountain stream, or watch the tiny *oopu* fish climb up a stream at the **Hawaii Nature Center** (© **808/244-6500;** p. 244) in beautiful Iao Valley, where you'll find some 30 hands-on, interactive exhibits and displays of Hawaii's natural history.

Wailuku

This historic gateway to Iao Valley (see below) is worth a visit, if only for a brief stop at the Bailey House Museum and some terrific shopping (see chapter 9).

Bailey House Museum ★   Missionary and sugar planter Edward Bailey's 1833 home—an architectural hybrid of stones laid by Hawaiian craftsmen and timbers joined in a display of Yankee ingenuity—is a treasure trove of Hawaiiana. Inside, you'll find an eclectic collection, from precontact artifacts like scary temple images, dogtooth necklaces, and a rare lei made of tree-snail shells to latter-day relics like Duke Kahanamoku's 1919 redwood surfboard and a koa-wood table given to President Ulysses S. Grant, who had to refuse it because he couldn't accept gifts from foreign countries. There's also a gallery devoted to a few of Bailey's landscapes, painted from 1866 to 1896, which capture on canvas a Maui we can only imagine today.

2375-A Main St. ⓒ **808/244-3326.** www.mauimuseum.org. Admission $7 adults, $5 seniors, $2 children 7-12, ages 6 and under free. Mon–Sat 10am–4pm.

Iao Valley ★

A couple of miles north of Wailuku, past the Bailey House Museum, where the little plantation houses stop and the road climbs ever higher, Maui's true nature begins to reveal itself. The transition from suburban sprawl to raw nature is so abrupt that most people who drive up into the valley don't realize they're suddenly in a rainforest. The walls of the canyon begin to close around them, and a 2,250-foot-high needlelike rock pricks gray clouds scudding across the blue sky. The moist, cool air and the shade are a welcome comfort after the hot tropic sun. This is Iao Valley, an eroded volcanic caldera in the West Maui Mountains whose great nature, history, and beauty have been enjoyed by millions of people from around the world for more than a century.

The 1833 home of missionary and sugar planter Edward Bailey is now a museum housing artifacts such as scary temple images, dogtooth necklaces, and Duke Kahanamoku's 1919 redwood surfboard.

Iao ("Supreme Light") Valley is 10 miles long and encompasses 4,000 acres. The head of the valley is a broad circular amphitheater where four major streams converge into Iao Stream. At the back of the amphitheater is rain-drenched Puu Kukui, the West Maui Mountains' highest point. No other Hawaiian valley lets you go from sea-coast to rainforest so easily. This peaceful valley, full of tropical plants, rainbows, waterfalls, swimming holes, and hiking trails, is a place of solitude, reflection, and escape for residents and visitors alike.

To get here from Wailuku, take Main Street; then turn right on Iao Valley Road to the entrance to the state park. The park is open daily from 7am to 7pm. Go early in the morning or late in the afternoon, when the sun's rays slant into the valley and create a mystical atmosphere. You can bring a picnic and spend the day, but be prepared at any time for a tropical cloudburst, which often soaks the valley and swells both waterfalls and streams.

The Iao Valley is an eroded volcanic caldera in the West Maui Mountains that is now home to a rainforest.

For information, contact the **Division of State Parks,** 54 S. High St., Room 101, Wailuku, HI 96793 (© **808/984-8109;** www.hawaiistateparks.org/parks/maui). The **Hawaii Nature Center ★**, 875 Iao Valley Rd. (© **808/244-6500;** www.hawaiinaturecenter.org), home of the Iao Valley Nature Center, features interactive exhibits and displays relating the story of Hawaiian natural history; it's an important stop for all who want to explore Iao Valley. Hours are daily from 10am to 4pm. Admission is $6 for adults and $4 for children 4 to 12. **Rainforest walks** are led Monday through Friday at 11:30am and 1:30pm, and Saturday and Sunday at 11am and 2pm. Wear closed-toe shoes (no sandals) suitable for an uneven trail. The cost, which includes a visit to the museum, is $30 for adults and $20 for children 5 and older (younger children not allowed). Book in advance.

You can take the loop trail into the massive green amphitheater of Iao Valley for free. The public walkway crosses the bridge of Iao Stream and continues along the stream itself. The .35-mile paved loop is an easy walk—you can even take your grandmother on this one. A leisurely stroll will allow you to enjoy lovely views of the Iao Needle and the lush vegetation. Others often proceed beyond the state park border and take two trails deeper into the valley, but the trails enter private land, and NO TRESPASSING signs are posted.

The feature known as **Iao Needle** is an erosional remnant consisting of basalt dikes. This phallic rock juts an impressive 2,250 feet above sea level. Youngsters play in **Iao Stream,** a peaceful brook that belies its bloody history. In 1790, King Kamehameha the Great and his men engaged in the battle of Iao Valley to gain control of Maui. When the battle ended, so many bodies blocked

Iao Stream that the battle site was named Kepaniwai, or "damming of the waters." An architectural heritage park of Hawaiian, Japanese, Chinese, Filipino, and New England–style houses stands in harmony by Iao Stream at **Kepaniwai Heritage Garden.** This is a good picnic spot, with plenty of tables and benches. You can see ferns, banana trees, and other native and exotic plants in the **Iao Valley Botanic Garden** along the stream.

LAHAINA & WEST MAUI

Olowalu

Most people drive right by Olowalu, on the Honoapiilani Highway 5 miles south of Lahaina; there's little to mark the spot but a small general store Iowalu ("many hills") was the scene of a bloody massacre in 1790. The Hawaiians stole a skiff from the USS *Eleanora,* took it back to shore here, and burned it for its iron parts. The captain of the ship, Simon Metcalf, was furious and tricked the Hawaiians into sailing out in their canoes to trade with the ship. As the canoes approached, he mowed them down with his cannons, killing 100 people and wounding many others.

Olowalu has great snorkeling around **mile marker 14,** where there is a turtle-cleaning station about 150 to 225 feet out from shore. Turtles line up here to have cleaner wrasses (small bony fish) pick off small parasites.

Historic Lahaina

Located between the West Maui Mountains and the deep azure ocean offshore, Lahaina stands out as one of the few places in Hawaii that has managed to preserve its 19th-century heritage while still accommodating 21st-century guests.

Lahaina.

In ancient times, powerful chiefs and kings ruled this hot, dry, oceanside village. At the turn of the 19th century, after King Kamehameha united the Hawaiian Islands, he made Lahaina the royal capital—which it remained until 1845, when Kamehameha III moved the capital to the larger port of Honolulu.

In the 1840s, the whaling industry was at its peak: Hundreds of ships called into Lahaina every year. The streets were filled with sailors 24 hours a day. Even Herman Melville, who later wrote *Moby-Dick,* visited Lahaina.

Just 20 years later, the whaling industry was waning, and sugar had taken over the town. The Pioneer Sugar Mill Co., which still stands but no longer operates today, reigned over Lahaina for the next 100 years.

Today, the drunken and derelict whalers who wandered through Lahaina's streets in search of bars, dance halls, and brothels have been replaced by hordes of tourists crowding into the small mile-long main section of town in search of boutiques, art galleries, and chic gourmet eateries. Lahaina's colorful past continues to have a profound influence. This is no quiet seaside village, but a vibrant, cutting-edge kind of place, filled with a sense of history—but definitely with its mind on the future.

See chapter 7 for details on the various cruises and outfitters operating out of Lahaina.

Baldwin Home Museum ★ The oldest house in Lahaina, this coral-and-rock structure was built in 1834 by Rev. Dwight Baldwin, a doctor with the fourth company of American missionaries to sail to Hawaii. Like many missionaries, he came to Hawaii to do good—and did very well for himself. After 17 years of service, Baldwin was granted 2,600 acres in Kapalua for farming and grazing. His ranch manager experimented with what Hawaiians called *hala-kahiki,* or pineapple, on a 4-acre plot; the rest is history. The house looks as if Baldwin has just stepped out for a minute to tend a sick neighbor down the street.

Master's Reading Room.

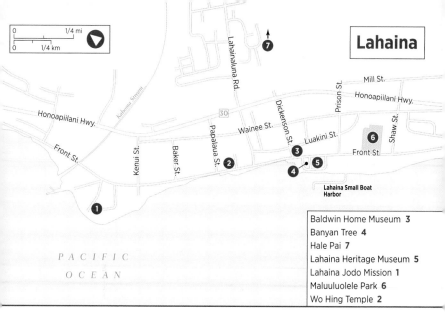

Baldwin Home Museum	**3**
Banyan Tree	**4**
Hale Pai	**7**
Lahaina Heritage Museum	**5**
Lahaina Jodo Mission	**1**
Maluuluolele Park	**6**
Wo Hing Temple	**2**

Next door is the **Master's Reading Room,** Maui's oldest building (included with museum admission). This became visiting sea captains' favorite hangout once the missionaries closed down all of Lahaina's grog shops and banned prostitution. By 1844, when hotels and bars started reopening, it lost its appeal. It's now the headquarters of the **Lahaina Restoration Foundation,** a plucky band of historians who try to keep this town alive and antique at the same time. Stop in and pick up a self-guided walking-tour map, which will take you to Lahaina's most historic sites.

120 Dickenson St. (at Front St.). ℂ **808/661-3262.** www.lahainarestoration.org. Admission $3 per person, $5 couple, children ages 12 and under free. Daily 10am–4pm.

Banyan Tree ☺ Of all the banyan trees in Hawaii, this is the greatest—so big that you can't get it all in your camera's viewfinder. It was only 8 feet tall when it was planted in 1873 by Maui sheriff William O. Smith to mark the 50th anniversary of Lahaina's first Christian mission. Now it's more than 50 feet tall, has 12 major trunks, and shades two-thirds of an acre in Courthouse Square.

At the Courthouse Building, 649 Wharf St.

Hale Pai When the missionaries arrived in Hawaii to spread the word of God, they found the Hawaiians had no written language. They quickly rectified the situation by converting the Hawaiian sounds into a written language. They then built the first printing press in order to print educational materials that would assist them on their mission. Hale Pai was the printing house for the Lahainaluna Seminary, the oldest American school west of the Rockies. Today, Lahainaluna is the public high school for the children of west Maui.

Lahainaluna High School Campus, 980 Lahainaluna Rd. (at the top of the mountain). ℂ **808/661-3262.** www.lahainarestoration.org/halepai. Free admission. Mon–Fri 10am–4pm.

Lahaina Heritage Museum Located on the second floor of the old Lahaina Courthouse, this museum tells the story of the history and culture of Lahaina. In addition to ever-changing exhibits, there are videos, live demonstrations by cultural artisans, "touch and feel" displays, and interactive exhibits.

648 Wharf St. ℂ **808/661-3262.** www.lahainarestoration.org. Free admission. Daily 9am–4pm.

Lahaina Jodo Mission This site has long been held sacred. The Hawaiians called it Puunoa Point, which means "the hill freed from taboo." Once a small village named *Mala* (garden), this peaceful place was a haven for Japanese immigrants, who came to Hawaii in 1868 as laborers for the sugar-cane plantations. They eventually built a small wooden temple to worship here. In 1968, on the 100th anniversary of Japanese presence in Hawaii, a Great Buddha statue (some 12 ft. high and weighing 3½ tons) was brought here from Japan. The immaculate grounds also contain a replica of the original wooden temple and a 90-foot-tall pagoda.

12 Ala Moana St. (off Front St., near the Mala Wharf). ℂ **808/661-4304.** Free admission. Daily during daylight hours.

Maluuluolele Park At first glance, this Front Street park appears to be only a hot, dry, dusty softball field. But under home plate is the edge of Mokuula, where a royal compound once stood more than 100 years ago—it's now buried under

WHERE TO park for free—
OR NEXT TO FREE—IN LAHAINA

Lahaina is the worst place on Maui for parking. The town was created and filled with shops, restaurants, and historic sites before the throngs of tourists (and their cars) invaded. Street parking is hit or miss. You can either drive around the block for hours looking for a free place to park on the street or park in one of the nearly 20 parking lots. I've divided the lots into three classes: free for customers, discount with validation, and pay.

Free for Customers: The three lots on Papalaua Street are all free for customers. The largest is the Lahaina Shopping Center lot, with 2 free hours. Next in size is the Lahaina Center, across the street (which allows 4 hr. free, but you must get validation from a store in the Lahaina Center). The smallest is the Lahaina Square lot at Wainee Street, which offers 2 free hours for customers.

Discount with Validation: Customers of the Wharf Cinema Center, located on Front Street, can get a discount by parking at either of the theater's two lots—both are between Dickenson and Prison streets, but one is on Wainee Street and the other on Luakini Street.

Pay: Lahaina is filled with pay lots ranging from 50¢ for a half-hour to all-day parking for $8 to $10. Pay lots on Front Street are located between Papalaua and Lahainaluna streets, on the corner of Dickenson Street, and underground at the 505 Front Street shopping center. Pay lots on Luakini Street are located near the Prison Street intersection and near the Lahainaluna Road intersection. Lahainaluna Road has several pay lots between Wainee and Front streets. Dickenson Street has three pay lots between Wainee and Luakini streets.

The Great Buddha statue was brought to Lahaina Jodo Mission from Japan.

Colorful decorations on the altar at the Wo Hing Temple.

tons of red dirt and sand. Here, Prince Kauikeaolui, who ascended the throne as King Kamehameha III when he was only 10, lived with the love of his life, his sister, Princess Nahienaena. Missionaries took a dim view of incest, which was acceptable to Hawaiian nobles in order to preserve the royal bloodline. Torn between love for her brother and the new Christian morality, Nahienaena grew despondent and died at the age of 21. King Kamehameha III, who reigned for 29 years—longer than any other Hawaiian monarch—presided over Hawaii as it went from kingdom to constitutional monarchy, and as power over the islands began to shift from island nobles to missionaries, merchants, and sugar planters. Kamehameha died in 1854 at the age of 39. In 1918, his royal compound, containing a mausoleum and artifacts of the kingdom, was demolished and covered with dirt to create a public park. The baseball team from Lahainaluna School now plays games on the site of this royal place, still considered sacred to many Hawaiians.
Front and Shaw sts.

Wo Hing Temple ★ The Chinese were among the various immigrants brought to Hawaii to work in the sugar-cane fields. In 1909, several Chinese workers formed the Wo Hing society, a chapter of the Chee Kun Tong society, which dates from the 17th century. In 1912, they built this social hall for the Chinese community. Completely restored, the Wo Hing Temple contains displays and artifacts on the history of the Chinese in Lahaina. Next door in the old cookhouse is a theater with movies of Hawaii taken by Thomas Edison in 1898 and 1903.
858 Front St. (btw. Wahie Lane and Papalaua St.). ℂ **808/661-3262.** www.lahainarestoration. org. Admission $2 per person, children ages 12 and under free. Sat–Thurs 10am–4pm; Fri 1–8pm.

START: **Front and Dickenson streets.**
FINISH: **Same location.**
TIME: **About an hour.**

Back when "there was no God west of the Horn," Lahaina was the capital of Hawaii and the Pacific's wildest port. Today it's a milder version of its old self—mostly a hustle-bustle of whale art, timeshares, and "Just Got Lei'd" T-shirts. I'm not sure the rowdy whalers would be pleased. But if you look hard, you'll still find the historic port town they loved, filled with the kind of history that inspired James Michener to write his best-selling epic novel *Hawaii.*

Members of the Lahaina Restoration Foundation have worked for 3 decades to preserve Lahaina's past. They have labeled a number of historic sites with brown-and-white markers; below, I provide explanations of the significance of each site as you walk through Lahaina's past.

From the Kahului Airport, take the Kuihelani Highway (Hwy. 38) to the intersection of Honoapiilani Highway (Hwy. 30), where you turn left. Follow Honoapiilani Highway to Lahaina and turn left on Lahainaluna Road. When Lahainaluna Road ends, make a left on Front Street. Dickenson Street is a block down (see the box on parking, above).

Begin your tour at the:

1 Master's Reading Room

This coral-and-stone building looks just as it did in 1834, when Rev. William Richards and Rev. E. Spaulding convinced the whaling-ship captains that they needed a place for the ships' masters and captains, many of whom traveled with their families, to stay while they were ashore. The bottom floor was used as a storage area for the mission; the top floor, from which you could see the ships at anchor in the harbor, was for the visiting ships' officers.

Next door is the:

2 Baldwin Home

Harvard-educated physician Rev. Dwight Baldwin, with his wife of just a few weeks, sailed to Hawaii from New England in 1830. Baldwin was first assigned to a church in Waimea, on the Big Island, and then to Lahaina's Wainee Church in 1838. He and his family lived in this house until 1871. The Baldwin Home and the Master's Reading Room are the oldest standing buildings in Lahaina, made from thick walls of coral and hand-milled timber. Baldwin also ran his medical office and his missionary activities out of this house. (See Baldwin Home Museum, p. 246, for information on hours and admission.)

On the other side of the Baldwin Home is the former site of the:

3 Richards House

The open field is empty today, but it represents the former home of Lahaina's first Protestant missionary, Rev. William Richards. Richards went on to become the chaplain, teacher, and translator to Kamehameha III. He was

1 Master's Reading Room
2 Baldwin Home
3 Richards House
4 Taro Patch
5 Hauola Stone
6 Brick Palace
7 Former *Carthaginian* site
8 Pioneer Inn
9 Banyan Tree
10 Courthouse
11 Fort
12 Canal
13 Government Market
14 Holy Innocents Episcopal Church
15 Hale Piula
16 Maluuluolele Park
17 Wainee Church
18 Wainee Cemetery
19 Hongwanji Mission
20 David Malo's Home
21 Old Prison
22 Episcopal Cemetery
23 Hale Aloha
24 Buddhist Church
25 Luakini Street

also instrumental in drafting Hawaii's constitution and acted as the king's envoy to the United States and England, seeking recognition of Hawaii as an independent nation. After his death in 1847, he was buried in the Wainee Churchyard.

From here, cross Front Street and walk toward the ocean, with the Lahaina Public Library on your right and the green Pioneer Inn on your left, until you see the:

4 Taro Patch

The lawn in front of the Lahaina Library was once a taro patch stretching back to the Baldwin Home. The taro plant was a staple of the Hawaiian

The Baldwin Home Museum.

diet: The root was used to make poi, and the leaves were used in cooking. At one time Lahaina looked like a Venice of the tropics, with streams, ponds, and waterways flooding the taro fields. As the population of the town grew, the water was siphoned off for drinking use.

The Pioneer Inn.

Walk away from the Lahaina Harbor toward the edge of the lawn, where you'll see the:

5 Hauola Stone

Hawaiians believed that certain stones placed in sacred places had the power to heal. *Kahuna* (priests) of medicine used stones like this to help cure illnesses.

Turn around and walk back toward the Pioneer Inn; look for the concrete depression in the ground, which is all that's left of the:

6 Brick Palace

This structure was begun in 1798 as the first Western-style building in Hawaii. King Kamehameha I had this 20 x 40-foot, two-story brick structure built for his wife, Queen Kaahumanu (who is said to have preferred a grass-thatched house nearby). Inside, the walls were constructed of wood and the windows were glazed glass. Kamehameha I lived here from 1801 to 1802, when he was building his war canoe, *Peleleu*, and preparing to invade Kauai. A handmade stone sea wall surrounded the palace to protect it from the surf. The building stood for 70 years. In addition to being a royal compound, it was also used as a meetinghouse, storeroom, and warehouse.

Behind you, dockside of the loading pier of the Lahaina Harbor, is the:

7 Former Site of the Carthaginian

This was once the site of a replica of a 19th-century brig that carried commerce back and forth to Hawaii, and, until 2004, served as a museum and exhibit of 19th-century boating and whaling. The *Carthaginian*, which had been plagued with numerous maintenance problems for years, has been removed from the slip, and the Lahaina Restoration Foundation is in the process of finding a replacement ship.

Directly opposite the *Carthaginian* site is the:

8 Pioneer Inn

Lahaina's first hotel was the scene of some wild parties at the start of the 20th century. George Freeland, of the Royal Canadian Mounted Police, tracked a criminal to Lahaina and then fell in love with the town. He built the hotel in 1901 but soon discovered that Lahaina wasn't the tourist mecca it is today. To make ends meet, Freeland built a movie theater, which was wildly successful. The Pioneer Inn remained the only hotel in all of west Maui until the 1950s. You can stay at this restored building today (p. 129).

From the Pioneer Inn, cross Hotel Street and walk along Wharf Street, which borders the harbor. On your left is the:

9 Banyan Tree

This ancient tree has witnessed decades of luau, dances, concerts, private chats, public rallies, and resting sojourners under its mighty boughs. It's hard to believe that this huge tree was only 8 feet tall when it was planted here.

Continue along Wharf Street. Near the edge of the park is the:

10 Courthouse

In 1858, a violent windstorm destroyed about 20 buildings in Lahaina, including Hale Piula, which served as the courthouse and palace of King Kamehameha III. It was rebuilt immediately, using the stones from the previous building. It served not only as courthouse, but also as custom house, post office, tax collector's office, and government offices. Upstairs on the second floor is the Lahaina Heritage Museum, with exhibits on the history and culture of Lahaina (free admission; open daily 9am–5pm).

Continue down Wharf Street to Canal Street. On the corner are the remains of the:

11 Fort

This structure once covered an acre and had 20-foot-high walls. In 1830, some whalers fired a few cannonballs into Lahaina in protest of Rev. William Richards's meddling in their affairs. (Richards had convinced Gov. Hoapili to create a law forbidding the women of Lahaina from swimming out to greet the whaling ships.) The fort was constructed from 1831 to 1832 with coral blocks taken from the ocean where the Lahaina Harbor sits today. As a further show of strength, cannons were placed along the waterfront, where they remain today. Historical accounts seem to scoff at the "fort," saying it appeared to be more for show than for force. It was later used as a prison, until it was finally torn down in the 1850s; its stones were used for construction of the new prison, Hale Paahao (see no. 21 below).

Cross Canal Street to the:

12 Canal

Unlike Honolulu with its natural deepwater harbor, Lahaina was merely a roadstead with no easy access to the shore. Whalers would anchor in deep water offshore, then board smaller boats (which they used to chase down

The Banyan Tree is the site of decades of luau, dances, concerts, and more.

and harpoon whales) to make the passage over the reef to shore. If the surf was up, coming ashore could be dangerous. In the 1840s, the U.S. consular representative recommended digging a canal from one of the freshwater streams that ran through Lahaina and charging a fee to the whalers who wanted to obtain fresh water. In 1913, the canal was filled in to construct Canal Street.

Up Canal Street is the:

13 Government Market

A few years after the canal was built, the government built a thatched marketplace with stalls for Hawaiians to sell goods to the sailors. Merchants quickly took advantage of this marketplace and erected drinking establishments, grog shops, and other pastimes of interest nearby. Within a few years, this entire area became known as "Rotten Row."

Make a right onto Front Street and continue down the street, past Kamehameha III Elementary School. Across from the park is:

14 Holy Innocents Episcopal Church

When the Episcopal missionaries first came to Lahaina in 1862, they built a church across the street from the current structure. In 1909, the church moved to its present site, which was once a thatched house built for the daughter of King Kamehameha I. The present structure, built in 1927, features unique paintings of a Hawaiian Madonna and birds and plants endemic to Hawaii, executed by DeLos Blackmar in 1940.

Continue down Front Street, and at the next open field, look for the white stones by the ocean, marking the former site of the "iron-roofed house" called:

15 Hale Piula

In the 1830s, the two-story stone building with a large surrounding courtyard was built for King Kamehameha III. However, the king preferred sleeping in a small thatched hut nearby, so the structure was never really completed. In the 1840s, Kamehameha moved his capital to Honolulu and wasn't using Hale Piula, so it became the local courthouse. The windstorm of 1858, which destroyed the courthouse on Wharf Street (see no. 10 above), also destroyed the iron-roofed house. The stones from Hale Piula were used to rebuild the courthouse on Wharf Street.

Continue down Front Street; across from the 505 Front Street complex is:

16 Maluuluolele Park

This sacred spot to Hawaiians is now the site of a park and ball field. This used to be a village, Mokuhinia, with a sacred pond that was the home of a *moo* (a spirit in the form of a lizard), which the royal family honored as their personal guardian spirit. In the middle of the pond was a small island, Mokuula, home to Maui's top chiefs. After conquering Maui, Kamehameha I claimed this sacred spot as his own; he and his two sons, Kamehameha II and III, lived here when they were in Lahaina. In 1918, in the spirit of progress, the pond was drained and the ground leveled for a park.

Make a left onto Shaw Street and then another left onto Wainee Street. On the left side, just past the cemetery, is:

17 Wainee Church

This was the first stone church built in Hawaii (1828–32). At one time the church could seat some 3,000 people, albeit tightly packed together, complete with "calabash spittoons" for the tobacco-chewing Hawaiian chiefs and the ship captains. That structure didn't last long—the 1858 windstorm that destroyed several buildings in Lahaina also blew the roof off the original church, knocked over the belfry, and picked up the church's bell and deposited it 100 feet away. The structure was rebuilt, but that too was destroyed—this time by Hawaiians protesting the 1894 overthrow of the monarchy. Again the church was rebuilt, and again it was destroyed—by fire in 1947. The next incarnation of the church was destroyed by yet another windstorm in 1951. The current church has been standing since 1953. Be sure to walk around to the back of the church: The row of palm trees on the ocean side includes some of the oldest palm trees in Lahaina.

Wander next door to the first Christian cemetery in Hawaii:

18 Waihee Cemetery

Established in 1823, this cemetery tells a fascinating story of old Hawaii, with graves of Hawaiian chiefs, commoners, sailors, and missionaries and their families (infant mortality was high then). Enter this ground with respect, because Hawaiians consider it sacred—many members of the royal family were buried here, including Queen Keopuolani, who was wife of King Kamehameha I, mother of kings Kamehameha II and III, and the first Hawaiian baptized as a Protestant. Among the other graves are those of Rev. William Richards (the first missionary in Lahaina) and Princess Nahienaena (sister of kings Kamehameha II and III).

Continue down Waihee Street to the corner of Luakini Street and the:

19 Hongwanji Mission

The temple was originally built in 1910 by members of Lahaina's Buddhist sect. The current building was constructed in 1927, housing a temple and language school. The public is welcome to attend the New Year's Eve celebration, Buddha's birthday in April (see "Maui, Molokai & Lanai Calendar of Events," p. 61), and O Bon Memorial Services in August.

Continue down Wainee Street. Just before the intersection with Prison Street, look for the historical marker for:

20 David Malo's Home

Although no longer standing, the house that once stood here was the home of Hawaii's first scholar, philosopher, and well-known author. Educated at Lahainaluna School, his book on ancient Hawaiian culture, *Hawaiian Antiquities,* is considered *the* source on Hawaiiana today. His alma mater celebrates David Malo Day every year in April in recognition of his contributions to Hawaii.

Cross Prison Street. On the corner of Prison and Waihee is the:

21 Old Prison

The Hawaiians called the prison Hale Paahao ("stuck in irons house"). Sailors who refused to return to their boats at sunset used to be arrested and taken to the old fort (see no. 11 above). In 1851, however, the fort physician told the government that sleeping on the ground at night made the prisoners ill, costing the government quite a bit of money to treat them—so the Kingdom of Hawaii used the prisoners to build a prison from the coral block of the old fort. Most prisoners here had terms of a year or less (those with longer terms were shipped off to Honolulu) and were convicted of crimes like deserting ship, being drunk, or working on Sunday. Today, the grounds of the prison have a much more congenial atmosphere, and are rented out to community groups for parties.

Continue down Waihee Street, just past Waianae Place, to the small:

22 Episcopal Cemetery

This burial ground tells another story in Hawaii's history. During the reign of King Kamehameha IV, his wife, Queen Emma, formed close ties with British royalty. She encouraged Hawaiians to join the Anglican Church after asking the Archbishop of Canterbury to form a church in Hawaii. This cemetery contains the burial sites of many of those early Anglicans.

Next door is:

23 Hale Aloha

This "house of love" was built in 1858 by Hawaiians in "commemoration of God's causing Lahaina to escape the smallpox," while it decimated Oahu in 1853, carrying off 5,000 to 6,000 souls. The building served as a church and school until the turn of the 20th century, when it fell into disrepair.

Turn left onto Hale Street and then right onto Luakini Street to the:

24 Buddhist Church

This green wooden Shingon Buddhist temple is very typical of myriad Buddhist churches that sprang up all over the island when the Japanese laborers were brought to work in the sugar-cane fields. Some of the churches were little more than elaborate false "temple" fronts on existing buildings.

On the side of Village Galleries, on the corner of Luakini and Dickenson streets, is the historical marker for:

25 Luakini Street

"Luakini" translates as a *heiau* (temple) where the ruling chiefs prayed and where human sacrifices were made. This street received its unforgettable name after serving as the route for the funeral procession of Princess Harriet Nahienaena, sister of kings Kamehameha II and III. The princess was a victim of the rapid changes in Hawaiian culture. A convert to Protestantism, she had fallen in love with her brother at an early age. Just 20 years earlier, their relationship would have been nurtured in order to preserve the purity of the royal bloodlines. The missionaries, however, frowned on brother and sister marrying. In August 1836, the couple had a son, who lived only a few short hours. Nahienaena never recovered, and died in December of that same year (the king was said to mourn her death for years, frequently visiting her grave at the Waihee Cemetery; see no. 18 above). The route of her funeral procession through the breadfruit and koa trees to the cemetery became known as "Luakini," in reference to the gods "sacrificing" the beloved princess.

Turn left on Dickenson and walk down to Front Street, where you'll be back at the starting point.

Winding Down 🍺

Ready for some refreshment after your stroll? Head to **Maui Swiss Cafe**, 640 Front St. (𝄐 **808/661-6776**), for tropical smoothies, great espresso, and affordable snacks. Sit in the funky garden area, or get your drink to go and wander over to the sea wall to watch the surfers.

A Whale of a Place in Kaanapali

Heading north from Lahaina, the next resort area you'll come to is Kaanapali, which boasts a gorgeous stretch of beach. If you haven't seen a real whale yet, go to **Whalers Village,** 2435 Kaanapali Pkwy., an oceanfront shopping center that has adopted the whale as its mascot. You can't miss it: A huge, almost life-size metal sculpture of a mother whale and two nursing calves greets you. A few more steps, and you're met by the looming, bleached-white skeleton of a 40-foot sperm whale; it's pretty impressive.

On the second floor of the mall is the **Whalers Village Museum** (𝄐 **808/661-5992;** www.whalersvillage.com/mallinfo.htm), which celebrates the "Golden Era of Whaling" from 1825 to 1860. Harpoons and scrimshaw are on display; the museum has even re-created the cramped quarters of a whaler's seagoing vessel. It's open during mall hours, daily from 10am to 6pm; admission is free.

The Scenic Route from West Maui to Central or Upcountry Maui: The Kahekili Highway

The usual road from west Maui to Wailuku is the Honoapiilani Highway (Hwy. 30), which runs along the coast and then turns inland at Maalaea. But those in search of a back-to-nature driving experience should go the other way, along the **Kahekili Highway (Hwy. 340)** ★. (*Highway* is a bit of a euphemism for this paved but somewhat precarious narrow road; check your rental-car agreement before you head out—

Whalers Village has adopted the whale as its mascot.

some companies don't allow their cars on this road. If it is raining or has been raining, skip this road due to mud and rock slides.) The road was named after the great chief Kahekili, who built houses from the skulls of his enemies.

You'll start out on the Honoapiilani Highway (Hwy. 30), which becomes the Kahekili Highway (Hwy. 340) after Honokohau, at the northernmost tip of the island. Around this point are **Honolua Bay** ★ and **Mokuleia Bay** ★, which have been designated as Marine Life Conservation Areas (the taking of fish, shells, or anything else is prohibited).

From this point, the quality of the road deteriorates, and you may share the way with roosters, goats, cows, and dogs. The narrow road weaves along for the next 20 miles, following an ancient Hawaiian coastal footpath and showing you the true wild nature of Maui. These are photo opportunities from heaven: steep ravines, rolling pastoral hills, tumbling waterfalls, exploding blowholes, crashing surf, jagged lava coastlines, and a tiny Hawaiian village straight off a postcard.

Halekii and Pihanakalani Heiau sit on a hill with a commanding view of central Maui and Haleakala.

Kahakuloa village church.

Just before **mile marker 20,** look for a small turnoff on the mauka ("*mow-kah*," meaning toward the mountain) side of the road, just before the guard-rail starts. Park here and walk across the road, and on your left you'll see a spouting **blowhole.** In winter, this is an excellent spot to look for whales.

About 3 miles farther along the road, you'll come to a wide turnoff providing a great photo op: a view of the jagged coastline down to the crashing surf.

Less than half a mile farther along, just before **mile marker 16,** look for the POHAKU KANI sign, marking the huge, 6 × 6-foot **bell-shaped stone.** To "ring" the bell, look on the side facing Kahakuloa for the deep indentations, and strike the stone with another rock.

Along the route, nestled in a crevice between two steep hills, is the picturesque village of **Kahakuloa ★** ("the tall hau tree"), with a dozen weather-worn houses, a church with a red-tile roof, and vivid green taro patches. From the northern side of the village, you can look back at the great view of Kahakuloa, the dark boulder beach, and the 636-foot Kahakuloa Head rising in the background.

At various points along the drive are artists' studios nestled into the cliffs and hills. One noteworthy stop is the **Kaukini Gallery,** which features work by more than two dozen local artists, with lots of gifts and crafts to buy in all price ranges. (You may also want to stop here to use one of the few restrooms along the drive.)

When you're approaching Wailuku, stop at the **Halekii and Pihanakalani Heiau,** which visitors rarely see. To get here from Wailuku, turn north from Main Street onto Market Street. Turn right onto Mill Street and follow it until it ends; then make a left on Lower Main Street. Follow Lower Main until it ends at Waiehu Beach Road (Hwy. 340) and turn left. Turn left on Kuhio Street and again at the first left onto Hea Place, and drive through the gates and look for the Hawaii Visitors Bureau marker.

These two *heiau,* built in 1240 from stones carried up from the Iao Stream below, sit on a hill with a commanding view of central Maui and Haleakala. Kahekili, the last chief of Maui, lived here. After the bloody battle at Iao Stream, Kamehameha I reportedly came to the temple here to pay homage to the war god, Ku, with a human sacrifice. Halekii ("house of images") is made of stone walls with a flat grassy top, whereas Pihanakalani ("gathering place of supernatural beings") is a pyramid-shaped mount of stones. If you sit quietly nearby (never walk on any *heiau*—it's considered disrespectful), you'll see that the view alone explains why this spot was chosen.

SOUTH MAUI
Maalaea

At the bend in the Honoapiilani Highway (Hwy. 30), Maalaea Bay runs along the south side of the isthmus between the West Maui Mountains and Haleakala. This is the windiest area on Maui: Trade winds blowing between the two mountains are funneled across the isthmus, and by the time they reach Maalaea, gusts of 25 to 30 mph are not uncommon.

This creates ideal conditions for **windsurfers** out in Maalaea Bay. Surfers are also seen just outside the small boat harbor in Maalaea, which has one of the fastest breaks in the state.

Maui Ocean Center ★★ ☺ This 5-acre facility houses the largest aquarium in the state and features one of Hawaii's largest predators: the tiger shark. Exhibits are geared toward the residents of Hawaii's ocean waters. As you walk past the three dozen or so tanks and numerous exhibits, you'll slowly descend from the "beach" to the deepest part of the ocean, without ever getting wet. Start at the surge pool, where you'll see shallow-water marine life like spiny urchins and cauliflower coral; then move on to the reef tanks, turtle pool, touch pool (with starfish and urchins), and eagle-ray pool before reaching the star of the show: the 100-foot-long, 600,000-gallon main tank featuring tiger, gray, and white-tip sharks, as well as tuna, surgeonfish, triggerfish, and numerous others. A walkway goes right through the tank, so you'll be surrounded on three sides by marine creatures. A very cool place, and well worth the time. Some new additions are a hammerhead exhibit and the Shark Dive Maui Program (Mon, Wed, and Fri); if you're a certified scuba diver, you can plunge into the aquarium with sharks,

The turtle pool at the Maui Ocean Center.

stingrays, and tropical fish while friends and family watch safely from the other side of the glass. *Helpful hint:* Buy your tickets online to avoid the long admission lines.

At the Maalaea Harbor Village, 192 Maalaea Rd. (the triangle btw. Honoapiilani Hwy. and Maalaea Rd.). ℭ **808/270-7000.** www.mauioceancenter.com. Admission $26 adults, $23 seniors, $19 children 3–12. Daily 9am–5pm (until 6pm July–Aug).

Kihei

Capt. George Vancouver "discovered" Kihei in 1778, when it was only a collection of fishermen's grass shacks on the hot, dry, dusty coast (hard to believe, eh?). A **totem pole** stands today where he's believed to have landed, across from the Aston Maui Lu Resort, 575 S. Kihei Rd. Vancouver sailed on to what later became British Columbia, where a great international city and harbor now bear his name.

West of the junction of Piilani Highway (Hwy. 31) and Mokulele Highway (Hwy. 350) is **Kealia Pond National Wildlife Preserve** (ℭ **808/875-1582**), a 700-acre U.S. Fish and Wildlife wetland preserve where endangered Hawaiian stilts, coots, and ducks hang out and splash. These ponds work two ways: as bird preserves and as sedimentation basins that keep the coral reefs from silting from runoff. You can take a self-guided tour along a boardwalk dotted with interpretive signs and shade shelters, through sand dunes, and around ponds to Maalaea Harbor. The boardwalk starts at the outlet of Kealia Pond on the ocean side of North Kihei Road (near mile marker 2 on Piilani Hwy.). Among the Hawaiian water birds seen here are the black-crowned high heron, Hawaiian coot, Hawaiian duck, and Hawaiian stilt. There are also shorebirds like sanderling, Pacific golden plover, ruddy turnstone, and wandering tattler. From July to December, the hawksbill turtle comes ashore here to lay her eggs. *Tip:* If you're bypassing Kihei, take the Piilani Highway (Hwy. 31), which parallels strip-mall-laden South Kihei Road, and avoid the hassle of stoplights and traffic.

Wailea

The dividing line between arid Kihei and artificially green Wailea is distinct. Wailea once had the same kiawe-strewn, dusty landscape as Kihei until Alexander & Baldwin Inc. (of sugarcane fame) began developing a resort here in the 1970s (after piping water from the other side of the island to the desert terrain of Wailea). Today, the manicured 1,450 acres of this affluent resort stand out like an oasis along the normally dry leeward coast.

A totem pole stands where Capt. George Vancouver is believed to have landed when he "discovered" Kihei in 1778.

The Wailea coastal nature trail stretches between the Fairmont Kea Lani and the grass of the Wailea Beach Marriott.

The Keawalai Congregational Church.

The best way to explore this golden resort coast is to rise with the sun and head for Wailea's 1.5-mile **coastal nature trail** ★, stretching between the Fairmont Kea Lani and the green grass of the Wailea Beach Marriott. It's a great morning walk on a serpentine path that meanders uphill and down past native plants, old Hawaiian habitats, and a billion dollars' worth of luxury hotels. You can pick up the trail at any of the resorts or from clearly marked SHORELINE ACCESS points along the coast. The best time to go is when you first wake up; by midmorning, the coastal trail is often clogged with joggers and later with beachgoers. As the path crosses several bold black-lava points, it affords vistas of islands and ocean. Benches allow you to pause and contemplate the view across Alalakeiki Channel, where you may see whales in season. Sunset is another good time to hit the trail.

Makena

A few miles south of Wailea, the manicured coast changes over to the wilderness of *Makena* (abundance). In the 1800s, cattle were driven down the slope from upland ranches and loaded onto boats that waited to take them to market. Now **Makena Landing** ★ is a beach park with boat-launching facilities, showers, toilets, and picnic tables. It's great for snorkeling and for launching kayaks bound for La Pérouse Bay and Ahihi-Kinau Natural Preserve.

From the landing, go south on Makena Road; on the right is **Keawalai Congregational Church** (✆ 808/879-5557), built in 1855 with walls 3 feet thick. Surrounded by ti leaves, which by Hawaiian custom provide protection, and built of lava rock with coral used as mortar, this Protestant church sits on its own cove with a gold-sand beach. It always attracts a Sunday crowd for its 9:30am Hawaiian-language service. Take time to wander through the cemetery; you'll see some tombstones with a ceramic picture of the deceased on them, which is an old custom.

A little farther south on the coast is **La Pérouse Monument ★**, a pyramid of lava rocks that marks the spot where French explorer Adm. Comte de la Pérouse set foot on Maui in 1786. The first Westerner to "discover" the island, he described the "burning climate" of the leeward coast, observed several fishing villages near Kihei, and sailed on into oblivion, never to be seen again; some believe he may have been eaten by cannibals in what is now Vanuatu. To get here, drive south past Puu Olai to Ahihi Bay, where the road turns to gravel. Go another 2 miles along the coast to La Pérouse Bay; the monument sits amid a clearing in black lava at the end of the dirt road.

La Pérouse Monument.

The rocky coastline and sometimes rough seas contribute to the lack of appeal for water activities here; **hiking** opportunities, however, are excellent. Bring plenty of water and sun protection, and wear hiking boots that can withstand walking on lava. From La Pérouse Bay, you can pick up the old King's Highway trail, which at one time circled the island. Walk along the sandy beach at La Pérouse and look for the trail indentation in the lava, which leads down to the lighthouse at the tip of Cape Hanamanioa, about a .75-mile round-trip. Or you can continue on the trail as it climbs up the hill for 2 miles, then ventures back toward the ocean, where there are quite a few old Hawaiian home foundations and rocky coral beaches.

HOUSE OF THE SUN: HALEAKALA NATIONAL PARK ★★★

At once forbidding and compelling, Haleakala ("House of the Sun") National Park is Maui's main natural attraction. More than 1.3 million people a year ascend the 10,023-foot-high mountain to peer down into the crater of the world's largest dormant volcano. (Haleakala is officially considered active, even though it has not rumbled since 1790.) That hole would hold Manhattan: 3,000 feet deep, 7½ miles long by 2½ miles wide, and encompassing 19 square miles.

The Hawaiians recognized the mountain as a sacred site. Ancient chants tell of Pele, the volcano goddess, and one of her siblings doing battle on the crater floor where *Kawilinau* (Bottomless Pit) now stands. Commoners in ancient Hawaii didn't spend much time here, though. The only people allowed into this sacred area were the *kahuna,* who took their apprentices to live for periods of time in this intensely spiritual place. Today, New Agers also revere Haleakala as one of the earth's powerful energy points, and even the U.S. Air Force has a not-very-well-explained presence here.

> ## Impressions
>
> "There are few enough places in the world that belong entirely to themselves. The human passion to carry all things everywhere, so that every place is home, seems well on its way to homogenizing our planet, save for the odd unreachable corner. Haleakala crater is one of those corners."
>
> —Barbara Kingsolver, the *New York Times*

But there's more to do here than simply stare into a big black hole: Just going up the mountain is an experience in itself. Where else on the planet can you climb from sea level to 10,000 feet in just 37 miles, or a 2-hour drive? The snaky road passes through big, puffy cumulus clouds to offer magnificent views of the isthmus of Maui, the West Maui Mountains, and the Pacific Ocean.

Many drive up to the summit in predawn darkness to watch the **sunrise over Haleakala;** writer Mark Twain called it "the sublimest spectacle" of his life. Others take a trail ride inside the bleak lunar landscape of the wilderness inside the crater or coast down the 37-mile road from the summit on a bicycle with special brakes (see "Biking," p. 234, and "Horseback Riding," p. 235). Hardy adventurers hike and camp inside the crater's wilderness (see "Hiking & Camping," p. 222). Those bound for the interior should bring their survival gear, for the terrain is raw, rugged, and punishing—not unlike the moon. However, if you choose to experience Haleakala National Park, it will prove memorable—guaranteed.

Just the Facts

Haleakala National Park extends from the summit of Mount Haleakala into the crater, down the volcano's southeast flank to Maui's eastern coast, beyond Hana. There are actually two separate and distinct destinations within the park: **Haleakala Summit** and the **Kipahulu** coast (see "Tropical Haleakala: Oheo Gulch at Kipahulu," p. 288). The summit gets all the publicity, but Kipahulu draws crowds, too—it's lush, green, and tropical, and home to Oheo Gulch (also known as Seven Sacred Pools). No road links the summit and the coast; you have to approach them separately, and you need at least a day to see each place.

WHEN TO GO At the 10,023-foot summit, weather changes fast. With wind chill, temperatures can be freezing any time of year. Summer can be dry and warm; winter can be wet, windy, and cold. Before you go, get current weather conditions from the park (℃ 808/572-4400) or the **National Weather Service** (℃ 866/944-5025;   www.prh. noaa.gov/hnl).

From sunrise to noon, the light is weak, but the view is usually free of clouds. The best time for photos is in the afternoon, when the sun lights the crater and clouds are few. Go on full-moon nights for spectacular viewing. However, even when the forecast is promising, the weather at Haleakala can change in an instant—be prepared.

Nene, a Hawaiian goose.

Haleakala National Park

Legend

- (i) Information
- △ Campground
- ▲ Primitive campsite
- 🏕 Picnic area
- 📞 Public telephone
- 🏠 Ranger station
- ♿ Wheelchair accessible

Haleakala Visitor Center **5**
Halemauu Trailhead **2**
Hosmer Grove **1**
Leleiwi Overlook **3**
Kalahaku Overlook **4**
Kaupo Trail **8**

Kipahulu Visitor Center **11**
Paliku Cabin & Campground **7**
Pipiwai Trail **10**
Sliding Sands Trailhead **5**
Summit (10,023 feet) **6**
Waimoku Falls **9**

The lower half of the Kaupo Trail is on private land. Permission to pass is extended to hikers as a courtesy.

A horseback ride in Haleakala's crater.

ACCESS POINTS Haleakala Summit is 37 miles, or a 1½- to 2-hour drive, from Kahului. To get here, take Hwy. 37 to Hwy. 377 to Hwy. 378. For details on the drive, see "The Drive to the Summit," below. Pukalani is the last town for water, food, and gas.

The **Kipahulu** section of Haleakala National Park is on Maui's east end near Hana, 60 miles from Kahului on Hwy. 36 (Hana Hwy.). Due to traffic and rough road conditions, plan on 4 hours for the one-way drive from Kahului. For complete information, see "Driving the Road to Hana," below. Hana is the only nearby town for services, water, gas, food, and overnight lodging; some facilities may not be open after dark.

At both entrances to the park, the admission fee is $5 per person or $10 per car, good for a week of unlimited entry.

INFORMATION, VISITOR CENTERS & RANGER PROGRAMS For information before you go, contact **Haleakala National Park,** P.O. Box 369, Makawao, HI 96768 (© **808/572-4400;** www.nps.gov/hale).

One mile from the park entrance, at 7,000 feet, is **Haleakala National Park Headquarters** (© **808/572-4400**), open daily from 7:30am to 4pm. Stop here to pick up information on park programs and activities, get camping permits, and, occasionally, see a nene (Hawaiian goose)—one or more are often here to greet visitors. Restrooms, a pay phone, and drinking water are available.

The **Haleakala Visitor Center,** open daily from sunrise to 3pm, is near the summit, 11 miles past the park entrance. It offers a panoramic view of the volcanic landscape, with photos identifying the various features, and exhibits that explain the area's history, ecology, geology, and volcanology. Park staff members are often on hand to answer questions. Restrooms and water are available.

Rangers offer excellent, informative, and free naturalist talks at 9:30, 10:30, and 11:30am daily in the summit building. For information on hiking (including guided hikes) and camping, including cabins and campgrounds in the wilderness itself, see "Hiking & Camping" (p. 222).

The Drive to the Summit

If you look on a Maui map, almost in the middle of the part that resembles a torso, there's a black wiggly line that looks like this: WWWWW. That's **Hwy. 378,** also known as **Haleakala Crater Road**—one of the fastest-ascending roads in the world. This grand corniche has at least 33 switchbacks; passes through numerous climate zones; goes under, in, and out of clouds; takes you past rare silversword plants and endangered Hawaiian geese sailing through the clear, thin air; and offers a view that extends for more than 100 miles.

Going to the summit takes 1½ to 2 hours from Kahului. No matter where you start out, you'll follow Hwy. 37 (Haleakala Hwy.) to Pukalani, where you'll pick up Hwy. 377 (which is also Haleakala Hwy.), which you'll take to Hwy. 378. Along the way, expect fog, rain, and wind. You may encounter stray cattle and downhill bicyclists. Fill up your gas tank before you go—the only gas available is 27 miles below the summit at Pukalani. There are no facilities beyond the ranger stations, so bring your own food and water.

Remember, you're entering a high-altitude wilderness area. Some people get dizzy due to the lack of oxygen; you might also suffer lightheadedness, shortness of breath, nausea, severe headaches, flatulence, or dehydration. People with asthma, pregnant women, heavy smokers, and those with heart conditions should be especially careful in the rarefied air. Bring water and a jacket or a blanket, especially if you go up for sunrise. Or you might want to go up to the summit for sunset, which is also spectacular.

As you go up the slopes, the temperature drops about 3° every 1,000 feet, so the temperature at the top can be 30° cooler than it was at sea level. Come prepared with sweaters, jackets, and rain gear.

At the **park entrance,** you'll pay an entrance fee of $10 per car (or $5 per person without a vehicle). About a mile from the entrance is **park headquarters,** where an endangered **nene,** or Hawaiian goose, may greet you with its unique call. With its black face, buff cheeks, and partially webbed feet, the gray-brown bird looks like a small Canada goose with zebra stripes; it brays out "nay-nay" (thus its name), doesn't migrate, and prefers lava beds to lakes. The unusual goose clings to a precarious existence on these alpine slopes. Vast populations of more than 25,000 once inhabited Hawaii, but hunters, pigs, feral cats

 The Legend of the House of the Sun

According to ancient legend, Haleakala got its name from a very clever trick that the demigod Maui pulled on the sun. Maui's mother, the goddess Hina, complained one day that the sun sped across the sky so quickly that her tapa cloth couldn't dry.

Maui, known as a trickster, devised a plan. The next morning he went to the top of the great mountain and waited for the sun to poke its head above the horizon. Quickly, Maui lassoed the sun, bringing its path across the sky to an abrupt halt.

The sun begged Maui to let go, and Maui said he would on one condition: that the sun slow its trip across the sky to give the island more sunlight. The sun assented. In honor of this agreement, the Hawaiians call the mountain Haleakala, or "House of the Sun."

To this day, the top of Haleakala has about 15 minutes more sunlight than the communities on the coastline below.

and dogs, and mongooses preyed on the nene; coupled with habitat destruction, these predators nearly caused its extinction. By 1951, there were only 30 left. Now protected as Hawaii's state bird, the wild nene on Haleakala number fewer than 250—and the species remains endangered.

Beyond headquarters are **two scenic overlooks** on the way to the summit; stop at Leleiwi on the way up and Kalahaku on the way back down, if only to get out, stretch, and get accustomed to the heights. Take a deep breath, look around, and pop your ears. If you feel dizzy or drowsy, or get a sudden headache, consider turning around and going back down.

Leleiwi Overlook ★ is just beyond mile marker 17. From the parking area, a short trail leads you to a panoramic view of the lunarlike crater. When the clouds are low and the sun is in the right place, usually around sunset, you may experience a phenomenon known as the "Specter of the Brocken"—you can see a reflection of your shadow, ringed by a rainbow, in the clouds below. It's an optical illusion caused by a rare combination of sun, shadow, and fog that occurs in only three places on the planet: Haleakala, Scotland, and Germany.

Two miles farther along is **Kalahaku Overlook ★**, the best place to see a rare **silversword.** You can turn into this overlook only when you are descending from the top. The silversword is the punk of the plant world, its silvery bayonets displaying tiny purple bouquets—like a spacey artichoke with attitude. This botanical wonder proved irresistible to humans, who gathered them in gunnysacks for Chinese potions and British specimen collections, and just for the sheer thrill of having something so rare. Silverswords grow only in Hawaii, take from 4 to 50 years to bloom, and then, usually between May and October, send up a 1- to 6-foot stalk with a purple bouquet of sunflower-like blooms. They're very rare, so don't even think about taking one home.

The Leleiwi Overlook affords a panoramic view of the lunarlike crater of Haleakala.

Silverswords only grow in Hawaii and take from 4 to 50 years to bloom.

Continue on, and you'll quickly reach the **Haleakala Visitor Center ★**, which offers spectacular views. You'll feel as if you're at the edge of the earth. But don't turn around here: The actual summit's a little farther on, at **Puu Ulaula Overlook ★** (also known as Red Hill), the volcano's highest point, where you'll find a mysterious cluster of buildings officially known as Haleakala Observatories, but unofficially called **Science City.** If you go up for sunrise, the building at Puu Ulaula Overlook, a triangle of glass that serves as a windbreak, is the best viewing spot. After the daily miracle of sunrise—the sun seems to rise out of the vast crater (hence the name "House of the Sun")—you can see all the way across Alenuihaha Channel to the often-snowcapped summit of Mauna Kea on the Big Island.

MAKING YOUR DESCENT When driving down the Haleakala Crater Road, be sure to put your car in low gear. That way, you won't destroy your brakes by riding them the whole way down.

MORE IN UPCOUNTRY MAUI

Come upcountry and discover a different side of Maui: On the slopes of Haleakala, cowboys, planters, and other country people make their homes in serene, neighborly communities like **Makawao** and **Kula,** a world away from the bustling beach resorts. Even if you can't spare a day or two in the cool upcountry air, there are some sights that are worth a look on your way to or from the crater. Shoppers and gallery hoppers might want to spend more time here; see chapter 9 for details.

On the slopes of Haleakala, Maui's farmers have been producing vegetables since the 1800s. In fact, during the gold rush in California, the Hawaiian farmers in Kula shipped so many potatoes that it was nicknamed Nu Kaleponi, a sort of pidgin Hawaiian pronunciation of "New California." In the late 1800s, Portuguese and Chinese immigrants, who had fulfilled their labor contracts with the sugar-cane companies, moved to this area, drawn by the rural agricultural lifestyle. That lifestyle continues today, among the fancy gentlemen's farms that have sprung up in the past 2 decades. Kula continues to grow its well-known onions, lettuce, tomatoes, carrots, cauliflower, and cabbage. It is also a major source of cut flowers for the state: Most of Hawaii's proteas, as well as nearly all the carnations used in leis, come from Kula.

To experience a bit of the history of Kula, turn off the Kula Highway (Hwy. 37) onto Lower Kula Road. Well before the turnoff, you'll see a white octagonal building with a silver roof, the **Holy Ghost Catholic Church** (✆ **808/878-1091**). Hawaii's only eight-sided church, it was built between 1884 and 1897 by Portuguese immigrants. It's worth a stop

More than 700 native and exotic plants reside at Kula Botanical Garden.

STOP & SMELL THE lavender

While in the upcountry Kula region, stop by **Alii Kula Lavender,** 1100 Waipoli Rd., Kula (✆ **808/878-3004;** www.alii kulalavender.com), which grows several different varieties of lavender, so one species of lavender is always in bloom. There are great tours to take while you're here. On the 30-minute **Lavender Garden Walking Tour** (daily at 9:30, 10:30, and 11:30am, and 1 and 2:30pm for $12 per person), you're served lavender herb tea with a lavender scone and given a garden and studio tour. My favorite, the **Combo Tour** ($37 per person,24-hr. advance reservation) combines the walking tour with a lunch basket, which includes a choice of lavender beverage, a delicious lavender-seasoned chicken wrap, lavender gourmet chips, fresh fruit, and a decadent lavender brownie. Seasonal events offered range from a fabulous Valentine's Day Luncheon to a woven-lavender-wand-making workshop in the summer. Be sure to stop by the store and look over the culinary products (lavender seasonings, dressings, scones, honey, jelly, and teas), bath and body goodies (lotions, soaps, bubble baths, bath gels), aromatherapy (oil, candles, eye pillows), and other items (T-shirts, gift baskets, and dried lavender).

to see the hand-carved altar and works of art for the Stations of the Cross, with inscriptions in Portuguese.

Kula Botanical Garden ★ You can take a self-guided, informative, leisurely stroll through more than 700 native and exotic plants—including three unique collections of orchids, proteas, and bromeliads—at this 5-acre garden. It offers a good overview of Hawaii's exotic flora in one small, cool place.

Hwy. 377, south of Haleakala Crater Rd. (Hwy. 378), ½ mile from Hwy. 37. © **808/878-1715.** www.kulabotanicalgarden.com. Admission $10 adults, $3 children 6–12, under 6 years free. Daily 9am–4pm.

Tedeschi Vineyards and Winery ★ On the southern shoulder of Haleakala is **Ulupalakua Ranch,** a 20,000-acre spread once owned by legendary sea captain James Makee, celebrated in the Hawaiian song and dance "Hula O Makee." Wounded in a Honolulu waterfront brawl in 1843, Makee moved to Maui and bought Ulupalakua. He renamed it Rose Ranch, planted sugar as a cash crop, and grew rich. Still in operation, the ranch is now home to Maui's only winery, established in 1974 by Napa vintner Emil Tedeschi, who began growing California and European grapes here and producing serious still and sparkling wines, plus a silly wine made of pineapple juice. The rustic grounds are the perfect place for a picnic. Pack a basket before you go, and enjoy it with a bottle of Tedeschi wine.

Across from the winery are the remains of the three smokestacks of the **Makee Sugar Mill,** built in 1878. You may do a double take at the people lounging on the front porch. On closer

A sign points the way to Tedeschi Vineyards and Winery.

 Touring the Surfing Goat Dairy Farm

Just beyond the sugar-cane fields, on the slopes of Haleakala, lies the **Surfing Goat Dairy,** 3661 Omaopio Rd., Kula (© **808/878-2870;** www.surfinggoat-dairy.com). Some 140 dairy goats blissfully graze the 42 acres and contribute the milk for 24 different cheeses, which are made every day. If you have kids in tow, they will love the 2-hour **Grand Dairy Tour** ($25; but call for dates, they do it about twice a month)—they get to be a goat herder for a day and even try to milk a goat. They can also play with the kids—goat kids, that is. Meanwhile,

mom and dad can learn how to make cheese and sample the different varieties made on the premises. Grand Dairy Tours are scheduled several times each month; call for information. If you don't have a lot of time, drop by for the 20-minute casual dairy tour (Mon–Sat 10am–5pm, Sun 10am–1pm) for just $7 a person. Or check out the Evening Chores and Milking Tour, Tuesday, Thursday and Saturday at 3:15pm for $12 per person. Be sure to sample the goat cheeses (off-the-charts terrific) and buy a bar or two of goat-milk soap.

inspection they are not "people," but the work of Maui artist Reems Mitchell who carved the mannequins on the front porch of the Ulupalakua Ranch Store: a Filipino with his fighting cock, a cowboy, a farmhand, and a sea captain, all representing the people of Maui's history.

Off Hwy. 37 (Kula Hwy.). ☏ **877/878-6058.** www.mauiwine.com. Free tastings daily 10am–5pm. Free tours at 10:30am, 1:30pm, and 3pm.

DRIVING THE ROAD TO HANA ★★★

Top down, sunscreen on, radio tuned to a little Hawaiian music on a Maui morning: It's time to head out to Hana along the Hana Highway (Hwy. 36), a wiggle of a road that runs along Maui's northeastern shore. The drive takes at least 3 hours from Lahaina or Kihei—but plan to take all day. Going to Hana is about the journey, not the destination.

There are wilder roads, steeper roads, and more dangerous roads, but in all of Hawaii, no road is more celebrated than this one. It winds 50 miles past taro patches, magnificent seascapes, waterfall pools, botanical gardens, and verdant rainforests, and ends at one of Hawaii's most beautiful tropical places.

The outside world discovered the little village of Hana in 1926, when the narrow coastal road, carved by pickax-wielding convicts, opened. The mud-and-gravel road, often subject to landslides and washouts, was paved in 1962, when tourist traffic began to increase; now more than 1,000 cars traverse the road each day, according to storekeeper Harry Hasegawa. That equals about 500,000 people a year, which is way too many. Go at the wrong time, and you'll be stuck in a bumper-to-bumper rental-car parade—peak traffic hours are midmorning and midafternoon year-round, especially on weekends.

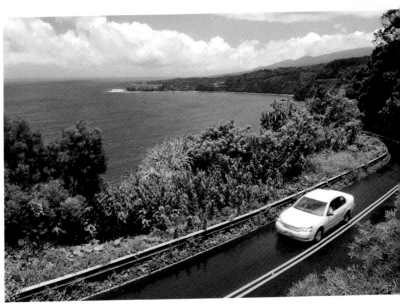

The Hana Highway runs along Maui's northeastern shore.

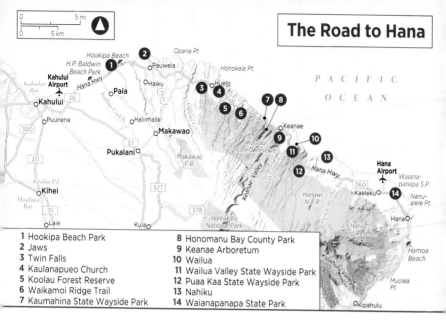

The Road to Hana

1 Hookipa Beach Park	8 Honomanu Bay County Park	
2 Jaws	9 Keanae Arboretum	
3 Twin Falls	10 Wailua	
4 Kaulanapueo Church	11 Wailua Valley State Wayside Park	
5 Koolau Forest Reserve	12 Puaa Kaa State Wayside Park	
6 Waikamoi Ridge Trail	13 Nahiku	
7 Kaumahina State Wayside Park	14 Waianapanapa State Park	

In the rush to "do" Hana in a day, most visitors spin around town in 10 minutes flat and wonder what all the fuss is about. It takes time to take in Hana, play in the waterfalls, sniff the tropical flowers, hike to bamboo forests, and marvel at the spectacular scenery; stay overnight if you can.

However, if you really must do the Hana Highway in a day, go just before sunrise and return after sunset: On a full-moon night, the sea and the waterfalls glow in soft white light, with mysterious shadows appearing in the jungle. And you'll have the road almost to yourself on the way back.

Tips: Forget your mainland road manners. Practice aloha. Give way at one-lane bridges, wave at oncoming motorists, and let the big guys in 4 x 4s have the right of way—it's just common sense, brah. If the guy behind you blinks his lights, let him pass. And don't honk your horn—in Hawaii, it's considered rude.

THE JOURNEY BEGINS IN PAIA Before you even start out, fill up your gas tank. Gas in Paia is expensive (even by Maui standards), and it's the last place for gas until you get to Hana, some 42 miles, 54 bridges, and 600 hairpin turns down the road.

A surfer takes a walk in Paia, a once-thriving sugar-mill town.

The former plantation village of Paia was once a thriving sugar-mill town. The mill is still here, but the population shifted to Kahului in the 1950s when subdivisions opened there, leaving Paia to shrivel up and die. But the town refused to give up and has proven its ability to adapt to the times. Now chic eateries and trendy shops stand next door to the mom-and-pop establishments that have been serving generations of Paia customers.

Plan to be here early, around 7am, when **Charley's ★**, 142 Hana Hwy. (*©* **808/579-9453**), opens. Enjoy a big, hearty breakfast for a reasonable price.

After you leave Paia, just before the bend in the road, you'll pass the Kuau Mart on your left; a small general store, it's the only reminder of the sugar-plantation community of **Kuau.** The road then bends into an S-turn; in the middle of the S is the entrance to **Mama's Fish House,** marked by a restored boat with Mama's logo on the side. Just past the truck on the ocean side is the entrance to Mama's parking lot and adjacent small sandy cove in front of the restaurant. It's not good for swimming—ocean access is over very slippery rocks into strong surf—but the beach is a great place to sit and soak up some sun.

WINDSURFING MECCA A mile from Mama's, just before mile marker 9, is a place known around the world as one of the greatest windsurfing spots on the planet, **Hookipa Beach Park ★**. *Hookipa* ("hospitality") is where the top-ranked windsurfers come to test themselves against the forces of nature: thunderous surf and forceful wind. World-championship contests are held here (see "Maui, Molokai & Lanai Calendar of Events," p. 61), but on nearly every windy afternoon (the board surfers have the waves in the morning), you can watch dozens of windsurfers twirling and dancing in the wind like colorful butterflies. To watch the windsurfers, do not stop on the

Surfers battle the mammoth waves at Jaws.

Twin Falls.

highway, but go past the park and turn left at the entrance on the far side of the beach. You can either park on the high grassy bluff or drive down to the sandy beach and park alongside the pavilion. Facilities include restrooms, a shower, picnic tables, and a barbecue area.

INTO THE COUNTRY Past Hookipa Beach, the road winds down into **Maliko (Budding) Gulch** at mile marker 10. At the bottom of the gulch, look for the road on your right, which will take you out to **Maliko Bay.** Take the first right, which goes under the bridge and past a rodeo arena (scene of competitions by the Maliko Roping Club in summer) and on to the rocky beach. There are no facilities here except a boat-launch ramp. In the 1940s, Maliko had a thriving community at the mouth of the bay, but its residents rebuilt farther inland after a strong tidal wave wiped it out. The bay may not look that special, but if the surf is up, it's a great place to watch the waves.

Back on the Hana Highway, as you leave Maliko Gulch, around mile marker 11, you'll pass through the rural area of **Haiku,** where you'll see banana patches, cane grass blowing in the wind, and forests of guava trees, avocados, *kukui* trees, palms, and Christmas berry. Just before mile marker 15 is the **Maui-Grown Market and Deli** (© **808/572-1693**), a good stop for drinks or snacks for the ride.

JAWS If it's winter and the waves are up (like 60 ft. or so), here's your chance to watch tow-in surfing off Pauwela Point at an area known as Jaws (because the waves will chew you up), where expert tow-in surfers (who use a personal watercraft to pull a surfer into waves that are bigger than what could be caught by traditional paddling) battle the mammoth waves. To get here, make a small detour off the Hana Highway by turning left at Hahana Road, between mile markers 13 and 14. After the paved road ends, the dirt road is private property (Maui Land & Pine), so you may have to hike in about a mile and a half to get close to the ocean. Practice aloha, do not park in the pineapple fields, and do not pick or even touch the pineapples. Be very careful along the oceanside cliffs.

At mile marker 16, the curves begin, one right after another. Slow down and enjoy the view of bucolic rolling hills, mango trees, and vibrant ferns. After mile marker 16, the road is still called the Hana Highway, but the number changes from Hwy. 36 to Hwy. 360, and the mile markers go back to 0.

A GREAT PLUNGE ALONG THE WAY A dip in a waterfall pool is everybody's tropical-island fantasy. A great place to stop is **Twin Falls ★**, at mile marker 2. Just before the wide, concrete bridge, pull over on the mountain side and park. There is a NO TRESPASSING sign on the gate. Although you will see several cars parked in the area and a steady line of people going up to the falls, be aware that this is private property and trespassing is illegal in Hawaii. If you decide that you want to "risk it," you will walk about 3 to 5 minutes to the waterfall and pool, or continue on another 10 to 15 minutes to the second, larger waterfall and pool (don't go in if it has been raining).

HIDDEN HUELO Just before mile marker 4 on a blind curve, look for a double row of mailboxes on the left side by the pay phone. Down the road lies a hidden Hawaii of an earlier time, where an indescribable sense of serenity prevails. Hemmed in by Waipo and Hoalua bays is the remote community of **Huelo ★**, which means "tail end, last." This fertile area once supported a population of 75,000; today only a few hundred live among the scattered homes here, where a handful of B&Bs and exquisite vacation rentals cater to a trickle of travelers (see p. 159 for my recommendations).

The only reason Huelo is even marked is the historic 1853 **Kaulanapueo Church.** Reminiscent of New England architecture, this coral-and-cement church, topped with a plantation-green steeple and a gray tin roof, is still in use, although services are held just once or twice a month. It still has the same austere interior of 1853: straight-backed benches, a no-nonsense platform for the minister, and no distractions on the walls to tempt you from paying attention to the sermon. Next to the church is a small graveyard, a personal history of this village in concrete and stone.

KOOLAU FOREST RESERVE After Huelo, the vegetation seems more lush, as though Mother Nature had poured Miracle-Gro on everything. This is the edge of the **Koolau Forest Reserve.** *Koolau* means "windward," and this certainly is one of the greatest examples of a lush windward area: The coastline here gets about 60 to 80 inches of rain a year, as well as runoff from the 200 to 300 inches that falls from farther up the mountain. You'll see trees laden with guavas, as well as mangoes, java plums, and avocados the size of softballs. The spiny, long-leafed plants are *hala* trees, which the Hawaiians used for weaving baskets, mats, and even canoe sails.

From here on out, there's a waterfall (and one-lane bridge) around nearly every turn in the road, so drive slowly and be prepared to stop and yield to oncoming cars.

DANGEROUS CURVES About ½ mile after mile marker 6, there's a sharp U-curve in the road, going uphill. The road is practically one-lane here, with a brick wall on one side and virtually no maneuvering room. Sound your horn at the start of the U-curve to let approaching cars know you're coming. Take this curve, as well as the few more coming up in the next several miles, very slowly.

Just before mile marker 7 is a forest of waving **bamboo.** The sight is so spectacular that drivers are often tempted to take their eyes off the

Kaulanapueo Church, from 1853, is notable for its New England-style architecture.

road. Be very cautious. Wait until just after mile marker 7, at the **Kaaiea Bridge** (literally "breathtaking view") and stream below, to pull over and take a closer look at the hand-hewn stone walls. Then turn around to see the vista of bamboo.

A GREAT FAMILY HIKE At mile marker 9, there's a small state wayside area with restrooms, picnic tables, and a barbecue area. The sign says KOOLAU FOREST RESERVE, but the real attraction here is the **Waikamoi Ridge Trail ★**, an easy .75-mile loop (*Waikamoi* means "waters of the king"). The start of the trail is just behind the QUIET TREES AT WORK sign. The well-marked trail meanders through eucalyptus, ferns, and *hala* trees.

SAFETY WARNING I used to recommend another waterfall, **Puohokamoa Falls,** at mile marker 11, but not anymore. Unfortunately, what was once a great thing has been overrun by hordes of not-so-polite tourists. You will see cars parking on the already dangerous, barely two-lane Hana Highway ½ mile before the waterfall. Slow down after mile marker 10. As you get close to mile marker 11, the highway becomes a congested one-lane road due to visitors parking on this narrow stretch. Don't add to the congestion by trying to park: There are plenty of other great waterfalls; just drive slowly and safely through this area.

CAN'T-MISS PHOTO OPS Just past mile marker 12 is the **Kaumahina State Wayside Park ★** (*kaumahina* means "moon rise"). This is not only a good pit stop (restrooms are available) and a wonderful place for a picnic (with tables and a barbecue area), but also a great vista point. The view of the rugged coastline makes an excellent shot—you can see all the way down to the jutting Keanae Peninsula.

Another mile and a couple of bends in the road, and you'll enter the Honomanu Valley, with its beautiful bay. To get to the **Honomanu Bay County Beach Park ★**, look for the turnoff on your left, just after mile marker 14, located at a point in the road where you begin your ascent up the other side of the valley. The rutted dirt-and-cinder road takes you down to the rocky black-sand beach. There are no facilities here. Because of the strong rip currents offshore, swimming is best in the stream inland from the ocean. You'll consider the drive down worthwhile as you stand on the beach, well away from the ocean, and turn to look back on the steep cliffs covered with vegetation.

MAUI'S BOTANICAL WORLD Farther along the winding road, between mile markers 16 and 17, is a cluster of bunkhouses composing the YMCA Camp Keanae. A ¼-mile down is the **Keanae Arboretum ★★**, where the region's botany is divided into three parts: native forest, introduced forest, and traditional Hawaiian plants, food, and medicine. You can swim in the pools of Piinaau Stream, or press on along a mile-long trail into Keanae Valley, where a lovely tropical rainforest waits at the end (see "Hiking & Camping" in chapter 7).

KEANAE PENINSULA The old Hawaiian village of **Keanae ★★** ("the mullet") stands out against the Pacific like a place time forgot. Here, on an old lava flow graced by an 1860 stone church and swaying palms, is one of the last coastal enclaves of native Hawaiians. They still grow taro in patches and pound it into poi, the staple of the old Hawaiian diet. And they still pluck opihi (limpet) from tide pools along the jagged coast and cast throw-nets at schools of fish.

The turnoff to the Keanae Peninsula is on the left, just after the arboretum. The road passes by farms as it hugs the peninsula. Where the road bends, there's a small beach where fishermen gather to catch dinner. A ¼ mile farther is the **Keanae Congregational Church** (✆ **808/248-8040**),

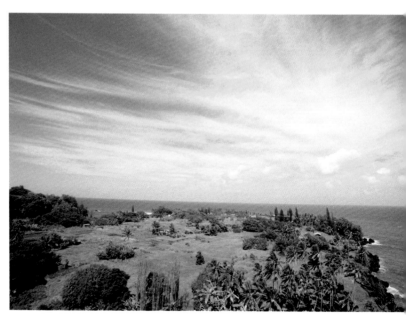

The Keanae lookout.

built in 1860 of lava rocks and coral mortar, standing in stark contrast to the green fields surrounding it. Beside the church is a small beachfront park, with false *kamani* trees against a backdrop of black lava and a roiling turquoise sea.

For an experience in an untouched Hawaii, follow the road until it ends. Park by the white fence and take the short 5-minute walk along the shoreline over the black lava. Continue along the footpath through the tall California grass to the black rocky beach, separating the freshwater stream, **Pinaau,** which winds back into the Keanae Peninsula, nearly cutting it off from the rest of Maui. This is an excellent place for a picnic and a swim in the cool waters of the stream. There are no facilities here, so be sure you carry everything out with you and use restrooms before you arrive. As you make your way back, notice the white PVC pipes sticking out of the rocks—they're fishing-pole holders for fishermen, usually hoping to catch ulua.

ANOTHER PHOTO OP: KEANAE LOOKOUT Just past mile marker 17 is a wide spot on the ocean side of the road, where you can see the entire Keanae Peninsula's checkerboard pattern of green taro fields and its ocean boundary etched in black lava. Keanae was the result of a postscript eruption of Haleakala, which flowed through the Koolau Gap and down Keanae Valley and added this geological punctuation to the rugged coastline.

FRUIT & FLOWER STANDS Around mile marker 18, the road widens; you'll start to see numerous small stands selling fruit or flowers. Many of these stands work on the honor system: You leave your money in the basket and select your purchase. I recommend stopping at **Uncle Harry's,** which you'll find just after the Keanae School around mile marker 18. His family sells a variety of fruits and juices here Monday through Saturday from 9am to 4pm.

WAILUA Just after Uncle Harry's, look for the Wailua Road off on the left. This will take you through the hamlet of homes and churches of Wailua, which also contains a shrine depicting what the community calls a "miracle." Behind the pink **St. Gabriel's Church** is the smaller, blue-and-white **Coral Miracle Church,** home of the **Our Lady of Fatima Shrine.** According to legend, in 1860 the men of this village were building a church by diving for coral to make the stone. But the coral offshore was in deep water and the men could only come up with a few pieces at a time, making the construction of the church an arduous project. A freak storm hit the area and deposited the coral from the deep on a nearby beach. The Hawaiians gathered what they needed and completed the church. After the church was completed, another freak storm hit the area and swept all the remaining coral on the beach back out to sea.

If you look back at Haleakala from here, on your left you can see the spectacular, near-vertical **Waikani Falls.** On the remainder of the dead-end road is an eclectic collection of old and modern homes. Turning around at the road's end is very difficult, so I suggest you just turn around at the church and head back for the Hana Highway.

Back on the Hana Highway, just before mile marker 19, is the **Wailua Valley State Wayside Park ★** (*wailua* means "two waters"), on the right side of the road. Climb up the stairs for a view of the Keanae Valley, waterfalls, and Wailua Peninsula. On a really clear day, you can see up the mountain to the Koolau Gap.

Fruit and flowers stands dot the roadside along the road to Hana.

For a better view of the Wailua Peninsula, continue down the road about ¼ mile. There's a pull-off area with parking on the ocean side.

PUAA KAA STATE WAYSIDE PARK You'll hear this park long before you see it, about halfway between mile markers 22 and 23. The sound of waterfalls provides the background music for this small park area with restrooms, a phone, and a picnic area. In fact, *Puaa Kaa* translates as "open laughter." There's a well-marked path to the falls and to a swimming hole. Ginger plants are everywhere: Pick some flowers and put them in your car so that you can travel with that sweet smell.

OLD NAHIKU Just after mile marker 25 is a narrow 3-mile road leading from the highway, at about 1,000 feet elevation, down to sea level—and to the remains of the old Hawaiian community of **Nahiku.** At one time this was a thriving village of thousands; today, the population has dwindled to fewer than 100—including a few Hawaiian families, but mostly extremely wealthy mainland residents who jet in for a few weeks at a time to their luxurious vacation homes. At the turn of the 20th century, this site saw brief commercial activity as home of the Nahiku Rubber Co., the only commercial rubber plantation in the United States. You can still see rubber trees along the Nahiku Road. However, the amount of rainfall, coupled with the damp conditions, could not support the commercial crop; the plantation closed in 1912, and Nahiku was forgotten until the 1980s, when multimillionaires "discovered" the remote and stunningly beautiful area.

At the end of the road, you can see the remains of the old wharf from the rubber-plantation days. Local residents come down here to shoreline fish; there's a small picnic area off to the side. Dolphins are frequently seen in the bay.

HANA AIRPORT After mile marker 31, a small sign points to the Hana Airport, down Alalele Road on the left. Commuter airline **Pacific Wings**

(📞 **888/575-4546;** www.pacificwings.com) offers four flights daily to and from Hana (from Kahului), with connecting flights from Kahului and traveling on to Honolulu. **Be warned:** There is no public transportation in Hana and there is no car rental service in Hana anymore.

WAIANAPANAPA STATE PARK ★★ At mile marker 32, just on the outskirts of Hana, shiny black-sand Waianapanapa Beach appears like a vivid dream, with bright-green jungle foliage on three sides and cobalt-blue water lapping at its feet. The 120-acre park on an ancient *aa* lava flow includes sea cliffs, lava tubes, arches, and the beach, plus 12 cabins, tent camping, picnic pavilions, restrooms, showers, drinking water, and hiking trails. If you're interested in staying here, see p. 164 for a review of the cabins; also see "Beaches" and "Hiking & Camping" in chapter 7.

THE END OF THE ROAD: HEAVENLY HANA ★★

Green, tropical Hana is a destination all its own, a small coastal village that's probably what you came to Maui in search of. Here you'll find a rainforest dotted with cascading waterfalls and sparkling blue pools, skirted by red- and black-sand beaches.

Beautiful Hana enjoys more than 90 inches of rain a year—more than enough to keep the scenery lush. Banyans, bamboo, breadfruit trees—everything seems larger than life in this small town, especially the flowers, such as wild ginger and plumeria. Several roadside stands offer exotic blooms for $1 a bunch. Just "put money in box." It's the Hana honor system.

A Look at the Past

The Hana coast is rich in Hawaiian history and the scene of many turning points in Hawaiian culture. The ancient chants tell of rulers like the 15th-century **Piilani,** who united the island of Maui and built fishponds, irrigation fields, paved roads, and the massive **Piilanihale Heiau,** which still stands today in **Kahanu Garden,** part of the **National Tropical Botanical Garden** (📞 **808/248-8912;** www.ntbg.org/gardens/kahanu.php). It was Piilani's sons and grandson who finished the *heiau* and built the first road to Hana from west Maui, not only along the coast, but also up the Kaupo Gap and through the Haleakala Crater. For information on visiting the garden, see "Hiking" under "Outdoor Activities," below.

In 1849, the cantankerous sea captain **George Wilfong** brought commerce to this isolated village when he started the first sugar plantation on some 60 acres. Because his harsh personality and set demands for plantation work did not sit well with the Hawaiians, Wilfong brought in the first Chinese immigrants to work his fields.

In 1864, two Danish brothers, **August** and **Oscar Unna,** contributed to the growth of the local sugar industry when they established the Hana Plantation. Four years later they brought in Japanese immigrants to labor in the fields.

By the turn of the 20th century, sugar wasn't the only crop booming in Hana (there were some six plantations in the area): Rubber was being commercially grown in Nahiku, wheat in Kaupo, pineapple in Kipahulu, and tobacco in Ulupalakua.

In the 1920s and 1930s, several self-sufficient towns lined the coast, each with its own general store, school, and churches; some had movie theaters as well. Hana has all of the above plus some 15 stores, a pool hall, and several restaurants.

One can only guess what those towns would have been like today if not for the huge tidal wave that hit the state on April 1, 1946. The damage along the Hana coast was catastrophic: The Keanae Peninsula was swept clear (only the stone church remained), Hamoa was totally wiped out, and entire villages completely disappeared.

After World War II, the labor movement became a powerful force in Hawaii. **C. Brewer,** owner of the largest sugar plantation in Hana, decided to shut down his operation instead of fighting the labor union. The closure of the plantation meant not only the loss of thousands of jobs, but also the loss of plantation-supplied homes and the entire plantation lifestyle. Thankfully, **Paul I. Fagan,** an entrepreneur from San Francisco who had purchased the Hana Sugar Co. from the Unna brothers in the 1930s, became the town's guardian angel.

Fagan wanted to retire here, so he focused his business acumen on the tiny town with big problems. Recognizing that sugar was no longer economically feasible, he looked at the community and saw other opportunities. He bought 14,000 acres of land in Hana, stripped it of sugar cane, planted grass, and shipped in cattle from his ranch on Molokai.

Next he did something that was years ahead of his time: He thought tourism might have a future in Hana, so he established an inn in 1946 that later became the **Hotel Hana-Maui.** Fagan also pulled off a public-relations coup: He brought the entire San Francisco Seals baseball team (which he happened to own) to Hana for spring training, and, more important, he brought out the sportswriters as well. The writers loved Hana and wrote glowing reports about the town; one even gave the town a nickname that stuck: "Heavenly Hana."

In 1962, the state paved the Hana Highway. By the 1970s, tourists had not only "discovered" Maui, but they were also willing to make the long trek out to Hana.

The biggest change to the local lifestyle came in December 1977, when television finally arrived—after a local cable operator spent 6 months laying cable over cinder cones, mountain streams, and cavernous gulches from one side of the island to the other. Some 125 homes tuned in to the tube—and the rural Hawaiian community was never the same. Today, Hana is inhabited by 2,500 people, many part Hawaiian.

Seeing the Sights

Most visitors zip through Hana, perhaps taking a quick look out their car windows at a few sights before buzzing on down the road. They might think they've seen Hana, but they definitely haven't experienced Hana. Allow at least 2 or 3 days to really let this land of legends show you its beauty and serenity.

Another recommendation: See Hana's attractions, especially the pools, ponds, waterfalls, and hikes, early in the day. You'll have them all to yourself. The day-trippers arrive in Hana around 11am and stay until about 4pm; that's when the area is overrun with hundreds of people in a hurry, who want to see everything in just a few hours.

As you enter Hana, the road splits about ½ mile past mile marker 33, at the police station. Both roads will take you to Hana, but the lower road, Uakea Road,

Uakea Rd.

Keanini Dr.

Keawa Pl.

Hana Town Rd.

Hana Hwy.

Hauoli Rd.

Hana Beach
Park

*Kauiki
Head*

*Red Sand
Beach*

Kaihalulu Bay

Mill Rd.

360

0   1/4 mi

0   1/4 km

is more scenic. Just before you get to Hana Bay, you'll see the old wood-frame **Hana District Police Station and Courthouse.** Next door is the **Hana Cultural Center & Museum** ★, 4974 Uakea Rd. (© **808/248-8622;** www. hookele.com/hccm), usually open daily from 10am to 4pm. This small building has an excellent collection of Hawaiian quilts, artifacts, books, and photos. Also on the grounds are Kauhala O Hana, composed of four *hale* (houses) for living, meeting, cooking, and canoe building or canoe storage.

Cater-cornered from the cultural center is the entrance to **Hana Bay** ★. You can drive right down to the pier and park. There are restrooms, showers, picnic tables, barbecue areas, and even a snack bar here. The 386-foot, red-faced cinder cone beside the bay is **Kauiki Hill,** the scene of numerous fierce battles in ancient Hawaii and the birthplace of Queen Kaahumanu in 1768. A short 5-minute walk will take you to the spot. Look for the trail along the hill on the wharf side, and follow the path through the ironwood trees; the lighthouse on the point will come into view, and you'll see pocket beaches of red cinder below. Grab onto the ironwood trees for support, as the trail has eroded in some areas. This is a perfect place for a secluded picnic, or you can continue on the path out to the lighthouse. To get to the lighthouse, which sits on a small island, watch the water for about 10 minutes to get a sense of how often and from which direction the waves are coming. Between wave sets, either swim or wade in the shallow, sandy bottom channel or hop across the rocks to the island.

Hotel Hana-Maui.

To get to the center of town, leave Hana Bay, cross Uakea Road, and drive up Keawa Place; turn left on Hana Highway, and on the corner will be the **Hotel Hana-Maui,** the now-luxurious hotel established by Paul Fagan in 1946. On the green hills above Hotel Hana-Maui stands a 30-foot-high white cross made of lava rock. Citizens erected the cross in memory of Paul Fagan, who founded the Hana Ranch

Above Hotel Hana-Maui is Fagan's Rock, a memorial to Paul Fagan, the hotel's founder.

as well as the hotel and helped keep the town alive. The hike up to **Fagan's Cross** provides a gorgeous view of the Hana coast, especially at sunset, when Fagan himself liked to climb this hill (see p. 230 for details).

Back on the Hana Highway, just past Hauoli Road, is the majestic **Wananalua Congregation Church.** It's listed on the National Register of Historic Places not only because of its age (it was built in 1838–42 using coral stones), but also because of its location, atop an old Hawaiian *heiau.*

Just past the church, on the right side of the Hana Highway, is the turnoff to the **Hana Ranch Center,** the commercial center for Hana, with a post office, bank, general store, the Hana Ranch Stables, and a restaurant and snack bar (see "Hana Ranch Restaurant," p. 199). But the real shopping experience is across the Hana Highway at the **Hasegawa General Store ★** (p. 303), a Maui institution, which carries oodles of merchandise from soda and fine French wines to fishing line and name-brand clothing, plus everything you need for a picnic or a gourmet meal. This is also the place to find out what's going on in Hana: The bulletin board at the entrance has fliers and handwritten notes advertising everything from fundraising activities to classes to community-wide events. Don't miss this unique store.

Outdoor Activities

Hana is one of the best areas on Maui for ocean activities; it also boasts a wealth of nature hikes, remote places to explore on horseback, waterfalls to discover, and even lava tubes to investigate.

For more information on the lava tubes, see **Hana Lava Tube** (© **808/248-7308**), on p. 237; for details on horseback riding, see **Maui Horseback Tours at Maui Stables** (© **808/248-7799**), on p. 236. If you're a tennis player, you can take advantage of the free public courts located next to the Hotel Hana-Maui, available on a first-come, first-served basis.

BEACHES & OCEAN ACTIVITIES

Hana's beaches come in numerous varieties—white, black, gray, or red sand; perfectly shaped coves, crescents, or long stretches—and they're excellent for just about every kind of ocean activity you can think of. If you'd like to snorkel or kayak, or venture out on your own at one of my favorite beaches:

HANA BAY The waters in the Hana Bay are calm most of the time and great for swimming. There's excellent snorkeling and diving by the lighthouse. Strong currents can run through here, so don't venture farther than the lighthouse. See "Seeing the Sights," above, for more details on the facilities and hikes here.

RED SAND BEACH The Hawaiian name for this beach is Kaihalulu ("roaring sea"). It's truly a sight to see. The beach is on the ocean side of Kauiki Hill, just south of Hana Bay, in a wild, natural setting on a pocket cove, where the volcanic cinder cone lost its seaward wall to erosion and spilled red cinders everywhere to create the red sands. Before you put on your bathing suit, there are three things to know about this beach: You have to trespass to get here (which is against the law); due to recent heavy rains, there have been several serious injuries on the muddy, slippery terrain (enter at your own risk; it can be extremely dangerous); and nudity (also illegal in Hawaii—arrests have been made) is common here.

If you are determined to go, ask for permission at the Hotel Hana-Maui. And ask about conditions on the trail (which drops several stories down to the ocean rocks). To reach the beach, put on solid walking shoes (no flip-flops) and walk south on Uakea Road, past Haoli Street and the Hotel Hana-Maui, to the

Hana Bay.

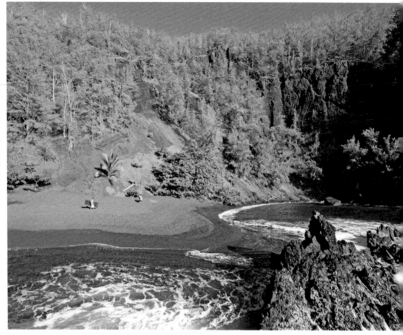

Red Sand Beach.

parking lot for the hotel's Sea Ranch Cottages. Turn left and cross the open field next to the Hana Community Center. Look for the dirt trail and follow it to the huge ironwood tree, where you turn right (do not go ahead to the old Japanese cemetery). Use the ironwood trees to maintain your balance as you follow the ever-eroding cinder footpath a short distance along the shoreline, down the narrow cliff trail (do not attempt this if it's wet). The trail suddenly turns the corner, and into view comes the burnt-red beach, set off by the turquoise waters, black lava, and vivid green ironwood trees.

The lava outcropping protects the bay and makes it safe for swimming. Snorkeling is excellent, and there's a natural whirlpool area on the Hana Bay side of the cove. Stay away from the surge area where the ocean enters the cove.

KOKI BEACH ★ One of the best surfing and boogie-boarding beaches on the Hana Coast lies just a couple of miles from the Hasegawa General Store in the Oheo Gulch direction. There is a very strong rip current here, so unless it is dead calm and you are a strong swimmer, do not attempt to swim here. However, it's a great place to sit on the white sand and watch the surfers. The only facility is a big parking area. To get here, drive toward Oheo Gulch from Hana, where Hwy. 36 changes to Hwy. 31. About 1½ miles outside of Hana, turn left at Haneoo Road.

HAMOA BEACH ★★ For one of Hana's best beaches—great for swimming, boogie boarding, and sunbathing—continue another ½ mile down the Haneoo Road loop to Hamoa Beach. There is easy access from the road down to the sandy beach, and facilities include a small restroom and an outdoor shower.

The large pavilion and beach accessories are for Hotel Hana-Maui guests.

WAIOKA POND Locally, this swimming hole in a series of waterfalls and pools is called Venus Pool. Unfortunately, it has become overrun with impolite tourists who park on the narrow highway, tear down the fence, and aren't very considerate about cleaning up their trash. The land owner, Hana Ranch, has put up NO TRESPASSING signs and is enforcing trespassing laws. (Getting arrested is not a great way to spend your vacation.) I recommend you skip this pond and keep driving to Haleakala National Park down the road. The park has adequate parking as well as restrooms. If you hike just 10 to 15 minutes upstream from the national park's parking lot, you will find much better pools and most likely have them to yourself.

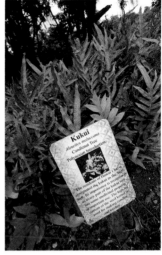

Kahanu Garden.

HIKING

Hana is woven with hiking trails along the shoreline, through the rainforest, and up in the mountains. See p. 229 for a discussion of hiking in Waianapanapa and up to Fagan's Cross.

Another excellent hike that takes you back in time is through Kahanu Garden and to **Piilanihale Heiau ★★**, one of the largest ancient Hawaiian temples in the state. To get here, look for mile marker 31 on the Hana Highway, make a left on to Ulaino Road, and drive a little over a mile down the paved road (which turns into a dirt road but is still drivable) to the first stream bed (about 1½ miles). If the stream is running with water, do not cross it, as you most likely will get stuck; turn around and go back. If you can forge the stream, cross it and park on the right side of the road by the huge breadfruit trees. The trees are part of the **Kahanu Garden ★★** (✆ **808/248-8912**), owned and operated by the **National Tropical Botanical Garden** (www.ntbg.org). Admission is $10 for adults and free for children 12 and under. The garden is open Monday through Friday from 10am to 2pm. Allow an hour and a half for the self-guided tour. Be sure to wear comfortable walking shoes and long pants, and bring mosquito repellent, a hat for shade, and water. The guided tours are Saturday at 10am and cost $25 per person (children 12 and under free). Reserve in advance at ✆ **808/248-8912** or www.ntbg.org/gardens/kahanu-tours.php.

The 122 acres here encompass plant collections from the Pacific Islands, concentrating on plants of value to the people of Polynesia, Micronesia, and Melanesia. Kahanu Garden contains the largest known collection of breadfruit cultivars from more than 17 Pacific Island groups and Indonesia, the Philippines, and the Seychelles.

The real draw here is the Piilanihale Heiau (see "A Look at the Past," above). Believed to be the largest in the state, it measures 340 feet x 415 feet, and it was built in a unique terrace design not seen anywhere else in Hawaii. The walls are some 50 feet tall and 8 to 10 feet thick. Historians believe that Piilani's two sons and his grandson built the mammoth temple, which was dedicated to war, sometime in the 1500s.

Just Beyond Hana

TROPICAL HALEAKALA: OHEO GULCH AT KIPAHULU ★★

If you're thinking about heading out to the so-called Seven Sacred Pools, out past Hana at the Kipahulu end of Haleakala National Park, let's clear this up right now: There are more than seven pools—about 24, actually—and *all* water in Hawaii is considered sacred. It's all a PR campaign that has spun out of control into contemporary myth. Folks here call the attraction by its rightful name, **Oheo Gulch ★★★**, and visitors sometimes refer to it as Kipahulu, which is actually the name of the area where Oheo Gulch is located. No matter what you call it, it's a beautiful sight. The dazzling series of pools and cataracts cascading into the sea is so popular that it has its own roadside parking lot.

Even though Oheo is part of Haleakala National Park, you cannot drive here from the summit. Even hiking from Haleakala to Oheo is tricky: The access trail out of Haleakala is down Kaupo Gap, which ends at the ocean, a good 6 miles down the coast from Oheo. To drive to Oheo, head for Hana, some 60 miles from Kahului on the Hana Highway (Hwy. 36). Oheo is about 30 to 50 minutes beyond Hana, along Hwy. 31. The Hwy. 31 bridge passes over pools near the ocean; the other pools, plus magnificent 400-foot Waimoku Falls, are reachable via an often-muddy, but rewarding, hour-long uphill hike (see "Hiking & Camping at Kipahulu [near Hana]," p. 227). Expect showers on the Kipahulu coast. The admission fee is $5 per person or $10 per car.

The **Kipahulu Ranger Station** (☏ **808/248-7375**) is staffed from 9am to 5pm daily. Restrooms are available, but there's no drinking water. Kipahulu rangers offer safety information, exhibits, books, and a variety of walks and hikes year-round. Check with the park rangers before hiking up to or swimming in the pools, and always keep one eye on the water in the streams; the sky can be sunny near the coast, but floodwaters from Kipahulu Valley can cause the pools to rise 4 feet in less than 10 minutes.

There are a number of hikes in the park, and tent camping is allowed. See "Hiking & Camping at Kipahulu (near Hana)," on p. 227, for details.

LINDBERGH'S GRAVE

A mile past Oheo Gulch on the ocean side of the road is **Lindbergh's Grave.**

Oheo Gulch is a dazzling series of pools and cataracts cascading into the sea.

Charles Lindbergh's gravesite.

First to fly across the Atlantic Ocean, Charles A. Lindbergh (1902–74) found peace in the Pacific; he settled in Hana, where he died of cancer in 1974. The famous aviator is buried under river stones in a seaside graveyard behind the 1857 **Palapala Hoomau Congregational Church,** where his tombstone is engraved with his favorite words from the 139th Psalm: "If I take the wings of the morning and dwell in the uttermost parts of the sea . . . "

EVEN FARTHER AROUND THE BEND

Be careful, as the road here is unpaved all the way to the fishing village of **Kaupo.** It narrows to one lane at times, wandering in and out of valleys with sharp rock walls and blind bends hugging the ocean cliffs. You may encounter wild pigs and stray cows. About 6 miles and about 60 minutes from Oheo Gulch, you'll see the restored **Huialoha Congregationalist "Circuit" Church,** originally constructed in 1859. Across from the church and down the road a bit is the **Kaupo Store** (© 808/248-8054), which marks the center of the ranching community of Kaupo. Store hours are officially Monday through Friday from 7:30am to 4:30pm, but in this arid cattle country, posted hours often prove meaningless. The Kaupo Store is the last of the Soon family stores, which at one time stretched from Kaupo to Keanae.

From the Kaupo Store, the landscape turns into barren, dry desert. In the lee of Haleakala, this area gets little rain. There are no phones or services until you reach **Ulupalakua Ranch** (p. 271), where there are a winery, general store, and gas station, which is likely to be closed.

Between mile markers 29 and 30, look for the ancient lava flow that created an arch as it rolled down Haleakala. Keep an eye peeled for cattle—this is open-range country. Eventually the road will wind uphill, and suddenly the forest and greenery of Ulupalakua come into sight. From here, you're about 45 minutes from Kahului.

9

SHOPS & GALLERIES

M aui is a shopaholic's dream as well as an arts center, with a large number of resident artists who show their works in dozens of galleries and countless gift shops. Maui is also the queen of specialty products, an agricultural cornucopia that includes Kula onions, upcountry protea, Kaanapali coffee, and many other tasty treats that are shipped worldwide.

As with any popular visitor destination, you'll have to wade through bad art and mountains of trinkets, particularly in Lahaina and Kihei, where touristy boutiques line the streets between rare pockets of treasures. If you shop in south or west Maui, expect to pay resort prices, clear down to a bottle of Evian or sunscreen.

With a well-heeled flourish, the **Shops at Wailea,** an upscale shopping-and-restaurant complex, opened in south Maui in 2001. The 16-acre complex features more than 50 shops and five restaurants, including Louis Vuitton, Tiffany, Gap, Banana Republic, and a few locally well-known stores like Ki'i Gallery. This is resort shopping much in the vein of **Whalers Village** in Kaanapali, where shopping and restaurant activity is concentrated in a single oceanfront complex.

Don't ignore central Maui, home to some first-rate boutiques. Watch the quaint town of **Wailuku,** which is poised for a resurgence. It has its own antiques alleys, and a major promenade on Main Street is in the works. The **Kaahumanu Center,** in neighboring Kahului, is becoming more fashionable by the month.

Upcountry, the boutiques of **Makawao** are worth seeking out, despite some attitude and high prices. The charm of shopping on Maui has always rested in the small, independent shops and galleries that crop up in surprising places.

CENTRAL MAUI
Kahului

Kahului's best shopping is concentrated in two places. Almost all of the shops listed below are at one of the following centers:

The formerly rough-around-the-edges **Maui Mall,** 70 E. Kaahumanu Ave. (𝄢 **808/871-1307;** www.mauimall.com), is the place of everyday retail, from **Longs Drugs** and **Whole Foods** to **Tasaka Guri Guri** (the decades-old purveyor of inimitable icy treats that are neither ice cream nor shave ice, but something in between) and Kahului's largest movie theater, a 12-screen megaplex that features current releases as well as art-house films.

Queen Kaahumanu Center, 275 Kaahumanu Ave. (𝄢 **808/877-3369;** www.queenkaahumanucenter.com), a 10-minute drive from the Kahului Airport on Hwy. 32, offers more than 100 shops, restaurants, and theaters. It covers all the bases, from arts and crafts to a **Foodland** and everything in between: a thriving food court; the island's best beauty supply, **Lisa's Beauty Supply & Salon** (𝄢 **808/877-6463**), and its sister store for cosmetics, **Madison Avenue Day**

Spa and Boutique (✆ 808/873-0880); mall standards like **Sunglass Maui, Radio Shack,** and **Local Motion** (surf- and beachwear); and standard department stores like **Macy's** and **Sears.**

Cost Less Imports Natural fibers are ubiquitous in this corner of the Maui Mall. Home accessories include lauhala, bamboo blinds, grassy floor and window coverings, shoji-style lamps, burlap yardage, baskets, Balinese cushions, Asian imports, *noreng* (Japanese folk curtains), and made-on-Maui soaps and handicrafts. A good source of tropical and Asian home decor. At the Maui Mall. ✆ **808/877-0300**. www.costlessimports-online.com.

Duck Soup 👕 Way, way off the beaten path lies this warehouse full of Asian and Indonesian treasures. Owners Judy Bruder and Sandi Stoner definitely have an eye for spotting the unusual and chic. Most of their buying trips to Indonesia are for interior designers, homeowners, and hotels, but they also bring back some incredible jewelry, handbags, and art, all at prices that will put a smile on your face. The location is a bit tricky; call first for directions and note that it is only open Wednesday through Saturday. Off Mokulele Hwy. (Hwy. 311), about a mile from Puunene, near the Maui Animal Shelter and the Central Maui Baseyard. ✆ **808/871-7875**.

Maui Swap Meet After 17 years on a parcel of land next to the Kahului post office, the popular Maui Swap Meet finally outgrew its home. In 2008, it moved to the Maui Community College campus, in Kahului, where there is room enough for 300 vendors and plenty of parking. Every Saturday from 7am to 1pm, vendors spread out their wares in booths and under tarps, in a festival-like atmosphere that is pure Maui with a touch of kitsch. The colorful Maui specialties include vegetables from Kula and Keanae, fresh taro, plants, proteas, crafts, household items, homemade ethnic foods, and baked goods, including some fabulous fruit breads. Now students at the community college sell artwork and ceramics; the culinary-arts program has prepared food for sale. Between the cheap Balinese imports and New Age crystals and incense, you may find some vintage John Kelly prints and 1930s collectibles. Admission is 50¢, and if you go early while the vendors are setting up, no one will turn you away. At Maui Community College, in an area bounded by Kahului Beach Rd. and Wahine Pio Ave. (access via Wahine Pio Ave). ✆ **808/244-3100**.

EDIBLES

The **Whole Foods Market** and **Longs Drugs** in the Maui Mall, **Foodland** in the Kaahumanu Center, and **Safeway** at 170 E. Kamehameha Ave. will satisfy your ordinary grocery needs. On Saturday, you may want to check out the **Maui Swap Meet** (see above).

Down to Earth Natural Foods, 305 Dairy Rd. (✆ **808/877-2661**), a health-food staple for many years, has fresh organic produce, a bountiful salad bar, sandwiches and smoothies, vitamins and supplements, fresh-baked goods, snacks, whole grains, and several packed aisles of vegetarian and health foods.

Wailuku

Located at the gateway to Iao Valley, Wailuku is the county seat, the part of Maui where people live and work. Wailuku's attractive vintage architecture, smattering of antiques shops, and mom-and-pop eateries imbue the town with a down-home charm noticeably absent in Maui's resort areas. The community spirit fuels festivals throughout the year and is slowly attracting new businesses, but Wailuku is still a work in progress. It's a mixed bag—of course, there's junk, but a stroll along Main and Market streets usually turns up a treasure or two.

Bailey House Museum Shop For made-in-Hawaii items, Bailey House is a must-stop. It offers a thoroughly enjoyable browse through authoritative Hawaiiana, in a museum that's one of the finest examples of missionary architecture, dating from 1833. Gracious gardens, rare paintings of early Maui, wonderful programs in Hawaiian arts and culture, and a restored hand-hewn koa canoe await visitors. The shop, a small space of discriminating taste, packs a wallop with its selection of remarkable gift items, from Hawaiian music to exquisite woods, traditional Hawaiian games to pareu and books. Prints by the legendary Hawaii artist Madge Tennent, lauhala hats, hand-sewn pheasant hatbands, jams and jellies, Maui cookbooks, and an occasional Hawaiian quilt are some of the treasures to be found here. At the Bailey House Museum, 2375-A Main St. ✆ **808/244-3326.**

Bird of Paradise Unique Antiques Owner Joe Myhand loves furniture, old Matson liner menus, blue willow china, kimonos for children, and anything nostalgic that happens to be Hawaiian. The furniture ranges from 1940s rattan to wicker and old koa—those items tailor-made for informal island living and leisurely moments on the lanai. Myhand also collects bottles and mails his license plates all over the world. The collection ebbs and flows with his finds, keeping buyers waiting in the wings for his Depression glass, California pottery from the 1930s and 1940s, old dinnerware, perfume bottles, vintage aloha shirts, and vintage Hawaiian music on cassettes. 56 N. Market St. ✆ **808/242-7699.**

Brown-Kobayashi Graceful living is the theme here. Prices range from a few dollars to the thousands in this 750-square-foot treasure trove. The owners have added a fabulous selection of antique stone garden pieces that mingle quietly

FARM FRESH: maui's farmers' markets

Maui's produce has long been a source of pride for islanders. Check out the following farmers' markets around the island (http://hawaii.gov/hdoa/add/farmers-market-in-hawaii/Maui.pdf):

o **Maui's Fresh Produce Farmer's Market,** at the Queen Kaahumanu Center, Kahului (✆ **808/298-4289**), on Tuesday, Wednesday, and Friday from 7am to 4pm, is the place to find a fresh, inexpensive selection of Maui-grown fruit, vegetables, flowers, and plants. They do have baked goods.

o **Maui Mall Farmers' Market & Craft Fair** is at the Maui Mall, Kahului (✆ **808/871-1307**), on Tuesday, Wednesday, and Friday from 7am to 4pm.

o **Farmers' Market of Maui–Honokowai,** on lower Honoapiilani Rd., across from the Honokowai Park (near Haku Hale Pl.; ✆ **808/669-7004**) is every Monday, Wednesday, and Friday from 7 to 11am.

o **Kihei Farmers' Market** at Suda Store on Kiehi Road in Kihei, is Monday, Wednesday, and Friday from 8am to 4pm.

MAUI'S OWN: ocean vodka

If you're looking for a souvenir of your fabulous Maui trip to take home, or a unique gift for friends, Maui has its own vodka, called Ocean Vodka. Produced by Hawaii Sea Spirits, this ultrapremium brand is not only USDA-certified to contain organic ingredients, but also the water comes from 3,000 feet beneath the ocean off the Kona coast of the Big Island. The deep-sea water is harvested by KOYO USA, producers of MaHaLo Hawaii Deep Sea Water. The desalinated water has become widely popular in Japan, where people swear it has provided beneficial health effects (so far, no scientific studies have backed up this claim). The MaHaLo water is shipped to Maui, where it is blended with organic corn and rye to produce this one-of-a-kind vodka. It's available at restaurants, bars, hotels, and retail shops (for a complete list, see www.oceanvodka.com).

with Asian antiques and old and new French, European, and Hawaiian objects. Although the collection is eclectic, there is a strong cohesive aesthetic that sets Brown-Kobayashi apart from other Maui antiques stores. Japanese kimonos and obi, Bakelite and Peking glass beads, breathtaking Japanese lacquerware, cricket carriers, and cloisonné are among the delights here. Exotic and precious Chinese woods (purple sandalwood and *huanghuali*) glow discreetly from quiet corners, and an occasional monarchy-style lidded milo bowl comes in and flies out. 38 N. Market St. © **808/242-0804.**

Gottling Ltd. Karl Gottling's shop specializes in Asian antique furniture, but you can also find smaller carvings, precious stones, jewelry, netsuke, opium weights, and more. I saw a 17th-century Buddha lending an air of serenity next to a 150-year-old Chinese cabinet. Ming Dynasty ceramics, carved wooden apples ($15), and a Persian rug ($65,000) give you an idea of the range of possibilities here. 34 N. Market St. © **808/244-7779.**

Sandell 🏛 Since the early 1970s, artist, illustrator, and cartoonist David Sandell has been commenting on Maui through his artwork. Don't miss the opportunity to stop by this shop and "talk story" with the talented artist, who watched Maui go from undiscovered to discovered. His work—from original oils to prints to T-shirts—makes excellent souvenirs to take home. 133 Market St. © **808/249-2456** or 808/249-0234.

EDIBLES

Located in the northern section of Wailuku, **Takamiya Market,** 359 N. Market St. (© **808/244-3404**), is much loved by local folks and visitors with adventurous palates, who often drive all the way from Kihei to stock up on picnic fare and mouthwatering ethnic foods for sunset gatherings. Unpretentious home-cooked foods from East and West are prepared daily and served on plastic-foam plates. From the chilled-fish counter come fresh sashimi and poke, and among the renowned assortment of prepared foods are mounds of shoyu chicken, tender fried squid, roast pork, kalua pork, laulau, Chinese noodles, fiddlehead ferns, and Western comfort foods, such as corn bread and potato salad. Fresh produce and paper products are also available, but it's the prepared foods and fresh-fish counter that have made Takamiya a household name in central Maui.

WEST MAUI

Lahaina

Lahaina's merchants and art galleries go all out from 7 to 9pm every Friday, when **Art Night** brings an extra measure of hospitality and community spirit. The Art Night openings are usually marked with live entertainment and refreshments, plus a livelier-than-usual street scene.

If you're in Lahaina on the second or last Thursday of the month, stroll by the front lawn of the **Baldwin Home Museum,** 120 Dickenson St. (at Front St.), for a splendid look at the craft of lei making and an opportunity to meet the gregarious seniors of Lahaina. In a program sponsored by AARP, they gather from 10am to 4pm to demonstrate lei making, to sell their floral creations, and, equally important, to socialize. (It doesn't happen in the winter when flowers aren't blooming; best to call ✆ **808/661-3262** to confirm.)

What was formerly a big, belching pineapple cannery is now a maze of shops and restaurants at the northern end of Lahaina town, known as the **Lahaina Cannery Mall,** 1221 Honoapiilani Hwy. (✆ **808/661-5304;** www.lahaina cannerymall.com). Find your way through the T-shirt and sportswear shops to coffee at **Starbucks.** At the recently expanded food court. **L & L Drive-Inn** serves up plate lunches near Greek, pizza, Vietnamese, and Japanese food booths. For film, water, aspirin, groceries, sunscreen, and other things you can't live without, nothing beats **Longs Drugs** and **Safeway** (open 24 hr.), two old standbys. **Footprints Maui** may surprise you with its selection of footwear, everything from running shoes to inexpensive sandals.

The **Lahaina Center,** 900 Front St. (✆ **808/667-9216;** www.lahaina center.com), is still a work in progress. It's located north of Lahaina's most congested strip, where Front Street begins. Across the street from the center, the sea wall is a much-sought-after front-row seat to the sunset. There's plenty of free validated parking and easy access to more than 30 shops, a salon, restaurants, a nightclub, and a four-plex movie-theater complex. **Ruth's Chris Steak House** has opened its doors here, and **Hard Rock Cafe** serves lunch and dinner and offers nighttime live music on weekdays. Among the shopping stops: **Hilo Hattie** (a dizzying emporium of aloha wear), **ABC Discount Store,** and a dozen other recreational, dining, and entertainment options.

The conversion of 10,000 square feet of parking space into the re-creation of a traditional Hawaiian village, called **Hale Kahiko,** is a welcome touch of Hawaiiana at the Lahaina Center. With the commercialization of modern Lahaina, it's easy to forget that it was once the capital of the Hawaiian kingdom and a significant historic site. Hale Kahiko features three main houses, called *hale:* a sleeping house, the men's dining house, and the crafts house, where women pounded *hala* (pandanus) strips to weave into mats and baskets. Construction of the houses consumed 10,000 square feet of ohia wood from the island, 20 tons of pili grass, and more than 4 miles of hand-woven coconut sennit for the lashings. Artifacts, weapons, a canoe, and indigenous trees are among the authentic touches in this village; you can take a free guided tour daily between 9am and 6pm.

Banana Wind Tucked into the Lahaina Cannery, this whimsical store has everything from T-shirts to woven baskets, candles, pareus, shells, and even carved wooden banana trees (just $6,000 and very tricky to transport in your luggage). This is the place to find some great souvenirs to take back home. At the Lahaina Cannery Mall, 1221 Honoapiilani Hwy. ℂ **808/661-1600.**

Lahaina Arts Society Galleries With its membership of more than 185 Maui artists, the nonprofit Lahaina Arts Society is an excellent community resource. Changing monthly exhibits in the Banyan Tree and Old Jail galleries offer a good look at the island's artistic well: two-dimensional art, fiber art, ceramics, sculpture, prints, jewelry, and more. In the shade of the humongous banyan tree in the square across from Pioneer Inn, "Art in the Park" fairs are offered every second and fourth weekend of the month (check calendar on website). 648 Wharf St., Ste. 103. ℂ **808/661-3228.** www.lahaina-arts.com.

Lei Spa Maui Expanded to include two massage rooms and shower facilities, this day spa offers facials and other therapies. About 95% of the beauty and bath products sold here are made on Maui, and that includes Hawaiian Botanical Pikake shower gel, *kukui* and macadamia-nut oils, Hawaiian potpourris, mud masks with Hawaiian seaweed, and a spate of rejuvenating potions for hair and skin. Aromatherapy body oils and perfumes are popular, as are the handmade soaps and fragrances of torch ginger, plumeria, coconut, tuberose, and sandalwood. Scented candles in coconut shells, inexpensive and fragrant, make great gifts. 505 Front St. ℂ **808/661-1178.**

Lahaina Art Night.

Hale Kahiko is a re-creation of traditional Hawaiian village.

Maggie Coulombe 🎁 Imagine a high-fashion store with the unique designs of Maggie Coulombe in the midst of Lahaina. You'll find Maggie's latest couture, jersey, linen, pareu, and shoes, plus accessories, jewelry, purses, and a few surprises. 505 Front St. © **808/662-0696.** www.maggiecoulombe.com.

Martin Lawrence Galleries The front is garish, with pop art, kinetic sculptures, and bright, carnivalesque glass objects. Toward the back of the gallery, however, there's a sizable inventory of two-dimensional art and some plausible choices for collectors of Keith Haring, Andy Warhol, and other pop artists. The originals, limited-edition graphics, and sculptures also include works by Marc Chagall, Pablo Picasso, Joan Miró, Roy Lichtenstein, and other noted artists. At the Lahaina Market Place, 126 Lahainaluna Rd. © **808/661-1788.** www.martinlawrence.com.

Old Lahaina Book Emporium What a bookstore! Chockablock with used books in stacks, on shelves, on counters, and in the aisles, this place is a browser's dream. More than 25,000 quality used books are lovingly housed in this shop, where owner JoAnn Carroll treats both books and customers well. Prices are low, and the selection is diverse, everything from *Li'l Abner* to *Genius and Lust,* old *Mad* magazines, *Aphrodisiac Cookery, Bhagavad Gita, A History of Bicycles,* and *The Cockroach Combat Manual.* The store is 95% used books and 100% delight. Specialties include Hawaiiana, fiction, mystery, sci-fi, and military history, with substantial selections in cookbooks, children's books, and philosophy/religion. You could pay as little as $2 for a quality read, or a whole lot more for that rare first edition. Books on tape, videos, the classics, and old guitar magazines are among the treasures of this two-story emporium. 834 Front St. © **808/661-1399.** www.oldlahainabookemporium.com.

Peter Lik Gallery Australian photographer Peter Lik is known for his spectacular panoramic photos, and his gallery is a lot like his art: spacious, eye-catching, and full of surprises. Stop by just to see his incredible vistas. Even if you can't afford one of his photos, there are posters, cards, books, and other items for sale. 712 Front St. © **808/661-6623.** www.peterlik.com.

Village Galleries in Lahaina The nearly 30-year-old Village Galleries is the oldest continuously running gallery on Maui, and it's esteemed as one of the few galleries with consistently high standards. Art collectors know this as a respectable showcase for regional artists; the selection of mostly original two- and three-dimensional art offers a good look at the quality of work originating on the island. The newer contemporary gallery offers colorful gift items and jewelry. Village Gift & Fine Art, 120 Dickenson St. (© **808/661-5559**), and The Master's Reading Room at the Baldwin House, 120 Dickenson St. (© **808/661-3262**). An additional location is at the Ritz-Carlton Kapalua, 1 Ritz-Carlton Dr. (© **808/669-1800**).

Kaanapali

I am somewhat disappointed with upscale **Whalers Village,** 2435 Kaanapali Pkwy. (© **808/661-4567;** www.whalersvillage.com). Although it offers everything from whale blubber to Prada and Ferragamo, it's short on local shops, and parking at the nearby lot is expensive. The complex is home to the **Whalers Village Museum** (p. 257), with its interactive exhibits, 40-foot sperm-whale skeleton, and sand castles on perpetual display, but shoppers come for the designer thrills and beachfront dining. You can find most of the items featured here in the shops in Lahaina and can avoid the parking hassle and the high prices by skipping Whalers Village.

If you do decide to check out Whalers Village, don't miss my favorite store: **Lahaina Printsellers** has a selection of antique prints, maps, paintings, and engravings, including 18th- to 20th-century cartography, all of which offer great browsing and gift potential. You can also find an expanded **Reyn's** for aloha wear, and **Cinnamon Girl,** a hit in Honolulu for its matching mother-daughter clothing. Another mainstay of the village is the busiest **ABC** store in the state, with everything from suntan lotion to takeout sandwiches to cold beer. Once you've stood under the authentic whale skeleton at the museum, you can blow a bundle at **Louis Vuitton, Coach,** or any of the more than 60 shops and restaurants that have sprouted up in this open-air shopping center. Despite obvious efforts to offer more of a balance between Island-made and designer goods, the chain luxury boutiques still dominate. Whalers Village is open daily from 9:30am to 10pm.

Ki'i Gallery Some of the works are large and lavish, such as the Toland Sand prisms for just under $5,000 and the John Stokes handblown glass. Those who love glass in all forms, from handblown vessels to jewelry, will love a browse through Ki'i. I found Pat Kazi's work in porcelain and found objects, such as the mermaid in a teacup, inspired by fairy tales and mythology, both fantastic and compelling. The gallery is devoted to glass and original paintings and drawings; roughly half of the artists are from Hawaii. At the Grand Wailea Resort (📞 **808/874-3059**) and the Shops at Wailea (📞 **808/874-1181**). www.kiigallery.com.

Sandal Tree It's unusual for a resort shop to draw local customers on a regular basis, but the Sandal Tree attracts a flock of footwear fanatics who come here from throughout the islands for rubber thongs and Top-Siders, sandals and dressy pumps, athletic shoes and hats, designer footwear, and much more. Sandal Tree also carries a generous selection of Mephisto and Arche comfort sandals, Donald J Pliner, Anne Klein, Charles Jourdan, and beachwear and casual footwear for all tastes. Accessories range from fashionable knapsacks to avant-garde geometrical handbags—for town and country, day and evening, kids, women, and men. Prices are realistic, too. At Whalers Village, 2435 Kaanapali Pkwy. 📞 **808/667-5330**. Also at the Shops at Wailea, 3750 Wailea Alanui Dr., Wailea (📞 **808/874-9006**); and the Hyatt Regency Maui Resort, 200 Nohea Kai Dr., Kaanapali (📞 **808/661-1234**).

Totally Hawaiian Gift Gallery This gallery makes a good browse for its selection of Niihau shell jewelry, excellent Hawaiian CDs, Norfolk pine bowls, and Hawaiian quilt kits. Hawaiian quilt patterns sewn in Asia (at least they're honest about it) are labor-intensive, less expensive, and attractive, although not totally Hawaiian. Hawaiian-quilt-patterned gift wraps and tiles, perfumes and soaps, handcrafted dolls, and koa accessories are of good quality, and the artists, such as Kelly Dunn (Norfolk wood bowls), Jerry Kermode (wood), and Pat Coito (wood), are among the tops in their fields. Whalers Village, 2435 Kaanapali Pkwy. 📞 **808/667-4070**. www.totallyhawaiian.com.

Honokowai, Kahana & Napili

Those driving north of Kaanapali toward Kapalua will notice the **Honokowai Marketplace,** on Lower Honoapiilani Road, only minutes before the Kapalua Airport. It houses restaurants and coffee shops, a dry cleaner, the **Times Supermarket,** a few clothing stores, and the sprawling **Hawaiian Interiors.**

Nearby **Kahana Gateway** is an unimpressive mall built to serve the condominium community that has sprawled along the coastline between Honokowai and Kapalua. If you need women's swimsuits, however, **Rainbow Beach**

Swimwear is a find. It carries a selection of suits for all shapes, at lower-than-resort prices, slashed even further during the frequent sales. **Hutton's Fine Jewelry** offers high-end jewelry from designers around the country (lots of platinum and diamonds), reflecting discerning taste for those who can afford it. Tahitian black pearls and jade are among Hutton's specialties.

Kapalua

Honolua Store Walk on the old wood floors peppered with holes from golf shoes and find your everyday essentials: bottled water, stationery, mailing tape, jackets, chips, wine, soft drinks, paper products, fresh fruit and produce, and aisles of notions and necessities. With picnic tables on the veranda and a takeout counter offering deli items—more than a dozen types of sandwiches, salads, and budget-friendly breakfasts—there are always long lines of customers. Golfers and surfers love to come here for the morning paper and coffee. 502 Office Rd. (next to the Ritz-Carlton Kapalua). ✆ **808/669-6128.**

Village Galleries Maui's finest artists exhibit their works here and in the other two Village Galleries in Lahaina. Take heart, art lovers: There's no clichéd marine art here. Translucent, delicately turned bowls of Norfolk pine gleam in the light, and George Allan, Betty Hay Freeland, Fred KenKnight, and Pamela Andelin are included in the pantheon of respected artists represented in the tiny gallery. Watercolors, oils, sculptures, handblown glass, Niihau shell leis, jewelry, and other media are represented. The Ritz-Carlton's monthly Artist-in-Residence program features gallery artists in demonstrations and special hands-on workshops that are free, including materials. At the Ritz-Carlton Kapalua, 1 Ritz-Carlton Dr. ✆ **808/669-1800.**

SOUTH MAUI

Kihei

Kihei is one long strip of strip malls. Most of the shopping here is concentrated in the **Azeka Place Shopping Center** on South Kihei Road. Fast foods abound at the Azeka center. Across the street, there's another Azeka, called **Azeka Place II,** which houses several prominent attractions, including the **Coffee Store** and a cluster of specialty shops with everything from children's clothes to shoes, sunglasses, and swimwear. Also on South Kihei Road is the **Kukui Mall,** with movie theaters, fast eats, and a few other visitor-oriented stores.

WAILEA

CY Maui Women who like flowing clothing in silks, rayons, and natural fibers will love this shop, formerly the popular Manikin in Kahului. If you don't find what you want on the racks of simple bias-cut designs, you can have it made from the bolts of stupendous fabrics lining the store. Except for a few hand-painted silks, everything here is washable. At the Shops at Wailea, 3750 Wailea Alanui Dr. ✆ **808/891-0782.** www.cymaui.com.

Fairmont Store This chic boutique in the Fairmont Kea Lani stands out due to the careful eye of buyer Lynett Clark, who has an excellent sense of fashion. Here you'll find Michael Stars and Glima T-shirts, Yellow Box and Matisse sandals, Sophia and Chloe jewelry, Helen Kaminski hats, and a range of clothing by Citron, Sigrid Olsen, and Betsey Johnson. It's definitely worth your time to browse this airy and well-lit shop, with a truly helpful staff. At the Fairmont Kea Lani Maui, 4100 Wailea Alanui Dr. ✆ **808/875-4100,** ext. 810.

Grand Wailea Shops The sprawling Grand Wailea Resort is known for its long arcade of shops and galleries tailored to hefty pocketbooks. Stop by the Napua Gallery, which houses the private collection of the resort owner. Ki'i Gallery (p. 298) is luminous with studio glass and exquisitely turned woods, and Sandal Tree (p. 298) raises the footwear bar. At the Grand Wailea Resort, 3850 Wailea Alanui Dr. ✆ **808/875-1234.**

The Shops at Wailea This is the big shopping boost that resortgoers have been awaiting for years. The high-end shops sell expensive souvenirs, gifts, clothing, and accessories for a life of perpetual vacations. Chains rule (Gap, Louis Vuitton, Banana Republic, Tiffany, Crazy Shirts, Honolua Surf Co.), but there is still fertile ground for the inveterate shopper in the nearly 60 shops in the complex. **Martin & MacArthur** (furniture and gift gallery) has landed in Wailea as part of a retail mix that is similar to Whalers Village. 3750 Wailea Alanui Dr. ✆ **808/891-6770.**

UPCOUNTRY MAUI

Makawao

Besides being a shopper's paradise, Makawao is the home of the island's most prominent arts organization, the **Hui No'eau Visual Arts Center** ★, 2841 Baldwin Ave. (✆ **808/572-6560;** www.huinoeau.com). Designed in 1917 by C. W. Dickey, one of Hawaii's most prominent architects, the two-story, Mediterranean-style stucco home that houses the center is located on a sprawling 9-acre estate called Kaluanui. A legacy of Maui's prominent *kamaaina* (old-timers) Harry and Ethel Baldwin, the estate became an arts center in 1976. Visiting artists offer lectures, classes, and demonstrations, all at reasonable prices, in basketry, jewelry making, ceramics, painting, and other media. Classes on Hawaiian art, culture, and history are also available. Call ahead for schedules and details. The exhibits here are drawn from a wide range of disciplines and multicultural sources, and include both contemporary and traditional art from established and emerging artists. The gift shop, featuring many one-of-a-kind works by local artists and artisans, is worth a stop. Hours are Monday through Saturday from 10am to 4pm.

Collections This longtime Makawao attraction is showing renewed vigor after more than 2 decades on Baldwin Avenue. It's one of my favorite Makawao stops, full of gift items and spirited clothing reflecting the ease and color of island living. Its selection of sportswear, soaps, jewelry, candles, and tasteful, marvelous miscellany reflects good sense and style. Dresses (including up-to-the-moment Citron in cross-cultural and vintage-looking prints), separates, home and bath accessories, sweaters, and other good things make this a Makawao must. 3677 Baldwin Ave. © **808/572-0781.**

Gecko Trading Co. Boutique The selection in this tiny boutique is eclectic and always changing: One day it's mesh T-shirts in a dragon motif, the next it's Provence soaps and antique lapis jewelry. I've seen everything from handmade crocheted bags from New York to hammered-tin candle holders from Mexico, plus clothing from Spain and France, collectible bottles, toys, and shawls. The prices are reasonable, the service is friendly, and it's more homey than glammy— not as self-conscious as some of the other local boutiques. 3621 Baldwin Ave. © **808/572-0249.**

Holiday & Co. Attractive women's clothing in natural fibers hangs from racks, while jewelry to go with it beckons from the counter. Recent finds include elegant fiber evening bags, luxurious bath gels, easygoing dresses and separates, Dansko clogs, shawls, soaps, aloha shirts, books, picture frames, and jewelry. 3681 Baldwin Ave. © **808/572-1470.**

Hot Island Glassblowing Studio & Gallery You can watch the artist transform molten glass into works of art and utility in this studio at the Makawao Courtyard, where an award-winning family of glass blowers built its own furnaces. It's fascinating to watch the shapes emerge from glass melted at 2,300°F (1,260°C). The colorful works range from small paperweights to large vessels. Four to five artists participate in the demonstrations, which begin when the furnace is heated, about a half-hour before the studio opens at 9am. 3620 Baldwin Ave. © **808/572-4527.**

Hurricane This boutique carries clothing, gifts, accessories, and books that are two steps ahead of the competition. Tommy Bahama aloha shirts and aloha print dresses; the Nick & Zoe line; work by local artists; a notable selection of fragrances for men and women; and hard-to-find, eccentric books and home accessories are part of the Hurricane appeal. 3639 Baldwin Ave. © **808/572-5076.**

The Mercantile The jewelry, home accessories (especially the Tiffany-style glass-and-shell lamps), dinnerware, Italian linens, plantation-style furniture, and clothing here are a salute to the good life. There's exquisite bedding, rugs, hand-carved armoires, slipcovers, and a large selection of Kiehl's products. The clothing—comfortable cottons and upscale European linens—is for men and women, as are the soaps, which include Maui Herbal Soap products and some unusual finds from France. Maui-made jams, honey, soaps, ceramics, and Jurlique organic facial and body products are among the new winners. 3673 Baldwin Ave. © **808/572-1407.**

Sherri Reeve Gallery & Gifts If you want to take a little bit of the beauty of Maui home with you, stop by this open-air gallery. Artist Sherri Reeve grew up in Hawaii (the local phone book featured her art on the cover one year), and she has captured the vibrant color and feel of the islands. You can find everything from inexpensive cards, hand-painted tiles, and T-shirts to original works and limited editions. 3669 Baldwin Ave. © **808/572-8931.** www.sreeve.com.

Viewpoints Gallery Maui's only fine-arts cooperative showcases the work of 20 established artists in an airy, attractive gallery located in a restored theater with a courtyard, glass-blowing studio, and restaurants. The gallery features two-dimensional art, jewelry, fiber art, stained glass, paper, sculpture, and other media. This is a fine example of what can happen in a collectively supportive artistic environment. 3620 Baldwin Ave. ✆ **808/572-5979.** www.viewpointsgallerymaui. com.

EDIBLES

Working folks in Makawao pick up spaghetti and lasagna, sandwiches, salads, and changing specials from the **Rodeo General Store,** 3661 Baldwin Ave. (✆ **808/572-7841**). At the far end of the store is the oenophile's bonanza, a superior wine selection housed in its own temperature-controlled cave.

In the more than 6 decades that the **T. Komoda Store and Bakery,** 3674 Baldwin Ave. (✆ **808/572-7261**), has spent in this spot, untold numbers have creaked over the wooden floors to pick up Komoda's famous cream puffs. Old-timers know to come early, before they're sold out. Then the cinnamon rolls, doughnuts, pies, and chocolate cake take over. Pastries are just the beginning: Poi, macadamia-nut candies and cookies, and small bunches of local fruit keep the customers coming.

East Maui

SHOPS & GALLERIES

Fresh Flowers in Kula

Like anthuriums on the Big Island, proteas are a Maui trademark and an abundant crop on Haleakala's rich volcanic slopes. They also travel well, dry beautifully, and can be shipped worldwide with ease. Among Maui's most prominent sources is **Sunrise Protea** (✆ **808/876-0200;** www.sunriseprotea.com), in Kula. It offers a walk-through garden and gift shops, friendly service, and a larger-than-usual selection. Freshly cut flowers arrive from the fields on Tuesday and Friday afternoons. You can order individual blooms, baskets, arrangements, or wreaths for shipping all over the world. (Next door, the Sunrise Country Market offers fresh local fruits, snacks, and sandwiches, with picnic tables for lingering.)

Proteas of Hawaii (✆ **808/878-2533;** www.proteasofhawaii.com), another reliable source, offers regular walking tours of the University of Hawaii Extension Service gardens across the street in Kula.

Outside of Kula, the Saturday-morning **Maui Swap Meet** (p. 292) is among the best and least expensive places for tropical flowers of every stripe.

EAST MAUI

On the Road to Hana: Paia

Hemp House Clothing and accessories made of hemp, a sturdy, eco-friendly fiber, are finally making their way into the mainstream. The Hemp House has as complete a selection as you can expect to see in Hawaii, with "denim" hemp jeans, lightweight linenlike trousers, dresses, shirts, and a full range of sensible, easy-care wear. 16 Baldwin Ave. ✆ **808/579-8880.**

Maui Crafts Guild The old wooden storefront at the gateway to Paia houses crafts of high quality and in all price ranges, from pit-fired raku to bowls of Norfolk pine and other Maui woods, fashioned by Maui hands. Artist-owned and -operated, the guild claims 25 members who live and work on Maui. Basketry, hand-painted fabrics, jewelry, beadwork, traditional Hawaiian stonework, pressed flowers, fused glass, stained glass, copper sculpture, banana-bark paintings, and pottery of all styles are displayed in the two-story gift gallery. Upstairs, sculptor Arthur Dennis Williams shows his breathtaking work in wood, bronze, and stone. Everything can be shipped. **Aloha Bead Co.** (© **808/579-9709**), in the back of the gallery, is a treasure trove for bead workers. 69 Hana Hwy. © **808/579-9697.** www.mauicraftsguild.com.

Maui Hands Maui hands have made 90% of the items in this shop/gallery. Because it's a consignment shop, you'll find Hawaii-made handicrafts and prices that aren't inflated. The selection includes paintings, prints, jewelry, glass marbles, native-wood bowls, and tchotchkes for every budget. This is an ideal stop for made-on-Maui products and crafts of good quality. 84 Hana Hwy. © **808/579-9245.** www.mauihands.com. Additional locations in Kaanapali at the Hyatt Regency, 200 Nohea Kai Dr. (© **808/667-7997**), and Lahaina Old Town, 612 Front St. (© **808/667-9898**).

Moonbow Tropics If you're looking for a tasteful aloha shirt, go to Moonbow. The selection consists of a few carefully culled racks of the top labels in aloha wear, in fabrics ranging from the finest silks and linens to Egyptian cotton and spun rayons. Some of the finds: aloha shirts by Tori Richard, Reyn Spooner, Kamehameha, Paradise Found, Kahala, and other top brands. Silk pants, silk shorts, vintage-print neckwear, and an upgraded women's selection hang on colorful racks. The jewelry pieces, ranging from tanzanite to topaz, rubies to moonstones, are mounted in unique settings made on-site. 36 Baldwin Ave. © **808/579-8592.** www.moonbowtropics.com.

Hana

Hana Coast Gallery 🎁 This gallery is a good reason to go to Hana: It's an aesthetic and cultural experience that informs as it enlightens. Tucked away in the posh Hotel Hana-Maui, the gallery is known for its high level of curatorship and commitment to the cultural art of Hawaii. There are no jumping whales or dolphins here, and except for a section of European and Asian masters, the 3,000-square-foot gallery is devoted entirely to Hawaii artists, whose sculptures, paintings, prints, feather work, stonework, and carvings are featured in displays that are so natural, they could well exist in someone's home.

In response to the ongoing revival of the American Crafts Movement, director-curator Patrick Robinson (of impeccable artistic integrity) has expanded the selection of koa-wood furniture with a Hawaiian/Japanese influence. Stellar artists Tai Lake from the Big Island and Randall Watkins from Maui are among those represented. Connoisseurs of hand-turned bowls will find the crème de la crème of the genre here: J. Kelly Dunn, Ron Kent, Todd Campbell, Ed Perrira, and Gary Stevens. You won't find a better selection elsewhere under one roof. The award-winning gallery has won accolades from the top travel and arts magazines in the country and has steered clear of trendiness and unfortunate tastes. At the Hotel Hana-Maui. © **808/248-8636.** www.hanacoast.com.

Hasegawa General Store Established in 1910, immortalized in song since 1961, burned to the ground in 1990, and back in business in 1991, this legendary store is indefatigable and more colorful than ever in its fourth generation in business. The aisles are choked with merchandise: coffee specially roasted and blended for the store, Ono Farms organic dried fruit, fishing equipment, every tape and CD that mentions Hana, the best books on Hana to be found, T-shirts, beach and garden essentials, baseball caps, film, baby food, napkins, and other necessities for the Hana life. Hana Hwy. © **808/248-8231.**

10

MAUI AFTER DARK

C entered around the $32-million Maui Arts & Cultural Center (MACC), in Kahului (© **808/242-7469**; www. mauiarts.org), the performing arts are alive and well on this island. The MACC remains the island's most prestigious entertainment venue, a first-class center for the visual and performing arts. Bonnie Raitt has performed here, as have Hiroshima, Pearl Jam, Ziggy Marley, Tony Bennett, the American Indian Dance Theatre, the Maui Symphony Orchestra, and Jonny Lang, not to mention the finest in local talent. The center boasts a visual-arts gallery, an outdoor amphitheater, offices, rehearsal space, a 300-seat theater for experimental performances, and a 1,200-seat main theater. The center's activities are well publicized locally, so check the Maui News or ask your hotel concierge what's going on during your visit.

In Search of Hawaiian, Jawaiian & More

Nightlife options on this island are limited. Revelers generally head for **Casanova** (**www.casanovamaui.com**) in Makawao. Because they are in different parts of this spread-out island, you'll either have to drive a great distance to these clubs or explore what's happening in the major hotels near you. The hotels generally have lobby lounges offering Hawaiian music, soft jazz, or hula shows beginning at sunset.

The best of Hawaiian music can be heard every Wednesday night at 7:30pm at the Napili Kai Beach Resort's indoor amphitheater, thanks to the Grammy-winning **Masters of Hawaiian Slack Key Guitar Concert Series** (© **888/669-3858**; www.slackkey.com). The weekly shows present a side of Hawaii that few visitors ever get to see. Host George Kahumoku, Jr., introduces a new slack-key master every week. Not only is there incredible Hawaiian music and singing, but George and his guest also "talk story" about old Hawaii, music, and Hawaiian culture. Not to be missed.

At the Movies

The 12-screen movie megaplex at the **Maui Mall,** 70 E. Kaahumanu Ave. (© **808/249-2222**), in Kahului, features current releases. In June, the not-to-be-missed **Maui Film Festival ★★★** (© **808/572-3456** or 579-9244; www. mauifilmfestival.com) puts on nights of cinema under the stars in Wailea (see "The Best Place in the World to See a Movie," below). The Maui Film Festival also presents "Academy House" films for the avant-garde, ultrahip movie buff Wednesday nights at the **Maui Arts & Cultural Center,** 1 Cameron Way (just off Kahului Beach Rd.), Kahului, usually followed by live music and poetry readings.

MAUI AFTER DARK

Introduction

FACING PAGE: Luau, Maui style.

A display at the Maui Arts & Cultural Center.

Film buffs can check the local newspapers to see what's playing at the other theaters around the island: the **Kaahumanu Theatres,** at the Kaahumanu Center, in Kahului (🕿 **808/873-3137**); the **Kukui Mall Theater,** 1819 S. Kihei Rd., in Kihei (🕿 **808/874-8624**); the Wallace Theaters at the **Wharf Cinema Center,** 658 Front St., in Lahaina (🕿 **808/249-2222**); and the **Front Street Theatres** at the Lahaina Center, 900 Front St. (🕿 **808/249-2222**).

At the Theater

It's not Broadway, but Maui does have live community theater at the **Iao Theater,** 68 N. Market St., in Wailuku (🕿 **808/242-6969** for the box office and program information or 808/244-8680 or the dinner theater option with Café O'Lei; www.mauionstage.com). Shows range from locally written productions to well-known plays and musicals.

WEST MAUI: LAHAINA, KAANAPALI & KAPALUA

The **Hard Rock Cafe,** 900 Front St., Lahaina (🕿 **808/667-7400**), occasionally offers live music, so it wouldn't hurt to call to see if something's up. Usually it features mainland bands, normally on weekends after 10pm. Cover ranges from $20 to $50.

You won't have to ask what's going on at **Cheeseburger in Paradise,** 811 Front St., Lahaina (🕿 **808/661-4855**), the two-story green-and-white building at the corner of Front and Lahainaluna streets. Just go outside and you'll hear it. Loud, live tropical rock blasts into the streets and out to sea nightly from 4:30 to 10pm (no cover).

Other venues for music in west Maui include the following:

- **Hula Grill,** in Whalers Village, Kaanapali (✆ **808/667-6636**), has live music (usually Hawaiian) from 3 to 5pm and again from 6:30 to 8:30pm nightly.

- **Kimo's,** 845 Front St., Lahaina (✆ **808/661-4811**), has live musicians at various times; call for details.

- **Lahaina Pizza,** 730 Front St., Lahaina (✆ **808/661-0700**), offers live music from 6:30 to 8:30pm Thursday through Saturday nights.

- **Leilani's on the Beach,** in Whalers Village, Kaanapali (✆ **808/661-4495**), has live music from 3 to 5pm Friday through Sunday; the styles range from contemporary Hawaiian to rock.

- **Maui Brewing Co.,** in the Kahana Gateway Shopping Center, Kahana (✆ **808/669-3474**), has live music Wednesday and Saturday nights from 9:30pm to 12:30am.

- **Moose McGillycuddy's,** 844 Front St., Lahaina (✆ **808/667-7758**), offers a DJ some nights from 5:30 to 8:30pm; the schedule varies, so call for details.

- **Pineapple Grill,** 200 Kapalua Dr., Kapalua (✆ **808/669-9600**), features Hawaiian music on Friday and jazz on Saturday from 7 to 10pm.

- **Pioneer Inn,** 658 Wharf St., Lahaina (✆ **808/661-3636**), offers a variety of live music Tuesday and Wednesday nights starting at 6pm.

- **Sansei Seafood Restaurant & Sushi Bar,** 600 Office Rd., Kapalua (✆ **808/669-6286**), has karaoke on Thursday and Friday from 10pm to 1am.

- **Sea House Restaurant,** at the Napili Kai Beach Resort, Napili (✆ **808/669-1500**), has live music from 7 to 9pm nightly.

The historic Iao Theater hosts Maui's rich community theater tradition.

THE BEST PLACE IN THE WORLD TO SEE A movie

Imagine lounging on a comfy beach chair on the island of Maui watching the stars come out in the night sky. As soon as it gets dark enough, the biggest outdoor screen you've ever seen comes to life with a film premiere. This has to be the best place in the entire world to watch movies.

If you're headed to Maui in June, plan your travel dates around the **Maui Film Festival** (℃ **808/572-3456** or 579-9244; www.mauifilmfestival.com), which always starts the Wednesday before Father's Day. This is an event you won't want to miss. The 5-day festival features nightly films in the "Celestial Cinema," an under-the-stars, open-air "outdoor theater" on the Wailea Golf Course. The event features premieres and special advance screenings on a 50-foot-wide screen in Dolby Digital Surround Sound. Festival organizer and film producer Barry Rivers selects "life-affirming" films that often become box-office hits.

In addition to the 5 days and nights of films, film workshops, and film-

maker panels, there's also terrific food: a Taste of Chocolate night, a Taste of Wailea (with Maui's top chefs creating exquisite culinary masterpieces), and a host of other foodie events. For the family, there's a Father's Day concert of contemporary Hawaiian music, a sand-sculpture contest, and picnics. And for those interested in Hawaii culture, the festival presents TheStarShow, where live images of celestial objects are projected onto the screen, as experts in Polynesian astronomy and cultural history take the audience on a tour of the night sky and Polynesian navigational lore.

As Rivers puts it: "Rising stars, shooting stars, movie stars, all under the stars."

A Night to Remember: Luau, Maui Style

Most of the larger hotels in Maui's major resorts offer luau on a regular basis. You'll pay about $65 to $92 to attend one. Don't expect it to be a homegrown affair prepared in the traditional Hawaiian way. There are, however, commercial luau that capture the romance and spirit of the luau with quality food and entertainment in outdoor settings.

Maui's best choice is indisputably the nightly **Old Lahaina Luau** (℃ **800/248-5828** or 808/667-1998; www.oldlahainaluau.com). On its 1-acre site just ocean side of the Lahaina Cannery, at 1251 Front St., the Old Lahaina Luau maintains its high standards in food and entertainment in a peerless ocean-front setting. Local craftspeople display their wares only a few feet from the water. Seating is provided on lauhala mats for those who wish to dine as the traditional Hawaiians did, but there are tables for everyone else. There's no fire dancing in the program, but you won't miss it (for that, go to the **Feast at Lele,** p. 170). This luau offers a healthy balance of entertainment, showmanship, authentic high-quality food, educational value, and sheer romantic beauty. (No watered-down mai tais, either; these are the real thing.)

The luau begins at sunset and features Tahitian and Hawaiian entertainment, including various forms of hula and an intelligent narrative on the dance's rocky course of survival into modern times. The entertainment is riveting, even for jaded locals. The food, served from an open-air thatched structure, is as much Pacific Rim as authentically Hawaiian: *imu*-roasted kalua pig, baked mahimahi in Maui-onion cream sauce, guava chicken, teriyaki sirloin steak, lomi salmon, poi, dried fish, poke, Hawaiian sweet potato, sautéed vegetables, seafood salad, and the ultimate taste treat, taro leaves with coconut milk. The cost is $92 for adults, $62 for children 12 and under.

Ulalena: Hula, Myth & Modern Dance

The buzz in Lahaina is all about **Ulalena ★**, Maui Theatre, 878 Front St., Lahaina (✆ **877/688-4800** or 808/661-9913; www.ulalena.com), a riveting evening of entertainment that weaves Hawaiian mythology with drama, dance, and state-of-the-art multimedia capabilities in a multimillion-dollar theater. Polynesian dance, original music, acrobatics, and chant, performed by a local and international cast, combine to create an evocative experience that often leaves the audience speechless. It's interactive, with dancers coming down the aisles, drummers and musicians in surprising corners, and mind-boggling stage and lighting effects that draw the audience in. Some special moments: the goddesses dancing on the moon, the white sail of the first Europeans, the wrath of the volcano goddess Pele, the labors of the field-worker immigrants. The story unfolds seamlessly; at the end, you'll be shocked to realize that not a single word of dialogue was spoken. Performances are held Tuesday, Wednesday, Friday, and Saturday at 6:30pm. Tickets are $60 to $79 for adults, $40 to $59 for children 12 and under.

Maui-Style Magic

A very different type of live entertainment is **Warren & Annabelle's,** 900 Front St., Lahaina (✆ **808/667-6244;** www.warrenandannabelles.com), a

A traditional performance at the Old Lahaina Luau.

Ulalena is a riveting evening of entertainment that weaves Hawaiian mythology with drama, dance, and state-of-the-art multimedia capabilities.

Nightlife in Maui begins at sunset, when all eyes turn westward to see how the day will end. And what better way to take it all in than over cocktails? With its view of Molokai to the northwest and Lanai to the west, Kaanapali and west Maui boast panoramic vistas unique to this island. In south Maui's resort areas of Wailea and Makena, tiny Kahoolawe and the crescent-shaped Molokini islet are visible on the horizon, and the West Maui Mountains look like an entirely separate island. No matter what your vantage point, you are likely to be treated to an astonishing view.

In Kaanapali, park at Whalers Village and head for **Leilani's on the Beach** (📞 808/661-4495) or **Hula Grill** (📞 808/667-6636), next to each other on the beach. Both have busy, upbeat bars and tables bordering the sand. These are happy places for great people-watching, gazing over at Lanai, and enjoying mai tais and margaritas. Hula Grill's Barefoot Bar appetizer menu is a cut above. Leilani's has live music Friday through Sunday from 3 to 5pm, while at Hula Grill the happy hour starts at 3pm, with live music from 3 to 5pm and hula at 8pm.

Now, Lahaina: It's a sunset-lover's nirvana, lined with restaurants that have elevated mai tais to an art form. If you love loud rock, head for **Cheeseburger in Paradise** (📞 808/661-4855). A few doors away, the **Lahaina Fish Company** (📞 808/661-3472) and **Kimo's** (📞 808/661-4811) are magnets all day long and especially at sunset, when their open decks fill up with revelers.

At the southern end of Lahaina, in the 505 Front Street complex, **Pacific'O** (📞 808/667-4341) is a solid hit, with a raised bar, seating on the ocean, and a backdrop of Lanai across the channel. A few steps away, sister restaurant **I'O** shares the same vista, with an appetizer menu that includes smoked sashimi, cowboy ribs, and thai curry asparagus soup, and a curved bar that will wow you as much as the drop-dead-gorgeous view.

In Wailea, the restaurants at the Shops at Wailea, including the highly successful **Tommy Bahama** (📞 808/875-9983) and **Longhi's** (📞 808/891-8883), are noteworthy additions to the beachfront retail-and-dining scene. **Ferraro's** and **Spago** (📞 808/874-8000), both at the neighboring Four Seasons Resort Wailea, have great sunset views to go with their Italian and Pacific Rim menus. Farther south, in Makena, you can't beat the Maui Prince's **Molokini Bar & Grill** (📞 808/874-1111), with its casual elegance and unequaled vista of Molokini islet on the ocean side and, on the mauka side, a graceful, serene courtyard with ponds, rock gardens, and lush foliage. Adding to the setting is the appetizer menu, which comes from the Prince Court kitchen. From 5:30 to 9:30pm nightly, the *pupu* menu features a Molokini sampler platter for two: honey-glazed baby back ribs, chicken yakitori, and shrimp and crab spring rolls. Don't forget the upcountry view: **Kula Lodge** (📞 808/878-2517) has a phenomenal one that takes in central Maui, the West Maui Mountains (looking like Shangri-La in the distance), and the coastline. Dinner begins at 4pm, so you can take in the sunset over Cajun ahi, New York steak, seafood fra Diablo, braised pork ribs, and other country-comfort fare.

Nightlife in Hana is pretty sparse. The only exception is the **Hotel Hana-Maui** (✆ 808/248-8211), which features Hawaiian music in the Paniolo Lounge Wednesday through Sunday from 7 to 9:30pm, and hosts a dinner hula show every Friday from 7 to 7:45pm in the Main Dining Room.

magic/comedy cocktail show with illusionist Warren Gibson and "Annabelle," a ghost from the 1800s who plays the grand piano (even taking requests from the audience) as Warren dazzles you with his sleight-of-hand magic. Appetizers, desserts, and cocktails are available (either as a package or a la carte). Check-in is at 5 and 7:30pm. The show-only price is $56; the show plus gourmet appetizers and dessert costs $95. You must be 21 to attend.

The **Kaanapali Beach Hotel** has a wonderful show called **Kupanaha** (✆ 808/661-0011; www.kupanaha.com) that is perfect for the entire family. It features the renowned magicians Jody and Kathleen Baran and their entire family, including child-prodigy magicians Katrina and Crystal. The dinner show includes magic, illusions, and the story of the Hawaii fire goddess, Pele, presented through hula and chant performed by the children of the Kano'eau Dance Academy. The shows are Tuesday through Thursday and Saturday; tickets are $79 to $89 for adults, and $39 to $55 for children 6 to 12. Prices include dinner (entree choices include Island fish, roasted stuffed chicken, steak and shrimp, and a vegetarian dish, with a children's menu available).

SOUTH MAUI: KIHEI-WAILEA

The Kihei, Wailea, and Maalaea areas in south Maui also feature music in a variety of locations:

- **Capischi,** at the Diamond Resort, 555 Kaukahi St., Wailea (✆ 808/879-2224), has live music Friday and Saturday from 7 to 10pm.
- **Kahale's Beach Club,** 36 Keala Place, Kihei (✆ 808/875-7711), offers a potpourri of live music nightly at 6:30pm; call for details.
- **Life's a Beach,** 1913 S. Kihei Rd., Kihei (✆ 808/891-8010), has nightly live music; call for times.
- **Lobby Lounge,** at the Four Seasons Resort Maui at Wailea (✆ 808/874-8000), features nightly live music from 5 to 11pm.
- **Lulu's,** 1945 S. Kihei Rd., Kihei (✆ 808/879-9944), offers entertainment most nights, call for schedule, cover charges, and times.
- **Mulligan's on the Blue,** 100 Kaukahi St., Wailea (✆ 808/874-1131), has live music nightly. Call for times and cover or check it out at www.mulligans ontheblue.com.
- **Sansei Seafood Restaurant & Sushi Bar,** in Kihei Town Center (✆ 808/879-0004), has karaoke Thursday through Saturday from 10pm to 1am.
- **South Shore Tiki Lounge,** 1913 S. Kihei Rd., Kihei (✆ 808/874-6444), has live music Wednesday through Monday from 4 to 6pm, and dancing from 10pm to 2am.
- **Sports Page Bar,** 2411 S. Kihei Rd., Kihei (✆ 808/879-0602), has live music or a DJ Friday and Saturday nights starting at 9pm.

UPCOUNTRY MAUI

Upcountry in Makawao, the party never ends at **Casanova,** 1188 Makawao Ave. (✆ **808/572-0220**), the popular Italian ristorante where the good times roll with the pasta. The newly renovated bar area has large booths, all the better for socializing around the stage and dance floor. If a big-name mainland band is resting up on Maui following a sold-out concert on Oahu, you may find its members setting up for an impromptu night here. DJs take over on Wednesday (ladies' night); on Friday, and Saturday, live entertainment or a DJ draws fun-lovers from even the most remote reaches of the island. Entertainment starts at 10pm and continues to 1:30am (check the website, www.casanovamaui.com, for schedules and cover charges). Expect good blues, rock 'n' roll, reggae, jazz, Hawaiian, and the top names in local and visiting entertainment. Elvin Bishop, the local duo Hapa, Los Lobos, and many others have taken Casanova's stage. The cover is usually $5 to $10. Go Sunday afternoons, from 2:30 to 5:30pm, for excellent live jazz.

PAIA & CENTRAL MAUI

In central Maui, **Café Marc Aurel,** 28 N. Market St., Wailuku (✆ **808/244-0852;** www.cafemarcaurel.com), is the place for a range of eclectic music, from folk to Hawaiian to ethnic, and even some open-mic nights; call for information. The **Kahului Ale House,** 355 E. Kamehameha Ave., Kahului (✆ **808/877-9001;** www.alehouse.net), offers live music on Monday through Thursday, and live DJs Friday through Sunday. Times vary; call or check the website for schedule and cover charges.

In Paia, **Charley's Restaurant,** 142 Hana Hwy. (✆ **808/579-8085**), features an eclectic selection of music from country and western (Willie Nelson has been seen sitting in) to fusion/reggae to rock 'n' roll; call for details. Also in Paia, the **Moana Bakery & Cafe,** 71 Baldwin Ave. (✆ **808/579-9999**), has everything from Hawaiian music to cool jazz to sizzling Latin to swing; call for details.

10

Upcountry Maui

MAUI AFTER DARK

WATCH FOR THE green flash

If you're gathered in a crowd on Maui watching a sunset, you may hear someone call out: "Green flash!" If you're lucky, you may get to see it yourself.

The romantic version of the story is the green flash happens when the sun kisses the ocean good night (honeymooners love this version). The scientific version is not quite as dreamy: Light bends as it goes around the curve of the earth. When the sun dips beneath the horizon, it is at the far end of the spectrum. So this refraction of the sun's light, coupled with the atmosphere on the extreme angle of the sunset on the horizon, causes only the color green to be seen in the color spectrum just before the light disappears.

Here's how to view the green flash: First, it has to be a clear day, with no clouds or haze on the horizon. Second, the sun has to set on the ocean (if it sets behind an island, you won't see the flash). Keep checking the sun as it drops. If the conditions are ideal, just as the sun drops into the blue water, a "flash" or laserlike beam of green will appear to shoot out for an instant.

MOLOKAI, THE MOST HAWAIIAN ISLE

Born of volcanic eruptions 1.5 million years ago, Molokai remains a time capsule on the dawn of the 21st century. It has no deluxe resorts, no stoplights, and no buildings taller than a coconut tree. Molokai is the least developed of all the islands, making it especially attractive to adventure travelers and peace seekers.

Molokai lives up to its reputation as the most Hawaiian place chiefly through its lineage; there are more people here of Hawaiian blood than anywhere else. This slipper-shaped island was the birthplace of hula and the ancient science of aquaculture. An aura of ancient mysticism clings to the land here, and the old ways still govern life. The residents survive by fishing and hunting wild pigs and axis deer on the range. Some folks still catch fish for dinner by throwing nets and trolling the reef.

Modern Hawaii's high-rise hotels, shopping centers, and other trappings of tourism haven't been able to gain a foothold here. The lone low-rise resort on the island, Kaluakoi—built 30 years ago, now closed and empty—was Molokai's token attempt at contemporary tourism.

Not everyone will love Molokai. The slow-paced, simple life of the people and the absence of contemporary landmarks attract those in search of the "real" Hawaii. I once received a letter from a New York City resident who claimed that any "big city resident" would "blanche" at the lack of "sophistication." This is a place where Mother Nature is wild and uninhibited, with very little intrusion by man. Forget sophistication; this is one of the few spots on the planet where one

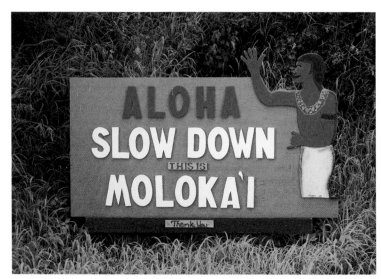

PREVIOUS PAGE: The cliffs of Molokai's north shore. ABOVE: A little friendly advice for Molokai's visitors.

Molokai

WEST END
- Moomomi Dunes Preserve **1**
- Maunaloa

NORTH COAST
- Palaau State Park
- Kalaupapa Peninsula
- Kalaupapa Historical Park
- Kalaupapa **9**
- Kalae
- Kualapuu
- Molokai Airport
- Hoolehua

PALI COAST
- Mokapu I.
- Lae O Kapaihu Pt.
- Kaunakakai **10**
- Kamiloloa
- One Alii Beach
- Kamehameha V Hwy.
- Kamalo
- Pukoo **16**
- Pauwalu
- Waialua
- Murphy's Beach
- Sandy Beach

EAST END
- Halawa Valley
- Halawa Beach
- Cape Halawa

Kaiwi Channel
Kaloha Channel
Pailolo Channel
PACIFIC OCEAN

Ilio Pt.
Kepuhi Bay
Papohaku Beach
Kapukahehu Beach
Kepuhi
Manalo Gulch
Kahaiko Gulch
Waihanau Gulch

5 mi
5 km

- Ancient Fishponds (from Kaunakakai to Waialua) **15**
- Coffees of Hawaii Plantation Store **4**
- Ililiopae Heiau **16**
- Ironwood Hills Golf Course **5**
- Kalaupapa Lookout **7**
- Kalaupapa National Historical Park **9**
- Kamakou Preserve **12**
- Kapuaiwa Coconut Grove/Kiowea Park **10**
- Kaunakakai Wharf **11**
- Molokai Mule Ride **8**
- Molokai Museum and Cultural Center **6**
- Molokai Ranch **2**
- Moomomi Dunes **1**
- Palaau State Park **7**
- Phallic Rock **7**
- Purdy's All-Natural Macadamia Nut Farm **3**
- R. W. Meyer Sugar Mill **6**
- St. Joseph's Catholic Church **13**
- Smith Bronte Landing Site **14**

can stand in awe of the island's diverse natural wonders: Hawaii's highest water-fall and greatest collection of fishponds; the world's tallest sea cliffs; sand dunes, coral reefs, rainforests, and hidden coves; and gloriously empty beaches.

EXPLORING THE "MOST HAWAIIAN" ISLE Only 38 miles from end to end and just 10 miles wide, Molokai stands like a big green wedge in the blue Pacific. This long, narrow island is like yin and yang: One side is a flat, austere, arid desert; the other is a lush, green, tropical Eden. Three volcanic eruptions formed Molokai; the last produced the island's "thumb"—a peninsula jutting out of the steep cliffs of the north shore like a punctuation mark on the island's geological story.

On the red-dirt southern plain, where most of the island's 7,000 residents live, the rustic village of **Kaunakakai** ★ looks like the set of an old Hollywood western, with sun-faded clapboard houses and horses tethered on the side of the road. Mile marker 0, in the center of town, divides the island into east and west.

Eastbound, along the **coastal highway** ★★★ named for King Kamehameha V, are Gauguin-like, palm-shaded cottages set on small coves or near fishponds; spectacular vistas that take in Maui, Lanai, and Kahoolawe; and a fringing coral reef visible through the crystal-clear waves. This is the place to stay if you are looking for a quiet, relaxing vacation in "old Hawaii."

Out on the sun-scorched West End, overlooking a gold-sand beach with water usually too rough to swim in, is the island's lone destination resort, **Kaluakoi** (where the hotel is currently closed). The old hilltop plantation town of **Maunaloa** has been a ghost town since 2008, when the Molokai Ranch closed the expensive lodge (and dining room), the movie theater, restaurant, and a retail store. Cowboys no longer ride the range on **Molokai Ranch,** a 65,000-acre spread, which was also closed in 2008.

Elsewhere around the island, in hamlets like **Kualapuu,** old farmhouses with pickup trucks in the yards and sleepy dogs under the shade trees stand amid row crops of papaya, coffee, and corn—just like farm towns in Anywhere, USA.

But that's not all there is. The "backside" of Molokai is a rugged wilderness of spectacular beauty. On the outskirts of **Kaunakakai,** the land rises gradually from sea-level fishponds to cool uplands and the Molokai Forest, long ago stripped of sandalwood for the China trade. All that remains is an indentation in the earth shaped like a ship's hull, a crude matrix that gave them a rough idea of when they'd cut enough sandalwood to fill a ship (it's identified on good maps as *Luanamokuiliahi,* or Sandalwood Boat).

The land inclines sharply to the lofty mountains and the nearly mile-high summit of Mount Kamakou, then ends abruptly with emerald-green cliffs, which plunge into a lurid aquamarine sea dotted with tiny deserted islets. These breathtaking 3,250-foot **sea cliffs** ★★, the highest in the world, stretch 14 majestic miles along Molokai's north shore, laced by waterfalls and creased by five valleys once occupied by early Hawaiians who built stone terraces and used waterfalls to irrigate taro patches.

Long after the sea cliffs were formed, a tiny volcano erupted out of the sea at their feet and spread lava into a flat, leaflike peninsula called **Kalaupapa** ★★★—the 1860s leper exile where Father Damien de Veuster of Belgium devoted his life to care for the afflicted. A few people remain in the remote colony by choice, keeping it tidy for visitors. As we went to press, the Catholic Church was on the verge of announcing sainthood for Father Damien, if granted, Kalaupapa, and all of Molokai may become a haven for spiritual pilgrims.

WHAT A VISIT TO MOLOKAI IS REALLY LIKE There's plenty of aloha on Molokai, but the so-called "friendly island" remains ambivalent about vacationers. One of the least-visited Hawaiian islands, Molokai welcomes about 50,000 to 70,000 visitors annually on its own take-it-or-leave-it terms; it never wanted to attract too big of a crowd, anyway. A sign at the airport offers the first clue: SLOW DOWN, YOU ON MOLOKAI NOW—wisdom to heed on this island, where life proceeds at its own pace.

Rugged, red-dirt Molokai isn't for everyone, but those who like to explore remote places and seek their own adventures should love it. The best of the island can be seen only on foot, bicycle, mule, horseback, kayak, or boat. The sea cliffs are accessible only by sea in summer (when the Pacific is calm) or via a 10-mile trek through the Wailau Valley—an adventure only a handful of hardy hikers attempt each year. The great **Kamakou Preserve** is open just once a month, by special arrangement with the Nature Conservancy. Even **Moomomi,** which holds bony relics of prehistoric flightless birds and other creatures, requires a guide to divulge the secrets of the dunes.

Those in search of nightlife have come to the wrong place; Molokai shuts down after sunset. The only public diversions are softball games under the lights of Mitchell Pauole Field, movies at Maunaloa, and the few restaurants that stay open after dark, often serving local brew and pizza.

The "friendly" island may enchant you as the "real" Hawaii of your dreams. On the other hand, you may leave shaking your head, never to return. Regardless of how you approach Molokai, remember our advice: Take it slow.

ORIENTATION

Arriving

BY PLANE Molokai has two airports, but you'll most likely fly into **Hoolehua Airport,** which everyone calls "the Molokai Airport." It's on a dusty plain about 6 miles from Kaunakakai town. Twin-engine planes offer daily service. Commuter airlines Pacific Wings started operating a discount airline, **PW Express** (© **888/866-5022** or 808/873-0877; www.pacificwings. com) with two daily nonstop flights between Molokai and Honolulu, and one daily flight between Kahului, Maui, and Molokai (there are three direct flights from Honolulu and two from Kahului daily into Kalaupapa). Another inexpensive air carrier is **Mokulele Airlines** (© **808/426-7070;** www.mokuleleairlines.com). Another interisland carrier is **Island Air** (© **800/652-6541** from the mainland or 800/652-6541 interisland; www. islandair.com), with 5 to 10 direct flights a day from Honolulu. I must say that I have gotten less than sterling service from Island Air; their reservations system (or customer service, depending on who is blaming whom) has left me stranded in mid-route, not once, but twice!

BY BOAT You can travel across the seas by ferry from Maui's Lahaina Harbor to Molokai's Kaunakakai Wharf on the *Molokai Princess* (© **877/500-6284** or 808/667-6165; www.mauiprincess.com). The 100-foot yacht, certified for 149 passengers, is fitted with the latest generation of gyroscopic stabilizers, making the ride smoother. The ferry makes the 1-hour-and-45-minute journey from Lahaina to Kaunakakai daily; at press time a one-way ticket cost $42 plus a fuel surcharge of $12 for a total of $54 adults (half prices for kids ages 3 to 12, under 3 years are free). Be sure to check what the current fuel charge is before you go. Or you can choose to tour the island from two different package options: Cruise-Drive, which includes round-trip passage and a rental car; or the Alii Tour, which is a guided tour in an air-conditioned van plus lunch.

Visitor Information

Contact the **Molokai Visitors Association,** P.O. Box 960, Kaunakakai, HI 96748 (© **800/800-6367** from the U.S. mainland and Canada, or 808/553-3876; www.molokai-hawaii.com), or stop by their office in The Moore Center, 2 Kamoi St., Ste. 200, Kaunakakai. The staff can give you all the information you need on what to see and do while you're on Molokai.

The Island in Brief

KAUNAKAKAI ★

Kaunakakai is the closest thing Molokai has to a business district. Friendly Isle Realty and Friendly Isle Travel offer islanders dream homes and vacations; Rabang's Filipino Food posts bad checks in the window; antlered deer-head trophies guard the grocery aisles at Misaki's Market; and Kanemitsu's, the town's legendary bakery, churns out fresh loaves of onion-cheese bread daily. With its Old West–style storefronts laid out in a 3-block grid, Kaunakakai is a town from the past. At the end of Wharf Road is Molokai Wharf, a picturesque place to fish, photograph, and just hang out.

Kaunakakai is the dividing point between the lush, green East End and the dry, arid West End. On the west side of town stands a cactus and on the east side of town, there's thick, green vegetation.

THE NORTH COAST ★★

Upland from Kaunakakai, the land tilts skyward and turns green, with scented plumeria in yards and glossy coffee trees all in a row, until it blooms into a true forest—and then abruptly ends at a great precipice, falling 3,250 feet to the sea. The green sea cliffs are creased with five V-shaped crevices so deep that light is seldom seen (to paraphrase a Hawaiian poet). The north coast is a remote, forbidding place, with a solitary peninsula—**Kalaupapa ★★★**—that was once the home for exiled lepers (it's now a National Historical Park). This region is easy on the eyes but difficult to visit. It lies at a cool elevation, and frequent rain squalls blow in from the ocean. In summer the ocean is calm, providing great opportunities for kayaking, fishing, and swimming, but during the rest of the year, giant waves come rolling onto the shores.

THE WEST END ★

This end of the island, once home to **Molokai Ranch,** is miles of stark desert terrain, bordered by the most beautiful white-sand beaches in Hawaii. The rugged rolling land slopes down to Molokai's only destination resort, **Kaluakoi,** a cul-de-sac of condos clustered around a 3-decades-old seafront hotel (closed for a decade now) near 3-mile-long Papohaku, the island's biggest beach. On the way to Kaluakoi, you'll find **Maunaloa,** a 1920s-era pineapple-plantation town that's been a ghost town since the Molokai Ranch closed all its operations in 2008. The West End is dry, dry, dry. It hardly ever rains, but when it does (usually in the winter), expect a downpour and lots of red mud.

THE EAST END ★★★

The area east of Kaunakakai becomes lush, green, and tropical, with golden pocket beaches and a handful of cottages and condos that are popular with thrifty travelers. With this voluptuous landscape comes rain. However, most storms are brief (15-min.) affairs. Winter is Hawaii's rainy season, so expect more rain from January to March, but even then, the storms usually are brief and the sun comes back out.

Beyond Kaunakakai, the two-lane road curves along the coast past piggeries, palm groves, and a 20-mile string of fishponds as well as an ancient *heiau* (temple), Damien-built churches, and a few contemporary condos by the sea. The road ends in the glorious **Halawa Valley ★**, one of Hawaii's most beautiful valleys.

[Fast FACTS] MOLOKAI

Molokai and Lanai are both part of Maui County. For **local emergencies,** call ☎ **911.** For nonemergencies, call the **police** at ☎ **808/553-5355,** the **fire department** at ☎ **808/553-5601,** or **Molokai General Hospital,** in Kaunakakai, at ☎ **808/553-5331.**

Downtown Kaunakakai has a **post office** (☎ **808/553-5845**) and several banks, including the **Bank of Hawaii** (☎ **808/553-3273**), which has a 24-hour ATM.

GETTING AROUND

Getting around Molokai isn't easy if you don't have a rental car, and rental cars are often hard to find here. On holiday weekends (see "When to Go" in chapter 3), car-rental agencies simply run out of cars. Book before you go. There's no municipal transit or shuttle service, but a 24-hour taxi service is available (see below).

CAR-RENTAL AGENCIES Rental cars are available from **Alamo,** (☎ **877/222-9075;** www.alamo.com), located at the Molokai Airport. **National** has a rental desk at the Hotel Molokai (☎ **877/222-9058** or 808/553-3596; www.nationalcar.com).

TAXI & TOUR SERVICES Molokai Off-Road Tours & Taxi (☎ **808/553-3369;** www.molokai.com/offroad) offers regular taxi service, an airport shuttle ($32 for one or two people one-way to Kaunakakai). Also available is **Midnight Taxi** (☎ **808/658-1410;** $29 to Kaunakakai)

FROMMER'S FAVORITE molokai experiences

Riding a Mule into a Leper Colony.
Don't pass up the opportunity to see this hauntingly beautiful peninsula. Buzzy Sproat's mules (p. 343) go up and down the 3-mile Kalaupapa Trail to Molokai's famous leper colony. The views are breathtaking: You'll see the world's highest sea cliffs (over 300 stories tall) and waterfalls plunging thousands of feet into the ocean. If you're afraid of heights, catch the views from the Kalaupapa Lookout.

Venturing into the Garden of Eden.
Drive the 30 miles along Molokai's East End. Take your time. Stop to smell the flowers and pick guavas by the side of the road. Pull over for a swim. Wave at every car you pass and every person you see. At the end of the road, stand on the beach at Halawa Valley and see Hawaii as it must have looked in A.D. 650, when the first people arrived on the islands.

Celebrating the Ancient Hula. Hula is the heartbeat of Hawaiian culture, and Molokai is its birthplace. Although most visitors to Hawaii never get to see the real thing, it's possible to see it here— once a year, on the third Saturday in May, when Molokai celebrates the birth of the hula at its **Ka Hula Piko Festival.** The daylong affair includes dance, music, food, and crafts. For details, contact the Moloka'i Visitor Association (ⓒ **800/800-6367** or 808/553-3876; www.molokai-hawaii.com).

Strolling the Sands at Papohaku. Go early, when the tropical sun isn't so fierce, and stroll this 3-mile stretch of unspoiled golden sand on Molokai's

West End. It's one of the longest beaches in Hawaii. The big surf and riptides make swimming somewhat risky, but Papohaku is perfect for walking, beachcombing, and, in the evening, sunset watching.

Traveling Back in Time on the Pepeopae Trail. This awesome hike takes you through the Kamakou Preserve (p. 335) and back a few million years in time. Along the misty trail (actually a boardwalk across the bog), expect close encounters of the botanical kind: mosses, sedges, violets, lichens, and knee-high ancient ohia.

Soaking in the Warm Waters off Sandy Beach. On the East End, about 20 miles outside Kaunakakai—just before the road starts to climb to Halawa Valley—lies a small pocket of white sand known as Sandy Beach. Submerging yourself here in the warm, calm waters (an outer reef protects the cove) is a sensuous experience par excellence.

Snorkeling among Clouds of Butterflyfish. The calm waters off Murphy (Kumimi) Beach, on the East End, are perfect for snorkelers. Just don your gear and head to the reef, where you'll find lots of exotic tropical fish, including long-nosed butterflyfish, saddle wrasses, and convict tangs.

Kayaking along the North Shore. This is the Hawaii of your dreams: waterfalls thundering down sheer cliffs, remote sand beaches, miles of tropical vegetation, and the wind whispering in your ear. The best times to go are late March and early April, or in summer, especially August to September, when the normally galloping ocean lies down flat.

Watching the Sunset from a Coconut Grove. Kapuaiwa Coconut Grove/ Kiowea Park (p. 338), off Maunaloa Highway (Hwy. 460), is a perfect place to watch the sunset. The sky behind the coconut trees fills with a kaleidoscope of colors as the sun sinks into the Pacific. Be careful where you sit, though: Falling coconuts could have you seeing stars well before dusk.

Sampling the Local Brew. Saunter up to the Espresso Bar at the Coffees of Hawaii Plantation Store (p. 351) in Kualapuu for a fresh cup of java made from beans that were grown, processed, and packed on this 450-acre plantation. While you sip, survey the vast collection of native crafts.

Tasting Aloha at a Macadamia Nut Farm. It could be the owner, Tuddie Purdy, and his friendly disposition that make the macadamia nuts here taste so good. Or it could be his years of practice in growing, harvesting, and shelling them on his 1½-acre farm. Either way, Purdy produces a perfect crop. See how he does it on a short, free tour of Purdy's All-Natural Macadamia Nut Farm (p. 339) in Hoolehua, just a nut's throw from the airport.

Talking Story with the Locals. The number-one favorite pastime of most islanders is "talking story," or exchanging experiences and knowledge. You can probably find residents more than willing to share their wisdom with you while fishing from the wharf at Kaunakakai, hanging out at Molokai Fish & Dive (p. 350), or having coffee at any of the island's restaurants.

Posting a Nut. Why send a picturesque postcard to your friends and family back home when you can send a coconut? The Hoolehua Post Office (p. 338) will supply the free coconuts if you'll supply the postage (which averages $9–$13 for a mainland-bound coconut).

WHERE TO STAY

Molokai is Hawaii's most affordable island, especially for hotels. And because the island's restaurants are few, most hotel rooms and condo units come with kitchens, which can save you a bundle on dining costs.

The downside is that there aren't too many accommodations options on Molokai—mostly B&Bs, condos, a few quaint oceanfront vacation rentals, and a motel-like hotel. For camping on Molokai, hardy souls can pitch their own tent at the beach or in the cool upland forest (see "Hiking & Camping," later in this chapter). I've listed my top picks below; for additional options, contact **Molokai Vacation Properties,** P.O. Box 1979, Kaunakakai, HI 96748 (✆ **800/367-2984** or 808/553-8334; fax 808/553-3783; www.molokai-vacation-rental.com). *Note:* Taxes of 12.42% will be added to your hotel bill. Parking is free.

Kaunakakai

MODERATE

Hotel Molokai ★ ☺ Since the closing of the Lodge at Molokai Ranch, this nostalgic Hawaiian motel-like complex is the only hotel on the island. The modest hotel is composed of a series of modified A-frame units, nestled under coco palms along a gray-sand beach that has a great view of Lanai but isn't good for swimming. Several years ago the entire hotel underwent a $1-million renovation, from repaving the parking lot to redoing the kitchen. The interiors of all the rooms have been upgraded and look fresh. This is a modest budget hotel—the rooms have all the necessities but aren't fancy. Be sure to ask for a room with a ceiling fan; most rooms have a lanai. The mattresses are on the soft side, the sheets thin, and the bath towels rough, but you're on Molokai. The kitchenettes have coffeemakers, toasters, pots, and a two-burner stove. The front desk is open only from 7am to 9pm; late check-ins or visitors with problems have to go to security.

Kamehameha V Hwy. (P.O. Box 1020), Kaunakakai, HI 96748. ✆ **877/553-5347** or 808/553-5347. Fax 800/477-2329. www.hotelmolokai.com. 54 units. $159–$179; $199 with kitchen; from $249 double suite. Extra bed/crib $25. AE, DISC, MC, V. **Amenities:** Fairly good and reasonably priced restaurant w/bar; babysitting; bike rentals; outdoor pool; watersports equipment rentals. *In room:* A/C, TV, fridge, hair dryer, Internet $10/day, kitchenette (in some rooms).

Molokai Shores Suites ☺ Basic units with kitchens and large lanais face a small gold-sand beach in this quiet complex of three-story Polynesian-style buildings, less than a mile from Kaunakakai. Alas, the beach is mostly for show (offshore, it's shallow mud flats underfoot), fishing, or launching kayaks, but the swimming pool and barbecue area come with an ocean view, and the spacious units make this a good choice for families. Well-tended gardens, spreading lawns, and palms frame a restful view of fishponds, offshore reefs, and neighbor islands. The central location is a plus. There's no daily maid service. I have received some letters complaining about the lack of maintenance and cleanliness; the management swears that they are taking steps to correct these deficiencies. On my most recent visit, the grounds and units I saw were clean and well maintained. However, keep in mind that these units are individually owned (as well as managed by various management companies).

Kamehameha V Hwy. (P.O. Box 1037), Kaunakakai, HI 96748. ✆ **800/367-5004** or 808/553-5954. Fax 808/553-5954. www.castleresorts.com. 102 units. $169–$199 1-bedroom apt (sleeps up to 4); $250 2-bedroom apt (up to 6). Discounted rates for weekly and extended stays, plus

Where to Stay & Dine on Molokai

ACCOMMODATIONS

A'ahi Place **6**
Aloha Beach House **9**
Country Cottages at
  Pu'u O Hoku Ranch **10**
Dunbar Beachfront Cottages **7**
Hotel Molokai **4**
Ka Hale Mala Bed &
  Breakfast **5**
Ke Nani Kai Resort **1**
Molokai Shores **3**
Paniolo Hale **1**

DINING

Hotel Molokai **4**
Kamoi Snack-n-Go **2**
Kanemitsu's Bakery &
  Restaurant **2**
Mana'e Goods & Grindz **8**
Molokai Drive-Inn **2**
Molokai Pizza Cafe **2**
Outpost Natural Foods **2**
Paddlers' Inn **2**
Sundown Deli **2**

corporate, military, and senior discounts and Internet-only specials. AE, DISC, MC, V. **Amenities:** Putting green. *In room:* TV, fridge, kitchen, Wi-Fi.

INEXPENSIVE

A'ahi Place *✦* Just outside of the main town of Kaunakakai and up a small hill lies this dream vacation cottage, complete with a wicker-filled sitting area, a kitchen, and two full-size beds in the bedroom. Two lanais make great places to just sit and enjoy the stars at night. The entire property is surrounded by tropical plants, flowers, and fruit trees. You can choose to forgo breakfast or for $10 more per night (for two) get all the fixings for a continental breakfast (homegrown Molokai coffee, fresh-baked goods, and fruit from the property) placed in the kitchen. For those who seek a quiet vacation with no phone or TV to distract you, this is the place. And for those who wish to explore Molokai, the central location is perfect.

P.O. Box 2006, Kaunakakai, HI 96748. © **808/553-8033.** www.molokai.com/aahi. 1 unit. $75–$85 double. Continental breakfast $10 extra. Extra person $20. 3-night minimum. No credit cards. *In room:* Fridge, kitchen, no phone.

Ka Hale Mala Bed & Breakfast *✦* In a subdivision just outside town is this large four-room unit, with a private entrance through the garden and a Jacuzzi just outside. Inside, you'll find white rattan furnishings, room enough to sleep four, and a full kitchen. The helpful owners, Jack and Cheryl, meet all guests at the airport like long-lost relatives. They'll happily share their homegrown, organic produce; we recommend paying the extra $10 each for breakfast here. The owners can also supply a couple of bikes and snorkel and picnic gear.

7 Kamakana Place (P.O. Box 1582), Kaunakakai, HI 96748 (off Kamehameha V Hwy., before mile marker 5). ©/fax **808/553-9009.** www.molokai-bnb.com. 1 unit. $80 double without breakfast; $90 double with breakfast. Extra person $15 without breakfast; $20 with breakfast. No credit cards. **Amenities:** Jacuzzi. *In room:* TV, fridge, kitchen.

The West End

MODERATE

Paniolo Hale ★ 🎁 Tucked into a verdant garden on the dry West End, this condo complex has the advantage of being next door to a white-sand beach and a golf course. The two-story, old Hawaii ranch-house design is airy and homey, with oak floors and walls of folding-glass doors that open to huge screened verandas, doubling your living space. All are spacious and well equipped, with full kitchens and washer/dryers.

The whole place overlooks the Kaluakoi Golf Course, a green barrier that separates these condos from the rest of the rapidly fading Kaluakoi Resort. Out front, Kepuhi Beach is a scenic place for walkers and beachcombers, but the seas are too hazardous for most swimmers. A pool, paddle tennis, and barbecue facilities are on the property, which adjoins open grassland countryside.

As with most condominiums in a rental pool, the quality and upkeep of the individually owned units can vary widely. When booking, spend some time talking with the friendly people at Molokai Vacation Properties so that you can get a top-quality condo that has been renovated recently.

Lio Place (next door to Kaluakoi Resort), Kaluakoi, HI 96770. Reservations c/o Molokai Vacation Properties, P.O. Box 1979, Kaunakakai, HI 96748. © **800/367-2984** or 808/553-8334. Fax 808/553-3783. www.molokai-vacation-rental.com. 77 units. $120–$150 double studio; $135–$195

1-bedroom apt (sleeps up to 4); $275 3-bedroom apt (up to 6), $65–$150 cleaning fee. 3-night minimum; 1-week minimum Dec 16–Jan 3. AE, MC, V. **Amenities:** Nearby golf course; outdoor pool. *In room:* TV, fridge, kitchen.

INEXPENSIVE

Ke Nani Kai Resort ★ ☺ This place is great for families, who will appreciate the space. The large apartments are set up for full-time living with real kitchens, washer/dryers, attractive furnishings, and breezy lanais. There's a huge pool, a volleyball court, tennis courts, and golf on the neighboring Kaluakoi course. These condos are farther from the sea than other local accommodations but are still just a brief walk from the beach. The two-story buildings are surrounded by parking and garden areas. The only downside: Maid service is only every third day.

In the Kaluakoi Resort development, Kaluakoi Rd., off Hwy. 460 (P.O. Box 289), Maunaloa, HI 96770. Reservations c/o Molokai Vacation Properties, P.O. Box 1979, Kaunakakai, HI 96748. ℂ **800/367-2984** or 808/553-8334. Fax 808/553-3783. www.molokai-vacation-rental.com. 100 units. $105–$135 1-bedroom apt (sleeps up to 4); $125–$185 2-bedroom apt (up to 6), $75–$95 cleaning fee. 3-night minimum. AE, DC, DISC, MC, V. **Amenities:** Golf course; Jacuzzi; outdoor pool; 2 tennis courts. *In room:* TV, high-speed Internet, fridge, kitchen.

The East End

MODERATE

Aloha Beach House ★★ 🏠 Book this place! Here is the "Hawaii" of your dreams. This Hawaiian-style beach house sits right on the white-sand beach of Waialua on the lush East End. Perfect for families, this impeccably decorated, two-bedroom, 1,600-square-foot beach house has a huge open living/dining/kitchen area that opens to an old-fashioned porch for meals or just sitting in the comfy chairs and watching the clouds roll by. It's fully equipped, from the complete kitchen (including a dishwasher) to a library of videos to all the beach toys you can think of. It's close to Mana'e Goods and Grindz (p. 328).

Located just after mile marker 19. Reservations c/o The Rietows, P.O. Box 79, Kilauea, HI 96754. ℂ **888/828-1008** or 808/828-1100. Fax 808/828-2199. www.molokaivacation.com. 1 unit. $230–$290 double, plus one-time cleaning fee of $175. Extra person $20 plus additional cleaning fee. 2-night minimum. No credit cards. *In room:* TV, fridge, kitchen.

Country Cottage at Pu'u O Hoku Ranch ★ ☺ *Pu'u o Hoku* ("Star Hill") Ranch, which spreads across 14,000 acres of pasture and forests, is the last place to stay before Halawa Valley—it's at least an hour's drive from Kaunakakai along the shoreline. Two acres of tropically landscaped property circle the ranch's rustic cottage, which boasts breathtaking views of rolling hills and the Pacific Ocean. The wooden cottage features comfortable country furniture, a full kitchen, two bedrooms (one with a double bed, one with two twins), two bathrooms, and a separate dining room on the enclosed lanai. TVs and video players are available on request. Stargaze at night, watch the sunrise in the morning, and hike, swim, or play croquet in the afternoon. For larger parties, there's a four-bedroom, three-bathroom house (sleeps up to eight) on the property. Kids will have plenty of room to run around and explore.

Kamehameha V Hwy., at mile marker 25. Reservations: P.O. Box 1889, Kaunakakai, HI 96748. ℂ **808/558-8109.** Fax 808/558-8100. www.puuohoku.com. 2 units. $140 double, plus $75 cleaning fee. Extra person $20. 2-night minimum. MC, V. *In room:* TV/video player (available on request), fridge, kitchen.

Dunbar Beachfront Cottages ★★ ☺ This is one of the most peaceful, com-fortable, and elegant properties on Molokai's East End, and the setting is simply stunning. Each of these two green-and-white plantation-style cottages sits on its own secluded beach (good for swimming)—you'll feel like you're on your own pri-vate island. Each cottage sleeps up to four (great for a family), and comes with a full kitchen, ceiling fans, tropical furniture, a large furnished deck (perfect for whale-watching in winter), and views of Maui, Lanai, and Kahoolawe across the channel. Kamehameha V Hwy., past mile marker 18. Reservations c/o Matt and Genesis Dunbar, HC01 Box 738, Kaunakakai, HI 96748. ⓒ **800/673-0520** or 808/558-8153. www.molokai-beachfront-cottages.com. 2 units. $170 cottage (sleeps up to 4), plus one-time $75 cleaning charge. 3-night minimum. No credit cards. *In room:* TV, fridge, kitchen.

WHERE TO DINE

The good news is that on Molokai, you won't find long lines at overbooked, self-important restaurants. The bad news is that Molokai's culinary offerings are spare.

A lot of people like it that way and acknowledge that the island's character is unchangeably rugged and natural. But a few years ago, when the renovated Hotel Molokai unveiled a tropical fantasy of an oceanfront dining room, the island-ers thought this was the height of culinary pleasure. And it quickly became the island's busiest restaurant.

Even with these new developments, Molokai has retained its glacial pace of change. The culinary offerings of the island are dominated by mom-and-pop eat-eries, most of them fast-food or takeout places and many of them with a home-cooked touch. Personally, I like the unpretentiousness of the island; it's an oasis in a state where plastic aloha abounds. But sybarites, foodies, and pampered oenophiles had best lower their expectations upon arrival.

You'll even find a certain defiant stance against the trappings of modernity. Although some of the best produce in Hawaii is grown on this island, you're not likely to find much of it served in its restaurants, other than in the takeout items at Outpost Natural Foods, or at the Molokai Pizza Cafe (one of the most pleas-ing eateries on the island), and the Hotel Molokai. The rest of the time, content yourself with ethnic or diner fare—or by cooking for yourself. The many visitors who stay in condos find that it doesn't take long to sniff out the best sources of produce, groceries, and fresh fish to fire up at home when the island's other dining options are exhausted. The "Edibles" sections in "Shopping" (later in this chapter) will point you in the right direction.

Molokai's restaurants are inexpensive or moderately priced, and several of them do not accept credit cards. Regardless of where you eat, you certainly won't have to dress up. In most cases, we've listed just the town rather than the street address because, as you'll see, street addresses are as meaningless on this island as fancy cars and sequins. Reservations are not accepted unless otherwise noted.

Note: You'll find the restaurants reviewed in this chapter on the "Where to Stay & Dine on Molokai" map on p. 323.

Kaunakakai

INEXPENSIVE

Hotel Molokai ★ AMERICAN/ISLAND On the ocean, with a view of Lanai, torches flickering under palm trees, and tiny fairy lights lining the room and the neighboring pool area, the Hotel Molokai's dining room evokes the romance of a South Seas fantasy. It's a casual room and provides the only nightlife in Kaunakakai (see "Molokai After Dark," later in this chapter) and the most pleasing ambience on the island. Lunch choices consist of the basics; most promising are salads (Big Island organic greens) and sandwiches, from kalua pig to grilled mahimahi. As the sun sets and the torches are lit for dinner, the menu turns to heavier meats, ribs, fish, and pasta. Try the fresh catch, kalbi ribs, barbecued pork ribs, New York steak, or the lip-smacking coconut shrimp. Temper your expectations of culinary excellence and you're sure to enjoy a pleasing dinner in an atmosphere that's unequaled on the island.

On Kamehameha V Hwy. © **808/553-5347.** Reservations recommended for dinner. Main courses $9-$15 lunch, $15-$25 dinner. AE, DC, MC, V. Daily 7am-2pm and 6-9pm; bar until 10:30pm.

Kamoi Snack-N-Go ICE CREAM/SNACKS The Kamoi specialty: sweets and icy treats. Ice cream made by Dave's on Oahu comes in flavors such as green tea, litchi sherbet, *ube* (made from Okinawan sweet potato), haupia, mango, and many others. Lines form for the cones, shakes, sundaes, and popular Icee floats served at this tiny snack shop. If the ice cream doesn't tempt you, maybe something in the aisles full of candies will. It's takeout only; no tables.

In Kamoi Professional Center. © **808/553-3742.** Ice cream $2.25-$3.75; sundaes $4-$5. MC, V. Mon-Fri 11am-9pm; Sat 9am-9pm; Sun noon-9pm.

Kanemitsu's Bakery & Restaurant ★ BAKERY/DELI Morning, noon, and night, this local legend fills the Kaunakakai air with the sweet smells of baking. Taro lavosh is the hot seller, joining Molokai bread—developed in 1935 in a cast-iron, kiawe-fired oven—as a Kanemitsu signature. Flavors range from apricot-pineapple to coconut or strawberry, but the white, wheat, cheese, sweet, and onion-cheese breads are classics. The bread mixes offer a way to take Molokai home. In the adjoining coffee shop/deli, the hamburgers and egg-salad sandwiches are popular and cheap.

Kanemitsu's has a life after dark, too. Whenever anyone on Molokai mentions "hot bread," he's talking about the hot-bread run at Kanemitsu's, the surreal late-night ritual for die-hard bread lovers. Those in the know line up at the bakery's back door beginning at 10pm, when the bread is whisked hot out of the oven and into waiting hands. You can order your fresh bread with butter, jelly, cinnamon, or cream cheese, and the bakers will cut the hot loaves down the middle and slather on the works so it melts in the bread. The cream-cheese-and-jelly bread makes a fine substitute for dessert.

79 Ala Malama St. © **808/553-5855.** Most items less than $5.50. AE, MC, V. Restaurant Wed-Mon 5:30am-noon; bakery Wed-Mon 5:30am-5pm.

Molokai Drive-Inn AMERICAN/TAKEOUT It's a greasy spoon, but it's one of the rare drive-up places with fresh akule (mackerel) and ahi (when available), plus fried saimin at budget-friendly prices. The honey-dipped fried chicken is a favorite among residents, who also come here for the floats, shakes, and other artery-clogging choices. But don't expect much in terms of ambience: This is a fast-food takeout counter, and it doesn't pretend to be otherwise.

Kaunakakai. © **808/553-5655.** Most items less than $11. No credit cards. Sun-Thurs 6am-10pm; Fri-Sat 6:30am-10:30pm.

Molokai Pizza Cafe ★ PIZZA This gathering place serves excellent pizzas and sandwiches that have made it a Kaunakakai staple as well as one of my favorite eaties on the island. The best-selling pies are the Molokai (pepperoni and cheese), the Big Island (pepperoni, ham, mushroom, Italian sausage, bacon, and vegetables), and the Molokini (plain cheese slices). Pasta, sandwiches, and the new addition of "gourmet" hamburgers on homemade buns round out the menu. My personal fave is the vegetarian Maui pizza, but others tout the fresh-baked submarine and pocket sandwiches and the gyro pocket with spinach pie. Sunday is prime-rib day and Wednesday is Mexican. Coin-operated cars and a toy airplane follow the children's theme, but adults should feel equally at home with the very popular barbecued baby back rib plate and the fresh-fish dinners.

In Kahua Center, on the old Wharf Rd. ℂ **808/553-3288.** Large pizzas $17–$29. No credit cards. Sun 11am–10pm; Mon–Thurs 10am–10pm; Fri–Sat 10am–11pm.

Outpost Natural Foods ★ VEGETARIAN The healthiest and freshest food on the island is served at the lunch counter of this health-food store, around the corner from the main drag on the ocean side of Kaunakakai town. The tiny store abounds in Molokai papayas, bananas, herbs, potatoes, watermelon, and other local produce, complementing its selection of vitamins, cosmetics, and health aids, as well as bulk and shelf items. The salads, burritos, tempeh sandwiches, tofu-spinach lasagna, and mock chicken, turkey, and meatloaf served at the lunch counter are testament to the fact that vegetarian food need not be boring. A must for health-conscious diners and shoppers.

70 Makaena Place. ℂ **808/553-3377.** Entrees $6–$10. AE, DISC, MC, V. Mon–Thurs 9am–6pm; Fri 9am–4pm; Sun 10am–5pm. Closed Sat.

Paddlers' Inn AMERICAN/LOCAL This local diner, with everything from burgers to steak, recently added breakfast (with specials like homemade biscuits with sausage gravy). If you want to meet local residents, come to this friendly place. Lunch is generally filled with hungry diners grinding on ⅓-pound all-beef burgers, big sandwiches, or plate lunches. Vegetarians will find a few items here, but not a lot. Call ahead for dinner specials. Later the small cafe becomes a hot spot for Molokai entertainment (p. 353).

10 Mohala St. ℂ **808/553-5256.** Breakfast $5–$12, lunch $8–$15, dinner entrees $10–$30. AE, DC, DISC, MC, V. Daily 7am–9pm, bar until 11pm.

Sundown Deli ★ DELI From "gourmet saimin" to spinach pie, Sundown's offerings are home-cooked and healthful, with daily specials that include vegetarian quiche, vegetarian lasagna, and club sandwiches. The sandwiches (like smoked turkey and chicken salad) and several salads (Caesar, Oriental, stuffed tomato) are served daily, with a soup that changes by the day (clam chowder, Portuguese bean, cream of broccoli). Vitamins, T-shirts, and snacks are sold in this tiny cafe, but most of the business is takeout.

145 Puali St. (across the st. from Veteran's Memorial Park). ℂ **808/553-3713.** Sandwiches, soups, and salads $3.95–$7.50. AE, MC, V. Mon–Fri 7:30am–3:30pm.

The East End

INEXPENSIVE

Mana'e Goods and Grindz ★ AMERICAN Formerly the Neighborhood Store, this place has a new name, but it's still the same quick-stop market/lunch counter. It's nothing fancy, and that's what I love about it. Near mile marker 16 in the Pukoo area en route to the East End, this tiny store appears like a mirage, complete with large parking area and picnic tables. The place serves omelets, Portuguese sausage, and other breakfast specials (brunch is very popular), then segues into sandwiches, salads, mahimahi plates, and varied over-the-counter lunch offerings, served on paper plates with plastic utensils. Favorites include the mahimahi plate lunch, the chicken katsu, and the Mexican plate, each one with a tried-and-true home-cooked flavor. There are daily specials, ethnic dishes, and some vegetarian options, as well as burgers (including a killer veggie burger), saimin, and legendary desserts. Made-on-Maui Roselani ice cream is a featured attraction. A Molokai treasure, this is the only grocery store on the East End (see "Shopping," later in this chapter).

Pukoo. ☎ **808/558-8498.** Most items less than $10. MC, V. Mon–Fri store hours 6:30am–6pm, Sat–Sun 6:30am–5pm; food service Mon–Tues and Thurs–Fri 9am–5pm, Wed 9am–3pm, Sat–Sun 7am–5pm.

BEACHES

With imposing sea cliffs on one side and lazy fishponds on the other, Molokai has little room for beaches along its 106-mile coast. Still, a big gold-sand beach flourishes on the West End, and you'll find tiny pocket beaches on the East End. The emptiness of Molokai's beaches is both a blessing and a curse: The seclusion means no lifeguards on any of the beaches. See the "Molokai" map on p. 315 for locations of these beaches.

Kaunakakai

ONE ALII BEACH PARK

This thin strip of sand, once reserved for the *alii* (chiefs), is the oldest public beach park on Molokai. You'll find One Alii Beach Park (*One* is pronounced

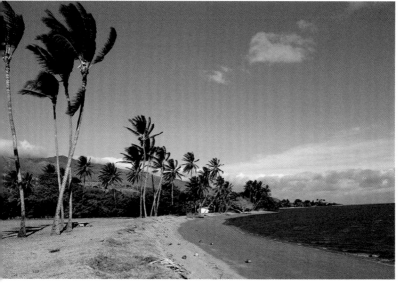

One Alii Beach Park.

o-nay, not *won*) by a coconut grove on the outskirts of Kaunakakai. Safe for swimmers of all ages and abilities, it's often crowded with families on weekends, but it can be all yours on weekdays. Facilities include outdoor showers, restrooms, and free parking.

The West End

KEPUHI BEACH

Golfers see this picturesque golden strand in front of the Kaluakoi Resort and Golf Course as just another sand trap, but sunbathers like the semiprivate grassy dunes; they're seldom, if ever, crowded. Beachcombers often find what they're looking for here, but swimmers have to dodge lava rocks and risk riptides. And look out for errant golf balls. There are no facilities or lifeguards, but cold drinks and restrooms are handy at the resort.

PAPOHAKU BEACH ★★

Nearly 3 miles long and 300 feet wide, gold-sand Papohaku Beach is one of the biggest in Hawaii (17-mile-long Polihale Beach on Kauai is the biggest). It's great for walking, beachcombing, picnics, and sunset watching year-round. The big surf and riptides make swimming risky except in summer, when the waters are calmer. Go early in the day when the tropic sun is less fierce and the winds are calm. Facilities include outdoor showers, restrooms, picnic grounds, and free parking.

The East End

HALAWA BEACH PARK ★

At the foot of scenic Halawa Valley is this beautiful black-sand beach with a palm-fringed lagoon, a wave-lashed island offshore, and a distant view of the

Kepuhi Beach.

Papohaku Beach.

West Maui Mountains across the Pailolo Channel. The swimming is safe in the shallows close to shore, but where the waterfall stream meets the sea, the ocean is often murky and unnerving. A winter swell creases the mouth of Halawa Valley on the north side of the bay and attracts a crowd of local surfers. Facilities are minimal; bring your own water. To get here, take King Kamehameha V Highway (Hwy. 450) east to the end.

MURPHY BEACH PARK (KUMIMI BEACH PARK)

In 1970 the Molokai Jaycees wanted to create a sandy beach park with a good swimming area for the children of the East End. They chose a section known as Kumimi Beach, which was owned by the Pu'u o Hoku Ranch. The beach was a dump—literally. The ranch owner, George Murphy, gave his permission to use the site as a park, and the Jaycees cleaned it up and built three small pavilions, plus picnic tables and barbecue grills. Officially, the park is called the George Murphy Beach Park (shortened to Murphy Beach Park), but some old-timers still call it Kumimi Beach, and, just to make things really confusing, some people call it Jaycees Park.

No matter what you call it, this small park is shaded by ironwood trees that line a white-sand beach. It's generally a very safe swimming area. On calm days snorkeling and diving are great outside the reef. Fishermen also frequently come here to look for papio and other island fish.

SANDY BEACH ★

Molokai's most popular swimming beach—ideal for families with small kids—is a roadside pocket of gold sand protected by a reef, with a great view of Maui and Lanai. You'll find it off the King Kamehameha V Highway (Hwy. 450) at mile marker 20. There are no facilities—just you, the sun, the sand, and the surf.

Halawa Beach Park.

WATERSPORTS

The best place to rent beach toys (snorkels, boogie boards, beach chairs, fishing poles, and more) is **Molokai Fish & Dive,** Kaunakakai (© **808/553-5926;** www.molokaifishanddive.com), where you can rent snorkeling gear, fishing gear, even ice chests here. This is also a hot spot for fishing news and tips on what's running where.

For general advice on the activities listed below, see "Special-Interest Trips" in chapter 3.

Body Boarding (Boogie Boarding) & Bodysurfing

Molokai has only three beaches that offer ridable waves for body boarding and bodysurfing: Papohaku, Kepuhi, and Halawa. Even these beaches are only for experienced bodysurfers, due to the strength of the rip currents and

Sandy Beach.

undertows. You can rent boogie boards with fins for just $5 a day or $20 a week at **Molokai Outdoors Activities** (© **877/553-4477** or 808/553-4477; www. molokai-outdoors.com).

Ocean Kayaking

During the summer months, when the waters on the north shore are calm, Molokai offers some of the most spectacular kayaking in Hawaii. However, most of Molokai is for the experienced kayaker only. You must be adept in paddling through open ocean swells and rough waves.

Molokai Outdoors Activities (�C **877/553-4477** or 808/553-4477; www.molokai-outdoors.com), has a "downwinder" tour: six miles of Molokai's reef as you paddle down wind ($89, plus $10 for lunch per person). They also rent kayaks; rates start at $26 a day.

Scuba Diving

Want to see turtles or manta rays up close? How about sharks? Molokai resident Bill Kapuni has been diving the waters around the island his entire life; he'll be happy to show you whatever you're brave enough to encounter. You can book him through **Molokai Fish & Dive** (℃ **808/553-5926;** www.molokaifishanddive. com), which offers scuba-diving trips from $135 (two-tank dive) to $275 (three-tank dive).

Snorkeling

When the waters are calm, Molokai offers excellent snorkeling; you'll see a wide range of butterflyfish, tangs, and angelfish. Good snorkeling can be found—when conditions are right—at many of Molokai's beaches (see the box titled "Molokai's Best Snorkel Spots," below). **Molokai Fish & Dive,** Kaunakakai (℃ **808/553-5926;** www.molokaifishanddive.com), rents mask, snorkel, and fins for $10 for 24 hours.

Murphy Beach Park.

For snorkeling tours on a boat, Walter Naki of **Molokai Action Adventures** (☏ 808/558-8184) offers leisurely snorkeling, diving, and swimming trips in his 21-foot Boston whaler for $50 per person for a 4- to 6-hour custom tour.

Sportfishing

Molokai's waters can provide prime sporting opportunities, whether you're looking for big-game sportfishing or bottom fishing. The number-one person we recommend is Capt. Clay, of **Hallelujah Hou Fishing** (☏ 808/336-1870; www.hallelujahhoufishing.com). Capt. Clay, who also is a minister and the nicest guy you may ever meet, leads light-tackle guided fishing trips on his 24-foot power catamaran. The price is $395 to $495 for up to four adults for a half-day. He provides all tackle and bottled water; you bring the sunscreen. If you catch something, he'll even filet your fish for dinner. **Note:** There's no "head" (toilet) on the boat.

Most of Molokai is for experienced kayakers only, though summer months offer calm waters on the north shore.

When customers are scarce, Capt. Joe Reich goes commercial fishing, so he always knows where the fish are biting. He runs **Alyce C Sportfishing** out of Kaunakakai Harbor (☏ 808/558-8377; ace@aloha.net). A full day of fishing for up to six people is $550, three-quarters of a day is $500, and a half-day is $450. You can usually persuade him to do a whale-watching cruise during the winter months.

For fly-fishing or light-tackle reef-fish trolling, contact Walter Naki at **Molokai Action Adventures** (☏ 808/558-8184). A full-day trip in his 21-foot Boston whaler, for up to four people, is $400.

Molokai Fish & Dive, Kaunakakai (☏ 808/553-5926; www.molokaifishanddive.com), has fishing tours for $400 for a half-day, and $600 for a full day.

For deep-sea fishing, contact **Fun Hogs Hawaii,** who books through Molokai Outdoors Activities (see below) for fishing excursions on a 27-foot, fully equipped sportfishing vessel. Prices are $365 for six passengers for 4 hours, $417 for 6 hours, and $521 for 8 hours.

Surfing

Depending on the time of year and the wave conditions, Molokai can offer some great surfing for the beginner, as well as the expert. **Molokai Outdoors Activities** (☏ 877/553-4477 or 808/553-4477; www.molokai-outdoors.com)

Most Molokai beaches are too dangerous for snorkeling in winter, when big waves and strong currents are generated by storms that sweep down from Alaska. From mid-September to April, stick to Murphy Beach Park (also known as Kumimi Beach Park) on the East End. In summer, roughly May to mid-September, the Pacific Ocean turns into a flat lake, and the whole west coast of Molokai opens up for snorkeling. Mike Holmes, of Molokai Ranch & Fun Hogs Hawaii, says the best spots are as follows:

Kawaikiunui, Ilio Point, and **Pohaku Moiliili** (West End) These are all special places seldom seen by even those who live on Molokai. You can reach Kawaikiunui and Pohaku Moiliili on foot after a long, hot, dusty ride in a four-wheel-drive vehicle, but it's much easier and quicker to go by sea. See above for places to rent a kayak and get advice. It's about 2 miles as the crow flies from Pohaku Moiliili to Ilio Point.

Kapukahehu (Dixie Maru) Beach (West End) This gold-sand family beach is well protected, and the reef is close and shallow. The name *Dixie Maru* comes from a 1920s Japanese fishing boat stranded off the rocky shore. One of the Molokai Ranch cowboys hung the wrecked boat's nameplate on a gate by Kapukahehu Beach, and the name stuck. To get here, take Kaluakoi Road to the end of the pavement, and then take the footpath 300 feet to the beach.

Murphy (Kumimi) Beach Park ★ (East End) This beach is located between mile markers 20 and 21, off Kamehameha V Highway. The reef here is easily reachable, and the waters are calm year-round.

not only will know where the waves are, but they also rent gear: soft surfboards for $19 a day. Good surfing spots include Kaunakakai Wharf in town, Hale O Lono Beach and Papohaku Beach on the West End, and Halawa Beach on the East End.

HIKING & CAMPING
Hiking Molokai's Pepeopae Trail

Molokai's most awesome hike is the **Pepeopae Trail ★★**, which takes you back a few million years. On the cloud-draped trail (actually a boardwalk across the bog), you'll see mosses, sedges, native violets, knee-high ancient ohia, and lichens that evolved in total isolation over eons. Eerie intermittent mists blowing in and out will give you an idea of this island at its creation.

The narrow boardwalk, built by volunteers, protects the bog and keeps you out of the primal ooze. Don't venture off it; you could damage this fragile environment or get lost. The 3-mile round-trip takes about 90 minutes to hike—but first you have to drive about 20 miles from Kaunakakai, deep into the Molokai Forest Reserve on a four-wheel-drive road. *Warning:* Don't try this with a regular rental car. Plan a full day for this outing. Better yet, go on a guided nature hike with the **Nature Conservancy of Hawaii,** which guards this unusual ecosystem. For information, write to the Nature Conservancy at 1116 Smith St., Ste. 201, Honolulu, HI 96817. No permit is required for this easy hike. Call ahead (✆ **808/553-5236;** www.nature.org) to check on the condition of the ungraded, four-wheel-drive, red-dirt road that leads to the trail head and to let people know that you'll be up there. To get here, take Highway 460 west from Kaunakakai for 3½ miles and turn right before the Maunawainui Bridge onto the unmarked Molokai Forest Reserve Road (sorry, there aren't any road signs). The pavement ends at the cemetery; continue on the dirt road. After about 2 to 2½ miles, you'll see a sign telling you that you are now in the Molokai Forest Reserve. At the Waikolu Lookout and picnic area, which is just over 9 miles on the Molokai Forest Reserve Road, sign in at the box near the entrance. Continue on the road for another 5 miles to a fork in the road with the sign PUU KOLEKOLE pointing to the right side of the fork. Do not turn right; instead, continue straight at the fork, which leads to the clearly marked trail head. The drive will take about 45 minutes.

Hiking to Kalaupapa ★★

This hike to the site of Molokai's famous leper colony is like going down a switchback staircase with what seems like a million steps. You don't always see the breathtaking view because you're too busy watching your step. It's easier going down (surprise!)—in about an hour, you'll go 2½ miles, from 2,000 feet to sea level. The trip up sometimes takes twice as long. The trail head starts on the mauka (inland) side of Highway 470, just past the Mule Barn. Check in here at 7:30am, get a permit, and go before the mule train departs. You must be 16 or older (it's an old state law that kept kids out of the leper colony) and should be in good shape. Wear good hiking boots or sneakers.

Hiking the West End

Molokai Outdoors Activities (✆ **877/553-4477** or 808/553-4477; www.molokai-outdoors.com) offers an all-day (6–8 hr.) Halawa Cultural hike full of historical information on East Molokai. The hike is rated intermediate to advanced, with a distance of 2.2 miles. It has two river crossings, and

A tree carving in the Molokai Forest Preserve.

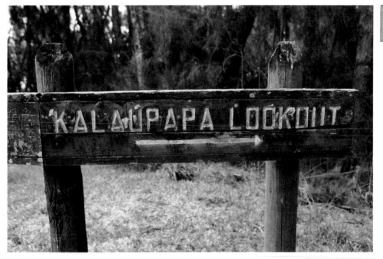

A sign points the way to the Kalaupapa Lookout.

some rocky areas along the trails, with possible fallen trees after a storm. The cost is $78 per person.

Molokai Fish & Dive (𝄐 808/553-5926; www.molokaifishanddive.com) offers a hike back into Halawa Valley for $69 (p. 350).

Camping

Bring your own camping equipment, as none is available for rent on the island.

AT THE BEACH

One of the best year-round places to camp on Molokai is **Papohaku Beach Park ★**, on the island's West End. This drive-up seaside site makes a great getaway. Facilities include restrooms, drinking water, outdoor showers, barbecue grills, and picnic tables. Groceries and gas are available in Maunaloa, 6 miles away. Kaluakoi Resort is a mile away. Get camping permits by contacting **Maui County Parks Department,** 700 Halia Nakoa St., Wailuku, HI 96793 (𝄐 808/553-3204; www.co.maui.hi.us). Camping is limited to 3 days, but if nobody else has applied, the time limit is waived. The cost is $5 a person per night Monday through Thursday and $8 Friday through Sunday.

IN AN IRONWOOD FOREST

At the end of Highway 470 is the 234-acre piney woods known as **Palaau State Park ★★**, home to the Kalaupapa Lookout (the best vantage point for seeing the historic leper colony if you're not hiking or riding a mule in). It's airy and cool in the park's ironwood forest, where many love to camp at the designated state campground. Camping fees for Hawaii state parks are $5 per campsite per night, and you'll need a permit from the **State Division of Parks** (𝄐 808/587-0300; www.hawaiistateparks.org/camping/maui.cfm). At press time, the State Parks Department is in the process of converting their system to online, so by 2011 phone information may not be available. For more on the park, see p. 341.

GOLF & OTHER OUTDOOR ACTIVITIES

Golf

Golf is one of Molokai's best-kept secrets: It's challenging and fun, tee times are open, and the rates are lower than your score will be. **Ironwood Hills Golf Course,** off Kalae Highway (☏ **808/567-6000**), is located just before the Molokai Mule Ride Mule Barn, on the road to the Lookout. Built in 1929 by Del Monte Plantation for its executives, it's one of the oldest courses in the state. This unusual course, which sits in the cool air at 1,200 feet, delights with its rich foliage, open fairways, and spectacular views of the rest of the island. *Tip:* After teeing off on the 6th hole, just take whatever clubs you need to finish playing the hole and a driver for the 7th hole, and park your bag under a tree. The climb to the 7th hole is steep—you'll be glad that you're only carrying a few clubs. Greens fees are $31 for 18 holes.

Bicycling

Molokai is a great place to see by bicycle. The roads are not very busy and there are great places to pull off the road and take a quick dip.

 Molokai Bicycle, 80 Mohala St., Kaunakakai (☏ **808/553-3931;** www. bikehawaii.com/molokaibicycle), offers bike rentals for $18 a day, or $80 a week, including a complimentary helmet and lock. Owner Phillip Kikukawa is schoolteacher, so call him in late afternoon when he's in the shop.

Tennis

The only two tennis courts on Molokai are located at the **Mitchell Paaole Center,** in Kaunakakai (☏ **808/553-3204**). Both are lit for night play and are available free on a first-come, first-served basis, with a 45-minute time limit if someone is waiting. You can also rent tennis rackets ($5 a day, $24 a week) and balls ($3 a day, $12 a week) from **Molokai Outdoors Activities** (☏ **877/553-4477** or 808/553-4477; www.molokai-outdoors.com).

SEEING THE SIGHTS

Note: You'll find the following attractions on the "Molokai" map on p. 315.

In & Around Kaunakakai

Kapuaiwa Coconut Grove/Kiowea Park ★ ☺ This royal grove—1,000 coconut trees on 10 acres planted in 1863 by the island's high chief Kapua'iwa (later, King Kamehameha V)—is a major roadside attraction. The shoreline park is a favorite subject of sunset photographers and visitors who delight in a hand-lettered sign that warns: DANGER: FALLING COCONUTS. In its backyard, across the highway, stands Church Row: seven churches, each a different denomination—clear evidence of the missionary impact on Hawaii.
Along Maunaloa Hwy. (Hwy. 460), 2 miles west of Kaunakakai.

Post-A-Nut ★ Postmaster Gary Lam will help you say "Aloha" with a Molokai coconut. Just write a message on the coconut with a felt-tip pen, and he'll send it via U.S. mail. Coconuts are free but postage averages $9 to $13 for a mainland-

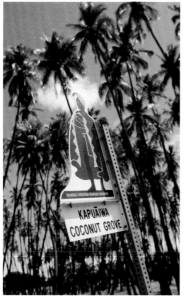
Kapuiwa Cocnut Grove.

bound coconut. Gary mails out about 3,000 per year and likes to decorate them with colorful stamps.

Hoolehua Post Office, Puu Peelua Ave. (Hwy. 480), near Maunaloa Hwy. (Hwy. 460). ✆ **808/567-6144.** Mon–Fri 8:30am–noon and 12:30–4pm.

Purdy's All-Natural Macadamia Nut Farm (Na Hua O'Ka Aina) ★ 👬
The Purdys have made macadamia-nut buying an entertainment event, offering tours of the homestead and giving lively demonstrations of nutshell-cracking in the shade of their towering trees. The tour of the 70-year-old nut farm explains the growth, bearing, harvesting, and shelling processes.

Lihi Pali Ave. (behind Molokai High School), Hoolehua. ✆ **808/567-6601.** www.molokai-aloha.com/macnuts. Free admission. Mon–Fri 9:30am–3:30pm; Sat 10am–2pm. Closed holidays.

The North Coast

Even if you don't get a chance to see Hawaii's most dramatic coast in its entirety—not many people do—you shouldn't miss the opportunity to glimpse it from the **Kalaupapa Lookout** at Palaau State Park. On the way, there are a few diversions (arranged here in geographical order).

EN ROUTE TO THE NORTH COAST

Coffees of Hawaii The defunct Del Monte pineapple town of Kualapuu is rising again—only this time, coffee is the catch, not pineapple. Located in the cool foothills, Coffees of Hawaii has planted coffee beans on 600 acres of former pineapple land. The plantation irrigates the plants with a high-tech, continuous water-and-fertilizer drip system. You can see it all on the self-guided walking tour or the Morning Espresso Tour, which is lead by a guide from the plantation and gives you a tour of the sorting facility and processing procedures. The less physically motivated should try the Mule Drawn Wagon tour, great for a family. The 2-hour tour is lead by a guide and two mules (Moana and Leila or Lilo and Loke) through the coffee fields and around the reservoir. The Plantation Store sells arts and crafts from Molokai. Stop by the Espresso Bar for a Mocha Mama, an intoxicating blend of coffee, ice cream, and chocolate that will keep you going all day—maybe even all night.

1630 Farrington Ave., (near the junction of Hwy. 470), Kualapuu. ✆ **877/322-FARM** (3276) or 808/567-9490, ext. 26. www.coffeesofhawaii.com/plantations/molokai. Mon–Fri 7am–5pm; Sat 8am–8pm; Sun 8am–5pm. Self-guided tour free. Morning Espresso Tour Mon–Fri 11am, $25 adults, $10 kids 5–10 years, under 5 free. Mule Drawn Wagon Tour Tues and Fri 8am and 1pm, $40 adults, $12 kids 5–10, under 5 free.

ESPECIALLY FOR kids

Flying a Kite (p. 352) Not only can you get a guaranteed-to-fly kite at the **Big Wind Kite Factory** (📞 **808/552-2364**) in Maunaloa, but kite designer Jonathan Socher offers free kite-flying classes to kids, who'll learn how to make their kites soar, swoop, and, most important, stay in the air for more than 5 minutes.

Spending the Day at Murphy (Kumimi) Beach Park (p. 331) Just beyond Waialua on the East End is this small wayside park that's perfect for kids. You'll find safe swimming conditions, plenty of shade from the ironwood trees, and small pavilions with picnic tables and barbecue grills.

Molokai Museum and Cultural Center En route to the California Gold Rush in 1849, Rudolph W. Meyer (a German professor) came to Molokai, married the high chieftess Kalama, and began to operate a small sugar plantation near his home. Now on the National Register of Historic Places, this restored 1878 sugar mill, with its century-old steam engine, mule-driven cane crusher, copper clarifiers, and redwood evaporating pan (all in working order), is the last of its kind in Hawaii. The mill also houses a museum that traces the history of sugar growing on Molokai and has special events, such as wine tastings, taro festivals, an annual music festival, and occasional classes in ukulele making, loom weaving, and sewing. Call for a schedule.

Meyer Sugar Mill, Hwy. 470 (just after the turnoff for the Ironwood Hills Golf Course and 2 miles below Kalaupapa Overlook), Kalae. 📞 **808/567-6436.** Admission $3.50 adults, $1 children and students. Mon–Sat 10am–2pm.

Coffee plants.

Molokai's north coast.

Palaau State Park ★ This 234-acre piney-woods park, 8 miles out of Kaunakakai, doesn't look like much until you get out of the car and take a hike, which literally puts you between a rock and a hard place. Go right, and you end up on the edge of Molokai's magnificent sea cliffs, with its panoramic view of the well-known Kalaupapa leper colony; go left, and you come face to face with a stone phallus.

If you have no plans to scale the cliffs by mule or on foot (see "Hiking & Camping," earlier in this chapter), the **Kalaupapa Lookout** ★★★ is the only place from which to see the former place of exile. The trail is marked, and historic photos and interpretive signs will explain what you're seeing.

It's airy and cool in the ironwood forest, where camping is free at the designated state campground. You'll need a permit from the **State Division of Parks** (℃ **808/587-0300;** www. hawaiistateparks.org/camping/maui. cfm). Not many people seem to camp here, probably because of the legend associated with the **Phallic Rock** ★. Six feet high and pointed at an angle that means business, Molokai's famous Phallic Rock is a legendary fertility tool: According to Hawaiian legend, a woman who wishes to become pregnant need only spend the night near the rock and, *voilà!*

Phallic Rock.

Phallic Rock is at the end of a well-worn uphill path that passes an ironwood grove and several other rocks that vaguely resemble sexual body parts. No mistaking the big guy, though. Supposedly, it belonged to Nanahoa, a demigod who quarreled with his wife, Kawahuna, over a pretty girl. In the tussle, Kawahuna was thrown over the cliff, and both husband and wife were turned to stone. Of all the phallic rocks in Hawaii and the Pacific, this is the one to see. It's featured on a postcard with a tiny, awestruck Japanese woman standing next to it. At the end of Hwy. 470.

THE LEGACY OF FATHER DAMIEN: KALAUPAPA NATIONAL HISTORICAL PARK ★★★

Kalaupapa, an old tongue of lava that sticks out to form a peninsula, became infamous because of man's inhumanity to victims of a formerly incurable contagious disease.

King Kamehameha V sent the first lepers—nine men and three women—into exile on this lonely shore, at the base of ramparts that rise like temples against the Pacific, on January 6, 1866. By 1874, more than 11,000 lepers had been dispatched to die in one of the world's most beautiful—and lonely—places. They called Kalaupapa "The Place of the Living Dead."

Leprosy is actually one of the world's least contagious diseases, transmitted only by direct, repetitive contact over a long period of time. It's caused by a germ, *Mycobacterium leprae*, that attacks the nerves, skin, and eyes, and is found mainly, but not exclusively, in tropical regions. American scientists found a cure for the disease in the 1940s.

Before science intervened, there was Father Damien. Born to wealth in Belgium, Joseph de Veuster traded a life of excess for exile among lepers; he devoted himself to caring for the afflicted at Kalaupapa. Horrified by the conditions in the leper colony, Father Damien worked at Kalaupapa for 11 years, building houses, schools, and churches, and giving hope to his patients. He died on April 15, 1889, in Kalaupapa, of leprosy. He was 49.

A hero nominated for Catholic sainthood, Father Damien is buried not in his tomb next to Molokai's St. Philomena Church but in his native Belgium. Well, most of him anyway. His hand was recently returned to Molokai, and was reinterred at Kalaupapa as a relic of his martyrdom.

This small peninsula is probably the final resting place of more than 11,000 souls. The sand dunes are littered with grave markers, sorted by the religious affiliations—Catholic, Protestant, Buddhist—of those who died here. But so many are buried in unmarked graves that no accurate census of the dead exists.

Kalaupapa is now a National Historical Park (© 808/567-6802; www.nps.gov/kala) and one of Hawaii's richest archaeological preserves, with sites that date from A.D. 1000. About 60 former patients chose to remain in the tidy village, where statues of angels stand in the yards of whitewashed houses. The original name for their former affliction, leprosy, was officially banned in Hawaii by the state legislature in 1981. The name used now is "Hansen's disease," for Dr. Gerhard Hansen of Norway, who discovered the germ in 1873.

Kalaupapa welcomes visitors who arrive on foot, by mule, or by small plane. Father Damien's St. Philomena church, built in 1872, is open to visitors, who can see it from a yellow school bus driven by resident tour guide Richard Marks, an ex-seaman and sheriff who survived the disease. You won't be able to roam

Ruins of the leper colony at Kalaupapa.

freely, and you'll be allowed to enter only the museum, the crafts shop, and the church.

MULE RIDES TO KALAUPAPA ★★★ The first turn's a gasp, and it's all downhill from there. You can close your eyes and hold on for dear life, or slip the reins over the pommel and sit back, letting the mule do the walking down the precipitous path to Kalaupapa National Historical Park.

Even if you have only 1 day to spend on Molokai, spend it on a mule. This is a once-in-a-lifetime ride. The cliffs are taller than a 300-story skyscraper, but Buzzy Sproat's mules go safely up and down the narrow 3-mile trail daily, rain or shine. Starting at the top of the nearly perpendicular ridge (1,600 ft. high), the surefooted mules step down the muddy trail, pausing often on the 26 switchbacks to calculate their next move—and always, it seems to me, veering a little too close to the edge. Each switchback is numbered; by the time you get to number four, you'll catch your breath, put the mule on cruise control, and begin to enjoy Hawaii's most awesome trail ride.

The mule tours are offered once a day Monday to Saturday (the park is closed Sun) starting at 8am, and they last until about 3pm. It costs $175 per person for the all-day adventure, which includes the round-trip mule ride, a guided tour of the settlement, a visit to Father Damien's church and grave,

If you have only 1 day to spend on Molokai, spend it on a mule.

lunch at Kalawao, and souvenirs. To go, you must be at least 16 years old and physically fit. Contact **Molokai Mule Ride ★★★**, 100 Kalae Hwy., Ste. 104, on Highway 470, 5 miles north of Highway 460 (✆ **800/567-7550,** or 808/567-6088 btw. 8 and 10pm; www.muleride.com). Advance reservations (at least 2 weeks ahead) are required.

SEEING KALAUPAPA BY PLANE The fastest and easiest way to get to Kalaupapa is by hopping on a plane and zipping to Kalaupapa airport. From here, you can pick up the same Kalaupapa tour that the mule riders and hikers take. **Molokai Mule Ride** (see above) will pick you up at the Kalaupapa airport and take you to some of the area's most scenic spots, including Kalawao, where Father Damien's church still stands, and the town of Kalaupapa. The package includes round-trip airfare from Honolulu, hotel pickup, guided mule tour, entry permits, Historical Park tour, and a picnic lunch for $319 per person, two-person minimum.

If you are coming from Maui, your choices are either by ferry (where you will hike in and back out in 1 day) or take the mule ride, but you will have to overnight due to the ferry's schedule. It might be possible to charter a shuttle to the top of the path down through **Molokai Fish & Dive** (✆ **808/553-5926**).

If you are on Molokai and want to fly directly into Kalaupapa, Molokai Mule Ride will book you from the Molokai Airport to Kalaupapa and include entry permits, Historical Park tour with Damien Tours, and a light picnic lunch for $130 per person, two-person minimum.

SEEING KALAUPAPA BY FERRY/HIKING From Maui, take the *Molokai Princess* ferry to Molokai (✆ **800/275-6969** or 808/667-6165; www.mauiprincess.com), where you are met and transported by van to the top of the 1,700-foot sea cliffs. Here you hike down the 3-mile trail to the Kalaupapa National Historical Park; at the park, you are met by Damien Tours and given a van tour of the peninsula, during which you'll visit Father Damien's St. Philomena Church, see his early gravesite, and hear the stories of struggle and courage of the residents of Kalaupapa. Before you sign up, be aware that there are a couple of problems: one, you have to hike back up the 1,700-foot cliffs, where you are picked up by the van and returned to the ferry dock for the trip back to Maui. This fabulous experience really should be undertaken only by the physically fit (it will take about an hour hiking down and another 90 min. to hike back up). And the second problem is that because of the ferry schedule, you will have to spend the night on Molokai. Cost for ferry is $109, plus transportation from the ferry dock to the top of the sea cliffs and return, tour, and lunch, which adds an additional $277 (participants must be 16 years and older).

The West End

MAUNALOA

In the first and only urban renewal on Molokai, the 1920s-era pineapple-plantation town of Maunaloa is now a ghost town.

ON THE NORTHWEST SHORE: MOOMOMI DUNES

Undisturbed for centuries, the Moomomi Dunes, on Molokai's northwest shore, are a unique treasure chest of great scientific value. The area may look like just

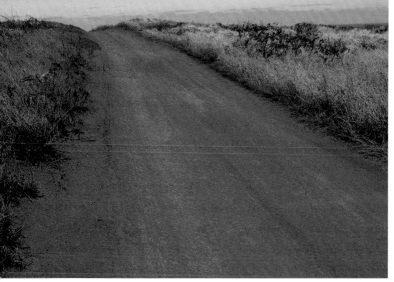
The Moomomi Dunes.

a pile of sand as you fly over on the final approach to Hoolehua Airport, but Moomomi Dunes is much more than that. Archaeologists have found adz quarries, ancient Hawaiian burial sites, and shelter caves; botanists have identified five endangered plant species; and marine biologists are finding evidence that endangered green sea turtles are coming out from the waters once again to lay eggs here. The greatest discovery, however, belongs to Smithsonian Institute ornithologists, who have found bones of prehistoric birds—some of them flightless—that existed nowhere else on earth.

Accessible by jeep trails that thread downhill to the shore, this wild coast is buffeted by strong afternoon breezes. It's hot, dry, and windy, so take water, sunscreen, and a windbreaker.

At Kawaaloa Bay, a 20-minute walk to the west, there's a broad golden beach that you can have all to yourself. **Warning:** Due to the rough seas, stay out of the water. Within the dunes, there's a 920-acre preserve accessible via monthly guided nature tours led by the **Nature Conservancy of Hawaii;** call ✆ **808/553-5236** for an exact schedule and details.

To get here, take Highway 460 (Maunaloa Hwy.) from Kaunakakai; turn right onto Highway 470, and follow it to Kualapuu. At Kualapuu turn left on Highway 480 and go through Hoolehua Village; it's 3 miles to the bay.

The East End

The East End is a cool and inviting green place that's worth a drive to the end of King Kamehameha V Highway (Hwy. 450). Unfortunately, the trail that leads into the area's greatest natural attraction, Halawa Valley, is now off-limits.

ONE OF HAWAII'S MOST POWERFUL ANCIENT TEMPLES: ILIILIOPAE HEIAU

Out on the East End, you bump along a dirt trail through an incredible mango grove, bound for an ancient temple of human sacrifice. This temple of doom—right

Alii Fish Pond.

out of *Indiana Jones*—is Iliiliopae, a huge rectangle of stone made of 90 million rocks, overlooking the once-important village of Mapulehu and four ancient fish-ponds. You trek under the perfumed mangoes, then head uphill through a kiawe forest filled with Java plums to the *heiau* (temple), which stands across a dry stream bed under cloud-spiked Kaunolu, the 4,970-foot island summit.

One of Hawaii's most powerful *heiau,* this ancient temple attracted *kahuna* (priests) from all over the islands. They came to learn the rules of human sacri-fice at this university of sacred rites. Contrary to Hollywood's version, historians say that the victims here were always men, not young virgins, and that they were strangled, not thrown into a volcano, while priests sat on lauhala mats watching silently. Spooky, eh?

This is the biggest, oldest, and most famous *heiau* on Molokai. The mas-sive 22-foot-high stone altar is dedicated to Lono, the Hawaiian god of fertil-ity. The *heiau* resonates with *mana* (power) strong enough to lean on. Legend says Iliiliopae was built in a single night by a thousand men who passed rocks hand over hand through the Wailau Valley from the other side of the island; in exchange for the *ili'ili* (rock), each received a *'opae* (shrimp). Others say it was built by *menehune,* mythic elves who accomplished Herculean feats.

King Kamehameha V Highway (Hwy. 450), at mile marker 15, Kaunakakai, HI 96748.

KAMAKOU PRESERVE

It's hard to believe, but close to the nearly mile-high summit here, it rains more than 80 inches a year—enough to qualify as a rainforest. The Molokai Forest, as it was historically known, is the source of 60% of Molokai's water. Nearly 3,000 acres, from the summit to the lowland forests of eucalyptus and pine, are now held by the Nature Conservancy, which has identified 219 Hawaiian plants that grow here exclusively. The preserve is also the last stand of the endangered *olomao* (Molokai thrush) and *kawawahie* (Molokai creeper).

To get to the preserve, take the Forest Reserve road from Kaunakakai. It's a 45-minute, four-wheel-drive trip on a dirt trail to Waikolu Lookout Campground; from here, you can venture into the wilderness preserve on foot across a boardwalk on a 1½-hour hike (see "Hiking Molokai's Pepeopae Trail," earlier in this chapter). For more information, contact the **Nature Conservancy** (© **808/553-5236;** www.nature.org).

EN ROUTE TO HALAWA VALLEY

No visit to Molokai is complete without at least a passing glance at the island's **ancient fishponds,** a singular achievement in Pacific aquaculture. With their hunger for fresh fish and lack of ice or refrigeration, Hawaiians perfected aquaculture in A.D. 1400, before Christopher Columbus "discovered" America. They built gated, U-shaped stone and coral walls on the shore to catch fish on the incoming tide, then would raise them in captivity. The result: a constant, ready supply of fresh fish.

The ponds, which stretch for 20 miles along Molokai's south shore and are visible from Kamehameha V Highway (Hwy. 450), offer insight into the island's ancient population. It took something like a thousand people to tend a single fishpond, and more than 60 ponds once existed on this coast. Some are silted in by red-dirt runoff from south coast gulches; others have been revived by folks who raise fish and seaweed.

The largest, 54-acre **Keawa Nui Pond,** is surrounded by a 3-foot-high, 2,000-foot-long stone wall. **Alii Fish Pond,** reserved for kings, is visible through the coconut groves at One Alii Beach Park (p. 329). From the road, you can see **Kalokoeli Pond,** 6 miles east of Kaunakakai on the highway.

Our Lady of Sorrows Catholic Church, one of five built by Father Damien on Molokai and the first outside Kalaupapa, sits across the highway from a fishpond. Park in the church lot (except on Sun) for a closer look.

St. Joseph's Catholic Church The afternoon sun strikes St. Joseph's Church with such a bold ray of light that it looks as if God is about to perform a miracle. This little 1876 wood-frame church is one of four Father Damien built "topside" on Molokai. Restored in 1971, the church stands beside a seaside cemetery, where feral cats play under the gaze of a Damien statue amid gravestones decorated with flower leis.

King Kamehameha V Hwy. (Hwy. 450), just after mile marker 10.

A statue of Father Damien stands outside St. Joseph's Catholic Church.

Smith Bronte Landing Site In 1927 Charles Lindbergh soloed the Atlantic Ocean in a plane called *The Spirit of St. Louis* and became an American hero. That same year, Ernie Smith and Emory B. Bronte took off from Oakland, California, on July 14, in a single-engine Travelair aircraft named *The City of Oakland,* headed across the Pacific Ocean for Honolulu, 2,397 miles away. The next day, after running out of fuel, they crash-landed upside-down in a kiawe thicket on Molokai, but emerged unhurt to become the first civilians to fly to Hawaii from the U.S. mainland. The 25-hour-2-minute flight landed Smith and Bronte a place in aviation history—and a roadside marker on Molokai. King Kamehameha V Hwy. (Hwy. 450), at mile marker 11, on the makai (ocean) side.

HALAWA VALLEY ★

Of the five great valleys of Molokai, only Halawa, with its two waterfalls, golden beach, sleepy lagoon, great surf, and offshore island, is easily accessible. Unfortunately, the trail through fertile Halawa Valley, which was inhabited for centuries, and on to the 250-foot Moaula Falls has been closed for some time. There is one operator who conducts hikes to the falls (see box below).

You can spend a day at the county beach park (described under "Beaches" earlier in this chapter), but do not venture into the valley on your own. In a kind of 21st-century *kapu,* the private landowners in the valley, worried about slip-and-fall lawsuits, have posted NO TRESPASSING signs on their property.

halawa valley: A HIKE BACK IN HISTORY

"There are things on Molokai, sacred things, that you may not be able to see or may not hear, but they are there," says Pilipo Solotario, who was born and raised in Halawa Valley and survived the 1946 tsunami that barreled into the ancient valley. "As Hawaiians, we respect these things."

If people are going to "like Molokai," Solotario feels it is important that they learn about the history and culture; that is part of the secret of appreciating the island.

"I see my role, and I'm nearly 70 years old, as educating people, outsiders, on our culture, our history," he said at the beginning of his cultural hike into his family property in Halawa Valley. "To really appreciate Molokai, you need to understand and know things so that you are *pono,* you are right with the land and don't disrespect the culture. Then, then you see the real Molokai."

Solotario and his family, who own the land in the valley, are the only people allowed to hike into Halawa. They lead daily tours, which begin at the County Park pavilion, with a history of the valley, a discussion of the Hawaiian culture, and a display of the fruits, trees, and other flora you will be seeing in the valley. Along the hike, Solotario stops to point out historical and cultural aspects, including chanting in Hawaiian before entering a sacred *heiau.* At the waterfalls visitors can swim in the brisk pool water. Cost for the 4-hour tour is $69. Contact **Molokai Fish & Dive** (✆ **808/553-5926;** www.molokaifish anddive.com). Bring insect repellent, water, a snack, and a swimsuit. Don't forget your camera.

Note that if you venture away from the county park into the valley on your own, you are trespassing and can be prosecuted.

Hike into Halawa Valley and experience its two waterfalls, golden beach, sleepy lagoon, great surf, and offshore island.

For a closer look at Halawa Falls, you'll have to hike in with a tour guided by Pilipo Solotario, who owns the land in the valley.

To get to Halawa Valley, drive north from Kaunakakai on Highway 450 for 30 miles along the coast to the end of the road, which descends into the valley past Jersalema Hou Church. If you'd just like a glimpse of the valley on your way to the beach, there's a scenic overlook along the road: After Pu'u o Hoku Ranch at mile marker 25, the narrow two-lane road widens at a hairpin curve, and you'll find the overlook on your right; it's 2 miles more to the valley floor.

SHOPPING

Kaunakakai

Molokai Surf, Molokai Island Creations, and **Lourdes** are clothing and gift shops close to one another in downtown Kaunakakai, where most of the retail shops sell T-shirts, muumuu, surf wear, and informal apparel. For food shopping, there are several good options. Because many visitors stay in condos, knowing the grocery stores is especially important. Other than that, serious shoppers will be disappointed, unless they love kites or native wood vessels. The following are Kaunakakai's notable stores.

Bamboo Pantry It's hard to believe this creative kitchenware, cutlery, and specialty foods store is located in the heart of Kaunakakai. Molokai is changing, and this store proves it, with "gifts for the home" including everything from dishes, woven baskets, glassware, and high-end pots and pans to gourmet food. 17 Ala Malama St. ✆ **808/553-3300.**

Imamura Store Wilfred Imamura, whose mother founded this store, recalls the old railroad track that stretched from the pier to a spot across the street. "We brought our household things from the pier on a hand-pumped vehicle," he recalls. His store, appropriately, is a leap into the past, a marvelous amalgam of precious old-fashioned things. Rubber boots, Hawaiian-print tablecloths, Japanese tea plates, ukulele cases, plastic slippers, and even coconut bikini tops line the shelves. But it's not all nostalgia: The Molokai T-shirts, jeans, and palaka shorts are of good quality and inexpensive, and the pareu fabrics are a find. In Kaunakakai. ✆ **808/553-5615.**

Molokai Drugs David Mikami, whose father-in-law founded this pharmacy in 1935, has made this more than a drugstore. It's a gleaming, friendly stop full of life's basic necessities, with generous amenities such as a phone and a restroom for passersby. Here you'll find the best selection of guidebooks, books about Molokai, and maps, as well as greeting cards, paperbacks, flip-flops, and every imaginable essential. The Mikamis are a household name on the island, not only because of their pharmacy, but also because the family has shown exceptional kindness to the often economically strapped Molokaians. In Kamoi Professional Center. ✆ **808/553-5790.**

Molokai Fish & Dive Here you'll find the island's largest selection of T-shirts and souvenirs, crammed among fishing, snorkeling, and outdoor gear that you can rent or buy. Find your way among the fishnets, boogie boards, diving equipment, bamboo rakes, beach towels, postcards, juices and soft drinks, and staggering miscellany of this store. One entire wall is lined with T-shirts, and the selection of Molokai books and souvenirs is extensive. The staff is happy to point out the best snorkeling spots of the day. In Kaunakakai. ✆ **808/553-5926.** www.molokai fishanddive.com.

Molokai Surf This wooden building houses a selection of skateboards, surf shorts, sweatshirts, sunglasses, T-shirts, footwear, boogie boards, backpacks, and a broad range of clothing and accessories for life in the surf and sun. 130 Kamehameha V Hwy. ✆ **808/553-5093.**

Take's Variety Store If you need luggage tags, buzz saws, toys, candy, cloth dolls, canned goods, canteens, camping equipment, hardware, batteries, candles, pipe fittings, fishing supplies—whew!—and other products for work and play, this 55-year-old variety store is the answer. You may suffer from claustrophobia in the crowded, dusty aisles, but Take's carries everything. In Kaunakakai. ✆ **808/553-5442.**

EDIBLES

For fresh-baked goods, see the review of Kanemitsu's Bakery & Restaurant on p. 327.

Friendly Market Center You can't miss this salmon-colored wooden storefront on the main drag of "downtown" Kaunakakai, where people of all generations can be found just talking story in the Molokai way. Friendly has an especially good selection of produce and healthy foods—from local poi to Glenlivet. Blue-corn tortilla chips, soy milk, organic brown rice, a good selection of pasta sauces, and Kumu Farms macadamia-nut pesto, the island's stellar gourmet food, are among the items that surpass standard grocery-store fare. In Kaunakakai. ✆ **808/553-5595.**

Misaki's Grocery and Dry Goods Established in 1922, this third-generation local legend is one of Kaunakakai's two grocery stores. Some of its notable items: chopped garlic from California, fresh luau leaves (taro greens), fresh okra, Boca Burgers, large Korean chestnuts in season, gorgeous bananas, and an ATM. The fish section includes akule and ahi, fresh and dried, but the stock consists mostly of meats, produce, baking products, and a humongous array of soft drinks. Liquor, stationery, candies, and paper products round out the selection of this full-service grocery. In Kaunakakai. ℂ **808/553-5505.**

Molokai Wines & Spirits This is your best bet on the island for a decent bottle of wine. The shop offers 200 labels, including Caymus, Silver Oak, Joseph Phelps, Heitz, Bonny Doon, and a carefully culled European selection. *Wine Spectator* reviews are tacked to some of the selections and the snack options include imported gourmet cheeses, salami, and Carr's biscuits. In Kaunakakai. ℂ **808/553-5009.**

En Route to the North Coast

Coffees of Hawaii Plantation Store and Espresso Bar This is a fairly slick—for Molokai—combination coffee bar, store, and gallery for more than 30 artists and craftspeople from Hawaii. Sold here are the Malulani Estate and Muleskinner coffees that are grown, processed, and packed on the 500-acre plantation surrounding the shop. (See p. 339 for details on plantation tours.) The gift items are worth a look: pikake and plumeria soaps from Kauai, perfumes and pure beeswax candles from Maui, koa bookmarks and hair sticks, pottery, woods, and baskets. Hwy. 480 (near the junction of Hwy. 470), Kualapuu. ℂ **800/709-BEAN** (2326) or 808/567-9023.

Molokai Museum Gift Shop This restored 1878 sugar mill sits 1,500 feet above the town of Kualapuu. It's a considerable drive from town, but a good

 THE PERFECT molokai souvenir

It's small, it's easy to pack and take back home, and it's made only on Molokai. It's Molokai salt. The Hawaii Kai Corporation (www.hawaiikaico.com) has two product lines featuring sea salt: the gourmet **Soul of the Sea** ($20–$30 for 12 oz.) and the **Palm Island Premium** ($4–$5 for 6 oz.). Soul of the Sea salt is hand-harvested from some of the cleanest ocean water in the state, hand-processed and hand-packed on Molokai. It comes in three varietals: Papohaku White, Kilauea Black, and Haleakala Red. While making Soul of the Sea salt, Hawaii Kai Corporation got a byproduct they call Ocean Essence, which they blend with Molokai salt and restore trace minerals lost in the heating process. The result is Palm Island Gourmet, which comes in White Silver, Red Gold, or Black Lava.

cause for those who'd like to support the museum and the handful of local artisans who sell their crafts, fabrics, cookbooks, quilt sets, and other gift items in the tiny shop. There's also a modest selection of cards, T-shirts, coloring books, and, at Christmas, handmade ornaments made of lauhala and koa. Meyer Sugar Mill, Hwy. 470 (just after the turnoff for the Ironwood Hills Golf Course, and 2 miles below Kalaupapa Overlook), Kalae. ✆ **808/567-6436.**

EDIBLES

Kualapuu Market This market, in its third generation, is a stone's throw from the Coffees of Hawaii store. It's a scaled-down, one-stop shop with wine, food, and necessities—and a surprisingly presentable, albeit small, assortment of produce, from Molokai sweet potatoes to Ka'u navel oranges in season. The shelves are filled with canned goods, propane, rope, hoses, paper products, and baking goods, reflecting the uncomplicated, rural lifestyle of the area. In Kualapuu. ✆ **808/567-6243.**

The West End

Big Wind Kite Factory & the Plantation Gallery ★★ Jonathan and Daphne Socher, kite designers and inveterate Bali-philes, have com-

Airplanes

Some of the colorful wares at Big Wind Kite Factory.

bined their interests in a kite factory/import shop that dominates the commercial landscape of Maunaloa, the reconstituted plantation town. Maunaloa's naturally windy conditions make it ideal for kite-flying classes, which are offered free when conditions are right. The adjoining Plantation Gallery features local handicrafts such as milo-wood bowls, locally made T-shirts, Hawaii-themed sandblasted glassware, baskets of lauhala and other fibers, and Hawaiian-music CDs. There are also many Balinese handicrafts, from jewelry to clothing and fabrics. In Maunaloa. ✆ **808/552-2364.**

A Touch of Molokai ★ Even though the Kaluakoi Hotel is closed, this fabulous shop remains open. It is well worth the drive. The surf shorts and aloha shirts sold here are better than the norm, with attractive, up-to-date choices by Jams, Quiksilver, and other name brands. Tencel dresses, South Pacific shell necklaces (up to $400), and a magnificent, hand-turned milo bowl also caught my attention. Most impressive are the handsome array of lauhala bags, all made on Molokai. Since there have been so many stores closing in this area, they now carry some groceries as well. At Kaluakoi Hotel & Golf Club. ✆ **808/552-0133.**

The East End

EDIBLES

Mana'e Goods and Grindz Formerly the Neighborhood Store 'N Counter, the only grocery on the East End sells batteries, aspirin, cookies, beer, Molokai produce, candies, paper products, and other sundries. There's good food pouring out of the kitchen for the breakfast and lunch counter, too. See p. 328 for the restaurant review. In Pukoo. ✆ **808/558-8498.**

MOLOKAI AFTER DARK

Hotel Molokai, in Kaunakakai (✆ **808/553-5347;** www.hotelmolokai.com), offers live entertainment by local musicians poolside and in the dining room every night. On Friday from 4 to 6pm is Aloha Fridays Night, when the musicians of Molokai who have been performing here for decades show you why people love their music and hula. With its South Seas ambience and poolside setting, it has become the island's premier venue for local and visiting entertainers. The **Paddlers' Inn** (✆ **808/553-5256**), also in Kaunakakai, recently has become a nightspot for live Hawaii music, comedy acts, and other entertainment. Call to see what's coming up.

12

LANAI, A DIFFERENT KIND OF PARADISE

L anai is not an easy place to reach. There are no direct flights from the mainland. It's almost as if this quiet, gentle oasis—known, paradoxically, for both its small-town feel and its celebrity appeal—demands that its visitors go to great lengths to get here in order to ensure that they will appreciate it.

12

LANAI

Introduction

Lanai (pronounced "Lah-*nigh*-ee"), the nation's biggest defunct pineapple patch, now claims to be one of the world's top tropical destinations. It's a bold claim because so little is here; Lanai has even fewer dining and accommodations choices than Molokai. There are no stoplights and barely 30 miles of paved road. This almost virgin island is unspoiled by what passes for progress, except for a tiny 1920s-era plantation village—and, of course, the village's fancy new arrivals: two first-class luxury hotels where room rates average $400-plus a night.

As soon as you arrive on Lanai, you'll feel the small-town coziness. People wave to every car, residents stop to "talk story" with their friends, fishing and working in the garden are considered priorities in life, and leaving the keys in your car's ignition is standard practice.

For generations, Lanai was little more than a small village, owned and operated by the pineapple company, surrounded by acres of pineapple fields. The few visitors to the island were either relatives of the residents or occasional weekend hunters. Life in the 1960s was pretty much the same as in the 1930s. But all that changed in 1990, when the Lodge at Koele, a 102-room hotel resembling an opulent English Tudor mansion, opened its doors, followed a year later by the 250-room Manele Bay, a Mediterranean-style luxury resort overlooking Hulopoe Bay. Overnight the isolated island was transformed: Corporate jets streamed into tiny Lanai Airport, former plantation workers were retrained in the art of serving gourmet meals, and the population of 2,500 swelled with transient visitors and outsiders coming to work in the island's new hospitality industry. Microsoft billionaire Bill Gates chose the island for his lavish wedding, booking all of its hotel rooms to fend off the press—and uncomplicated Lanai went on the map as a vacation spot for the rich and powerful.

But this island is also a place where people come looking for dramatic beauty, quiet, solitude, and an experience with nature. The sojourners who find their way to Lanai seek out the dramatic views, the tropical fusion of stars at night, and the chance to be alone with the elements.

They also come for the wealth of activities: snorkeling and swimming in the marine preserve known as Hulopoe Bay, hiking on 100 miles of remote trails, talking story with the friendly locals, and beachcombing and whale-watching along stretches of otherwise deserted sand. For the adventurous, there's horseback riding in the forest, scuba diving in caves, playing golf on courses with stunning ocean views, or renting a four-wheel-drive vehicle for the day and discovering wild plains where spotted deer run free.

FACING PAGE: **The beach at Manele Bay.**

In a single decade, a plain red-dirt pineapple patch has become one of Hawaii's top fantasy destinations. But the real Lanai is a multifaceted place that's so much more than a luxury resort—and it's the traveler who comes to discover the island's natural wonders, local lifestyle, and other inherent joys who's bound to have the most genuine island experience.

The Pineapple Island's Unusual Past

This old shield volcano in the rain shadow of Maui has a history of resisting change in a big way. Early Polynesians, fierce Hawaiian kings, European explorers, 20th-century farmers—the island has seen them all and sent most of them packing, empty-handed and broken. The ancient Hawaiians believed that the island was haunted by spirits so wily and vicious that no human could survive here. People didn't settle here until around A.D. 1400.

But those spirits never really went away, it seems. In 1778, the king of the Big Island, Kalaniopuu, invaded Lanai in what was called "the war of loose bowels." His men slaughtered every warrior, cut down trees, and set fire to all that was left except a bitter fern whose roots gave them all dysentery.

In 1802, Wu Tsin made the first attempt to harvest a crop on the island, but he ultimately abandoned his cane fields and went away. Charles Gay acquired 600 acres at public auction to experiment with pineapple as a crop, but a 3-year drought left him bankrupt. Others tried in vain to grow cotton, sisal, and sugar beets; they started a dairy and a piggery and raised sheep for wool. But all enterprises failed, mostly for lack of water.

Harry Baldwin, a missionary's grandson, was the first to succeed on Lanai. He bought Lanai for $588,000 in 1917, developed a 20-mile water pipeline between Koele and Manele, and sold the island 5 years later to Jim Dole for $1.1 million.

Dole planted and irrigated 18,000 acres of pineapple, built Lanai City, blasted out a harbor, and turned the island into a fancy fruit plantation. For a half-century, he enjoyed great success. Even Dole was ultimately vanquished, however: Cheaper pineapple production in Asia brought an end to Lanai's heyday.

The island still resembles old photographs taken in the glory days of Dole. Any minute now, you half expect to look up and see old Jim Dole himself rattling up the road in a Model-T truck with a load of fresh-picked pineapples. Only now, there's a new lord of the manor, and his name is David Murdock.

Of all who have looked at Lanai with a gleam in their eye, nobody has succeeded quite like Murdock, a self-made billionaire who acquired the island in a merger more than a decade ago. About 97% of it is now his private holding.

Murdock spent $400 million to build two grand hotels on the island: the Lodge at Koele, which resembles an English country retreat, and the Four Seasons Resort Lanai at Manele Bay, a green tile-roofed Mediterranean palazzo by the sea. Murdock recycled the former field hands into waitstaff, even summoning a London butler to school the natives in the fine art of service, and carved a pair of daunting golf courses, one in the island's interior and the other along the wave-lashed coast. He then set out to attract tourists by touting Lanai as "the private island."

Murdock is now trying to make all this pay for itself by selling vacation homes and condos, all in the million-dollar range, next door to the two resorts.

The redevelopment of this tiny rock should have been a pushover for the big-time tycoon, but island-style politics have continually thwarted his schemes.

Lanai

GO SLOW, a sun-faded sign at Dole's old maintenance shed once said. Murdock might have heeded the warning because his grandiose plans are taking twice as long to accomplish as he had expected. Lanai is under the political thumb of many who believe that the island's precious water supply shouldn't all be diverted to championship golf courses and Jacuzzis, and there remains opposition from Lanaians for Sensible Growth, who advocate affordable housing, alternative water systems, and civic improvements that benefit residents.

Lanai residents might have lived in a rural setting, but they certainly haven't been isolated. Having watched the other islands in Hawaii attempt the balancing act of economic growth and the maintenance of an island lifestyle, the residents of Lanai are cautiously welcoming visitors, but at a pace that is still easy for this former plantation community to digest.

ORIENTATION
Arriving

BY PLANE No matter where you're coming from, you'll have to make a connection in Honolulu (on Oahu) or Kahului (on Maui), where you can catch a plane for the 25-minute flight to Lanai's airport. You'll touch down in Puuwai Basin, once the world's largest pineapple plantation; it's about 10 minutes by car to Lanai City and 25 minutes to Manele Bay.

Commuter airline offering service to Lanai are: **Go Airlines** (✆ 888/435-9462; www.iflygo.com) and **Island Air** (✆ 800/323-3345 from the mainland, 800/652-6541 interisland, or 808/565-6744; www.islandair.com), with daily flights from Honolulu. *Note:* Island Air has left me stranded mid-route twice.

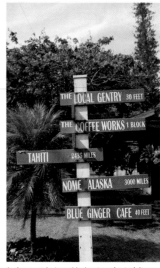
A signpost in Lanai helps to orient visitors.

BY BOAT A round-trip on **Expeditions Lahaina/Lanai Passenger Ferry** (✆ 800/695-2624 or 808/661-3756) takes you between Maui and Lanai for $30 adults and $20 children, each way. The ferry runs five times a day, 365 days a year, between Lahaina (on Maui) and Lanai's Manele Bay harbor. The 9-mile channel crossing takes 45 minutes to an hour, depending on sea conditions. Reservations are strongly recommended; call or book online. Baggage is limited to two checked bags and one carry-on.

Visitor Information

Lanai Visitors Bureau, P.O. Box 631436, Lanai City, HI 96763; or 431 Seventh St., Ste. A, Lanai City (✆ 800/947-4774 or 808/565-7600; fax 808/565-9316; www.visitlanai.net), and the **Hawaii Visitors & Convention Bureau** (✆ 800/GO-HAWAII [464-2924] or 808/923-1811; www.gohawaii.com) provide brochures, maps, and island guides.

The Island in Brief

Inhabited Lanai is divided into three parts—Lanai City, Koele, and Manele—and two distinct climate zones: hot and dry, and cool and misty.

Lanai City (pop. 3,200) sits at the heart of the island at 1,645 feet above sea level. It's the only place on the island where you'll find services. Built in 1924, this plantation village is a tidy grid of quaint tin-roofed cottages in bright pastels, with tropical gardens of banana, lilikoi, and papaya. Many of the residents are Filipino immigrants who once worked the pineapple fields. Their clapboard homes, now worth $500,000 or more (for a 1,000-sq.-ft. home, built in 1935, on a tiny 5,000-sq.-ft. lot), are excellent examples of historic preservation; the whole town looks like it's been kept under a bell jar.

Around Dole Park, a charming village square lined with towering Norfolk and Cook Island pines, plantation buildings house general stores selling basic necessities, a post office (where people stop to chat), two banks, three restaurants, an art gallery, an art center, a whimsical shop, and a coffee shop that outshines any Starbucks. A victim of "progress" was the local one-room police station with a jail that consisted of three blue-and-white wooden outhouse-size cells with padlocks. It's now a block from the square with "modern facilities," including regulation-size jail cells.

In the nearby cool upland district of **Koele** is the Lodge at Koele (now managed by the Four Seasons Resort), standing alone on a knoll overlooking pastures and the sea at the edge of a pine forest, like a grand European manor.

The other bastion of indulgence, the Four Seasons Resort Lanai at Manele Bay, is on the sunny southwestern tip of the island at **Manele.** You'll get more of what you expect from Hawaii here—beaches, swaying palms, mai tais, and the like.

[Fast FACTS] LANAI

Lanai is part of Maui County. In case of **emergencies,** call the police, fire department, or ambulance services at ✆ 911, or the **Poison Control Center** at ✆ 800/222-1222. For nonemergencies, call the **police** at ✆ 808/565-6428.

For emergency dental care, call **Dr. Nora Harmsen** (✆ 808/565-6418). If you need a doctor, contact the **Straub Lanai Family Health Center** (✆ 808/565-6423) or the **Lanai Community Hospital** (✆ 808/565-8450).

For a weather report, call the **National Weather Service** at ✆ 808/565-6033.

The Lahaina Passenger Ferry shuttles visitors between Maui and Lanai five times a day, 365 days a year.

GETTING AROUND

With so few paved roads here, you'll need a four-wheel-drive vehicle if you plan to explore the island's remote shores, its interior, or the summit of Mount Lanaihale. Even if you have only a day on Lanai, rent one and see the island. Both standard cars and four-wheel-drive vehicles are available at the **Dollar Rent-A-Car desk** at **Lanai City Service/Lanai Plantation Store,** 1036 Lanai Ave. (© **800/533-7808** for Dollar reservations, or 808/565-7227 for Lanai City Service). Expect to pay about $139 to $169 a day for a four-wheel-drive jeep.

Warning: Gas is expensive on Lanai, and those four-wheel-drive vehicles get terrible mileage. Because everything in Lanai City is within walking distance, it makes sense to rent a jeep only for the days you want to explore the island.

Though it's fun to rent a car and explore the island, it is possible to stay here and get to the beach without one. The two big resort hotels run shuttle vans to the Four Seasons Resort Lanai at Manele Bay; from there, you can walk to Hulopoe Beach. When you want to return, you just catch the hourly shuttle (it may run on the half-hour from Four Seasons Resort Lanai at Manele Bay) back to Lanai City. The shuttle picks up at Hotel Lanai as well and will take guests to town, the airport, and the golf courses. There is a one-time charge of $45 per person for Four Seasons guests and $35 per person for Hotel Lanai guests.

If you're staying elsewhere, you can walk to everything in Lanai City. Or you can most likely get a ride back up to Lanai City with a local resident from the airport. Whether or not you rent a car, sooner or later you'll find yourself at Lanai City Service/Lanai Plantation Store. This all-in-one grocery store, gas station, rental-car agency, and souvenir shop serves as the island's Grand Central Terminal—you can pick up information, directions, maps, and all the local gossip here.

WHERE TO STAY

The majority of the accommodations are located "in the village," as residents call Lanai City. Above the village is the luxurious Lodge at Koele (now managed by Four Seasons), while down the hill at Hulopoe Bay are two options: the equally luxurious Four Seasons Resort Lanai at Manele Bay or tent camping under the stars at the park.

In addition to the choices listed below, consider a vacation home rental like **Hale O Lanai,** in Lanai City (© **808/247-3637;** www.myhawaiibeachfront.com). It has a fully equipped two-bedroom vacation rental that sleeps up to six; rates range from $115 to $135, plus a $45 to $65 cleaning fee.

Don't forget to add 12.42% in taxes to all accommodations bills. Parking is free.

Expensive

Four Seasons Resort Lanai at Manele Bay ★★★ The well-known luxury hotel chain Four Seasons took over management of this 236-unit oceanside resort after a $50-million makeover. Every Four Seasons resort is spectacular, but this one really stands out. Located on a sun-washed southern bluff overlooking Hulopoe Beach, one of Hawaii's best stretches of golden sand, this U-shaped hotel steps down the hillside to the pool and the beach, and then fans out in oceanfront wings separated by gardens with lush flora, man-made waterfalls, lotus ponds, and streams. On the other side, it's bordered by golf greens. The place is a real oasis against the dry Arizona-like heat of Lanai's south coast.

Designed as a traditional luxury beachfront hotel, it features open, airy rooms, each with a breathtaking view of the big blue Pacific. Murals depicting scenes from Hawaiian history, sea charts, potted palms, soft camel-hued club chairs, and hand-woven kilim rugs fill the lobby. Redone in the clean, crisp style of an elegant Hawaiian resort, the oversize guest rooms have 40-inch flatscreen TVs, huge marble bathrooms, and semiprivate lanais. This resort is much less formal than the Lodge at Koele up the hill and attracts more families. Speaking of families, in addition to the "Kids for All Seasons" child-care programs, the hotel features a teen center with video games, computers, a small pool table, and a 54-inch TV.

The spa offers a variety of massages, facials, wraps, and scrubs (don't miss the signature Ali'i banana-coconut scrub). In addition, the Four Seasons has added a 1,500-square-foot fitness center (with one of the best ocean views in the resort) that has the latest cardiovascular and strength-training equipment, free weights, and a wood-floored studio for classes (spinning, yoga, Pilates, and meditation).

1 Manele Bay Rd., P.O. Box 631380, Lanai City, HI 96763. © **800/321-4666** or 808/565-2000. Fax 808/565-2483. www.fourseasons.com/lanai. 236 units. $295–$795 double; from $1,000 suite. Extra person $100. Children under 18 stay free in parent's room. Numerous packages available. AE, DC, MC, V. Airport shuttle $45 round-trip. **Amenities:** 4 restaurants (Ihilani, p. 363; Hulopoe Court, p. 363; Ocean Grill, p. 364; and the Challenge at Manele Clubhouse, p. 364); bar w/breathtaking views; babysitting; children's program; concierge; fitness center w/classes; golf at the Jack Nicklaus–designed Challenge at Manele; Jacuzzi; large outdoor pool; room service; full spa; tennis courts; complimentary snorkeling equipment. *In room:* A/C, TV/DVD, hair dryer, minibar, Wi-Fi ($13 per day).

Four Seasons Resort Lanai, The Lodge at Koele ★★★ After some $50

million in renovations, the Four Seasons took over the management of the former Lodge at Koele. This inn, which resembles a grand English country estate, was built in 1991 and needed the makeover. All 102 guest rooms were totally redone, a game room was added, the grounds have been spruced up, and a pagoda imported from China has been constructed on the sprawling English gardens' grounds (not my taste, but I'm sure it will be the backdrop for hundreds of wedding photos).

Inside, heavy timbers, beamed ceilings, and the two huge stone fireplaces of the Great Hall complete the look. Overstuffed furniture sits invitingly around the fireplaces, richly patterned rugs adorn the floor, and museum-quality art hangs on the walls. The guest rooms continue the English theme with four-poster beds, sitting areas (complete with window seats), formal writing desks, and bathrooms with oversize tubs. All rooms have signature Four Seasons beds, 42-inch flatscreen televisions, and high-speed Internet access.

The Four Seasons also retrained the staff to their level of excellent service. Don't expect the "sophisticated" service you'd get in most Four Seasons around the world—most of the staff have lived on Lanai for generations. Instead, you'll find a charming display of aloha spirit and a strong desire to make sure your vacation is perfect.

Before you reach for the phone, understand that this hotel is not located at the beach (see the Manele Bay resort, above), but rather in the cool mist of the mountains, on 21 acres at 1,700 feet above sea level, 8 miles inland from any beach. In the winter, temperatures can drop into the 50s (don't worry, the rooms have heat as well as air-conditioning). Most guests here are looking for relaxation: sitting on the rattan chairs on the porch, reading, watching the turkeys mosey across the manicured lawns, strolling through the Japanese hillside garden, or watching the sun sink into the Pacific.

There are plenty of activities here and at the sister resort down the hill, Manele, so you'll get the best of both hotels. Other pluses include shuttle to the golf courses, beach, and Four Seasons Resort Lanai at Manele Bay (for a one-time $45 fee), complimentary coffee and tea in the lobby, formal afternoon tea, and twice-daily maid service. Guests can take advantage of the croquet lawns, horseback riding, hiking trails, and garden walks.

1 Keomoku Hwy., P.O. Box 631380, Lanai City, HI 96763. ✆ **800/321-4666** or 808/565-4000. Fax 808/565-4561. www.fourseasons.com/lanai. 102 units. $295–$565 double; from $750 suite. Extra person $100. Children under 18 stay free in parent's room. Numerous packages available. AE, DC, MC, V. Airport shuttle $45 round-trip. **Amenities:** 2 restaurants (including the Main Dining Room, p. 363, and Terrace, p. 364); bar w/live music; babysitting; bike rentals; children's program; concierge; fitness room; golf at Greg Norman–designed Experience at Koele (p. 373); Jacuzzi; outdoor pool; room service; tennis courts; complimentary snorkeling equipment at Four Seasons Resort Lanai at Manele Bay. *In room:* A/C, TV/DVD, fridge, hair dryer, minibar, Wi-Fi ($13 per day).

Moderate

Hotel Lanai ★ ☺ This hotel lacks the facilities of the two resorts described above, but it's perfect for families and other vacationers who can't afford to spend $345 to $445 (and up) a night. In fact, if you're looking for the old-fashioned aloha that Lanai City is famous for, this is the place to stay. Built in the 1920s for VIP plantation guests, this clapboard plantation-era relic has retained its quaint character and lives on as a country inn.

The entire hotel underwent renovations several years ago—repainting, remodeling, and a general sprucing up. The guest rooms, although extremely small, are clean and outfitted with Hawaiian quilts, wood furniture, and ceiling fans (but no air-conditioning or TVs). The most popular are the lanai units, which feature a shared lanai with the room next door. All rooms have private shower-only bathrooms. The one-bedroom cottage, with a TV and bathtub, is perfect for a small family.

The hotel serves as a down-home crossroads where total strangers meet local folks on the lanai to drink beer and talk story or play the ukulele and sing into the dark, tropical night. Often a curious visitor in search of an authentic experience will join the party and discover Lanai's very Hawaiian heart. Guests have the use of the shuttle to both Four Seasons Resorts, the golf courses (at which they get the same lower rates given to guests at the two resorts), and the beach for a one-time $35 fee.

828 Lanai Ave. (P.O. Box 630520), Lanai City, HI 96763. ✆ **800/795-7211** or 808/565-7211. Fax 808/565-6450. www.hotellanai.com. 11 units. $99–$149 double; $179 cottage double. Rates include continental breakfast. Extra person $50. AE, MC, V. Unlimited shuttle service for entire stay $35. **Amenities:** Excellent restaurant (Lanai City Grille, p. 365); intimate bar; access to 2 resort golf courses on the island; nearby tennis courts; complimentary snorkeling equipment.

WHERE TO DINE

Lanai is a curious mix of innocence and sophistication, with strong cross-cultural elements that liven up its culinary offerings. You can dine like a sultan on this island, but be prepared for high prices. The tony hotel restaurants require deep pockets, and there are only a handful of other options.

Note: You'll find the restaurants reviewed in this chapter on the map on p. 357.

Very Expensive

Ihilani ★★★ ITALIAN A number of top Hawaii chefs (such as Philippe Padovani and Edwin Goto) have added bits of their own style to the resort's inspiring menu, which melds Mediterranean with Island cuisine. The result is one of Lanai's top gourmet restaurants. The latest incarnation of this classy, formal restaurant, overlooking the resort and the ocean beyond, is traditional Italian cuisine. Try the perfect homemade gnocchi. My other favorites include the osso buco, duck and root vegetable orecchiette, and shutome alla puttanesca with artichoke purée and a spicy tomato and caper sauce. Be sure to leave room for the scrumptious desserts.

At the Four Seasons Resort Lanai at Manele Bay. ⓒ **808/565-2296.** www.fourseasons.com/manelebay/dining. Reservations strongly recommended. Resort attire recommended. Set menu $61 2 courses with dessert, $69 3 courses, $81 3 courses and dessert. AE, DC, MC, V. Tues–Sat 6–9:30pm.

Main Dining Room ★★★ NEW AMERICAN The former Formal Dining Room has been revamped under the Four Seasons management and has a new menu. However, they did retain the relaxing setting, with a roaring fire, bountiful sprays of orchids, sienna-colored walls, and a team of waitstaff serving in hushed voices. The menu highlights American favorites. The appetizers are so tempting, you could make a meal from the variety of choices: seared diver scallops with sweet spring pea blini, foie gras and black truffle parfait, and lava rock–seared Lanai venison. The entrees vary according to the season; when I dined here, the menu included Maui lavender honey–roasted duck breast, mustard-and-herb-roasted rack of lamb, and a buttered poached lobster from the Big Island. The service is impeccable, the atmosphere relaxing. But don't forget your platinum credit card—you'll need it.

At the Four Seasons Resort Lanai, The Lodge at Koele. ⓒ **808/565-4580.** www.fourseasons.com/koele/dining. Reservations required. Resort attire recommended; collared shirts and closed-toe footwear requested for men. Main courses $43–$59. AE, DC, MC, V. Fri–Tues 6–9:30pm.

Expensive

Hulopoe Court ★★ HAWAII REGIONAL This is the Manele Bay's informal dining room. It serves one of the best breakfast buffets I've seen in Hawaii, with everything from an omelet station to breakfast meats, daily pancakes, potatoes, rice, and local tropical fruit. The dinner menu showcases the culinary influences in the islands, Pacific Islands, Chinese, Portuguese, and Japanese, with dishes like steamed onaga with pork lau lau, Kung Pau chicken, shrimp with Piri Piri sauce and oven-baked miso cod.

At the Four Seasons Resort Lanai at Manele Bay. ⓒ **808/565-2290.** www.fourseasons.com/manelebay/dining. Reservations recommended for dinner. Resort attire recommended. Breakfast main courses $17–$24, buffet $30–$34; dinner main courses $20–$33. AE, DC, MC, V. Daily 7–11am and Sat–Wed 6–9:30pm.

Ocean Grill ★ SEAFOOD The former Pool Grille has been remodeled and expanded, and is now open for lunch and dinner. Located just off the pool, the casual, open-air, Hawaii-style bistro serves interesting lunches like wraps and sandwiches (such as a veggie panini with mushrooms, red peppers, mozzarella cheese, zucchini), a great selection of salads (including a yummy smoked scallop and fresh orange, arugula, and spinach), and a range of entrees such as *kalua* pork and cheese quesadilla or mahimahi fish and chips. At dinner, watch the sun set and the stars come out as you dine on fresh local fish, steak, free-range chicken, or small-plate entrees such as Hawaiian kampachi, crab cakes, lobster, and red-curry chowder.

At the Four Seasons Resort Lanai at Manele Bay. © **808/565-2092.** www.fourseasons.com/manelebay/dining. Main courses $12–$21 lunch, $32–$49 dinner. AE, MC, V. Sun, Mon, Thurs, and Fri 11am–5pm and 5:30–9pm.

Terrace ★★ AMERICAN Located next to the Main Dining Room in the Lodge at Koele, between the 35-foot-high Great Hall and a wall of glass looking out over prim English gardens, this wonderful spot is the Lodge's "casual" dining room. The Terrace is far from your typical hotel restaurant—the menu may be fancy for comfort food, but it does, indeed, comfort. Hearty breakfasts of waffles and cereals, fresh pineapple from the nearby Palawai Basin, Paniola rancheros, and traditional Benedict make a grand start to the day. Dinner choices include flank steak, meatloaf, roasted pork loin, fresh fish of the day, and a vegetarian selection (ricotta and local mushroom risotto with basil and truffle oils).

At the Four Seasons Resort Lanai, The Lodge at Koele. © **808/565-4580.** www.fourseasons. com/koele/dining. Reservations recommended. Resort attire recommended. Full breakfast $16–$40, lunch $14–$21, dinner main courses $23–$40. AE, DC, MC, V. Daily 7–11am breakfast, 11am–2pm lunch, 6–9:30pm dinner.

Moderate

The Challenge at Manele Clubhouse ★ PACIFIC RIM The view from the alfresco tables here may be the best on the island, encompassing Kahoolawe, Haleakala (on Maui), and, on an especially clear day, the peaks of Mauna Kea and Mauna Loa on the Big Island. You can lunch on salads and sandwiches (Asian tuna salad with grilled ahi, turkey club sandwich, clubhouse burgers with caramelized onions and cheese) or on more substantial entrees, ranging from fish and chips to kalbi beef. The clubhouse is casual, the view of the ocean is awe-inspiring, and it's a great gathering place.

At the Challenge at Manele Golf Course. © **808/565-2230.** www.fourseasons.com/manelebay/dining. Reservations recommended. Main courses $11–$20. AE, DC, MC, V. Daily 11am–3pm.

The Experience at Koele Clubhouse AMERICAN This tiny eatery overlooks the verdant, rolling hills of the Experience at Koele Golf Course. Most of your fellow diners will have just finished a round of golf; you can join them at one of a handful of tables inside or on the lanai overlooking the pastoral view. Soups, salads, and oversized sandwiches rule here, everything from a delicious portobello mushroom on toasted focaccia bread to open-faced chicken salad (with a yummy mango-avocado salsa), smoked turkey club, or charbroiled cheddar burger.

At the Experience at Koele Golf Course. © **808/565-4605.** www.fourseasons.com/koele/dining. Main courses $10–$20. AE, DC, MC, V. Wed–Sun 10am–3pm.

Lanai City Grille ★★ CAJUN/COUNTRY Celebrated Maui chef Bev Gannon (Haliimaile General Store, Joe's Restaurant) redesigned the menu in this cute eatery, where the decor consists of pine-paneled walls, chintz curtains, and a fireplace. The menu sticks to whatever is in season and fresh that day, from the fish and seafood to meats and rotisserie chicken.

At the Hotel Lanai, 828 Lanai Ave., Lanai City. € **808/565-7211.** www.hotellanai.com. Reservations recommended. Main courses $23–$40. AE, MC, V. Wed–Sun 5–9pm.

Inexpensive

Blue Ginger Cafe COFFEE SHOP Famous for its mahimahi sandwiches and inexpensive omelets, Blue Ginger is a very local, very casual, and very reasonably priced alternative to Lanai's fancy hotel restaurants. The four tables on the front porch face the cool Norfolk pines of Dole Park and are always filled with locals who talk story from morning to night. The offerings are solid, no-nonsense, every-day fare: fried saimin (no MSG), very popular burgers on homemade buns, and mahimahi with capers and mushrooms. Blue Ginger also serves a tasty French toast made with homemade bread and a surprisingly good stir-fried vegetable dish.

409 Seventh St. (at Ilima St.), Lanai City. € **808/565-6363.** Breakfast and lunch items under $15, dinner main courses under $17. No credit cards. Mon and Thurs–Fri 6am–8pm; Tues–Wed 6am–2pm; Sat–Sun 6:30am–8pm.

Canoes Lanai LOCAL This ma-and-pa eatery may have changed its name (it used to be Tanigawa's), but it remains the landmark that it's been since the 1920s. In those days, the tiny storefront sold canned goods and cigarettes; the 10 tables, hamburgers, and Filipino food came later. This hole in the wall is a local institution, with a reputation for serving local-style breakfasts. The fare—fried rice, omelets, short stack, and simple ham and eggs—is more greasy spoon than gourmet, but it's definitely budget friendly.

419 Seventh St., Lanai City. € **808/565-6537.** Reservations not accepted. Breakfast items under $9, sandwiches $4–$8, burgers $3–$7. No credit cards. Daily 6:30am–1pm.

Coffee Works ★ COFFEEHOUSE Oahu's popular Ward Warehouse coffee-house has opened a branch on Lanai, with a menu of espresso drinks, ice cream (including local brands), and a small selection of pastries. It's Lanai City's gathering place, a tiny cafe with tables and benches on a pleasing wooden deck just a stone's throw from Dole Park. Formerly a plantation house, the structure fits in with the surrounding plantation homes in the heart of Lanai City. There are some nice gift items available, including T-shirts, tea infusers, teapots, cookies, and gourmet coffees.

604 Ilima St., Lanai City (across from the post office). € **808/565-6962.** Most items under $8. AE, DC, DISC, MC, V. Mon–Sat 7am–1:30pm.

Pele's Other Garden ★★ DELI/BISTRO Owners Mark and Barbara have turned this small sandwich shop into a popular full-scale deli and bistro. Daily soup and menu specials, excellent pizza, fresh organic produce, and special items such as top-quality black-bean burritos make Pele's Other Garden a Lanai City must. Sandwiches are made as wraps or with whole-wheat, rye, sourdough, or French bread, all baked on the island and delivered fresh daily. In the evening, you can dine on china at cloth-covered tables, and the menu expands to include pastas (bow-tie pasta with butterflied garlic shrimp, fettuccine with smoked salmon), pizza, and salads. Beer and wines by the glass (from $6) and a full bar were recently added.

Dole Park, 811 Houston St., Lanai City. © **888/764-3354** or 808/565-9628. www.pelesother garden.com. Main courses $7.50–$12 lunch, $17–$20 dinner, pizza from $9. AE, DISC, MC, V. Mon–Fri 11am–3pm and Mon–Sat 5–8pm (bar menu 4:30–6:30pm).

BEACHES

If you like big, wide, empty, gold-sand beaches and crystal-clear, cobalt-blue water full of bright tropical fish—and who doesn't?—go to Lanai. With 18 miles of sandy shoreline, Lanai has some of Hawaii's least crowded and most interesting beaches.

Hulopoe Beach ★★★

In 1997, Dr. Stephen Leatherman of the University of Maryland (a professional beach surveyor who's also known as "Dr. Beach") ranked Hulopoe the best beach in the United States. It's easy to see why. This palm-fringed, gold-sand beach is bordered by black-lava fingers, protecting swimmers from ocean currents. In summer, Hulopoe is perfect for swimming, snorkeling, or just lolling about; the

---

FROMMER'S FAVORITE
lanai experiences

Snorkeling Hulopoe Beach. Crystal-clear waters teem with brilliant tropical fish off one of Hawaii's best beaches. There are tide pools to explore, waves to play in, and other surprises—like a pod of spinner dolphins that often makes a splashy entrance.

Exploring the Garden of the Gods. Eroded by wind, rain, and time, these geologic badlands (p. 375) are worth visiting at sunrise or sunset, when the low light plays tricks on the land—and your mind.

Hiking the Munro Trail. The 11-mile Munro Trail (p. 376) is a lofty, rigorous hike along the rim of an old volcano. You'll get great views of the nearby islands. Take a four-wheel-drive vehicle if you want to spend more time on top of the island.

Four-Wheeling It. Four-wheeling is a way of life on Lanai because there are only 30 miles of pavement on the whole island. Plenty of rugged trails lead to deserted beaches, abandoned villages, and valleys filled with wild game.

Camping under the Stars. The campsites (p. 373) at Hulopoe Beach Park are about as close to the heavens as you can get. The crashing surf will lull you to sleep at night, and chirping birds will wake you in the morning. If you're into roughing it, this is a great way to experience Lanai.

Watching the Whales at Polihua Beach. Located on the north shore, this beach—which gets its name from the turtles that nest here—is a great place to watch for whales during the winter months.

Hulopoe Beach.

water temperature is usually in the mid-70s (mid-20s Celsius). Swimming is usually safe, except when swells kick up in winter. The bay at the foot of the Four Seasons Resort Lanai at Manele Bay is a protected marine preserve, with schools of colorful fish and spinner dolphins. Humpback whales cruise by here in winter. Hulopoe is also Lanai's premier beach park, with a grassy lawn, picnic tables, barbecue grills, restrooms, showers, and ample parking. You can camp here, too.

HULOPOE'S TIDE POOLS Some of the best lava-rock tide pools in Hawaii are found along the south shore of Hulopoe Bay. These miniature SeaWorlds are full of strange creatures such as asteroids (sea stars) and holothurians (sea cucumbers), not to mention spaghetti worms, Barber Pole shrimp, and Hawaii's favorite local delicacy, the opihi, a tasty morsel also known as the limpet. Youngsters enjoy swimming in the enlarged tide pool at the eastern edge of the bay. When you explore tide pools, do so at low tide. Never turn your back on the waves. Wear tennis shoes or reef walkers, as wet rocks are slippery. Collecting specimens in this marine preserve is forbidden, so don't take any souvenirs home.

Polihua Beach ★

So many sea turtles once hauled themselves out of the water to lay their eggs in the sunbaked sand on Lanai's northwestern shore that Hawaiians named the beach here *Polihua,* or "egg nest." Although the endangered green sea turtles are making a comeback, they're seldom seen here now. You're more likely to spot an offshore whale (in season) or the perennial litter that washes up onto this

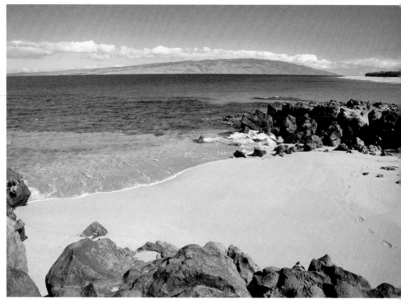

Polihua Beach

deserted beach at the end of Polihua Road, a 4-mile jeep trail. This strand is ideal for beachcombing (those little green-glass Japanese fishing-net floats often show up here), fishing, or just being alone. There are no facilities except fishermen's huts and driftwood shelters. Bring water and sunscreen. Beware of the strong currents, which make the water unsafe for swimming.

Shipwreck Beach ★

This 8-mile-long windswept strand on Lanai's northeastern shore—named for the rusty ship *Liberty* stuck on the coral reef—is a sailor's nightmare and a beachcomber's dream. The strong currents yield all sorts of flotsam, from Japanese hand-blown-glass fish floats and rare pelagic paper nautilus shells to lots of junk. This is also a great place to spot whales from December to April, when the Pacific humpbacks cruise in from Alaska. The road to the beach is paved most of the way, but you really need a four-wheel-drive to get down here.

Shipwreck Beach.

The rusty ship *Liberty* is stuck on the coral reef.

WATERSPORTS

Lanai has Hawaii's best water clarity because it lacks major development, it has low rainfall and runoff, and its coast is washed clean daily by the sea current (known as "The Way to Tahiti"). But the strong sea currents pose a threat to swimmers, and there are few good surf breaks. Most of the aquatic adventures—swimming, snorkeling, scuba diving—are centered on the somewhat protected south shore, around Hulopoe Bay.

The only outfitter for watersports is **Trilogy Lanai Ocean Sports ★★★** (𝄏 **888/MAUI-800** [628-4800]; www.visitlanai.com).

Sailing & Snorkeling

Trilogy Lanai Ocean Sports (see above), which has built a well-deserved reputation as the leader in sailing/snorkeling cruises in Hawaii, offers both a morning and an afternoon **snorkel sailing trip** on board its luxury custom sailing catamarans or its 32-foot jet-drive rigid aluminum-inflatable vessel. The trips along Lanai's protected coastline sail past hundreds of spinner dolphins and into some of the best snorkeling sites in the world for $203 (half-price for children 3–15) and include lunch, sodas, snorkel gear, and instruction.

If you just want to snorkel on your own, Hulopoe is Lanai's best snorkeling spot. Fish are abundant in the marine-life conservation area. Try the lava-rock points at either end of the beach and around the lava pools.

Scuba Diving

Two of Hawaii's best-known dive spots are found in Lanai's clear waters, just off the south shore: **Cathedrals I** and **II,** so named because the sun lights up

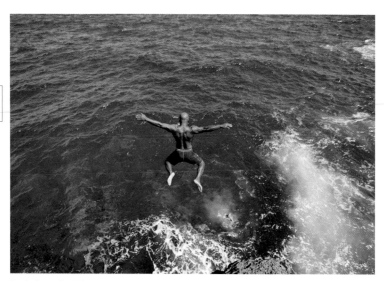

Fun in the surf at Hulopoe Bay.

an underwater grotto like a magnificent church. **Trilogy Lanai Ocean
Sports** (see above for contact information) offers several kinds of sailing, diving, and snorkeling trips on
catamarans and from its new 32-foot
high-tech jet-drive ocean raft. It has its
own version of "sunrise services" at the
Cathedrals—not only is this the best
time of day to dive this incredible area,
but there are virtually no other dive
boats in the water at this time. Cost is
$169 to $199 for a two-tank dive, $79
for nondivers. Beach dives are available for $95 (one-tank dive) for certi-
fied divers and $95 for an introductory
dive for noncertified divers.

A scuba diver explores in the waters off Lanai.

Sportfishing

**Spinning Dolphin Charters of
Lanai** (© **808/565-7676;** www.
sportfishinglanai.com) offers sportfishing on a 36-foot catamaran. It will take up
to six passengers for $700 for 4 hours ($110 for each additional hour), or you can
share a boat for $150 each for 4 hours.

Surfing

If you've ever wanted to learn how to surf, let instructor Nick Palumbo, a surfing champion, take you on a four-wheel-drive surfing safari to a secluded surf

spot. He'll have you up and riding the waves in no time. His **Lanai Surf School & Surf Safari** (📞 **808/306-9837;** www.lanaisurfsafari.com) offers a package that includes a 2½-hour lesson with surfboard, four-wheel-drive transportation, refreshments, and "a really good time" for $175 per person.

Whale-Watching

During whale season, from December to April, **Trilogy Lanai Ocean Sports** (see above for contact information) takes passengers out on its 26-passenger, rigid-hulled inflatable boat, a 32-foot jet-drive Zodiac named *Manele Kai,* for a 2-hour ocean adventure that explores some of the remote and unspoiled sites in Hawaii. Lanai is also home to one of Hawaii's largest schools of spinner dolphins and a haven for North Pacific humpback whales. The captains and crew are Certified Island Naturalists who make each trip educational as well as entertaining, and they can usually find these wonderful and playful mammals. The cost is $75 (half-price for children 3–15), which includes soft drinks.

HIKING & CAMPING

Hiking

A LEISURELY MORNING HIKE

The 3-hour self-guided **Koele Nature Hike** starts by the reflecting pool in the backyard of the Lodge at Koele and takes you on a 5-mile loop through Norfolk Island pines, into Hulopoe Valley, past wild ginger, and up to Koloiki Ridge, with

Do the Koele Nature Hike in the morning, by afternoon the clouds usually roll in, marring visibility at the top and increasing your chance of being caught in a downpour.

The Munro Trail leads to a spectacular view of Molokai, Maui, Kahoolawe, the peaks of the Big Island, and, on a clear day, Oahu.

its panoramic view of Maunalei Valley and of Molokai and Maui in the distance. You're welcome to take the hike even if you're not a guest at the Lodge. The path isn't clearly marked, so ask the concierge for a free map. Do this hike in the morning; by afternoon, the clouds usually roll in, marring visibility at the top and increasing your chance of being caught in a downpour.

THE CHALLENGING MUNRO TRAIL

This tough 11-mile (round-trip) uphill climb through the groves of Norfolk pines is a lung-buster, but if you reach the top, you'll be rewarded with a breathtaking view of Molokai, Maui, Kahoolawe, the peaks of the Big Island, and—on a really clear day—Oahu in the distance. Figure on 7 hours. The trail begins at Lanai Cemetery along Keomoku Road (Hwy. 44) and follows Lanai's ancient caldera rim, ending up at the island's highest point, Lanaihale. Go in the morning for the best visibility. After 4 miles, you'll get a view of Lanai City. The weary retrace their steps from here, while the more determined go the last 1.25 miles to the top. Die-hards head down Lanai's steep south-crater rim to join the highway to Manele Bay. For more details on the Munro Trail—including information on four-wheel-driving it to the top—see "Five Islands at a Single Glance: The Munro Trail" (p. 376).

A SELF-GUIDED NATURE TRAIL

This self-guided nature trail in the Kanepuu Preserve (described below) is about a 10- to 15-minute walk through eight stations, with interpretive signs explaining the natural or cultural significance of what you're seeing. The trail head is clearly marked on the Polihua Road on the way to the Garden of the Gods. Kanepuu is one of the last remaining examples of the type of forest that once covered the dry lowlands throughout the state. There are some 49 plant species here that are found only in Hawaii. The **Nature Conservancy** (𝄢 **808/572-7849**) conducts guided hikes every month; call for details. At press time, the Kanepuu Preserve was closed but had plans for reopening, with guided hikes soon. I would definitely call the Maui Conservancy office to confirm in advance. There are also plans to re-construct the self-guided trails and signage, which have fallen into serious disrepair, but no dates or projections.

GUIDED HIKES

The **Lodge at Koele** (𝄢 **808/565-4552;** www.fourseasons.com/lanai) offers a 2½-hour Koloiki Ridge nature hike through 5 miles of the upland forests of Koele at 11am daily. The fee is $25. It's considered moderate, with some uphill and downhill hiking.

Camping at Hulopoe Beach Park

There is only one legal place to camp on Lanai: **Hulopoe Beach Park,** which is owned by Castle and Cooke Resorts. To camp in this exquisite beach park, with its crescent-shaped white-sand beach bordered by kiawe trees, contact Dony Haban–Park Manager, Castle and Cooke Resorts, P.O. Box 630310, Lanai City, HI 96763 (𝄢 **808/559-7841**). There's a $25 registration fee, plus a charge of $10 per person, per night. Hulopoe has eight campsites; each can accommodate up to five people. Facilities include restrooms, running water, showers, barbecue areas, and picnic tables.

GOLF & OTHER OUTDOOR ACTIVITIES

Golf

Cavendish Golf Course 🎁 This quirky par-36, 9-hole public course lacks not only a clubhouse and club pros, but also tee times, scorecards, and club rentals. To play, just show up, put a donation into the little wooden box next to the first tee, and hit away. The 3,071-yard, E. B. Cavendish–designed course was built by the Dole plantation in 1947 for its employees. The greens are a bit bumpy, but the views of Lanai are great and the temperatures usually quite mild.

Next to the Lodge at Koele in Lanai City. No phone. Greens fees $5–$10 suggested donation.

The Challenge at Manele ★★ This target-style, desert-links course, designed by Jack Nicklaus, is one of the most challenging courses in the state. Check out the local rules: "No retrieving golf balls from the 150-foot cliffs on the ocean holes 12, 13, or 17," and "All whales, axis deer, and other wild animals are considered immovable obstructions." That's just a hint of the unique experience you'll have on this course, which is routed among lava outcroppings, archaeological sites, kiawe groves, and ilima trees. The five sets of staggered tees pose a challenge to everyone from the casual golfer to the pro. Facilities include a clubhouse, pro shop, rentals, practice area, lockers, and showers.

Next to the Four Seasons Resort Lanai at Manele Bay. 𝄢 ***808/565-2222.*** Greens fees $225 ($210 for guests).

The Experience at Koele ★★ This traditional par-72 course, designed by Greg Norman with fairway architecture by Ted Robinson, has very different front and back 9 holes. Mother Nature reigns throughout: You'll see Cook Island and Norfolk pines, indigenous plants, and lots of water—seven lakes, flowing streams, cascading waterfalls, and one green (the 17th) completely surrounded by a lake. All goes well until you hit the signature hole, number 8, where you tee off from a 250-foot elevated tee to a fairway bordered by a lake on the right and trees and dense shrubs on the left. After that, the back 9 holes drop dramatically through ravines filled with pine, koa, and eucalyptus trees. The grand finale, the par-5 18th, features a green rimmed by waterfalls that flow into a lake on the left side. To level the playing field, there are four different sets of tees. Facilities include a clubhouse, pro shop, rentals, practice area, lockers, and showers.

Next to the Lodge at Koele in Lanai City. ℂ **808/565-4653.** Greens fees $225 ($210 for guests). Closed Mon–Tues.

Biking

The **Lodge at Koele** (ℂ **808/565-4552**) rents mountain bikes for $10 an hour.

Horseback Riding

Horses can take you to many places in Lanai's unique landscape that are otherwise unreachable. The **Four Seasons Lanai Resort's Stables at Koele** (ℂ **808/565-4424**) offers various daily rides (9am and 1:30pm), including slow, gentle group excursions starting at $105 for a 2-hour **Paniolo Trail Ride,** which takes you into the hills surrounding Koele. You'll meander through guava groves and ironwood trees; catch glimpses of axis deer, quail, wild turkeys, and Santa Gertrudis cattle; and end with panoramic views of Maui and Lanai. Private 2-hour rides can be arranged for $170 per person; 1½-hour sunset rides go for $200 per person. Kids will love the 10-minute pony rides; parents will love the price of $15 per person. Long pants and closed-toe shoes (like running shoes) are required, and safety helmets are provided. Bring a jacket—the weather is chilly and rain is frequent. Children must be at least 9 years old and 4 feet tall, and riders cannot weigh more than 225 pounds.

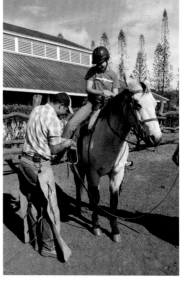

Tennis

Public courts, lit for night play, are available in Lanai City at no charge; call ℂ **808/565-6979** for reservations. If you're staying at the Lodge at Koele or at Manele Bay, you can take advantage of the Lodge's three new Premiere Cushion outdoor hard courts, with complimentary use of Wilson racquets, balls, and bottled water. You're also invited to experience the tennis

Horses allow you a chance to visit landscapes that are otherwise unreachable on Lanai.

center at the Four Seasons Resort Lanai at Manele Bay, which offers a full pro shop, use of a ball machine, and weekly tennis mixers and tournaments. Courts are $20 per person for hotel guests (not open to nonguests). For information, call ✆ **808/565-2072.**

SEEING THE SIGHTS

You'll need a four-wheel-drive vehicle to reach all the sights listed below. Renting a jeep is an expensive proposition on Lanai—from $139 to $179 a day—so I suggest renting one just for the day (or days) you plan on sightseeing; otherwise, it's easy enough to get to the beach and around Lanai City without your own wheels. For details on vehicle rentals, see "Getting Around" (p. 360).

Note: You'll find the following attractions on the map on p. 357.

Garden of the Gods ★

A dirt four-wheel-drive road leads out of Lanai City, through the now uncultivated pineapple fields, past the Kanepuu Preserve (a dry-land forest preserve teeming with rare plant and animal life) to the so-called Garden of the Gods, out on Lanai's north shore. This rugged, barren, beautiful place is full of rocks strewn by volcanic forces and shaped by the elements into a variety of shapes and colors—brilliant reds, oranges, ochers, and yellows.

Ancient Hawaiians considered this desolate, windswept place an entirely supernatural phenomenon. Scientists, however, have other, less colorful

---

 ESPECIALLY FOR kids

Exploring Hulopoe Tide Pools (p. 367) An entire world of marine life lives in the tide pools on the eastern side of Hulopoe Bay. Everything in the water, including the tiny fish, is small—kid size. After examining the wonders of the tide pool, check out the larger swimming holes in the lava rock, perfect for children.

Hunting for Petroglyphs (p. 377) The Luahiwa Petroglyph Field, located just outside Lanai City, is spread out over a 3-acre site. Make it a game: Whoever finds the most petroglyphs gets ice cream from the Pine Isle Market.

Listening to Storytellers Check with the Lanai Library, on Fraser Avenue near Fifth Street, in Lanai City (✆ **808/565-7920**), to see if any storytelling or other

children's activities are scheduled. The events are usually free and open to everyone. Usually held on Fridays at 10am with Aunty Chelsea, but good to call ahead.

---

explanations. Some call the area an "ongoing posterosional event"; others say it's just "plain and simple badlands." Take a four-wheel-drive ride out here and decide for yourself.

Go early in the morning or just before sunset, when the light casts eerie shadows on the mysterious lava formations. Drive west from the Lodge on Polihua Road; in about 2 miles, you'll see a hand-painted sign that'll point left down a one-lane, red-dirt road through a kiawe forest to the site.

Five Islands at a Single Glance: The Munro Trail ★

In the first golden rays of dawn, when lone owls swoop over abandoned pineapple fields, hop into a four-wheel-drive and head out on the two-lane blacktop toward Mount Lanaihale, the 3,370-foot summit of Lanai. Your destination is the Munro Trail, the narrow, winding ridge trail that runs across Lanai's razorback spine to the summit. From here, you may get a rare Hawaii treat: On a clear day, you can see all of

The Garden of the Gods sits on Lanai's north shore.

the main islands in the Hawaiian chain except Kauai.

When it rains, the Munro Trail becomes slick and boggy with major washouts. Rainy-day excursions often end with a rental jeep on the hook of the island's lone tow truck—and a $250 tow charge. You could even slide off into a major gulch and never be found, so don't try it. But in late August and September, when trade winds stop and the air over the islands stalls in what's called a *kona*

Perfect for a Rainy Day: Lanai Art Center

A perfect activity for a rainy day in Lanai City is the **Lanai Art Center,** 339 Seventh St., located in the heart of the small town. Top artists from across Hawaii frequently visit this homegrown art program and teach a variety of classes, ranging from raku (Japanese pottery), silk printing, silk screening, pareu making (creating your own design on this islanders' wrap), gyotaku (printing a real fish on your own T-shirt), and watercolor drawing to a variety of other island crafts. The cost for the 2- to 3-hour classes is usually in the $15 to $70 range (materials are extra). For information, call ✆ **808/565-7503** or visit www. lanaiart.org.

Along the Munro Trail.

condition, Mount Lanaihale's suddenly visible peak becomes an irresistible attraction.

When you're on Lanai, look to the summit. If it's clear in the morning, rent a four-wheel-drive vehicle and take the Munro Trail to the top. Look for a red-dirt road off Manele Road (Hwy. 440), about 5 miles south of Lanai City; turn left and head up the ridge line. No sign marks the peak, so you'll have to keep an eye out. Look for a wide spot in the road and a clearing that falls sharply to the sea.

From here you can see Kahoolawe, Maui, the Big Island of Hawaii, and Molokini's tiny crescent. Even the summits show. You can also see the silver domes of Space City on Haleakala in Maui; Puu Moaulanui, the tongue-twisting summit of Kahoolawe; and, looming above the clouds, Mauna Kea on the Big Island. At another clearing farther along the thickly forested ridge, all of Molokai, including the 4,961-foot summit of Kamakou and the faint outline of Oahu (more than 30 miles across the sea), are visible. You actually can't see all five islands in a single glance anymore because a thriving pine forest blocks the view. For details on hiking the trail, see "Hiking & Camping" (p. 371).

Luahiwa Petroglyph Field

Lanai is second only to the Big Island in its wealth of prehistoric rock art, but you'll have to search a little to find it. Some of the best examples are on the outskirts of Lanai City, on a hillside site known as Luahiwa Petroglyph Field. The characters you'll see incised on 13 boulders in this grassy 3-acre knoll include a running man, a deer, a turtle, a bird, a goat, and even a rare curly-tailed Polynesian dog (a latter-day wag has put a leash on him—some joke).

To get here, take the road to Hulopoe Beach. About 2 miles out of Lanai City, look to the left, up on the slopes of the crater, for a cluster of reddish-tan boulders (believed to form a rain *heiau,* or shrine, where people called up the gods Ku and Hina to nourish their crops). A cluster of spiky century plants marks the spot. Look for the Norfolk pines on the left side of the highway, turn left on the dirt road that veers across the abandoned pineapple fields, and after about 1 mile, take a sharp left by the water tanks. Drive for another ½ mile and then veer to the right at the V in the road. Stay on this upper road for about ¼ mile; you'll come to a large cluster of boulders on the right side. It's just a short walk up the cliffs (wear walking or hiking shoes) to the petroglyphs. Exit the same way you came. Go between 3pm and sunset for ideal viewing and photo ops.

A 1903 clapboard church in Keomoku Village.

Kaunolu Village

Out on Lanai's nearly vertical, Gibraltar-like sea cliffs is an old royal compound and fishing village. Now a National Historic Landmark and one of Hawaii's most treasured ruins, it's believed to have been inhabited by King Kamehameha the Great and hundreds of his closest followers about 200 years ago. It's a hot, dry, dusty, slow-going, 3-mile four-wheel-drive from Lanai City to Kaunolu, but the mini-expedition is worth it. Take plenty of water, don a hat for protection against the sun, and wear sturdy shoes.

Ruins of 86 house platforms and 35 stone shelters have been identified on both sides of Kaunolu Gulch. The residential complex also includes the Halulu Heiau temple, named after a mythical man-eating bird. The king's royal retreat is thought to have stood on the eastern edge of Kaunolu Gulch, overlooking the rocky shore facing Kahekili's Leap, a 62-foot-high bluff named for the mighty Maui chief who leaped off cliffs as a show of bravado. Nearby are burial caves, a fishing shrine, a lookout tower, and many warrior-like stick figures carved on boulders. Just offshore stands the telltale fin of little Shark Island, a popular dive spot that teems with bright tropical fish and, frequently, sharks.

Excavations are underway to discover more about how ancient Hawaiians lived, worked, and worshipped on Lanai's leeward coast. Who knows? The royal fishing village may yet yield the bones of King Kamehameha. His burial site, according to legend, is known only to the moon and the stars.

Kanepuu Preserve

This ancient forest on the island's western plateau is so fragile, you can visit only once a month, and even then only on a guided hike. Kanepuu, which has 48 species of plants unique to Hawaii, survives under the Nature Conservancy's protective wing. Botanists say the 590-acre forest is the last dry lowland forest in Hawaii; the others have all vanished, trashed by axis deer, agriculture, or "progress." Among the botanical marvels of this dry forest are the remains of *olopua* (native olive), *lama* (native ebony), *mau hau hele* (a native hibiscus), and the rare *'aiea* trees, which were used for canoe parts.

Due to the forest's fragile nature, guided hikes are led only 12 times a year, on a monthly, reservations-only basis. Contact the **Nature Conservancy Oahu Land Preserve** manager at 1116 Smith St., Ste. 201, Honolulu, HI 96817 (📞 **808/537-4508**).

Off the Tourist Trail: Keomoku Village

If you're sunburned lobster red, have read all the books you packed, and are starting to get island fever, take a little drive to Keomoku Village, on Lanai's east coast. You'll really be off the tourist path here. All that's in Keomoku, a ghost town since the mid-1950s, is a 1903 clapboard church in disrepair, an overgrown graveyard, an excellent view across the 9-mile Auau Channel to Maui's crowded Kaanapali Beach, and some very empty beaches that are perfect for a picnic or a snorkel. This former ranching and fishing village of 2,000 was the first non-Hawaiian settlement on Lanai, but it dried up after droughts killed off the Maunalei Sugar Company. The village, such as it is, is a great little escape from Lanai City. Follow Keomoku Road for 8 miles to the coast, turn right on the sandy road, and keep going for 5¾ miles.

SHOPPING

Central Bakery ★ 🎁 This is the mother lode of the island's baked delights—the bakery that is, well, central to Lanai's dining pleasure. If you've noshed on the fantastic sandwiches at the Terrace at the Lodge at Koele or any of the stellar desserts at the Lodge's Main Dining Room or at the Four Seasons Resort Lanai at Manele Bay, you've enjoyed goodies from Central Bakery. The bakery supplies all breads, all breakfast pastries, specialty ice creams and sorbets, all banquet desserts, and restaurant desserts on the island. Although it's not your standard retail

The Lanai Art Center offers classes in an array of mediums including woodworking, painting, ceramics, and photography.

outlet, you can call in advance, place your order, and pick it up. The staff prefers as much notice as possible (preferably 48 hr.). Breads (most priced at $6.50) range from walnut onion to roasted potato bacon to olive onion. The bakery also has cookies (chocolate chip, oatmeal, coconut—all for $2), brownies, muffins, croissants (including chocolate croissants), Danishes, and scones, plus an assortment of breakfast pastries (pineapple turnover, hazelnut roll, mascarpone apricot Danish, pistachio chocolate roll, and others). All orders and pick-ups now go through Richard's Market (see below), 434 8th St., Lanai, *C* **808/565-3780.**

Dis 'N Dat ★★ 🎁 Dis (Barry) and Dat (Susie) visited Lanai from Florida to look at buying a retirement home. They found their home and moved to Lanai to retire. Retirement didn't last. A few years later, outgoing Barry and his wife started searching for unusual, finely crafted teak and exotic wood sculptures and carvings. Along the way, they took a shine to mobiles and wind chimes—the more outrageous, the better. Then they started collecting handmade jewelry, stained glass, and unique garden ornaments and home decor. All this led to this eclectic store, which you have to see to believe. Meeting Barry is worth the trip alone. You'll find T-shirts, pottery, ceramics, batik scarves, hula lamps and whimsical dragonfly lamps, woven baskets, and even waterfalls. This is also the biggest collection of Hawaii slipper necklaces, earrings, anklets, and bracelets. You can't miss the vivid green shop with hanging chimes and mobiles leading the way to the front door. 418 Eighth Ave. (at Kilele St.), Lanai City. *C* **866/DIS-N-DAT** (347-6328) or 808/565-9170.

International Food & Clothing This store sells the basics: groceries, housewares, T-shirts, hunting and fishing supplies, over-the-counter drugs, wine and liquor, paper goods, and hardware, and even has a takeout lunch counter. I was pleasantly surprised by the extraordinary candy and bubble-gum section, the beautiful local bananas in the small produce section, the surprisingly extensive selection of yuppie soft drinks (Sobe, Snapple, and others), and the best knife-sharpener I've seen. 833 Ilima Ave., Lanai City. *C* **808/565-6433.**

Lanai Art Center ★ 🎁 This wonderful center was organized in 1989 to provide a place where both residents and visitors can come to create art. The center offers classes and studio time in ceramics, painting and drawing, calligraphy, woodworking, photography, silk and textile painting, watercolor, and glass. There's an impressive schedule of visiting instructors, from writers to folk artists (quilting, lei making, and instrument making) to oil painters. Check out the reasonably priced classes (generally in the $25 range) or browse the gallery for excellent deals on works by Lanai residents. 339 Seventh St., Lanai City. *C* **808/565-7503.** www.lanaiart.org.

Lanai Marketplace Everyone on Lanai, it seems, is a backyard farmer. From 7 to 11am or noon on Saturday, they all head to this shady square to sell their dewy-fresh produce, home-baked breads, plate lunches, and handicrafts. This is Lanai's version of the green market: petite in scale (like the island) but charming, and growing. Dole Park, Lanai City.

The Local Gentry ★★ 🎁 Jenna (Gentry) Majkus's wonderful boutique was the first of its kind on the island, featuring clothing and accessories that are not the standard resort-shop fare. (Visiting and local women alike make a beeline for this store.) You'll find fabulous silk aloha shirts by Kahala, mermaids and hula girls, inexpensive sarongs, and fabulous socks. There are also great T-shirts, jewelry, bath products, picture frames, jeans, and offbeat sandals. The most recent additions are wonderful children's clothes. 363 Seventh St., Lanai City. (C) **808/565-9130.**

Mike Carroll Gallery If he is on the island, you'll find Mike Carroll at work here on his original oil paintings. After a successful 22-year career as a professional artist in Chicago, Carroll moved to Lanai and has been painting the beauty and the lifestyle of the island ever since. You'll find an extensive selection of his original work, some limited editions, prints and note cards, plus a dozen or so of Maui's and Lanai's top artists and even some locally made, one-of-a-kind jewelry. 443 Seventh St., Lanai City. (C) **808/565-7122.** www.mikecarrollgallery.com.

Pine Isle Market A local landmark for two generations, Pine Isle specializes in locally caught fresh fish, but you can also find fresh herbs and spices, canned goods, electronic games, ice cream, toys, zoris, diapers, paint, cigars, and other basic essentials of work and play. The fishing section is outstanding, with every lure imaginable. 356 Eighth St., Lanai City. (C) **808/565-6488.**

Richard's Market The Tamashiros' family business has been on the square since 1946; not much has changed over the years. Richard's is a general store with a grocery section, paper products, ethnic foods, meats (mostly frozen), liquor, toys, film, cosmetics, fishing gear, sunscreens, clothing, kitchen utensils, T-shirts, and other miscellany. Half a wall is lined with an extraordinary selection of fish hooks and anglers' needs. Aloha shirts, aloha-print zoris, fold-up lauhala mats, and gourmet breads from the Central Bakery (see above) are among the countless good things at Richard's. 434 Eighth St., Lanai City. (C) **808/565-3780.**

LANAI AFTER DARK

The only regular nightlife venues are the Lanai Playhouse, at the corner of Seventh and Lanai avenues in Lanai City, and the two resorts, the Lodge at Koele and Four Seasons Resort Lanai at Manele Bay.

The **Lodge at Koele** has stepped up its live entertainment. In front of the manorial fireplaces in the Great Hall, local artists serenade listeners, who sip port and fine liqueurs while sinking into plush chairs, with contemporary Hawaiian, classical, and other genres of music. The special programs are on weekends, but some form of nightly entertainment takes place throughout the week, from 5:30 to 9:30pm. Down at the Manele Bay Resort, **the Ahi Ahi Lounge** also has live entertainment nightly from 7:30 to 9:30pm.

Occasionally, special events will bring in a few more nightlife options. During the annual **Pineapple Festival,** generally the first weekend in July, some of Hawaii's best musicians arrive to show their support for Lanai (see "Maui, Molokai & Lanai Calendar of Events" on p. 61). The **Aloha Festival** (www.alohafestivals.com) takes place in the end of September or the first week in October, and the **Christmas Festival** is held on the first Saturday in December. For details on these festivals, contact the **Lanai Visitors Bureau,** P.O. Box 631436, Lanai City, HI 96763; or 431 Seventh St., Ste. A, Lanai City; (C) **800/947-4774** or 808/565-7600; fax 808/565-9316; www.visitlanai.net.

13

FAST FACTS

[Fast FACTS] MAUI

Area Codes All of the Hawaiian Islands are in the **808** area code. Note that if you're calling one island from another, you'll have to dial "1-808" before the local number (and you'll be billed long-distance rates).

Business Hours Most offices are open Monday through Friday from 8am to 5pm. Bank hours are Monday through Thursday from 8:30am to 3pm and Friday from 8:30am to 6pm; some banks are open on Saturday as well. Shopping centers are open Monday through Friday from 10am to 9pm, Saturday from 10am to 5:30pm, and Sunday from noon to 5 or 6pm.

Cellphones See "Staying Connected," p. 91.

Dentists Emergency dental care is available at **Kihei Dental Center,** 1847 S. Kihei Rd., Kihei (✆ **808/874-8401**), and at **Aloha Lahaina Dentists,** 134 Luakini St. (in the Maui Medical Group Bldg.), Lahaina (✆ **808/661-4005**).

Doctors The **West Maui Healthcare Center,** Whalers Village, 2435 Kaanapali Pkwy., Ste. H-7 (near Leilani's on the Beach), Kaanapali (✆ **808/667-9721**), is open 365 days a year; no appointment is necessary. In Kihei, call **Urgent Care Maui,** 1325 S. Kihei Rd., Ste. 103 (at Lipoa St., across from Star Market), Kihei (✆ **808/879-7781**).

Drinking Laws The legal age for purchase and consumption of alcoholic beverages is 21; proof of age is required and often requested at bars, nightclubs, and restaurants, so it's always a good idea to bring ID when you go out.

Bars are allowed to stay open daily until 2am; places with cabaret licenses are able to keep the booze flowing until 4am. Grocery and convenience stores are allowed to sell beer, wine, and liquor 7 days a week.

Do not carry open containers of alcohol in your car or any public area that isn't zoned for alcohol consumption. The police can fine you on the spot. And nothing will ruin your trip faster than getting a citation for DUI ("driving under the influence"), so don't even think about driving while intoxicated.

Driving Rules See "Getting There & Getting Around," p. 67.

Electricity Like Canada, the United States uses 110 to 120 volts AC (60 cycles), compared to 220 to 240 volts AC (50 cycles) in most of Europe, Australia, and New Zealand. Downward converters that change 220 to 240 volts to 110 to 120 volts are difficult to find in the United States, so bring one with you.

Embassies & Consulates All embassies are located in the nation's capital, Washington, D.C. Some consulates are located in major U.S. cities, and most nations have a mission to the United Nations in New York City. If your country isn't listed below, call for directory information in Washington, D.C. (☎ **202/555-1212**), or check www. embassy.org/embassies.

The embassy of **Australia** is at 1601 Massachusetts Ave. NW, Washington, DC 20036 (☎ **202/797-3000;** www.usa.embassy.gov.au). There are consulates in New York, Honolulu, Houston, Los Angeles, and San Francisco.

The embassy of **Canada** is at 501 Pennsylvania Ave. NW, Washington, DC 20001 (☎ **202/682-1740;** www.canadianembassy.org). Other Canadian consulates are in Buffalo (New York), Detroit, Los Angeles, New York, and Seattle.

The embassy of **Ireland** is at 2234 Massachusetts Ave. NW, Washington, DC 20008 (☎ **202/462-3939;** www.embassyofireland.org). Irish consulates are in Boston, Chicago, New York, San Francisco, and other cities. See the website for a complete listing.

The embassy of **New Zealand** is at 37 Observatory Circle NW, Washington, DC 20008 (☎ **202/328-4800;** www.nzembassy.com). New Zealand consulates are in Los Angeles, Salt Lake City, San Francisco, and Seattle.

The embassy of the **United Kingdom** is at 3100 Massachusetts Ave. NW, Washington, DC 20008 (☎ **202/588-7800;** www. ukinusa.fco.gov.uk/en/). Other British consulates are in Atlanta, Boston, Chicago, Cleveland, Houston, Los Angeles, New York, San Francisco, and Seattle.

Emergencies Dial ☎ **911** for **police, fire,** or **ambulance.** Police district stations are located in Lahaina (☎ **808/661-4441**) and in Hana (☎ **808/248-8311**). For the **Poison Control Center,** call ☎ **800/362-3585.**

Gasoline (Petrol) At this writing, average prices for regular gas in Maui are about $3.79 per gallon. Note that taxes are already included in the printed price. One U.S. gallon equals 3.8 liters or .85 imperial gallons. Fill-up locations are known as gas or service stations.

Holidays Banks, government offices, post offices, and many stores, restaurants, and museums are closed on the following legal national holidays: January 1 (New Year's Day), the third Monday in January (Martin Luther King, Jr., Day), the third Monday in February (Presidents' Day), the last Monday in May (Memorial Day), July 4 (Independence Day), the first Monday in September (Labor Day), the second Monday in October (Columbus Day), November 11 (Veterans' Day/Armistice Day), the fourth Thursday in November (Thanksgiving Day), and December 25 (Christmas). The Tuesday after the first Monday in November is Election Day, a federal government holiday in presidential-election years (held every 4 years, and next in 2012).

State and county offices are also closed on local holidays. For more information, go to "Holidays" and "Maui, Molokai & Lanai Calendar of Events" in the "When to Go" section of chapter 3, on p. 58.

Hospitals In central Maui, **Maui Memorial Hospital** is at 221 Mahalani, Wailuku (📞 **808/244-9056**). East Maui's **Hana Medical Center** is on the Hana Highway (📞 **808/248-8924**). In upcountry Maui, **Kula Hospital** is at 204 Kula Hwy., Kula (📞 **808/878-1221**).

Insurance For information on traveler's insurance, trip cancellation insurance, and medical insurance while traveling, please visit www.frommers.com/planning.

Internet Access On every island, branches of the **Hawaii State Public Library System** have free computers with Internet access. To find your closest library, check **www.librarieshawaii.org**. There is no charge for use of the computers, but you must have a Hawaii library card, which is free to Hawaii residents and members of the military. Visitors have a choice of two types of cards: a $25 nonresident card that is good for 5 years (and may be renewed for an additional $25) or a $10 visitor card ($5 for children age 18 and under) that is good for 3 months but may not be renewed. To download an application for a library card, go to **www.librarieshawaii.org/services/libcard.htm**.

To find Internet cafes in Maui, check **www.cybercaptive.com** or **www.cybercafe.com**.

If you have your own laptop, every **Starbucks** in Hawaii has Wi-Fi. For a list of locations, go to **www.starbucks.com**. To find other public Wi-Fi hotspots, go to **www.jiwire.com**; its Hotspot Finder holds the world's largest directory of public wireless hotspots.

Legal Aid If you are "pulled over" for a minor infraction (such as speeding), never attempt to pay the fine directly to a police officer; this could be construed as attempted bribery, a much more serious crime. Pay fines by mail, or directly into the hands of the clerk of the court. If accused of a more serious offense, say and do nothing before consulting a lawyer. Here the burden is on the state to prove a person's guilt beyond a reasonable doubt, and everyone has the right to remain silent, whether he or she is suspected of a crime or actually arrested. Once arrested, a person can make one telephone call to a party of his or her choice. International visitors should call their embassy or consulate.

Mail At press time, domestic postage rates were 28¢ for a postcard and 44¢ for a letter. For international mail, a first-class letter of up to 1 ounce costs 98¢ (75¢ to Canada and Mexico); a first-class postcard costs the same as a letter. For more information, go to **www.usps.com** and click on "Calculate Postage."

In Lahaina, there are post offices at the Lahaina Civic Center, 1760 Honoapiilani Hwy., and at the Lahaina Shopping Center, 132 Papalaua St. In Kahului, there's a branch at 138 S. Puunene Ave., and in Kihei, there's one at 1254 S. Kihei Rd.

If you aren't sure what your address will be in the United States, mail can be sent to you, in your name, c/o General Delivery at the main post office of the city or region where you expect to be. (Call 📞 **800/275-8777** for information on the nearest post office.) The addressee must pick up mail in person and must produce proof of identity (driver's license, passport, and such). Most post offices will hold your mail for up to 1 month, and are open Monday through Friday from 8am to 6pm, and Saturday from 9am to 3pm.

Always include zip codes when mailing items in the U.S. If you don't know your zip code, visit www.usps.com/zip4.

Measurements See the chart on the inside front cover of this book for details on converting metric measurements to nonmetric equivalents.

Newspapers & Magazines The island's daily newspaper is the ***Maui News,*** P.O. Box 550, Wailuku, HI 96793 (✆ **808/244-3981;** www.mauinews.com).

Publications for visitors include *This Week Maui* (www.thisweek.com), *Maui Visitor Magazine* (www.visitormagazines.com), and *101 Things to Do.*

Passports For an up-to-date, country-by-country listing of passport requirements around the world, go to the "International Travel" tab of the U.S. State Department at **http://travel.state.gov**. International visitors to the U.S. can obtain a visa application at the same website. ***Note:*** Children are required to present a passport when entering the United States at airports. Allow plenty of time before your trip to apply for a passport; processing normally takes 4 to 6 weeks (3 weeks for expedited service) but can take longer during busy periods (especially spring). And keep in mind that if you need a passport in a hurry, you'll pay a higher processing fee.

For Residents of Australia You can pick up an application from your local post office or any branch of Passports Australia, but you must schedule an interview at the passport office to present your application materials. Call the **Australian Passport Information Service** at ✆ **131-232,** or visit the government website at www.passports.gov.au.

For Residents of Canada Passport applications are available at travel agencies throughout Canada or from the central **Passport Office,** Dept. of Foreign Affairs and International Trade, Ottawa, ON K1A 0G3 (✆ **800/567-6868;** www.ppt.gc.ca). ***Note:*** Canadian children 16 and younger must travel with their own passport.

For Residents of Ireland You can apply for a 10-year passport at the **Passport Office,** Setanta Centre, Molesworth Street, Dublin 2 (✆ **01/671-1633;** www.irlgov.ie/iveagh). Those under age 18 and over 65 must apply for a 3-year passport. You can also apply at 1A South Mall, Cork (✆ **21/494-4700**), or at most main post offices.

For Residents of New Zealand You can pick up a passport application at any New Zealand Passports Office or download it from the website. Contact the **Passports Office** at ✆ **0800/225-050** (in New Zealand) or 04/474-8100, or log on to www.passports.govt.nz.

For Residents of the United Kingdom To pick up an application for a standard 10-year passport (5-year passport for children under 16), visit your nearest passport office, major post office, or travel agency, or contact the **United Kingdom Passport Service** at ✆ **0870/521-0410** or go to www.ukpa.gov.uk.

Police In an emergency, dial ✆ **911** for police. For nonemergencies, call the district station in Lahaina (✆ **808/661-4441**) or Hana (✆ **808/248-8311**).

Smoking It's against the law to smoke in public buildings, including airports, shopping malls, grocery stores, retail shops, buses, movie theaters, banks, convention facilities, and all government buildings and facilities. There is no smoking in restaurants, bars, and nightclubs. Most bed-and-breakfasts prohibit smoking indoors, and more and more hotels and resorts are becoming nonsmoking even in public areas. Also, there is no smoking within 20 feet of a doorway, window, or ventilation intake (so no hanging around outside a bar to smoke—you must go 20 ft. away).

Taxes The United States has no value-added tax (VAT) or other indirect tax at the national level. Every state, county, and city may levy its own local tax on all purchases, including hotel and restaurant checks and airline tickets. Hawaii state general excise tax is 4%. The hotel-occupancy tax is 7.25%, and hoteliers are allowed by the state to tack on an additional .1666% excise tax. Thus, expect taxes of about 11.42% to be added to your hotel bill.

Telegraph, Telex & Fax **Telegraph** and **telex** services are provided primarily by **Western Union** (☎ **800/325-6000;** www.westernunion.com). You can telegraph (wire) money, or have it telegraphed to you, very quickly over the Western Union system, but this service can cost as much as 15% to 20% of the amount sent.

Most hotels have **fax machines** available for guests' use (be sure to ask about the charge to use them). Many hotel rooms are wired for guests' fax machines. A less expensive way to send and receive faxes may be at stores such as the **UPS Store** (formerly Mail Boxes Etc.).

Telephones See "Staying Connected," p. 91.

Time The continental United States is divided into **four time zones:** Eastern Standard Time (EST), Central Standard Time (CST), Mountain Standard Time (MST), and Pacific Standard Time (PST). Alaska and Hawaii have their own zones. For example, when it's 9am in Los Angeles (PST), it's 7am in Honolulu (HST), 10am in Denver (MST), 11am in Chicago (CST), noon in New York City (EST), 5pm in London (GMT), and 2am the next day in Sydney.

Daylight saving time is in effect from 2am on the second Sunday in March to 2am on the first Sunday in November, except in Arizona, Hawaii, the U.S. Virgin Islands, and Puerto Rico. Daylight saving time moves the clock 1 hour ahead of standard time. Note that when the rest of the U.S. observes daylight saving time, Hawaii is 3 hours behind the West Coast and 6 hours behind the East Coast.

Tipping Tips are a very important part of certain workers' income, and gratuities are the standard way of showing appreciation for services provided. (Tipping is certainly not compulsory if the service is poor!) In hotels, tip **bellhops** at least $1 per bag ($2–$3 if you have a lot of luggage) and tip the **chamber staff** $1 to $2 per day (more if you've left a disaster area for him or her to clean up). Tip the **doorman** or **concierge** only if he or she has provided you with some specific service (for example, calling a cab for you or obtaining difficult-to-get theater tickets). Tip the **valet-parking attendant** $1 every time you get your car.

In restaurants, bars, and nightclubs, tip **service staff** 15% to 20% of the check, tip **bartenders** 10% to 15%, tip **checkroom attendants** $1 per garment, and tip **valet-parking attendants** $1 per vehicle.

As for other service personnel, tip **cab drivers** 15% of the fare, tip **skycaps** at airports at least $1 per bag ($2–$3 if you have a lot of luggage), and tip **hairdressers** and **barbers** 15% to 20%.

Toilets You won't find public toilets or "restrooms" on the streets in most U.S. cities but they can be found in hotel lobbies, bars, restaurants, museums, department stores, bus stations, and service stations. Large hotels and fast-food restaurants are often the best bet for clean facilities. If possible, avoid the toilets at parks and beaches, which tend to be dirty; some may be unsafe. Restaurants and bars in resorts or heavily visited areas may reserve their restrooms for patrons.

Visas For information on U.S. visas, go to **http://travel.state.gov** and click on "Visas." Or go to one of the following websites:

Australian citizens can obtain up-to-date visa information from the **U.S. Embassy Canberra,** Moonah Place, Yarralumla, ACT 2600 (☎ **02/6214-5600**), or by checking the U.S. Diplomatic Mission's website at http://usembassy-australia.state.gov/consular.

British subjects can obtain up-to-date visa information by calling the **U.S. Embassy Visa Information Line** (📞 **0891/200-290**) or by visiting the "Visas to the U.S." section of the American Embassy London's website at www.usembassy.org.uk.

Irish citizens can obtain up-to-date visa information through the **Embassy of the USA Dublin,** 42 Elgin Rd., Dublin 4, Ireland (📞 **353/1-668-8777**), or by checking the "Visas to the U.S." section of the website at http://dublin.usembassy.gov.

Citizens of **New Zealand** can obtain up-to-date visa information by contacting the **U.S. Embassy New Zealand,** 29 Fitzherbert Terrace, Thorndon, Wellington (📞 **644/472-2068**), or get the information directly from the website at http://wellington.us embassy.gov.

Visitor Information The **Maui Visitors Bureau** is at 1727 Wili Pa Loop, Wailu-ku, Maui, HI 96793 (📞 **800/525-MAUI** or 808/244-3530; fax 808/244-1337; www. visitmaui.com). **Molokai Visitors Association,** P.O. Box 960, Kaunakakai, HI 96748 (📞 **800/800-6367** from the U.S. mainland and Canada, 800/553-0404 interisland, or 808/553-3876; www.molokai-hawaii.com). **Lanai Visitors Bureau,** P.O. Box 631436, Lanai City, HI 96763; or 431 Seventh St., Suite A, Lanai City (📞 **800/947-4774** or 808/565-7600; fax 808/565-9316; www.visitlanai.net). The **Hawaii Visitors & Convention Bureau** (📞 **800/GO-HAWAII** or 808/923-1811; www.gohawaii.com) provide brochures, maps, and island guides.

Other great websites:

The Hawaiian Language website: **http://www.instanthawaii.com**

Maui Net: **www.maui.net**

Maui Island Current (arts and culture): **www.islandcurrents.com**

Wi-Fi See "Staying Connected," p. 91.

AIRLINE WEBSITES

MAJOR U.S. AIRLINES
(also flies internationally)

Alaska Airlines
www.alaskaair.com

American Airlines
www.aa.com

Continental Airlines
www.continental.com

Delta Air Lines
www.delta.com

go!
(interisland Hawaii only)
www.iflygo.com

Hawaiian Airlines
www.hawaiianair.com

Island Air
www.islandair.com

Mokulele Airlines
www.mokuleleairlines.com

Northwest Airlines
www.delta.com

United Airlines
www.united.com

US Airways
www.usairways.com

MAJOR INTERNATIONAL AIRLINES

Air Canada
www.aircanada.com

Air France
www.airfrance.com

Air New Zealand
www.airnewzealand.com

Air Pacific
www.airpacific.com

Air Tahiti Nui
www.airtahitinui-usa.com

Alitalia
www.alitalia.com

All Nippon Airways (ANA)
www.fly-ana.com

American Airlines
www.aa.com

British Airways
www.british-airways.com

China Airlines
www.china-airlines.com

Continental Airlines
www.continental.com

Delta Air Lines
www.delta.com

Hawaiian Airlines
www.hawaiianair.com

Japan Airlines
www.jal.co.jp

Korean Air
www.koreanair.com

Philippine Airlines
www.philippineairlines.com

Qantas Airways
www.qantas.com

United Airlines
www.united.com

US Airways
www.usairways.com

Virgin Atlantic Airways
www.virgin-atlantic.com

13

Airline Websites

FAST FACTS

INDEX

See also Accommodations and Restaurant indexes, below.

General Index

A

ABC (Kaanapali), 298
Access Aloha Travel, 81
Accommodations, 125–164. *See also* Accommodations Index
avoiding unpleasant surprises, 94
best, 13–18
best bed & breakfasts, 16–18
best luxury hotels and resorts, 13–15
best moderately priced, 15–16
best resort spas, 18–20
booking agencies, 95
Central Maui, 125–126
definition of "hotel," 93
East Maui, 158–160
Haiku, 159
Hana, 160–164
Honokowai, Kahana and Napili, 137–142
Huelo/Wailua, 159–160
Kaanapali, 132–136
Kahului, 125
Kapalua, 142–143
Kihei, 143–151
Kuau, 158
Kula, 156, 158
Lanai, 360–362
landing the best room, 97
Makena, 154–155
Molokai, 322–326
nickel-and-dime charges at high-priced hotels, 93
responsible tourism and, 87
saving on your hotel room, 95–97
South Maui, 143–155
surfing for hotels, 95
tipping, 386
Twin Falls, 159
types of, 93–94
Upcountry Maui, 155–156
Wailea, 151–154
Wailuku, 125–126
West Maui, 126–143
Activities & Attractions

Association of Hawaii Gold Card, 90
Activities desks, 90
Aeo, 42
African tulip trees, 38
Agricultural screening, 69
Ahi, 56
The Ahi Ahi Lounge (Lanai), 381
Ahihi-Kinau Natural Preserve, 216
Air travel, 67–70
agricultural screening, 69
interisland flights, 68
jet lag, 70
Molokai, 317
responsible tourism and, 87
Aku, 56
Alala, 42
Alexander & Baldwin Sugar Museum, 242
Alii Cab Co., 73
Alii Fish Pond (Molokai), 347
Alii Kula Lavender, 270
All Stings Considered: First Aid and Medical Treatment of Hawaii's Marine Injuries (Thomas and Scott), 77
Aloha Bead Co. (Paia), 303
Aloha Festivals, 64
Lanai, 381
Aloha Festivals Hoolaulea (Lahaina), 65
Aloha Lahaina Dentists (Maui), 382
Altitude sickness, 77
Alyce C Sportfishing (Molokai), 334
Ambulance, Maui, 383
American Airlines Vacations, 87
American Plan (AP), 96
America the Beautiful Access Pass, 81
America the Beautiful Senior Pass, 82
Angelfish, 43
Angel's trumpets, 38
Animal-friendly issues, 87
Anthuriums, 38
Area codes, 382
Art School at Kapalua, 299
Atlantis Adventures, 218, 241

ATMs (automated-teller machines), 74–75
Australia
embassy of, 383
passports, 385
visas, 386
Azeka Place II (Kihei), 299
Azeka Place Shopping Center (Kihei), 299

B

Baby's Away, 82
Bailey House Museum (Lahaina), 243
Bailey House Museum Shop (Lahaina), 293
Baldwin Beach (Lahaina), bodysurfing, 211
Baldwin Home Museum (Lahaina), 246, 250
shopping, 293
Baldwin Park, 206
Bamboo forest, 228, 276–277
Bamboo Pantry (Molokai), 349–350
Banana Wind (Lahaina), 296
Bank of Hawaii (Kaunakakai), 319
Banyan Tree Birthday Party (Lahaina), 62
Banyan Tree (Lahaina), 247, 253
Lighting of the (Lahaina), 65
Banyan trees, 38
Bay Course, 232
Beaches, 201–208. *See also specific beaches*
best, 2–5
East Maui, 206–208
Hana area, 285–287
Lanai, 366–368
Molokai, 329–331
camping, 337
nude, 80
responsible tourism, 84
South Maui, 204–205
West Maui, 201–204
Bed & Breakfast Hawaii, 95
Bed & breakfasts (B&Bs), 94, 96
etiquette at, 129

389

GENERAL INDEX

401

Accommodations

Restaurants

PHOTO CREDITS

p. i: © Marc Schechter / Photo Resource Hawaii; p. iii, iv, v, vi: © Ann Cecil / Lonely Planet Images; p. 1: © Cara Jalbert; p. 2: © Ryan Siphers; p. 4: © Ryan Siphers; p. 5: © Pacific Stock / SuperStock; p. 6: © Agustin Tabares; p. 7: © Ryan Siphers; p. 8: © Debra Behr / Alamy; p. 9: © Marco Garcia; p. 10: © Ron Dahlquist / Photolibrary; p. 11: © Reinhard Dirscherl / Agentur Bilderberg / Aurora Photos; p. 12: © Courtesy Kapalua Resort; p. 14: © Courtesy Four Seasons Hotels and Resorts; p. 15: © Courtesy Grand Wailea Resort Hotel & Spa; p. 16: © Marco Garcia; p. 17: © Courtesy Old Wailuku Inn at Ulupono; p. 18: © Courtesy Fairmont Kea Lani; p. 21: © Courtesy Sansei Seafood Restaurant & Sushi Bar; p. 23: © Courtesy Four Seasons Hotels and Resorts; p. 24: © Kristin Mills; p. 25: © Marco Garcia; p. 26: © Ryan Siphers; p. 28: © Val Kim / Photo Resource Hawaii; p. 30: © Douglas Peebles / Photolibrary; p. 31, left: © SuperStock; p. 31, right: © Greg Elms / Lonely Planet Images; p. 33: © Bettmann / Corbis; p. 34, left: © Hawaiian Legacy Archive / Pacific Stock / Photolibrary; p. 34, right: © Bettmann / Corbis; p. 35: © Schenectady Museum; Hall of Electrical History Foundation / Corbis; p. 37: © K.J. Historical / Corbis; p. 39: © Bruce Omori; p. 40, left: © Marco Garcia; p. 40, right: © Marco Garcia; p. 41: © Carla Jalbert; p. 42, left: © David Fleetham / Alamy; p. 42, right: © Douglas Peebles / Alamy; p. 44: © David Fleetham / Alamy; p. 45: © Stephen Frink Collection / Alamy; p. 47: © Courtesy Mutual Publishing; p. 51: © Paramount / The Kobal Collection; p. 52: © Marco Garcia; p. 53: © 20th Century Fox / The Kobal Collection; p. 55: © Ryan Siphers; p. 57: © Bill Heinsohn / Alamy; p. 100: © Ryan Siphers; p. 102: © Carla Jalbert; p. 104: © Ryan Siphers; p. 105: © Carla Jalbert; p. 108: © Kristin Mills; p. 110, left: © Ryan Siphers; p. 110, right: © Carla Jalbert; p. 112: © Agustin Tabares; p. 113: © Courtesy Maui Ocean Center; p. 114: © Ryan Siphers; p. 115: © Kristin Mills; p. 116: © Kristin Mills; p. 118: © Marco Garcia; p. 120: © Marco Garcia; p. 121: © Ron Dahlquist / Pacific Stock / Photolibrary; p. 122: © David Schrichte / Photo Resource Hawaii; p. 124: © Courtesy Hotel Hana-Maui; p. 165: © Ryan Siphers; p. 168: © Courtesy Roselani Ice Cream; p. 178: © Courtesy O'o Farm, photo by Anthony Martinez; p. 200: © Ryan Siphers; p. 202, left: © Ryan Siphers; p. 202, right: © Ryan Siphers; p. 205, left: © Ryan Siphers; p. 205, right: © Ryan Siphers; p. 206: © Kristin Mills; p. 207, left: © Carla Jalbert; p. 207, right: © Ryan Siphers; p. 208: © Ryan Siphers; p. 210: © Andre Jenny / Alamy; p. 211, top: © Ryan Siphers; p. 211, bottom: © Ryan Siphers; p. 212: © Carla Jalbert; p. 213: © Ryan Siphers; p. 216: © Ryan Siphers; p. 218: © Courtesy Atlantis Adventures; p. 219: © Kristin Mills; p. 220: © Bill Schildge / Pacific Stock / Photolibrary; p. 221: © Ryan Siphers; p. 223: © Carla Jalbert; p. 224: © Kristin Mills; p. 226: © Tor Johnson / Photo Resource Hawaii; p. 230: © Agustin Tabares; p. 231: © Ryan Siphers; p. 235, left: © Kristin Mills; p. 235, right: © Kristin Mills; p. 238: © Kristin Mills; p. 239: © David Fleetham / Alamy; p. 240: © Ryan Siphers; p. 242, top: © Carla Jalbert; p. 242, bottom: © Ryan Siphers; p. 243: © Carla Jalbert; p. 244: © Kristin Mills; p. 245: © Ryan Siphers; p. 246: © Ryan Siphers; p. 249, left: © Agustin Tabares; p. 249, right: © Ryan Siphers; p. 251: © Ryan Siphers; p. 252: © Ryan Siphers; p. 254: © Ryan Siphers; p. 258, top: © Ryan Siphers; p. 258, bottom: © Carla Jalbert; p. 259: © Ryan Siphers; p. 260: © Courtesy Maui Ocean Center; p. 261: © Ryan Siphers; p. 262, left: © Ryan Siphers; p. 262, right: © Ryan Siphers; p. 263: © Ryan Siphers; p. 264: © Annette Wagner; p. 266: © Kristin Mills; p. 268: © Ryan Siphers; p. 269: © Annette Wagner; p. 270, top: © Ryan Siphers; p. 270, box: © Carla Jalbert; p. 271: © Carla Jalbert; p. 272: © Reimar Gaertner / Insadco / AGE Fotostock; p. 273: © Carla Jalbert; p. 274: © Kristin Mills; p. 275: © Ryan Siphers; p. 277: © Ryan Siphers; p. 278: © Ryan Siphers; p. 280: © Agustin Tabares; p. 284, top: © Courtesy Hotel Hana-Maui; p. 284, bottom: © Agustin Tabares; p. 285: © Ryan Siphers; p. 286: © Ryan Siphers; p. 287: © Ryan Siphers; p. 288: © Ryan Siphers; p. 289: © Ryan Siphers; p. 290: © Marco Garcia; p. 294: © Carla Jalbert; p. 296, left: © Ryan Siphers; p. 296, right: © Ryan Siphers; p. 304: © Ryan Siphers; p. 306: © Kristin Mills; p. 307: © Kristin Mills; p. 309, left: © Courtesy of Ulalena at Maui Theatre; p. 309, right: © Courtesy Old Lahaina Luau; p. 313: © Pacific Stock / SuperStock; p. 314: © Pacific Stock / SuperStock; p. 320: © Marco Garcia; p. 329: © Marco Garcia; p. 330: © Marco Garcia; p. 331: © Marco Garcia; p. 332, top: © Marco Garcia; p. 332, bottom: © Marco Garcia; p. 333: © Marco Garcia; p. 334: © David Fleetham / Alamy; p. 335: © David Fleetham / Alamy; p. 336: © Marco Garcia; p. 337: © Marco Garcia; p. 339: © Marco Garcia; p. 340: © Marco Garcia; p. 341, top: © Caroline Commins / Alamy; p. 341, bottom: © Marco Garcia; p. 343, top: © Marco Garcia; p. 343, bottom: © Marco Garcia; p. 345: © Marco Garcia; p. 346: © Marco Garcia; p. 347: © Marco Garcia; p. 349, left: © Jon Ogata / Photo Resource Hawaii; p. 349, right: © Marco Garcia; p. 351:

NOTES